KEIRON PIM is the author of *Jumpin[g]* [...]
Rock'n'Roll Underworld, which was [...]
Prize and shortlisted in the Wales B[...]
written for the *Guardian*, the *Daily Telegraph* and the *Spectator*. He lives
in Norwich with his wife and three daughters.

'Absorbing ... A thoughtful, thorough, and sympathetic book, and a
necessary one. It has often been lamented that Roth's work, apart from
The Radetzky March, has for years been underread and neglected, and
that it has taken time for his novels to be translated ... *Endless Flight*
is a welcome aid for people like me who can't read Roth, or his critics
and biographers, in German, and for any English-language readers who
might want an introduction to his work. And now, more than ever, is
the time to read him' Hermione Lee, *New York Review of Books*

'Vivid ... convincing ... It is Keiron Pim's substantial achievement
in *Endless Flight* to have shown us the magnitude of Roth's struggle
in a turbulent era that has alarming parallels with our own' George
Prochnik, *Times Literary Supplement*

'[Pim's] effort to understand the man in full is profound and the result
feels definitive' Dorian Lynskey, *Guardian*

'Not every great historical figure is guaranteed a great biographer,
and not every great writer is so fortunate as to get written about by
someone who can pen their own great sentences as well. Thankfully,
Joseph Roth's fortunes have been revived by this extraordinary new
biography, a remarkable and penetrating study of his life and times'
Devorah Baum

'A novelist of genius, an anti-nationalist prophet in the wilderness, a
human being capable of the monstrous: *Endless Flight* does humane
and painstaking justice to all these aspects, and more, of Joseph Roth's
short, utterly compelling life' David Kynaston

'Lucid and perceptive ... A masterly and moving biography' Richard
Bratby, *Critic*

'Pim is scrupulous in his research and fair in his assessments ... The further Pim delves, the richer the picture becomes' Rachel Seiffert, *Prospect*

'Pim is particularly good on Roth's Jewishness ... A dark story, movingly told' David Herman, *Jewish Chronicle*

'Thrilling ... Pim's detective work, untangling Roth's tortured (sometimes maddening) contradictions, is enormously impressive, and his analysis of Roth's work is incisive and sometimes revelatory' Samantha Ellis, *Literary Review*

'Pim is worthy of the mammoth task at hand, chronicling the complex story of Roth's ultimately tragic life with sensitivity, intelligence, and some serious and revelatory research ... An important biography' Jane Graham, *Big Issue*

'It's incredible that it's taken this long for an English-language biography of Joseph Roth to appear – and incredibly fortunate that Keiron Pim has been the one to do it, evoking with compassion and depth the work and the world of one of the greatest of modern writers' Benjamin Moser

'A superb biography of Joseph Roth, the first in English, which more than does justice to its complex and contradictory subject ... A compelling and moving picture of Roth's extraordinary talent alongside his tragic contradictions and flaws' Dr Jon Hughes, Director of Research, University of London

'Pim has told this vital and singular story with the deft tenacity and the passionate flexibility of attitude and tone that it requires, and his book is a mighty achievement' Patrick Mackie

'Wonderful ... A propulsive journey through European, Jewish, and literary life between the wars' Adam Foulds

Endless Flight

The Life of Joseph Roth

KEIRON PIM

GRANTA

Granta Publications, 12 Addison Avenue, London W11 4QR
First published in Great Britain by Granta Books, 2022
This paperback edition published by Granta Books, 2023

The illustration credits on pp. 511–512 and the acknowledgements on
pp. 455–6 constitute an extension of this copyright page. As stated on p. 23
and p. 455, most of the translations of Joseph Roth's work in this volume
are by Michael Hofmann, and are reproduced by his kind permission.

A CIP catalogue record for this book is available from the British Library.

1 3 5 7 9 10 8 6 4 2

ISBN 978 1 78378 511 7
eISBN 978 1 78378 648 0

Typeset by M Rules
Printed and bound by CPI Group (UK) Ltd, Croydon, CR0 4YY

www.granta.com

For my parents, Malcolm and Claudia, with love and gratitude.

I have covered many miles. Between the place where I was born, and the towns and villages I have lived in in the last ten years — and lived in only, apparently, to leave them again — lies my life, amenable more readily to spatial than to chronological measurement. The years I have put behind me are the roads I have travelled. Nowhere, in no parish register or cadastre is there a record of my name or date of birth. I have no home, aside from being at home in myself.

Joseph Roth, letter to Gustav Kiepenheuer on his
fiftieth birthday, June 1930, trans. Michael Hofmann

[Joseph Roth] was one of the first to despair in those times. His characters were always in flight, and he predicted everyone would have to flee. His books are no more than pale reflections of what he produced during those conversations in the dark hours of the night. In visionary images he depicted what we all dreaded and then fell into self-absorption again. When he looked up, he might casually remark: 'It's all nonsense, folks. Don't take my agonies so seriously, I simply don't know how to live.'

Das Land, das ich verlassen musste, by Max Tau (Bertelsmann, 1961), trans. Eileen Walliser-Schwartzbart

There are only two things that can destroy a healthy man: love trouble, ambition, and financial catastrophe. And that's already three things, and there are a lot more.

Fechsung, by Peter Altenberg (S. Fischer, 1918),
trans. Clive James

CONTENTS

PRE-FIRST WORLD WAR EUROPE

GALICIA

OVAKIA

NGARY

TRANSYLVANIA

IA

ARIAN EMPIRE 1914

A Memory of Joseph Roth

In February 2020 I spoke on the telephone with the ninety-year-old Dan Morgenstern, a noted jazz writer and Emeritus Director of the Institute of Jazz Studies at Rutgers University in Newark, New Jersey. He has lived in the USA since 1947 but was born in Munich and raised in Vienna, the son of Soma Morgenstern, a novelist and close friend of Joseph Roth. Dan is, to the best of my knowledge, the last surviving person to have known Roth.

'Here's my own tiny glimpse of Joseph Roth. In October 1938, my mother and I visited my father, Soma Morgenstern, in Paris. Soma and Roth were teenagers when they first met, and they were friends until the very end. I remember the hotel where both my father and Roth were staying, the Hôtel de la Poste, not too far from the Jardin du Luxembourg, and I remember Roth very well for a boy of not yet nine. That first encounter, at the hotel where we also stayed, in his favourite spot in the lobby, I was scared by his voice, which, at that late stage, was ravaged by alcohol yet quite resonant. It was pretty loud and very hoarse. "Aarr-rrr-rrr!", like that!

'It was a typical French hotel: when you came in there was the check-in desk on the right, then there were tables in the lobby, there was the one that we would call in Vienna his *Stammtisch*, his regular table, where he always sat. It was a round table where there was room, in addition to his chair, for two or three other people to sit. And that was the way it was. People came by, the way they do in France, for a glass of wine. Roth would sit there from the time he got up in the morning, and he would call for a drink: "*Garçon!*" He knew the *garçon* quite well by then, so when he called out he would come with his drink, because he knew what he was drinking: some liqueur, it was always the same. He would yell and the guy would come.

'So I was a little scared but very quickly I found that he was very nice to me, extra-nice to me, and I think there were sentimental reasons for that, I was his close friend's son. We became friends, sort of. When I came down in the morning he would pat me on the head and feed me centimes to put in the pinball machine, and he would buy me drinks – not alcohol, usually tomato juice.

'It was clear to me that my father was very concerned about him. He didn't say anything to me but it was clear he was looking out for him. Making sure that he ate something, making sure he had a bath. My father would be physically supportive of him and see to it that he got to his room all right. Sometimes we'd go for a little walk, my father and I and Roth. He was not walking too well. He had a cane by his side there on the chair, and he used the cane to get up and shuffle across the room.

'Unfortunately, he was considered to have very little time left. I was not old enough to be a proper judge of that, but I could tell that he was not well. When we left Paris, I remember saying goodbye to him, and even at my age I had the feeling it was not very likely that I would see him again. I think he wished me a good journey. He would have patted me on the head. He was a bit like a friendly bear to me. I can still hear that voice and recall its rhythm when he called for a drink.'

Introduction

Pictures of the Little Town

The air grows chill, the mists descend!
'Tis in the evening first our home we prize . . .

Faust, Part One by Johann Wolfgang von Goethe

In the plains of western Ukraine that once lay within the Austrian crownland of Galicia, there is a town called Brody that looks as you would imagine it might if it were built up over centuries as a commercial and cultural centre, then stripped of all that enabled it to flourish and allowed to fade for a century, its decline intermittently accelerated by warfare on its streets. Weathered floral friezes decorate Habsburg-era shopfronts, and paint peels from the solemn-faced corbels that support rusty, iron-railed balconies. Its old marketplace is an empty strip of tarmac, its synagogue a ruin. In the middle of town there is a street called Vulytsya Zolota where clusters of dilapidated buildings from its heyday still stand, conspicuously delicate between lumpen concrete flats and shops of the post-war Soviet period. Number 18 is now a confectioner; at the end of the nineteenth century, along with the since-rebuilt Number 20, it belonged to a rich tailor who stitched bright uniforms for the soldiers of the Imperial and Royal Army. A narrow alley runs between the two buildings. If you walk through it to the street, you see a former bookshop fronted with bas-relief busts of once-eminent men and, to your left, the ghostly old Hotel Bristol, dirty-white as the snow that covers the town through the winter. The alley leads back to a patch of land where a house once stood, and in that house in September 1894 a young woman nursed her newborn child, not knowing whether the husband who had abandoned her would come home.

Vulytsya Zolota (formerly Goldgasse) in Brody; the alley
leading from the street to where Roth's childhood home
stood; the former tailor's premises at Numbers 18–20.

Later her family told stories – resentful tales about this strange
man they had never quite trusted, about how he had vanished when
Maria Grübel needed him and left them to support her and the child.
Nachum Roth was, they said, on a steam train rattling through the
German countryside towards Berlin when his behaviour began to

disturb the other passengers. The former rabbinical student worked as a grain buyer for a Hamburg export company, but in the past few days his life had collapsed. Someone he trusted had stolen his grain from a store in the Silesian town of Kattowitz. He had dashed there with Maria to find the goods, but failed; he left her in Silesia and travelled the 500 miles to Hamburg to pacify his employers, but failed; now, ashamed and facing ruin, he was heading back to Kattowitz to bring her home to Brody. The experience had shattered him. His grasp on reality had for some time been tenuous, but here in the train carriage he seemed deranged. When the train reached the next station, Roth was manhandled to the platform and transferred to a German psychiatric institution, from where he was handed on to relatives in Rzeszow, Galicia. They knew a nearby Hasidic wonder-rabbi reputed to have miraculous healing powers, so they sent Roth to him.

Maria returned alone to Brody and waited for her husband but heard nothing. On 2 September, in all likelihood at her father's house in the courtyard off Vulytsya Zolota, known then to German-speaking Jews as Goldgasse, she gave birth to a boy, but Nachum Roth did not come to meet him.* After some time, Maria's brother Salomon Grübel arranged a meeting at the rabbi's premises. On being introduced to Grübel, Roth began to laugh and for the duration of their encounter he barely stopped. Grübel noted his handsome, blond-bearded face, with the same luminous eyes that had come to distinguish his young son. Roth had no comprehension that he was a father. He lived with the rabbi for the rest of his life. Years later the son would write: 'He must have been a strange man, an Austrian scallywag, a drinker and a spendthrift. He died insane when I was sixteen. His specialty was the melancholy which I inherited from him. I never saw him. But I remember when I was four or five, I had a dream of a man in whom I saw my father. Ten or twelve years after that, I first saw a photograph of my father. I had seen the face before. He was the man in my dream.'[1]

---

*It is likely that Maria Roth gave birth at home but this cannot be stated with certainty as there are no surviving birth, marriage and death certificates from Brody during the 1890s.

This was almost certainly an invention, but we can believe that he dreamed of the parent he never met. Willing his lost father into some form of existence – trying to replace the irreplaceable with substitutes both real and imaginary – would preoccupy Joseph Roth for his entire life.

A grand Ukrainian city just east of midway between Prague and Kyiv has become a shorthand for the mutability of place and identity in eastern Europe. Prior to 1991 it spent half a century as Lvov, within the Soviet Socialist Republic of Ukraine. Before that, it was the Polish city of Lwów for three decades – some Poles today maintain it is only on loan to their neighbours – and for a few months in 1918 it was the capital of the West Ukrainian People's Republic. On a modern map it's called Lviv, but if you look at one from the early 1900s you'll find it called Lemberg,* lying in Galicia at the eastern edge of the Austro-Hungarian Empire. (At that time, its Yiddish-speaking population called it Lemberik.) On both maps, if you run your finger sixty miles further east-north-east you'll find Brody.† On the older one it's by the Galician border with the Russian Empire, on today's it is well within Ukraine. The phrase '*u kraina*' means 'borderland'. An old border town in a borderland. Regardless of where the lines lie on the maps, Brody has always been somewhere in between, its history one of transience and migration. Lying as it does on the road from Lviv to Kyiv, people stream through daily, and some stop for a generation or two. Its population today is around 23,000,‡ not so different from when the 1900 Austro-Hungarian census recorded 16,400 inhabitants, but its demography and fabric are much changed. That year, 72 per cent of the residents were Jewish. At the community's peak in the late nineteenth century this figure was above 80 per cent. In March 1881 outraged Russians had wrongly blamed Jews

---

* Subsequent references to this city will use the name from the period in question.
† Pronounced somewhere indefinably between 'bro-dee' and '*braw*-dee'.
‡ Russia's invasion of Ukraine in early 2022 occurred as this book was being prepared to go to print. Brody and Lviv both came under attack, and residents were among the many Ukrainians to flee the country. Descriptions of buildings and population figures may therefore be out of date by the time of publication.

for the murder of the reforming Tsar Alexander II, venting their fury through pogroms in 200 towns around their country, which spurred thousands of people to dash over the border into Brody.

The town became known as the Polish Jerusalem and had an especially high population of Hasidim, people with a murmured prayer for every stage of the day, who were drawn there because in the seventeenth century it had been home to the Baal Shem Tov, their spiritual leader. The late-nineteenth-century side streets grew clustered with *yeshivot*, small centres of religious study, where black-clad boys wearing skullcaps and sidelocks would debate Talmudic law and spill out on to the pavements chattering in Yiddish, the lingua franca of Jewish Europe. Three times a day, three-quarters of Brody's population turned to face the real Jerusalem and pray. Like every Galician *shtetl* it had its revered, mystical wonder-rabbis, or *tzaddikim*. The wonder-rabbi dispensed blessings, worked miracles and issued sage guidance for every dilemma imaginable, assisted by a coterie of Hasidim who brought his meals and prayed with him, admitted and withheld his visitors.

On one occasion in 1924 the renowned *Frankfurter Zeitung* journalist and author Joseph Roth, until recently based in Vienna but presently engaged in a tour filing dispatches from Poland and Ukraine, resolved to visit such a rabbi; he would later describe this phenomenon in a study of the eastern Jews. This *tzaddik* was reputed to intercede not merely between man and God, 'but between man and his fellow man, which is still harder'.[2] Roth arrived in time for the Jewish high holidays, when the rabbi would hold court. He rose at five o'clock while the chilly Galician fogs lifted and the horses shivered, and set off in a farm cart with five mothers and their small children. The women were poultry traders, clad in black woollen cloths, and all were bound for the rabbi. They reached the town as the sun rose on what became a warm, gleaming autumn morning and Roth saw that many others had preceded him, some sleeping in barns and passageways while they awaited their audience, others squatting on wooden planks that formed crude pavements by the muddy street. His detached descriptions of the town's squalor and the people's coarseness imply he was entering foreign territory.

As the appointed hour neared, the hordes thronged around the rabbi's home. A burly, copper-bearded Hasid served as a gatekeeper, gruffly keeping them at bay. Roth caught his eye. The journalist's fur coat and high riding boots helped set him apart. He asked to speak to the rabbi. The man advised him to write down his problem and the rabbi would read it and pray for him. Roth insisted but met more resistance: *Can you come back after the holidays?* Roth pleaded and was told to go around the house and in through the kitchen, where he found a merchant who had enough money to skip the queue. When Roth's turn came, he entered a simple room to find the rabbi – black-bearded, grey-eyed, bony-handed with 'sharp white nails'[3] – sitting at a table by a window overlooking a courtyard. The man glanced at Roth as he asked what he wanted, then looked out of the window again. 'I replied that I had heard much about his wisdom and had wanted to meet him,' Roth wrote. 'God is wise!' the rabbi said, beckoning the reporter to come close; at which he shook Roth's hand and bade him a warm 'Farewell!'.[4]

Roth knew such men's limitations of old. There were no answers here, except to less exacting people's questions. Still, some insistent part of him remained fascinated by their legends. His record of this trip formed part of a perspicacious survey from Paris to Russia, also examining Jewish life in Berlin and Vienna, published in 1927 as *The Wandering Jews* (*Juden auf Wanderschaft*). He writes of the eastern Jews with unflinching clarity, some disdain at their lack of refinement, but more often sympathy and affection verging on admiration for their refusal to assimilate. If he is wry in evoking the unsophisticated eastern Jewish world, he is vitriolic about the diluted Judaism he sees in the West, as practised by the old *shtetl*-dwellers' grandsons, who need a church-style 'organ to put them in the mood',* and whose 'God is a redaction of nature, their prayer a formula. And on top of that they're proud of it!'[5] His subsequent description of the eastern

---

* He could well have been writing about the beautiful and famous Neue Synagoge on Oranienburger Strasse in Berlin, known for its organ-led choral services and built in the Moorish style to suggest a romantic connection with the Sephardic Jewish tradition rather than the Ashkenazic ethnicity of its congregants.

Hasidim's exuberant ring-dancing on the Feast of the Torah tingles with their energy. But while he personalises the narrative, intermittently switching into the first person to describe such encounters, he holds something back. Eastern Jews are always described in the third person. When he writes 'we' and 'us', he means Germans and Austrians. He suggests that he stands within that collective, not the Jewish tribe. Only an informed reader would know that, far from diligently investigating an alien world, in visiting Galicia Joseph Roth was returning home.

The unnamed *shtetl* his book describes is Brody if it is anywhere; like much of Roth's 'non-fiction', some details are likely polished, others transplanted. He deals in facts of the poetic and psychological kind more than the literalities of journalism. Of the five chief elements of reportage – who, what, where, when and why – he concerns himself with the first, second and last; but even with the 'who', the few deft strokes with which he draws his characters rarely include adornments such as names. Extrapolation and analysis take precedence over chronology, location and narrative. He is forensic on specific human foibles, on glancing moments that summon a psychological landscape, but is broad-brush regarding place and time. The text is an amalgam of observation, polemic and memories old and new; and those of Brody are a defining ingredient.

'The little town lies in the middle of a great plain, not bounded by any hill or forest or river,' he writes. Well, Brody lies in a plain, but it is enclosed by woodland and to the west by the Boldurka River; the town's name comes from the Ukrainian for 'ford'. 'It runs out into the plain. It begins with little huts and ends with them. After a while the huts are replaced by houses. Streets begin. One runs from north to south, the other from east to west. Where they intersect is the marketplace.'[6] Yes, and in pre-war Brody the houses gathered around this muddy cobbled rectangle where the roads cross. 'At the far end of the north-south street is the railway station.' This is correct too, and the tracks recede to vanishing points in the east and west, towards Kyiv and Lviv.

The old railway station building at Brody after the First World War.

On the streets are millers, labourers, broad-backed water carriers and – in roles just as menial but imbued with a purpose beyond their meagre remuneration – what Roth terms 'members of a religious proletariat':[7] the Torah scribes, ritual butchers, and makers of prayer shawls and candles. This could well be Brody, and previous books on Roth have asserted that it is; but it could be anywhere in Galicia. There are no defining details. The *shtetl* he conjures has a dreamlike quality, existing in a succession of intense moments loosely strung together: telling exchanges between unnamed characters that are over before we know it, playing out in tangential locations. Is it Brody? In the words of Helen Chambers, a Roth scholar and Emeritus Professor of German Literature at St Andrews University, 'I don't even know how much sense it makes to ask that. I think that's a very difficult question. Because even when you read reportage which is ostensibly factual, it's often fiction, and you have to remember that these people' – Roth and fellow German-language authors-cum-journalists such as Theodor Fontane – 'are writers, so they'll construct what they think is a good narrative, and it'll draw on things that they actually knew. But you can't say: "This is Brody, and this is somewhere else." They'll transfer a church from one place to another place. And that goes on a lot more, I think, than people are aware of.'[8]

Better to term it as Roth does: the little town. Yes, the *shtetl* is Brody if it is anywhere; but it is everywhere and nowhere, and never was anywhere specific apart from the place in Joseph Roth's mind where his memory met his imagination.

Brody Castle, owned by the wealthy Potocki family.

In Roth's remembered Brody there is a barracks to house blue-uniformed Austro-Hungarian Imperial Army troops, an imposing fortress synagogue dating from the eighteenth century, and a mansion on the outskirts owned by the Potocki family of Polish nobility. There is a narrow, crepuscular clockmaker's shop where an hourly cacophony erupts as if many cities' bell towers are 'all caught and imprisoned'[9] within its gloomy confines, and where he recalls desiring a pocket-watch so he might measure the 'endless sea'[10] of time that stretches ahead in childhood, even though this notion prompts 'a shiver of curiosity and foreboding'[11] he only otherwise associates with the town's cemetery. There is a row of canvas-covered wooden stalls by a squat arcaded building that form the marketplace, or *rynek*. Pictures from the early twentieth century show the market busy with shawled women, horse-drawn carts, cloth-capped boys, laden horses, bearded men in heavy coats; and down the road we see a church with a dome and cupola, for the Orthodox Christian minority.

Postcard of Brody market from the late nineteenth
or early twentieth century.

In his 1974 German-language biography of Roth, the American
scholar David Bronsen noted of the market that 'More than twenty
wholesalers and 200 retailers, nearly all of them Jewish, traded in corn,
cattle, fur, wool from Russia, cotton, silk goods, scythes from Upper
Austria, leather, jewels, pearls, brushes and feathers.'[12] They scraped an
existence in the poorest region of Austria–Hungary. Whereas the other
provinces experienced some economic uplift with the nineteenth-century
spread of capitalism, Galicia's industrial growth stood at one-fifth that of
the rest of the empire. It formed a quarter of the empire's land mass and
of its population. Of its seven million inhabitants, in the year of Roth's
birth three million were illiterate. In 1890, three-quarters of Galicians
worked in agriculture and less than one-tenth in industry. Most farmers
grew potatoes and cereal or bred livestock. The soil was rich and fertile,
the lakes and rivers teemed with fish, but while the landowners flourished, little of the wealth trickled down to the workers. According to
the enticingly titled 1888 text *Galician Misery in Numbers*, by Stanisław
Szczepanowski, the average inhabitant of the province consumed only
half as much food as the typical European, and had 25 per cent of the
average European work capacity. Around 50,000 people died of starvation

every year. Malnutrition led to lethargy, which led to low productivity, then to poverty. The poorest people of all were known as 'see-traders', those who were so desperate they'd sell anything they saw. The market was only the visible surface of the Brody economy: lurking out of view were a multitude of smugglers, who trafficked goods and people across the Russian border, laying blankets on the ground before them in winter so as not to leave footprints in the snow. *U kraina*, the borderland, a place where it paid best to live unnoticed, where stealth, discretion, deceit and transgression were woven into the fabric of daily life.

The view from a Lviv-bound aeroplane descending over western Ukraine reveals the terrain that shaped these people's lives. It is the land that Joseph Roth describes in his finest novel, *The Radetzky March* (*Radetzkymarsch*), one of great fertile levels scattered with small cruciform towns that abut vast forests, which from the plane window look like drapes of green crushed velvet, stroked and scuffed. The land's gentle contours are described by brown ribbon-fields, dusted green with sprouting crops. It must be damp, for some fields segue via marshes into lakes. As you descend further, in the minute before the wheels judder on the runway, you might see solitary labourers hoeing or harvesting by hand, straight-legged and bent-backed. A tethered tan goat grazes a broad circle. A red-beaked white stork struts by the roadside. A farmer bumps down a rutted gravelly track on his horse-drawn cart, just as Roth travelled upon almost a century ago. And you land and disembark and explore and confirm that in certain ways this patch of eastern Europe is little changed. In late spring, the sultry atmosphere is recognisable from his books. On a warm evening, the moist air thickens with gnats as you stand at the outskirts of Brody by the tangled, nettle-strewn edge of a dark forest. On a plinth is a tall marble slab bearing a Star of David and an inscription in Hebrew, Ukrainian and English: 'In the memory of the holy martyrs – Jews that were ruthlessly killed by the Nazi murderers.' This is where in 1942 and 1943 hundreds of Brody's Jewish men, women, boys and girls were taken into the woods to be machine-gunned into mass graves. Their ancestors lie yards away in a cemetery of two-metre-tall tombstones engraved with Hebrew script and biblical illustrations. Thousands of others were deported from a ghetto in the town to Belzec death camp.

Decorated gravestones at the Jewish cemetery, Brody.

Jews awaiting deportation from Brody, 1943.

A dozen had tried to hide in the ruins of their Great Synagogue, where Maria* Grübel and Nachum Roth married in 1892 in a lavish ceremony paid for by her brothers. Swathes of slender red bricks are

---

* She was also known as Mania and Miriam, the Polish and Jewish versions of her name.

exposed amid crumbling plaster on the remaining walls. The upper storeys' runs of blind arcading are abruptly smashed at one end, a classical column and capital supports half an archway, foliage bursts from the brickwork. A long iron girder props the collapsed interior, which is riddled with fallen rafters and twisted metalwork. A cracked frieze of carved script commemorates the synagogue's restoration in 1903 after a fire in the mid-nineteenth century, at least for those visitors who read Hebrew. Through the glassless windows, you see birds flying high above.

Top: Postcard of the Great Synagogue, Brody, early twentieth century.
Bottom: Ruins of the Great Synagogue, 2019.

Rabbi Nachman Krochmal, a Jewish theologian and philosopher born in Brody in 1785, once called it the town 'where wisdom and wealth meet; the Torah and understanding, trade and faith'.[13] No Jews live there today, but the economic decline long preceded the Holocaust. From 1779 to 1879 it enjoyed the status of a 'free town', with trading rights that brought great prosperity. When this was rescinded, Brody declined; by the time of Joseph Roth's birth there was a sadness in the air, and it was becoming somewhere people moved from, not to. The melancholy remains, heightened by the stark absence of its Jews, and rendered more unsettling still by the town's jumble of overlain, superseded and faintly present identities. Take Vulytsya Zolota: the erstwhile Goldgasse to those residents who were oriented towards Vienna, and Ulica Złota to those of Polish heritage (literally the three meant the same, politically they represented competing ethnicities). Walk the street that the young Joseph Roth walked and, owing to two wars' street battles and bombing topped off by half a century of Soviet rule, the strangeness is increased by brutal juxtapositions in its architecture and street furniture. Habsburg arabesque railings, a green-tiled art nouveau dome on the chemist; plastic window frames, garish advertisements, shop signs scrawled in overexcited cursive fonts. Power lines and telephone wires lattice the blue midday sky, hanging over the town like a vast spiderweb. The modern world began to encroach on Brody in the early twentieth century: electric street lamps arrived in 1911, thirty years after London, Berlin and Paris, until when the night sky above the Habsburg-era town was navy-black and speckled with countless stars. The evenings were still, but not silent. You might hear a few moments' raucous conversation while a tavern's doors opened to let a crew of Imperial Army officers stagger back to the barracks, or the silhouetted chevrons of wild geese calling across the dusky sky, or, at the town's edges, the croaking of frogs from the marshes on the plain. Horses, traders, soldiers, smugglers and wonder-rabbis, innkeepers and a starry night from within the town's limits; beyond them marshland, frogs, geese, fields and dark forest. These were the features of a Brody childhood in the earliest 1900s and, if one moved on as so many did, one's adult nostalgia.

Old postcard of Goldgasse, Brody.

Visit the railway station today and you find the line spanned by a Soviet-era footbridge that gives a view over the town. Just over to the east you see a district known as Schwaby, reflecting its origin as a Swabian German colony populated by farmers and Protestant clergy. In the early twentieth century around 10 per cent of Galicians were of German extraction, their ancestors having been lured there by the Viennese government, which hoped these sober and hard-working people would improve the land and raise the cultural tone. On the occasions when Roth conceded that Brody was his birthplace, sometimes he would try to lessen the shame by claiming he was born in Schwaby, placing him within a German ethnic group known for their loyalty to Vienna and the Habsburgs.

Joseph Roth was far from alone in feeling ambivalent about his connection to Galicia. When he acknowledged his origins, it was often in a spirit of disarming humility, a sudden exhausted abandonment of an unsustainable performance. 'The more Western the origins of a Jew, the more Jews there are for him to look down on,' he once observed. 'The Frankfurt Jew despises the Berlin Jew, the Berlin Jew despises the Viennese Jew, the Viennese Jew despises the Warsaw Jew. Then there are Jews from all the way back in Galicia, upon whom they all look down, and that's where I come from, the lowest of all Jews.'[14]

The lowest of all Jews, looked down upon by everyone – including by himself as he scaled the social strata of the central and western European capitals, developing a split identity that straddled *de haut en bas* snobbery and self-disgust. It was an image that would gnaw at him throughout his life, even as literary acclaim placed him in high esteem. He would, dichotomous as ever, evoke his homeland in terms of shame and pride: he internalised his hosts' contempt for the east, rarely returning in person and obscuring his origins there, but wrote nostalgically of the place and its people in his fiction, more so the longer he stayed away.

Within Brody, though, his family were not the lowest of all Jews; they perched a couple of rungs up the social ladder, hanging on somewhere in the lower reaches of the middle class. He would always know financial hardship, but his poverty was of the genteel rather than proletarian variety, a mode that established itself in a childhood segregated from the neighbouring hoi polloi. Maria never encouraged him to think of Brody as a place to belong but rather to transcend. As Dennis Marks put it in his short study *Wandering Jew: The Search for Joseph Roth*, his 'possessive mother brought her son up to be a German Jew – or more accurately, an Austro-German Jew – rather than a Galitzianer'.[15] Anyone aspirational would look west rather than root themselves in a town that prompted embarrassment. The credulous '*Brodyer narunim*', or 'fools of Brody', were a Jewish comic archetype. With its penury and illiteracy the place was a byword for eastern backwardness, embodying all that was guaranteed to wrinkle the noses of the 'assimilated' Jews over to the west. From the perspective of a salon in Vienna, Brody lay beyond the eastern horizon and one could pretend it did not exist. To those such as Stefan Zweig, the *Ostjuden*[*] were an embarrassing distant branch of the family better ignored than embraced: the word 'Brody' summoned images of the squalid masses their ancestors had

---

[*] The term popularly used by German and Austrian Jews from the early twentieth century onwards to describe eastern European Jewry.

striven to leave behind. When the First World War arrived, writes
Volker Weidermann, 'In Vienna no one wanted to fight for Brody,
certainly not any intellectuals, and most certainly not Stefan Zweig.'[16]
But as a thirty-three-year-old Joseph Roth would drily remark in *The
Wandering Jews*, published in 1927 as he and Zweig embarked on one
of his life's defining friendships, 'Half of all the Jews who today speak
contemptuously or disparagingly of the East had grandfathers who
came from Tarnopol',[17] the nearby city in western Ukraine.

In 1937, Roth wrote a preface to a new edition of that book, which
was published into a darker world than the one that spawned its creation. If Roth had sensed the twilight a decade earlier, in the aftermath
of the Nuremberg Laws he knew night was falling. What, he asked
as he sat exiled in Paris, writing between gulps of brandy, 'is a man
without papers? Rather less, let me tell you, than papers without a
man!'[18] By now he was such a man, and again in this preface he analysed his own situation under the auspices of writing about others': in
this case, German Jewish émigrés, for whom 'life nowadays hangs from
a passport as it once used to hang by the fabled thread. The scissors
once wielded by the Fates have come into the possession of consulates,
embassies and plainclothesmen. No one loves victims, not even their
fellow victims. At most they are loved by holy and devout people, who
are as despised by this vulgarised world as the Jews are. Where can
they go? . . .

'Oh – the whole world thinks in such tired, worn, traditional clichés. It never asks the wanderer where he's going, only ever where he's
come from. And what matters to the wanderer is his destination, not
his point of departure.'[19]

Maria named her son after her grandfather, Moische Jossif Gräber,
whose surname presumably derived from his trade: he was a mon-
umental sculptor who lived near the cemetery. His children, among
them Maria's father Jechiel, modified the name to Grübel. At the
town's Jewish Register Office, Jechiel Grübel recorded the birth of
his grandson Moses Joseph Roth – but as the boy began to display a
preternatural wisdom and intelligence, he became known as 'Muniu',

a diminutive* of Solomon, as in the biblical king. Often the nickname was shorter still, just 'Mu'.

Many years later he would write of his earliest memories in a German periodical titled *Die Literarische Welt*. From the age of seven onwards, he said, his memories flowed in a near-continuous stream of recollection, but he recalled one incident from when he was three, divided from the rest so that 'this earliest experience seems to stand all alone, like a brightly lit scene surrounded by darkness, and therefore all the more luminous'.† It was a memory, he said, of the first sad moment of his life. Standing in his small bedroom he saw a blue winter sky, snow on the windowsill, 'a few intricate ice flowers on the right-hand window'. A short, elderly woman entered, her head and shoulders wrapped in a grey-brown shawl. His mother moved the bedding from his cradle to a brown armchair. Suddenly the old woman picked up the cradle and held it to her chest 'as if it were a thing of no particular weight or dimensions', spoke at length, '[flashed] her long yellow teeth', and left the house. 'I am left feeling sad, inconsolably helpless and sad,' he writes. 'I seem to understand that I have lost something irrecoverable. I have in a certain sense been robbed. I start to cry, and am taken to a large white bed, which is my mother's. There I fall asleep.' When he asked his mother a decade later, she could not recall the day, nor to whom she had given his cradle. 'I wasn't surprised, nor was I upset with her. She had merely missed the first grief of my life. She had no idea.' All that perturbed him was that she could not even

---

* Roth's Galician friend Józef Wittlin once remarked: 'The proximity of Romania must have had an effect on the exotic diminutive forms of the local first names too, which instead of the usual Polish -ek ending, came out as . . . Józiu, Biziu, Busiu, Filu, Fulu, Milu, Dziuniu, Maniu' and so on. 'My Lwów', in Józef Wittlin and Philippe Sands, *City of Lions* (Pushkin Press, 2016), Kindle edition.

† Impossible to verify this story, but it tells us how Roth viewed his childhood and wished it to be perceived by others: as a period that established the pattern by which his comforting metaphorical cradles – professional niches, spiritual homes – would suddenly vanish. Discussing 'The Cradle' in the *London Review of Books*, Michael Hofmann notes that 'It brings to mind what Roth said about his revered Heine: "Maybe he did make up the odd fact, but then he saw things the way they ought to be. His eye was more than visual apparatus and optic nerve."' Michael Hofmann, 'Conspiratorial Hapsburger', *London Review of Books*, vol. 9, no. 5, 5 March 1987, accessed at https://www.lrb.co.uk/the-paper/v09/n05/michael-hofmann/conspiratorial-hapsburger

remember whether it happened in summer or winter. 'I have the feeling that on that day, in that hour I became a grown-up – only briefly
perhaps, but long enough to be sad, as sad as a grown-up, and perhaps
for a better reason.'[20] It is easy to project retrospective knowledge on
to the blankness of an infant's face but, looking at photographs of the
boy aged three and four, it does seem he was precocious not only in his
intelligence but in his sadness.

Studio photographs of the young Moses Joseph Roth.

The house where Moses grew up and the streets beyond churned with
characters who crossed his withering gaze – the determined and forbidding Maria, the elderly Jechiel, a cast of passing aunts and uncles,
cameos from maids and tutors, and then the chancers, smugglers, 'fools
of Brody', market traders and innkeepers – but there was someone
missing. The gentleman from his dream, the handsome face in the
photograph. In his son's mind Nachum Roth became an ever-present
unknown, a mannequin to dress in varying guises, a screen on which
to project a riotous gallery of invented figures. The boy's imagined
relationship with his father is a picaresque, a frieze peopled with heroes
and cads, roués and aristocrats, decorated soldiers and dissipated artists,
some of them Nachum in multiple roles, others Moses himself, the pair
playing out intrigues and romances over time against the backdrop of

an Austro-Hungarian Empire in decline. Moses is born to a Russian mother just outside Brody in the German colony of Schwabendorf, a baptised Catholic of noble descent, the son of a Polish count; here is his father as a celebrated Viennese armament maker, and now an artist, now a railwayman, now a roguish army officer. The faces are the same, only the uniforms change. The boy ages and becomes Joseph,* a name less overtly Jewish than Moses. It is a *Rake's Progress* in which duplicitous characters vie for prominence. By the 1920s Joseph is himself an esteemed soldier like his fictional father, a hero of the First World War, a gallant lieutenant in the 24th Lancers of the Imperial and Royal Army who formed part of the military escort at Emperor Franz Joseph's burial. We see him as a fearless fighter on the eastern front, now as a prisoner of war in frozen Siberia, and now as he stands with pride to receive a trio of medals for service and valour.

This is Joseph Roth's dreamscape, an imagined world from which he plucked the stories that he told his readers and the lies he told his friends: his biographer David Bronsen concluded he was a 'mythomaniac'.[21] At different times he attributed each of these qualities and origins to himself and his father, but none was true.† Who Joseph Roth actually was is the subject of this biography; that and how, despite a torturous personal decline that paralleled the collapse of the civilised world, he drew from his multiple traumas to create works that endure owing to their conscience, percipience, ironic humour and naked humanity. Like Roth himself, his characters strain for agency in a tumultuous world like birds trying to fly through a gale.

Many of the memories of Roth in this book come from the interviews Bronsen conducted with his friends and family in the 1960s and 1970s. Others come from Soma Morgenstern and Géza von Cziffra's memoirs of their times with Roth. Morgenstern wrote his in the 1970s, and von Cziffra in the early 1980s. Both include dialogue

---

* The German pronunciation of Joseph Roth is approximately 'Yosef Rote', with an 'R' from the back of the throat.
† As we will see later, it is just possible – or at least not impossible – that he did indeed stand in the late emperor's military guard, though not as a lieutenant in the 24th Lancers.

remembered from more than forty years earlier, newly translated by Michael Struppek: their accounts of these conversations should be considered indicative of the content rather than entirely accurate. Most of the quotations from Roth's work come from translations by Michael Hofmann. They reveal to English speakers a voice by turns nimble and melancholic, wry and sceptical, in his correspondence often brusque and splenetic, and in his fiction consistently moral and perceptive. Translation turns a wall into a window; even glass has its distortions and no translation is perfect, but Hofmann's sensitive, coruscating renderings of Roth's prose during the past thirty years have revealed to anglophone readers his stature as one of the foremost twentieth-century European writers.

As a journalist Roth traced the continent's trajectory between the wars in prose of sublime lyricism, insight and empathy. As a novelist he produced the definitive elegy for Austria-Hungary in his masterpiece *The Radetzky March*, one of a half-dozen works that form a still-greater composite picture of the little town that he once called home. The closer we inspect the borderline between his fiction and non-fiction, the more it melts away, as does the border between his public work and private life. Across his oeuvre he is a poet of the marginalised, the alienated and the dispossessed: of those who sought refuge after their homelands were destroyed, of those whose fractured lives reflected his own. In a time when our social fabric is fraying once more, when displacement, migration and transience are again the norm and ugly reductive nationalisms threaten to overpower liberal aspirations, Roth speaks to us with as much urgency and power as he did to those who read him during his brief lifetime.

PART ONE

The nine-year-old Moses Joseph Roth with his mother, Maria.

Chapter One

I loved to make myself invisible. I used to dream of a cape
of invisibility ... I was capable of persuading myself that I
was invisible, although really I knew that everyone could
see me. I liked hiding. I was an expert at hide-and-seek, no
one ever found me.

'Youth', in *Collected Shorter Fiction of Joseph Roth*

Every day the family's neighbours saw Maria Roth lead her young son
Moses by hand on the short walk to the Baron Hirsch Grundschule
in Pfarrgasse, where she would wait for five hours until the end of the
school day, take his hand again and guide him back to the home they
shared with her father, Jechiel Grübel. The house no longer exists,
but the tailor's premises it stood behind at 18–20 Vulytsya Zolota are
partly intact. The tailor, Kalman Ballon, was a member of the town's
chamber of commerce and did a good trade in fitting out the soldiers
from the Brody garrison. 'In the small town from which Joseph Roth
came,' wrote Stefan Zweig in 1939, 'the Jews looked gratefully across
to Vienna; there, unreachable like a god in the clouds, dwelt the old,
the ancient Emperor Franz Joseph, and they praised and loved in reverence this distant emperor like a legend, they honoured and admired
the colourful angels of this god, the officers, the Uhlans and dragoons,
who brought a glimmer of bright colour into their lowly, dull, poor
world.'[1] Investigations in the Ukraine National Archives conducted
for this book by the Lviv-based researcher Alex Dunai revealed the
location of Roth's first home and the tailor's shop where these 'colourful angels' brightened what was otherwise a childhood of painful

absences.* Jechiel Grübel was widowed: his wife Rachel died giving
birth to their seventh child. Among the carved gravestones in the
old Brody cemetery stands one showing a broken tree with seven
forlorn birds. Maria and her sister Rebekka took on responsibility for
running the household and raising their younger siblings. Perhaps it
was grief that turned Jechiel's hair white in his late twenties, the age
when he sat for a portrait; that and his arduous life as a cloth merchant

who bought his goods in England and
sold them to tailors in Galicia. He was
also a Jewish scholar who studied under
the eminent conservative Brody rabbi
Salomon Kluger.

The Grübel aunts, uncles and cousins
were a constant presence in the young
Moses' life. Jechiel was in all likelihood primarily a Yiddish speaker. The
younger generations of his household
spoke some Yiddish too, and Maria sang

A portrait of Jechiel Grübel,
grandfather of Joseph Roth.

old Ukrainian songs when she was sad,
but German was her language of choice
at home: it was more dignified, befitting

her ambitions for her son. She ensured he received a good education.

---

* Further details of Alex Dunai's research may help future students of Roth's life.
He checked Galician business directories and *Szematyzms* (directories published from
1782 to 1914 listing Austrian administration officials, local professionals and members
of social, business, charitable and cultural organisations). These showed that Kalman
Ballon was on the board of the town's chamber of commerce from 1880 to 1906, and
the owner of a men's cloth retail shop and warehouse until at least 1913. Ballon's business partner was named Wolf Kramrisch. Land ownership records for 1879 revealed
that Ballon owned the house no. 765/766 on parcel of land no. 821. This property was
behind the business premises on Vulytsya Zolota. The alley between the buildings to
the property dates back at least to 1844, when it appears on the cadastral map. Dunai
explained: 'The majority of stone buildings one can see now in Brody have the same
dimensions as in 1844 because sizes were limited by the parcel number, and, which
is important, by old basements. Basements usually were made from stone, had deep
cellars and it was a common practice to construct a new building on the old base-
ment. The house on parcel no. 82 does not exist anymore ... but the buildings on
Vulytsya Zolota and even the original path between them are still there. It looks like
the building number 18 is original. Building number 20 looks like it was partially
reconstructed, especially the exterior.'

German was also the primary language at the *Grundschule*, which he attended from 1901 to 1905. The school day began at 8 a.m. and Moses sat on the right-hand side of the classroom with the other boys, while all the girls sat on the left. They learned some Polish and Ukrainian, and translated psalms and prayers from Hebrew. Until the 1890s most Galician Jewish boys had been taught by rabbis in religious *cheders*; then came the establishment of the free, state-supported Baron Hirsch schools, which taught a Jewish-oriented curriculum but delivered in German rather than Hebrew or Yiddish. The only part of the curriculum delivered in Hebrew was the Saturday morning religious service, held at the Great Synagogue. The rest of Moses' family were regular worshippers there too. Maria kept a kosher household, and they fasted on Yom Kippur. Under Jechiel's influence it was an Orthodox Jewish home. They were *frum*, devout believers who lived a religious life, as Moses recalled in 1912 in a few lines of verse in a letter to his cousin Willy Grübel:

And grandfather teaches me to pray
Right from the heart, pious and delicate
And I prayed so soulfully
Hot and honest before going to bed.

Jechiel Grübel died in 1907. A few months later Moses turned thirteen. It may be that his grandfather's death lessened his and Maria's obligation to Orthodox custom and freed them to identify further with German culture: having already eschewed *cheder* for the Hirsch school, now he rejected the traditional *bar mitzvah*. Moses instead underwent confirmation, an alternative preferred within the Reform Judaism tradition established in the early nineteenth century by Israel Jacobson, a wealthy German businessman. Later he would write that from the ages of fourteen to sixteen he was an atheist, because God was nowhere to be seen; then he concluded it was possible God was merely hiding from him. Whether or not he believed, he absorbed irrational ideas that would shape his adult outlook. He wavered between notions of God as covert and interventionist: the possibility of miracles possessed him. His friend Géza von Cziffra later wrote: 'Roth was as superstitious as a hag. Friday the thirteenth, a black cat crossing the path, a white horse or bird droppings on your hat – all signs of good or ill fate. If you mocked this, he would have metaphysical explanations. He would refer to the Hasidic belief in miracles held by the Orthodox Jews of his homeland, who saw logic as detrimental to faith.'[2] For the Hasidim, miracles were not a thing of the distant past: quite the opposite. 'Miracles no longer startled anyone,' wrote the Polish-American rabbi Abraham Heschel in 1967, looking back on the pre-war days, 'and it was no surprise to discover among one's contemporaries a man who attained contact with the Holy Spirit'.[3]

By the time of his childhood, the tensions in his family were a microcosm of the arguments raging across European Jewish culture. Within Germany and Austria assimilation seemed a viable prospect, albeit at an acknowledged cost: 'German Jews were not accepted as Jews, but were under pressure to acquire the educational and social characteristics of the German middle class, summed up in the word '*Bildung*'.* The great Moses Mendelssohn was seen as the example to follow,'[4] writes the Roth scholar Ritchie Robertson, referring to the eighteenth-century philosopher whose ideas informed the *Haskalah*, or Jewish Enlightenment – a rationalist, free-thinking movement some of whose principal figures lived in Brody, among them the aforementioned Rabbi Nachman Krochmal. Its adherents rejected mysticism: they accepted the idea of miracles as part of biblical legend but distanced themselves from the enduring Hasidic belief in their daily possibility. Mendelssohn was, in Amos Elon's words, 'One of the first practicing Jews to be fully assimilated into high German culture',[5] 'the first in a long line of assimilated German Jews who worshipped German culture and civilization',[6] and a man who in turn was widely admired by gentile Enlightenment thinkers in Berlin. German Jews 'celebrated, idealized and drew hope from'[7] such friendships.

Out on the distant eastern fringes of the Austro-Hungarian Empire the prospects of such assimilation were diminished. The author Karl Emil Franzos (1848–1904), a Galician-born Jew of Sephardic ancestry, examined the situation of eastern Orthodox Jews in a series of books

---

* Meaning the process of self-cultivation and education.

collectively titled *Aus Halb-Asien*, 'half-Asia' being his term for the great swathe of eastern Europe stretching down to the Black Sea. An advocate for Germanisation and assimilation, Franzos castigated the beliefs and practices of the *Ostjuden*. Antisemitic gentile German writers through the nineteenth century had depicted Jews both at home and to the east as alien or grotesque.* Jewish novelists, in turn, would often 'portray the Jews as possessing all the middle-class German virtues, in particular a warm domestic life', in fiction that 'tends to be sentimental, nostalgic and idyllic' and 'tones down the alien character of Jewish culture by representing it as quaint but perfectly intelligible'.[8]

The eastern Jews proved harder to defend from a German-normative perspective. Franzos criticised their customs as 'deplorable forms of oppression and obstacles to progress'. He 'inveighs against the traditional *kheyder*† school and the frequent brutality of its teachers', 'the custom of arranging marriages for children aged twelve or thirteen' and 'the activities of the *Fehlermacher*, whose business is to save young men from military recruitment by inducing illnesses or injuries'.[9] But he saved his most vicious attacks for Orthodox and in particular Hasidic rabbis, whom he held responsible for standing between the Jews and enlightenment, instead keeping their followers in Galician darkness. Many Jews felt themselves pulled in two directions by forces both without and within them. As Elon puts it, 'The duality of German and Jew – two souls within a single body – would preoccupy and torment German Jews throughout the nineteenth century and the first decades of the twentieth.'[10] These were the existential arguments playing out in and around eastern Jewish families who leaned towards German culture. They sank deep into Moses Joseph Roth's mind in his formative years, and would rage on unresolved throughout his life.

---

* 'German-Jewish writers had to assist the process of assimilation by contending against fictional conventions representing the Jews as irredeemably alien, like those in Droste-Hülshoff's *Die Judenbuche*, or as repulsive, dishonest and calculating, like Veitel Itzig in Freytag's *Soll und Haben* and Moses Freudenstein in Raabe's *Der Hungerpastor*.' Ritchie Robertson, 'Roth's *Hiob* and the Traditions of Ghetto Fiction', in *Co-Existent Contradictions: Joseph Roth in Retrospect: Papers of the 1989 Joseph Roth Symposium at Leeds University to Commemorate the 50th Anniversary of his Death*, ed. Helen Chambers (Ariadne Press, 1991), p. 186.
† An alternative spelling of *cheder*.

After Jechiel Grübel's death, Maria and her son moved from Goldgasse to a flat in Bahngasse,* taking in lodgers to help meet the rent. One of them, Moses Wasser, was a schoolmate of Roth's. 'It was a small, two-family wooden house at ground level with a plastered and gabled roof,' he later recalled. 'There was an apple tree in front of the house and in the garden a table where we sometimes ate in summer ... Roth and his mother's flat was furnished in a plain, middle-class style, but Roth himself always went neatly dressed.'[11]

By then he had progressed to the town's Royal Imperial Crown Prince Rudolf Gymnasium, one of only two German-speaking secondary schools in Galicia, the other being in Lemberg. He studied there from 1905 until 1913. The pupils came from three religious backgrounds: Judaism, Roman Catholicism and Eastern Orthodoxy. The headteacher was an antisemite who imposed quotas on the number of Jewish boys who could receive academic prizes, whereas none applied to Christians. Although Jewish teachers were in a minority, half the 700 pupils were Jewish, and in Roth's class of thirty-four pupils that proportion rose to two-thirds. Dr Oser Frost gave lectures on Jewish history and led pupils to the Great Synagogue, where they continued to attend the Saturday morning service. Roth and his peers also attended annual services there on 18 August, the birthday of Franz Joseph, Emperor of Austria-Hungary. In the space occupied today by mangled ironwork and weeds were held services of great ceremony and grandeur, attended by the district commissioner and the commander of the garrison.

For all that Jews formed a majority in Brody, they still felt looked down upon, Roth once recalled. 'And that was their own fault,' he claimed:

> In fact I had to suffer less repudiation than my fellow believers. I was the best pupil in my class, my Jewish classmates were envious, they were even hostile towards me. The others not so much, they were less ambitious at school. Their future was secured by the rank their parents held in society or by their fortunes. At least

---

* Like their house in Goldgasse, this property no longer exists.

that seemed to be the case. No one had imagined the war and its consequences. I even had a Catholic friend, or let's say something similar to a friend; we shared our way home. This friend told me something that will stay with me forever. It happened on a Sabbath, when no Jew is allowed to do any kind of work. Crown Prince Rudolf though did not make allowances for this, Jewish pupils had to go to school as everybody else. We were about to say our goodbyes after we walked home together. It was at the corner of Bahngasse, where I lived, and four orthodox Jews passed us. They wore long, black caftans which nearly touched the muddy ground of the road and black velvet hats, lined with sable fur. Nothing out of the ordinary in Brody, rather an everyday sight.

Roth said the four of them looked so alike in appearance and clothing that they could have been identical quadruplets:

Their noses and their overly long side curls had the same length. They were young and seemed to be in a hurry. They marched side by side in unison.

We gave way, my friend followed them with his gaze and asked: 'Now honestly, Moses, don't they look like fleeing scarecrows?' Since I did not reply he probed further: 'Can't the Jews dress like normal people?'

I shrugged and walked on, but silently agreed. For the very first time I questioned whether Jews behaved correctly towards their environment. I asked myself why they wore different clothes than the rest, why they had different habits, different traditions, different festivals? Why did they have to stand out from Austrians, Poles and Russians, even on the outside, though they inhabited the same country and the same city? For the first time I wondered if Jews had not to blame themselves for their isolation.[12]

The Crown Prince Rudolf Gymnasium is little changed. The same old corridors throng with boisterous, chattering children. Their footsteps echo from the dulled wooden flooring to the high vaulted ceilings, against large round windows and sage-green-painted heavy doors. But a small room now houses a display celebrating eminent alumni, five of whom are commemorated in a sculpture on the forecourt, where the steely dignity of Roth's visage is somewhat undermined by lavish streaks of bird droppings.

The *Gymnasium* in Brody, with a sculpture commemorating
Roth and other alumni.

Within this building the teenage Moses asserted his credentials as someone whose future lay beyond the town. He excelled in studying literature, cultivated an air of detachment and would do his classmates' homework for them, a characteristic display of simultaneous generosity and superiority. His German Literature master was a Polish Jew named Max Landau, with whom he formed a relationship that endured long after leaving the school. Roth was combative in classroom discussions and brilliant in his analysis, and Landau's admiration for him was plain to see. 'Now we will allow ourselves a treat,' he would declare to the class, before reading aloud an essay by his star pupil. Landau was a poet and nurtured Roth's ambitions in that field, treating his work with a seriousness that extended to giving him especial criticism in front of his classmates when he fell short of his potential: Landau considered his verse too Romantic at times and lacking in structural discipline.

For all his apparent self-confidence, Roth would later admit to having been a nervous student. He recalled his schooldays in an article titled 'From the Diary of the Schoolboy Joseph Roth', written in 1930 for a German newspaper. 'The foolish hope that had accompanied me from my first day at school right up to the eve of the leaving certificate examinations, that, certificate in hand, I would finally escape from the great and small shameful and degrading harassments of school was, sadly, disappointed by reality to a devastating degree ... Every book and every essay that I write [today], I deliver with the old familiar anxiety with which I used to accompany my exercise books on their perilous way some twenty or more years ago.'[13]

He masked his anxieties well. His demeanour was one of a young man more on a par with his teachers than his contemporaries. Landau and Roth differed in opinion on one major issue: the future of Galician culture and identity. Landau cleaved towards those of his Polish origins. Roth had little time for what were termed the 'Polish subjects', known collectively as '*Krajowka*'. He once remarked: 'My Polish only stretches from here to Cracow',[14] i.e., not far. German was, after all, the language of the civilised world. 'For the Eastern European Jew,' he once said, 'Germany is ... the land of Goethe and Schiller, of the German poets, familiar to every Jewish boy who is eager to learn ...' .[15]

But after Roth's admission to the school, one class after another switched from learning in German as the local Polish nobility reasserted its culture in this contested town. He belonged to the last year taught in German throughout. He must have felt he was at the end of an era. His identification with German and Austrian culture also elicited an admiration for the Habsburg rulers that his contemporaries found odd. One of them, named Abraham Pares, remembered a visit to Roth's home during their schooldays:

At the grammar school Roth made virtually no close contacts, either with the Catholic or the Jewish pupils. I too had little contact with him, though perhaps I was the only one who exchanged a few words with him now and then. So it happened that on one occasion he invited me home. He was in the fifth class at the time, so he was sixteen. I've never forgotten that visit. Roth received me in a large room where I first had to accustom myself to the dim light, for it was broad daylight outside. Roth's mother, a good-looking, imposing figure, paced up and down the room, hardly noticed me, and didn't even greet me, which made an eerie impression on me ... Roth himself had a serious and solitary air, but he was manifestly pleased by my visit. His first words were: 'Nobody visits us. My mother does not wish it. You're the first person to visit me here.' I told him that we Jewish pupils belonged to a Zionist society, which in actual fact was forbidden, but this didn't prevent us from holding lots of meetings in each other's houses. There we discussed Jewish culture and history, but there were also purely social occasions. When I asked him why he didn't join our society, Roth replied: 'I am for assimilation!' He must have noticed my amazement, for he immediately added: 'But not here.' (I can still remember how he pointed to the floor.) 'I'm not for assimilation with Poland but with Austria.' As soon as I heard that I had no further interest in Roth. I thought to myself, 'What do the Habsburgs have to do with us?' And I never visited him again.[16]

What had the Habsburgs to do with a couple of boys living on their empire's periphery, in an impoverished town more than 400 miles from the grandeur and refinement of Vienna? The remote ministers in the capital's vast, palatial Hofburg made decisions from afar over a land that most Viennese held in contempt – why would Jewish Galicians want to tighten rather than weaken this tenuous and onesided relationship? By now many people considered the Habsburgs a relic of the last century, somewhat absurd and ripe for ridicule. The ubiquitous description 'Kaiserlich und Königlich' – Imperial and royal – was abbreviated to 'k. und k.', which with the German pronunciation of 'k' suggested 'kaka' or excrement; in the Austrian writer Robert Musil's epic satire of the empire's last days, The Man Without Qualities, he renames it Kakania. It had been a long decline for one of the world's most powerful families. The Habsburg Empire stretched across 240,000 square miles of Europe and, aside from Austrians, its fifty million inhabitants included Czechs, Hungarians, Serbs, Croats, Bosnians, Slovenes, Romanians, the Italians of southern Tyrol and Trieste, the Poles and Ruthenians[*] in Galicia and the Russians in western Ukraine. For much of its existence the empire reached into even further-flung corners of Europe. Its beginnings lay in the thirteenth century with Rudolf I, King of Germany, a member of the Habsburg family who lived at Habsburg Castle in the Duchy of Swabia (now in Switzerland). From there, one of the great European dynasties unfolded and endured despite the odds for almost seven centuries. As Simon Winder puts it in his entertaining history of the Habsburgs, 'All empires are in some measure accidental, but theirs was particularly so, as sexual failure, madness or death in battle tipped a great pile of kingdoms, dukedoms and assorted marches and counties into their laps.'[17]

In 1282 Rudolf acquired the Duchy of Austria. In the fifteenth century Maximilian acquired the Netherlands by marriage. In a political manoeuvre to establish the Habsburg dynasty in Spain he had his son Philip, born in Bruges, married to a gifted Spanish princess named Joanna. Later she succumbed to depression and became known, somewhat unfairly, as Joanna the Mad – and, judging by his portraits, her husband's soubriquet may also have been inaccurate, although Philip the Handsome was good-looking by Habsburg standards.[†] When Charles V abdicated in 1556 (owing to ill-health, principally gout) the empire was divided into two, with his brother Ferdinand I ruling Austria, Hungary and Bohemia, and Charles's son Philip II ruling Spain, the Netherlands, Burgundy and parts of Italy. The latter arm of the dynasty ceased to exist in 1700 when Charles II died, reducing the Habsburg Empire to an agglomeration of territories in central and

---

[*] Eastern Slavs, including Ukrainians.
[†] Repeated intermarriage between the Austrian and Spanish branches meant the family became notoriously inbred, which notably presented itself in the form of a deformity known as the 'Habsburg jaw'. In the case of Charles II of Spain, it was so severe he struggled to eat or speak.

eastern Europe, chief among them Austria and Hungary. In 1804 it became known as the Austrian Empire.

In July 1848 came one of the empire's last major military victories, at the Battle of Custoza, where troops led by Field Marshal Joseph Radetzky defeated Sardinian insurgents attempting to overthrow the Austrian occupation; in his honour Johann Strauss immediately wrote the 'Radetzky March', which received its first public performance a few weeks later. The revolutions of that year threatened the empire, now ruled by Ferdinand I. In Hungary revolutionaries declared independence but said he would still be their king. When Ferdinand abdicated at the end of the year, a move intended to placate his rivals, he was replaced by the eighteen-year-old Franz Joseph I, who would go on to become one of Europe's longest-serving monarchs, ruling through the rest of the nineteenth century and onwards until his death in 1916. While Franz Joseph's long reign was largely stable, his personal life was tragic. His brother Maximilian was executed in Mexico, his wife Empress Elisabeth was assassinated and their son, Crown Prince Rudolf, died in a suicide pact with his lover in 1889. The Brody education authorities responded by naming the secondary school after him.

These years saw Austria's military fortunes begin to wane. In 1859 at the Battle of Solferino during the Second Italian War of Independence, 130,000 Austrian troops led by Franz Joseph were beaten decisively by the Franco-Sardinian Alliance. The emperor never again personally led his soldiers into battle. Then defeat in the Austro-Prussian War in 1866 prompted the *Ausgleich* between the Austrian and Hungarian areas of the empire and thus the creation of the Dual Monarchy. The Austro-Hungarian Empire had two parts, as you might expect – one ruled by the Austrians, the other by the Hungarians, with separate governments and laws – but they shared a foreign policy, an army and a ruler. Franz Joseph I was Emperor of Austria and King of Hungary, overseeing their seventeen crownlands; that of Galicia and Lodomeria took its name from the Latinised forms of Halych, part of medieval Ruthenia (now Ukraine), and the eleventh-century ruling prince, Vladimir.

Whatever its virtues or flaws, for one of its constituent peoples Austria-Hungary offered a home that could not be demarcated on national lines within its borders; those who harboured national ambitions instead looked across to Palestine. A growing number, like Roth's schoolmate Abraham, adhered to the Zionist movement founded in the late nineteenth century by Theodor Herzl, but that was little more than a pipe dream for now. While the Czechs and Ukrainians could seek to reassert their own territories within the empire, the Austro-Hungarian Jews had none to begin with: if it were to collapse, they would be stranded. In the absence of such dire circumstances as to make the case for a Jewish national home seem unanswerable, Austria-Hungary's continuation seemed the preferable option. Moreover, many Jews considered Franz Joseph philosemitic, or at least benign towards them. Jews in Brody liked to recall his words when, during a visit to the town, he stepped out on to a balcony and realised how many of them had gathered to pay homage: 'Now I know why I am called King of Jerusalem.'* They recalled how, four times over, the Viennese voted for the antisemite Karl Lueger as their mayor but Franz Joseph refused to appoint him, until on the fifth occasion Pope Leo XIII intervened to ensure the election of the man who would inspire Adolf Hitler. The story was often told of a time when the emperor visited a *shtetl* in Galicia and was greeted by a rabbi who gave a Hebrew blessing. One of the Imperial party said in a stage whisper: 'What is the point of that? Not a soul understands this Yiddish stuff!' He was correct, Franz Joseph could not comprehend a word of what had been said to him, but he looked at his underling and said: 'I understand the rabbi very well.'[18]

Joseph Roth would much later incorporate the scene in *The Radetzky March*. He would say that 'the only people the Habsburgs

---

* Following the *Ausgleich* in 1867, the emperor's full title was: 'Franz Joseph the First, by the Grace of God Emperor of Austria, Apostolic King of Hungary, King of Bohemia, King of Dalmatia, Croatia, Slavonia, Galicia and Lodomeria and Illyria; King of Jerusalem etc., Archduke of Austria; Grand Duke of Tuscany and Cracow, Duke of Lorraine, of Salzburg, Styria, Carinthia, Carniola and of Bukovina; Grand Prince of Transylvania; Margrave of Moravia; Duke of Upper and Lower Silesia, of Modena, Parma, Piacenza and Guastalla, of Oświęcim, Zator and Ćeszyn, Friuli, Ragusa [Dubrovnik] and Zara [Zadar]; Princely Count of Habsburg and Tyrol, of Kyburg, Gorizia and Gradisca; Prince of Trent [Trento] and Brixen; Margrave of Upper and Lower Lusatia and in Istria; Count of Hohenems, Feldkirch, Bregenz, Sonnenberg, etc.; Lord of Trieste, of Cattaro [Kotor], and over the Windic march; Grand Voivode of the Voivodeship of Serbia'.

could rely on were the Jews',[19] and in turn, for Roth and others of his mindset, the Habsburgs were the only people the Jews could rely on. As David Bronsen put it, Jewish intellectuals who agitated against the Habsburgs in the late nineteenth and early twentieth centuries were '[sawing] off the branch on which they were sitting'.[20] By Roth's adolescence the Habsburgs were struggling to keep their empire's patchwork stitched together in the face of rising nationalism. Franz Joseph was to his Jewish supporters a figure of reassuring solidity in a time of turmoil, someone unchanging and benign during the late nineteenth century, when pogroms across eastern Europe and Russia showed them time and again that hitherto-friendly neighbours could suddenly turn murderous.

Franz Joseph grew steadily older, his bushy whiskers turning grey. He was stolid, incurious, he didn't read books. He was determinedly bland — it was a standing joke that his response to places he visited and events he attended was always: '*Es war sehr schön. Es hat mich sehr gefreut.*' ('It was very nice. I was very pleased.') He had good reason for this, dating from the opening of the Vienna State Opera House, when he added his voice to the chorus of criticism over its appearance and thus spurred one of the humiliated architects to commit suicide. Since then the emperor had sought never to offend. He seemed all-encompassing, a comforting presence who embodied a supranational entity. The writer Bruno Schulz, another Galician Jew, once recalled: 'At that time the world was embraced on all sides by Franz Joseph I — and there was no way out to either side of him: at every horizon he rose up, in every corner this ubiquitous and inevitable profile appeared and sealed off the world like a gaol . . .'.[21]

Roth himself went a step further. To the end of his life he would rue the absence of his father and try to shoehorn the emperor into the vacant role, while also claiming that Franz Joseph performed a similar duty for all his scattered subjects. 'Without a father,' Roth's narrator reflects in 1939's *The Tale of the 1002nd Night* (*Die Geschichte von der 1002. Nacht*), 'not unnaturally, [a] boy grows up with disciplinary problems. What has been put in motion is the destruction of a life in its first bloom. Only the mercy of the Emperor himself can save a boy, a citizen and a future loyal soldier, from the full punishment demanded by the law.'[22] In Roth's world view, the omnipresence Bruno Schulz described takes on a more intimate, paternal quality. 'The father is called Franz Joseph, the First,' he wrote. 'The Emperor's arm stretches a very long way. From Trieste, Sarajevo, Mostar by way of Budapest, Vienna, Prague, Cracow, Lemberg all the way to Tarnopol and Czernowitz and beyond ... In all languages and peoples he lives in a variety of forms, and his private, improbable misfortune which already seems unreal makes him seem all the more legendary in the eyes of the simpler, geographically remote people.'[23] The people of Brody, in other words, or at least those who shared his reverence for this distant icon; Roth's nostalgic account dispenses with those such as his schoolmate who felt no affinity to the monarchy. If the late-Habsburg monarchy was by now a 'cold sun',[24] as he would later write, a cooling star whose rays just reached the Russian border, then he aspired to move west towards the source of the fading light.

The Dual Monarchy was a vast multinational home, and Franz Joseph I its human embodiment, a steady protector whose embrace held Roth secure along with all others within his empire. A father who embodied a fatherland. It is easy to see why he might appeal to a boy who suspected he might soon have neither; he had never had the former and, as the first decade of the twentieth century drew to a close, could feel the latter slipping into history.

Not only was Brody an embarrassment for those who left it behind, but within the town itself Maria and her son were marked out for another form of shame. The absence of a father lent them an air of tragedy and mystery, for no one knew what had become of the man, and Maria tersely resisted any enquiries. Insanity was so stigmatised – to be *meshugge* was thought a punishment from God – that she managed to keep the truth concealed. In its place, a rumour became accepted as fact among the townsfolk. It was decided that Nachum Roth had hanged himself. His wife and son were viewed with a mixture of curiosity and pity. Her loss would be why she was so protective of the boy, people concluded. Maria still accompanied her only child to school when he was a teenager and kept him apart from his contemporaries, instilling the belief that he was made for greater things. She only stopped walking him to the grammar school at his insistence when he grew too embarrassed. She kept his hair cropped short, a markedly Germanic style. She dressed him in the finest clothes she could, as if to advertise that they could cope perfectly well without his father. Her pride was palpable: he was her prized possession. As she possessed him, so she controlled him. They were a duo, tightly bonded by circumstance, but with an imbalance of feeling for one another: Maria smothered her son with maternal affection, and he sought to wrest himself free. He barely socialised with schoolmates, had no close friends to confide in and, as we've seen, it was rare she permitted anyone to visit him.

Hard work filled her days; she was a sturdy figure who loomed over her young son's childhood, casting a forbidding shadow as she did the housework. Many years later his friend Soma Morgenstern would write that Roth gives 'an exact portrait'[25] of his mother in his novel *Job*. When the main character's wife, Deborah Singer, scrubbed the floorboards every Friday, 'Her broad shoulders bobbed up and down in an even rhythm; her strong hands rubbed the length and breadth of each single board; and her fingernails sought in the cracks between the boards, scratched out the black dirt, and destroyed it with splashes of water from her pail. She crept through the bare blue whitewashed room like a broad, mighty and moveable mountain.'[26] Her adult son casts his mind back: 'I remember my mother. It was warm and soft with her, she had a very deep voice, and her face was big and round, like a whole world.'[27]

Maria was her son's world, and vice versa: he could hardly see beyond her imposing form, she was everywhere he looked; and she would not permit herself to look beyond him and their household. She knitted, cooked, laboured, prayed, devoted herself to his care, baked cakes that filled the house with a warm, sweet aroma he would always associate with home: these were the salient features of her life. Her solicitousness had the opposite of the intended effect. One of his cousins recalled for David Bronsen a series of charming remarks Roth made about mothers in general, prompted by his own upbringing:

'All mothers are stupid'; 'It ought to be possible to bring up mothers'; 'Mothers think it is a tremendous achievement to prepare a roast.'[28] Bronsen paraphrases another interviewee as saying that Maria, 'who sometimes appeared strikingly dressed, hardly ever socialised and was only ever seen in the street, apart from seeing to daily needs, going for walks with her little boy. The mother-son relationship appeared very intimate to outside observers, but sometimes it even seemed as if she did not want the carefully protected boy to go out on his own.'[29]

The adolescent Roth developed a profound ambivalence about his mother. Her company gave him comfort, and he would later say that the times he spent with her were the happiest of his life, but in the still of the night he would quietly get dressed, slip out of the house and walk the streets, just for a little freedom. Even years later, after her death, he would seek small forms of revenge against the woman whose all-consuming love stifled his liberty. He told friends and lovers that when he was born his mother had been too poor to buy a cradle – a lie, if his other story about his cradle's sale to an old lady is true – and instead he was laid on a window seat and forgotten until he turned blue with cold and almost died of pneumonia. The surest way of hurting her reputation was to portray her as she would have hated to be seen – as uncaring and neglectful, rather than a mother whose devotion knew no bounds.

The mother and son lived in the kind of fraught near-poverty that comes of perpetual straining to appear well-to-do. Maria's eldest brother Siegmund, a merchant in Lemberg, gave them money, but their margins were always vanishingly narrow. For all that the insular Hasidim drew the teenage Moses' disdain, they were, if nothing else, authentic and without pretension. He was torn between contempt and admiration. Dennis Marks notes that Maria's ambitions for her cherished son 'placed young Moses Joseph Roth half inside and half outside his Jewish origins – a position he occupied for the rest of his life'.[30] Encouraged by her, he developed an internal conflict that led him to reject his home and identity while never being sure of how to replace either. What some call inauthenticity, others call ambition. For some your true station is the one to which you were born; for others it is the place you have the potential to reach. To a boy who loved telling stories, her ambitious instinct might have appealed as the most interesting way to live, a programme for self-fulfilment. But to the sceptic in him who sought solidity and facts in a slippery world, it also felt inauthentic.

Michael Hofmann prefers to term the family 'not exactly poor',[31] noting the occasional visits to a Brody photographer's studio, the violin lessons and a maid when finances permitted, but he sets these intermittent displays of affluence against a backdrop of constant anxiety over money. Maria would have only the best for her son. Moses had become known for his conspicuous intelligence of the sort that is always on display because its owner has not yet found a satisfactory place in which to invest it. There was no work yet to speak for him, to broadcast his talents beyond his immediate world, so Moses spoke for himself.

Moses Joseph Roth, 1905.

He acquired the habit of ending his opinionated statements with the word '*faktisch!*' – 'that's a fact!' – until his family extended his nickname to 'Muniu-faktisch'. At the Crown Prince Rudolf Gymnasium he passed his exams with distinction, as he casually boasted in a pair of teenage letters to his cousin Resia Grübel, daughter of Siegmund. He had an intense imaginative life: he dreamed of sunparched cities, he devoured stories such as *Robinson Crusoe* that lifted him out of cold Galicia into exotic, far-off lands. He knew now that he wanted to be a writer, the surest way to stop his insights and opinions and inventions from evanescing, and to articulate his experiences to himself and share these distillations with strangers in the hope of forging connections that would tether him to the world. Moses knew he had sharp things to say and striking ways in which to say them. He already felt himself a detached onlooker as an only child, and savoured the respite from his domineering mother.

A photograph of him as a student suggests his personality was already moulded: there is an impatience in the way his eyes are looking over the photographer's shoulder, and a determined set to his pursed lips, but a hint of a smile on them too. There was, by now, a pronounced swagger to his demeanour, though it was often mitigated by tenderness and playful self-deprecation; even in adolescence he was paradoxical, and not in the way that many teenagers are determinedly contrary or seek to seem mysterious. Reading his early correspondence, you sense that the dichotomous personality he displayed as an adult is there already: that it is pathological, and there's a schism at his core. One thing you soon learn in attempting to understand Joseph Roth: he intentionally contradicts himself, using contradiction as a way of throwing people off the scent, of winning himself a moment's more freedom. Inconsistency is always to be expected in biography – people aren't equations, they don't always add up – but few subjects deploy it so deliberately as part of their survival kit.

In charting his thought you must seek the general trends rather than the repeated deviations. There is always a side to him that he doesn't present, kept in reserve, a trump card hidden in his hand: if you think you've placed him, he'll prove you wrong. In his last letter to Resia he had suggested he and Maria might visit her family in Lemberg, but 'that wasn't a serious inquiry: you shouldn't take everything seriously', he instructs her. 'I am a sworn enemy to etiquette.'[32] (He was not, Hofmann points out, saying that in truth Roth was 'Old World in his courtliness'.[33]) 'I'm not sure if I will be able to come, because I've been

Joseph Roth as a student in Vienna, 1914.

set some reading to do. It's all because I'm an "A" student, and more is required of us. Anyway, I know I won't be able to talk Mama into going, she never wants to leave the house. She seeks various pretexts for this, and since the help was discreetly "let go" yesterday, and there's little chance of finding a suitable replacement, the prospect of my visit has rather receded. Well, the sky won't fall down on top of us.'[34]

His airy tone speaks volumes: mentally he was leaving Brody, and he was impatient to escape for good to pursue his writing ambitions. A succession of letters from this period make plain his restlessness. To his aunt Rosia Grübel, mother of Resia and Paula, he wrote: 'Every young person dreams of happiness and greatness in the future, why shouldn't a writer?! Perhaps I'm building castles in the air? Well, aeroplanes have been built so I will be able to reach my airy palaces. But I hope they will stand on solid ground so that you will still be able to come and visit me there often. "The will is my god." And even the greatest goal can be reached through application and endurance.'[35]

Writing to his Uncle Willy in Nuremberg, he enquired after his news and the weather: 'Is it as cold there too? Here there is a hoar frost on all the roofs in the morning and it is bitterly cold at night. I hope I soon get away from Galicia.'[36] When Resia Grübel told him of her hectic social life in Lemberg, he assured her: 'That's how it ought to be. Of course in Brody there is none of that apart from a so-called "ball" which my class has organised, but which I won't go to, as it's not my society. – Otherwise it's very boring here."[37]

And he wrote to his cousin Resia again on 2 September 1912, a teasing, sincere, worldly-wise eighteen-year-old: 'I was very pleased to get your birthday congratulations; that's not just a manner of speaking either, I mean I felt a real, deep, inner, genuine-in-every-fibre pleasure. I know how devoted you are to me, and that you really are concerned for my welfare. It's not so hard to tell real feelings from false. I see you take delight in the way my writing is coming on, and I want to thank you for that especially. Thank you too for your wishes regarding my studies. This last year will soon be over, and after my final exams all the trials and tribulations of school will be behind me, and I will go on to the great school of life. Let's hope I earn equally good grades at that institution.'[38]

*

His chief rival for academic honours was a boy named David Schapiro, whose father, a landowner, was one of the richest men in Brody. Schapiro tried to outdo Roth, and prepared for the leaving examination in hope of gaining the distinction award, which the headteacher's diktat restricted to one Jewish boy. Roth and Schapiro had each to prepare an essay on the subject 'On Opportunism and Compromise'. The resulting pieces of work were discussed by the senior teachers. One, a Dr Schirmer, argued that in future years Schapiro would sit in the coffee houses reading the newspapers, and the best articles he would read in them would be by Joseph Roth. And so it was that Roth's leaving certificate, issued in May 1913, bore the words '*sub auspicii imperatoris*' – 'under the auspices of the emperor'. With this endorsement he took his first steps away from Brody, each taking him closer to the heart of the empire – but for now, his first stop would be only an hour from home. The eighteen-year-old set out for the little railway station, with its exposed stretch of tracks leading to the eastern and western horizon, towards Kiev and Lemberg. He took the train west.

The view looking west from
the bridge at Brody railway
station, 2019.

Chapter Two

It is good when our mothers are not there, with their doubtful, searching eyes, our mothers who are tired and tearful,
strict and frightening and yet sad, poor mothers, who understand nothing and chide us, and to whom we have to lie.
When they are not there, we do not have to give an account
of ourselves, nor must we fear the effect that account might
have, the need to lie and be discovered lying.

'The Blind Mirror', in *The Coral Merchant*

The Vulytsya Antona Chekhova* is a street in the centre of Lviv where
four-storey houses with a distressed, taupe-coloured façade bear ornate
balconies and pedimented windows that overlook broad, tree-lined
pavements. The heavy wooden door of Number 7 opens to reveal eight
purple-painted stone steps that rise to a hallway floored with patterned
tiles of cream, lilac and brown. Through glazed narrow double doors
a staircase twists back towards the front of the building. The ceiling
above the stairwell is painted with scrolls of flowers and foliage in
faded grey, jade and primrose-yellow. The chipped wooden handrail
is supported by an art nouveau balustrade, and as you tread the wide,
worn steps they croak like marshland frogs. After two flights comes a
landing, and the door to Flat 5 is on the left. Dust drifts through the
shafts of light from the window, and grey shadows of the staircase's
looping ironwork stretch across the matt parquet floor.

---

* This is its current name. Roth and the Grübels always referred to it by its previous
name, Ulica Hofmana.

Number 7, Vulytsya Antona Chekhova, Lviv –
the staircase and decorative floor tiles.

At a glance the scale and decoration confirm you are in a city. You are no longer in the *shtetl*. It is easy to see why Lviv was known as 'Little Vienna'. In 1256 King Daniel of Galicia founded what became the region's capital, naming it for his son Prince Lev, or Leo, and since then it has accrued a pride of wild-maned lions sculpted in marble and iron that glower at you everywhere: from the top of grand archways, as supports to balconies, guarding the cemetery, on the armrests of benches by the city hall. In the twenty-first century this palimpsestic city has a strange mystique. Its peeling pastel paintwork and crumbling façades hint at half-forgotten stories. The present here is a membrane pressed upon by a heavy past: you feel its weight without knowing its details. If you sit, to gather yourself after arriving, in the broad space before an opera house lit by sunshine that gilds its stone lions and columns, you sense that such a fine setting in an old city must have served as a focal point for its tumultuous history. Who congregated here, what transpired? Later you leaf through a history book and see that in 1942 the spot where you sat was occupied by reverent hordes watching the Nazi commandant Hans Frank give a speech that precipitated the liquidation of the Jewish ghetto, and the exquisite opera house formed a backdrop disfigured by swastika banners.

Today Lviv delights and chills you by turns. In 1913 its splendour had not yet been defiled by Nazi and Soviet occupation. Walking down what was then Ulica Hofmana and stepping through the door of Number 7 would make a newly arrived young person from the east feel they'd taken a step up in the world, as we can imagine Roth did when he trod this route that summer. Flat 5 was owned by Maria's brother Siegmund Grübel, who lived there with his wife Rosia and children Paula, Resia and Heinrich. Roth had often visited before in the summer holidays, but now he was to reside in the flat while reading Philology at the Imperial-Royal University of Lemberg, which was fifteen minutes' walk away via Ivana Franka Street and Pekarska Street. There was only one problem with living in his uncle's home, and that was his uncle.

Siegmund Grübel was a successful wholesaler in malt and hops, and the stark differences in their attitudes towards life and money became inescapable now that they were compelled to spend sustained periods together. Grübel had already paid for Roth's grammar school education, and now he was paying his university fees. Roth felt under pressure to display his gratitude to his uncle, who often reminded him that without his help he would still be in Brody. Roth hated feeling dependent on charity. Nor did he enjoy feeling patronised – a story told by a cousin suggests their relationship remained frozen in an adult-child dynamic long after Roth reached adulthood. Michael* Grübel said that, some years into his career as a writer, Roth met Siegmund by chance in a crowded Paris street and, soon after falling into conversation, the uncle could not help but shout: 'Muniu, what kind of behaviour is this?'[1]

For all that Lemberg represented a step up from Brody, Roth would ideally not have studied there. The family spoke Polish at home and it was the university's language of instruction. Roth's Polish remained imperfect and he wanted to develop his talent as a writer of German prose. His mother had forced him to Lemberg because her brother was

---

* Known as Miguel Grübel by the time Bronsen interviewed him, having moved to Mexico City.

willing to house him and pay his fees, but he wished he were in Vienna. He could not be unfaithful to the German language, he explained to his uncomprehending uncle, whom Roth considered a philistine who understood nothing but how to sell hops and malt. It is a measure of the antagonism Roth developed towards his uncle that a decade after lodging with the Grübels, he still felt the need to score a point against him. Written in 1923, the novel *Hotel Savoy* features two characters who owe something to Grübel. The more obvious is the narrator Gabriel Dan's uncle, Phöbus Böhlaug, a rich merchant whom Dan resents depending upon for money.

'Before me,' Dan relates, 'stands my uncle Phöbus Böhlaug and whispers to me, "A lot of good you've done! You're worth no more than your father! You good for nothing!"'[2] Which we can imagine echoes Siegmund Grübel's view of Roth's father after his abandonment of Maria, leaving Grübel to support his sister and nephew. Dan does not understand his mother's admiration for this oafish man, the way she looks on him 'as if he were someone very strange and royal, as if the same womb had not borne them both and the same two breasts suckled them'.[3] Later we're told that 'Phöbus Böhlaug greets me heartily and reproaches me for not visiting him. "I have no time these days," say I. "You no longer need money,"[4] answers Phöbus. Finally Dan mentions an occasion when 'my uncle Phöbus Böhlaug passes us, gives the first greeting and bows very low and I smile condescendingly at him, as if I were his uncle.'[5] How Roth must have enjoyed conjuring a scenario in which he could reverse the roles and make his all-powerful uncle feel the inferior one.

Then there's a chilly, tough American businessman named Henry Bloomfield, son of a Jechiel Blumenfeld; recall that Jechiel Grübel was the father of Siegmund, Maria and their siblings. News that the émigré Bloomfield is to return to Łódź,* his home town and the location of the titular hotel, prompts feverish anticipation. His generosity on previous visits is legendary. All hopes are in vain as he has only returned to visit his father's grave. Bloomfield greets strangers with the question:

---

* The approximate pronunciation is 'Woodge'.

'How goes it?', expressed 'not as if it were an enquiry, but a greeting. He was not interested.' He lacks warmth and human spirit; he calculates rather than grant the benefit of the doubt. 'No, it was not easy to extract money from Bloomfield,' concludes the narrator. While Grübel had financially supported his sister as she raised her son alone, we can imagine he took Böhlaug and Bloomfield's approach to the teenage boy whom he had accepted into his home; for that alone he expected explicit gratitude, and on top of this the boy wanted more money? A letter Roth wrote to his cousin Paula almost five years later indicates the relationship between him and his temperamental uncle. Roth had been ill and neglected to acknowledge some debt to Siegmund. 'Please tell your father – I'm writing to him under a separate cover – not to go off the deep end if I didn't send him a card. Does he need a postcard from me with a couple of lines of writing on it to prove my gratitude and devotion? Where would that take us! It's absurd to be so fixated on externals. I got sick, otherwise I would have written long ago.'[6] Given that 'externals' – displays of courtliness – were his default behaviour towards those he wished to impress, it seems he had no desire to impress his uncle, and preferred to nurse a grudge.

Michael Grübel, son of Siegmund's brother Heinrich, often came to the apartment around the time of Roth's admission to university. 'I was only six years old then,' said Michael. 'Roth, who seemed very serious to me, was always busy writing when I visited. Once I asked him: "Why do you write so much?" His answer astonished me: "To make the spring come."'[7] Perhaps time could not pass quickly enough that summer – or more likely for the teenage Roth 'the spring' was an optimistic and fertile state of mind, abundant in germinating ideas induced by immersion in his writing.

When he was not leaning over a notebook, he was exploring the city or spending time with a neighbour in the apartment block whom he came to hold in higher esteem than his older relatives. Helene von Szajnocha-Schenk (c.1863–1945) lived at Number 1, where her rooms served as an informal literary and musical salon. She was a French tutor, divorced from a professor at Kraków University. Her brother Dr Josef, Baron von Schenk, was a civil servant and politician who would become one of the Habsburg monarchy's last ministers of justice, and her father was president of the District Court in Czernowitz. She was of the kind of stock that appealed to Roth and contributed to his excitement on moving to the city; one didn't meet such people in Brody. In turn she liked him. She was aged around fifty and infirm, he was nineteen. They came to call each other 'mother' and 'son'. In sight of the uncle he had grown to dislike, and having distanced himself from his overbearing mother in Brody, Roth created ersatz family ties in place of the ones he'd rejected, a habit he would sustain. Roth's friend Józef Wittlin, who met von Szajnocha-Schenk five years later, said: 'Many an important decision for his life and his writing was made by Roth at the bedside of this sick old lady, whose mind was as young and fresh as the esprit of the French ladies in the Age of the Enlightenment.'[8]

Meanwhile, in autumn 1913 Maria Roth wrote a letter to the son she still called 'Muniu', pleading with him to write to her: 'My sweet child! Why do you keep me on tiptoes for weeks now, "letter will follow", it is like torture for me, longing to see this elaborate letter; from around you I hear about great success, but nothing from my dear child. Uncle Siegmund writes you live like a prince and you look splendid and still I wait day after day for a detailed letter from you, if you are really so happy, won't you give me that pleasure . . . Your longing mother sends heartfelt kisses, my precious child.'[9]

Roth was moving on, from Brody and from his mother. He kept out of the flat when he could and roamed the city in a spirit of journalistic enquiry. He travelled to the poorest quarters and interviewed people he encountered, trying to understand their lives, in all likelihood masquerading as a reporter despite having no published outlet for his writing. He seems to have done this when he spent 2–9 September 1913 in Vienna, marking his nineteenth birthday by attending a week of meetings at the 11th Zionist Congress. The thousands of participants ranged from Chaim Weizmann and Edmond de Rothschild through to Franz Kafka, who was unsettled by the atmosphere of 'endless shouting' and argument between Zionists, whom he characterised as typically having 'small round heads, [and] firm cheeks'.[10] 'Unrewarding speeches in German, a great deal of Hebrew,' [11] Kafka added, later referring to it as 'a totally alien event'.[12]

As Roth moved among the hordes, he claimed to be a newspaper correspondent. He listened in on debates concerning the intellectual and cultural basis for Zionism and recorded that there was discussion of setting up what would become Hebrew University in Jerusalem. In surveying the inhospitable atmosphere across Europe that had galvanised the campaign for a Jewish national home, Weizmann noted that western European universities were reducing access to eastern European Jews, and 1912–13 had seen German and Swiss universities introduce 'stringent measures'[13] to bar them from higher education. Many of the delegates were from Russia, and they would have had far worse tales to tell: of vicious blood libels and pogroms inspired by the Protocols of the Elders of Zion, the fabricated document purporting to reveal the workings of a Jewish ruling elite. Since their publication in 1903 the Protocols had circulated poison into people's minds across the Russian Empire.

The congress resolved that every participant should establish personal and commercial connections in Palestine. Roth knew well the delegates' concerns and was interested to hear their solutions. But he was not persuaded. His growing wariness over escalating nationalistic tensions in Ukraine and Poland meant he could no more support a Jewish nationalism than any other. Growing up among Hasidim, he had also absorbed the belief that Jews should only return to Israel upon the Messiah's arrival. It seems that a combination of political and theological reasons left him ill-disposed to the Zionist project. Having earlier told his schoolfriend in Brody of his allegiance to the Habsburgs rather than Zionism, now he moved towards the firm position he set out fourteen years later in *The Wandering Jews*.

Roth's thoughts there are worth quoting at length, because they summarise his eventual stance on one of his foremost concerns in early adulthood. He writes that the Orthodox eastern Jew 'detests the Zionist, who uses ridiculous European methods to try to set up a Judaism that doesn't deserve the name . . . There can be no compromise between that Orthodoxy and the kind of Zionism that will build roads even on the Sabbath. An Orthodox Hasid from the east will prefer a Christian to a Zionist. For the latter would change Judaism root and branch. His Jewish nation would be along the lines of a European state.'[14] By this he means a western European nation state, based on a way of thinking that is inimical to the mentality of the supranational tribes of eastern Europe. Just as the Armenians in the Caucasus were Muslims ahead of being 'Armenians', he says, so with the Jews: both ethnic groups, he notes, 'speak several languages, are themselves the product of several generations of mixed marriages, and fatherland is whichever country happens to conscript them'.[15]

[The notion of] nationality is a western concept. It was an invention of Western European scholars, who ever since have struggled to explain it. The old Dual Monarchy of Austria-Hungary gave them, apparently, their best evidence of nationalism in action.[*] In fact, if it had been at all well governed it could just as easily have provided evidence for the opposite ... The cradle of modern Zionism was Austria, was Vienna. It was founded by an Austrian journalist. No one else could have founded it. The Austrian parliament was where the representatives of the various nationalities sat [and formed] a battlefield for the various competing nationalisms. If the Czechs were promised a new school, the German community in Bohemia felt aggrieved. And if the Poles in East Galicia were given a Polish-speaking governor, then the Ruthenians felt their noses were out of joint. Every nationality within Austria-Hungary pressed its claims on the basis of its 'territory'. Only the Jews ('soil' was the word used in their case) had no territory of their own. In Galicia the majority of them were neither Poles nor Ruthenian. However, anti-Semitism was to be found equally among Germans and Czechs, Poles and Ruthenians, Magyars and Romanians in Transylvania. They managed to refute the proverb that says when two quarrel, the third is the winner. The Jews were always the third

---

[*] Roth wrote these lines almost a decade after the collapse of the Austro-Hungarian Empire.

party, and they always lost. Then they pulled themselves together and came out in favour of a Jewish nation of their own. They compensated for the lack of any 'soil' to call their own in Europe by aspiring to a home in Palestine.[16]

Well, he resolves, 'It's surely better to be a nation than to be mistreated by one. But it's a painful necessity all the same.'[17] He can see why his contemporaries have placed their faith in Jewish nationalism as an escape from European persecution. But he knows where nationalism leads and will not accept it as the solution to the Jewish question.*

The literary scholar and critical theorist Devorah Baum makes an acute point on the interrelation of geopolitics and Jewish self-perception at this juncture. She writes:

self-doubt could . . . be said to distinguish a historical moment that saw the position of the self becoming ever more tenuous: suddenly it was the case that a modern person could no longer necessarily expect his own status to resemble that of his parents. Little wonder, then, that the question of belonging was to become so integral to the concept of modern statehood. Nor, indeed, is it any accident that the so-called 'Jewish question', which hovered so menacingly over Jewish modernity, first arose during the period when Europe was forming its nation states.

The 'Jewish question' was primarily one of categorisation. To what category belonged the postemancipation Jew? Were the Jews still a religion? Or were they a race? Or a nation? Or a culture? Were they Asiatic or European? Were they ancients or moderns?

---

* Also known as 'the Jewish problem' – though, as Bernard Wasserstein notes, this term is flawed: before the Second World War, 'Jews and Christians alike spoke of the "Jewish Problem" but this was a misnomer for what should more properly have been called the Christian problem. In its essence, after all, anti-Semitism was a phenomenon that arose out of the failure of European Christendom to live up to the most fundamental teaching of its Jewish founder: "love thy neighbour as thyself." . . . [The] fons et origo of anti-Jewish ideology in Europe [is] the Christian concept of the Jews as a deicide nation and all that flowed from that in the teaching . . . of the church.' Bernard Wasserstein, *On the Eve: The Jews of Europe Before the Second World War* (Profile Books, 2013), pp. 31–2.

The lack of a unified response to this question suggested some strange ambivalence at the heart of Jewish identity, an ambivalence that put Jews in danger at a time of increasing nationalistic fervour. As Nietzsche was to put it ... : 'You shall be knowable, express your inner nature by clear and constant signs – otherwise you are dangerous ... We despise the secret and unrecognisable.' But a doubtful identity not only stimulates the predictable hatred of the herd for the stranger, it also provokes self-hatred in a world where knowing who one is and what one stands for is the key to social success.[18]

Geopolitical tensions strained at a Jewish psyche already torn between Jewishness and Germanness, forever asking itself the increasingly complex question of where the Jews belonged: one that gentiles were asking in more aggressive terms. All around him, the Jewish question was being discussed at increasing volume at the beginning of Roth's university career. He was unsure of the answer, but becoming certain it was not Zionism.

The university faculty where Roth was due to begin his degree is a bright and airy building around a grassy courtyard where students sit and read. Black-and-white-tiled corridors with white-painted walls lead to panelled wooden doors beneath oversized art deco fanlights. The building exudes calmness and is saturated with daylight. He seems to have spent little time here; not only did he struggle with the Polish language, but the campus had become a focal point for political tension. He often sought refuge on the opposite side of Shevchenka Avenue in the Café Roma. Café life appealed to him – a slowly sipped coffee, maybe a schnapps, a newspaper to read and critique; watching the students and professors come and go, striking up conversation with an acquaintance then returning to his thoughts, gazing out of the window, making notes in his tiny, impeccable handwriting. For a young man predisposed to feeling isolated and abandoned, working in public was preferable to being alone. It provided a form of solitude within company, an amenable balance of the two conditions, each offering a retreat from the other: if he tired of what he was writing he could strike up a conversation, if he tired of the conversation he could retreat into his thoughts under the auspices of continuing to work. Either way he was at a remove from the political difficulties at the university.

The tensions arose as Lemberg entered one of its identity crises, in which the Ukrainian majority sought to regain power from the ruling Polish minority. The Ukrainians were strengthening their national identity and reasserting their rights, for instance to be educated in their own language. Roth's university was a particular scene of contention. In 1907 a Ukrainian nationalist student, Myroslav Sichynsky, formed part of a group that destroyed lecture halls and assaulted a Polish lecturer. Between 1903 and 1908 Ukrainians tried to establish a separate university of their own. That five-year period concluded with Lemberg witnessing a pivotal assassination: Sichynsky shot dead the Viceroy of Galicia, a conservative and authoritarian Polish count named Andrzej Potocki,* in protest at the murderous suppression of Ukrainian peasants during the recent campaign for election to the Diet.†

This incident had deep antecedents: the Ruthenians had long been oppressed by the Polish Catholic landowners and had often uprisen, burning their mansions and beating them to death. Now the old enmity had resurfaced. Potocki's murder outraged the Poles of Lemberg and a furious mob tore through the city, vandalising Ukrainian institutions. As Józef Wittlin wrote: 'The entire Ruthenian people were tainted with the blood of the victim of this political assassination.'[19] The two groups' relationship in Lemberg and Galicia deteriorated from thereon, and by 1913 there was a profound enmity that would violently manifest again five years later during the Polish–Ukrainian War, the landgrab that followed the collapse of the Austrian and Russian empires. Such an atmosphere 'could only have been deeply alienating for someone like Roth', wrote the American scholar Sidney Rosenfeld, 'whose religious-ethnic heritage stamped him as an outsider to both of the contending national groups'.[20]

The ethnonational fault lines in this part of Austria-Hungary were manifesting in frightening fashion. Roth was an outsider at university

---

* A member of the family who owned Brody Castle.
† The Diets were the regional assemblies in the crownlands of Austria-Hungary.

and found little refuge in his uncle's home, where he felt like a suffered guest. That autumn, having barely started his degree, he made a relieved exit from the flat. Today there is a bas-relief plaque by the front door that bears this script beneath an excellent likeness of a bow-tied Roth: '*In diesem Haus weilte bei seinem Onkel der österreichische Schriftsteller Joseph Roth.*' ('In this house the Austrian writer Joseph Roth stayed with his uncle.') But as soon as possible he moved on, from 'Little Vienna' to the real thing.

On the opening page of *The Man Without Qualities*, Robert Musil depicts Vienna on an August day in 1913 when 'Automobiles shot out of deep, narrow streets into the shallows of bright squares. Dark clusters of pedestrians formed cloudlike strings. Where more powerful lines of speed cut across their casual haste they clotted up, then trickled on faster and, after a few oscillations, resumed their steady rhythm. Hundreds of noises wove themselves into a wiry texture of sound with barbs protruding here and there . . .'.[21] Scanning through the period's silent film footage* and still images, the latter notably by a street photographer named Emil Mayer, we can hear the barbs. Tram bells and vendors' cries over a white noise of conversation, footsteps, horses' hooves, wide-spoked cartwheels rumbling on flat cobbles. On the pavements women gesture and converse while selling produce from huge wicker baskets strapped to their waists, some filled with flowers, some with parsnips and onions. On a bright day around this time someone shot a few minutes' film from a tram veering round the Ringstrasse, passing the half-shadowed colonnade of the Vienna Opera, the monument to Admiral Tegetthoff, the Burgtheater. Pedestrians amble across the frame. A portly policeman in embroidered uniform and white-gloved hands directs the traffic, which moves in a mess of bisecting tangents: cars push across curving tramlines, streams of pedestrians flow and pause and flow between vehicles, horses pull carriages across fast-approaching trams, a road sweeper clears manure from one's path and ducks back again. Silhouetted ladies strut beneath

---

* Silent footage from 1911 held by Filmarchiv Austria, viewable here: https://www.youtube.com/watch?v=FbMwd1CHMhI Film shot from a tram in 1906 here: https://www.youtube.com/watch?v=pN6SrB6r3MA

parasols. Men stroll in fedoras and jackets, watch chains arcing across waistcoats. Barely an uncovered head is to be seen: peaked caps and boaters, plumed hats and headscarves. Blurred figures, some glancing at the passing camera.

Mayer's photographs clarify such characters in exquisite detail. A bowler-hatted old man stands by a horse and carriage, peering intently through wire-framed spectacles at the front page of *Die Neue Zeitung*, a Catholic-leaning newspaper. A shoe-shine boy hunches over the raised foot of a well-dressed woman, and his white hat picks out the gleam on his polished black boots. A suited man and a woman in an extravagantly feathered hat take coffee on the terrace of a café with geometrically leaded windows, their legs touching beneath the table. Two rows of brass buttons on a stout man's military greatcoat, four medals on his chest, and beneath his cap a pugnacious face with drooping moustache and bushy side-whiskers like Franz Joseph's. Young army officers banter in brocaded tunics and soft hats, each with a sword swinging from his belt. A sailor-suited boy at a fountain cups water in his hands. Couples waltz around an ice-skating rink, the women's black dresses flaring out as they spin past Mayer's camera, lit by soft orbs of lamplight on a misty evening.

In the decade preceding the First World War, this beautiful, self-regarding city's cultural life grew frantic as it accelerated towards its own demise. Its last days as a great Imperial capital saw the metropolis by the Danube abuzz with revolutionary thinkers in every aspect of the arts and sciences. Habsburg Austria's decline in power and status only inspired Vienna's intellectuals and artists to cultivate the life of the mind. As Frederic Raphael observes, the 1866 defeat to Bismarck's Prussia at Sadowa had a profound effect 'on the Viennese psyche ... Austria had already suffered preliminary humiliation by the French, under Louis-Napoleon, but Sadowa confirmed she would never again be a major player in the world's game. Yet conscious acceptance of Austria's vanished supremacy was repressed by the brilliance and brio of its social and artistic life. Who can be surprised that Adler's "discovery" of the inferiority complex, and of compensating assertiveness, was made in a society traumatised by dazzling decline? It was as if the city which spawned Arthur Schnitzler and Sigmund Freud feared to awake from its tuneful dreams to prosaic reality.'[22]

Writers, painters and composers were driven to brilliant achievement by intense competition and toxic rivalries. This city of one and three-quarter million people contained a rare concentration of geniuses, and the atmosphere was febrile and invigorating, born of a culture in a constant state of self-scrutiny and reinvention. In the year preceding the war one could sit in the Café Central in Herrengasse reading commentary in the *Neue Freie Presse*[*] on a novel by a member of the avant-garde *Jung Wien* literary movement, or on the so-called *Skandalkonzert* at which Arnold Schoenberg had conducted a performance of atonal expressionist music by radical composers of the Second Viennese School. The audience rioted and the organiser, Erhard Buschbeck, punched the operetta composer Oscar Straus, who said the smack on his jaw was the most harmonious sound he heard all evening.

If not the *NFP*, the city's most popular paper, perhaps a copy of Karl Kraus's journal *Die Fackel*,[†] in which he repeatedly lambasted the *Neue Freie Presse* for its corruption by commercial interests. *Die Fackel* carried no advertisements and was a pure conduit for Kraus's uncompromising world view; he was obsessive and fastidious in his proofreading, wanting no typographical errors to hinder the power of each issue's satirical assault on his readers' minds. Kraus was an acerbic, divisive presence whose enemies outnumbered his friends, but even his fiercest critics conceded he lent Viennese culture a rare stringency and moral seriousness – Joseph Roth, for example, who swung violently from idolising Kraus as a student, to writing after his death in 1936: 'I admit that I, who could not stand Karl Kraus, have learned a lot from him in

---

[*] Stefan Zweig: 'the *Neue Freie Presse* ... with its high-minded stance, its concentration on culture and its political prestige occupied much the same position throughout the entire Austro-Hungarian Monarchy as *The Times* did in England and *Le Temps* in France ... The editor, Moritz Benedikt, a man of inexhaustible energy and with a phenomenal talent for organisation, put all his positive daemonic energy into outshining all the German newspapers in the field of literature and culture.' Stefan Zweig, *The World of Yesterday: Memoirs of a European*, trans. Anthea Bell (Pushkin Press, 2011), p. 122.
[†] 'The Torch'.

my life ... From Karl Kraus after all I learned to tell the wheat from the chaff in the literary world.'[23] Schoenberg, meanwhile, sent Kraus a copy of his *Harmonielehre** with the inscription, 'I have learned more perhaps from you than one can learn if one is to remain independent.'[24] Walter Benjamin wrote of Kraus that 'Nothing is understood about this man until it has been perceived that ... everything – language and fact – falls, for him, within the sphere of justice.'[25] This attitude accorded with the young Roth's preoccupation with social justice and would inform the fixation on justice – or more often injustice – that later shaped his literary works.

The Café Central, Vienna, c.1900.

Kraus saw himself as the conscience of a decadent capital. He wrote much of *Die Fackel* in coffee houses, a feature of Vienna since the seventeenth century that formed a locus for intellectual conversation. Take an *Einspänner* coffee (served black in a glass, topped with

---

* Meaning 'Theory of Harmony', published in 1911.

whipped cream) at the Café Central and you might overhear writers such as Peter Altenberg, Arthur Schnitzler, Alfred Polgar, Hugo von Hofmannsthal and Stefan Zweig in impassioned debate at the next table; all were members of the *Jung Wien* movement. There was a fair chance you'd see Leon Trotsky there too, or Sigmund Freud (another figure of scorn for Roth, who later mocked him as 'the father-confessor of the beautiful Jewish women of Vienna'[26]); or, some years earlier, Theodor Herzl and his circle of Zionists; or, until his embittered departure in 1913, the young Adolf Hitler hawking his sterile watercolours of picturesque Vienna. Other residents of the city that year included Ioseb Dzhugashvili and Josip Broz, later better known as Joseph Stalin and Marshal Tito.

Around this congregation of geniuses and grotesques the city kept reimagining itself, just as its empire entered its death throes. Architects created buildings that rejected art nouveau flourishes and curlicues for a clean, modernist style, and the interiors' simple furnishings reflected this too. The Vienna Secession, an offshoot of the nouveau movement, comprised artists, designers and architects who, like Kraus, strove to create an honest artistic vision uncompromised by financial motivations. In the first issue of its journal, *Ver Sacrum*,* the literary critic Hermann Bahr wrote: 'Our art is not a combat of modern artists against those of the past, but the promotion of the arts against the peddlers who pose as artists and who have a commercial interest in not letting art bloom. The choice between commerce and art is the issue at stake in our Secession. It is not a debate over aesthetics, but a confrontation between two different spiritual states.'[27] The Secession's first president was Gustav Klimt; his paintings defined the moment's sensuality, and his protégé Egon Schiele's its angst and erotic fixations. Klimt and Schiele were often to be seen at the Café Museum on the corner of Friedrichstrasse and Operngasse, a café designed by Adolf Loos, another member of the Secession whose essay 'Ornament and Crime' influenced the architectural trend from fin-de-siècle decoration towards smooth, modernist lines. This was known as an artists' café,

---

* 'Sacred Spring'.

but writers were often seen there too: Elias Canetti, Robert Musil, the ubiquitous Kraus.

In his short story 'Buchmendel', set in the 1930s, Stefan Zweig evokes the atmosphere of these Viennese coffee houses. Seeking to escape a downpour, his narrator recounts that 'Luckily there is a café at almost every street-corner in the metropolis, and I made for the nearest,' not noticing its name as he dashes in from the rain. 'Since it was already late in the evening, the air, which would have been stuffy anyhow, was thick with tobacco-smoke ... Succumbing to the inertia which results from the narcotic atmosphere of the typical Viennese café', the narrator realises that this one is familiar. He scans the interior and at last finds a trigger for long-buried memories of a time before the First World War. 'A square box of a place, behind the bar – the card room ... There were two small billiard-tables, looking like silent ponds covered with green scum. In the corners, card tables, at one of which two bearded men of professorial type were playing chess. Beside the iron stove, close to a door labelled "Telephone," was another small table. In a flash, I had it! That was Mendel's place, Jacob Mendel's. That was where Mendel used to hang out, Buchmendel. I was in the Café Gluck!'[28]

Mendel was a book pedlar, so immersed in perusing his daily pile of hardbacks and periodicals that he had no regard for his tattered clothing or dirty fingernails, a ragged autodidact who formed part of the furniture in Zweig's fictional café: the marble-topped table, the kerosene lamps, the telephone, and Buchmendel sitting alone, 'his spectacled eyes fixed upon the printed page' but 'not altogether motionless, for he had a habit (acquired in the Jewish quarter of the Galician town from where he came) of rocking his shiny bald pate backwards and forwards and humming to himself as he read. There he studied catalogues and tomes, crooning and rocking, as Jewish boys are taught to do when reading the Talmud. The rabbis believe that, just as a child is rocked to sleep in its cradle, so are the pious ideas of the holy text better instilled by this rhythmical and hypnotising movement of head and body.'[29]

Jacob Mendel was an archetype of a familiar figure in pre-war

Vienna. Since the late nineteenth century thousands of Galician Jews had arrived and had a profound impact on its identity and culture, though this influence was far from universally admired within the city. The Christian Social Party mayor Karl Lueger had declared that: 'The Jews don't want "equality" but complete domination,' and claimed they were planning 'the establishment of an international alliance of banks with its seat in Washington' so as to 'publicly dictate its laws to the world'. Just as Russia had driven out its Jews, said Lueger, 'Should the Jews threaten our fatherland, we will show no mercy either.'[30] It had ever been thus. A rhyme dating from 1690 summarised the Viennese attitude towards those from the east:

If you go to Poland, what do you find?
A rough nobleman and a drunken swine
Many stinking Jews, plenty rats and mice
Scrawny little oxen, big fat lice.[31]

Viennese contempt for Galicia intensified during the reign of Empress Maria Theresa, when in 1772 Austria received the territory during the dismembering of Poland. An emissary she dispatched to this distant land reported that it was full of lice and Jews. In 1777, the empress wrote: 'In future no Jew shall be allowed to remain in Vienna without my special permission. I know of no greater plague than this race, which on account of its deceit, usury and avarice is driving my subjects into beggary. Therefore as far as possible, the Jews are to be kept away and avoided.'[32] Such loathing for Jews was not exclusive to gentiles. These ideas hung like bacteria in the air of Austrian society and were inhaled daily by all its inhabitants. Roth, one of 'the lowest of all the Jews', knew well that antisemitic snobbery and hatred were internalised by Jews themselves: he saw it in western Jews' attitude to the *Ostjuden*, and in his own feelings about his Jewishness. Likewise he knew that in such self-rejection, some Jews saw the possibility of freedom from their straitjacketed condition.

Of the artists and intellectuals mentioned above, most* were Jewish, and few were entirely comfortable with this. In the still of the night, lying unconscious in the city that elected Karl Lueger, the city where their Jewishness limited their professional prospects, the Viennese Jews' repressed desires emerged from the depths of their minds. In *The Interpretation of Dreams* Sigmund Freud describes a dream† ostensibly inspired by thwarted career aspirations; but as Carl E. Schorske notes, Freud's was surely not the only mind whose dreams 'revealed a disguised wish either not to be Jewish or to have the power to eliminate professional rivals'.[33] Mayer, Kraus and Schoenberg converted to Christianity, and its allure, coupled with ambivalence about his Jewishness, would prove one of the themes of Roth's life. A flavour of his contempt for the Jews' perceived lack of refinement comes in a remark in a 1916 letter from Vienna written to Paula Grübel: 'it's summer outside, and a holiday, and a scent of lime blossom has snuck in from somewhere, and perched on my windowsill. Alas, my neighbour is a Jewess, and scares away my lime blossom with her appalling squawks. Her voice is shrill, and smells of onions.'[34] The final line is at once brilliant and contemptible.

Roth's pronouncements on Jews are so contradictory that it is hard to resolve them into a coherent outlook. He describes them with respect and contempt, love and loathing. The same man who once termed them 'so stupid'[35] elsewhere rhapsodised about 'Jewish intelligence'; they were 'the weakest and far from loveliest of peoples' whom it takes 'a truly divine love to choose',[36] and yet an Orthodox 'Eastern Jew has within himself more humanity and more divinity than all the preachers can come up with in all the theological colleges of Western Europe'.[37] The only consistency discernible is that he is almost uniformly rude about western, 'assimilated' Jews, reliably furious with those on the left who 'sowed Marxism and reaped the swastika',[38] and equally scathing about the Zionists who would detach the Jews from Europe; while by turns, depending on his mood and his company,

---

* Schoenberg, Kraus, Altenberg, Schnitzler, Zweig, Freud, Trotsky, Canetti, Mayer.
† The 'Dream of the Uncle with the Yellow Beard'.

he admires and derides the eastern Jews for their dogged refusal to assimilate. The best way to marshal these views is to perceive them all as within a strained relationship to one's family. He will criticise his family, but will rear up if an outsider dares do the same. He is angry with his family, knows just how best to needle and hurt them, speaks *in extremis* of severing ties with them, and yet he loves them, even if he rarely tells them so. These are not exclusive positions.

The instinct towards Jewish self-loathing was hardly unusual. As Marjorie Perloff notes, a gallery of Viennese cultural figures, 'mostly of Jewish as well as provincial descent, came of age in one of the most anti-Semitic periods in modern European history, the paradox being that in their eagerness to be part of the larger cultural and artistic scene, they were themselves prone to anti-Semitism'. This manifested in 'The drive to "pass", to undergo such rituals as the *Karriere-Taufe* (career baptism)'.[*39] Conversion to Christianity seemed to many the only long-term solution to antisemitism – before settling on Zionism, Theodor Herzl proposed mass-baptism as the answer, and 'imagined himself leading thousands upon thousands of Austrian Jews in a long procession to St Stephen's Cathedral, there to liberate his persecuted, homeless people for ever from the curse of segregation and hatred'.[40] One's Jewishness, if not discarded with relief, seemed worth sacrificing for the anticipated dividends: Roth's literary idol Heinrich Heine described his conversion from Judaism to Protestantism almost a century earlier as 'the ticket of admission into European culture'. Later Roth would have occasion to ask, on seeing his second novel meet greater success in Russian translation than German, whether he was 'a German writer'.[41] As the Roth scholar Sidney Rosenfeld observes, 'The question was at least as old as Heinrich Heine. A century earlier, the Jewish Heine had confidently proclaimed in his *Buch der Lieder*, "I am a German poet / Renowned in German lands," while still knowing he was regarded as an outsider to Germandom and being wary about reviews mentioning his Jewishness.' To profess one's Germanness and obscure one's

---

* Another popular method of 'passing' was rhinoplasty – when the American actor Fanny Brice proudly underwent this procedure in 1923, Dorothy Parker noted she had 'cut off her nose to spite her race'.

Jewishness had long seemed politic; but eventually most Jews were disabused of the idea that they could transform into acceptable, authentic
Germans. 'Many others after Heine – among them the popular author
of village stories Berthold Auerbach (1812–82) and, most poignantly
of all, the novelist Jakob Wassermann (1873–1934) – came to know
the pain of rejection and despaired of it. The literary historian Adolf
Bartels (1862–1945), in fact, had made a career of tracing Jewish origins
and denouncing as un-German any writer possessed of them; in 1933
Bartels's obsession became the norm.'[42]

Worse than Heine's abnegation of his Jewishness were the attitudes
espoused by those such as Karl Kraus, a convert to Catholicism whom
Theodor Lessing termed 'that most brilliant example of Jewish self-
hate':[43] his criticisms of Moritz Benedikt, editor of the *Neue Freie Presse*,
employed vitriolic antisemitic language about Jewish dishonesty and
avarice.* The great Viennese moralist had a manic preoccupation with
alerting others to Jewish immorality. Still more grotesque was the
writer Arthur Trebitsch, who claimed he wasn't Jewish, tried to sue
people who said he was, gave viciously antisemitic lectures in German
cities, theorised that only Aryans could form original ideas and Jews
could only adapt and poison other people's, and, in his 1919 work *Spirit
and Judaism* (*Geist und Judentum*), argued that Jewish presence in Europe
damaged the spirit of the Aryan peoples, so the Jews must be forcibly
removed. In the 1920s he funded the Nazi Party, as Roth would allude
to in his first novel. It is little wonder, given the pervasive loathing for

---

* Kraus's best-known work, his epic anti-war play *Die Letzten Tage der Menschheit* (*The
Last Days of Mankind*), contains numerous examples of antipathy to Jews that encapsulate the wider phenomenon of Jewish antisemitism in the first third of the twentieth
century. In Act I there is what has been termed 'a most lurid description of a Jewish-
war profiteer: "A fat Jew from the Automobile Corps. His belly is a Moloch. His nose
is a sickle which drips blood. His eyes shine like carbuncles . . ." Throughout the first
half of the play the specific object of Kraus's venom, and his *Sündenbock* [scapegoat]
for the growing catastrophe, is a Viennese middle class, which Kraus represents as
overwhelmingly Jewish . . .'. Kraus says the greatest evil is the 'lying language' of the
Neue Freie Presse and its Jewish editor Moritz Benedikt. 'The evil here is specifically
Jewish. Indeed, Benedikt appears in the final Epilogue of the whole play as the Lord of
the Hyenas.' From William O. McCagg, 'Jewish Assimilation in Austria', in Robert S.
Wistrich (ed.), *Austrians and Jews in the Twentieth Century: From Franz Joseph to Waldheim*
(St Martin's Press, 1992), pp. 62–3.

Jews emanating not only from gentiles but also erstwhile members of their own community – an insistent, unending hatred from all directions – that many people tried to shed their Jewishness in a tactical bid for acceptance. But Schoenberg and Gustav Mahler's fates encapsulate their resulting disillusion. In the early 1920s Schoenberg learned painfully that his conversion to Protestantism in 1898 offered no immunity from antisemitic persecution. To the antisemite, conversion did not redeem the Jew but only confirmed his inauthenticity and mendacity: how very like a cowardly Yid to imagine he could squirm his way to safety by donning a new guise. 'I have at last learnt the lesson that has been forced upon me this year,' Schoenberg wrote, 'and I shall never forget it. It is that I am not a German, not a European, indeed perhaps scarcely even a human being (at least, the Europeans prefer the worst of their race to me), but that I am a Jew.'[44] He had reached the same conclusion as his mentor Mahler, an earlier Viennese convert to Catholicism: 'I am thrice homeless: as a Bohemian among Austrians, as an Austrian among the Germans, and as a Jew throughout the entire world. I am an intruder everywhere, welcome nowhere.'[45] Roth would later observe, in response to a book review that called him a one-off in German literature, that 'The feeling of not belonging anywhere, which has always been with me, was borne out.'[46] The notion of home – its provisional existence and sudden absence; the prospect of being made homeless in Europe and establishing a homeland in Palestine – would define the condition of European Jews in the first three decades of the twentieth century.

In leaving Galicia and securing a perch in the capital, the nineteen-year-old Joseph Roth hoped he had come home: he felt himself at the centre of his world, no longer peripheral but proximate to his revered emperor, intoxicated by the city's intellectual life and architectural grandeur. He arrived alone and rented a room in Leopoldstadt, the

Jewish quarter – his new address was 35 Rembrandtstrasse,* a short walk across the river to the Ringstrasse, where he surveyed the fine houses, the Parliament, the Palace of Justice and the University of Vienna. He had managed to transfer his degree here and enrol as a student of Philosophy and German Literature.

Any idealism soon soured. In the grand, refined heart of the empire he grew yet more conscious of his lowly origins. Vienna sparkled like sunlit snow, beautiful but cold. The atmosphere was unwelcoming; though escaping Lemberg removed him from the midst of Polish–Ukrainian aggression, this genteel city's disdain for Galician Jews reiterated the same question: how could he make himself appear worthy of respect? While he now lived in the capital, his surrounds in Leopoldstadt were familiar from life in Brody. He remained in a set-ting that felt like his old home, which we can imagine felt reassuringly familiar yet constrictive. He was surrounded by the *Ostjuden* about whom he felt so ambivalent in Galicia. Here they still wore caftans, spoke Yiddish, bought and sold goods, aspired to ascend from street selling to shopkeeping. Their children, however, had grander plans. Between 1912 and 1914 the proportion of the University of Vienna's students who were Jewish grew to 27.54 per cent, owing to this influx of students from the east, Roth among them. The traders' sons 'were already able to make the great leap'[47] and graduated from the University of Vienna to become 'lawyers, doctors, scholars, writers, propri-etors of department stores', who 'moved into the city centre or to the Alsergrund,† and belonged to a different world'.[48]

Their rapid success brings to mind the old Jewish joke: 'What's the difference between a tailor and a psychiatrist? A generation.' But it remained the case that professional success did not amount to social

---

* Claudio Magris on Roth's time here: 'The building is grey, surrounded by the drab-ness of the suburbs; the stairway is dark, and in the featureless courtyard is a stunted tree. Living in this building it cannot have been difficult to become a specialist in melancholy, the dominant note of Vienna and Mitteleuropa as a whole. Here is the sadness of boarding-school and barracks, the sadness of symmetry, of transience and disenchantment.' *Danube* (Collins Harvill, 1990), p. 193.

† A well-to-do district of Vienna, home at varying times to Franz Schubert, Ludwig van Beethoven and Sigmund Freud, who psychoanalysed his patients at his premises in Berggasse.

acceptance, and elements of both gentile and Jewish Vienna alike continued to scorn the Jews who had for decades contributed to the city's cultural flowering. Vienna promised a home for these people and formed the setting for the apogee of European Jewish culture, but ultimately would remind its Jews of their homelessness. Roth spoke for many when he observed that 'I have no home, aside from being at home in myself.'[49] But such a home's security depends on its being impervious to others' ill-founded yet vehement beliefs: for a Jew, it requires steely resolve not to admit at least some of the barrage of antisemitic ideas one is exposed to while moving through the world. Roth, like many Jews of his time, could not prevent the ingress of such notions into his psyche.

Orthodox Jews from Galicia at the Karmeliterplatz in
Vienna's second district, Leopoldstadt, in 1915.

Imagine, then, this combination of conditions and beliefs: that one's home is in one's head, but the toxic stereotypes peddled by antisem-ites are true enough to prompt self-rejection, that European nation states offer little security, but a Jewish national home is a suspect endeavour ... suddenly the prospect of 'home' vanishes, at least as a secure refuge. As Devorah Baum writes, 'there is no "at home" for the self-hater. To hate oneself is to have no "safe space" to return to, no comfortable way of withdrawing from the world into the shelter of a private sphere.'[50]

But consider too that for a writer such as Roth, the childlike desire for a safe and stable home is countered by a dissonant professional urge towards homelessness. 'I am a stranger in this town,' he once wrote, describing a departure from an unnamed hotel in an unnamed place. 'That is why I was so at home here.'[51] This is not a paradox. Roth is stimulated by the unfamiliar. He thrills at absorbing fresh material to analyse in his constant project to understand the world, to feel less daunted by its terrors and confusions. The interrogative mode is his preferred mindset. He needs a little discomfort to feel alert; too much comfort is soporific. When he starts to feel drowsy, it is time to move to somewhere that will reinstate this productive unease, which enables him to write and thus to articulate himself, resulting in a moment's relief from his angst and a glimpse of happiness. Returning to a state of homelessness becomes a homecoming.

By 1914 hostility to Austria-Hungary had grown fervent among nationalists in the Balkans. On the command of Emperor Franz Joseph, his heir Franz Ferdinand visited the region in June to observe military manoeuvres and open a state museum that would symbolise Austrian power. When the Serbian nationalist Gavrilo Princip shot Ferdinand and his wife, Sophie, on 28 June, Roth was in Vienna. He admired the 'linguistic grandeur' of the elderly emperor's declaration of war one month later: although Franz Joseph had hoped to 'devote the years which by God's grace still remain to Me to works of peace', he wrote that the 'machinations of an opponent filled with hatred compel Me to preserve the honour of My monarchy, to defend her reputation and her position of power, to secure her possessions after long years of peace and reach for the sword'.[52] Thirteen years on, Roth would recall the outbreak of fighting. 'The World War began in Sarajevo, on a balmy summer afternoon in 1914,' he wrote during a visit to the Balkan city. 'It was a Sunday; I was a student at the time. In the afternoon a girl came round. Girls wore plaits in those days. She was carrying a large yellow straw hat in her hand, it was like summer coming to call, with hay, grasshoppers and poppies. In her straw hat was a telegram, the first special edition I had seen, crumpled and terrible, a thunderbolt on paper. "Guess what," said the girl, "they've killed the heir to the throne. My father came home from the café. But we're not going to stay here, are we?"[53]

A fortnight after Franz Joseph's declaration of war, the Russian armies swarmed into Austria's eastern provinces. Lemberg was the setting in late summer for the Battle of Galicia, in which both sides incurred six-figure death tolls before Russia claimed victory in September and captured the city. Galician Jews were deported and executed on charges of being Austrian spies, and raped and murdered by Cossacks. Almost 400,000 Jewish refugees left the region for Hungary, Moravia, Bohemia and Vienna. There were more than 300 students from Brody alone at the University of Vienna in late 1914. Roth's entries on the Faculty of Arts' attendance rolls reveal the consequences of this mass migration on his new, would-be independent life in Vienna. 'Moses Joseph Roth' is entered on all five of the year's rolls. His nationality is recorded as Austrian. Birthplace and crownland: Brody, Galicia. Native language: German. Religion: Mosaic. Father's name, occupation and place of residence are left blank. And while the first answer to 'Name, Occupation and Place of Residence of Guardian' reads: 'S. Grübel, Lemberg, Merchant', the next four state: 'Maria Roth, private, presently Vienna, Wallensteinstrasse 14/16'.[54] In the late summer of 1914, Roth's mother joined that exodus of Galician Jews to Vienna and, accompanied by her sister Rivka Piczenik, moved into an apartment in the working-class Brigittenau neighbourhood to be reunited with her beloved son.

Around this time Roth took a trip back home to Galicia, where he saw his new friend and fellow student Soma Morgenstern. They visited a Jewish inn in Lemberg, the Zehngut, and discussed their desire to see Russia defeated. On seeing an elderly man enter the bar, Roth told Morgenstern how he envisaged himself in old age; they were young enough that the idea seemed a safely distant source of amused speculation. 'I'm a skinny old man,' he said. 'I wear a long black robe with long sleeves that almost cover my hands. It's autumn, and I take walks in a garden and think up devious plots against my enemies. Against my enemies and my friends too.'[55]

Back in Vienna, it seemed the university's library was overrun by Jewish refugees. 'Books had suddenly disappeared, there was general indignation, suspicion fell on the Jewish students from Galicia,' writes David Bronsen. 'Students' briefcases were more rigorously checked from now on, and access to reference catalogues was henceforth only granted to library staff. The local students avoided the Galicians or openly showed their displeasure at their presence. No Galician, least of all the hypersensitive Joseph Roth, remained unaffected by the atmosphere of the time.'[56] At times, young Jews left the lecture halls to be ambushed and beaten with clubs by antisemitic fellow students. In The Wandering Jews, Roth would take a swipe at 'The University of Vienna, where they impose quotas and bigotry . . . It is terribly hard to be an Eastern Jew, there is no harder lot than that of the Eastern Jew newly arrived in Vienna.'[57]

Roth did what most people would do in such hostile circumstances: he made every effort to fit in, though the degree to which he undertook this effort suggests he needed little excuse to disown his previous identity. He began to affect the mannerisms and style of a Viennese dandy. Some say he adopted a Viennese accent, others that he took pains not to: 'Our German had a high Viennese sound,' one of his tutors later recalled, whereas Roth 'spoke an emphatic High German. You could literally feel how he made an effort to speak very correct German.'*[58] Read in this light, the passages in The Wandering Jews where he chastises western Jews for parodying their host nations' practices and diluting their eastern origins take on an air of self-chastisement – 'And on top of that they're proud of it!' As was Roth. In a speech given in the early 1940s, his fellow university student Józef Wittlin recalled how Roth stood out. He arrived at lectures alone and sat apart from

---

* This mimicry did not amount to whole-hearted admiration for the culture of his host city. Roth adopted the costume and admired aspects of the Viennese character – the value placed on courtliness, for instance – but despaired of the city's inhabitants too, as he made plain in conversation with his cousin Michael Grübel: 'The Viennese has part of his brain missing, and it happens to be the very part containing the seat of the intelligence.'

the other students, a habit born of shyness which heightened his air of aloofness, and on first noticing him Wittlin felt insulted. 'Joseph Roth was one of those people whom you love or hate,' Wittlin said. 'He had many enemies but more friends. My friendship with him lasted nearly twenty-five years – after a hatred which endured about two weeks. I saw him for the first time in 1915 at the University of Vienna. He was my classmate in philosophy and together we attended the lectures of Walter Brecht, professor of German literature,' which Wittlin said were popular during the first year of the war, especially with female students. 'Few men attended and it was no wonder that those who did drew attention. Roth caught my eye. He was very thin and elegantly dressed. His light hair was parted in the middle and he seemed to me the prototype of the Viennese "*gigerl*".* And in his beautiful, ironic blue eye he wore a monocle. This was what irritated me. It is difficult to say whether Roth wore the monocle the better to see a world which at that time seemed charming and delightful to him, or whether he was ashamed of his love for the world and hoped to camouflage his admiration with a monocle which gave his sharp countenance an arrogant grimace.'

The nineteen-year-old Wittlin felt that this conceited stranger was staring at him in a deliberate affront. 'In the old world,' he explained, looking back on that pre-war era from thirty years' distance, 'to stare at a stranger ironically was almost an offence. The word for it was "fixation" ... I was especially sensitive in the matter of honour, and particularly with respect to the Germans. This German – which was what I considered Roth – is attempting to provoke me, I thought.'

Wittlin ran through the possible reasons – perhaps it was that he and his friends spoke Polish, or perhaps this man was a Christian Socialist antisemite. 'Suffice it to say that my reaction to Roth's provocation was just what you would've expected of a freshman in Old Austria. I possessed newly printed visiting cards inscribed "Stud. Phil.",' because he was a student of philosophy, and 'I was determined to fling my visiting card in the face of this arrogant youth and his monocle, if he did not

---

* A dandy man about town, related to the Italian *gigolo*.

stop his staring. This, of course, would have called for a duel. I was not even aware of my prospective adversary's name.'

Stefan Zweig described the code of honour that persisted among early-twentieth-century Viennese scholars in his memoir *The World of Yesterday*. 'Only in Germany and German-speaking Austria, where class consciousness still had the upper hand, did students cling tenaciously to privileges which had long ago lost any meaning,' he wrote. 'They even based their own student code of conduct on them.' Anyone who insulted them would be challenged to a duel if considered 'fit to give satisfaction', i.e. of sufficient social standing to merit 'the honour of crossing swords with one of those stupid, beardless boys'. In those times, said Zweig, 'to be considered a real student you had to have proved your courage, meaning you had fought as many duels as possible, and even showed the signs of those heroic deeds on your face in the form of duelling scars; unscarred cheeks and a nose without a nick in it were unworthy of an academic in the genuine German tradition.'[59] Jews were often denied the 'honour' of 'satisfaction' by gentile students in Alemannic fraternities, the cited reason being that Jews were cowards and unworthy of fighting.* According to Robert Wistrich, however, a significant factor was fear of humiliation: for reasons of self-defence Jewish students had become expert swordsmen and were too likely to emerge victorious.

Wittlin told a friend of his plan to retain his honour. The friend tried to cool Wittlin's temper and soon afterwards introduced him to another young Pole, who asked him whether he would 'care to meet an unusually brilliant German poet' whom this man knew from the Brody *Gymnasium*. Not only was Wittlin an aspiring writer, he had been born near Brody, and his father and uncles had attended the school,

---

* Jacob Wassermann, in his pained memoir *My Life as German and Jew*, details how German peers saw him as qualitatively, irredeemably different at a spiritual level, writing that 'those for whom I was and remained a Jew, wanted to make me understand that I could not give them satisfaction; that is, as a Jew. That as a Jew I was incapable of sharing their secret higher life, incapable of stirring their souls or becoming attuned to their character. They would not concede that I too bore the color and stamp of German life; they would not let the kindred principle approach them.' *My Life as German and Jew*, by Jacob Wassermann, trans. S. N. Brainin (Coward-McCann, 1933), p. 146.

so he was intrigued to meet this character. 'You can well imagine my facial expression when the lyricist turned out to be no other than the youth with the monocle, whom I had intended to challenge to a duel. Truthfully, I had pictured German poets as looking quite different.' The two became friends and corresponded for the rest of Roth's days. 'I have had many friends in my life,' Wittlin said, 'but Roth was the only one who ever called me a friend of his soul, "*Freund meiner Seele*".'[60] For many years they would end their letters with a couplet from one of Roth's early poems:

Hoch die Geige, hoch die Geige,
*Stille dummes Herz und Schweige.**

The books the students ingested under the guidance of Walter Brecht and through the other undergraduate courses† shaped Roth's tastes for life. He kept Wittlin apprised of his favourite discoveries. Wittlin recalled that Roth particularly loved Arthur Schnitzler, Hugo von Hofmannsthal, whose poems he could still recite two decades later, Stendhal, whom he read in German translation, and Joseph Conrad, of whom Roth would write that his books are 'turbulent like the sea and calm like the sea and deep like the sea'.[61] Later in life, though, he would credit Marcel Proust as his greatest influence. 'I learned a lot from Proust,' he told Soma Morgenstern, then confided in him that in fact: 'I learned most of all from Proust.' Why so secretive, wondered Morgenstern. 'One should never admit from whom one has learned,' said Roth. 'On the contrary, one should cover all traces.'[62]

---

* 'Raise the violin, raise the violin, / Silence, foolish heart, be silent.'
† Subjects included 'History of the German Novel and Related Genres', 'History of German Literature in the Last Third of the Nineteenth Century', 'History of the German Novel in the Eighteenth Century', studying Goethe and Schiller, 'Sixteenth-century Drama', 'Seminar in German Philology – Interpretation of Opitz', 'History of German Drama from the End of the Middle Ages to the English Comedians, with Elucidation from Various Dramatic Works', and so on. He also attended lectures in 'Psychology', 'The Psychology of Language', 'The History of Humanism', 'On Fallacies', 'The Interpretation and Definition of Musical Works', 'Exercises and Essays on Ethnography' and 'The Place of Venetian Art in the Context of the General Development of Art'.

Around his academic timetable and within his financial constraints, he began to establish a social life. As well as Wittlin, it was at this stage that he grew closer to Morgenstern, who found Roth's monocle an affectation but became an important friend. He also socialised with select members of his extended family. The first person he cleaved to in Vienna was a great-uncle, Joseph Czecher, a brother of his maternal grandmother. This lawyer's clerk in his sixties executed repossession orders and had a lifestyle that tallied well with Roth's. 'From six in the evening he sat in the coffee house,' writes Bronsen, 'playing cards until closing time and knocking back one glass after another. Several times a month Roth met up with his uncle, who was always under-slept but never out of sorts. They met in his coffee house on the corner of Nussdorferstrasse and Währingerstrasse. His uncle was animated in Roth's company and merrily recounted droll incidents in his life. Roth remained loyal to Czecher and on later visits to Vienna would always seek him out in his regular haunt. In March 1938, when Roth paid a last fleeting visit to Vienna, his uncle, by now in his 80s, was the only blood relation he went to see.'[63]

At 6 a.m. one day during his first year at the University of Vienna, Roth travelled to Schönbrunn Palace, the Habsburgs' vast rococo residence in the west of the city, to see the emperor leaving for the spa town of Bad Ischl. At last, the distant, unknowable father figure who had loomed over his Brody childhood stood there before him, in the flesh. 'And it really was the Emperor,' he wrote. 'There he came, old and bowed, tired ... and, so early in the morning, confused by the loyalty of his subjects, perhaps a little nervous too at the thought of the journey, in that state which was then referred to in the news-paper report as "the monarch's youthful freshness", and with the slow step of an old man which was called "elastic", almost tripping and with softly tinkling spurs, an old black and rather dusty officer's cap on his head, such as was still worn in the days of Radetzky ... The young lieutenants despised this style of cap. The Emperor was the only member of the army who held so strictly to the regulations. For he *was* an Emperor.'[64]

It is said that he made another pilgrimage during these months. He found an address for the author Stefan Zweig, travelled to the apartment and stood outside, gazing at the door, hoping that Zweig might emerge; but he did not. After a time, Roth walked away.

It was a time when he hoped to build literary connections and develop as a writer but found himself frustrated. A few years later he would tell his cousin Fred Grübel in Leipzig how disappointed he had been by his German courses, saying he wanted poetry but received 'scholarly discipline'.[65] The only lecturer he admired was Professor Brecht, whose structural analysis of the novels they studied Roth regarded as his most valuable experience at university. He was happy, though – a student friend said that life 'seemed beautiful and magical to him then',[66] and his letters show an optimism that the world functioned with sufficient justice to repay effort and investment. In one, undated but from late 1915, he writes to his cousin Paula in playful, confident tones. He alludes to the pride he takes in his dress, spits out a few dislikeable contemptuous remarks about women, and makes light of his continued financial hardship while letting on in faux-casual terms that he has probably had some poems published.* He had offered them to *Österreichs Illustrierte Zeitung* in August 1915.

Unfortunately, Mme Sun has had a toothache these past few days. She's wrapped her face in black cloths. From time to time a bit of white cotton wool peeps out. And now it's gone and started raining. M. Wind, my friend, has married Mme Cloud. I attended their wedding, a jolly affair. Now Mme Cloud is giving birth to their children on a daily basis: small and great Showers. What a to-do. I must ask the wind to desist, because his sons will insist on spoiling my creases. And you know how sacrosanct *they* are ... Ever since October 1st, the library has been open all day. Soon lectures will begin. This year, Brecht is giving a course on classical drama (less

---

* Paula took a great interest in his poetry and amassed a collection of around 150 early poems, which she intended to publish after his death, but around half were lost during the early years of the Second World War – some as Paula attempted to escape from France, others when Józef Wittlin's flat in Warsaw was bombed.

interesting, unfortunately). Then the girl students will show up, with their earnest expressions and tousled hair. Anxious faces, like a three-day rain. How I hate those women! Though students are no more women than streetwalkers are . . .

I have poems due to appear in *Österreichs Illustrierte Zeitung*, if they haven't come out already. I haven't the cash or inclination to go to a café or to invest in a copy. Either would set me back 60 hellers. If you wouldn't mind, perhaps you can see if they've run something of mine . . . What do you think about money? I don't think it's worth bothering about. If I had it, I would chuck it out the window. Money's the opposite of women. You think highly of a woman until you've got her, then when you get her, you feel like chucking her out (or at least you ought). Whereas money you despise as long as you don't have it, and then you think very highly of it . . . Things are all right. I myself am better than all right. My heart is heavy and my pockets are light. Mind you, if my pockets were as heavy as my heart, then my heart would be as light as my pockets.

This is an early example of his finding poetic inspiration in the relationship between money and well-being. The twenty-year-old signs off this letter to his cousin with a fond nod to their childhood: 'Greetings, Muniu Faktisch'.[67]

Österreichs Illustrierte Zeitung published the poems, wistful juvenilia that speak of some lingering preoccupations in early adulthood: memories of childhood anxiety, his mother's protection, the accelerating passage of time, the abandonment of his homeland in search of one where he would feel more at home. They are credited to 'Joseph Roth'; by now he had abandoned the 'Moses', except among family. The first is titled '*Welträtsel*', or 'The World's Mystery':

Sterne gibt's, die ewig scheinen wollten
    Stars there are, that wished to shine for ever,
Und doch verglüh'n . . .
    But they have faded . . .

Wolken gibt's, die eher weinen sollten

    Clouds there are, that rather should have wept,

Und weiterzieh'n . . .

    And they move on . . .

Steine gibt's, die viel zu fragen wüssten,

    Stones there are, that could ask many things,

Doch keiner spricht . . .

    But none speaks . . .

Menschen gibt's, die sich was fragen müssten,

    People there are, that should ask something of themselves,

Und sagen's nicht . . .

    And say it not . . .[68]

The second was titled '*Wo?*', or '*Where?*':

Ich war einmal ein kleines Kind,

    Once I was a very small child,

Das angstgequält zur Mutter floh,

    Who fled to his mother in anguish

Wenn durch den Schornstein fuhr der Wind –

    When the wind went through the chimney –

Ich weiss nicht wo . . .

    I know not where . . .

Ich hab einmal gëhort ein Lied,

    Once, I heard a little song,

Das klang so zart and und müde so.

    So tender and weary its sound.

Als ich von meiner Heimat schied –

    When I parted with my homeland –

Ich weiss nicht wo . . .

    I know not where . . .

Es hat einmal mein Herz gebebt,

   Once, I had a trembling heart,

Mohnblumen brannten lichterloh,

   Poppies were burning all ablaze,

Ich hab einmal ein Gluck erlebt . . .

   Once, I experienced some joy . . .

Ich weiss nicht wo . . .

   I know not where . . .[69]

In December the paper printed Roth's first published piece of prose. 'War Stories from the Autumn Wind' ('Herbstwindes Kriegsgeschichten') is a beautiful, dreamlike little collection of tableaux from the war, as narrated by 'my friend the wind'; evidently the imagery he used in the letter to Paula Grübel remained on his mind. As the Roth scholar Ingeborg Sültemeyer-von Lips has noted, the conceit reveals 'Roth's affinity with Heine'.[70] The wind blows from east to west, north to south and back, and it sees beauty, ugliness, joy and sadness; and 'at night it sometimes knocks on my windowpanes and tells me stories', Roth explains. The wind gusts by a train full of wounded and dying soldiers, and down a dirty Polish street where a grey-bearded Jew hangs from a gallows erected by jeering Cossacks, to Germany and Russia, until it blows over a battlefield where a friend's corpse lies; and from here it drifts to the dead boy's *Heimatstadt*, his home town, and to his house, where through a window it sees his unsuspecting mother alone in her lamp-lit parlour, writing a letter to her 'dear son'.[71]

Roth had parted from his *Heimat* and, in his sadder moments, dreamed of homecomings, whether physical or spiritual. The word is usually translated as 'home' or 'homeland', but these do not suggest the depth of the German term. *Heimat* is the familiar territory where one's soul best fits, where one can behave naturally without feeling conscious of others' gaze, where one feels safe, as an insider rather than an alien. It is a fount of spiritual and psychological comfort, not merely a physical location. To be distanced from such a home brings the sensation of *Heimweh*, homesickness. To be exiled is to enter a condition of *Heimatlosigkeit*, homelessness. When Roth in English translation refers to 'home', he means a place where he can be his true self, where the foundations of his identity formed in his Galician childhood are within reach even though he has transformed himself into an urbane metropolitan; that they still exist and he knows where.

Roth became Walter Brecht's favourite pupil, and Brecht a mentor to him: another academic father-figure, assuming the role held in Brody by Max Landau. He and Wittlin were less taken with Brecht's assistant Dr Heinz Kindermann, who largely ignored them and 'in [whose] heart . . . cherished perfect hatred for Slavs and Jews', as Wittlin put it. This year, 1916, as the war Vienna had launched brought food and clothing shortages, soaring inflation and rising crime to the city, Roth continued to focus on his writing and produced his first short story we know of. Titled '*Der Vorzugsschüler*', 'The Honours Student', it traces the rise of a Dr Anton Wanzl, a callous, scheming, ambitious academic, inspired by Kindermann. Roth derives palpable pleasure from describing Wanzl's downfall, when his 'underlying weakness, so long suppressed by sheer force of will, suddenly manifested itself. Anton Wanzl was laid low by pneumonia . . . He died after weeks of terrible suffering.'[72]

'Today looking back,' Wittlin reflected in the early 1940s, 'it strikes me that Kindermann was the classic prototype of the Nazi, which he apparently became.'[73] As late as 1932, Roth evidently retained his animosity towards his lecturer. *The Radetzky March* features a pathetic, insincere German lieutenant named Kindermann whose faults are listed at length – among them a squeaky voice, a 'rather feeble interest in the opposite sex', and an insubstantiality such that 'you felt you could put your hands through him as through a wispy, sunny, evening mist. Everything he said was gauzy and transparent . . . He sat at the table, like a cheerful zero.'[74] The novel barely contains a reference to him without a jibe: a generous portion of revenge served ice-cold almost two decades later.

Brecht's influence on Roth extended beyond literary ideals to his vision for Austria. As Michael Hofmann observes, he 'advanced an idea of Austria not as a corrupt and negligible appendage ripe for a tacit or explicit Anschluss . . . but as an older, better form of Germany'.[75] Roth confided in Brecht that his dream now was to emulate him as an academic teacher of German. He would later say that he had just taken the teaching qualification exam when the war started and disrupted his studies – but this is impossible, for it was necessary to have completed eight semesters and Roth had only six, and his name does not appear in the Imperial and Royal Examination Board's register of newly qualified teachers either before or after 1918. However, he did gain work as a private tutor, which gave him access to the households of the Viennese upper classes. Later he put his experiences into a short story titled 'The Private Tutor' ('Der Hauslehrer'), in which the narrator describes meeting a genteel woman in a railway carriage. He leaves his homeland to teach in the capital. 'No one accompanied me, I did not have to take my leave, say farewells nor wave goodbye. I turned my back on my home town. I looked with scorn on its spires, the panorama of the town lay before me like some picture postcard which meant nothing to me.'[76]

Roth calculated that admission into such people's rarefied realm would consolidate his new life beyond Galicia. This proved a formative period, giving him a template for the primary persona he would adopt for the rest of his life. His habits, adopted from the mid-1920s in Germany, of sending yellow roses to female friends and travelling by first-class rail, arose in imitation of such families' lifestyle. Likewise, writes Bronsen, 'the walking sticks Roth used in Berlin and Paris, the narrow officer's trousers he was in the habit of wearing since his army days, the hand-kissing and the chivalry – all these habits . . . remained with him from these years of contact with the metropolis on the Danube'.[77]

'Self-hatred can arise when the face you see in the mirror isn't the one you want,' observes Devorah Baum,

> when the body you wash in the bath isn't the kind you imagine others want, when you seem to have the wrong accent, the wrong name, the wrong parents. What you lack is the power of self-determination: your personhood has been determined impersonally by forces beyond your control. And so, given that who you are or appear to be isn't really you, you may well decide to alter these

things, whether through marriage, name change, surgery, or any of the various measures people resort to in order to disassociate themselves from family, history, body, roots. You reinvent yourself, becoming the person you would much rather be, the person you feel you are. But is this new self really you? Not according to the voice that whispers constantly inside your head: 'What if the old me resurfaces? What if my mask slips?'[78]

The courtly Viennese Roth strained to keep the mask in place. His peers were aware of the game he was playing: his friend Hermann Kesten would call him a '*Maskenspieler*', which Rosenfeld defines as 'a dissembler or player of divers roles'.[79] This was not a dishonorable deceit, more a survival tactic demanded by an antisemitic environment, but one forced upon him that he could turn into a pleasure. He enjoyed discovering new facets of his personality, testing which felt sustainable, which he might pull off convincingly in public. He contained a continuum of selves. He grew adept at, then relished, flitting between them as the circumstances required. Later he would expand on this in a novel where a character 'remembered the lunatic in his village at home, who never tired of asking everyone he met: "How many are you? Are you *one*?" No, one wasn't just *one*. One was ten people, twenty, a hundred. The more opportunities life gave us, the more beings it revealed in us. A man might die because he hadn't experienced anything, and had been just *one* person all his life.'[80]

He knew the potential loss entailed in adopting personae that might bring social gain. As he sought to gain a foothold in Vienna, he met with the dilemma faced by any ambitious and talented Jew. If attempting integration into a higher social stratum had a personal cost, he hoped it might prove a speculation that would reap dividends. Again, as Mahler and Schoenberg had found, social progress for a European Jew entailed expending a portion of one's authentic self in the hope that the invented self would offer a more comfortable condition. But to sustain a performance when under gentile scrutiny was one matter; to resolve one's inner sense of inauthenticity quite another. 'Every kind of assimilation,' Roth would write later, 'however superficial, is a flight or an attempt at flight from the sad community of the persecuted; is an attempt to reconcile contradictions which nevertheless exist.'[81] The schoolboy Roth who had urged assimilation with the Austrians was learning that an eastern Jew could disguise his *shtetl* self in Viennese society but had to maintain a constant effort to 'pass'* while quelling the ever-present internal contradictions between the old and the new selves. This eagerness to please was ultimately tragic, as he knew. When Roth later wrote that 'the Berlin Jews, long since lapsed, go on celebrating their holiest festivals in a kind of shamefaced secrecy, but Christmas publicly, and for all to see',[82] his tone is scornful. He had not long been in his dreamed-of Vienna before he realised that Jews in his position would remain in a perpetual condition of flight, rather than ever feel they had arrived.

---

* Devorah Baum again: 'lack of self-determination ... curses the inauthentic Jew to the life of a showman who, over the course of incessant theatrical appearances, could at any time forget one of his lines – as in the classic joke in which a Jew in a posh restaurant is doing a great job of "passing" until asked, "What would Sir like for his entrée?" "Oh, anything, as long as it's *treif*" [not kosher].' *Feeling Jewish (A Book for Just About Anyone)* (Yale University Press, 2017), p. 43.

Chapter Three

We were outfitted for life, only for death to greet us.

The White Cities, in *Report from a Parisian Paradise*

As the fighting raged between the Imperial Army and the Russians on the eastern front, and while around them one young man after another departed for battle, Roth and Józef Wittlin took pride in remaining in Vienna. They were pacifists, and Roth had started contributing to *Abend*, an anti-war newspaper. Driven by anger at the war and concern for the oppressed, at university Roth discarded his attachment to the Habsburg monarchy and embraced socialism, also toying with anarchism. He embraced the socialist cause with characteristic vigour and idealism, and among the many competing facets of his personality, the part that sympathised with the Habsburgs now withdrew from view. He was adamant that he would not help the ruling class pursue their military interests. His uncle Heinrich Grübel, along with the wife of the editor of the *Neues Wiener Journal*, concocted a ruse to avoid him being conscripted. They suggested that Roth describe himself as working for that pro-government, pro-war paper, whose editor would vouch for him as an indispensable member of staff. Roth disapproved of this form of deceit: 'It is not my way. I cannot say that I work for the *Neues Wiener Journal* when I work for the *Abend*.'[1]

At this time Roth and Wittlin revered Karl Kraus for the furious contempt in which he held the war's perpetrators. 'We considered the war a crime,' said Wittlin, 'committed by emperors and royal generals and ministers against an innocent lamb – which was what we romantically thought of humanity at the time.' Gradually their pacifist position became unsustainable. Soma Morgenstern arrived in Vienna on leave, dressed in his uniform, and Roth was impressed, feeling ashamed and conspicuous in civilian clothes. By 1916 he found it harder to take pride in his moral position when the streets of Vienna were increasingly populated by men crippled by their time at the front line; worse still were the friends who did not return at all. In Wittlin's words, 'as the war dragged on killing many of our close friends we grew weary of our café rebellions. We despised all the healthy Kindermanns,' their supercilious lecturer, 'who were spared the horrors of war and whose careers were not interrupted, while at Isonzo and Piave our Galician, Czech, Moravian and Bukovinian friends were perishing.'[2]

Lingering in Vienna, Roth and Wittlin were confronted with the casualty lists from those battles between the Austro-Hungarian and Italian armies in what's now Slovenia, and with the news of devastation in Galicia. At the same time, Roth's private tuition work faded away. As he wrote later, 'When the war broke out, I lost my pupils, one by one.' He said he had been teaching the children of lawyers who habitually neglected their wives; and as Roth told it, he charmed and courted the wives, accepting gifts of clothing and evenings in their opera house boxes. 'They were my mothers,' he said. 'I loved them dearly.' Then the lawyers 'joined up, their wives grew moody and patriotic, and began to express a preference for war-wounded. I volunteered for the 21st Jaegers.'[3]

The story of his admission into the army is more convoluted than he let on. He and Wittlin, who would become a Nobel Prize-nominated novelist and poet, were twice rejected. As Wittlin put it, 'the Imperial Royal Army ... scorned us as notorious weaklings [and] refused us service in its famous regiments', which they found humiliating; but they were determined to join up, not only for reasons of conscience but because they suspected the experience would improve their writing. As Roth and Wittlin were born in Galicia, they should have served in the 80th Infantry Regiment, stationed in the Hungarian town of Rima-Szombat.* A transfer to the more desirable, Vienna-based 21st Jaegers required some work behind the scenes. They turned to Wittlin's uncle,

---

* Now Rimavská Sobota, Slovakia. As is common with military regiments, the barracks was intentionally positioned far from the region its soldiers called home.

a military doctor with the rank of general, who wrote them a glowing reference, which went to the appropriate commanding officer. Subject to permission from their home regiment, they would be admitted to the Jaegers. This required the two young men to make the 220-mile trip from Vienna to Rima-Szombat. There they were inspected by a doctor who was perplexed by their request. 'The physician of the 80th regiment considered us insane,' said Wittlin. In the doctor's view their feeble physiques meant they were unfit for active service, and he suggested they enlist for clerical work. They were adamant they had to fight, as Wittlin later explained: 'We were of the opinion that the only appropriate place for a poet in wartime was in service in the "front line". For there one can gain acquaintance with life and death, even as a pacifist.'[4] Roth's biographer Wilhelm von Sternburg also makes the plausible suggestion of a less romantic motive: a reaction against the antisemitic press's claims that Jews were shirking military service. Whatever the reason, they persuaded the bemused doctor, who eventually declared them both fit for life on the front. Roth and Wittlin returned to Vienna feeling triumphant.

In a set of autobiographical notes cited by David Bronsen, Roth gave his version of the romantic, tragic fate he had in mind when enlisting. His enthusiasm was not so much for the war but, as if viewing it from afar as a narrator, the way it might shape his life story. 'I volunteered, I was rejected, because I was too weak,' but he 'had a longing for the war. I sought out an excuse for myself to head, together with many others, for some goal or other, if it brought ruin what did that matter? I went into the war, like confirmed bachelors who cannot bear their loneliness and enter into marriage. Now I was no longer alone. Now we were all going, thousands, millions of us – and it was a matter of indifference to me whether our enterprise was pointless or had some point.'[5]

The army records show that 'Roth, Moses Josef, b. 1894 in Brody' had a 'medical examination in Vienna 31.5.1916. Number 1264 passed suitable for territorial reserve, reported for duty 28.8.1916.'[6] Wittlin would describe such an examination twenty years later in his novel *The Salt of the Earth*, which earned him his Nobel Prize nomination: 'For the first time in many years we were not being judged according to the way we dressed. On the contrary, today we were only worth anything without our clothes. Only as naked bodies could we display our greatest merits. All they were interested in was whether we were fit. They looked at our teeth as you look horses in the mouth at the sales; they looked us over from the front, they checked us over from behind, tapping our bellies to make sure our innards were not infested with worms.'[7]

After the three-month wait, Roth and Wittlin entered the military school in Vienna. They hoped to keep attending university in their free time, but this proved impossible. Roth had to abandon his degree.

It took only one week for their optimism about army life to evaporate. 'There were too many military *Vorzugsschüler*, careerists and informers,' Wittlin recalled. 'The atmosphere was unbearable. The weak were persecuted, human dignity was trod upon. The cult of heartlessness and stupidity blossomed and vulgarity appeared to be a social obligation.'[8] Their superiors were abusive, they found the discipline depressing and, on serving alongside more robust fellow soldiers, they grew self-conscious of their physical frailty.

But the experience satisfied Roth's expectations in one sense: now he could feel proud rather than embarrassed if he saw friends such as Soma Morgenstern. In his military uniform, with yellow braid on the lower arms and buttoned upturned collar, Roth was 'fit company for a girl on the Schwarzenbergplatz or in the Prater'.[9] He enjoyed parading in public view, sensing the spectators' admiration. For a man who considered himself ugly, to feel gazed upon with reverence was a pleasant novelty.

Roth in uniform – detail from a group picture at the 21st Feldjäger battalion training school, 1916.

For all that he relished subsuming himself into a tribe, he never quite abandoned his self-consciousness. 'I enjoyed the harmonious sound of marching feet and I heard my own above all,' he wrote. 'I was a good soldier. I loved the drill. I loved it because it forced me to experience something indescribably, inexhaustibly stupid – and with what precision – together with the others. I hated the comrades who couldn't do the drill or who had an aversion to the military. Those were the finest human beings. But I was filled with hostility for them if, on a particular command, their rifle barrels stuck out of line with the others. I couldn't help this feeling, which I tried to combat.'[10]

One of their superiors made an especial impression and fulfilled their hope of gaining good material for their writing. In *The Salt of the Earth*, Wittlin described how 'Some lieutenant at the one-year service school, wanting to express utter contempt for one of his trainees and to convince him of the total worthlessness of his existence, would exclaim: "I'll shoot you, and not even a dog will bark for you!"'[11] Recalling that time, Wittlin said: 'Heartlessness and apathy flourished, meanness was a social duty. In later years Roth and I often thought back to those days. Sergeant Marek stuck in our minds particularly clearly: he appeared to us years later like a miniature version of "the great Führer" of Germany. He even looked like him.'[12]

Roth gave this account of the same man: 'After all that I've said about myself, it will not surprise anyone that I wanted to become an officer very quickly. I could not bear the NCOs who were my superiors, no more than previously I had been able to stand my teachers and later my professors.* I can remember them, there were two of them who were in charge of the recruits, they were called Marek and Türling. The first had black hair and moustache, red cheeks, small brown eyes. They had the brown brightness of beer glasses held up to a lamp. I don't know whether he applied pomade to his hair and moustache, or if it was a natural oil that his body produced every day and that penetrated not only his skin but also his uniform, especially the buttons and the silver medal on his chest. He had already distinguished himself in the face of the enemy. That's why he was allowed to remain so long in the

---

* Not quite true – as we've seen, there were always certain teachers and professors with whom he formed a tight bond, those who took a paternal interest in guiding his talent.

hinterland, training recruits.'[13] Wittlin said that 'Colonel Marek' was
the mocking nickname that some of the recruits gave the sergeant on
account of his self-important attitude. He became the model for the
character of that name who runs the cavalry cadets' school where Carl
Joseph von Trotta trains in *The Radetzky March*.

Roth and Wittlin made a friend in a fellow soldier who was the
opposite of all that they had come to despise about the army. 'In the
21st battalion of the Feldjaegers Roth and I had the good fortune to
meet the noblest person we were ever to come upon in our lives,' said
Wittlin. 'He was a young Pole, Ludwig Brudzinski. Roth considered
him a saint till the end of his days. Brudzinski had also been a philosophy student at the University of Vienna. Neither Roth nor I had ever
met any other person who sparkled with such unworldly goodness as
he. This goodness harmonised with a deep intelligence and aesthetic
taste. "*Der Brudzinski wird nicht lange leben*," Roth used to say to me.
"People like him don't live long in this kind of a world."'[14]

The three would often meet in the evenings at Brudzinski's apartment near the Johann Strauss Theatre. Brudzinski would change into
civilian dress before their arrival, out of concern that his uniform
would summon memories of the day's traumas. 'Those were unforgettable evenings,' said Wittlin. 'We read our writings, Brudzinski his
essays on art and archaeology, Roth his stories and poems, and I my
never-published or produced dramas. Brudzinski was our ideal critic.
His vast knowledge never oppressed us . . . Modesty was a natural trait
with him . . . I remember how Roth once asked me as we watched the
sleeping Brudzinski – "Do you see the halo shining around his cap?"'
A world that still contained such people could not be beyond saving.
During the First World War, this was what passed for optimism.

On the evening of 21 November 1916, at the age of eighty-six and
after a sixty-eight-year reign, Emperor Franz Joseph I died from pneumonia in the Schönbrunn Palace. Roth claimed to have participated in
the funeral, on 30 November. 'When he was laid to rest, I stood, one
of his many soldiers from the Viennese garrison in the new field-grey
uniform, which we were to wear into battle a few weeks later, a link
in the long chain that lined the streets.'[15] It is possible he did: silent

monochrome newsreel footage shows that the cortège included dozens of Imperial Army soldiers, some marching and others on horseback, and many more forming a thin barrier between the procession and onlookers, but the focus is too soft to identify faces. The funeral was a performance of such profound grief and solemnity it seems the attendees, consciously or otherwise, were mourning the empire as much as the emperor. Black-clad soldiers in black-tasselled hats riding black horses sporting black plumes; white-caped guards astride grey horses; slow-walking women in black veils and gowns, like black ghosts; the coffin borne across Josefsplatz to the Imperial Crypt beneath the Capuchin Church, where it would rest in one of over 100 sarcophagi holding Habsburgs from back to the seventeenth century.

Roth reflected a decade later: 'At the time that Emperor Franz Joseph died, I was already a "revolutionary", but I shed tears for him. I was a one-year volunteer in a Vienna regiment, a so-called elite unit, that stood by the Kapuzinergruft as a guard of honour, and I tell you, I was crying. An epoch was buried.'[16] He viewed the funeral as a valediction for Austria-Hungary itself. 'The sense of devastation caused by the knowledge that a historic day was passing encountered the ambivalent grief at the end of a fatherland which itself had brought up its sons to oppose it,' he wrote. 'And as I condemned it, I began already to regret its passing. And while I bitterly measured the closeness of death to which my emperor was sending me, I was moved by the ceremonial with which the majesty that was Austria-Hungary was being borne to its grave. I recognised clearly the senselessness of his last years, but it was undeniable that this senselessness was a piece of my childhood. The cold sun of the Habsburgs had been extinguished, but it was a sun . . .'.[17]

Franz Ferdinand's nephew Karl assumed the role of emperor, but the Habsburgs' days were numbered, their already crumbling empire now irreparably fractured by the war Franz Joseph had launched. What was intended as a short campaign to save his monarchy had turned into an embarrassing saga in which Austria had grown increasingly reliant on German military and financial support. There is little evidence for Roth's claim, fifteen years later, to have participated in the fighting. In 1932 he would assert in a letter to Professor Otto Forst de Battaglia, a summary of his career that contains some of his most often-quoted lines of putative autobiography, that he 'volunteered for the front in 1916, and from 1917 to 1918 fought on the eastern front'. The latter assertion is almost certainly untrue. 'I was made lieutenant and decorated with the Silver Cross, the Merit Cross, and the Karl Truppen Cross.'* These are lies. (Géza von Cziffra once saw him show off a silver medal, but their mutual friend Egon Erwin Kisch later explained how Roth acquired it: 'Bought it at a junk dealer!'[18]) 'My service was initially with the 21st Jaegers, then the 24th Land Reserve.' Half true – there seems to be no record of him transferring to the Land Reserve. 'The most powerful experience of my life was the war and the end of my fatherland, the only one I have ever had: the Dual Monarchy of Austria-Hungary. To this date I am a patriotic Austrian and love what is left of my homeland as a sort of relic.' Among the truest words he ever wrote: the war collapsed his world and the emperor's death was a pivotal moment, for while he had grown infuriated by the ailing empire's maladministration, what followed left him in no doubt as to the flawed institution's value in holding Europe together. Then he returns to the realm of fantasy: 'I spent six months in a Russian prisoner of war camp, fled, and fought for two months in the Red Army, then two months' flight and return home.'[19]

David Bronsen could find Roth's name nowhere in the Austrian War Ministry's records of prisoners of war. During early 1918, the period when he later claimed to have been held captive in Russia, he wrote a letter to Paula Grübel from Vienna, where he had apparently attended a poetry reading, a show at the Volkstheater and a violin recital. Roth evidently still played the instrument, for he tells Paula that the performer, Bronisław Huberman, 'played a Bach etude with skill, *froideur*, and physical exertion', and Schubert's 'Ave Maria' in 'such a way that I can't possibly torture you with it anymore. Divine.'[20] On 19 April he obtained a military travel ticket for the Imperial Royal Austrian State Railways in Lemberg. It seems safe to say he was not a

---

* The Karl-Truppenkreuz, or Karl Troop Cross, was awarded to 651,000 soldiers for serving at the front for at least twelve weeks.

prisoner of war in Russia for three months, let alone that he mounted a daring escape from a PoW camp.

In fact, after his training ended in early 1917 it seems he was stationed first in Moravia, then spent most of the war in Lemberg or elsewhere in Galicia, censoring letters and working for a military newspaper, the *Illustrierte Kriegs-Zeitung*.*

The Central Powers[†] had regained control of the region in mid-1915, a German-led offensive driving the Russians into a mass withdrawal from the eastern front, in what became known as their Great Retreat. The Austrian War Archive corroborates that 'Joseph Roth, as a voluntary recruit in the area of the 32nd Division of the Infantry, was put to work in 1917 in the press section. The 32nd Division at that time was under the Böhm-Ermolli[‡] army group in the Lemberg district.'[21] On 24 August 1917, he wrote two letters to Resia and Paula Grübel, who still lived in the city, that shed light on his activities and feelings. In the letter to Resia, who had been depressed, he gives sympathetic advice and says he can empathise: 'I too am not floating over the earth as you imagine, at the very most I'm swimming, and that in Galician bogs.' He adds: 'You are right. It was fine when we were free and without a care. What did we know of life? This cruel war has silenced our youth. If we survive it, we will be mature individuals. But the youth that one has within is strong, even if one lives to be 80.' Elsewhere he says: 'You don't have the energy either, which Paula possesses in full measure.'

It is no surprise, given that aside, that his letter to Paula has a different tone, pitched at a capable adult on his own level, although she was the younger sister. His address is given as 'Field Post 632', which he only describes in the letter as 'some Augean *shtetl* in East Galicia'.

---

* Roth worked on the editorial staff in the first half of 1917. The richly illustrated magazine was published bilingually in German and Hungarian, and was intended to glorify its commanders, relay reports of heroic deeds, and entertain the troops with riddles, poetry, short stories and jokes.

† The coalition of Austria-Hungary, Germany, the Ottoman Empire and Bulgaria.

‡ Eduard Freiherr von Böhm-Ermolli (1856–1941), a general in the Austro-Hungarian Army who fought largely in Galicia and attained the rank of field marshal by the end of the war.

Austrian archival records reveal that this field post was in Plesniany, a *shtetl* forty miles south of Brody.

'Grey filth, harbouring one or two Jewish businesses,' he notes. 'Everything's awash when it rains, and when the sun comes out it starts to stink. But the location has one great advantage: it's about six miles behind the lines. Reserve encampment. Materially, I'm not so well off as I used to be. Our newspaper is failing, and once the aura of reporter has faded away, there'll be nothing left of me but a one-year volunteer.* And I'll be treated accordingly. But for the likes of me that doesn't really matter. The main thing is experience, intensity of feeling, tunnelling into events. I have experienced frightful moments of grim beauty.'[22] In a *Frankfurter Zeitung* article seven years later he expanded on this: 'We have seen mass graves, mouldy hands protruding out of filled-in pits, thighs on barbed wire and burnt-out skulls besides latrines.'[23]

It is moot whether he participated in fighting, but he saw the after-math. If he and Józef Wittlin wanted experiences that would give them literary material, their wish had been granted. For years afterwards Roth's books would explore the prospects of men who had seen such things reintegrating into post-war civilian life.

At this time he used the Grübels' apartment in Lemberg as a postal address, and must have travelled there often to collect mail. He not only visited his relatives, but also Frau von Szajnocha-Schenk, whom he still called 'Mother'. Sons' relations with maternal figures continued to preoccupy him. During 1917 he wrote the most striking of his early poems, titled 'Mothers'. It opens with a train carrying grieving mothers to the battlefields, where they search 'for the skeletons of the dead sons they wanted to kiss'. The lines are written in an expressionist style that feels overwrought but sincere, a heartfelt cry from a young writer who had distanced himself from his own mother and seems to be covertly using this topic to acknowledge her pain. He gives voice to a bereft woman crying out:

---

* Characteristic of Roth to have an eye on the role's cachet, and the effect its antici-pated loss would have on his own standing.

I have born him from my womb, I have nourished him on my
breasts, I have taught him his first babble . . .

I've lost him . . . lost . . . lost . . .

My son!

My child![24]

During his time working for the military newspaper he also wrote
short unsigned reports for *Der Abend*, and in January and February
1918 may have contributed, again anonymously, to a pacifist Viennese
weekly journal called *Der Friede:** Wochenschrift für Politik, Wirtschaft und
Literatur*. The latter title's aim, only stated explicitly after censorship
rules were lifted in 1919, was that after 'a few million powerless people
have been hounded into war, misery and the grave . . . by a few dozen
powerful brutes' and 'the warlike attempts to make Europe German
and Austrian have failed, we now want to try to make Germany and
Austria European'.[25] Its socialist, pacifist founder Benno Karpeles
was a former correspondent of the Social Democratic Party-affiliated
Arbeiter-Zeitung in London, where he had known Friedrich Engels.
Others among *Der Friede*'s approximately 200 contributors included
Alfred Polgar, Robert Musil and Peter Altenberg. Roth also had poems
published in the *Prager Tagblatt* this year – for instance a description of
a shell-shock victim ('Nervenchok') and another that captures his and
other soldiers' weariness and *Heimweh* at the close of the war:

They all have this tired strange look in their pale faces:

In their eyes trembles a shy, staggering foreboding of home and
peace . . .

They all carry on their tired feet the dust of wandering years:

They have travelled through many countries and have not yet
found their way home . . .

Sometimes only their cheeks redden when they hear glad tidings, and they sit together and exchange whispering speeches of
sweet longing . . .

---

* Meaning 'Peace'.

Their hard, torn hands are folded in humility, and childhood-
worn words grasp them silently in prayer: Lord, make an end! – O
Lord, make an end![26]

By now the pride and self-regard Roth cultivated when sporting
his uniform on the safety of the parade ground had been evaporated
by war, leaving him frail and timid. Fred Heller, one of *Der Friede*'s
editors, recalled a visit by Roth that summer:

In 1918, in the last year of the war, a young soldier in a worn uniform came into the editorial offices ... I received him because at
that time I had recently returned home wounded and had joined
the editorial staff of the pacifist journal. My personal impression
was of a poor, undernourished, shivering individual, whose old
uniform made him look even more pitiful. He had two poems with
him. Would we print them? Out of pity for the poor devil I read
the verses at once, although our literary editor was Alfred Polgar,
who generally took a long time to come to a decision. The young
soldier's verses were quite beautiful. Full of enthusiasm I assured
him that the poems would definitely appear in our periodical and
he thanked me profusely.

Eight days later a poem of Joseph Roth's was published for
the first time. And from then on the newly discovered poet often
came to me and told me about his unhappy youth and spoke of his
uncertain future, when the war came to an end. Should he become
a writer? Had he enough talent? I encouraged him, I believed in
him, but I tried to persuade him to write not just poems but little
stories too, for what he related orally was original and gripping.
But Joseph Roth could not extricate himself from lyric poetry.[27]

In fact, quite aside from his story 'The Honours Student', in which
he wrought fictional revenge on his erstwhile university lecturer, Roth
had already had a short story published. Titled 'Barbara', it appeared
in April 1918 in *Österreichs Illustrierte Zeitung*, the paper that had published his early poems three years earlier. Over nine pages it charts the

eponymous woman's life, from being married off by her uncle, to her husband's death that leaves her raising their only child alone, through to a visit by this self-absorbed son, Philip, as she lies dying. There are passages where it seems plain that Roth is addressing his guilt towards his mother. At one stage she considers remarrying, having fallen deeply in love, but eventually tells her suitor, Peter Wendelin: 'It cannot be. On account of the child!' Barbara was 'almost consumed by love for her boy',[28] he writes:

> Philip had grown, and was going to school. He came home with good reports, and Barbara was proud of him. She had the idea her son had some special destiny, and she was determined to do all she could so that he could study ... Barbara had great ambitions for her son. She didn't want all her sacrifices to have been in vain ...
>
> She walked with a stoop, even when she didn't have a bundle to carry. The work weighed heavily on her. But a smile played round her bitter mouth each time she saw her son ... [The son] saw her working, but that seemed perfectly natural to him, he didn't have the fineness of perception required to discern the sorrow that was in his mother's heart, and that was in every one of the sacrifices she made for him.

On her deathbed, she tries to tell him about Wendelin, but Philip is not interested. He yawns. It does not occur to him that this woman, who raised him single-handed, might have wished her life to turn out otherwise; that she might have quietly hoped to find another husband who would love and support her, but never indulged such possibilities for fear of neglecting him. Roth's story reads like an attempt to empathise with his mother and offer a conciliatory gesture safely conducted at a double remove: through fictionalising her, and from several hundred miles' distance.

Perhaps at this time he lacked the confidence to let on to Fred Heller that he also dabbled in fiction. The war had aged him prematurely. Melancholy replaced optimism, the dandy *gigerl* now looked timid and shabby. Among other factors, for all his conflict over his Jewishness, he had grown angry about the dilemma the war posed for Europe's Jews. The American writer Barbara Probst Solomon, a distant relative of Roth,[*] summarises his view well: she writes of his 'rage that Jews had to fight in the armies of countries where they were mistreated, in which they had few rights; and worse, where they were put in the shameful positions of murdering their relatives; who because of migration or an unreal, flaky, porous border were on the other side. It was almost as though they were participating in an inchoate civil war with themselves. And the Europeans understood that. If Jews openly made a point of their trauma at killing their co-religionists they were in danger of being considered spies – "enlightened" France had sent Dreyfus[†] to Devil's Island.'[29]

This general source of angst weighed upon him, but in the final months of the war Roth suffered a specific blow that caused acute pain. His friend Ludwig Brudzinski, the fellow soldier whom Roth so admired, could bear the horrendous bloodshed no longer and, in Józef Wittlin's words, 'is thought to have hastened his own death during a raging epidemic of the Spanish flu. He was no more than 23 at the time.' The world ushered in by this war was not, it transpired, one that could accommodate the kind of gentle, refined characters whom Roth revered.

The most powerful experience of my life was the war and the end of my fatherland, the only one I have ever had: the Dual Monarchy of Austria-Hungary. The warm, all-surrounding, comforting setting for his childhood, his metaphorical cradle, was gone as surely as the one taken from his home when he was an infant. He would later reflect on the trauma of this rupture from the perspective of seven years' distance, on visiting

---

[*] Her father, Anthony Probst, was a cousin of Roth's. See: https://www.tabletmag.com/sections/arts-letters/articles/notes-on-joseph-roth

[†] Captain Alfred Dreyfus: the twelve-year-long 'Dreyfus Affair' commenced in 1894 when he was wrongly convicted of treason for passing military secrets to the German Embassy, imprisoned for almost five years on the Devil's Island penal colony, and only finally pardoned and exonerated in 1906. The Jewish officer's alleged treachery sparked antisemitic riots and the scandal divided French society. It was a significant factor in convincing Theodor Herzl that the Jews' future lay in establishing their own state outside Europe.

somewhere that stirred memories of exotic places he'd dreamed of when a boy: 'If you find your childhood dreams, you become a child again. It was more than I dared hope. Because my childhood is quite irrecoverably remote from me, separated by a global conflagration, a world on fire. My childhood was nothing more than a dream itself. It was expunged from my life; years that hadn't disappeared, but were dead and buried.'[30]

The empire's untenability was clear before the cessation of fighting. From the moment the Allies' victory looked probable, nationalists across Austria-Hungary grew emboldened in their demands for independence. The Italian victory in June 1918 at the Battle of the Piave River confirmed Austria's terminal weakness, when after losing 90,000 men the Imperial Army retreated and around one-third of its troops – 448,000 men, including twenty-four generals – were taken captive. Soldiers from the lands ruled over by the Habsburgs refused to keep fighting a doomed battle on behalf of a supranational entity that no longer existed other than on paper. Strikes and famine crippled the economy, leftist parties in Vienna and Budapest agitated on behalf of ethnic minorities' self-determination, and mutinies thwarted what remained of the army.

In autumn 1918 the edifice collapsed. On 28 October the Czechs took control of Prague, capital of the Austro-Hungarian Kingdom of Bohemia, and a day later they and the Slovaks established Czechoslovakia. The next day saw the Slavs in the south of the empire proclaim the State of Slovenes, Croats and Serbs. On 31 October the Aster Revolution in Hungary led to Count Mihály Károlyi, a long-time advocate of separation from Austria, taking control of the First Hungarian People's Republic. After a reign of two years, Emperor Karl was compelled to accept the dissolution of the Austro-Hungarian union, Habsburg rule now going the same way as the Romanovs' and the Hohenzollerns' in Russia and Germany. Swathes of central and eastern Europe were proclaiming independence or handed to new rulers. In Galicia, the west became part of the Republic of Poland, and on 1 November the Ukrainians in the east declared the West Ukrainian People's Republic, which endured until the following July. This schism prompted the Polish-Ukrainian War, which Poland won, leading to its annexation of the rest of the region. In June 1919 the Treaty of Versailles delivered the reunion of Poland after a century of its division between the now-vanished Austrian, German and Russian monarchies. The short-lived Ukrainian republic had been notable for its respectful treatment of its Jewish minority; the new Polish administration was avowedly antisemitic. And now, on account of his birth in Galicia, Joseph Roth learned that he had become a Polish national. He immediately left his final military posting, which was probably still in Galicia, for Vienna, where he began trying to apply for Austrian nationality.

The war defined his future in another respect: it enriched the persona he would play in civilian life. Having assumed the guise of a Viennese gentleman before the war, he progressed to claiming that he left the Austro-Hungarian Army as an officer, though there is no evidence to suggest this. Regardless, in the post-war period he adopted the appropriate style of dress and courtly manner, and played the role convincingly. Later he peppered his speech with military sayings, a couple of favourites being: 'You have to know who you can lie in the trenches with' and, to those he wished to compliment, 'I'd be happy to be on guard duty with you.' When trying to impress the recipients of his letters, he would even sign off: 'Joseph Roth, Lieutenant of the Imperial and Royal Army, ret'd.'

He had a tortuous journey from Galicia back to Vienna, as he described to his young cousin Michael Grübel, who had remained in the city during the war. Roth had tried to return to Lemberg but couldn't, finding it occupied by Poland and encircled by West Ukrainians, so he went to Brody, which was occupied by the West Ukrainian Republican Army, who wanted to enlist him to fight. Then he crossed the Carpathians and ran into another war, between Czechoslovaks and the West Ukrainians, who again wanted him to sign up – so he hastily made for Hungary, and from there returned to Vienna in late March 1919.

On his return he lived for the first months in a state of poverty, subsisting day to day 'from hand to mouth'.[31] He wrote a couple of pieces on cinema for *Die Filmwelt* magazine, and placed an article in the *Prager Tagblatt* that described a war-wounded man whose 'gait is a zigzag ... the symbol of a present that staggers with a broken back between revolutions, world views and social orders'.[32] Roth's existence in this disordered world was lonely and impoverished without family to fall back on. His mother and uncle Siegmund had returned home to Galicia, though not to Brody, which remained unsafe and would receive another battering in the Polish-Soviet War that followed the First World War. The little town was devastated by repeated assaults, as Isaac Babel recorded in his diary in July 1920. His terse notes sketch the ruination to desolate effect:

The Ukraine in flames ... This morning Brody was taken, again the surrounded enemy managed to get out ... Brody at dawn, all this is horrifying: barbed wire everywhere, burned-out chimneys, a bloodless city, drab houses, word has it there are goods to be had, our men won't hold back, there were factories here, a Russian military cemetery, and, judging by the nameless lonely crosses on the graves, these were Russian soldiers ...

The town is destroyed, looted. A town of great interest. Polish culture. An old, rich, distinctive, Jewish population. The terrible bazaars, the dwarves in long coats, long coats and *peyes*, ancient old men. Shkolnaya Street, nine synagogues, everything half-destroyed ... a bearded, talkative Jew [speaks of] the Cossacks' looting of the town, of the humiliations inflicted by the Poles ... Trenches, destroyed factories ... The high road, barbed wire, cut-down forests, and dejection, boundless dejection.[33]

Ruined buildings in Brody after the First World War.

Roth was back in Vienna alone, impoverished, traumatised and uncertain of his way forward. Without the support of a father or siblings, and with a mother so overbearingly protective he felt compelled to distance her to develop his individuality, he had emerged near-defenceless into an adult life that commenced brusquely with a two-year immersion into the horror of war, a traumatic experience regardless of how sustained his time at the front line. He had to find shields to numb the world's blows. Friends who could bolster his self-esteem. The affirmation of readers' and editors' praise. Enough income to keep his habitual poverty at bay. But most reliably, during the war he had found a new way of dulling pain. At the beginning of April 1917 he was on leave in Vienna, reporting for the *Abend* on the ongoing trial of Dr Josef Kranz, former president of the Allgemeine Depositenbank, who was charged with forcing up prices. One night in the street he saw a friend, who was astonished when Roth ran up and embraced him in a state of desperate drunkenness. Alcohol filled critical gaps in his armoury: it granted a shy, sensitive young man self-confidence and a fleeting resilience. Then its effects wore off, until the next drink.

*

In post-war Vienna, the economically shattered capital of a drastically diminished land, returning soldiers took such work as they could. Roth later claimed that he fell into journalism through a combination of poverty and accident, though in truth he had been set on this path for some years. 'One day I became a journalist, out of despair at the total inability of any profession to fulfil me,'[34] he reflected just over a decade later. On another occasion he offered this self-critical account of how he began his career: 'because I didn't have any money, I started to write for the papers. They printed my nonsense. I lived off it. I became a writer.'[35]

His career as a staff writer began thanks to the support of editors whom he had met while freelancing during the war. Fred Heller, formerly of the pacifist *Der Friede*, gave this account. 'The war was over. Roth had to decide on a civilian profession. I had in the meantime gone over to the editorial staff of a Vienna daily and now suggested to Roth that he should try his hand as a reporter.'[36] This publication was *Der Neue Tag* (*The New Day*), whose overweight, cigar-smoking editor Dr Benno Karpeles had previously edited *Der Friede*. The title spoke of his aspiration to draw a line under the war years and fashion a sprightlier, fairer Austria. The paper was to be an alternative to the *Neue Freie Presse*, which professed to be liberal and internationalist but had been an aggressive advocate of the war, and which he felt had a 'damaging stranglehold ... on the educated middle classes'.[37] Its reputation lay ruined beyond repair for those of Karpeles' political inclination. He had been a Social Democrat and founded the paper on leaving the party, distancing himself from its Marxist rhetoric and advocating 'a nonpartisan approach to building the new Austria, one that also acknowledged the value of tradition and historical structures'.

Karpeles was far from alone in feeling a need to interpret and shape the new Vienna; as Roth observed, the city at this time saw 'daily papers and magazines shooting up like mushrooms from the ground of public opinion after the downpour of the revolution'.[38] Karpeles sought to capture a sector of this contested market by attracting popular writers such as Egon Erwin Kisch, Anton Kuh, Richard Bermann and arts editor Alfred Polgar, another who had transferred from *Der*

Friede. Alongside them the paper featured a roster of promising young writers. On 20 April 1919, it published Roth's article 'The Island of the Unhappy', describing his visit to the Steinhof, Vienna's psychiatric hospital. He roamed its grounds and observed the residents: a woman

Roth in 1920 at the beginning of his journalistic career.

singing a sad song while walking with her arms extended before her, pushing an invisible perambulator; a man squatting on the ground to draw circles in the hard earth; now and then a grinning face that peered out through iron-barred windows. He was plainly keen to understand the causes of mental illness, as we might expect of a young man who had been deprived of a father by such a condition. And as a socialist angered by the inequality and injustice bedevilling post-war Vienna, he was receptive to an explanation proffered by a recovered inmate awaiting release: hunger. Poverty and malnutrition had led to people being admitted when starvation led to cognitive malfunction. 'One suspects his housemates of denying him the food he deserves in order to feed himself, becomes raving mad, lashes out. Another loses the ability to think at all, stares blearily before him: he is hungry.'[39] It was one answer to the question of madness that had hung over Roth since childhood; what he could not know at this stage was how mental illness and this institution on the western out-skirts of Vienna would haunt him in his future.

Between then and 30 April 1920 he would contribute around 140 pieces, almost one-fifth of them under the heading '*Wiener Symptome*' ('Viennese Symptoms'), and many with the byline 'Josephus', making pertinent reference to the Jewish historian Flavius Josephus, who took the Romans' side in the Jewish War and assimilated into Roman soci-ety. He was, as Wilhelm von Sternburg observes, perceived as a Jew by the Romans and a Roman by the Jews. The would-be assimilator Roth was growing cognisant of his marginal position between societies. Still, he seemed well set to entrench himself within Vienna: for the first time he had a regular income, and the formerly ragged ex-soldier also had a smart new suit after Karpeles paid for him to visit a tailor.

In these articles he sketches the subject of ex-soldiers' return to civilian life that would dominate his first novels. In one he writes of a general who returns to Vienna after the war: 'At pains to see into the future, he sees the past ... He was a general, in the framework of the brigade. He was "complete" when others saluted him. He was *never* an individual. Always a constituent part. Like a head, a rifle butt, a kit bag, a waterproof jacket. He found completion in the obedience of the others. Now he is a leftover, a fragment, a brigadier without a brigade ...'.[40]

In another, published in *Der Neue Tag* on 1 August 1919, he finds a microcosm of post-war Viennese life in a poignant, absurd image he observed in the city centre. 'To the many scenes of war misery in Vienna a new one was added, a few days ago.'

A man returned from the war in the form of a hinge – invalid with shattered spine – moves almost inexplicably through Kärntner Strasse,* selling newspapers. A dog sits on his back.

A clever, well-trained dog, riding on his own master, and making sure he doesn't lose a single paper ...

Once there were sheepdogs who watched herds of sheep, and guard-dogs that guarded houses. Today there are mandogs who watch invalids, mandogs the logical consequence of submissive men ... When he remembers what happened when he relied on other men, a man is happy to put his trust in a dog. Is there anything so sad as this sight, which seems so emblematic? All around stroll the war-profiteers with their X-ray vision, and in the midst of everything a mounted dog. The human race has lost, all hail to the animal. We have been through the war that was the last hurrah of cavalry, and at the end of it dogs ride around on men.[41]

---

* Then, as now, Vienna's main shopping street, running between the city's two main squares, Karlsplatz and Stephansplatz.

Such passages – lyrical, ironic, morally engaged, suffused with melancholy – owe much to his association during this period with Alfred Polgar.* Born Alfred Polak into a Jewish family in Leopoldstadt, Polgar was twenty years older than Roth. As part of the *Jung Wien*, the writing movement who congregated at the Café Central before the war, he became known as the 'Master of the Miniature', working in the Viennese style of feuilleton developed by fellow member Peter Altenberg. The style had attained immense cachet in the Austrian capital by the early twentieth century: in Stefan Zweig's words, 'As Vienna saw it, an author writing in the feuilleton on the front page had his name carved in marble.'[42] The feuilleton, literally 'small page', had a history extending back to early-nineteenth-century France, the term first appearing in a newspaper titled *Journal des débats*, where it formed a lighter adjunct to political commentary. It developed into an inherently metropolitan form – extrapolating from one of the deluge of minor human interactions that unfold daily in city life, and written to a length that accommodated the busy urban reader's attention span. After the First World War, the form seemed yet more attuned to the modern condition.

Polgar sensed that this 'tempestuous epoch, agitated by calamities never experienced before', was heading into a worrying future at 'dazzling speed'. 'At such a time,' he asked, 'who wants to be burdened with superfluous baggage? Ballast has to be discarded – and what doesn't turn out to be ballast? The shortest line from point to point is the rule of the fleeting hour.'[43] The style felt especially resonant and appropriate in the defeated Axis powers' disoriented, traumatised cities, according to the German Studies scholar Andreas Huyssen, who notes that defeat 'wrought radical transformations in political and urban experiences in Austria and Germany that had no match in the older European capitals, which returned to a new normal'.[44] The feuilleton was by then well established as a form that could capture the intense flux and

---

* Claudio Magris summed up Polgar's wry, mordant world view and the city that gave rise to it: 'Live and let live is the old Viennese attitude, a sort of easy-going tolerance that doesn't take much, as Alfred Polgar said, to become the cynical indifference of "die and let die".' Claudio Magris, *Danube*, p. 190.

disorienting strangeness of modern city life. 'These feuilleton texts,' says Huyssen, '. . . sought to capture the visceral feeling of acceleration and compression, social conflict, and cultural upheaval that defined urban existence. In their focus on dream images, ghostly appearances, surreal memories, and urban phantasmagorias, they largely shunned the realistic description, typical of older urban sketches like those of Louis Sébastien Mercier in the eighteenth century . . . [The style] was kick-started with Baudelaire in post-revolutionary Paris, capital of the nineteenth century, as Benjamin called it.'

Baudelaire's best-known description of the *flâneur*, written almost sixty years earlier in a Parisian newspaper, summarises not only Roth's method but the service it performed for him as he sought a niche in post-war Vienna. 'The crowd is his element, as the air is that of birds and water of fishes,' Baudelaire proclaimed. 'His passion and his profession are to become one flesh with the crowd. For the perfect *flâneur*, for the passionate spectator, it is an immense joy to set up house in the heart of the multitude, amid the ebb and flow of movement, in the midst of the fugitive and the infinite. To be away from home and yet to feel oneself everywhere at home; to see the world, to be at the centre of the world, and yet to remain hidden from the world . . .'.[45]

What Baudelaire did for mid-nineteenth-century Paris, feuilletonists such as Polgar did for early-twentieth-century Vienna, which like Berlin had expanded significantly faster in the fin-de-siècle period than the French capital or London.

Polgar and Roth independently gravitated towards similar sources of material: hotels and their staff, the Jewish theatre in Moscow, Grock the clown, national borders, dancing-girl revues. Roth would acknowledge Polgar in print as his role model. 'Polgar writes little stories without plots, and observations without résumés. He doesn't need any actual "content", because every one of his brilliantly deployed words is full of content. No occasion is too slight for him. It is precisely in the slightest of occasions that he shows his mastery. He polishes the everyday until it becomes extraordinary.'[46] That final sentence describes Roth's best journalism too. The style that emerged in these first pieces was not so much one of reporting but responding. Roth presents his subjective impressions with an authority that compels the reader to accept his perspective as that of one who can freely peer into others' souls. He writes journalism as an omniscient third-person narrator. For this reason and because he sometimes polishes away certain inconvenient facts to smooth out the story, his reporting has the aura of fiction. None of the conventions of journalistic duty – relaying the facts of what happened, when, where and why – weighed on Roth's mind while attending the scene of a newsworthy incident. His 'report' on a fire at the Third Coffee House in the main avenue of the Prater was actually an attempt to convey the melancholic atmosphere of the burnt-out building. In this he may have succeeded, but his editor at *Der Neue Tag*, on noting that the article provided no date, time or insight into the cause of the blaze, asked Roth's colleague and good friend Stefan Fingal to write a replacement.

These minor frustrations aside, in Fred Heller's assessment Roth's recruitment to the newspaper was an immediate success. Roth 'wrote his reports as lyrically ironic articles, which certainly in style still owed something to Alfred Polgar, but took on a distinctive flavour of their own with their subtle, intelligent and humane observations'.[47] He was by turns spiky and softly poetic, disarming and seducing the reader, coaxing them towards him, reminding them he could bite, then drawing them close again. One from 22 June 1919 showed him dissatisfied with both Austria's present and past: the post-war republic may have 'become a brand new state, but it's still cobbled together with miserable old Habsburg planks'.[48] Another was titled '*Seifenblasen*', or 'Soap Bubbles', published on 10 September 1919, the day that Austria signed the Peace Treaty of Saint-Germain and acknowledged the dissolution of its empire, its responsibility for starting the war, and its new form as a republic. Roth would himself use the term 'soap bubbles' as a general description of his feuilletons, but here he put the image to specific use, ranging between the innocence of children he saw on the Viennese streets and the machinations of geopolitical players.

'I saw children blowing soap bubbles,' he writes. 'Not in 1913 – yesterday. They were real soap bubbles. A little bottle full of soapy water, a straw, four children and a quiet alleyway in the bright sunshine of a summer morning. The soap bubbles were big, beautiful, rainbow-coloured globes and they swam lightly and gently through the blue air. There was no doubt: these were real soap bubbles. Not the soap bubbles of patriotic phraseology risen up from the muddy puddles of war editorials, the nationalist party, or the press corps, but beautiful, rainbow-coloured soap bubbles.'[49] In Roth's hands the bubbles become symbolic of the return to a state of affairs when children can once again play safely in the street, even as a traumatised post-war Vienna rings to the sound of ephemeral, hyperbolic speech from political rhetoricians; and it is plain that Roth identifies with the children, seeing in them a sincerity sorely lacking among political actors of the time.

Moments like this – microcosms spied in the city's quiet side streets and relayed with sweet lyricism – lend the journalism he produced in Vienna an intimacy that would not be apparent later in cities where he was less concerned to assimilate. 'Here he plays the Austrian,' writes David Bronsen, 'uses Austrianisms in his newspaper articles, shows how familiar he is with all the backstreets and obscure corners of the city, but suffers too at her misery and fate.'[50] Yes – and 'plays' is the critical word, because Roth is still acting the Viennese sophisticate, adopting a well-practised posture that convinces others, though not the stubborn part of his own mind that still tethered his identity to Brody. The Austro-Hungarian Army officer who had laid down his rifle and picked up a pen was a role he grew into, that he could perform with conviction and authority, to the point where he now seemed convinced of his talent. '[Through] the daily work as a journalist,' said Heller, 'Roth had acquired a routine and self-confidence. Now the eternally hesitant, sceptical and pathologically self-critical Roth believed in himself and his ability. A little later he was anything but modest – success went to his head . . .'.[51]

This outward show of self-regard did not mean that he had silenced his inner critic – his tendency now to boast of his talent suggests a fear that it was not self-evident – nor that he had quelled his psychological pain. The problem that became apparent during the war re-emerged around this time. Newspaper colleagues who only knew him as the well-dressed provider of elegant copy were shocked to hear that he'd recently been found on several occasions lying drunk and semi-conscious in the street.

An article from the 20 July 1919 edition of *Der Neue Tag* plays with the idea that the bridge over the River Leitha in Bruck-Kiralyhida represented the hyphen between the Austrian and Hungarian versions of the town's name. Roth was thinking about hyphenated identity, a concept instrumental to understanding his life and work. He was at times, often simultaneously, an Austro-Hungarian, an Austrian-German, a Jewish-Austrian and a Catholic-Jew, who claimed to be the son of a Polish count and a Ukrainian Jew, or an Austrian railway official and a Russian Jew. There is nothing to suggest Roth was anything but 100 per cent Jewish, but his repeated claim of a gentile father shows he wished to be seen as a mixture of ethnicities. A person who straddles borders, as a bridge links the banks of a river. He presented himself as a man of mixed heritage, an individual embodiment of his beloved Habsburg Empire that accommodated multiple coexistent identities. But hyphenated identities can prove fragile, an unstable foundation on which to construct a self: sometimes you think you're a member of one tribe, sometimes the other, sometimes both, often neither.

The question of Roth's nationality in the newly configured post-war Europe continued to press on him. He had had no success yet in claiming Austrian citizenship, which left him vulnerable to victimisation by nationalists who were now clamouring for Galician Jews in Vienna to return home. Later Roth noted that the Viennese had used and spat out their Jews, who had taken 'to smuggling. They brought flour, meat, and eggs from Hungary ... They made life easier for the Viennese. They were locked up for it.' Now they found little backing from any political quarter. 'When the war was over, they were repatriated, sometimes forcibly. A Social Democratic provincial governor had them thrown out. To Christian Socialists, they are Jews. To German nationalists, they are Semitic. To Social Democrats, they are unproductive elements.'[52] Roth was quite alone, unsupported and apparently unwanted. He had to prove himself the Austrian that he had always proudly considered himself to be, rather than a disposable drain on Vienna's resources. A potential solution presented itself by way of an assignment for *Der Neue Tag* that formed a change from his usual fare. Roth was given the title 'special correspondent' and sent to report from German West Hungary, a newly designated region granted to Austria in the Treaty of Saint-Germain. Because the Hungarians there objected, a referendum had been called to decide its status. Roth filed his copy as requested, but had another task to complete before he departed. During his research he met a priest who had no hesitation in giving him a certificate of baptism. The forged document gave his place of birth as Schwaben, a village in German West Hungary. Roth hoped dearly that this 'proof' of his birth in a region that remained Austrian territory would prove a breakthrough in his ongoing attempt to gain an Austrian passport, but instead he would remain in limbo for another two years, a stateless individual trying vainly to assert who he was in a region undergoing a violent identity crisis.

In 1919 the twenty-four-year-old Roth, looking back on a childhood that had slipped beyond reach, obscured by the war that had erupted at the cusp of his adult life, wrote this assessment of his youthful religious feelings:

> I hated the devil. But I only believed shyly in god. I knew for a fact that he did not exist, and yet I prayed to him.
>
> For two years, from my fourteenth to my sixteenth year, I was an atheist. I looked up, and I knew there was only blue air. But I had completely failed to notice that god hadn't disappeared, so much as merely relocated, from the sky to some other place, I didn't know where, but probably quite close to me. That no one ruled the world was quite clear to me, but I had a sense that someone was looking out for me personally. I prayed often, and my prayers were very short ... The one to whom I was praying always helped, he never punished. Yes, and neither did I shrink from asking his help with my low, almost criminal, but certainly sinful undertakings. He helped, too. I would have denied him

for ever. But the more eagerly did I believe in him. He was there like a reality.

It took two years for my personal god to turn into the god of the world and lord of the universe. I knew, from our old comradeship, that he was well-disposed to me. I wasn't scared of him. I trusted him. And if something bad happened to me, it wasn't punishment, but a sort of masked or dissembled form of grace.[53]

Did Roth truly believe in God, or did he wish others to see him as a believer? He was in most other respects pathologically sceptical. He does not couch his belief in terms of adherence to an established religion; instead we get the sense that this solitary, doubtful, half-orphaned young man had constructed an idiosyncratic belief system that fostered feelings of company and vindication. The Lord was not so much his shepherd as his accomplice. It is notable that this personal theology rested upon believing God had faith in him, as much as him having faith in God. He was by now openly disparaging of his Jewishness – though loyally defensive in the face of gentile antisemitism – and increasingly enchanted by the Catholicism of Viennese high society. As Michael Hofmann has argued, Catholicism's appeal may have lain, perversely enough, in its parallels with Judaism. 'Roth's religion was always an enigma ... and if his contemporaries weren't certain of it, it must be at least as baffling to us now,' he writes. 'Still, I have a sense that, in a cultural if not a doctrinal way, he equated Catholicism with Judaism so that Catholicism is either the local variant or else the permissive, universal vehicle for Judaism ... And certainly what later provokes Roth's ire* ... is the failure of Catholicism to remain universal, its reversion or perversion to schism and racism ... and the collapse thereby of his deeply desired, eccentric personal equation: Catholicism = Judaism.'[54]

To Roth, Catholicism shared Judaism's transcendence of national borders and likewise served to foster a pan-European culture that

---

* Hofmann cites three examples of this: *The Wandering Jews*, and the essays 'The Latin Renaissance' and 'The Frenchman on Wotan's Oak'.

was anathema to nationalists. So if they were alike, why Catholicism rather than Judaism? Catholicism was the religion of Viennese and Galician-Polish nobility. Andrea Manga Bell, one of the most important people in his later life, said: 'Roth became Catholic out of snobbery. I don't think he was moved by it.'[55] Perhaps Catholicism was Judaism unshackled, Judaism without the perceived vulgarity, without the reek of the *shtetl*, without the querulousness, redolent of well-spoken nobility rather than voices that 'smelled of onions': Judaism minus all those elements that were abrasive to the sensitive Roth, replacing them with stillness, sweet incense, choral song and the possibility of grace for sinners. That he later described himself as 'a Catholic with a Jewish intelligence' may suggest that he associated one mindset with emotion and the other with reason, and thus conceptualised the inner tussle we all experience as between two competing religions.

Regardless of how he attempted to weld them into a coherent entity, it seems quite possible that the root of Roth's admiration for religion lay not so much in a conviction that God exists as in recognising the psychological value of faith. By the end of his researches in the 1960s and 1970s, David Bronsen was convinced that Roth was an atheist. Roth's friend Géza von Cziffra concurred, citing a conversation they had in Stephansplatz in Vienna by the cathedral where Herzl once dreamed of mass-conversions of Jews. 'He came out of the cathedral and held out his hand to me with a serious face. "If God dwells anywhere, it is here." Before I could say anything, he asked me: "Do you believe in God at all, Ensign?* I know He doesn't exist, but still I believe in Him. Paradoxical, isn't it?"'[56]

Whether or not there is a God, the concept offered Roth a mooring that could tether him to the world, prevent him slipping too far adrift. There are obvious parallels with his quasi-religious attitude towards Austria-Hungary and its late emperor – for our Father who art in Heaven, so for the paternal protector who ruled over the vanished

---

* Von Cziffra had served in the army and Roth regarded him as a military comrade.

fatherland of his vanished childhood.* Roth had multiple absences to
fill: he sought God, a father and a fatherland. He was not convinced
that any of these could be found, but knew that the search granted
direction to his life. This way, a condition of endless flight could be
inverted into a constant pursuit. If he was chasing what he suspected
deep down to be a religious illusion, just as he chased an Austrian
identity he knew he could never quite inhabit, then at least he was not
only fleeing but pursuing; not only pushed by persecutors but pushing
his life's course, regaining control. Futile it may have been, but morally
preferable to passivity and inertia.

*Oh – the whole world thinks in such tired, worn, traditional clichés. It never
asks the wanderer where he's going, only ever where he's come from.* It was of
profound existential importance to Roth that he should feel himself
working towards certain destinations both spiritual and social. Roth
pursued God while doubting His existence, and pursued acceptance
in Vienna while harbouring no illusions about his hosts. He had little
hope of resolving these tasks; what mattered was that he tried and,
within the circumstances forced upon him, the trying lent him dignity.
For a stateless man, so crushed by the scale of suffering and beleaguered
by living in solitary poverty, dignity was at a premium in the aftermath of the First World War, which, he later observed, 'people call the
"World War", and in my view rightly, and not for the usual reason,
that the whole world was involved in it, but rather because as a result
of it we lost a whole world, our world . . .'.[57]

Having lost a world, he stood at the dawn of the 1920s determined
to build a new one.

---

* Roth undoubtedly conceptualised the monarchy in religious terms. When, in
a famous passage in 'The Bust of the Emperor', he likened the empire to 'a large
house with many doors and many rooms for many different kinds of people', his
imagery originated in the Bible. As Sidney Rosenfeld observes, Count Morstin's
words 'echo John 14:2. The Martin Luther Bible reads: "*In meines Vaters Hause sind
viele Wohnungen*" . . . [in English] the New Standard Revised Version reads: "In
my Father's house there are many dwelling places" . . . the source is easily recog-
nizable.' Rosenfeld, *Understanding Joseph Roth* (University of South Carolina Press,
2001), p. 100.

PART TWO

Friedl and Joseph Roth in France, 1925.

Chapter Four

'Now you're exaggerating,' say I to Zwonimir. 'You have to
do that or they don't believe you,' says he.

Hotel Savoy

One day in late 1919 while sitting with Stefan Fingal in the Café
Herrenhof in Herrengasse, his favourite haunt since earning a regular
income, Roth's gaze drifted to one of
the girls at the next table and lingered
there. The two men struck up a conversation with her and her friend. She
was nineteen years old, innocent and
a little shy but lively, sweet-natured
and gracious. When she smiled at his
jokes, dimples formed in her cheeks.
She had delicate features, wide eyes,
full lips and dark hair that swept
across her brow. Roth found her
enchanting. When the girls had to
leave, he followed them out on to the
street and asked who she was. 'I'm
Polish,' she said teasingly, adopting a
Polish accent. Roth asked again, and

The women's salon in the Café
Herrenhof, Vienna, in 1914.

she conceded that her name was Friederike, but everyone called her

Friedl. What was her address?, he asked, and she told him: Am Tabor 15, in Leopoldstadt.*

Roth could hardly wait to call on her. When he did, Friedl introduced him to her mother and father, Siegmund (known as Selig) and Jenny (née Jente Torczyner), and younger sisters Hedy and Erna. Their

surname was Reichler. They knew Brody, he had no need to gloss over his origins; the parents had moved in the 1890s from Galicia to Vienna. The visit passed off well, but Roth left dejected. The most important detail he garnered from getting to know the family was that Friedl was engaged to be married. Her intended husband was an occasional contributor to *Der Neue Tag*, a tall, slender man named Hanns Margulies.

Roth persevered. Hedy Reichler, who was twelve at the time, later recalled how he began to visit their

Friedl Reichler, *c*.1920.

apartment every evening, to sit and talk with the family while drinking vast amounts of tea. He was typically in high spirits and keen to impress. Hedy came to look on him as a big brother, and soon fell into addressing him with the informal *du*. Once she complimented him on the watch he was wearing. 'Do you want it?' he replied. 'You can have it!,'[1] and he handed it to her. On another occasion she arrived with wet feet after walking home in the rain, whereupon Roth escorted her to a shoe shop and bought her a new pair of shoes. It didn't pain him

---

* A location where Roth's story touches upon the author's ancestors: at this time my grandmother Ilse Epstein and her sister Lisbeth lived nearby at Am Tabor 22 with their parents Arnold and Edith. The Epsteins remained there until they had to flee in the late 1930s; Friedl's family were there until 1935. It seems plausible the two families knew of each other. Perhaps my ancestors were even acquainted with Roth owing to his regular visits to the apartment across the street. There is no way of knowing, as they are all long gone: Lisbeth is the only one I knew, and she died in 1996 when I was eighteen.

to act generously; he enjoyed being able to help those around him, and if at this time it curried favour with Friedl's family then so much the better. He remained as generous years later, by which time he no longer needed to impress Hedy: when she asked him to show her his new cigarette case, he handed it over saying: 'You can keep it. I buy everything by the hundred.'

His persistence paid off. Once Roth had made it plain that he was serious about Friedl, she ended her engagement. So in late 1919 began one of the happiest periods in Roth's life. He was the rising star of *Der Neue Tag*, he had by his side a young woman so pretty it was hard to believe she was his, and his confidence was expanding by the day. Back in the Café Herrenhof, to which the Viennese literati who hitherto met at the nearby Café Central transferred en masse after the war, he gained a reputation for cockiness and arrogant wit. His 'sonorous, brittle voice' rang out over the hubbub, and after only a few years in the city his delivery had modulated into the 'sluggish German of the distinguished Austrian'.[2] The café on Herrengasse became Roth's living room at this time. He would sit and write his feuilletons, offering a running commentary on his work to those who joined him for a coffee, or browse a newspaper, picking at every element from the content to the typography. As Michael Hofmann observes, he 'was a newspaperman all his life', and of the relatively few 'photographs that exist of him, a surprising number show him holding a newspaper or reading one'.[3]

Often Friedl would sit at his side, though her demeanour varied depending on whether they had company. When they were alone she could be effervescent, but when someone else pulled up a chair she usually lapsed into passive silence due to social anxiety, reminiscent of his mother's. In front of Roth's newspaper colleagues she became self-conscious and apprehensive. Roth respected her intuition, but she had limited schooling and lacked confidence among these educated people who had an informed opinion on any matter that crossed their view. At first this disparity held an appeal for Roth. He was flattered by this beautiful young woman's interest in him and enjoyed caring for her, offering advice, comfort and wisdom as a man six years her senior. His joy at being in love softened his lifestyle and his work. He cut down his drinking, and his writing changed. In a column from this time, he described how he 'packed the seconds full of the happiness of my love' and the 'minutes with the over-abundance of my heart'.[4] His personal optimism emboldened his political idealism, as is apparent in a sketch from 21 March 1920 when he surveyed the youthful post-war generation now emerging into view. '*These* young people will not know beery humour nor carnival Germanness, no medieval fancy dress and no reactionary politics. *These* young people will not, in blind obedience and bloodlust, march into wars for puppets! They will love life and work and produce a generation that is remote from crackpot ideology and hollow kitsch, from hate-enraged nationalism and slavish idolatry[;] standing firm in the middle of the day, bridging borders and uniting worlds, they will ensure the upward development of humanity.'[5] At this time, his optimism outweighed his realism and the comment is notable for describing specifically what would happen, even as he claimed it would not. He was still young, and he was in love with someone of that younger generation in whom he had such faith.

Then Friedl asked him to marry her, and something changed. He prevaricated and said he would rather wait. The idea of marriage chafed at his need for freedom to pursue sudden whims. He liked to control the people close to him, for fear that they would abandon him if left to their own devices, but he could not countenance being under someone's control – moreover, under a woman's. He had spent his first eighteen years in that condition. They resolved to continue as they were, Roth having made vague assurances about marrying in future, but Friedl was dissatisfied and the issue remained unresolved when this period of comfortable stability abruptly ended. *Der Neue Tag* ceased publication on 30 April 1920, after only thirteen months, owing to its unsustainably high production costs. Its demise had been rumoured in the preceding weeks and Roth had drawn up an escape plan: he decided he must move to Paris, and began frantically practising his French. It was made clear to him, however, that this would be an unwise career move – he had no contacts there and remained far from fluent in the language – so he thought again. Remaining in Vienna did not seem viable. He sought other work there but soon concluded that Alfred Polgar, the paper's erstwhile arts editor, was correct that the city was 'dried up by economic straits that had buried everything under sand'.[6] Later he would remark that 'Inflation drove me out of Vienna, one could no longer live there. I left,' he said, for 'where there was some money to be made.'[7]

As the comment suggests, he left alone. Departing without Friedl was not such a wrench; where at first her faithful attachment to him had seemed endearing, now he sought to move as he pleased, unencumbered. Like anyone at times, but more often than most, he grew wistful for the freedoms we trade for the security of love. He said goodbye to Friedl, promising he would see her again, but now she reinstated her engagement to Hanns Margulies. Moritz Scheyer, an editor at the *Neue Wiener Tagblatt*, remembered a telling line from a column Roth contributed to the paper: 'If you are suffering great pain, it is a good idea to change where you are staying.'[8] If life hurts in one location, sever your ties and move to another, hoping that new stimuli will spark excitement and refresh the mind, if not resolving then at least distracting from the pain. He couldn't stay in Vienna, he shouldn't go to Paris, and he wouldn't consider a regressive move back to the east. With reluctance he settled on a solution.

'Who in all the world goes to Berlin voluntarily?'[9] he asked rhetorically a few years later. His point was that the city exerted a magnetic pull that drew people in despite their reservations. You had to go there. It lured you then burned you, like a flame to a moth. There was another pull too: in a letter written a decade later he would tell a publisher that he was 'forced to go by the love of a married woman and my fear of losing my freedom, which was worth more to me than my uncertain heart'.[10] Judging by Soma Morgenstern's remarks in his memoir of his friendship with Roth, this woman was 'a doctor, a Russian Jewess, older than him', who 'loved him very much, at a time when Roth was still young and completely unknown, and he returned her great love'.[11] Her name was Sylvia Zappler. How and when they met, and if Friedl knew about her, remains unknown. What can be said is that the twenty-five-year-old Roth doubted whether Friedl was the right woman to marry.

As Vienna stagnated, the spring of 1920 saw its impoverished artists and writers look north. The warm months were the best time to arrive and find your feet. 'I'm going to Berlin in the summer,' he told his cousin Fritz Grübel, 'because in the summer you can sleep on a park bench and eat your fill on a bag of cherries.'[12] On 1 June, Roth and Stefan Fingal left Vienna on a train bound for what had just become the third-biggest city in the world, the great metropolis of the Weimar Republic.

The Weimar years formed a riotous interstitial period between monarchy and dictatorship. Since the republic's birth after the German Revolution at the end of the war, its Social Democrat president, Friedrich Ebert, had attempted to unite and stabilise a broken country that sought a scapegoat for its humiliation. The new Germany promised all adults democratic rights and a Bill that enshrined freedom and equality. There was something nobly flawed and unsustainable in the republic's conception, but the 1920s saw Berlin reach its cultural highwater mark amid a devastating economic crisis. Roth arrived at the right time, just as the decade began in which Berlin gathered a manic and forbidding energy: life there could be debauched, intense, prone to violent twists and turns, often terrifying, but never dull.

The city was not much to look at, but it made you feel alive; its strengths were the opposite of post-war Vienna's. Its architecture loomed where Vienna's charmed. Even before Weimar, Berlin had a mercurial quality that was at once fascinating and maddening: in 1910 the art critic Karl Scheffler called it a city doomed to a constant state of flux ('*immerfort zu werden und niemals zu sein*',[13] 'always to become and never to be'). The city was heading somewhere fast, but who knew where. An uneasy charge hung in the air: political protests often degenerated into brawls, assassinations were so common as to seem normalised. The conference that founded the republic had only been held in the genteel town of Weimar because the capital was too dangerous.

Despite the unforgiving callousness and moral ugliness of Berlin in the 1920s, it was a proving ground where the ambitious went to become the best they could be. The Weimar Republic's self-destructive flaws – an honourable commitment to proportional representation that ensured weak government in the Reichstag, yet a constitutional article that would permit a president in vaguely specified times of 'emergency' to abandon democracy and rule by dictatorial decree – lent an air of ephemerality, a transient excitement that came from living in a period that had better be enjoyed while it lasted. Weimar was a curious mixture of post-war chaos and compromise dressed in unattainably high ideals that lent it a haunting capacity for failure. Even its naming seemed to signify an idealism at odds with grinding reality. As Michael Hofmann writes, 'One has to imagine the United States or Britain defeated in war, having taken enormous casualties, under part-occupation, and saddled with reparations in a punitive peace treaty that assigned them the guilt for the war, then, bethinking themselves of their finer traditions, naming their government and new constitution after a town that seemed to offer some literary precedent, as it might be "Walden" or "Stratford-on-Avon".'[14]

Roth arrived in a city that had two months earlier witnessed the Kapp Putsch, a failed attempt by nationalists to overthrow the republic. Tensions were high that summer, and Berlin made little effort to ease his entry. He would soon suffer a series of experiences that formed an unshakeable impression. First he was refused a residence permit, despite Fingal receiving one within two days of their arrival.

Fingal was born in the Balkans, which distinguished him in the German authorities' view from someone born in Galicia. This incident would provide material for *The Wandering Jews*, where in the section on Berlin Roth writes: 'It has a Jewish district ... where emigrants come who want to get to America via Hamburg or Amsterdam. This is where they often get stuck. They haven't enough money. Or their papers are not in order. (Again: papers! Half a Jew's life is consumed by the futile battle with papers.)'[15] He applied again, and somehow persuaded the Berlin bureaucracy this time to accept him as a resident.

Now he needed to find somewhere to live. Inflation was less catastrophic than in Vienna, but rents were prohibitively high. He placed a classified advertisement in a newspaper seeking a home for a 'gentleman

[who] will pay punctually and guarantees irreproachable manners, orderliness and attitude'[16] and, once he had found somewhere (the address is unknown), he began to revive his professional life. Securing a job did not daunt him: Roth had built a strong reputation, had good contacts, and the city had an extraordinary twenty daily newspapers. More than 20,000 new books were published there per year. Berlin had supplanted Vienna as the epicentre of German-language printed culture, and there was no more stimulating or productive place to live for anyone writing in German.

He explored the city looking for work. The newspaper district lay between Lindenstrasse and the Jerusalem Church south of Dönhoffplatz. Knocking on doors and looking up contacts paid off. Arnold Höllriegel, a former colleague on *Der Neue Tag* in Vienna, had also moved to Berlin and wrote for the culture section of the liberal *Berliner Tageblatt*. Now Roth started to contribute to those pages too. They were edited by Erich Vogeler, and the theatre critic was Alfred Kerr. In July 1920 he wrote the first of a series of 'cuttingly sarcastic'[17] film reviews for the *Freie Deutsche Bühne*. Meanwhile *Die Neue Berliner Zeitung* became the first Berlin daily title to employ him on a casual basis. The paper had been founded on the day in 1919 when Rosa Luxemburg and Karl Liebknecht were shot. Alongside reviewing and his characteristically impressionistic pieces, this role gave him further opportunities to travel. The summer of 1920 soon saw him filing front-line dispatches from the conflict between Poland and Russia.

Once installed in Berlin, he tried to kindle his relationship with Sylvia Zappler. 'They were determined to get married,' wrote Soma Morgenstern. 'Unfortunately, that was impossible. The woman was married and her husband opposed a divorce. "You want to marry my wife? Can you support a wife?", shouted the very little (and of course very bellicose) husband. "I don't want to support her," said Roth, "I want to marry her."' Morgenstern added: 'He often portrayed Dr Sylvia Zappler in his novels. It is astonishing that he was never aware that in doing so he portrayed his mother at the same time. It is a crying shame that they never married. This woman would have kept him from drinking . . . She had a broad, open, good-natured Slavic face. She wasn't pretty. Joseph Roth seemed secure and optimistic in her presence.'[18]

In February 1921 the *Berliner Börsen-Courier* became Roth's main source of income. It was a financial paper noted also for its theatre coverage. Its editor was Dr Emil Faktor, a Jew from Prague, who was simultaneously editor-in-chief and arts editor. Roth began to contribute feuilletons, many depicting a solitary man roaming Berlin absorbing its sights and sounds, feeling distant from but fascinated by what he witnesses. 'One thing,' he wrote, 'is certain: 'that I am a loner in this unfamiliar city and that when I walk along the streets in the morning a shudder of homelessness assails me in the midst of such homelike surroundings.' The ordinary individual 'did not know that bliss too . . . is enjoyed most intensively, if you remain alone'.[19]

He moved through the city veering between bliss and righteous anger. He explored tirelessly on foot and relayed to readers what he saw, much of it appalling. Everything was on display, there was no film of gentility. Berlin was coarse, brutal, raw with life. The overt poverty repelled and saddened him. His early sketches saw him processing this tumultuous city. In one simply titled 'Going for a Walk', he begins: 'What I see, I see. What I see* is the day in all its absurdity and triviality.'[20] He saw a girl framed in an open window; a horse harnessed to a cab 'not knowing that horses originally came into the world without cabs';[21] a man collecting cigarette butts in the shadows of a city square; an old beggar piping a tin trumpet on the Kurfürstendamm; a war cripple who finds a lady's lost nail file and begins to use it, absently conferring on himself a touch of dignity; a dog perplexed by why the lively bouncing ball he just chased down now lies static on the pavement. 'It's only the minutiae of life that are important,'[22] Roth concludes. In writing of what he saw, he provided a mirror in which Berlin could scrutinise itself, and presented his readers with an indictment of Weimar life.

---

* Hence the title of Michael Hofmann's collected translations of Roth's Berlin reports, *What I Saw: Reports from Berlin 1920–33*.

He gravitated towards those who elicited his sympathy, the oppressed and impoverished, and the refugees who'd been washed up here by the currents sweeping westwards across eastern Europe. He set to work tenderly documenting their situation and condition. He wrote of a Hungarian named Fürst Géza who couldn't get to Hamburg for want of papers, and was stranded in a Jewish refugees' boarding house on Grenadierstrasse that 'smells of dirty laundry, sauerkraut and masses of people. Bodies all huddled together lie on the floor like luggage on a railway platform. A few old Jews are smoking their pipes. Their pipes smell of scorched horn. Squealings and screechings of children in the corners. Sighs disappear down the cracks between the floorboards. The reddish sheen of an oil lamp battles its way through a veritable wall of smoke and sweat.'[23] German firms wouldn't give these people jobs, but 'the only way they pose any sort of threat is if they are *not* allowed to work', when 'of course they *will* become black marketeers, smugglers and common criminals'.[24] He saw the costs of exploitation – of capitalists' pressure on their workers, of wealthy families' contempt for their house staff, as seen in the case of the *Oberstleutnant* who threw his maid over the banister because she'd dropped some plates, leaving her so injured that 'it was easy to mistake her for the broken crockery'.[25] He saw children playing with marbles that sparkled in the sunlit street. He saw children in a sandbox in Schiller Park, and declared that 'Sand is something that God invented especially for small children, so that in their wise innocence of what it is to play, they may have a sense of the purposes and objectives of earthly activity. They shovel the sand into a tin pail, then carry it to a different place, and pour it out. And then some other children come along and reverse the process, taking the sand back whence it came. And that's all life is.'[26]

He saw a grand hotel lobby in which he could sit for an hour, with toecaps newly polished by the shoe-shine man on Unter den Linden, passing himself off as one of the millionaire residents. The younger ones when seated '[gave] their trousers a little tweak at the knees to show off their silk socks'; the older kept a 'freshly guillotined cigar clenched so expectantly between their teeth that a waiter leaps by with tails aflutter, in mid-air striking a match on the emery board so as to have it ready when he alights', an image that seems at once to relish the solicitude of a fine hotel's staff while the socialist in him raises an eyebrow at their obsequiousness in the face of wealth. The men 'smell of new leather luggage and English shaving cream and coal', while the women 'disperse gentle hints of a Russian scent across the room';[27] and Roth tingled with wistfulness in his transient proximity to money before leaving the hotel. He teased a misanthropic parable from a moment on the rain-soaked Kurfürstendamm, when a woman slipped, was hit by a car and dropped her umbrella, which was calmly stolen by a passer-by. 'I had never supposed that people's decency was a match for their self-interest. But that their meanness was even greater than their curiosity, that was brought home to me by this incident, which shows that it isn't that difficult to strip the pillow off someone's deathbed, and sell the feathers on the next corner.' Berlin's ruthlessness is here captured in a split second and a sentence. As for the woman, she soon overlooked her fortune in not being more severely injured: she 'now wept for the loss of her umbrella and was not at all grateful that her limbs were intact. As evidenced here, people come in two sorts: unscrupulous and plain dim.'[28]

He saw in March 1921 a throng of people at the then sixty-metre-tall Victory Column by the Reichstag, speculating on who tried to blow it up with dynamite two days earlier: 'A nationalist says it must have been a communist. A communist pops up and says that he suspects the nationalists.'[29] The nationalist was correct: the failed attack formed part of a communist uprising* against the Weimar Republic that ended in defeat, weakening the left and strengthening the right. He saw the famous cabarets and nights of expressionist theatre, written by playwrights such as Ernst Toller who believed their commitment to political drama could combat nationalist thuggery. He saw photographs of corpses at the police station, where foreigners had to attend the Alien Registration Office (though he doesn't mention this is why he was there). The unidentified dead, apparently unmissed, their bodies

---

* The 'March Action', led by organisations including the Communist Party of Germany (KPD) and the Communist Workers' Party of Germany (KAPD).

unceremoniously interred and their monochrome likenesses kept in a cabinet in case one day someone should notice they'd gone. 'Thousands of unknown people die in the city ... They were never part of the weave of a society or community – a city has room for many, many lonely people.'[30] Perceptive readers would have placed Roth among them. Pictures of bloated drowned bodies like 'badly mummified Egyptian kings',[31] a solitary young man beaten to death in October 1921 in a scrap of wasteland off Spandauer Strasse. 'God, beyond the clouds, watches the conflagration of a world war quite unmoved,' notes the recovering ex-soldier. 'Why would he choose to get involved over one poor individual?'[32] Roth feels that a more honest world would give these photos equal prominence to the happy images he sees in photographic studios' windows or on the news reels: 'Life isn't as serenely beautiful as the Pathé News would have you believe.'[33]

He saw burglars conferring in the Café Dalles while a policeman looked on. He saw other policemen counting the minutes until they were off duty and could slip into a red-light bar for an hour, and a plainclothesman in a criminal haunt whose grooming and bearing undid his camouflage: 'in mufti but uniformed, incognito and unmistakable, the tips of his moustache giving away his loyal service and watchman's vigilance ... looking out for anyone with any hesitation about him'.[34] He saw panhandlers and street sweepers playing cards and drinking at the Tippel Pub on Linienstrasse, where an old dog lay stretched out by an iron stove, unfazed by the sound of cards being slapped down on tables. He frequented the city's dive bars around Alexanderplatz and saw pimps and prostitutes. He saw a girl at 11 p.m. on Mulackstrasse who 'patrols up and down, like a pendulum in her regular unceasing motion, as if she'd been set going by some invisible clockwork'.[35] He saw another shivering in Albert's Cellar on Weinmeisterstrasse, where habitués dozed undisturbed for hours by daytime, who opened her mouth to speak and revealed she had no teeth, while her pimp 'had a mouth full of fillings – a treasure chest, not a mouth'.[36] In the Gipsdiele on Gipstrasse – which became a favourite place to drink – he met another sex worker who had just got a gold filling and would cackle at anything to show it off: 'Erna laughs at the saddest things.'[37] Silk socks, gold dentistry; no one's advertisements of their status escaped Roth's all-seeing eye. He befriended a cast of workers, crooks and prostitutes there; another known as Bavarian Annie had just returned after a mysterious absence. 'She claims she was banged up in prison, but I don't believe her. I'm sure she was banged up another way ... and is back from the hospital but is embarrassed to say so.'[38]

Albeit laced with jaunty asides and delivered with brio, Roth's prose had grown fundamentally tender; his empathy had expanded since he expressed his casual contempt for 'streetwalkers' in his letter to cousin Paula five years earlier. Now he saw damaged humans trying to retain the remnants of their dignity. Forlorn people straining to kindle faint sparks of happiness. He found human foibles in the city's grimiest corners. He found more to admire in the Berliner lowlifes' gruff honesty and lack of affectation than among the prissy hypocrites of the Viennese bourgeoisie.

As had become his acknowledged technique since working under Alfred Polgar, he sought to identify – and succeeded with extraordinary regularity – fleeting moments with universal implications. 'I have to reduce every event with world-history status to a personal level in order to feel its greatness and to sense its effect,'[39] he wrote in the *Berliner Börsen-Courier* in 1921. 'Feel' is important here: he distils experience to high concentration to sense its effects more powerfully, like wine into brandy. What he felt, so did his readers: nothing was lost in transmission. His heady prose teemed with the boisterous energy and melancholic undertow, the sunlight and gloom, of the city he had made his home.

Still the question of his citizenship was unresolved. From Berlin Roth wrote a letter to the Viennese Ministry of the Interior setting out his case for being granted Austrian nationality. While the forged birth certificate from Schwaben in German West Hungary had failed to prove his case, he persisted with claiming a Swabian connection. The letter is riddled with fabrications, though these were not sheer fantasy or mischief-making, but more likely an understandable calculation to avoid signalling his Jewishness and the true nature of his military service to the antisemitic bureaucrats in the ministry. He claimed he was

> the son of a Galician and a German [who was] born in my mother's home of Szwaby (Schwabendorf) near Brody (a former German colony which, after gradual Polonisation, merged with the Brody district), without having been baptised in any denomination and thus without having been registered. I was brought up by my father's relatives who lived in Poznan, and I completed my second- ary school studies partly privately in Vienna, partly at the German Rudolf-Gymnasium in Brody ... I was in the field for five and a half months (Jäger 21 and Schützen 24) and reached the ensign's rank. I am a German writer and journalist by profession, known in Austria and in Berlin from my professional activities, and I am appreciated in literature circles as a German writer ...

> My whole existence is based on the personal freedom, condi- tioned by German–Austrian citizenship, to act within my cultural circle and would be shaken by a condemnation to homelessness. I therefore ask for the formal recognition of that citizenship which I believe I have long since acquired spiritually through my being and work.[40]

On 8 June 1921 he at last received the news he had been awaiting, and was granted Austrian nationality. The document gave his place of birth as Szwaby, though someone had added by hand 'allegedly',[41] owing to his failure to submit a birth certificate. His application had been supported by his drinking companion Hugo Schulz, a Social Democrat-supporting journalist who was working at the Austrian legation in Berlin. Schulz confirmed he had known Roth in Vienna and that he had served in the Imperial and Royal Army. Another letter from a colleague of Schulz's added that Roth 'makes a completely German impression'. Had he not had this assistance and his attempts been prolonged a few months more, he would not have succeeded at all. In autumn 1921, prompted by the number of Galician Jews who had remained in Vienna after the war, the minister of the interior issued a decree: 'Since the Jews are without question different in race from the majority of the population, I have issued an order that not a single application be granted.' Just in time Roth had acquired a piece of paper that agreed he was who he said he was, freed him from 'condemnation to homelessness', and allowed him to apply for an Austrian passport. He was free to move, free to travel. The new Europe lay before him, ripe for investigation.

For more than a year and a half Roth wrote letters to Friedl at her parents' apartment in Vienna. On occasion they visited one another. Finally she wrote to him asking for a decision on the question of their marriage. She remained engaged, at her parents' instigation, to Hanns Margulies, but she still thought of him. 'I can't forget you, but I have to marry,'[42] she wrote. Roth thought hard before making his decision, probably informed more by his sense of honour, his affection for her, his pride in her beauty and his concern for her well-being than by a conviction that it was a wise move. In early 1922 he wrote to his mother for the first time in years to tell her that he and Friedl intended to wed. Maria replied that she disapproved, though we do not know why. Perhaps she had grown understandably curmudgeonly towards an only child who barely contacted her; perhaps, too, the engagement seemed a final rejection, in which he confirmed that he'd transferred the focus of his affection from his mother to his fiancée. Maria had grown deeply lonely, with no intellectual interests, only seeing close family and struggling with ill-health. Her son brushed aside her reservations and pressed ahead with plans for the wedding.

Then he heard from his relatives in Lwów that his mother was seriously ill, with cancer of the womb. She had to go into hospital in the city for a hysterectomy, but to no avail. Roth arrived after the operation to find her on her deathbed. Later he concocted an account of those final moments designed to convey her maddening concern towards him, so all-consuming that it endured to the last. He claimed that on noticing that his shirt was torn, his mother got up and repaired it, then she painfully laid herself down again and died. What is true is that he requested, and gained permission, to see her womb in the hospital laboratory. Now he could picture just where he had come from. Sometimes he told friends he'd taken it away and kept it pickled in a jar. Later he informed Józef Wittlin that his mother's pain had been intolerable and death was a happy release: cool platitudes from a writer usually distinguished by his empathy, which only reveal his emotional distance from the woman who had given all she had to raise him. She left him few material possessions, but among them were some he would treasure: a lockable wooden box which contained his childhood prayer book and *tefillin*, the black cubic leather boxes containing Torah verses that are worn by Orthodox Jews. The verses are a reminder that at the time of the Exodus, God delivered the Jews from slavery – that He does not look on impassively from Heaven, but intervenes on Earth.

A few days after Maria's death, he and Friedl were married. Roth

The Pazmanite Temple, or
Synagogue of Leopoldstadt,
in Vienna.

arrived in Vienna on 2 March 1922 and stayed with her parents in Am Tabor. Three days later they became husband and wife at the Pazmanite Temple in Leopoldstadt, built eight years earlier and considered the most beautiful synagogue in Vienna. It was an Orthodox marriage, officiated by Rabbi Dr Funk before two witnesses, Friedl's father Siegmund and Roth's uncle Heinrich Grübel. His cousin Michael Grübel was his only other relative present. All other members of the wedding party were friends and family of the bride. Afterwards they travelled to Lwów, where he introduced Friedl to the extended Grübel family and to Frau von Szajnocha-Schenk, whom he still looked up to as a mother. From now on he also began to address Siegmund and Jenny Reichler as '*Vater*' and '*Mutter*', adding them to his roster of honorary parents who might fulfil the roles vacated by a father he'd never known and a mother he'd forced into estrangement long before her death. Roth sought to normalise his view of his mother – he wrote of 'the eternal, cruel law of nature' that forces mothers and sons to become 'strangers, ever more strangers'[43] – hiding his fierce individual compulsion to cultivate and protect his personal liberty.

Roth returned to Berlin, while Friedl waited in Vienna until he had found them somewhere to live. Within a few days of arriving in the city, he befriended an actor named Alfred Beierle. The two hit it off immediately and embarked on a three-day drinking binge, working their way through the bars of Berlin. 'I have many debts,' Roth confided in Beierle at one point. 'No money at all. No flat. I'm living in a hotel.' 'Come,' said Beierle, 'move in with me.' Then Roth added hesitantly: 'And a girl in Vienna.' 'Bring her here,'[44] said Beierle. So he did, and Friedl joined Roth and his new drinking buddy for a spell living in Beierle's flat at Mommsenstrasse 66. How she felt about this can only be guessed, but it wasn't long before the newly married couple moved to an apartment in Schöneberg, the first home either of them had had to call their own. Roth barely knew what to do. He was like a captive animal. His later publisher Gustav Kiepenheuer observed him there: 'Once for a short time he had rented an apartment, and I saw him in the enormous, gloomy Berliner room, his hands in his coat pockets as if he were walking up and down in a waiting room, on the look-out for the signal that his train was ready to depart.'[45] Later Roth would remark of his preference for the freedom of hotel living: 'Of course it's too expensive, and a nasty habit of mine. But I hate flats. A flat is something final. A crypt.'[46]

They lived next door to a Viennese radical socialist journalist named Bruno Frei and saw him almost every day at first, whether in each other's homes or at venues such as the Akademie Ball or the theatre. Friedl was, in Frei's view, 'one of the most beautiful women I've ever met. Roth loved her very much.'[47] She was sweet, witty and exuded coquettish charm. The newly married couple were almost inseparable. Roth also took advantage of her dutiful attitude by asking her to deliver his articles to the *Berliner Börsen-Courier* office and return with his fees. One from spring 1922 offered him the opportunity to reflect on mother-son relationships and maternal self-sacrifice without acknowledging that he had just lost his mother. He was working through his feelings in public but at a remove, filtered through others' experiences, a method that offered some catharsis without impinging on his keenly defended privacy.

On 24 April, Roth reported, a nineteen-year-old labourer named Franz Zagacki received a five-year prison sentence for a sustained attack on his mother while she peeled potatoes, trying to kill her 'first with an axe, then by asphyxiation, and finally by stabbing her'.[48] Leaving her for dead, Zagacki stole her wallet, paid off his debts, bought cigarettes, invited his friends and his girlfriend – who was complicit in the act – to a party in the woman's flat, then went out to celebrate. The mother survived and testified in court that she had forgiven her son, who wasn't to blame and had merely been led astray by bad company. As she lay recovering in hospital she had '[trembled] for the well-being of her son, and if she had had the strength and if her lust for life had not prevailed when she was near death, then she would have remained quietly under the bedding in which he had tried to asphyxiate her, in order to spare him'.[49] Now she would bring him provisions in prison, Roth speculates; but he goes on to use the story as a proxy to empathise with how a devoted, estranged mother might reflect on her lot in quiet moments spent alone. During her day's labours, between 'the scrubbing of the floorboards and the chopping of the kindling, there will be a brief, secretive folding of her hands. And each time she sits down to peel potatoes, as when the axe struck her, she will cry from pain'; and yet, still thinking of her beloved son, she will feel 'a kind of shy pride' based 'simply on the fact of the boy's existence'.[50]

On 24 June 1922 German nationalists from the Organisation Consul movement, which comprised men who'd previously plotted the failed Kapp Putsch, assassinated Walther Rathenau, a Jewish industrialist and liberal politician who was negotiating with Soviet Russia in his capacity as foreign minister. This made him, in their eyes, complicit in the spread of communism. Roth wrote a column deploring his murder. From Leipzig, where the conspirators' trial was held, he captured Germany's atmosphere and direction: 'You get to know the character and attitude of a German town at night. And also the police. At night Leipzig consists of Rathenau-murderers and those who want to become Rathenau-murderers. Three nights in a row I heard student groups parading through the streets.' They emerged from a brothel in Goldhahngässchen, he said, the heart of the red-light district. 'The Germanic youth shouted: *Down with the Jewish Republic. Ebert is a pig*,' referring to the Social Democratic president. 'About a hundred people from Leipzig passed by and put up with it. A patrolman swayed up and down, royal cotton wool in his ears.'[51]

Rathenau's was one of hundreds of killings the Organisation Consul perpetrated; it followed their shooting of finance minister Matthias Erzberger the previous August, for negotiating the Armistice and supporting the commitment to pay reparations to the Allies. On the streets of Berlin the 5,000-strong terrorist group targeted anyone they deemed an opponent of their agenda: this being 'warfare against all anti-nationalists and internationalists; warfare against Jewry, Social Democracy and Leftist-radicalism; [and] fomentation of internal unrest in order to attain the overthrow of the anti-nationalist Weimar constitution'.[52] They acted with near-impunity. Of the 350-plus killings they committed, only twenty-seven resulted in convictions, and the sentences were generally light owing to right-wing judges' sympathy with their cause.

In 1919 Alfred Wiener[*] had written a pamphlet titled 'Prelude to Pogroms?', in which he chillingly depicted the militias' growing strength as they blamed the post-war poverty and chaos on the country's Jews.[†] Fifteen years to the day before *Kristallnacht*, news reached England of a pogrom in Berlin. The *Jewish Chronicle* reported that 'bands of hooligans raided every large shop in the Grenadierstrasse in the Jewish quarter' where there were numerous black-market currency exchangers. Thousands of rioters yelling 'Death to the Jews', 'among whom women were prominent, attacked the Jews with the utmost fury,

---

[*] Later an anti-Nazi activist and founder of the institution in London that, after the Second World War, would become the Wiener Holocaust Library.
[†] Published in 2021 by Granta Books and the Wiener Library in *The Fatherland and the Jews: Two Pamphlets by Alfred Wiener, 1919 and 1924*.

and seemed to be endeavouring literally to tear them to pieces. Large numbers of police arrived, but did nothing to prevent the looting, which they watched with laughing approval,' until eventually they arrested the Jews to protect them from the attackers. The crowd swelled from 10,000 to 30,000 as they marauded into the financial district. There they cried 'Death to the Jewish speculators!' and stripped Jews naked in the street to 'beat [them] senseless'. 'There can be no doubt,' the *Jewish Chronicle* concluded, 'that the attacks were pre-arranged by German Nationalists, and that the atmosphere requisite for the outbreak was created by the unremitting anti-Semitic agitation of the Conservative Press.'[53]

While the streets of Berlin grew more fraught, in their flat in Schöneberg the new Herr and Frau Roth remained insulated by their love. On 28 August 1922 Roth wrote a letter to Paula Grübel that laid bare his feelings for Friedl, while inadvertently hinting at the unhealthy dynamic in their relationship. 'I would never have believed that I could feel such a constant affection for a little girl. I love the way she shies away from confessions, her feeling of fear and love together, her heart that always fears what it loves.'[54] He noted that she was scared of people. For now, reassuring and guiding a pathologically timid 'little girl' gave him a paternal glow. He enjoyed the role of fatherly dispenser of advice, a mode he had slipped into with ease since adolescence. He gave Paula his thoughts on the subject of a man who was courting her, but whom she was rejecting because of lack of 'shared intellectual interests'. 'Every productive man, even if he is one-sided, is worthy of love. Please open your heart *wider* than you have and live life to the full.'[55] Roth had opened his heart wide and relaxed his guard. The caution of his late teens and early twenties was suspended; if opening himself to love also meant leaving himself vulnerable to loss, he had the confidence now to take the gamble.

Joseph and Friedl Roth in Berlin.

In his professional realm, however, Roth was beginning to feel dismay. The next month saw an incident at the *Berliner Börsen-Courier* that set a precedent for how he would relate to his nominal superiors, although Roth left little doubt that he considered them lucky to employ him. Tensions between him and Emil Faktor came to a head. While Roth was indebted to his editor, he felt under-appreciated. Faktor was an authoritarian character, described by his staff as 'fuddy-duddy' and 'the inventor of artificial boredom', someone who could make the most interesting subject tedious. Roth requested a higher salary – inflation caused by Germany paying its war reparations had started to hit hard in Berlin – and said he felt inhibited in expressing his political opinions. Elsewhere he was becoming known for his left-wing commentary; this year had seen him begin to write for the city's socialist daily *Vorwärts*, where his byline, '*Der rote Joseph*', was a play on his name that emphasised his 'red' politics. The *BB-C*, however, obliged him to stifle his views. Its editors were unimpressed by his cheek. He received a rise but also a reprimand for disrespecting the newspaper. On 17 September Roth handed in his notice. A letter of explanation to his colleague Herbert Ihering, the *BB-C*'s theatre critic, stated that he could no longer 'share the outlook of a bourgeois readership and remain their Sunday chatterbox if I am not to deny my socialism on a daily basis'.[56]

As the Roth scholar Jon Hughes has put it, 'his early sensitivity to the threat presented by right-wing *völkisch* tendencies in Germany was . . . remarkable, and yet Roth's claim . . . that he had fallen out with Faktor for political reasons, and in particular because Faktor did not share his "Socialist" views, has long since been exposed as another example of Roth's myth-making and exaggeration. He was never in the strict sense a "Socialist".' Anyone who knew Roth well was aware that, while sincere in his yearning for social justice, he was the kind of socialist who preferred to advocate for the proletariat from such distance that he couldn't smell them.* Later, in a novel, he would describe a character with exactly his attitude to revolution: '"It's no lie," he would say in the halls which stank of beer, pipe tobacco and sweat, "that it's easier to die for the masses than live with them."'[57] 'However,' as Hughes concludes, this 'commitment to justice, and to human dignity as a fundamental right, is a characteristic of all of Roth's work, and in this less theoretical sense his references to "Socialism" are understandable.'[58]

Roth portrayed his resignation as a matter of pure principle, an idealistic gesture. While he must have felt politically compromised, this was mingled with petulance at feeling slighted. His delicate ego influenced his decision-making and he took an option that cast an egocentric overreaction to a grievance as occupation of the moral high ground. Ultimately such behaviour punished him more than the newspaper. He had little other work. He and Friedl found themselves short of money again. Roth had a long-term solution in mind, though. He realised he needed to look beyond journalism if he were to achieve his intellectual ambitions. His notebook from the time contains a plan for a play, which would focus on a set of aristocrats in Dresden against a backdrop of a sudden revolution. He also drafted the beginning of a novel, around fifty pages in which numerous weddings are held. He

---

* He would later admit that while he resented the rich, he was 'incapable of solidarity with the poor. They seemed stupid and clumsy to me. I dreaded any sort of coarseness. It made me very happy when I found an authoritative confirmation of my instincts in Horace's *odi profanum vulgus*.' *A Life in Letters*, trans. and ed. Michael Hofmann (Granta Books, 2013), p. 151. A reference to the Latin poet's third book of *Odes*, which begins: 'I hate the vulgar crowd, and keep them away: / grant me your silence' (trans. A. S. Kline).

knew he could not abandon journalism – he would require a regular income – but his plan now was to become a novelist. In Berlin during the final weeks of 1922 he began secretively writing another book, often working in the small back room of a patisserie in Potsdamer Strasse. His neighbour Bruno Frei approached him there and asked what he was working on, to which Roth would only respond: 'I'm just trying out something different.'[59]

On the evening of Thursday, 28 December, Roth went to the theatre. By 11.30 p.m. he still hadn't returned home, and back at their apartment Friedl lay in bed worrying. Outside in the dark city another wild night played out across the cabarets and dive bars: burlesque dancers titillating punters at an erotic revue, crooks and prostitutes carousing, and somewhere among all this her beloved 'Muh', no doubt enjoying an after-theatre drink in a crowded bar, talking about things she did not quite understand with people she did not trust. He might have been in the Schneider Café on the corner of the Kurfürstendamm and Schlüterstrasse, where Géza von Cziffra knew him as a voluble storyteller dominating the conversation at the regulars' table, regaling friends with tales of the people and places he'd known back in the east, where part of him always remained; he had no desire to return there for good, but Galicia gave him a well of stories to draw upon in the right company. 'His reunion with Galicia was his favourite topic,' said von Cziffra, 'he vividly described the towns and villages he visited and the people he met came alive in his stories.'[60] Later still, he might weave down the Kurfürstendamm to the corner of Joachimsthaler Strasse and take a booth alongside fellow night owls at Mampes Gute Stube, a bar where he could drink and write into the small hours.

All was quiet in the flat in Schöneberg, but Friedl could not quieten her mind. She decided to get up and write to her cousin-in-law Paula Grübel, with whom she had become friendly; that she owed Paula a letter was one of innumerable matters causing her anxiety. The letter reveals her husband's seriousness about his new writing project, and exposes contrasts in his and Friedl's characters that hint at cracks in their relationship. His irritability contrasts with her timidity, and his self-absorbed focus on work with her sweet, nervous urge to reassure her in-laws they shouldn't feel affronted by the couple's recent lack of communication. She was worried about her health, Roth's whereabouts tonight, that Siegmund Grübel might be cross with him, what Paula might think of her for not corresponding in a while. 'Don't be annoyed by the long silence,' she asks. 'My arm got very bad, and hurt a lot. The swelling's only just starting to go down. Today I was unwell again – I had a terrible cough. I followed your advice, hot bath, aspirin, sweating; now I'm feeling better.' 'Muh,' she says, is 'terribly busy. He's working very hard on his novel, which Frau Szajnocha will have told you about. It makes him moody, so he can't write letters. Please apologise for him to your father, and put in a good word for him.'

She asks after Frau von Szajnocha-Schenk, passes on greetings from a mutual friend, and says that Siegmund Grübel mentioned a jeweller named Pume Torczyner. 'Please tell him that's my grandmother, my mother's maiden name was Torczyner. All roads lead to Brody!' She signs off by asking Paula to send best regards to her parents, 'and many kisses, Friedl'. By the time she finishes the letter, half an hour has passed. She adds a postscript: '12 o'clock already, and Muh's still not back, what do you say to that?! Shocking!!!!'[61]

Roth immersed himself in his book where possible, but he needed to sustain his monthly wage. The only solution was to find another newspaper that would take him on. While inflation was rocketing in Berlin, the economy had stabilised in Vienna. Many Viennese were now returning home. By the winter of 1922–3 Roth had begun planning to join them, and soon afterwards he and Friedl left Berlin. If, as Michael Hofmann puts it, Roth 'hated Berlin but permitted it to exercise him',[62] doing so had the desired effect: he left as a stronger, sharper, bigger-hearted writer than the one who had arrived there two years earlier. It was no wrench to leave a city descending into savagery, where the contempt for his place of origin was if anything more vehement than he'd witnessed in Vienna. To Berliners, nowhere else in eastern Europe provoked quite the same scorn or curl of the lip as Galicia.

The Vienna he returned to felt different. The Austrian capital had changed, but so had he – three years ago he was a near-unknown attempting to leave the war behind and establish a career in journalism; now he had a reputation as an admired contributor to prominent Berlin newspapers. He found it easier this time to penetrate the Viennese newspaper industry, and from 18 June 1923 his byline appeared regularly in publications such as the *Wiener Sonn- und Montags-Zeitung*, the *Neues 8-Uhr-Blatt* and *Der Tag*. While he held himself in higher esteem now, he also saw Vienna as diminished. The grand capital of the vast Austro-Hungarian Empire had been reduced to a pretty but fading city in a small nation state nestling between larger and more powerful neighbours. German politics continued to preoccupy him, even at this distance. They felt more consequential than those playing out here. There was increasing talk of an *Anschluss*, by which the diminished Austria would regain its strength by unification with Germany; this view occurred across the political spectrum, even among Social Democrat supporters in Austria and liberal German newspapers such as the *Frankfurter Zeitung*, though Roth did not share their enthusiasm.

He analysed German politics in his journalism whenever he could, and continued to contribute to German newspapers; evidently he did not burn his bridges with the *Berliner Börsen-Courier* because it ran an entertaining piece by him on 25 February 1923 on one of his enduring fascinations, the Panopticum, or exhibition of topical waxworks, which presented an opportunity to take a swipe at a form of photography that met with his disapproval. 'Never has a memorial industry so stripped its objects of all dignity as the panoptical one ... The only achievement of the panopticum was the unintentional ridiculousness with which it atoned for the pathos of this world, and turned it into a kind of Fun House gallery. This is because the chief characteristic ... its frightening verisimilitude, is finally ridiculous. It is the – actually profoundly unartistic – impulse to produce exterior likeness rather than inner truth: the same impulse as naturalistic photography ...'.[63] His submissions to Viennese papers, meanwhile, largely concerned whimsical oddities he'd noticed on his travels around town.

In the Café Rebhuhn in Goldschmiedgasse, his new favourite haunt, he would spend most afternoons working while sitting with Friedl at a corner table that granted a vantage point over the room. Between

2 p.m. and 4 p.m. the coffee house attracted a crowd of journalists, and Roth would write for those couple of hours, completing his latest assignment while looking up now and then to chat with friends and discuss the last piece he'd had published. Friedl remained happy enough, just so long as Roth was content. She was aged twenty-three now and he was twenty-nine. At other times they would walk together in the Vienna Stadtpark, where on one occasion they bumped into Oskar Maurus Fontana, a fellow writer who had already had his debut novel published. Roth and Friedl were sitting and eating corn on the cob, and when Fontana sat beside them Friedl smiled and said: 'As you can see, we live on corn.'[64] They discussed their budding literary careers, and when Fontana made to leave, Roth assumed a reassuring air of omniscience and assured him they would both find the fame they desired, without allowing this recognition to deviate them from their artistic paths.

While by day he could be seen among the journalists at the Café Rebhuhn, in the evenings he fraternised with the literary crowd in the Café Herrenhof, among peers such as Franz Werfel, Hermann Broch, Anton Kuh and Milena Jesenská, the Czech writer and journalist, perhaps best remembered now as Franz Kafka's lover. Around this time his attitude towards the Habsburg monarchy changed. During the evenings spent debating politics and literature in the café he thrashed out a revised position. From being an avowed left-winger who instinctively opposed conservatism and saw the elderly emperor as an anachronistic relic, Roth retained his sympathies for the downtrodden and oppressed while increasingly recognising him as an embodiment of a more humane era. The coarser German and Austrian political life became, the more the old order of his childhood stood in relief as a period of civilisation. If Franz Joseph were staid and bland compared with the demagogues attempting to dominate the political realm, that was no bad thing. And at a time when nationalism was rising, the vast Habsburg Empire appealed to his internationalism. An Imperial form of union it might have been, but it had stitched together many patches across a great swathe of Europe that were now fraying at the seams. Roth had arrived at the conclusion held by the late Crown

Prince Rudolf after whom his school was named: that a multinational Austria was 'an idea of enormous importance to the civilization of the world. Because the present execution of this idea is, to put it diplomatically, not altogether harmonious, it does not mean that the idea itself is wrong.'[65]

Roth's republican-to-royalist transition (which in any case reinstated his adolescent admiration for the monarchy) was not so unusual. Others among his circle who made the same journey were the editor Benno Karpeles and historian Karl Tschuppik, who became a firm friend of Roth's until his death in 1937. Tschuppik played a crucial role in advancing Roth's career at this time. Money remained tight despite his elevated status; the comment to Fontana about subsisting on corn was only partly made in jest. He asked Tschuppik, who used to edit the liberal *Prager Tagblatt* newspaper, to recommend him to his younger brother Walter, who edited the paper now. The paper had published Roth's poems during the war, and occasional pieces since 1921; now he aimed to become a regular contributor. Roth made his first trip to Prague in late summer 1923 to stay with Walter Tschuppik and his wife Tanja. She told Bronsen of the first time they met: 'The first thing that struck me was how well-groomed Roth was. He had turned up in a pink and white checked shirt, which was quite out of the ordinary in those days. With his light eyes, reddish fair hair and rosy complexion it would never have occurred to me that he was Jewish. He was attractive and slim and one soon noticed his need to be charming and amusing.' He read her palm and 'spun such convincing tales'[66] that she was not surprised when he claimed he could foretell the future.

Roth would go on to have hundreds of articles published in the *Prager Tagblatt*, many of which had already appeared in other papers. The first, on 9 February 1923, was a report from Berlin previously included in the *Neue Berliner Zeitung* and *Frankfurter Zeitung*. Following it were a series of eyewitness dispatches and analyses of German politics filed from across the country: Chemnitz, Cologne, Düsseldorf, Hamburg and Wiesbaden. Roth established himself as a brave and radical voice who lambasted German writers for their silence 'about all things that concern Germany's welfare, employment, the bread and death* of its people, [and] about the barbaric character of public life'.[67] He stopped in Prague between his trips to Berlin, and Friedl stayed there with him at the Pension Flora. Roth got to know the city's character well, and it came to feel like home – more so than anywhere else, he later claimed. Brody had never felt like home; Lemberg was a stop en route to Vienna; the Austrian capital disabused him of the notion that arriving there was a homecoming; he had had no expectations of a warm welcome in Berlin. Prague was different. In 1929, he would recommend a friend to the editor of the *Prager Tagblatt* by calling him 'eager to learn and well brought up and ironic enough to understand the tone of our spiritual home, Prague'.[†68]

While there, he continued work on the novel that he'd been writing in the Berlin patisserie. Whereas most writers demand seclusion and silence so they can concentrate, Roth had by now established that he preferred to work in public. Aside from being unable to bear loneliness, being surrounded by life stimulated him. A hum of chatter, strangers recounting stories at the next table, Roth peering discreetly through briefly open windows into other lives, then warmly receiving the arrival of friends at his table: this would remain his modus operandi. A decade later the Swiss writer Carl Seelig requested a meeting and received this reply: 'Please come here on any day, even if I'm writing, I don't mind. Good company encourages me.'[69] Once when he sat in a café with the playwright Ödön von Horváth and Géza von Cziffra, he broke off their conversation to say:

'I want to work now, gentlemen, feel free to talk.' They remained silent, at which Roth chided them: 'Don't you have anything to say to each other?'

'Does it not distract you when we talk?' asked von Horváth.

'On the contrary, it distracts me if you don't talk,' Roth explained.

'Well, I really don't get it,' said von Cziffra. 'You have a nice desk in your room with a bottle of Barack on it, and surely your wife sits silently in a corner while you write.'

---

* A rhyming saying in German, *Brot und Tod*.
† Written with reference to Pierre Bertaux, 'one of the most charming Frenchmen and my friend'.

'But that's it!' Roth exclaimed. 'The quieter she sits, the louder she is.' He continued: 'It's torture to know a silent woman is sitting behind you. A situation which creates a bad conscience, which makes men slaves in marriage.'[70] He paused, then laughed and returned to his work.

Most writers find that words entering their ears distract from the ones already forming in their mind, but that is not how Roth's operated. He could not resist disparaging writers who worked differently, as Soma Morgenstern described when recalling a conversation at a Paris hotel. It 'took place in the small reading room of the hotel which, as I was soon to find out, had become Roth's study. Here he sat for hours ... and wrote. It was here that he received his visits. And wrote. Here he read the newspapers. And wrote ... He had always had the habit of writing in public. He already did so in Vienna, where he preferred to write in a quiet coffee house ... And this habit of writing in public had become his working method.' After their conversation ended, Roth told Morgenstern: 'You can find me here whenever you feel like it. You can't disturb me. I always have time. Only untalented people do not have time.' He could not resist a barb at their mutual friend Hermann Kesten, the butt of many of Roth's jokes. Kesten, he said, 'never has time. I've always got time.'*[71]

In the cafés and hotel lobbies of Prague he had time to reflect on the scenes he'd witnessed during his recent travels and deploy them in his novel. As Roth roamed Germany, seeing agitators whipping up crowds wherever he went, some sporting swastika armbands, others the Soviet star, he scrutinised their psychology and diverted his conclusions into this side-project. Roth walked through streets populated by men like Theodor Lohse, anti-hero of his work in progress. Angry men who had been discharged from the defeated army and found themselves adrift, seeking to apportion blame. Men who found themselves ejected from the solid structure of the military into the disarming freedom of

---

* To a degree this is swagger on Roth's part. When up against deadline to finish a novel, he resented interruption, as he wrote to Stefan Zweig in 1930 before leaving Berlin: 'For the past three days I've been back on *Job*, and find myself continually interrupted: by farewell visits ... Never have I cared less about people. Never did they seem more intrusive and less inclined to leave me alone.' *A Life in Letters*, p. 143.

civilian life, bereft of reference points. Men whose attempts to make sense of the post-war chaos entailed imagining hierarchies constructed by Jewish manipulators. Men whose resentment found focus in the spread of the 'stab-in-the-back' myth, which held that Germany did not lose the war on the battlefield but due to betrayal by civilians at home, especially Jewish conspirators and republicans who led the German Revolution of 1918–19 that culminated in the monarchy's replacement by the Weimar democracy. Men who were in thrall to received ideas about Jewish cowardice, expressed in the notion that Jewish soldiers were underrepresented on the front line and overrepresented in the safe higher echelons (a survey conducted by the German Army with the intention of proving this showed the opposite to be true and was therefore suppressed). Men who were in the ascendant in the new Germany, just as they claimed to be oppressed by Jewish and communist power. Men who imagined that in voicing these antisemitic ideas they were breaking a Jewish stranglehold and speaking brave truths, rather than regurgitating old lies.

Roth was grimly compelled to write about the dangerous characters he could see emerging all around him; as he once said, it was only by writing about the world that he could understand it. If he could understand the fascists' psychology, and moreover help others understand it, then he might help counter it. On 6 October 1923 the Viennese *Arbeiter-Zeitung*, the official newspaper of the Austrian Socialist Party, carried an announcement: from the next day it would run a serialisation of the first novel by Joseph Roth, incorrectly described as a German author. From then until 6 November *The Spider's Web* (*Das Spinnennetz*) appeared in twenty-eight instalments.

After the war's end, Theodor Lohse returns to the poky flat in Berlin occupied by his mother and sisters, by whom he is 'tolerated rather than welcomed'; they will never quite forgive him 'for having failed – he who had twice been mentioned in despatches – to die a hero's death as a lieutenant'.[72] Instead Lohse was a burden, a young law student who 'lived amid his family like some aged grandfather who would have been revered in death but who is scorned because he's still alive'. He gets free vegetables from the Reserve Officers' Cooperative and shares them with his ungrateful relatives. He always was inarticulate: he could rarely find the right words even before the numbing trauma of front-line combat. If only he could make them understand that his situation as an impoverished student is not of his own making, that the Jews and the communists bear responsibility for creating such a society. The whole Jewish plot was written in *The Protocols of the Elders of Zion*, and here it was playing out before his eyes, as they subverted the state, destroyed the army, had the police in their pocket, persecuted nationalists, fomented revolution, betrayed the Kaiser and conspired to establish the republic. It wasn't as if his late father hadn't warned Theodor and his sisters about Jewish mendacity and cowardice, a notion reinforced by Theodor's experience in the army, that honest institution where for once Jews could not swindle their way to senior positions.

'During the war they had been classified as unfit for active service, and were to be found as writers in field hospitals and area headquarters,'[73] Roth writes, in a line that is pure autobiography. What was worse, alongside his legal studies Lohse has to work for a Jew – a rich jeweller named Efrussi, who employs him as tutor to his son. The boy reminds Lohse of a Jewish rival at school, Glaser, who effortlessly surpassed him at the top of the class despite Lohse's strivings. Lohse lusts after Efrussi's young second wife, who is 'a lady: Jewish, but a lady',[74] but he knows she is unattainable and lacks the confidence even to try to seduce her – if only he were still a lieutenant! Instead of pursuing Frau Efrussi, he sates himself with impoverished women he picks up in the street: rough women in grubby clothes, with callused hands and tough faces. 'Girls with wide hips were Theodor's special delight. He loved to find a refuge and a home in women.' (To Roth, sex offered another prospect of a sensation of 'home', more subject to his own agency than the vagaries of geopolitics and the movements of national borders.) 'After the consummation he liked to be mothered by the all-embracing, to lay his head between big, kindly breasts.'[75] Without wishing to read too much into an author's sexual psychology, it is difficult not to notice, on reading all Roth's novels, the profusion of instances in which the descriptions that summon up his female characters include an appraisal of their breasts – 'lively breasts',[76] 'spongy, droopy' breasts,[77] 'flaccid breasts',[78] a peasant girl's 'large full breasts ... trembling with cold and arousal under a wet blouse',[79] 'breasts which are small and pointed and tremble continuously like young frozen animals',[80] breasts of 'bursting fullness' and 'broad, burgeoning, limitless softness',[81] and more besides – and this fixation, coupled with the description of Lohse's ideal woman in *The Spider's Web*, reinforces a suspicion that he yearned for a comforting mother figure to replace the one he rejected. Sylvia Zappler was such a woman, Friedl Roth was not; her anxiety paralleled his mother's, but there the similarity ended. He played the senior role in their marriage, offering his 'little girl' paternal guidance; not having one himself, he keenly appreciated a father's importance and could act like one to the person he loved the most.

With every journey between Lohse's spartan flat and the Efrussis' mansion, the injustice of it all burns hotter. He feels inadequate and emasculated, lusting after passing girls whose eyes would have lingered on him were he still in uniform, but who now don't even notice his presence. Whenever he walks through the Brandenburg Gate he fantasises that he is on horseback before an adoring crowd, rather than forlorn and alone. His situation echoes Roth's own nightmare scenario: 'No escape beckoned to him, and flight was impossible.'[82] Lohse resolves to make his mark on the world immediately around him. People think of him as harmless. He will show them! He meets the Efrussis' acquaintance Dr Trebitsch, a Jewish antisemite named after a similar character Roth knew of in Vienna; the real-life Trebitsch* had links to the Nazi newspaper the *Völkischer Beobachter*, and here it is called the *Nationaler Beobachter*. At first the inattentive Lohse is lazily distracted by Trebitsch's splendid beard while he speaks at length in the Efrussis' house, and registers little of what he's saying – then Trebitsch mentions his friend Prince Heinrich, and Lohse perks up. 'I was a lieutenant in the regiment of His Highness, Prince Heinrich!'[83] After a night out drinking together the prince makes sexual advances on Lohse, who complies to win his favour; doing so strengthens

---

* The aforementioned Arthur Trebitsch, the Jewish antisemite described in Chapter One.

Lohse's already considerable self-disgust. The prince refers him back to Trebitsch, who is connected to the right-wing underground in Weimar Berlin, and so Lohse is introduced to a quasi-military secret organisation titled S II, which parallels the real-life nationalist militia Organisation Consul. Now he has purpose and an outlet for his ambition. Lohse embarks on a pursuit of power with chilling ruthlessness, murdering a rival S II member named Klitsche, overseeing the brutal suppression of a revolt by Polish farm workers (an incident based on a 1921 uprising in Upper Silesia), and infiltrating a fictionalised version of the communist cell that attempted to blow up the Victory Column. After Lohse betrays them, he stands proudly beside the police while his newly arrested 'comrades' file past and spit in his face.

The novel's strength lies in its exploration of the nationalist mindset. We are left in no doubt of Lohse's inadequacies, his sense of powerlessness that manifests in aggressive demonstrations of power, his avarice and cunning that parallel the traits of the imagined Jew in his head, and his timid cultural tastes of the sort that would later fuel the Nazis' rejection of 'degenerate art'. He rises through the S II and comes into contact with the National Socialists. He attends meetings where drunken boorish nationalists 'ate and cheered with their mouths full of cabbage and pigs' knuckles';[84] you can feel the refined Roth's disgust at these oafs. He moves through a war-ruined Berlin populated by grotesques and unfortunates of the sort Roth had seen there, but the brusque misanthropic summaries of what Lohse sees lack the tender scrutiny of Roth's journalistic portraits: 'Greybeards were trampled underfoot in the streets, women hawked their sick bodies, beggars brandished their infirmities, the rich flaunted their wealth, painted young men made their living on the streets, the seedy silhouettes of workers shuffled to work like corpses long buried but sentenced to drag on and on the curse of their earthly working days.'[85] There was hunger, poverty, talk of a general strike. Still, as Roth notes in a line that feels more in accord with his own voice, amid all this strife and unrest 'there was enough money for schnapps, and the drunk feel no hunger'.[86]

Lohse grows frustrated by the strictures of undercover work, how it precludes him from receiving the admiration accorded to the National

Socialists' leader. 'Hitler was a menace. Was Theodor Lohse a menace? The newspapers spoke of Hitler's name every day. When did one see Theodor's name?'[87] Published in late 1923, *The Spider's Web* is the first novel to mention Hitler. In his coldly ambitious drive for power at the expense of his rivals for prominence in the nascent nationalist movement, Lohse weaves a metaphorical spider's web, then finds himself ensnared in it.* Eventually the author, too, traps himself in a web born of his own contradictions. Much of the book ridicules the risible thinking of the antisemitic mindset, but its climax is engineered by a Jewish character who is a Nazi fantasy made flesh. Dangerously clever and manipulative, the double agent Benjamin Lenz embodies Roth's conflicted attitude towards his Jewishness. Lenz is a vivid projection of Roth's self-loathing. He is the first of Roth's furtive Jewish go-betweens who'll commit treachery for an envelope of banknotes. He is also Roth's first avatar – like later manifestations such as Nikolai Brandeis in *Right and Left* and Count Chojnicki in *The Radetzky March*, he peers into souls, and sees the world with sunlit clarity where others squint through fog.

Lenz is antisemitic, but then again he is anti–everything but himself, a self-worshipping misanthrope with equal loathing for 'Europe, Christianity, Jewry, Monarchy, Republics, Philosophy, Political Parties, Ideas and Nations'.[88] He is slippery and unknowable, a duplicitous Jew who flits across borders and works cunning machinations that appear to benefit others but ultimately serve only his own agenda. Lohse finds Lenz copying secret party documents but cannot expose him because Lenz would in turn reveal to Lohse's nationalist peers his responsibility for Klitsche's death. Lohse is left paralysed and impotent, in an inconclusive ending of the sort that would characterise Roth's early

---

* A couple of years after this book, Roth would write a few lines that illuminate his choice of imagery: 'I've never been sentimental. Ever since I've been able to think, I've thought mercilessly. As a boy I fed flies to spiders. Spiders have remained my favourite creatures. Of all insects [*sic*] they and cockroaches have the most intelligence. They rest at the centres of circles of their own devising, and depend on chance to feed them. All other animals hunt for their prey. But the spider is a sensible, even a wise creature, because it has understood that the desperate hunting and chasing that other species go in for is useless, and that only waiting is profitable.' *Report from a Parisian Paradise*, trans. Michael Hofmann (W. W. Norton, 2004), p. 69.

works. Some critics have concluded that it was unfinished. Certainly the climax is dissatisfying, and Roth knew it. Such pleasure as he took in having this first novel published must have been mitigated by this and by the tension involved in its production, for as the first parts appeared in the newspaper he was still working on the later chapters. This showed: for all *The Spider's Web*'s flashes of brilliance the story has an air of being written on the hoof, with so many of its incidents incorporating Roth's experiences as a travelling reporter. It would not be published as a book until 1967. As Sidney Rosenfeld writes, the fact that 'Roth himself referred to his next novel, *Hotel Savoy*, as his first, could well attest to his own awareness that, for all of its inherent interest, *The Spider's Web* is structurally and stylistically flawed'.[89]

Whatever the novel's literary merit, its topicality would have resonated with newspaper readers over the few days after they finished reading. The serialisation in the Viennese *Arbeiter-Zeitung* concluded on 6 November.* On 8 November in Munich, Adolf Hitler and General Ludendorff attempted to overthrow the Weimar Republic by launching what became known as the Beer Hall Putsch.

Roth could smell the decay of German society. A faint but inescapable stench hung in the air almost wherever he travelled in late 1923. Early that year the French had marched into and occupied the Ruhr industrial area, in response to Germany falling behind with war reparations; now they were plundering resources, helping themselves to German coal, fostering resentment and violence. Roth moved back to Berlin to join the *Frankfurter Zeitung*, the Jewish-owned liberal paper that would become the mainstay of his journalistic career over the coming decade, and seems immediately to have embarked on a flurry of journeys around the country. Winter arrived but, as he noted in one of his most significant and prescient newspaper columns of this period, the climate felt mild, as if governed by some 'compensatory mechanism'

---

* The alternative view, floated by Wilhelm von Sternburg, is that this is no coincidence, and that the *Arbeiter-Zeitung* editors cancelled the serialisation of this potentially inflammatory story after the Hitler coup and subsequent political violence. The fact that the novel's 'ending' is abrupt would support this theory.

that ameliorated the cold grip of economic collapse and far-right violence. He saw window displays in banks where 'endless Reichsmark notes' were exhibited not as useable currency but as 'curiosities'.

In Dresden he bribed an impoverished policeman to talk, and heard how he'd been unemployed, set out into the countryside to find work, had his only pair of trousers ripped by a farm dog and stitched them crudely back together with a length of rope, 'for want of thread'. In Leipzig he saw a smartly dressed undertaker whose gleaming appearance and foreboding air as 'intercessor between this world and the next', an 'agent of eternity', were undermined by the fact he travelled everywhere by bicycle, being unable to afford a tram ticket let alone a hearse. In Chemnitz railway station, a hungry conductor sat polishing off a half-eaten box of liqueur chocolates a rich lady left behind in a train carriage: 'What to a passenger was a frippery, to him is a necessity. If it had been a dry crust of bread he had picked up – the effect couldn't have been more abject.' And in the West End of Berlin he saw a pair of teenage boys strolling along a busy road, 'arm in arm, like a pair of drunks', bellowing a boisterous song:

> Down, down, down with the Jewish republic,
> Filthy Yids,
> Filthy Yids!

No one on the street seemed too bothered. 'In Germany,' Roth observed in a passage that confirms his acute grasp of the country's character and destination, 'the convictions of high-school boys are respected. That's how law-abiding people are in Berlin. And that discipline is heading for a tragi-comic ending. Whether it's a schoolboy treating us to his political views on the Jewish republic or a conductor so hungry he wolfs down a box of chocolates – they are so laughable and tragic that no visitor could understand. No one understands Germany. *It is the least understood nation in Europe.*'

He described how a Japanese student's matriculation at Berlin University involved a rector named Professor Roethe declaring: 'We have accepted you, even though you are foreign. Thank God we are not dependent on your friendship . . .' Roth connected the schoolboys' and the professor's behaviour as aspects of the same decline; one boorish, the other genteel, both subject to the same mental malaise, the same feverish sickness. 'That's the way people in a fever rave,' he wrote. 'Anyone who has sat at the bedside of a sick patient will know the hours are not all pathos and anguish. The sick man will talk all kinds of nonsense, ridiculous, trivial, unworthy of himself and his condition. He is missing the regulating consciousness. That is just what is missing in Germany: the regulating consciousness.'[90]

When Hitler was put on trial for high treason in late February 1924, it was expected that this would spell the end for his political career and his National Socialist movement. Instead he spent three weeks in court in Munich exploiting the opportunity to make himself a martyr and establish his position as a figurehead for those who detested the republic. Joseph Roth looked on aghast from Berlin. Evidently he could freelance for other titles alongside his new role at the *Frankfurter Zeitung* – it's hard to imagine him accepting any other scenario – because one week into the trial, he wrote a piece for the Berlin socialist daily *Vorwärts* that expressed his horror at fascism's apparently inexorable journey towards acceptance in German life. 'The tombs of world history are yawning open in Munich and all the corpses one thought interred are stepping out,' Roth wrote. 'A grotesque dream is forming – and all Germany accepts this miracle with indifference, as if it was self-evident.'[91] Hitler left the courtroom with a short custodial sentence and a vastly increased profile, and the evil so disturbingly depicted in *The Spider's Web* consolidated its presence in the reality of 1920s Germany.

Chapter Five

He was almost thirty now. To him the thirtieth year marked
the last stage on the road to greatness. If one hadn't become
an important figure by then, it was too late. Then the whole
of life lost its point.

Right and Left

Joseph Roth's early books fit within a genre in post-war German literature known as *Heimkehrerromane*, novels that describe the situation of
soldiers returning home. But what of those who no longer had a home,
who were welcomed back not with open arms but indifference – those
who found themselves alone and adrift, whose ambition had reduced
to little more than finding a temporary perch to call their own, there
to take stock and relaunch their lives? Roth's second novel examines a
man in such a predicament.

After three years in a Siberian prisoner-of-war camp, Gabriel Dan
works his way back across Russia as a peripatetic labourer until one morning, he arrives in Łódź, wearing a dead comrade's breeches and an old
pair of boots. He knows the town, he has family living here. His 'parents
were Russian Jews' – presumably both, like Roth's, are dead – but he has
a rich uncle he wishes to tap for money. Dan seeks only to pause in the
Polish city, to raise funds for his continued journey westwards to Vienna,
and his home in Leopoldstadt. He stands outside the Hotel Savoy,* seeing

---

* The Hotel Savoy is a real hotel. It stands on Traugutta Street in central Łódź.
Built in 1911, it catered for those drawn to a fast-expanding industrial city. In
2012 it hosted a site-specific performance of a non-linear play based on Roth's
Hotel Savoy. Scenes were performed simultaneously around the hotel, from the top
floors down to the kitchen and backyard, and the audience moved between them at
will, assembling their own version of the story. See: https://culture.pl/en/article/
hotel-savoy-in-lodz-labyrinth-of-history-and-exile

it as 'more European than any other hotel in the east',[1] and decides to pass through these 'gates of Europe'. A hotel, to Gabriel Dan just as to his creator, is an opportunity to 'strip off an old life' and feel free. In his former life Dan was 'a soldier, a murderer, a man almost murdered, a man resurrected, a prisoner, a wanderer';[2] but here he can be anonymous. Here he can be good. He can make himself anew, just as a hotel room is daily made anew. Entering the hotel, he enters a different world.

A hotel is a tolerant multinational space, a micro-Habsburg Empire housing workers and residents of many nations, fostering an internationalist spirit that made Roth feel at home. Hotels drew from him a greater loyalty than he felt to any nation (he once described a favourite in a port city* as 'The hotel that I love like a father-

Hotel Savoy, Łódź, c.1912–16.

land'[3]). To live in hotels is to become, in Roth's later self-description, a '*Hotelpatriot*', an international traveller whose allegiance is not to a country but to a condition. Roth had no interest in expressing himself through owning a house and furnishing it to his tastes; he had no tastes where such things were concerned. 'I have never – long before the catastrophe [of Nazism] – had any understanding of furniture and the like. I shit on furniture. I hate houses,'[4] he wrote in a letter towards the end of his life. In a hotel the décor, not being of your own choosing or taste, does not define you. It has an anaesthetic quality. The paintings and ornaments do not stimulate memories of people, places and experiences; you are disconnected from your context, a dangerous freedom offering liberation but also rootlessness (Roth lived at the fulcrum of these two states, fate and his own ornery spirit tilting him either way).

---

* Probably the Hôtel Beauvau in Marseilles, but he does not give its name in this article.

Dust and detritus do not accrue to reinforce the self-criticism that you cannot handle domestic responsibilities. You are free of mundane obligations, free to focus on professional priorities. Your relationships with fellow residents do not rest upon observing social niceties and doing a share of chores. Staff will attend you without expectation of your attending on them in turn. All social obligations are dropped in exchange for money, the key to freedom. Money is the only currency in Roth's preferred form of home; it replaces what we might term social expenditure, the investments of time and effort we make in sustaining interpersonal relationships.

In place of a bickering partner or ungrateful children, a hotel offers a ready-made ersatz family – of porters, concierges, maids and waiting staff – who are obliged, in return for your cash, to treat you with deference and courtesy, however familiar they have grown with your character flaws. Roth, ever alert for paternal figures, found them in every hotel he visited. 'The look with which the doorman welcomes me is more than a father's embrace,' he wrote in describing that favourite hotel. 'As though he actually were my father, he discreetly pays my taxi out of his own waistcoat pocket, saving me from having to think about it.'[5] A hotel family treats you with respect, unlike one's birth family. If they don't, you can complain; if that doesn't work, you can leave at a moment's notice and move on to another hotel, another family.

He had been thinking about hotels for some time, an inevitable consequence of the increase in travel that came with his rising stature as a journalist, but they had loomed over him since childhood when he walked along Brody's Goldgasse and saw the imposingly decorative Hotel Bristol. In December 1923, as *Hotel Savoy* took shape in his mind, he filed a companion piece for the *Prager Tagblatt* that sits alongside his earlier 'Millionaire for an Hour' as a study of the blend of transience, genteel deceit and repetition that characterises hotel life. In 'Hotel Kopřiva' he describes a hotel in Prague with his usual eye for the paradox, pragmatism and compromise that underlie even the shiniest of surfaces in society. A good hotel is a conjuring trick, he implies, a sleight of hand: it conducts itself with the apparent serenity of a gliding swan whose feet paddle hard beneath the surface.

'The "Hotel Kopřiva" is always full,' he reports. 'And yet, one almost always finds room in it. There are hotels in which the law of solid geometry is suspended and replaced by another law, which goes as follows: "A room that already has one traveller in it may under certain circumstances accommodate a second." It is to this law that the "Hotel Kopriva" owes its wealth; and to the circumstance that it doesn't show itself to its visitors first, its unchallenged standing. Many hotel managers could learn from it. Complaints do not exist where they cannot be made. There is no such thing as inaudible dissatisfaction. It is true therefore to say that all its guests are fully satisfied with the "Hotel Kopriva".'[6] From this wry but grounded analysis, Roth goes on to essay the constituent elements of this hotel – its travelling salesmen, snoring sleepers, fawning staff, the tinny bombast of a blaring gramophone, its symbiotic relation with the railway station – then spin them into a remarkable fantasy, in which the piece ascends into a disturbing vision of an awry clockwork world, a demented machine accelerating out of control:

Tobacco smoke hangs under the ceiling. And no one has any time. Everyone is between arrival and departure. The 'Hotel Kopriva' is always between trains. Its eighty rooms and hundred and twenty beds whirl round and round. The 'Hotel Kopriva' doesn't exist. It merely seems to exist. The gramophone tumbles upstairs and down. The sample cases fly through the air. The manager rushes from room to room. The room-service waiter runs to the train. The porter is knocked for six. The manager is the room-service waiter. The porter is the manager. The room-service waiter is the porter. The room numbers are departure times. The clock is a timetable. The visitors are tied to the station on invisible elastics. They bounce back and forth. The gramophone sings train sounds. Eighty makes a hundred and twenty. A hundred and twenty rooms trundle through eighty beds.[7]

Whatever happens next, we can assume it involves further acceleration into chaos. The sleight of hand has failed, occult truths are
revealed. The piece closes at its climax in the way that we awake
sharply, heart thudding, from a disturbing dream, carrying long into
our day a renewed sense that our present ordered reality could collapse.

There is no hint of disorder in Roth's second novel's opening
descriptive passages, in which the pleasure he took from the aesthetics
and novelty of hotels is palpable. The Hotel Savoy, to Gabriel Dan,
'holds out the promise of water, soap, English lavatories, a lift, cham-
bermaids in white caps, a chamberpot gleaming like some precious
surprise in the little brown-panelled night cupboard; electric lamps
blooming in shades of green and rose, like flowers from their calyx;
bells which ring at the push of a button; and beds plump with eider-
down, cheerful and waiting to receive one's body'.[8] Escorted by a lift
boy, Dan ascends to the sixth floor. There he investigates his virgin
room: he will 'turn the light on and off a couple of times, open the
door of the cupboard for night-time use', and find that 'the mattress
gives beneath my hand and bounces back, water sparkles in its carafe,
the window gives on to a courtyard in which cheerfully coloured
laundry is flapping, children are shouting and hens are wandering at
will'.[9] The luxuriant sentences cosset the reader as a good hotel does
its guests.

What unfolds from there is, again, like a disconcerting dream: the
hotel turns out to house the strangest collection of characters, and the
ex-prisoner of war's hopes of a few quiet days' rest evaporate. The
hotel is a gilded cage. Its seven floors are analogous with society's
strata: the lower floors house the wealthy residents, and the upper
ones – pervaded by steam from the laundry – the poor, who wheeze
and stoop in their cramped quarters. There are 864 rooms in 'this
house in which strangers live, eat and starve alongside one another,
only separated by paper-thin walls and ceilings'.[10] Dan is in room 703.
Above him he hears pacing at night and resolves to investigate. The
restless occupant turns out to be a pretty young woman to whom Roth
applies a few generalisations he had drawn from his marriage. Stasia
is a dancer at the hotel's cabaret. They toy with one another but Dan

never makes an advance, and eventually she sleeps with his cousin and rival Alexander. 'I realise now that women are aware of everything that goes on in us, but nonetheless wait for the spoken word,' Roth has Dan say. 'God built hesitation into the soul of women.' Elsewhere he notes that he understands Stasia, and knows that 'Women make their mistakes not out of carelessness or frivolity, but because they are very unhappy.' We can imagine Friedl absorbing these pronouncements by her husband's narrator, brooding on them, keeping her thoughts to herself.

Alexander is a privileged figure of the sort whose unearned superiority Roth especially resented. On arriving in Łódź, Dan's first interaction with the Böhlaug family sees the shabbily dressed wanderer pressed into accepting their charity in the form of Alexander's cast-off suit. He appreciates the suit, but not the deliberate reminder of their differing status. From the war Dan has harsh memories of 'nights out in the freedom of the snowfields, of nights on watch at the outposts, of white nights in the Ukraine, when I was freezing and the rockets blazed across the sky tearing it like red and fiery wounds';[11] then he roamed desolate and sore-footed across the frozen fields of eastern Europe on his long journey west. Alexander, however, gained a transfer to the comfortable army service corps and emerged quite unscathed to study in Paris. He's back home in Łódź for a spell now, resplendent in a better Parisian suit, canary-yellow gloves and a felt hat, 'a poem of a hat in a delicate, pale, indescribable shade, carefully dented in the middle'.[12] He smells of mouthwash, brilliantine and scented cigarettes. At one stage he greets Dan with a '[raised] forefinger to the brim, like an officer returning the salute of an army cook',[13] the kind of power display that never escaped the insecure Roth's notice. He and his father Phöbus Böhlaug are, as Sidney Rosenfeld notes, exemplars of the hollowed-out westernised Jews whom Roth would three years later chastise in *The Wandering Jews*.

As Dan settles into his temporary home, he grows intrigued by the curious cast thrown together by fate to dwell here. The lift attendant, Ignatz, is a wily character with 'scornful eyes, yellow as beer';[14] the manager, a mysteriously absent man named Kaleguropulos; at the denouement we learn they are one and the same person. (Roth likens Kaleguropulos' eyes to beer bottles throughout, just as he had earlier described his parade sergeant Marek's having the 'brown brightness of beer glasses held up to a lamp', and in his October 1923 feuilleton about Schiller Park he states that 'rosehips look like fat red little liqueur bottles'.[15] By the early 1920s his perception was influenced by a drinker's bias.) Kaleguropulos exploits his poorest residents, even lending them money by pawning their own luggage. The cases remain in the owners' rooms and are locked by Ignatz, who does the rounds every morning to check they have not been tampered with. A group of unnamed girls pawn their trunks and 'end up naked in the clutches of Frau Jetti Kupfer',[16] who presses them into dancing forlornly in the Savoy's revue bar.

The upper storeys house rootless eastern Jews, whom Roth casts here as a benighted tribe who '[f]or thousands of years [have] been wandering in narrow alleys'.[17] One is the nervous, shrunken Abel Glanz; another is Hirsch Fisch, who spends his working days asleep, dreaming the correct lottery numbers, which he then bets upon and wins. He does this for others, too: 'Many people have become rich through Fisch's dreams and live on the first floor of the Savoy,' including industrialists and currency speculators. 'Out of gratitude they pay for his rooms.'[18]

When his cousin Alexander decides to step up his pursuit of Stasia by moving into the hotel, Dan has a dilemma. Alexander wants his room – he offers to pay for Dan to relocate, whether locally or to 'Vienna, Berlin or even Paris', which would free him from relying on his uncle's goodwill and enable him to travel onwards. He knows he should be thrilled and relieved. But he also knows this will allow Stasia to 'fall prey to Alexander from Paris' . . . and so, feeling pensive, he drinks 'one schnaps [sic] after another', such that 'the more I drank the more melancholy I became, and the thought of traveling further and the thought of freedom vanished into thin air'.[19]

All around them, soldiers pour into the hotel from Russia 'as if the revolution, like some active crater, were spitting them out like lava into the West'.[20] Roth's imagery is elemental and primal. The population of post-war eastern Europe is subject to currents, weather, tectonic forces. Soldiers are like lava, like rain driving hard across the continent, or like fish: they 'come in groups, many at a time. They come in shoals, like certain fish at certain times of year. They flow westwards, these returning soldiers.' They form 'an endless river of grey in this grey town. Their canteens rattle like the rain in the runnels. A great homesickness emanates from them, a longing which drives them onward, the overwhelming memory of home.'[21]

The soldiers' westward flow after the First World War replicated the journey civilian Jews had long been making before the war. The post-war period offered a topical way for Roth to explore for a general readership the subject of migration and assimilation that had concerned him and fellow Galicians for some time. Both groups coursed into Vienna and Berlin and tried to integrate. The soldiers believed they were returning to their old home, unaware of how it and they had changed into something new; the Jews had hoped to find a new home but met old prejudices; both found themselves disabused of their illusions, and remained adrift.

Among these seekers of a home that may not even exist beyond memory is Zwonimir Pansin, a Croat peasant whom Dan fought alongside. Pansin is the novel's most vivid character, by turns lachry-mose and pugnacious, a boundless spirit whose enthusiastic response to anything that impresses him is 'America!'. Back in their army days, Dan recalls, 'When a billet was good he said "America". When a position had been well fortified he said "America". Of a "fine" first lieutenant he would say "America", and because I was a good shot* he would say "America" when I scored bullseyes.' He has a winning pragmatism, too, scheduling himself time to cry for his dead cow at night '"because I have no time during the day".'[22]

With the characters assembled, two threads develop – the rumours of a workers' strike and revolution grow until they culminate in the

---

* Roth was, perhaps surprisingly, an excellent shot according to his friend Soma Morgenstern, who recalled him putting to use the skills he'd gained in the army by winning prizes at a fairground shooting gallery.

story's fiery climax, and amid this the town buzzes with anticipation of another arrival, that of prodigal son Henry Bloomfield. News that the now-American businessman is to return prompts feverish anticipation. His generosity on previous visits is legendary. Dan gains a job as his secretary – 'America!' exclaims Pansin – assessing the townspeople's requests, most of which are in vain. The 'prodigal son' actually has more of the air of a long-absent father to the town, finally returned but silent, unyielding, withholding largesse, unwilling to fulfil his pleading children's wishes.

He has come primarily to visit his father Jechiel Blumenfeld's grave. Again, Roth gives him a line that he will return to in *The Wandering Jews*: compare Bloomfield's observation that 'I am an Eastern Jew and, to us, home is above all where our dead lie'[23] with Roth's still bleaker conclusion in the latter book: 'Eastern Jews have no home anywhere, but their graves may be found in every cemetery.'[24] While the rich industrialists who populate the lower floors of the Savoy nurse futile hopes of Bloomfield's assistance and speculate over when he'll arrive, the beggars in the Łódź cemetery know when and why he will appear: they are savvy enough to note the death dates of all wealthy former residents and anticipate the descendants' arrival on anniversaries. Their reward is a flurry of banknotes. This is the journalist in Roth speaking, who knew his best information was gleaned from poor people on the ground rather than those wielding power in high office.

It is the poor and exploited who bring about the story's dramatic (and rushed) conclusion. After Bloomfield unexpectedly '[takes] flight in total silence . . . in the dark of the night'[25] having sensed what is to come, Zwonimir Pansin and many others storm the hotel, seeking to root out industrialists. Someone hurls a grenade in the lobby, killing the porter. The workers invade, police and the army follow, a riotous clash ensues and soon the hotel is ablaze, with many residents trapped inside. Given his disappearance, it is assumed that Pansin is among the many ex-soldiers who die. This, in *Der rote Joseph*'s irate view, summed up the proletarian ex-serviceman's lot: get maimed for the ruling class, limp west in search of refuge, find it, get burnt alive. Gabriel Dan and Abel Glanz take a train west the next evening, its carriages packed with more returning soldiers, these ones southern Slavs. Post-war eastern Europe is evidently a land where these *Heimkehrer* are in limitless supply: some die, more arrive. Glanz speaks of what he'll do when he reaches New York, and Dan thinks to himself: 'America; that is what Zwonimir would have said, just America.'[26]

America, the book's final word, and one that has recurred in *Hotel Savoy* as a symbol of hope and progress. Weimar Berlin had a cultural infatuation with the USA, apparent in its jazz clubs, the way German cinemagoers flocked to see the new Hollywood movies, the rapturously received visits by stars such as Charlie Chaplin and Josephine Baker, and the flapper-style '*Bubikopf*' bobbed hairstyle popular with so many women, among them Friedl Roth. Pansin's preoccupation with the USA raises the question of Roth's relationship to the Weimar years' *Neue Sachlichkeit* movement, usually translated as New Objectivity. This reaction against the angst of expressionism asserted a pragmatic, energetic engagement with the world, a can-do attitude embodied by America, the country whose loans were strengthening the Weimar economy. Romantic idealism made way for a new sobriety, emotion for fact. Coined in 1923 by gallerist Gustav Hartlaub with regard to the emerging style of German painting – notable exponents included Max Beckmann and Otto Dix – the term came to encompass a general spirit also discernible in the period's literature and music.

Critics have debated how *Hotel Savoy* relates to *Neue Sachlichkeit*; Roth only explicitly declared his attachment to the movement in 1927 in his *Flight Without End* (*Die Flucht ohne Ende*), which includes a brief introduction claiming that 'I have invented nothing, made up nothing. The question of "poetic invention" is no longer relevant. Observed fact is all that counts.'[27] Here in 1924 *Hotel Savoy* appears to be an avowedly subjective work. As Roth's biographer David Bronsen notes, the story begins with the pronoun 'I' and the word occurs thirty-three times in the first sixteen paragraphs, on ten occasions as the opening word of the paragraph. Like Roth's feuilletons, the novel proposes what some would term 'subjectivity' as the most reliable source of truth, a matter that now increasingly preoccupied him in the face of the *Neue Sachlichkeit* trend towards professed objectivity. The following year he would write a letter to an editor swiping at a fellow journalist and claiming 'my so-called subjectivity is in the highest degree objective. I can smell things he won't be able to see for another ten years.'* Likewise, his foreword to *The Wandering Jews* a couple of years later would include a pre-emptive assertion that the book was 'not interested in those "objective" readers who peer down with a cheap and sour benevolence from the rickety towers of their Western civilisation upon the near East and its inhabitants'.[29] Much like numerous passages in *The Wandering Jews*, the first-person narration of *Hotel Savoy* has a subjective, dreamlike quality that mixes the accurately observed upheaval of post-war Europe with poetic extrapolation and disarming flashes of surrealism. Roth portrays the admiration for America apparent in the 'objective' *Neue Sachlichkeit* movement, in Weimar society in general and among eastern Jews – to whom Ellis Island had for decades offered a prospect of sanctuary – while doggedly retaining, for now, the stance that his own supposedly 'subjective' perceptions were truer than any produced by writers who claimed to attain objectivity in their work.

The novel appeared first in newspaper serialisation – this time in the *Frankfurter Zeitung* from February to March 1924 – and later in the year as a book issued by the Berlin publisher Die Schmiede, which around this time would also publish Alfred Döblin and the recently deceased Franz Kafka.

The Jewish-run publishing house was founded in 1921, and run with more enthusiasm than nous; by the end of the decade it had filed for bankruptcy. Roth's editor, Rudolf Leonhard, was an informed and sympathetic sounding-board for the material treated by his author: he had fought first in the war before turning pacifist and being summoned to a court martial, then as a communist alongside Rosa Luxemburg in

---

* Letter to Benno Reifenberg, 16 May 1925. The journalist in question was an O. A. Palitzsch. Roth is amusingly scathing about Palitzsch's 'objectivity': 'He makes allowances for me! Me, a poet! That much-vaunted North German "objectivity" is a mask for his lack of instinct, for his nose that isn't an organ of sense but a catarrh dispenser.' *A Life in Letters*, p. 39.

the German Revolution. Die Schmiede failed to entice the German reading public to buy *Hotel Savoy* in significant numbers, but in the Soviet Union a Russian translation published by a Leningrad-based workers' press would find remarkable success. The next year a jovial Roth could wryly report: 'My book has been translated into Russian 4 times. I have 200,000 Russian readers. And 4½ in Germany. Does that make me a German writer? I'd say of those 4½, 2½ are Russian Jews anyway.'[29]

Géza von Cziffra, who would later find success as a filmmaker, had his first encounter with Roth at this time at the Romanisches Café, in a neo-Romanesque building on the corner of Tauentzienstrasse and Budapesterstrasse. One day 'a sickly-looking person' accosted him outside the toilet door:

'You are the Géza von Cziffra who writes in the *Welt am Abend*, aren't you?'

'Occasionally,' von Cziffra replied.

'Give me fifty pfennigs!' the stranger demanded energetically, holding out his hand.

Von Cziffra asked if he needed it to buy a coffee.

'On the contrary! Make it quick or I'll pee my trousers.' He explained that he owed the café so much money that they would not lend him another pfennig. Von Cziffra gave him a mark and the man disappeared into the toilet. He asked Red Richard, the café's hunchbacked, flame-haired newspaper waiter,* who it was he'd just met.

'His name is what I look like,' he said, pointing to his hair, 'Roth, Joseph Roth.'

'A *Schnorrer*?'† asked von Cziffra.

'Why no! He's a journalist and he's written a book too. When he has money, he throws it out with both hands, and then he's broke for days.'

---

* The subject of Roth's article 'Richard Without a Kingdom', which describes him here and in his previous employment at the rival Café des Westens, published in the *Neue Berliner Zeitung 12-Uhr-Blatt* on 9 January 1923. See *What I Saw*.
† Yiddish, someone who lives off the generosity of others.

'So broke that he hasn't got fifty pfennigs?'

'Old Kalle is mad at him,' Red Richard explained, referring to the café's owner. 'Roth has already puked all over his shop a couple of times. You see, he drinks like a fish.'

A few days later von Cziffra was back in the Romanisches Café when Roth reappeared and placed the mark he owed on his table, with a copy of *Hotel Savoy*.

'You know God and the world,' he told von Cziffra, 'and I don't know anyone here. The guys are boycotting me. I'm sure you can persuade some of your friends to write a review of my book.'

'Surely that's what your publisher should do.'

The publisher, Roth replied, 'has a lot of enemies, and they are now my enemies too'.[30]

With the book complete, Roth fitted in a dash up to the German Baltic coast to file a sketch for the *Frankfurter Zeitung* in which he surveys the lively resorts and spas at the dawn of the summer season, and contrasts their sunlit beauty with the locals' tales of 'harsh, white, unending winters' spent trapped indoors by snowdrifts, when the gas and electricity fail, and those who make it outside find the wells frozen and the gales overwhelming. In the sea's 'swelling and ebbing crash' on the shore he hears something of the simultaneous push-and-pull that 1920s society enacts on his novels' transient characters, and which he felt himself in his perpetual motion around central Europe: 'the kiss of the wave which combines coming and going, arrival and departure, greeting with the pain of separation'.[31] He alludes to the historic prevalence of far-right politics in these resorts* and advises visitors averse to swastikas to head for Baabe, where the mayor will not tolerate such grotesque adornments to his town. Roth looks out again to sea, which remains 'clean and untouched by the childish and violent games of men. You gaze at the infinity of water and sky, and

---

* Michael Hofmann: 'there is a late shadow cast over this enthusiastic piece by the phenomenon of "Bäder-Antisemitismus", the anti-semitism prevalent in some North German resorts from about 1890. Roth handles it discreetly and a little disdainfully, but it's very evidently there.' *The Hotel Years*, p. 22.

forget. The wind that billows out the swastika banner does so in all innocence. The wave in which it is reflected isn't to blame for its own desecration. So foolish are people,' he notes in closing, 'that even in sight of these eternal things, they do not shrink in awe.'[32]

He must have received copies of *Hotel Savoy* by 14 July, judging by a letter Friedl wrote from Berlin to Paula Grübel announcing that she and Roth were soon to depart for Prague and then Kraków, where they hoped Paula might come to meet them. After politely requesting information on the current cost of living in Poland, Friedl asks her to pass on their customary regards to her neighbour Frau von Szajnocha-Schenk and say that 'I'll send off a copy of *Hotel Savoy* this week.'[33] A day later Roth wrote a joshing, peremptory follow-up that reiterates the difference between his and Friedl's temperaments, and suggests his exuberance in the wake of the book's publication:

Dear Paula,

Friedl wrote you yesterday. But knowing how unreliable you are, I will repeat both her content, and her instruction to write back ASAP. I am going to Poland for <u>work</u>. What is the level of the <u>Polish mark</u>? I have 800 German marks. Can you work out the exchange? Can I live off it for 3 days <u>in Kraków</u>? Can you meet me there? I can barely stammer a word of Polish any more. Inform Frau Szajnocha, Wittlin, Mayen! Then I will travel to Austria with you, and perhaps even farther afield, depending on <u>money</u>. Am bringing books. Looking forward very much to clapping eyes and ears on you again.[34]*

---

* This name has previously been incorrectly transcribed as Mayer; Roth is referring here to Józef Mayen, a Polish actor, director and broadcaster from Lwów.

Letter to Paula Grübel, with Roth's illustrations of his friends and relatives.

He decorates the letter's margins with a playful little sequence of cartoons: of himself in the train, Lwów Station, his cousin offering an embrace with the caption 'Paula hugs him', Frau von Szajnocha-Schenk extending a hand to him, a table set for supper, and the coterie of relatives and friends he looks forward to seeing (seemingly everyone but the resented Uncle Siegmund). At the bottom right he walks upright and proud with Friedl. While Roth had reinvented himself into a sophisticated metropolitan so far as his friends in Berlin and Vienna could see, for Paula back in Lwów he still signed off the letter with the nickname from his lost Galician childhood: *Warmest best regards ALL ROUND. Your Mu.*

*

Most authors would see producing their debut novel and a deluge of well-received newspaper articles filed from across central Europe as a good year's work. Some might say two novels isn't so hard when they are relatively short: *The Spider's Web* and *Hotel Savoy* amount to around 250 pages between them.* Yet few would write three books within nine months. With his thirtieth birthday looming, this is what Roth achieved in July 1924 with the publication of *Rebellion* (*Die Rebellion*), first in newspaper serialisation again and then between covers, thus concluding an impressive opening salvo to his literary career. In characteristic accelerated fashion, he had managed to fit his own opening period as a writer – the trio of titles that are now seen collectively as his 'early works' – into one year. The final of these titles concerns Andreas Pum, a disabled soldier akin to those forlorn specimens Roth's feuilletons had described hobbling around Berlin, Vienna or Lemberg. The newspaper this time was *Vorwärts*, for which *Rebellion* made a good fit: it was the writer who sometimes styled himself *Der rote Joseph*'s most committedly socialist novel. It was also his best book yet.

That one year saw a remarkable maturation in his work. As Hofmann remarks in his introduction, its predecessors are 'marked by a charming inattentiveness that was to beset Roth in many of his novels', by which characters are introduced late or their fates left unresolved, when their brilliant creator's lively mind skipped elsewhere. 'Early Roth,' he writes, '... is like a manic juggler, picking up characters, incidents, objects, keeping them in the air with speed and dexterity, then distractedly letting them go as he stoops to collect different ones. This doesn't happen in *Rebellion*.'[35] It was written with a new control and attention to detail, balancing brilliance and diligence. There are beguiling changes of pace, a mixture of tempi that would become characteristic of Roth's fiction: ruminative and lyrical sentences that unwind and resolve, then a brisk, reportage-style, single-sentence paragraph that pushes the reader on to the next instalment of plot – an authorial flick of the wrist as if to remind us we are being told a story

---

* In English translation, and around 180pp in German.

by a storyteller, and he is in control.* That said, significant elements of its plot are lifted without acknowledgement directly from a real court case from 1923, so Roth's achievement should be seen more in terms of execution and imaginative empathy than pure invention of a story that seems so well to capture the inequities of Weimar society.

The novel opens with Andreas Pum† in the 24th Military Hospital – geographically on the outskirts of an unnamed city that could be Berlin or Vienna, metaphorically on the cusp between military and civilian life – seeking to reintegrate into society after having 'lost a leg and been given a medal'.[36] He develops an involuntary trembling before the work permit licensing board for just long enough (a miracle!) to acquire the papers allowing shell-shock victims to play the barrel organ in the street. Now that he has the right papers, like Roth after securing his Austrian citizenship, he is a different man, focused ahead rather than always glancing over his shoulder. They are a talisman enabling him to move through the world impervious to the attentions of police officers or malevolent neighbours, or so it seems.

The novel examines Pum's relations to God and the state, and charts a journey from compliance to rebellion in both religious and secular terms. It concerns a man who frames the secular world in quasi-religious terminology, perceiving the government as unimpeachable and just, blurring together his reverence for a deity, a distant and all-powerful secular ruler and the land he rules, in ways that parallel Roth's attitude towards Franz Joseph I, His Imperial and Royal Apostolic Majesty: like all Habsburg rulers, the emperor was deemed an apostle of Christ, ordained by God. 'What were they grumbling about?' Pum

---

* His influences in this respect might have predated journalism and also derive from the culture surrounding him in Brody. The Polish-American rabbi Abraham Heschel on Talmudic commentators: 'Just as their thinking was distinguished by a reaching out for the most subtle, so their mode of expression, particularly that of those engaged in mystic lore, was marked by a tendency towards terseness. Their sayings are pointed, aiming at reaching an idea in one bound, instead of approaching it gradually and slowly. They offered the conclusion and omitted the premises. They spoke briefly, sharply, quickly, and directly; they understood each other in a hint.' Roman Vishniac, *Polish Jews: A Pictorial Record* (Schocken Books, 1965), p. 12.

† Jon Hughes points out that the name 'Pum' is a self-referential joke: in Russian Cyrillic the equivalents of the letters 'P' and 'm' are pronounced 'R' and 't', so the name becomes a version of Rot(h).

asks of fellow *Heimkehrer* who felt mistreated by the government. 'They had no God, no Emperor, no Fatherland.'[37] Those soldiers who complain of the war's injustices meted out upon them are dismissed as 'no better than heathens'. Over the course of the novel, religious scepticism comes to seem more reasonable than faith.

Rebellion is a study of how a life can collapse while God looks on, just as a society can wither while its population goes about its mundane business. Recall Roth's newspaper column in March 1924, written while he was also working on this novel, stating that in the Nazis' emergence 'A grotesque dream is forming – and all Germany accepts this miracle with indifference.' In *Rebellion* he compares secular and divine indifference: 'Did God live beyond the stars? Could he bear to watch man's misery and not intervene? What went on behind that icy blue? Was the world ruled by a tyrant, whose injustice was as boundless as the heavens themselves?'[38] The prospects and consequences of a miraculous intervention by a hitherto absent God now preoccupied him; *Rebellion* is the first of several novels to demonstrate this.

At the beginning Pum believes in a just deity, who 'handed out shrapnel, amputations, and medals to the deserving'.[39] By the end he is interrogating God and chastising Him for His apparent indifference to suffering and injustice. Likewise, he returns from the war with faith in the government. He has been promised a prosthetic leg. The government's provision of artificial limbs – replenishing what its citizens sacrificed in its honour – shows its generosity, its commitment to justice.

That this does not transpire proves to be the least of his humiliations. What unfolds is akin to the biblical story of Job that Roth had absorbed as a child, played out in a devastated post-war city: a simple man is tested by one trial after another, and it remains to be seen whether he will succumb to his misery or experience a miraculous delivery from his predicament.

For Pum's new world to collapse, first it must be built. Roth briskly constructs his new post-war life. He lodges with a young couple named Klara and Willi, and falls asleep to the sound of them having sex. He needs to find his own home. Pum dreams of 'stout, broad-hipped

widows, with a well-stacked shelf of bosom', and in Katerina Blumich
he finds one. She is another of Roth's physically daunting maternal
figures of sexual desire akin to his former paramour Sylvia Zappler: a
'broad, mighty and moveable mountain' like Deborah Singer in *Job*,
and like Maria Roth. Andreas's own mother, we later learn, was widowed at a young age. Like Joseph Roth by 1924, like Gabriel Dan, both
Pum's parents are dead and he has no family. But now this solitary man
has the woman of his dreams in his life. He can barely countenance
that his story has taken such a happy twist. It seems too good to be
true. 'This sort of thing didn't happen every day, it wasn't a common
occurrence, it was a miracle.'[40] Another miracle, already. Andreas seems
to have God on his side.

Soon he has all he could wish for: a wife, a sweet stepdaughter, an
honest living, even a donkey he names Mooli, bought to carry his
hurdy-gurdy and lighten his load. His only anger is reserved for those
malcontent 'heathens' among his peers whose noisy protests disturb
his quiet life. The two-years-married Roth has his narrator offer this
observation: 'The heart yearns eventually for the regulated calm of
a lawful wedded life. We weary of forever travelling hopefully, so
to speak, to still our natural desire for the warmth and proximity
of a female form. Our profession already makes us homeless. We
need a home, sweet home, from which occasional forays are not to
be excluded, silently to be forgiven us.'[41] Pum finds a home in his
marriage. His love insulates him in the same way as did Roth's with
Friedl – when encountering Katharina's neighbour Vinzenz Topp, who
also desires her, Pum notices nothing awry 'because he was living in a
new and numbing blissfulness, which armours us against the offences
and hurts of the world, and, like a kindly veil, obscures the wickedness
of mankind'.[42]

But a third of the way through the book, a hitherto undetected
factor starts to exert its influence. Michael Hofmann comments that:
'Over time and many books, Roth's preoccupation shifted or clarified
from social justice to fate. In *Rebellion*, a squared circle, both are present, the one still, the other already.'[43] Beyond Andreas Pum's field of
vision, a troubled stranger's path starts to converge with his own. As

Roth's narrator has it, Pum might have lived out his years in bliss were it not for the intervention of this man, 'compelled by a blind Fate to be a hapless tool in the hand of the devil, who on occasion, all unbeknown to us, comes between ourselves and the Almighty; so that we are still sending our prayers up to Him in the comforting certainty that He is there, watching over us – and are astonished not to be heard by Him'.[44] It feels like an allusion to Roth's own enduring conversation with God, and now in the mid-1920s he acknowledges the overwhelming sense that his interlocutor is no longer listening, leaving him speaking into a void. As the critic Susan Miron has noted, 'if God has abdicated responsibility for events in Roth's fictional universe, His stand-in, Fate ... appears ready to leap in and take charge'.[45]

Herr Arnold is a wealthy businessman, a director of a successful haberdashery firm. He is solid, broad-shouldered, manly and heavy-footed, barks out his words, has a fulsome red moustache that distracts from his crooked nose. His life is a paragon of order. He dresses well, he is in good health, his wife is faithful, they have the son and daughter he wished for, and he has, we are told, no poor relatives who might disturb this tranquillity with irritating requests for financial support. We cannot help but suspect again that Roth's thoughts dwelled upon his uncle Siegmund Grübel while summoning this rich, tight-fisted character. There are but two factors that cause a hidden internal unease. One, that the society around him seems bent on destabilising the order he so values (the one thing he has in common with Pum, both men aspiring to a steady life, not impinged upon by political agitators). Two, that as Roth drily observes he was 'reaching that age when a paterfamilias requires a little erotic variety to restore his inner equilibrium'.[46] So he determines to make a move on his young secretary, Veronika Lenz, who is 'as good as engaged' but will surely not be able to resist his charms.

It turns out she can. When he tries to kiss and grasp her she pushes him away, but he is too strong and pulls her closer. She is repulsed by 'the tufts of reddish hair that sprouted from his ears', and smells 'the odour of cigar smoke and human fat that escaped through the crack between the man's neck and his shirt-collar'.[47] In trying to kiss her, he bites her on the cheek. She lurches back and spits in his face, then storms out of the office. The next morning her lover – a music-hall birdsong impersonator no less; the indignity of it for an esteemed man such as Herr Arnold! – turns up at the office, politely giving notice that Veronika has quit her job and he intends to open a prosecution.

The infuriated Arnold decides to visit his lawyer, who turns out to be away in court. He broods over dinner in a restaurant. He stalks the darkening streets thinking of the couple, with the special form of aggrieved hatred reserved for those who compel us to examine our flaws. The conceited businessman is confronted by his own weakness: how feeble the structure of his life, how easily it might now tumble down. His destiny is in his new enemies' hands. Lit by the glow of lamplight, a 'cripple' crosses his path and earns his scorn for wearing a sandwich board proclaiming: 'Comrades, the plight of the war-wounded is dire! The government is sitting on its hands!' Another one faking injury for sympathy and to defraud the honest taxpayer, no doubt. And the word 'Comrades' smacked of anarchism, of those damned Russian Jews with their bombs and insurrections. Andreas Pum would share his contempt for this so-called heathen's ingratitude. But when Herr Arnold decides to take a tram home and stands on the running board, his bulky form taking up most of the entrance, he is in no mood to move when Pum attempts to board. Now here's another phoney 'disabled' veteran, thinks Arnold, this one with a leg purport-edly missing, crutches, and a gleaming medal pinned to the chest of his uniform. A disgruntled Andreas squeezes past him but then refuses to proceed into the carriage, and remains standing by his unwelcome new acquaintance. Arnold declares to all in earshot that this is another conman, another scheming Bolshevik. He even demonstrates how easy it to feign loss of a limb by hiding a bended leg within one's trousers. The other passengers emit a cacophony of cries – they concur that this man is doubtless a fraud, a communist, a spy, a Jew ... The conductor intervenes, having read about the rich pickings such men extract from people more gullible than he. Where, he demands, are Andreas's papers?

Andreas's first mistake is to refuse the request, reasoning that the man has no right: he's a conductor, not a policeman, and besides he should ask for the other man's papers too. The conductor grabs Andreas, who sees red and begins to swing his crutches wildly around his head, hitting the conductor and Herr Arnold. This is his second mistake. Outside the stalled tram a crowd assembles, and from within it − another 'miracle'[48] − emerges a policeman. He ends up taking Andreas's permit, and it is as if that piece of paper were propping up a house of cards.

The collapse begins. Andreas tells Katharina, who stands looming over him; seen from this unflattering angle, she suddenly seems a stranger. As he recounts the incident hoping for her sympathy, instead he watches aghast as her nostrils flare, and she emits low, bestial growls before erupting in fury. She calls him a 'wretched cripple!'. Pum is floored, devastated, left trembling and dazed. He spends the night in his donkey's shelter, not knowing that his wife has already run to her neighbour in search of legal advice and ended up in bed with him. He still believes the world is just, so he must have done something to deserve this − but what? He examines his conscience, like the biblical Job, with 'the urgency of someone looking through his pockets for his missing wristwatch'.[49] Perhaps his sin is his self-absorption.

Soon he must go to court. He feels calm, for he still has faith in the world's justice. If he explains what happened, he will be freed, regain his permit and perhaps even see his tormentors jailed. But Andreas does not understand the law. He understands almost nothing of his situation or fate. He does not know that 'not only the Courts, but also the Police are entitled to levy fines'. He has no idea that, as Roth's narrator remarks, 'The laws lie open like traps on the paths we poor bastards walk.'[50] He is oblivious to what is happening to him. 'The great grinding wheels of the State were getting to grips with the citizen Andreas Pum,' Roth writes, 'and, before he even realised it, he was being slowly and comprehensively crushed.'[51]

No one is telling lies about Andreas Pum, but he is thwarted from speaking the truth. There is, still, an obvious parallel with Kafka's *The Trial*, posthumously published by Die Schmiede a year after *Rebellion* but written in 1914–15. There is no evidence that Roth knew Kafka's novel while writing *Rebellion*, and it does not share *The Trial*'s night-marish absurdity, but both addressed their authors' feeling that, by the early twentieth century, individual agency had become as nothing when fate and the modern state combined to place someone within the mechanisms of the justice system, rendering the innocent individual ensnared by the law and, like a fly in a cobweb, only apt to grow more entangled when he fights to free himself. Roth returns to the imagery of his debut novel towards the end of *Rebellion*: 'The authorities sit there like spiders, lurking in the fine mesh of ordinances, and it's only a matter of time before we fall prey to them.'[52] This time the web is spun by the state rather than a malign individual, and eventually, after being detained by the police and thus missing his court appearance, Andreas Pum is entrapped in prison.

During six weeks in jail he ages rapidly – when he sees himself in a mirror for the first time in weeks, he recoils at the sight of a man with a yellow, wrinkled face, white hair and a white beard. Even his blue eyes have turned green. It is a biblical image again befitting Job: 'And thou hast filled me with wrinkles, they are my witnesses; and my leanness riseth up for me, giveth its testimony to my face.'[53] Removed from a biblical context it feels more fitting for a fable than a novel hitherto written in realist mode, but this accelerated decline makes plausible Pum's final collapse and the novel's extraordinary end. He reconnects with Willi and finds that the unscrupulous entrepreneur is becoming quite the man about town. Willi finds just the job for the near-unemployable Andreas: he starts work as a toilet attendant at the Café Halali, doling out soap and towels, receiving tips, conversing with a talking parrot and surrounded by mirrors that reflect his wizened face wherever he looks. The image of death closes in on him, and the novel climaxes. Pum appears in court again, having been disabused of his illusions about the state's beneficence and divine connection. 'The government, as we now see, is no longer something high above us and remote from our lives. Rather, it has all the earthly weaknesses, and no line to God.'[54] He rebels, rejecting everything he held dear and abandoning his instinctive deference: he disregards the laws that he assumed were created by 'wiser heads than mine'. He loses his faith, his obedience, his patriotism. 'Facing death,' writes Roth, 'he clung to life in order to rebel: against the world, against the authorities, against the Government, against God.'[55]

Andreas has died in the café's lavatories. The courtroom where we see him now is a divine one. The judge whom Andreas must address is God, who combines royalty and judiciary, an all-powerful divine figure in a secular setting. 'He had an impassive face of granite majesty, like a dead emperor's', as 'grey as weathered sandstone'.[56] His voice is velvety, his eyes are as old as the world, he can see across millennia. Andreas realises he is standing before his maker. This prompts a confrontation that recalls Roth's own querulous relationship with his erstwhile accomplice. Andreas issues a diatribe against a deity whom he must not only 'deny' but 'revile'. This two-page monologue is a startling, vehement attack on God. 'You are the master of millions of worlds, and yet don't know what to do,' Pum declares. 'How impotent You are in your omnipotence! You have billions of accounts, and make mistakes in individual items? What kind of God are You? Is Your cruelty a wisdom that it is beyond us to comprehend – then how flawed You made us!' He concludes: 'I don't want Your mercy! I want to go to Hell.' He repeats himself under questioning from God. 'I want to go to Hell!'[57]

So concludes a novel that dwells on the question of God's intervention in our lives. The final scene echoes Pum's appearance before the work permit board in the book's second chapter. There he trembled before man, now he stands bold before God. The question for Roth appears not to be whether miracles happen, an enduring influence on him of the Brody Hasidim, but whether their appearance will be timely. A miracle in the wrong time and place is worse than none at all. It suggests a sly God who is less on one's side than one might imagine. Andreas Pum's allocation of miracles was dispensed too early.

Back in the material world, his body is taken from the toilet and later to the Anatomical Institute. Willi comes to say goodbye before the cadaver is dissected and he almost cries, then remembers a cheery tune that diverts his feelings elsewhere, before he leaves on pressing business. He must recruit another old man to work in the toilets.

*

Karl Kraus published an article in *Die Fackel* in January 1924 describing the case of Heinrich Reinthaler, a disabled organ grinder in Vienna who had been charged the previous summer with insulting a public official and a private citizen. He was prevented from appearing in court because, at the due time, he was being detained by the police. His incomprehension of the law aggravated his situation, and he was unfairly sentenced to three weeks in prison. Kraus made plain his view that the legal system was itself criminal. 'Without doubt, Roth found both the core motif and the theme for his novel in the case of Heinrich Reinthaler,' states Sidney Rosenfeld. 'While he could have learned of it from a newspaper report, he may just as well have discovered it in *Die Fackel*.'[58] Although Roth came to dislike Kraus, he credited him as an important influence on his morality and literary discipline, and this unacknowledged debt was a further reason for gratitude.

Reading the reports that resulted from the trip to the east that Roth mentioned in his July letter to Paula Grübel illustrates how beautifully he wrote about phenomena others perceived as ugly. He explored the towns, looked out over the landscape from a train window, saw the fields and highways he had once walked in uniform and had more recently imagined Gabriel Dan traversing towards the Hotel Savoy. A poignantly insistent tone runs through his recollections, born of a sense that others are already forgetting the horrors of the last war as they march towards the next: 'Many baggage trains have flogged down these roads, gun carriages left deep tracks, the horses sank down to the saddle – I remember it, I was there.'[59]

The ex-soldier's memories grew stark juxtaposed with the place where they originated, for he found it barely recognisable. The fields were healing over, the scars of trenches and craters obscured by swathes of maize nourished on his old comrades' remains. Where his depressed wartime letters spoke of Augean *shtetls* and of Galician mud like 'grey filth', writing now from eight years' distance he sees tarnished beauty, having been moved to wistfulness by the battlefields' gradual return to farmland, by how everything is sucked into history's maw: horror, beauty, fallen comrades, everything, gulped into the past and now gone. 'From a distance the mud has a sheen like dirty silver,'[60] he observed, and 'At night you might take the roads for murky rivers, in which the sky with the moon and stars are reflected a thousandfold, as in a dirty, distorting crystal.'[61] The three-part series, published from 22 to 24 November 1924 in the *Frankfurter Zeitung* as 'Journey Through Galicia' (*'Reise durch Galizien'*), rebutted his fellow Berliners' derision for the region. The first piece, 'People and Places', opens with a provocation: 'The country has a bad reputation in Western Europe. Our complacent culture likes to associate it with squalor, dishonesty and vermin. But while it may once have been the case that the East of Europe was less sanitary than the West, to say so today is banal; and anyone doing so will have said less about the region he claims to be talking about than the originality he lacks.'[62]

Over the first two articles he lays out Galicia's merits and difficulties. In 'People and Places', out in the rural towns he sees Jews carefully negotiating the aggressive Christianity that surrounds them: 'fields on the left, fields on the right; on the right is the picture of Jesus, on the left a saint's shrine, and between them go the Jews with lowered heads, careful not to touch the cross, and to avoid the saint, between the Scylla and the Charybdis of the alien, deliberately ignored faith'.[63] In the second, he goes to Lwów and reminisces on the polyglot city, setting its German, Ukrainian and Yiddish past against its Polish-dominated present. He recalls working for the military newspaper there. The third piece was filed from Lwów again, but is different and extraordinary. It is almost entirely descriptive, offering no analysis or argument. What it describes is a 'macabre procession of disabled war veterans through the streets',[64] a grim brigade of Andreas Pum's fellow sufferers parading through the City of Lions. It conjures a scene from a horror movie. It is grotesque and quite chilling, a measure apart from anything else in Roth's oeuvre. The ex-soldiers were following the funeral cortège for their comrade Jana Kosa, who, on 6 June 1924 in Lwów, addressed the Union of Disabled Veterans of the Polish Republic, concluded his speech with a cheer for the republic, then shot himself in the head. Newspapers around the world reported this public suicide, but not the ensuing spectacle that Roth observed on the day of his burial.

'The funeral procession consisted of all the invalids of the city,' Roth wrote, and he counted 1,000 men:

All the fragments, all the former human beings, the limping, the blind, the ones without arms, the ones without legs, the paralysed, the shaking, the ones without faces and the ones with destroyed spines ... the ones who had lost their memory and would not recognise themselves ... No invalid stayed at home. Who could limp, limped; who could crawl, crawled, and the ones who could not move at all lay on a huge truck ...

Instead of the healthy, even rhythm of marching soldiers you could hear the uneven knocking of crutches on cobblestones, a music of wood and stone, mixed with the squeaking and creaking of artificial limbs. From the throats of the sick rose sounds of difficult breathing and harrumphing, a mumbling and groaning ... Behind the blind followed the ones with only one arm, and behind them the ones without arms, and then the ones whose heads were shaking. Next came a huge lorry which radiated such horror that you could not hear its clatter. For the view silenced all sounds and a soundless pity cried in such deafening way that no one would hear the rumble of wheels. This carriage came straight out of a ghastly fantasy of hell itself. There were cripples, whose faces were one gaping red hole, framed by white bandages, red scars instead of ears. There stood lumps of meat and blood, soldiers without any limbs, torsos in uniform ... There were men hurling their fingers in the air like dead bundles of bone on strings and others whose faces were torn sideways, to the left and right, and others whose faces looked behind as if their heads were twisted backwards. The front was the back, they looked constantly rearwards as if their past had cursed them to look back on the terror they experienced. All this was a dreamlike vision of the colour red and rotting flesh and running spine fluid and broken vertebrae. Right at the back sat the elite of horrors. A man with a neck like an extended accordion, long and wrinkled. His head fell behind with each agitation of the car ... Completely loose was his head, a heavy pumpkin on a thin chain of withered skin.

Some of the men had their mouths half open in 'a never-ending smile'. They smiled 'about the dead and the world, the road, the houses and the watching crowd. Yes, there was a crowd, people stopped and gazed and did not move.' Rain grew heavier, the wind got up, and 'a dark blue cloud', 'massive and bulky', stretched out a tip at the front 'like a shredded finger, directing the cripples to the cemetery'.[65]

When Roth's novels describe ex-soldiers' return to civilian life, we are to understand that their attempted transition begins from a realm that inflicted such traumas to the bodies and minds of thousands of men. Society wants to forget them, they are too hideous and painful to contemplate. Issues discussed at the meeting where Kosa killed himself included a proposal to convert Lwów's 'House of Invalids' care home into private apartments and shunt the residents out into the country-side. It was easier not to look at these men. Easier to pretend they did not exist. Dignitaries should have been invited to the funeral and it should have been held in a major city like Geneva, Roth contended, but instead it was 'in remote eastern Galicia!'.[66] Half-ignored men in a half-ignored land. Roth was there to remind German readers of these people and places.

In this time of contested and shifting borders he used this series of articles to place Galicia decisively within Europe – not somewhere beyond the frontier, however much some would want it to be, not even a 'half-Asia' where the two continents merge, but part of the European continuum. 'Has Europe come to an end here?' he asks in the opening piece. 'No, it hasn't. The connection between Europe and this half-banished land is vital and unbroken. In the bookshops I saw the latest literary titles from France and England.'[67] Galicia still has its problems, to be sure. 'But it has its own delights,' he writes in conclusion, 'its own songs, its own people, and its own allure: the sad allure of the place scorned.'[68]

That first article amounts to a heartfelt defence of Roth's native land, not that readers of the *Frankfurter Zeitung* would have known this. He mentions having known Galicia before the war, but that is all. This series seems in retrospect a rehearsal for the self-defensive strategy he would pursue on a grander scale in *The Wandering Jews*; the conceptual link between the two is strengthened by the fact that he probably visited the wonder-rabbi in the unnamed *shtetl* during this trip to Galicia, which the book describes with feigned unfamiliarity. He will defend Galicia on its own merits, point out inaccuracies in its depiction, scorn those westerners who look down on the east – but never admit personal pride, because he cannot face the stigmatic shame. He will say people from Galicia have every reason to be proud; he will not say he is one of them. It is another literary sleight of hand, in which Roth distracts the reader from what he is hiding. While they look away, he plots his next move.

He needed to, for by late 1924 life as an eastern Jew in Weimar Germany felt untenable. He was sensitive enough to detect what was coming while others continued to go about their business. Not for the first time, Roth's position was that of a man on a cliff edge who feels the ground start to crack and crumble beneath his feet. He must run to firmer terrain and hope the fissures do not spread in that direction. Two months after President Friedrich Ebert's death in February 1925, the German people headed to the polls to choose between the Centre Party candidate Wilhelm Marx and the wartime dictator Hindenburg, the man who promulgated the antisemitic 'stab-in-the-back' myth as the reason for the nation's defeat under his leadership. A man wrapped in the discarded black, white and red flag of the German Empire and monarchy, an icon of the radical right; an anti-democrat at the head of the new democracy. The prospect appalled Roth to the point of fury. The seventy-seven-year-old Hindenburg may have been a reluctant leader, more a symbolic than a dynamic figure, but Roth could see what his election augured for Germany's future. Max Krell, a publishing acquaintance, met Roth in Leipzig at the time of the vote. 'On the decisive day,' said Krell, 'he said: "If it's Hindenburg, I'm leaving, I know what will follow this decision." When in the morning I saw the black, white and red flags and not those of the Republic, Roth was already on the train to Paris.'[69]

Chapter Six

Here you find a childhood, your own and Europe's.
Nowhere do you feel so easily at home. And even the one
who leaves the country behind takes with him the best that
a homeland has to offer: the memory of it, homesickness.

The White Cities

The windows of the Hôtel de la Place de l'Odéon look out from
between blue shutters over an eighteenth-century Parisian plain dominated by the eponymous neoclassical theatre, before which roads spear
out like compass points, tempting the visitor to pursue every angle into
the Left Bank. To the hotel's right runs the Rue de l'Odéon, which was
home in the early twentieth century to a community of Anglophone
authors and the Shakespeare and Company bookshop; in 1922 its
owner, Sylvia Beach, published *Ulysses* by James Joyce, who dubbed
the area 'Stratford-on-Odéon'. The gorgeously sombre twin-towered
church of Saint-Sulpice stands 200 yards to the west, and its chimes
call to the hotel over the dark-windowed Parisian attics. Cafés, galleries
and fine restaurants for the wealthy, bistros to suit the budgets of the
district's writers and artists. Nearby is the vast Jardin du Luxembourg,
with its elegant parterre, statues of royalty, Medici Fountain and a basin
where children sail model boats. The Sorbonne is a couple of minutes
away, and a short walk brings you to the Pont Saint-Michel, with its
view down the Seine to Notre Dame. A sentence Joseph Roth wrote a
few months later concerning the southern town of Tournon surely also
applied to his arrival in the Place de l'Odéon: 'I love finding myself in
the broad centres of towns, those squares and places from which the
streets radiate out in different directions, so they are not only a centre
but a beginning.'[1]

On 16 May 1925, Roth sat in this hotel and wrote the first of two letters that, judging by the available evidence, pinpoint the apex of his happiness. The recipient was Benno Reifenberg, the *Frankfurter Zeitung*'s feuilleton editor, who had become a friend. Their relationship

The Hôtel de la Place de l'Odéon, 6, Place de l'Odéon, Paris.

mixed the personal and professional to sometimes awkward effect. In the first letter, over the course of around 600 words, you would barely guess they were colleagues; it is only in his final line that Roth asks Reifenberg to expedite a payment he is owed. Nor would you guess that its writer had a depressive mindset, unless you suspected from the prose's intensity a bipolar tendency. The letters are rhapsodic, euphoric, ecstatic. They are the pure expression of a wanderer's belief that he has found his home.

Joseph Roth had discovered a sensation akin to that of his idol Heine, who remarked that 'if you asked a fish how it felt in water, it would say, "Like Heine in Paris."' Not only Paris, though: wherever Roth visited in France that summer triggered feelings of delight, admiration and sheer love for a place and its people such as he had never before experienced.

Paris, 16 May 1925

Dear Mr Reifenberg,

I fear this letter may give you the impression that I am so besotted with Paris, and with France, that I have lost the balance of my mind. Be assured, therefore, that I am writing to you in full possession of my sceptical faculties, with all my wits about me, and running the risk of making a fool of myself, which is just about the worst thing that could

happen to me. I feel driven to inform you personally that Paris is the
capital of the world, and that you must come here. Whoever has not
been here is only half a human, and no sort of European. Paris is free,
intellectual in the best sense, and ironic in the most majestic pathos. Any
chauffeur is wittier than our wittiest authors. We really are an unhappy
bunch. Here everyone smiles at me, I fall in love with all the women,
even the oldest of them, to the point of contemplating matrimony. I
could weep when I cross the Seine bridges, for the first time in my life
I am shattered by the aspect of buildings and streets, I feel at ease with
everyone, though we continually misunderstand each other in matters of
practicalities, merely because we so delightfully understand each other in
matters of nuance. Were I a French author, I wouldn't bother printing
anything, I would just read and speak. The cattle drovers with whom I
eat breakfast are so cultivated and noble as to put our ministers of state to
shame, patriotism is justified (but only here!), nationalism is an expression
of a European conscience, any poster is a poem, the announcements in a
magistrate's court are as sublime as our best prose, film placards contain
more imagination and psychology than our contemporary novels, soldiers
are whimsical children, policemen amusing editorialists.[2]

The city overwhelmed him with its spirit, its charm and gentle
beauty. Later he would write that 'the morning in Paris is drawn with
a soft pencil. The dispersed smoke of factories blends with the invisible
residues of silvery gas lamps and hangs above the façades of the houses.'[3]
If German policemen tended to strut or march, here they 'strolled,
not like policemen, but like idlers with all the time in the world'.[4]
Paris had a grace and languor that set his soul at ease. The strength
of his reaction surely owed much to the contrast in his surroundings:
he had switched from the cold, war-ravaged east with its parades of
ambulant corpses to a warm metropolis populated by chic Parisians.
He and Friedl had arrived just in time for the International Exposition
of Modern Industrial and Decorative Arts (*L'Exposition internationale des
arts décoratifs et industriels modernes*), which ran from April to October
and featured brave new designs by architects such as Le Corbusier,
giving rise to the abbreviation 'art deco'. Though he did not yet fully

understand the language, its tones and cadences seduced him; and
besides, all around him were German-speaking intellectuals to meet,
such as the philosopher and critic Walter Benjamin. The city's enduring
liberalism appealed as it would to anyone aghast at the rise elsewhere
of nationalism and fascism in the past three years: Mussolini had often
stated that fascism opposed everything the French Revolution stood
for. At every level – aesthetic, intellectual, sensual, spiritual – Paris
had captivated him. If one still caught a whiff of antisemitism in the
air twenty years since the end of the Dreyfus Affair, this residue was
preferable to the explicit loathing playing out on the streets of the
Germany he had left behind.

Now a second letter, written 400 miles south in Avignon on 1
August. This time he must first attend to business: having had no
acknowledgement of half a dozen submitted feuilletons, he confesses
to a terror that they have been lost in the post (this will become a fixation) and begs Reifenberg's indulgence in 'perpetrating such a breach of
decorum as to ask you in a personal letter to send me confirmation [of
receipt] at the Hotel de l'Odeon', from where Roth's correspondence
is being forwarded.* Logically he then allows that if Reifenberg has not
received the articles, he might not get this letter either.

> But even if you don't, I still hope you will somehow sense that I am
> enjoying – seems wrong, quaking, yearning, crying – the best days of my
> life. I shall never be able to describe what has been vouchsafed to me here.
> You will probably best assess the scale of my good fortune by the way I
> see how small and powerless I am, and yet seem to live thousandfold. I

---

* Later, having begged news of his 'missing' feuilletons and evidently received an
apologetic response, Roth rows back in conciliatory terms. 'No one can know about
the level of my agitation – constant and powerful – about everything under the sun.
Of course I exaggerate. When I write in that vein, you shouldn't take it seriously.'
Again, the playful acknowledgement of his exaggerative streak: see also the remark
to Max Tau that forms an epigraph to this book ('It's all nonsense, folks. Don't take
my agonies so seriously, I simply don't know how to live') and the early letter to Paula
Grübel ('. . . that wasn't a serious inquiry: you shouldn't take everything seriously . . .').
All three remarks display his tendency to disarm then reassure – by which time the
initial point has been made and remains in his interlocutor's mind. Roth knows what
he's doing.

love the rooftops, the stray dogs that run around the streets, the cats, the
wonderful tramps with their red leather complexions and young eyes,
the women who are so terribly thin, with long legs and bony shoulders
and yellow skin, the child beggars, the mix of Saracen, French, Celtic,
German, Roman, Spanish, Jewish, and Greek. I am at home in the
Palace of the Popes, all the beggars live in the most wonderful castles, I
should like to be a beggar and sleep in its doorways. Everything we do in
Germany is so stupid! So pointless! So sad! Come to me in Avignon, and
I promise you you'll never set another article of mine. I'm learning French
poems by heart for the fun of it. Kiss your wife's hand, greet your son
from me in a way he'll understand, and write a personal letter to your old
*   Joseph Roth*

Aside from his overwhelming joy, the two letters offer several points
worth noting. The foremost concerns Friedl. The first letter includes
an aside asking that Reifenberg contact her to lift her spirits: she is ill
again, and this time Roth fears she has a lung complaint. From this
time, references to her ill-health litter his correspondence. She was less
at ease in France; while Roth began to pick up the language, she did
not. He spent the evenings carousing on the boulevards, she stayed in
the hotel. Their marriage had already begun to show signs of strain
in public: if they were in a café and Friedl seemed more interested
in conversation with someone else at the table, or if he felt she was
criticising him in front of friends, he was liable to storm out in a rage.
He needed to control her. He wanted to reshape her into his preferred
form of woman, pliant, decorous and deferential. Their friend Ludwig
Marcuse, the German-Jewish philosopher, blamed Roth for attempting
to make Friedl into something she wasn't. 'In the beginning I knew
Friedl as a charming, intelligent, very amusing Viennese girl,' he said.
'But Roth's type was the elegant, reserved lady, and he moulded his
wife until he . . . robbed her of all naturalness. She had to play her role
according to his directions, and he destroyed her. Although sexually
she was quite lively and spirited,' by which Marcuse meant she was naturally flirtatious, 'she was not permitted to let this show. In public, she
had to appear distant and correct.'[5] It is little surprise that the strain she

was under had begun to manifest in illness. Marcuse, incidentally, gave a sharp description of the Roth he knew in the 1920s, who was 'then still a slight, blond and clean-shaven young man' who was 'a hundred years old on the inside'[6]. Living alongside him was ageing Friedl, too.

Marcuse gave another insight into the couple's changing relationship in conversation with Géza von Cziffra. Von Cziffra had recently met Friedl. She was loitering on the Kurfürstendamm outside Mampes Gute Stube, Roth's favourite bar in Berlin, as Roth and von Cziffra approached. 'When we crossed the "Ku'damm",' von Cziffra wrote, 'I saw a woman pacing up and down in front of the pub. Roth, who did not seem to have very good eyesight, only spotted her a little later. He laughed. "She is too afraid to enter on her own though every single waiter knows her."'[7]

Von Cziffra went to shake her hand. 'I could barely feel her hand when she offered it to greet me. She did not say a single word, only looked at me timidly. When we entered the pub, she stayed silent. Roth ordered her a mocha liqueur and cognacs for me and himself. Roth did all the talking.' When he left the table, von Cziffra tried to strike up a conversation.

'How do you like Berlin?'

'Oh, very well,' she said quietly.

'Are you here for the first time?'

'Oh, no. I have been here several times.'

Von Cziffra observed in his memoir that: 'It was not difficult to put her in that group of shy women who begin every sentence with an apologetic: "Oh."'[8] Alfred Beierle and Marcuse joined them at their table. They expressed surprise at seeing Friedl in her husband's favourite bar for once. Yes, she said, it was her first time there. Von Cziffra was puzzled. When the couple had departed, he asked why Roth had lied that she was a regular.

Marcuse corrected him: 'He does not lie, he invents.'

'Well, well,' said a confused von Cziffra, 'he invents when he is at his desk, but ...'

Marcuse interrupted him: 'As well as in real life. He reinvents his whole life. He is a gifted observer, but still he can never recount the things he experiences the way he experienced them. Sometimes he invents only minuscule details, sometimes he turns everything upside down. He does not see people the way they are, but the way he wants them to be. Especially the ones he likes. I am not a psychiatrist, but I know Joseph. I can imagine what's in his head. Let me, for example, analyse why he would claim that the waiters at Mampe know Friedl well.

'He loves his wife, but he suffers because she is not interested in art and literature. She can't keep up with him and his friends; if he takes her out, she sits in silence and if asked only answers with: "Oh yes," or: "Oh no." He suffers because of this but would never admit it. He invents character traits for his wife, which she does not possess. Before I met her, he told me she was the life of every party, she was well read and as witty as Madame de Staël. On the first day of our acquaintance, I told her about being compared with Baroness de Staël by her husband. "Oh, yes?" she asked, and looked at me with wide eyes. "Who is this Madame Staël?" And then I knew everything.'

Beierle intervened: 'Ludwig is right. Joseph would love to see his wife sitting here like on a throne day after day, witty and sparkling. Since that is impossible, he keeps her at home. But for himself he keeps the fiction intact. What he told you was nothing but the expression of his fantasy – Friedl at our usual table, admired by friends and served by waiters full of respect for her.'

'Complicated,'[9] said von Cziffra to his friends. It was all he could think to say.

In the midst of Roth's greatest happiness, his early letters from Paris also repeatedly acknowledge a melancholy prompted by comparison with the land he has left, and with which he still identified, however willingly. It wouldn't be Roth if he didn't measure his happiness against his sadness, and the recipients of his compliments against those who faced his criticisms. Even in his happiest moments his sadness was not gone, only outweighed. Germany had become the source and symbol of all that was awry in 1920s Europe. With this move to France, the country would never again form his permanent residence; as the Roth scholar Ingeborg von Sültemeyer-von Lips noted of this moment: '*Im Grunde beginnt hier ein freiwilliges Exil.*'[10] ('Basically, here begins a voluntary exile.') When he said of Germans that 'We really are an unhappy bunch,' and 'Everything we do in Germany is so stupid! So pointless! So sad!', the pronoun implies that the German Reifenberg should number Roth among his compatriots, a people to whom Roth had in truth always felt an outsider. An exile, though, is a departure from one's homeland. Germany was never home in the first place, though it was politic to treat it as such; this, then, was less an exile than another flight. It was a flight not only from a place but from himself, from his foundational persona, the Germanophile man his mother brought him up to become. He felt betrayed and bereft. To reject Germanic culture was to reject who he thought he was – so who would he be now?

It was a frustration that this German mindset seemed irreconcilable with the openness of spirit that he experienced in France. In the first letter he mentions that 'I feel terribly sad because there are no bridges between certain races.' Whether he saw himself as a metaphorical bridge or a hyphen, Roth aspired to connect people through their common humanity, to foster internationalism over nationalism. 'There will never be a connection between Prussia and France. I am sitting in a restaurant, the waiter greets me, the waitress gives me a smile, while the Germans I am with are frosty to the manager and the errand boy. They give off a ghastly rigidity, they breathe out not air but walls and fences, even though their French is better than mine. Why is it? It's the voice of blood and Catholicism. Paris is Catholic in the most urbane sense of the word, but it's also a European expression of universal Judaism. You must come here!'[11]

The mentions of race and blood snag our attention, and pause us for longer if this letter is read alongside Roth's prose from the same time. Take the sections on Lyons, Avignon and Tarascon in his proposed book *The White Cities* (*Die weissen Städte*), a poetic travelogue through the Midi. In the Lyons section he writes lovingly of the poorest residents as '*das Volk*', 'the people', and in their physiognomy claims to discern a Roman influence – it is plain to anyone perceptive, he asserts, that 'they go back to "antiquity" and that historic blood runs in their veins'.[12] In discussing 'cosmopolitan' Avignon, he offers his belief that where 'there is much mixing of races, it is the female descendants that gain the most in terms of attractiveness'.[13] In Tarascon, 'The most different bloods mingled here, and here was created the wonderful cosmopolitan mixture of races that characterises the European South.'[14]

As the Roth scholar Jon Hughes notes, 'the frequent references to 'Volk' and 'Blut' [blood] in Die weissen Städte [The White Cities] are bizarrely reminiscent of the anti-Semitic vocabulary of the extreme right, though of course the narrator advocates precisely the opposite of the goal of racial "purity". In fact the use of such vocabulary and argumentation is not an unusual phenomenon in German-Jewish, and particularly in Zionist discourse from the first decades of the century.'

More than Roth unthinkingly deploying terminology that was *au courant*, Hughes argues, we should understand this as 'a conscious reaction against the use to which such words are customarily put in both far-right and Zionist discourse'.[15] In his comment about the women of Avignon, he praises the merits of combining what the Nazis saw as pure bloodlines. What they would term miscegenation, he sees as an enrichment of the individual, more ingredients thrown into the recipe. That piece culminates in a rapturous plea for race-mixing, which he credits to Avignon's lure as an important Catholic city, bringing together and combining diverse peoples: Celts, Romans, Gauls, Germans, Phoenicians. The result was not the loss of character that contemporary 'European nations' feared, nor a merging into 'grey mush': 'people aren't pigments, and the world is not a palette! The more mixing, the more characteristics!'[16] The more hyphenation in individual and collective identities, the better. Roth is subverting 'the rhetoric of fatalism, separatism, racism and utopianism'; he 'uses repeatedly the concept of "race", only to claim that we are simultaneously all races and thus, ultimately, of no single one in particular. In this as in other aspects of the trip, he seeks to break down customary boundaries.'[17]

Consider that phrase 'a European expression of universal Judaism'. This is Roth developing what Michael Hofmann termed 'his deeply desired, eccentric personal equation: Catholicism = Judaism',[18] having identified France as a wellspring of that pan-European tolerant Catholic spirit which paralleled Judaism's transcendence of national borders and shamed Germany's aggressive insularity. As he would emphasise in the Avignon piece, he saw Catholicism as a motor for the enrichment of European culture. The Roth scholar Sidney Rosenfeld writes that

'in Avignon he discovered to his profound delight an incomparably humane European Catholic culture which had assimilated into the present diverse ancient races while nourishing the individuality of each'.[19] In this sense, Catholicism seems a spiritual analogue for the supranational Habsburg Empire. 'Nationalism' in Roth's France is a proud identification with a nation whose principles are liberty, equality and fraternity, all of which assume tolerance and trust – so, a nationalism that subverts itself, hardly nationalism at all. It is the heart of the European ideal, hence

Roth in 1925 on a railway platform in the South of France.

his assertion that you're not fully European if you haven't visited. 'Hug your little boy for me,' he instructs Reifenberg. 'He must learn French. It will make a European of him.'[20]

France equals Europe, and Germany the ruin of Europe: France is open, fluid, receptive; Germany insular, steely, self-certain. France is sensual, Germany is ascetic; France is rapturous subjectivity, Germany is cool, futile 'objectivity'. In a later letter to a French literary critic, he would approvingly contrast 'French Europeans of your stamp' with the 'American Germans in whose midst I write'.[21] France equals European gentility, Germany has the brashness of the American culture to which it had become so attached. In Jon Hughes's words, Germany for Roth 'embodies the West's fear of the ambivalent and the indefinable, its reliance upon systems in which there are only friends and enemies.

France, by contrast, functions in the text* as the embodiment of all that Germany denies – the ambiguous, the mixed, the freedom to be an individual, a part of no system, a perpetual stranger.'[22]

These comparisons between Germany and France pepper Roth's correspondence of the time. Shortly after arriving in Paris, he confesses to having messed up his visa extension, saying that Friedl came to the rescue by visiting the Interior Ministry to resolve this 'bureaucratic hoopla': 'Frenchmen will do anything for a woman. Germans just get impatient . . .'.[23] That comes from one of a series of letters to Bernard von Brentano, who had just, with Roth's assistance, become the Berlin correspondent for the *Frankfurter Zeitung*. These letters, over the course of 1925, show the best of Roth in his personal relationships, revealing how he took the younger Brentano under his wing. Roth schools him in how to write – and because he wishes to help develop a raw talent, to grant a genuine favour rather than flatter his ego by suggesting his talent is fulfilled, the advice is blunt and candid. He scolds Brentano for not expressing himself clearly – 'call a spade a spade and I'll understand you better'[24] – and while Brentano has conveyed his gratitude for Roth's influence on his work, Roth snaps back that it has plainly been insufficient, for 'you continue to make such tangled confessions. A clear profanity would suit me better. And you as well. It's not only when one has nothing to say that one should shut up, but also when one is unable to express it clearly. You will never attain artistic perfection unless, at the instant you reach for your pen and paper, you are sober as if someone had emptied a bucket of water over your head.' On another occasion Roth instructed him: 'Work harder! Three pieces a week. Practise that manner that's eye-catching and load-bearing at the same time.'[25] This last phrase captures the defining quality of Roth's best work: it has beauty and substance in equal measures. The exchanges give a flavour of Roth's version of kindness, a sharp expression of the truest version: to give friends valuable advice rather than cosset their egos.

---

* Hughes is referring here to *Die weissen Städte*, but the point also applies to his feuilletons and letters of the time.

There is another telling phrase to note in these letters. He signs off to Brentano on 14 June the same way as he would to Reifenberg on 30 August: 'Your old Joseph Roth'. Were it only to Brentano, we might see this as an ironic acknowledgement of his *de haut en bas* tone towards the six-years-younger man; but no, this is to become his default valediction. For all his happiness, for all the renewed spring in his step, at the age of thirty, Roth feels old. Not only physically weary (his liver is 'already packing up'[26]), but someone from a past era, a pre-war character, out of kilter with these strident times.

The letters to Brentano, his junior, are markedly different from those to Reifenberg, his editor. One has a devil-may-care air where he shows little concern for the younger man's feelings, the other a more respectful tone – still scabrous at times but never towards the recipient. As a liberal German journalist with a Jewish father and Catholic mother, Reifenberg understood Roth's dismay with his country's direction. Roth knew that he would not be offended by invective towards Germans. As for the Austrians, they were worse ... well, stupider. He describes the delegates at the Social Democratic Congress in Marseilles: '200 Germans, 100 Austrians. The latter a nasty perversion of Germans. The Austrians look like Germans who have understood nothing. As vile as a Prussian is when he's taking his pleasure, that's how ghastly the Austrian is all his life. Degenerate *boches*.'[27] Roth's reverence for Austria derived from what it had been in the fast-receding past: in the tolerant multinational entity it represented before the war, in the old-fashioned courtliness associated with its Imperial Army's officer class, and certainly not in the behaviour of Austrians in the 1920s.

Four days earlier Roth had written to Brentano from the same town, calling the *Frankfurter Zeitung* abject and immoral for apparently not printing his articles that criticised the Weimar Republic. He threatens to go to Mexico; to be free again, as he was for twenty years of his life. He says he doesn't care about an income or a 'bourgeois base',[28] for such banalities only make him ill. He does not aspire to wealth, but does care about money in that he knows his worth, feels disrespected in having to beg for what he is owed, and cannot bear the strain of poverty, the constant struggle to keep his head above water. Not just his head, besides: Friedl travels with him wherever he goes, and she always seems to be unwell these days, quite incapable of adding to their income. If the newspaper's publisher Heinrich Simon 'wants to be a coward, then I'll demand that he pay me properly for his cowardice. If he doesn't want to publish me, I want to see money.'[29]

Finally, he returns yet again to his fixation on Germany. He sets about the country with vigour and palpable relief at no longer being there. He can speak his mind, lobbing these explosive missives at Berlin while standing well back. From Paris, the summit of European civilisation, to look at Germany feels like peering down from a tall tower to 'some sort of gulch'[30] at the bottom. 'German is a dead language,'[31] he says of the language he writes in. He spoke half a dozen languages to varying degrees, but none of the others well enough to create literature. He is compelled to express himself in the language of those who despise him and whom he despises. What was once to him the language of civilisation now bespeaks barbarism. It is painful to write in German but he thinks in German, so he must; Roth now hates the way his thoughts and words take form in his mind and issue from his mouth and his pen. If his home is his head, even home is growing cold and inhospitable. There was another home, though, a warmer one that he could visit every evening.

In late August he and Friedl were in Marseilles, staying at the Hôtel Beauvau in the old port. The hotel faces the sea. The harbour is 'a city of ships',[32] oil slicks coat the water that slaps their hulls, the breeze wafts an 'intoxicating cosmopolitan smell'[33] that blends herring, anthracite and turpentine. Roth looks out over the thronging quay, the turbid water, the powder-blue sky, the constant arrival of boats importing new personalities to dissect, the constant departure of others he might hop on to on a whim, to reassert his freedom. 'There are 700 vessels in the port,' he informs Reifenberg on 26 August. 'I've half a mind to suddenly take one of them. My wife cries every day, if it weren't for her, I'd be long gone. It's the first time I've had a feeling for the presence of my wife. It's only in a port you know you're married,' he observes, one of the toughest aperçus he would put to paper.[34] In a place offering such scope for escape he felt the chains of the commitment he'd made. Roth was landbound, his movement restricted by someone who would barely leave their hotel room. There was always something wrong with her. She was ill again, now in bed with a fever, 'brought on by the climate, obviously'. But while Roth could not sail away, he could leave Friedl locked in the room while he spent a night in the old port's bars and terraces. 'That's the world I feel really at home in. My maternal forefathers live there. We're all kin there. Every onion seller is my uncle.'*35

This home is a condition brought on by an atmosphere of camaraderie, the transient sensation of tight and precious fraternity with strangers that comes at the apex of a night's drinking. The next morning, this home has vanished, become a memory, replaced by nausea and self-loathing.

The Hôtel Beauvau (right) and the quay at Marseilles, c.1900.

*

---

* An early instance of Roth not merely defending his drinking but advocating alcohol as a social leveller, a case he would make right to the end – take his late short story 'The Leviathan', in which his narrator proclaims that 'once we have got a drink or two inside us, all good honest men are our brothers, and all lovely women our sisters – and there is no difference between farmer and merchant, Jew and Christian; and woe to anyone who says otherwise!' *Collected Shorter Fiction*, trans. Michael Hofmann (Granta Books, 2002), pp. 266–7.

Roth had had the move to France in mind since the beginning of the year, a moment when he sought to reconfigure his working life as both a novelist and journalist. The status quo felt untenable: the newspaper wanted too much of him, his publisher had proved unsatisfactory, the national atmosphere had grown toxic. On 22 January 1925 he wrote from Berlin to a Dr Erich Lichtenstein, a rival publisher to Der Schmiede, airily advising him that they might have cause to do business with one another given his dissatisfaction with the promotion, presentation and payment for his novels thus far. 'I am told you are sometimes to be found in Berlin,' he informed Lichtenstein. 'I will be here until March, and thereafter in Paris.'[36] He let on to this stranger – while begging discretion – that he doubted Der Schmiede would accept his new terms, whereupon he would need a new publisher more deserving of his talents. At the same time, he had engineered a move out of Germany while remaining employed by the *Frankfurter Zeitung*. He would relocate to Paris and become the paper's 'Special Correspondent' in France, filing dispatches as he explored the country. The firm suggested to him that this roving reporter brief could develop into a permanent position as Paris correspondent. For now, he was to explore France, writing on whatever took his fancy. '[W]rite just exactly what you want, pay no regard to anything,'[37] the office reassured him once he was there.

The resulting work forms the peak of what we could call Roth's 'lyric journalism'. Elsewhere he writes with greater force, summoning a furious intensity of prose that slaps the reader in the face; with sharper irony in surveying metropolitan foibles with an eyebrow raised; or with heart-rending sadness in forming a conduit for his fellow soldiers' trauma. Nowhere else does he achieve such a consistent level of limpid beauty. Nowhere else does he immerse the reader so deep into the world. Nowhere does he write with such joy, nor such love for humanity.

You can feel the way the southern sunlight soaked into his soul. Its clarity and warmth infuse his sentences. The scenes he paints grow brighter and bolder. Their colours glow. There are no German clouds to cast shade in this Provençal sky, it is pure blue, day after

day, and the landscape's colours are constant too: white stone, green
bushes and tapering cypress trees. Only the terrain's form changes –
vertiginous here, undulant there. The sun unstintingly illuminates
places and people. He is in Marseilles during the Socialist Congress
attended by German and Austrian acquaintances. 'It's a terrible thing
to see those people in this setting,' he told Brentano. 'The sun shows
how much dust there is on them.'[38] Everything looks clearer, everyone becomes scrutable in the forensic light of southern France, even
the grey denizens of smoky offices in Berlin. Walking the terrain
around Avignon, the sharp contrast of light and shade reveals details
that would be hazy in damp, overcast climes. In this light every foray
becomes revelatory. 'I realise I have only ever walked in foggy countries ... Here, for the first time, I walked with joy.'[39] A piece about
Lyons opens with a description of a pivotal moment in his eight-hour
journey south, which exposes the psychological change wrought
upon him – from Paris's congestion into vast open space, from a grey
northern cityscape to brilliant colour and pervasive heat, from a locus
of agitated self-questioning modernism into rural simplicity. You
emerge from a tunnel into 'an abruptly southerly scene', he writes:
one of 'Precipitous slopes, split rocks revealing their inner geology, a
deeper green, soft, pale-blue smoke of a stronger, decidedly cerulean
hue.' A couple of white clouds on the horizon. No breeze. Mercury
rising on the thermometer. Relentless sunlight glazing rockfaces.
'All things have sharper edges; the air is still; its waves don't flatter
the fixed forms. Each has its unalterable contours. Nothing hovers
and havers between here and there. There is perfect conviction in
everything, as if the objects were better informed about themselves
and the position they took up in the world. Here you don't wonder.
You don't have a hunch. You know.'[40]

He takes this mindset around the south as he composes a series
of feuilletons published between September and November in the
Frankfurter Zeitung under the collective title 'In the French Midi'.*

---

* In German: '*Im mittäglichen Frankreich*', or roughly 'In France at midday', a play on
the French Midi region.

From Vienne to Marseilles, Nîmes to Nice, he writes with unsurpassed confidence and clarity, in a state of receptivity and articulacy. In Nice he measures up the gilded population of the Riviera in a few succinct phrases: it looks 'as if it had been dreamed up by society novelists and populated by their heroes',[41] who must spend fortunes in Monte Carlo to summon some excitement into their lives. 'The rest of us get Monte Carlo calling on us every day; our whole lives are games of roulette.'[42] In the letter of 26 August, he tells Benno Reifenberg he has seen a bullfight for the first time and notes its gruesomeness. He is disgusted. This presumably is what he refers to in a piece about the Roman arena at Nîmes, published on 12 September, where he mentions that in the evenings the arena becomes an outdoor cinema, 'a rather more cultured thing than a bullfight'. Mothers bring their babies, who 'lie on their backs under the night sky, with open mouths as though to swallow the stars'.

The stars prove more alluring to Roth than Cecil B. DeMille's 1923 film *The Ten Commandments*. Meteors streak across the navy firmament in different colours, arcs and paces. Now he is enraptured. 'Sometimes it's as though the heavens opened and showed us a glimpse of red-gold lining.' Perhaps God was there, after all. Perhaps Roth has an answer to the question he asked in *Rebellion* of whether He lives beyond the stars. 'Then the split quickly closes, and the majesty is once more hidden for good.'[43] Roth realises that constellations remind us of childhood – because 'it was only as a child that one gazed at them so raptly',[44] back in the comfortable days before notions of eternity came to trigger thoughts of life's brevity, before one became self-absorbed, time-conscious, distracted from considering the eternal by tomorrow's copy deadline, so preoccupied with earthly mundanities as to manage but a few seconds' skyward contemplation before fretting about the hotel bill.

From the sun-warmed stone steps of the Nîmes amphitheatre he sees the same stars that twinkled over Brody two decades earlier. They hint at once of deep time and childhood nostalgia, a clash of time-perceptions. Crane your head back, and time buckles and distorts. Moments from the past separated by centuries converge in the present:

the ancient starlight that completes its journey* across the universe to our eyes; the childhood memories that suddenly appear within tantalising reach, then are gone. In gazing up, Roth gazes backwards in time, rediscovering a lost self that had been eclipsed by the war. 'There you are, so remote from your childhood, and yet you meet it again. That's how small the world is. And if you think some of it is foreign, you're mistaken. Everywhere is home.'[45] In this moment, reconnecting with his memories of Brody, finding a thread between the present and a lost time and place, his brittleness softened by the summer evening's lingering warmth, the entire world becomes his home.

This sanguinity infuses the sketches he produced while roaming the south. There is so often an air of reflection after the event; of looking back, taking stock, living in a retrospective mode . . . a sense of recovery. Read them and you can hear him exhale. As usual the erstwhile '*rote Joseph*' is drawn towards the working people who prop up the rest of society. He remained a socialist by instinct, even if he was more circumspect now than his political peers about what was unfolding in Russia eight years on from the Revolution. In Lyons he spent evenings sitting with labourers in their district by the Rhône, for it is 'only among the poor that one can get a sense of what an evening is. For everyone else evening is an extension of their day. For the poor it signifies peace and rest. They sit outside their doors, they wander slowly down to the river and watch the water. The enormous fatigue of the day drops from their hard hands.'[46]

Recovery, reflection, reconnection, a sense of being at home in the world and reunited with his inner child, and a hope that France would be Europe's salvation. For all that Friedl's health, Germany's political state and his travails with the *Frankfurter Zeitung* rendered him fraught, at a deeper level he developed a calmness and tentative optimism: that he had found his place in the world, and that France formed a bulwark against nationalism. These were the conditions that elicited the happiness he poured out in his letters that summer. It was during these

---

* In many cases centuries-long, though some astronomical bodies visible to the naked eye are much older. The faint light we receive from the Andromeda galaxy is around two and a half million years old.

weeks that Roth wrote those lines reflecting on how 'If you find your childhood dreams, you become a child again'; on how his 'childhood [had been] quite irrecoverably remote from me', and 'nothing more than a dream itself', 'expunged from my life'.[47] At the age of thirty, seven years after the war that severed him from childhood, and after spending the first half of the 1920s frantically establishing his career, he could at last pause, ruminate and revive his connection with who he had been before the great obliterating trauma of the First World War.

Along the way, the idea took hold that he should write something more substantial, more permanent. This was the second professional reason for remaining in France. He began to draft a book, ostensibly non-fiction, though on closer examination it is more complex. In a letter to Reifenberg on 30 August he sketched out his idea for *The White Cities*, mentioning that his French tour would be over in a fortnight and he had accrued enough material for something bigger and deeper than the 'In the French Midi' feuilletons. He sought Reifenberg's advice on whether this should be 'a wholly "subjective" book, in other words something completely objective. The confession of a young, resigned, sceptical human being, at an age where he is completely indifferent whether he sees something new to him or not, travelling somewhere.'[48] He aspires to explore the 'last vestiges of Europe, places that are innocent of the ever more apparent Americanisation and Bolshevisation of our continent'.[49] An examination of those slivers of Europe pinched between the tectonic plates of capitalism and communism. The book would be 'a guide to the soul of its writer, as much as of the country he's passing through. What do you think of the idea? It's very creative, more than a novel.'[50]

He proposed to spend a fortnight writing the book, during which he would produce no feuilletons for the *Frankfurter Zeitung*, then come to Frankfurt to discuss payment with Reifenberg. Lack of money was pressing hard again. He should have been paid 600 marks plus 300 in expenses for the trip, but this had not yet transpired. Raising the subject might not be politic, he conceded, but not doing so would be cowardly. Had he been in Berlin, he would have asked for a raise owing to the inflation; but he was not, and did not intend to return to Germany during 1925. So he was at an impasse. He floats the possibility of his resignation, making clear he would rather stay. While he is not 'sufficiently sentimental to believe in categories like future, family, etc.', he 'is sufficiently sentimental to feel devotion to this house and this newspaper, the last vestiges of the old humanistic culture. I am being straight with you – this is *entre nous*. I know perfectly well I couldn't work for any other German paper. I know none would have me. And I still couldn't go back to Germany. It's a tragedy, not a passing fancy.' The country was turning into a nightmare. If that were his day-to-day reality, he would go insane. 'Everything affects me personally. If they lock up Becher,* it's me that's behind bars. I don't know what would happen. I'm capable of shooting someone, or throwing bombs, I don't think I'd last very long. I risk my life when I return to Germany. Physically, I can't do it.'[51]

He needed to write this book. He needed to remain in France, needed a project that would pay him to do so, and needed to articulate the deluge of ideas and images that the country had stimulated. Reifenberg thought he should go ahead. Writing at great speed, in the impulsive mode he believed produced his best work (and which he contrasts with the slow, scientific, methodical approach of German authors), Roth drafted a manuscript comprising eight studies of southern towns and cities† framed by an introduction and a closing note. Each is around twice the length of a typical Roth feuilleton, and most close by cueing up the next, tracing his progress around the south. The title derives from the exotic white cities about which he fantasised as a boy, and which he hopes to conjure into reality. From a hillside by Lyons he can see 'the full extent of the first of my white cities. Yes, this is how it was in my dreams. It's all still standing: the shimmering houses; the white walls bathed in sunlight; the flat, iridescent rainbow roofs; the skipping chimney flues puffing out little blue clouds like little building blocks for heaven.'[52] Resonating across the city he hears the 'heavy chime' of bells from medieval church towers.

---

* Johannes Becher (1891–1958), writer and member of the Independent Social Democratic Party.
† Lyons, Vienne, Tournon, Avignon, Les Baux, Nîmes and Arles, Tarascon and Beaucaire, and Marseilles.

He walks for three days to Tournon down the banks of the Rhône, where he sees anglers 'as taciturn as the fish that so rarely permit themselves to be caught'.[53] In Vienne he concludes that the town was long deceased but had 'died in the fullness of her beauty'.[54] Near Avignon he notes that the terrain has no forests, which are 'where a landscape hides its secrets. This landscape has no secrets.'[55] In Les Baux he roams a ruined castle that had been hewn from a chalky outcrop. In Arles the old buildings are alive with centuries of inhabitation, and 'Old walls, like old violins, acquire more sonority with every year.' This too is a white city, but Arles's is 'of the silvery whiteness of age, not the festive whiteness of everlasting joy'.[56] But Avignon is the whitest of the white cities, 'a stone garden full of stone flowers', a place whose 'houses, churches, and palaces were not built, they grew'. Here, the 'walls rustle like trees. Their stone is white and as endlessly tragic as anything infinite.'[57]

The introduction develops the observations on the French and German mentalities that he set out in his letters. He returns to the imagery of 'walls and fences' he associated with the German outlook in his 16 May letter to Reifenberg, and works it into a rationale for the book.

'I was curious to see how things looked on the other side of the fence that surrounds us. Because we are surrounded by a fence, those of us whose job it is to speak to the German world.' He writes this knowing full well that clambering over the fence into France would be seen by many Germans as a betrayal, a stab in the back. He doesn't care. He has found a place where he can be himself. 'On the other side of the fence, I recovered myself . . . On the street and in society I look just the way I do at home.' Home is where you need not wear a mask or perform. 'Yes, and I *am* at home there. I know the sweet freedom of not seeming to be anything more than what I am. I don't represent, I don't exaggerate, I don't deny. And even so I don't catch the eye. In Germany it's practically impossible not to catch the eye unless I playact, unless I deny, unless I exaggerate. And I am given the difficult task of choosing how I would like to appear.'[58]

He works through and presents his philosophy of writing, one that is now confirmed as entirely counter to the modish *Neue Sachlichkeit* – that his subjective appraisal of a single transient moment was truer and more honest than the 'objective' and would-be definitive study produced by the conventional German approach, that of the 'good observer'. The revelatory light in the Midi offers unsurpassed clarity, sounds carry true and far through the dry air – and he will convey exactly what his senses tell him, having certain knowledge of his own passing perceptions in that instant of a world in flux, rather than feel obliged to strive for the false certainty of the German fixation on objective labels, categorisations and definitions. 'It's the mark of a narrow world that it mistrusts the undefined. It's the mark of a wider one that it permits me to be.' The Germans want the world pinned down. Here in France people are more fluid, less uptight. They know the futility of the 'definitive' study set down by a writer who 'meets everything with open but inflexible eyes', who presents a snapshot as if it were a history. 'And by the time he's set down his impression, the world has moved on . . . Our familiar concepts no longer match the realities. The realities no longer fit the tight clothes we've put them in.'[59]

In many respects he is strikingly honest about his philosophy here, but this introduction should not be read as non-fiction. Jon Hughes argues that the narrator should be seen as a fictional Roth. 'Yet the narrative self created in the opening pages of *Die weissen Städte* is not to be equated with the author, just as the narrators of *Die Flucht ohne Ende* and *Zipper und sein Vater* [*Zipper and His Father*], who actually sign themselves "Joseph Roth", should also be distinguished from their creator. The distinction is signalled by several key differences. For example, their narrator is apparently German, not Austrian, and his claim that he has only ever been capable of "*prazise Formulierungen*" [precise formulations], and not poetry, does not apply to Roth, whose first literary experiments took the form of poetry, not prose.'[60] When Roth claims that the German preference for literality over ambiguity is 'why we don't understand the world, and why it doesn't understand us',[61] he is placing himself within the German collective pronoun, just as he did in his letter to Reifenberg. Having fled Germany, it remained politic to assure those he left behind that he still identified as a citizen.

The introduction concludes with a description that sketches the landscape he will proceed to explore in detail, and expresses Roth's confidence that if he can remain here, he will be content. This land is not lit by the old, cool sun of the dying Habsburgs, but by a life-giving force. 'The sun is young and strong, the sky is lofty and deep blue, the trees dark green, ancient, and pensive. And broad white roads that have been drinking in and reflecting the sun for hundreds of years, lead to the white cities with flat roofs, which are as they are to prove that even elevation can be harmless and benign, and that you never, ever fall into the black depths.'[62]

The book was not published. No one read it in Roth's lifetime. The *Frankfurter Zeitung* turned it down. Perhaps a paean to France was too out of tune with the German national mood at a time when the Treaty of Versailles had granted France such vital territories as the coal-rich Saarland. In November 1925 he told Bernard von Brentano that he'd offered it to a Berlin publisher called Dietz, which had just published two novellas he'd written: *April* and *The Blind Mirror* (*Der blinde Spiegel*). They would reject it too. Elsewhere in the same letter he talks newspaper business with his colleague. The firm cannot afford to give him a pay rise, nor to send him on 'any more jaunts, they all cost money'. He has 'half a mind to quit'.[63] His hopes rest on one possibility: gaining a permanent position as the paper's Paris correspondent. Roth had previously been all but assured of the job, which would secure him in the country where he felt at home and demonstrate the paper's respect for his work. In late 1925 Roth learned that another man was now in contention for the role. Friedrich Sieburg (1893–1964) joined the *FZ* in 1923. He was a contributor to the politics pages, and a nationalist: he would later become a National Socialist and, after leaving the *FZ* in 1942, remain in Paris as the press attaché to Otto Abetz, German ambassador to Vichy France. Roth mentions to Brentano that 'there is as yet no Paris correspondent in place'[64] because the *FZ* editors are hoping to save money by combining two jobs in one, a reporter who will double as feuilleton writer. These words are the first signpost that point towards his reacquaintance with the black depths.

*

Another letter to Bernard von Brentano is undated but must be from early 1926, judging by a reference to an unwanted impending trip to the Ruhrgebiet, the industrial region in western Germany that was powering the recovering Weimar economy.* The resulting dispatches appeared in March of that year. They are soaked in melancholy. Roth wanted to stay in France, and instead was sent to rain-lashed, chilly, industrial Germany where, to cite one article's title, 'Smoke Joins Up the Towns'. The voice in these feuilletons is quiet, morose, surly. He writes of sitting in a bar drinking kirsch, waiting for a tram to arrive, then taking a gloomy journey through dead towns: not preserved in full bloom like Vienne, just decaying. It's a tedious trip that allows plenty of time to read the notices within the vehicle: 'TWENTY SEATS; NO SPITTING. I have half a mind to.'[65] The tone is depressive but mild compared with how he felt inside. The letter to Brentano is a frightening insight into Roth's torment during this period when the newspaper seemed determined to wrest him away from the one place that had made him happy, back to the place that caused him such despair. 'Germany is making me ill. Every day I feel more hatred, and I could choke on my own contempt. Even the language is loathsome to me. A country's provinces give it away like nothing else. The fake elegance, the loud voices, the yahoos, the silence, the respect, the impertinence.'[66]

There was worse to come as the letter progressed. This is how it felt to be Joseph Roth in early 1926:

> My dear friend, I'm becoming more and more solitary ... Even my wife is withdrawing from me, for all her love. She is normal, and I am what you'd have to call insane. She doesn't react as I do, with vehemence, with trembling, she's less sensitive to atmosphere, she is sensible and straightforward. Anything and everything is capable of provoking me. The conversation at another table, a look, a dress, a walk. It's really not 'normal'. I'm afraid I'm going to have to forswear society, and break off all ties. I no longer believe anything I'm told. I see through a magnifying

---

* Wages and exports were rising, and within a couple of years industrial production levels would be higher than before the war.

glass. I peel the skins off people and things to see their hidden secrets — after that, you really can't believe anything. I know, before the object of my scrutiny knows, how it will adapt, how it will evolve, what it will do next. It might change utterly. But my knowledge of it is such that it will do exactly what I think it will do. If it occurs to me that someone will do something vicious or low, he goes and does it. I am becoming dangerous to ordinary decent people because of my knowledge of them.

It makes for an atrocious life. It precludes all of love and most of friendship. My mistrust kills all warmth, as bleach kills most germs. I no longer understand the forms of human intercourse. A harmless conversation chokes me. I am incapable of speaking an innocent word. I don't understand how people utter banalities. How they manage to sing. How they manage to play charades. If only the traditional forms still applied! . . . I can't participate. All I can do is talk very cleverly with other very clever people. I am starting to hate decency, where — as is so often the case — it's paired with limited intelligence. The merely decent are beginning to hate me back. It can't go on. It can't go on.

My novel is coming along.[67]

The novel was *Flight Without End*. Its hero, Franz Tunda, was a man 'becoming more and more solitary'. As the wrangle over the Paris job unfolded at excruciating pace over the first four months of the year, Roth had in Tunda a new fictional avatar by which to articulate his existential position. He would need this outlet, for the reversal in his fortunes was too painful to leave unexpressed.

By 30 December Roth had returned to Frankfurt, from where he wrote to Brentano that he faced a rival for the job in Sieburg, who was 'Apparently a better writer than he is a character.' Roth explained: 'They still haven't made up their minds. Anyway, my Paris stint is under threat, because the firm would say, why have more than one feuilletonist, if he can do political reports as well. I told Reifenberg I wasn't going to stand idly by while they pulled the rug out from under my feet. He thought I ought to go on the road and do some work. But of course I am far too worried to leave the building, now there's all these rumours flying around.'[68]

In early 1926 the management tried to placate Roth with the offer that he report from Italy instead, but he demurred. At the beginning of April, he wrote to Reifenberg saying he intended to resign and remain in Paris. On 7 April Reifenberg replied pleading with him to stay, calling his proposed departure 'the gravest blow I have experienced in the course of these early years',[69] and explaining the newspaper management's position. He assured Roth that they wanted to keep him as an employee 'come what may', and that what or when he wrote was of little concern: they knew any journalism he produced would merit publication. They had a new proposal for him, that he should become feuilleton correspondent in Moscow, and take on a tour of Spain too, if he liked. They were uncertain whether he felt confident enough speaking Russian, however, and Reifenberg reiterated that Italy was his preferred destination for Roth, for the newspaper had not yet given due coverage to the rise of Mussolini and fascism. He requested that Roth make a decision soon, and informed him that Sieburg would start work in Paris on 1 May.

Roth wrote to Brentano the next day, saying that although he did not want to 'surrender to the firm that has treated me badly', neither did he want to reject the Moscow opportunity out of pique. 'I am thinking my position through very carefully.' Whatever the outcome, his 'trust in this Jewish firm is shaken, and nothing remains but my friendship with Reifenberg'.[70] He wrote to Reifenberg the day after, begging for time to consider his options, and employing a military analogy as was his wont with male friends he respected. 'I am terribly cast down, I can't answer you yet, I beg you for around 8–10 days' grace. To leave you behind in the firm is like leaving a brother on the field. Believe me! You have no idea how much I stand to lose in both personal and career terms if I have to leave Paris.'[71]

He was also less sure about Friedl's mental state than he had let on in the letter in which he said she was 'normal' and he 'insane'. His growing concern about her reliability came to a head this year during a visit to the German author René Schickele's home in Badenweiler. While Roth was deep in conversation, a servant informed him that the postman was outside with a large sum of money. Roth was expecting

3,000 marks from the newspaper. He dispatched Friedl to collect it while he continued talking, and thought no more of it until they went to bed that night, when Friedl handed over 2,000 marks. Where was the rest?, Roth wondered. 'Well, you know the postman who brought the money was so poor,' Friedl said, 'so I gave him 1,000 marks.'[72] Roth resolved to monitor her closely.

While he considered his future at the *Frankfurter Zeitung*, he filed a feuilleton that says much about his state of mind. Titled 'Report from a Parisian Paradise', it is a near-hallucinatory account of an after-midnight visit to a Montmartre nightclub – down beneath a sign formed from electric bulbs 'the blue of blue pansies', 'of vivid dreams and of cigarette smoke', down a staircase between mirrored walls, down into a subterranean pit rammed with a cosmopolitan crowd dancing to a band whose instruments comprise piano, saxophone, flute, accordion, violin and a drum; but Roth doesn't dance, he sits back, sucks on a cigarette and drinks Calvados, until the room sways and time starts to distort: it 'doesn't trickle, it surges and billows'. He gazes into his glass, and explains to his readers the apple brandy's hue can vary from 'golden brown as autumn leaves' to 'soft yellow like amber', depending on its age. At times its taste resembles cognac, at others 'the blossoms of otherworldly fruits'. He fixates on time and tries to understand it. How it slows and bursts ahead; how suddenly he had aged, how at thirty-one he was now 'old Joseph Roth'. Another Calvados. He is well the worse for wear by the time the room's lighting flicks to golden orange and the accordionist performs a mournful tune that transports Roth back to 'Slavic summer nights', back to the old songs his mother sang when she was sad. The accordion is an evening instrument, he says. It has the quality of a sunset, but one 'without sun: the end of the world'. Soon everyone listening 'knows they are lost', and soon everyone 'would like to cry'.[73]

On 22 April he gave the *Frankfurter Zeitung* his decision, and a good deal else into the bargain. What hurt, he explained, was the multiple ways in which he personally, and the feuilleton form, had been disrespected and undervalued. He knew Sieburg was an excellent writer – but so was Roth, and why could not they retain the two men in Paris, if they so valued his service? Apparently Sieburg did not want him there – but why prioritise his needs over Roth's? What did it say of their commitment to the feuilleton that they felt Sieburg could hammer these pieces out as an afterthought to his political reporting? Did they not understand that the feuilleton was every bit as important, if not more so? Underlying this may have been a concern that the paper's feuilleton section had lately grown more political and 'objective' under the influence of *Neue Sachlichkeit*. Roth already felt defensive about his commitment to subjectivity, and the imposition of a writer from the politics pages would have embodied this feeling of being encroached upon, of having his approach to writing denigrated. And if it transpired that in fact Sieburg was to write mainly feuilletons, then why not just give Roth the job, as first suggested? It made no sense. 'I won't be gotten rid of just because it happens to suit a colleague. It's like a curse: how can the *FZ* not manage to retain two such gifted journalists as Mr Sieburg and me. I love this paper, I serve it, I am useful to it. No one asks my opinion when it occurs to someone to have me removed from Paris.'[74]

The paper misunderstood the importance of his work and its value to readers, and persisted 'in thinking of Roth as a sort of trivial chatterbox that a great newspaper can just about run to. Wrong. I don't write "witty glosses." *I paint the portrait of the age.* That ought to be the job of the great newspaper. I'm a journalist, not a reporter; I'm an author, not a leader writer.'[75] This kind of writing was what gave an eminent newspaper its value, and the editors needed to 'stop kidding themselves' that they could 'grip readers and win subscribers' with 'a fancy-pants article on the situation in Locarno', where in late 1925 European leaders had agreed treaties with the Weimar Republic intended to prevent Germany from ever again going to war.

He had wanted a new contract. 'Stenographers and telephonists get contracts – I don't. I asked for a raise. My pay is among the lowest in the company. I submit a book. It's turned down.' Their rejection of *The White Cities* still hurt. Other publications wooed him but he remained loyal, and this was how the *Frankfurter Zeitung* treated him in return. 'It really is an art to take someone as willing, and useful, and loyal as me, and alienate him.'[76]

So, to his decision. He would withdraw his resignation. Out of Moscow, Italy and Spain, only Moscow would do, but he might wish to take on the other roles in future. 'You will understand that my reputation as a journalist is paramount to me. It will be damaged by my departure from Paris, and my replacement by Mr Sieburg. Only a series of Russian reportages can rescue my good name.'[77]

His subsequent requests show him scrabbling to regain control from this undignified position. It had been a profound humiliation, a devastating blow that collapsed the new post-war world he thought he'd built for himself, leaving him floored, uncertain of anything, disinclined to trust anyone; in Michael Hofmann's words, 'This wasn't a career reverse, it was a moral and epistemological catastrophe.'[78] First he requested the office's help with obtaining a Russian visa. Then he would require a period of convalescence,

The former *Frankfurter Zeitung* office at 5, Place du Panthéon, Paris.

for he had developed a skin disease that required around three weeks to heal. He painted an unflattering self-portrait in another letter to Reifenberg that brings to mind the skin complaint suffered by Job when God tests his faith: Roth was so covered in hideous red boils that he only left home after dark, he itched all over and worked through the night so he couldn't lie in bed scratching himself, and he reeked of the sulphurous ointment he'd smeared all over his body. Once recovered, he would take his leave, but he proposed to expand the trip: he would travel east to explore not only Moscow but Kiev and Odessa, and remain in the country throughout 1926, until the Russian winter began to bite.

Chapter Seven

I am quite unfitted to hold down a job anywhere unless they were to pay me for getting angry with the world. I am not even in harmony with any of the ruling ideologies.

Flight Without End

It was midnight in Moscow in the frozen depths of December 1926, and the ice-covered streets glinted with reflected lamplight as Walter Benjamin travelled by sleigh to Joseph Roth's hotel. He had been tired when they spoke by telephone at 11.30 p.m., but Roth explained he must depart the next day, so his invitation for a late dinner would be their only opportunity to meet. The sleigh ride proved a tonic; the sound of the horses' hooves, the ethereal glide over snow and the cold night air on his face revived Benjamin's senses. When he set foot inside the grand hotel, they were stimulated further: he was confronted by colourful bars and buffets, two great palm trees that reached only halfway to the high ceiling, a loud brass band and an elegant, spacious dining room where he found Roth awaiting him at a table. The two men drank vodka, ate cold meats and compote, and fell deep into conversation. They had been acquainted in Paris but not spoken at such length before coinciding in Moscow, where Benjamin was analysing the new Russian society while pursuing his infatuation with Asja Lācis, a Latvian Bolshevik journalist who lived in the city.

Roth began to read the Marxist philosopher the article he was composing, which the *Frankfurter Zeitung* would publish over 18 and 19 January 1927 with the title '*Die Schule und die Jugend*'. The 4,000-word piece opened with a discussion of the Soviet authorities' attempts to address mass illiteracy. The past seven years had seen countless experiments in revolutionary education, and new schools established which any foreign visitor would be proudly shown around by locals; yet still a great many Russians could neither read nor write, he said. 'For the time being,' Roth wrote, 'the question is still not: what are the successes of the new educational method in Soviet Russia? It is still: how many illiterates does Soviet Russia have?' For the answer one might wish to turn to statistics, but Soviet statistics, he wryly noted, were not always accurate. Anecdotally he could report that all around the country he had witnessed 'illiteracy courses' where people could make 'arduous acquaintance' with the Cyrillic alphabet: in factories, workers' homes, sanatoriums, clubs, prisons and barracks. The effort was impressive – but what information would people absorb here if they learned to read? In describing the components of the education system he mentions a university lecture he attended in Leningrad, at which he saw students who could not write grammatical sentences. This was no great hindrance in the new Russia, though: 'The young man who cannot form a simple sentence, can probably chair a meeting, make a financial report, quote or even write one of the usual newspaper articles of today – because all the parts of an article, a speech, a report are ready made; the phrases, the ideology, the arguments are all disposable in tins, you don't need to cook, nor prepare anything. For sure this young man knows who is an exploiter and who is exploited, what socialisation is and a political reaction, he knows about the "*bourgeois* ideology" and the miners' strike in England. But he just cannot form a simple sentence',[1] Roth said, because he is trained not to think for himself.

The young Russian of 1926 must not only march, drum, organise and lead, says Roth. He must imbibe ideology, become a model to his peers, and call meetings in which '"resolutions are declared" – "against" or "for" a teacher, a book, a theatre performance'. 'You have no idea how difficult it is to be a citizen,' Roth concluded. 'You must visit factories to learn about "life", because "life" is of course the "rolling wheel" and the intensity of life is measured by the number of "smoking chimneys".'[2] This was not Roth's vision of a socialist world. It bore no resemblance to his ideal society. After eating, the two men adjourned to his suite to continue their discussion. As they drank and talked into the small hours, the conversation grew more intense.

Benjamin found himself scanning the room as Roth held forth. A table was littered with remnants of a 'lavish tea' for at least three people. 'Roth apparently lives in grand style,' wrote Benjamin in his diary, for 'the hotel suite – which is just as European in its appointments as is the restaurant – must cost a great deal, as did the fact-gathering tour that took him all the way to Siberia, the Caucasus and Crimea.'

Once Roth had finished reading the article, Benjamin urged him to make his political position clear. 'The long and the short of it: he had come to Russia as a (nearly) confirmed Bolshevik and was leaving it a royalist,'[3] Benjamin wrote. 'As usual, the country is left footing the bill for the change in colour that occurs in the convictions of those who arrive here as scintillating reddish-pink politicians (under the banner of "left-wing" opposition or idiotic optimism).'[4] Benjamin did not like Roth's politics, and nor for that matter did he like his face, which was 'riddled with many wrinkles and has an unpleasant, prying appearance'. In all, he was unimpressed. 'When I look back over the entire evening, Roth makes a worse impression on me than he did in Paris,' he decided. 'Or rather – more likely – I was already aware of these things in Paris, though they were still hidden, whereas this time they struck me as clear as day.'[5]

Their encounter came at the end of four months in which Roth had traversed Russia in a state of overwhelming freedom. He had set off in July and left Friedl in Berlin. His novels' popularity in Russian translation meant he was well known already, and the newspapers welcomed him as a great friend of the USSR. By the time he left, having published a series of seventeen weekly reports collectively titled 'Reise in Russland' ('Journey Through Russia'), they spoke of him as an enemy. Wherever he went, he wrote: in trams and trains, cafés and bars, hotel bedrooms and lobbies. Ceaseless production and testing of his analyses, a near-perpetual outflow of words in meticulous script in notebooks. He would later tell Stefan Zweig: 'I think I can only understand the world when I'm writing, and the moment I put down my pen, I'm lost.'[6] Changing relations between Germany and the Soviet Union would have been one issue to analyse: his visit came in the aftermath of the April 1926 Treaty of Berlin, in which Europe's two post-war pariah states agreed a non-aggression pact. This was in response to the recent Locarno Treaties that had seen Germany break its diplomatic isolation, normalise relations and agree a non-aggression pact with France and Belgium, which had left the Soviets concerned as to Germany's allegiances.

As he tells it in letters to Reifenberg and Brentano, he lived between extremes while roaming the vast country following his will – three or four days a week were spent in a near-vagrant state, subsisting on little money, eating black bread and onions, then 'the remaining days, admittedly, I spend in the best hotels I can find'.[7] The *Frankfurter Zeitung* heard nothing from him for two months. He cut himself off from all he had left behind. He spent a week walking through Chuvash villages. He explored Minsk and Belarus, and journeyed through the Caucasus mountain paths on muleback and bumpy carts. He got soaked in a Stalingrad hotel room when a downpour collapsed the ceiling, and found his entrance to a hotel in Samara barred by an irate goat. He cruised down the long, wide Volga on a mail steamer crammed with people from every ethnicity and stratum within Soviet society, and looked out across the flat river plain at primitive villages of huts and domed churches, then to soft hills and the distant steppe.

At the end of August, on the deck of that boat, he wrote Benno Reifenberg a letter that offered his perplexed colleagues some explanation. He was living in 'continual fear' given that the newspaper had been 'paying me since JULY and has received no copy', but he had 'been unable to write anything till now. I was overwhelmed, famished, continually shaking . . . If one were to set foot on a different star, things couldn't be more different or more strange.' In any case, whatever the company had been paying him wasn't enough. 'I have no money. I need 42 marks per diem, excluding travel and the vast tips a visitor is obliged to leave. I am experiencing incredible things. Almost more than I can put down, in terms of fullness and intensity.'[8] He doesn't say what they are. He sounds stunned, not a common tone in Roth's letters. The rapid succession of alien experiences he'd had to process was such, he later wrote to Brentano, that after three months he felt he'd been away from Europe twice as long. It only reinforced his self-conception as a

European, 'a man of the Mediterranean if you will, a Roman and a Catholic, a Humanist and a Renaissance man'.[9] Perhaps the 'incredible things' were not specific incidents, more the overwhelming immensity of the Soviet experiment that played out wherever he looked. 'There's no doubt that a new world is being born in Russia,' he told Reifenberg. 'For all my scepticism, I am happy to be able to witness it.'[10]

The boat would take him down the great river to the coastal city of Astrakhan, which proved less than incredible – the place stank of fish, he told *Frankfurter Zeitung* readers a few weeks later, though it was 'flies not fishes that make up ninety-eight per cent of the fauna'[11] here. In a café he updated local women on the latest fashions from Warsaw and discussed the recent Treaty of Berlin: 'Doubts people in Astrakhan had about a war involving Poland, Russia and Germany I was able to allay at length.'[12] He journeyed down to the Caspian Sea port of Baku, in the oilfields of Azerbaijan. He explored Ukraine, from eastern Kharkov down to Odessa.

In Kyiv he sat shivering in his hotel room, his numb hand scratching notes in his diary: 'It has become cold, a terrible north wind is blowing, the hotel is not heated ... I am already wearing two shirts and two pairs of stockings.'[13] At night he walked the streets of Odessa collecting observations for what would form the final section of *The Wandering Jews* when it was published as a long essay by Die Schmiede in 1927. The violent, visceral loathing of Jews becoming normalised on the streets of Weimar Germany had moved Roth to set out an affectionate defence of the eastern Jewish world that had once been his home. The misery in the Moldovanka district prompted the most lyrical passage in a book where straight description and analysis predominate. He sees a legion of beggars, crowded houses-cum-workshops where babies swing in cradles while their parents labour, a few burly dockers who look at odds with the neurasthenic majority of their fellow Jews. 'The evening there is a curse, the rising moon a mockery. A thick fog presses down like a condemnation.' The yellow light from the windows 'doesn't spread brightness but a kind of gloom'.

Bleakness prevails, for now at least. There may be cause for hope. The Jewish question is being addressed here in Soviet Russia.

Antisemitism still exists but the antisemite faces disgrace. It is 'the only country in Europe where antisemitism is scorned' and 'Jews are entirely free citizens', with full rights. In all of Jewish history, such a 'sudden and complete liberation is unexampled'. To be sure, this had entailed the loss of religious rights experienced by all faiths – synagogues were being converted into workmen's clubs, and *cheders* were banned – but the Jews are a people who exist beyond their religion. Aren't they? The Revolution did not address perennial questions that pressed harder in this time of sharpened national identification. 'Are the Jews a nation like any other, or are they more or less; are they a religious community, a tribal community, or do they merely share certain intellectual features?' (This cues up a romanticised portrayal of the Jewish peasant who stands apart from primitive gentile peasants, for behind his plough he is silently contemplating Einstein's relativity theory.) 'And is it possible to regard a people that has preserved itself in Europe purely by its religion and its historical separation as a "people", and leave religion out of it?'[14]

Who actually were these people? In the 1920s, as in the twenty-first century, as since time immemorial, even the Jews couldn't agree. If they were hard to define, they were hard for outsiders to know. If they were hard to know, they were easier to fear, and therefore to hate: we can vilify a horde of strangers quicker than an individual acquaintance. Taking away their religion did not automatically bring them into the fold. If they remained unassimilated, they were viewed across a separating barrier, a wall or fence: they were maddeningly hard to reach. So the Jews, set at a remove from this host society just like any other, still forming an unknowable mass, remained susceptible to loathing. Secular, Soviet Russia could shame the antisemite and excise Christian theological antisemitism; but the preconditions for other varieties of Jew-hatred remained in place, whatever the communists' ambitions. Roth did not appear to see this. While he left Russia disabused of any faith in communism and retreating towards the monarchism of his youth, he finished *The Wandering Jews* with a jarring paragraph suffused with blasé optimism. He noted that Jews were not fleeing Russia as they did when they spilled over the border into Brody; now they were settling there. In Soviet Russia, the Jews would wander no more.

'Once the Jewish question is solved in Russia,' Roth proclaimed, 'then it is on the way to being solved everywhere ... The piety of the population is declining rapidly. The stronger barriers of religion are falling, replaced by the weaker ones of nationality. If this process continues, the age of Zionism will have passed, along with the age of antisemitism – and perhaps even that of Judaism itself. It is a development that will be welcomed in some places and regretted in others. But everyone should take notice as one people is freed from the stain of suffering and another from the stain of cruelty. The victim is freed from his torments and the bully from his compulsion. This is a great accomplishment of the Russian Revolution.'[15]

Roth seems remarkably comfortable with the notion that Russia might solve the Jewish question by erasing Judaism – by removal of religious rights, not extermination of the Jews, but either way they would disappear as a distinct people. Perhaps the prospect appealed at a personal level. A liberating thought, that a body might lose its Jewishness. If only he could enact the same purge upon himself.

'When he was in Russia he had a woman, and his wife found out about it. Roth told me this,'[16] his friend Joseph Gottfarstein recalled in 1961. Who this woman was, and when Friedl found out, are not recorded. Presumably she can only have discovered after his return, but a series of excerpts from a diary he kept during his journey through Russia reveal his emotional state during this period, hinting at guilt and a determination to treat her better on his return home.

> 25 September, Saturday, Odessa
> Sent off article on new bourgeois today, Friedl telegraphed, cold, clear, unpleasant, guessing.

> 26 September, Sunday, Odessa
> ... Think about Friedl all day, why hasn't she answered the telegram? She may not be in Vienna. Mail in Moscow still hasn't come here.

For some days now I have loved Friedl more than ever. Yes, I'm beginning to love her. She was a very little girl when I was a very green boy. Has she grown with me? Sometimes it seems to me that she has grown faster. Her photograph tells me too little. I have forgotten what she looks like.

But today it seems to me that she has an incredible charm. I am curious to know it.

27 September, Monday, Odessa
Friedl written, by airmail. No answer to telegram, live in great fear . . . I love Friedl more with every day we are away. When I married her, I was smart and good. I reproach myself for treating her badly. But I am full of love for her, even if I don't know it, and I am with her, never against her. She is cooler than you think, more selfish than I would have thought, more naive than she admits. But her coolness is fresh, her egotism is natural, her naivety lovely and gentle and not a disturbing, banal naivety, but an arrangement of incessant delightful misunderstandings.

29 Wednesday
I am quite beside myself. I have telegraphed Friedl again. The mail from Moscow is not forwarded to me. Perhaps Friedl is not in Vienna. But then she must have someone there who could telegraph me. What should I do? I could still send a telegram to Frau Szajnocha, perhaps I will if there is no message the day after tomorrow. The devil take this journey. One cannot travel when one's heart is bound to someone. I can already see that I won't earn anything from this journey. I went only to be able to give Friedl something. I'll never leave her again. I can't smoke the cigarettes any more. They affect the palate more than the nerves. They make it dry and thirsty. They are like the dust of Astrakhan and Baku.

I am at a loss. There is no answer from Friedl. I can't speak, I can't write, I can't read. The darkest imaginings beset me. I reproach myself with the most absurd things. It is so easy to love passionately, the object of my love must only cause me pain. I did not think myself capable of passion; I also believe it is more a passion of the nerves than of the soul. Nevertheless, it is clear to me that I love her, that I

*cannot compare any woman with her, and I am determined to adore
her from now on. Tomorrow is the last day of September, I heard from
Friedl in mid-August, it's been a long time, seven weeks, it seems like
seven months.*

Thursday, 30 September
Today, finally, telegram from Friedl and post.

Monday, 4 October
. . . Friedl's letter has not yet arrived . . .

Wednesday, 6 October
. . . Friedl's letter finally arrived yesterday . . .

Saturday, 6 November
Nobody writes to me, I live in a great loneliness . . . Friedl writes nothing.

Friday, 12 November
*There was nothing from Friedl except a telegram. She hasn't written
anything for 15 days, so she hasn't thought of me.*[17]

Solitary travel brought an inevitable corollary, loneliness. Having
shaken himself free, he felt acute isolation and regret. He missed Friedl
dreadfully and began to appreciate her virtues he had taken for granted.
He complained that his friends rarely returned his letters either. The
familiar childhood sensation of abandonment recurred. Every day he
met new strangers, but he was far from the people he loved. It seemed
his friends didn't care enough to write. He hadn't heard back from
Brentano for a while, and feared he'd misjudged the younger man's
character: 'I pride myself on not being wrong about people,' he told
Reifenberg in a letter from Odessa. 'Anything but that . . . My isolation is enormous, unendurable. I need a letter now and again. People,
people, all day long, politicians, journalists. No women. Hence the
isolation. Nothing but men is like a desert full of sand.'[18]

As he travelled, he alternated between reading Lenin and Victor

Hugo; one book for the land where he was, the other for the city he now called home. It was starting to call for him now. 'I long for Paris, I have never given up on it, ever, I am a Frenchman from the East, a Humanist, a rationalist with religion, a Catholic with a Jewish intelligence, an actual revolutionary. What an oddity!'[19] More to the point, by the time of his meeting with Walter Benjamin he had been apart from Friedl for almost half a year. By October, as his weekly reports began to appear in the *Frankfurter Zeitung*, she had broken her silence and made her presence felt, but not in a reassuring way. 'My wife is coming ever nearer,' he told Reifenberg,* 'writing me strange love letters: lots of grumpy, dissatisfied, almost angry reviews of my articles. Perhaps she means *me* and doesn't know it.'[20] Perhaps she couldn't bring herself to be direct. As the fragmentary diary he kept reveals, after October she stopped writing to him again. He needed to return to her.

The good news on heading home was that the trip had produced a legacy beyond the journalism and material for the last chapter of *The Wandering Jews*. For one thing, first-hand experience of the new Russia had clarified his political views, as he noted in his diary while in Odessa on 25 September. 'The longer I am here, the less likely a revolution in the West seems to me. More and more I believe that Marx simply forgot to take into account several very important factors.' For instance, that reduced working hours and increased leisure time would subdue rebellious thoughts; that 'One loves life but hates the factory owner, but one does not love class more than life'; that the typical worker is 'a man of nature' for whom 'a walk in the sun drives away all rebellious thoughts'; that revolutionaries were foolish to persist in holding the 'stupid pious bourgeois proposition of the blessing of labour'. 'The bourgeois world,' Roth wrote, 'has gone to its ruin on this; the socialist world will not be able to maintain such a gigantic common lie.'[21]

He shared his concerns for Russia's future direction over drinks with Soma Morgenstern in Berlin soon after his return. At Mampes

---

* This undated letter is thought to have been written in October 1926 and would correspond with the terse diary entry for 6 October.

Gute Stube he ordered a schnapps called Mampediktiner. 'I was surprised that Roth was able to drink a schnapps that was so horribly named,' wrote Morgenstern. 'But the schnapps was good. And Roth had a lot to tell. He was back from his trip to Russia. All his sympathies for Russia were blown away. I asked him if he had seen Trotsky. "Trotsky," he said, "anyone can see now.* He is finished, and so is the Russian Revolution." Every newspaper reader knew that. I knew that, too. What I wanted to know from him was his opinion on whether antisemitism would now begin in Russia too. We agreed that it never stopped among the people. The question was only whether the party, led by Stalin, would not now also start again with antisemitism.' In Morgenstern's recollection, they both suspected it would, which implies Roth was less naïve than *The Wandering Jews'* conclusion suggests. 'As far as I can see in retrospect,' said Morgenstern, '... Roth was the first to smell antisemitic motives in the slander against Trotsky and to denounce them as such. In contrast to Trotsky himself.'[22]

As well as having progressed his political position, Roth had a couple of new ideas for novels. One would trace the rise of a revolutionary modelled on Trotsky: this was *The Silent Prophet* (*Der stumme Prophet*), which he would never complete, and would be published posthumously after scholars pieced together a combination of drafts. Another was more personal, born of the introspection and reflection enabled by this prolonged spell on his own. 'It's a boon that I have come to Russia,' he told Brentano in September 1926. 'I should never have gotten to know myself otherwise. Finally I have the subject for the book that only I can write ... It will be the novel I've waited for for so long ... You would be amazed if I were to tell you the story. But you will get to read it in a year's time.'[23] That proved an optimistic schedule – this book sounds like *Job*, which would emerge four years later. Before he could start thinking of that, he had another novel to complete. He spent Christmas with Józef Wittlin in Poland, reunited with Friedl in Berlin – how happily, we do not know – then made trips to Prague, Vienna and Frankfurt before returning to Paris, 'flat

---

* But there is no evidence that Roth did actually meet him.

broke', to confront the book's flaws and 'add another 40 pages or so of Parisian meat to the bones'.[24]

'I am the son of an Austrian railway official (took early retirement and died insane) and a Russian–Polish Jewess,' Roth claimed five years later when he wrote to Professor Otto Forst de Battaglia. Of his war years, he said: 'I was made lieutenant ... I spent six months in a Russian prisoner of war camp, fled, and fought for two months in the Red Army, then two months' flight and return home ... *Flight Without End* is largely autobiographical.'[25] He was and did none of those things, but his next novel, completed in spring 1927, echoes the fictional autobiography presented in this letter. After the foreword, in which Roth seems to adhere to *Neue Sachlichkeit* principles by claiming the story features no 'poetic invention' but only 'observed fact',* he proceeds to narrate it under his own name, often in the first person. This is, however, a fictional 'Joseph Roth', like the narrator of *The White Cities*. As this 'Roth' tells the story of his friend, interpolated with Tunda's diary entries and letters to 'Roth', we see two fictional versions of the same man discuss one another. *Flight Without End* is two of Joseph Roth's imagined selves talking aloud, a method he used to process and analyse the revelatory experience of a trip to Russia without which he would 'never have gotten to know myself'.

Born in 1894, Lieutenant Franz Tunda is the son of an Austro-Hungarian Army major and a Polish Jewish woman. He grows up in a small Galician garrison town and in 1914 joins the army in Vienna, where he dreams of parading in triumph down the Ringstrasse to the rhythm of the 'Radetzky March'. After escaping from a prisoner-of-war camp in Siberia with the help of a Polish farmer named Baranowicz, he obtains a false birth certificate that states he is the Pole's younger brother, born in Łódź. He remains there until spring 1919, when Baranowicz brings news of peace and the German revolution, at which Tunda begins to trek west for Vienna, where he hopes his fiancée still

---

* For which reason Roth's claim, two years later in an article titled 'Long Live the Poet', that critics had misinterpreted the novel by deeming it a work of *Neue Sachlichkeit* seems especially perverse.

awaits him. But he is ambushed by the Red Army and corralled into fighting for them in the Caucasus, and eventually she marries another man. Meanwhile he falls in love with Natasha Alexandrovna, a fiery communist, and travels with her band of revolutionaries. So the scene is set for another examination of how a returning soldier might resume his life after being derailed by the war.

Numerous locations from Roth's travels during 1926 crop up in the narrative. In Samara, Tunda is presented with a priest and five peasants who stand accused of torturing Red Army men to death. Without compunction, he has them tied up and shot, their corpses left on display. He fights in Ukraine and by the Volga, tramps through the mountains of the Caucasus and moves to Baku, where he settles down with a woman named Alja, aspects of whose behaviour resemble Friedl's increasingly withdrawn and otherworldly mien. She was 'beautiful and placid', she 'moved around as if cloaked in silence',[26] 'it seemed as if she was unable to long for anything outside her field of vision. Instead of refusal or rejection, she shook her head.'[27] She 'received him like a quiet room',[28] her 'reserve damped the noise of the world and slowed the passage of the hours'.[29] Tunda takes himself down to Baku's harbour in the evenings and sits in silence looking out over the water, unable to shake the belief that, having passed the age of thirty, 'the most important part of his life lay behind him'.[30] It is easy to imagine that Roth did the same, and that as he gazed out at the Caspian Sea he reflected on how he might address his wife's difficulties on his return to Paris.

Tunda finds himself caught between worlds, 'in a state of endless preparation for nothing'.[31] He works for the Soviet state as a photographic ethnographer of the Caucasian peoples, but the former revolutionary knows he is 'under constant surveillance, without knowing by whom'.[32] In a letter to the 'Roth' narrator, Tunda describes Soviet life in terms we could imagine Roth levelling at Walter Benjamin during their conversation in his hotel suite, or to the receptive Soma Morgenstern over a late-night schnapps at Mampes Gute Stube bar soon after his return from Russia. Wherever you work, Tunda says, you know someone in the office is a member of the secret police, be it the charwoman, the secretary, the facilities manager or a learned professor. 'They all, without exception, call you Comrade. You, too, call all of them Comrade. But you suspect each one of being a spy and realise at the same time that each takes you for a spy.'[33]

Tunda leaves Alja and moves to Vienna, but when he learns his erstwhile fiancée has married another man he drifts on to Germany. He travels between Berlin and a town on the Rhine where he lives with his brother, an orchestra conductor, who hosts a party to introduce him to prominent local cultural figures. This gives Roth the opportunity to write a savage scene satirising the kind of parties he had to attend back in Germany, such as one described in a letter to Bernard von Brentano: 'A fancy dress ball where everyone pretended not to know one another, and where all those who wanted to, rapidly got acquainted. A few didn't – and remained tiddly ridiculous outsiders. I was the only one with more pride than the counts and bankers. I sat there silently. [Frankfurter Zeitung editor Heinrich] Simon crept around me, my look drove him away, he saw bombs ticking in my eyes. A stench of living bourgeois corpses.'[34] Roth had come to hate Simon, who 'doesn't like me and takes the worse state of the newspaper as a pretext to get rid of me'.[35] Presumably Roth had identified him as responsible for Sieburg's appointment in Paris. As Michael Hofmann comments, Roth 'in those days was like an open knife, a mixture of prophet, revolutionary, and sociopath'.[36] Lampooning these tedious people in Flight Without End was a safer way of detonating bombs that might otherwise explode in a real-world setting.

Finally Tunda comes to Paris, where in early 1927 Roth sat writing the book's last ten short chapters. In a letter to Benno Reifenberg on 23 April, he says that he doesn't consider 'the novel is at all flawless'[37] and is expanding the ending. These final pages are its most beautiful, by turns joyous and sad: they say something of Roth's pleasure at returning home, but also of Tunda's melancholy in a city that did not feel like home (the only significant divergence in the author's and character's attitudes). His money runs out. He appeals to a President Marcel de K for financial assistance and receives it, but this dignitary will never

again hold him in high esteem. Having been raised and schooled thanks
to the financial support of his uncle, the constantly impoverished Roth
is beginning to consider the pros and cons of requesting money from
friends, balancing pragmatism against dignity. Tunda ends the book
with less sense of purpose than at the outset; at least then he had a
mission, to head west and find his fiancée. Now he is in the west, and
he is quite alone.

'Tunda walked through the bright streets with a great void in his
heart, feeling like a released convict on his first emergence to freedom ... He was not at home in this world. Where then? In the mass
graves.'[38] This is, by some distance, the bleakest *Heimat* Roth has
yet considered. By the grave of the Unknown Soldier at the Arc de
Triomphe, Tunda felt 'as if he himself lay there in the ground, as if we
all lay there, all those of us who set out from home and were killed
and buried, or who came back but never again came home – for it is a
matter of indifference whether we are buried or alive and well. We are
strangers in this world, we come from the realm of the dead.'[39]

Tunda stood in the Place de la Madeleine, 'in the centre of the capital of the world', and had no idea what to do. 'He had no occupation,
no desire, no hope, no ambition, and not even any self-love. No one
in the world was as superfluous as he.'[40] Those are the narrator's final
words. There is no resolution, no hint of his future's direction. All we
can surmise is that it will continue in the vein of his past, and Franz
Tunda's life will remain one of flight without end.

Steel-blue mountains rose on the horizon and larks flew in the blue
Albanian sky over green meadows garlanded with telegraph lines
strung between trees which transmitted 'journalistic reports – the
twitterings of political sparrows – to Europe'.[41] Friedrich Sieburg
would have noted the slight. Roth travelled through this lush landscape
to a house where he passed between saluting sentries before meeting
an aide in an anteroom, a prelude to an audience with a man who'd
had numerous rivals murdered on his rise to power. President Ahmet
Zogu, who would crown himself King Zog of Albania the following
year, received his guest with cool good manners. He was honoured to

entertain an emissary from Germany's great *Frankfurter Zeitung*, and he only asked one thing of any reporter to whom he granted an interview: that they report the truth.

'The truth, I replied, was relative,' Roth told his readers in the resulting article published on 29 May 1927. 'Something that was true to one person could be a falsehood to another. Certainly, German reporters were obsessed with the need for truthfulness.' In the event, Zogu could hardly complain of being misquoted in the piece. He wasn't quoted at all. 'I had no particular questions for him – I could answer them all for myself,' Roth explained. 'Interviews are an alibi for a journalist's lack of ideas.'[42]

The article instead sketched Zogu's situation as a young ruler surrounded by older, savvier advisers and a team of bodyguards whose loyalty would in all

Roth in traditional local dress during his travels through Albania.

likelihood follow the weather in a country known for its turbulent political climate. It was one of a short series on Albania, a newsworthy location since becoming a protectorate of Italy, which intended to use it as a gateway to exert control over the Balkans. The country bored Roth, though he found its lawlessness grimly compelling. This was a state where the traditional response to dishonour was murder. Such a moral code, he observed, turned almost all citizens into fugitives or corpses. He met a man who had tried to avenge a friend's death but instead shot someone innocent, who happened to have seven brothers who were now hunting him down. For three months this man had lived in expectation of imminent death; but in the meantime, he continued to pursue the person he intended to kill in the first place.

Over the three decades to come, King Zog himself would go on to become embroiled in around 600 such blood feuds and survive fifty-five assassination attempts.* The Albanian culture of vendetta was a topic, however, that Roth preferred not to dwell upon. He remarked that it 'may well appear worth investigating' when '[v]iewed from the distance of Berlin',[43] but faded into the background once you were in Albania, which reads like a swipe at colleagues back in Germany who had tried to influence his choice of subject during this trip to the Balkans. On the way he spent a week in Belgrade and visited Sarajevo, where he wrote his piece recalling the sunny day when a girl carrying a telegram like a 'thunderbolt on paper' told him of the outbreak of war.

Aloof superiority had become his default setting in the professional sphere. He exuded assurance and style: he was invariably elegant, usually in a grey suit with waistcoat, gaiter trousers as worn by Austrian officers, a brown Loden coat, leather gloves, a leather hat, a pressed white shirt and a cane, which at this stage he only needed for the late-night stagger from the bar to his hotel room. He was clean-shaven, in which respect this year's *The Wandering Jews* reveals a conflict between his urbane presentation and his inner self: the beardless Jew 'no longer sports the badge of his people', he wrote. 'He attempts, perhaps unconsciously, to ape those happy Christians who are not mocked or persecuted.'[44] He remained a prolific reporter, but he would file his copy from Albania only when he saw fit. While travelling from Skutari to Tirana with *Berliner Tageblatt* journalist Hans Kloetzel, his friend dared to enquire: 'How many articles have you written, Roth?'

'None!'

'And what do your readers say?'

'Remember, Kloetzel: at the *Frankfurter Zeitung* you don't write for the reader, but for posterity!'

When a brusque telegram arrived from Frankfurt asking when he was going to file some copy, Kloetzel responded: 'Was that posterity?'[45]

In June 1927 Joseph and Friedl Roth moved to the Hôtel Helvetia at 23, Rue de Tournon, Paris. She still took pleasure in his professional

---

* He died of natural causes in Paris in 1961, where he and Roth were reunited for half a century – both were buried at the Cimetière de Thiais, until Zog's remains were repatriated to Albania in 2012.

success, and he in her beauty; he gladly spent his money on buying her fashionable dresses, shoes and gloves, though once when she spent too long admiring herself in the mirror he snapped and called her a 'stupid'[46] narcissist. That summer Roth had to write a feuilleton from chichi, snooty Deauville on the Normandy coast, then he and Friedl would travel back down to revisit Marseilles and the south. While he awaited *Flight Without End*'s publication that autumn by the Kurt Wolff Verlag in Munich, he wrote his next book. On completing it in August he wrote from Grenoble to tell Benno Reifenberg: 'My new novel is wonderful. (Keep it under your hat: I'm ashamed to tell anyone else.)'[47] He'd decided against the fraught business of hammering out another book against deadline for newspaper serialisation – he 'couldn't after all muster the strength

The cover of *Zipper und Sein Vater* (*Zipper and his Father*), 1928.

or the brazenness' – and instead, what he'd done at his own leisure was 'write one called *Zipper and His Father*. I'm looking forward to reading it to you!'[48] He was correct: *Zipper* is indeed a wonderful novel, in terms of characterisation and atmosphere his most impressive yet.

Roth would go on to dedicate it to the ever-patient Reifenberg, the emollient between him and the *Frankfurter Zeitung*'s senior editors. His two titular characters are drawn in detail with affecting tenderness; they have a new depth and nuance, they seem to possess inner lives as well as vivid physical presence. Of the two, it is the older man who leaves the stronger impression on the reader's imagination. Joseph Roth's first thoroughly realised, deeply imagined, three-dimensional character is a father – which figures, as he had been imagining such a character all his life. The opening paragraph leaves any reader who knows something of Roth's biography with little doubt that the voice here is a plaintive one issuing from the author's time as a small, sad boy who looked on with envy at peers who had fathers. The first eleven words are autobiographical, and the subsequent words are so touching and sincere that they feel every bit as authentic. This boy not only wants affection but guidance and discipline, all the diverse facets of parental love. He wants to feel rooted, to have a solid paternal presence as a fixed reference point in life.

'I had no father – at least, I never knew my father – but Zipper had one. This earned my friend my special respect, as if he had owned a parrot or a St Bernard. When Arnold said: "Tomorrow I'm going to the Kobenzl* with my father," I would wish that I too had a father. I could have held his hand, copied his signature, been scolded, punished, rewarded, caned by him. At times I wanted to urge my mother to marry again, because even a stepfather would have been worth having. The state of things, however, did not permit it."[49]

The story is again told by a 'Joseph Roth' – a first-person narrator who only reveals his name on the final page – and it recounts the lives of his friend Arnold Zipper and his unnamed father. It is another *Heimkehrerroman* concerned with the fate of homecoming soldiers, but with important differences from the preceding four. For one, it begins before the war instead of in its aftermath, the better to convey how the great rupture could alter a character's personality and destiny. Two, it examines a parent-child relationship, whereas Andreas Pum, Gabriel Dan and Franz Tunda were all parentless and *The Spider's Web* only touches on Theodore Lohse's strained post-war relationship with his mother. It is also another work in the *Neue Sachlichkeit* mode, written with purported veracity by the 'Roth' narrator who presents himself as the faithful eyewitness reporter of the Zipper family's story.

The Zipper family – Herr and Frau Zipper, and their sons Arnold and Caesar – receive the 'Roth' narrator as a regular dinner guest at their suburban Viennese home, in which the focal point is the salon. The critic Sidney Rosenfeld gives a perfect summary of its atmosphere and symbolism: 'Steeped in constant twilight, smelling of moth balls, crammed with the bric-a-brac of sunken yesterdays, and reserved for

---

* An area of hills outside Vienna, giving picturesque views over the city.

Sunday use only, the Zipper salon reflects a life invested in the quest for bourgeois respectability, but crowned only with the most modest and ephemeral of successes.'[50] The Zippers' is the most detailed home yet described in a Roth novel, and it forms the setting for the first half of the book. Old Zipper is a violin maker and travelling salesman, and this is his domain. He is domineering but likeable, fond of practical jokes, obsessed with timepieces, a would-be polymath interested in geography, history, great literature and the natural sciences ('His reverence for medicine was only equalled by his mistrust of doctors'[51]) but above all, music. He is an atheist. Music is his religion. He has perfect pitch and it was said he might have been a professional violinist. Perhaps this is why, despite his energy, warmth and humour, those who observe him at close quarters (such as 'Roth') now and then glimpse a great sorrow. There was 'something of the tragic clown about him'. He was 'so sad, as sad as a room which has been emptied, as sad as a sundial in shadow, as sad as a stripped railway coach standing on a rusty line'.[52] His ambitions were thwarted by the onerous task of hauling himself up from the proletariat, but he has invested his hopes in Arnold, a scholarly boy who can do no wrong in his eyes. Photographs of the cherished son hang on the walls of the salon, several reminiscent of Roth's childhood pictures: dressed in a sailor's costume; seated on a horse; holding a violin ... 'Arnold at all ages, in all sorts of clothes and in every situation; Arnold, Arnold, Arnold.'[53] Caesar, on the other hand, is unacademic and wayward.

Arnold and the narrator start to make their way in life, by respectively studying Law and Philosophy. Then Gavrilo Princip shoots Franz Ferdinand, a moment refreshed in Roth's memory by his recent visit to Sarajevo, and, much to his wife's consternation, Old Zipper is all for sending his sons to war. 'We'll show them a thing or two! The Crown Prince was a swine, but what's that to do with the Serbs? We would have dealt with him ourselves. They'll see now that we're not to be messed about with.'[54]

The two friends go off to fight, as does Caesar. Arnold and Roth do not see one another for six months, after which Arnold 'seemed so changed in his civilian clothes that I felt I was meeting him again after many years'.[55] His trauma is mental, but Caesar's is physical: he loses a leg and joins the ranks of disabled veterans. He argues with his father over who gets to read the newspaper, and starts to trash the house with his crutches, a scene overly reminiscent of *Rebellion*. 'An ambulance was sent for. Caesar lapsed into delirium and died a few days later.'[56] Even by Roth's standards this is an abrupt conclusion to a character's story. Sometimes he dispatches his characters as if he has been holding the catch to a trapdoor beneath them and wants to remind the reader he is in control.

Reunited in Vienna after the war, Arnold and Roth walk and talk through the night, only parting at dawn, at which hour 'we felt less nervous of our houses, which we had so longed for during the war and in which we no longer felt at home'.[57] Arnold replaces this former home with an artists' and writers' coffee house, where he becomes a silent habitué, watching others play cards. No one knows who he is or what he is doing there, but he becomes part of the setting.

He needs to find a new job, but proves too timid to succeed as a salesman of old military uniform. Old Zipper, who is proud of his contacts, gains him a position at the Ministry of Finance, where Arnold stagnates and acquires 'a real horror of solitude',[58] such as Roth had while travelling alone through Russia. He steers clear of his parents' home, shying away from the father who urged him off to war and engineered him a soul-destroying job in its aftermath, and spends every evening in the coffee house. Roth describes this place in a page of sustained brilliant detail that brings the reader into an early-twentieth-century Viennese café – the carbide lamps throwing 'scalloped shadows' over the tables, the clink of glasses and occasional 'dry tap'[59] of a chessman falling on the board, the quiet glide of billiard balls on baize – illustrating how familiar he'd grown with these home-from-home settings during the previous decade.

When Arnold vanishes, those who'd become accustomed to his silent presence are mystified. It transpires he has fallen in love with Erna Wilder, a childhood sweetheart. He had long cherished her memory but doubted they would see one another again, then fate realigned their paths at a juncture when he had grown inert and would embrace any prospect of a new direction. 'I finally came to the conclusion,' remarks the narrator, 'that Arnold had fallen in love out of despair, like one of those people whose nature is to strive against alcohol, and who in despair become drinkers.'[60] Certainly Arnold appears addicted to her. This hitherto ghostly figure gains a feeling of solid purpose: to advance his lover's career. Erna is now an aspiring actress and he follows devotedly, dutifully in the wake of her thrusting ambition: around the provincial theatres, to Berlin, then into a job as the film editor of a small newspaper, so that he can pass on insider information to help her become a Hollywood star. He puts up with her contempt for him, and even with her repeated affairs with men and women. He follows her to Nice, and she deserts him. Old Zipper is dead now, and Arnold belatedly turns his talent as a violinist into a musical career, though not with the dignity his father would have wanted: he acts as the accompanist to the famous clown Lock (modelled on Grock, about whom Roth had written as a journalist), then winds up in vaudeville as a solo performer. Old Zipper never considered himself a sad clown, but young Zipper is all too aware that he now fits this description.

The final few pages have a change in register. Roth introduces a mysterious new character, Eduard P, a mutual friend of his and Arnold's. His appearance feels belated and abrupt, his characterisation hazy – and probably Roth felt as much, for in a letter to Reifenberg he proposed to cut this 'somewhat mystical conversation',[61] but he never did. They discuss their friend's life, and Eduard argues that fathers today are unsatisfactory: complacent and lacking in understanding of the sacrifices and hardships of Roth's generation. What good were fathers, what were they but a source of trouble?, asks the novelist whose psyche was scarred by never having had one. The ideas here seem salvaged from a passage in the unpublished *The White Cities*.[62] 'All our fathers are responsible for our bad luck,' Eduard claims:

> Our fathers belong to the generation which made the war. They gave their watch-chains and their wedding rings in exchange for

iron ones.* Ah! What patriots they were! … Just think back: you came back, you, the unluckiest generation of the modern era. What had happened? Your fathers had had time to get new children on the girls who were actually meant for you. You'd hardly come home before your fathers were sitting again in the chairs they'd had at the outbreak of war. They made the newspapers, public opinion, the peace treaties, politics. You young people were a thousand times more competent, but exhausted, half dead and needing to rest. You had no means of earning a living. It made no difference whether you had lived or died. And to *what* did you come home? To your parents' houses![63]

But the Roth-narrator simply says: 'Had I had a father, I would not have blamed him.'[64]

The book closes with a letter from 'Roth' to Arnold, a *Neue Sachlichkeit* device that sets out the author's credentials as an eyewitness observer. He urges Arnold to pursue his musical ambitions despite their generation's disadvantages. He gives the advice with which most artists console themselves: that their work is establishing itself beyond view, in ways they may never perceive, becoming part of the cultural air that people inhale, to enact some subtle alteration on the world. This conclusion feels like Roth warding off the sense of futility that haunted his self-perception as a writer, however well-reputed he was becoming. We are to understand that Roth, too, is a sad clown who is compelled to stand on stage and perform for a cloth-eared audience, in his case not French café diners but German newspaper readers. But after a decade of hard work he is girding himself for more – Roth tells the reader and himself that he won't give up, however tired he feels, however alone and in despair, however old before his time. 'Just carry on trying in vain to play,' he instructs Arnold, 'just as I shall never give up writing in vain. "In vain", which means: *apparently* in vain. For, as you know yourself, there does exist somewhere a region in which the traces of

---

* A reference to the *Eisernerzeit*, or 'Iron Time', when citizens were encouraged to trade their precious jewellery for iron substitutes to assist the war effort.

our playing are recorded, illegibly, but in some strange way effectively, if not today, then years hence, and if not years hence, then millennia hence. Probably it will not be known whether I wrote or you played, or vice versa. But in the spiritual content of the atmosphere, which is more powerful than its content of electricity, there will float the distant echo of your single notes, beside the equally distant echo of a thought which I must once have written down.'[65]

The cover of *Juden Auf Wanderschaft* (*The Wandering Jews*), 1927.

In September 1927 Roth was in the picturesque Swiss hillside village of Glion, near Montreux, from where he wrote to Stefan Zweig, who had praised *The Wandering Jews* after its publication by Die Schmiede in the spring.

'Dear esteemed Mr Zweig,' he wrote, 'I've been in debt to you for an unconscionably long time. You sent me kind words on my Jewish book. I thank you for them.'[66] Roth had established the connection he'd hoped for since the time he loitered outside Zweig's home as a student in Vienna. So began a friendship that would shape the remainder of his life.

By this time Zweig had become one of the world's best-known writers, if not one of its best-regarded. He was born in 1881 into wealth, the son of secular Jewish parents, and grew up in comfort in Vienna. After studying there and in Berlin he became known as a translator and biographer, and it was the latter form that brought him success, though to many his prose had the air of the rich dilettante. It was a challenge for the millionaire author to know how to spend his time and money, and one pleasing method was to find ways to fill his hilltop mansion on Salzburg's Kapuzinerberg. He collected things whose proximity stimulated him: autograph music manuscripts (Mozart, Bach), antiquarian books, Beethoven's desk, people with a greater talent than his own.

He always had the diffident bourgeois's urge towards those who lived harder lives at higher stakes: he observed of himself that 'Perhaps the very fact that I came from a solidly established background, and felt to some extent that this "security" complex weighed me down, made me more likely to be fascinated by those who almost recklessly squandered their lives, their time, their money, their health and reputation . . .'.[67]

Zweig is less remarkable for his own artistry than for what he connotes, namely the bohemian Viennese coffee-house culture and its network of eminent cosmopolitans he moved among from the fin-de-siècle to the entre-deux-guerres period. Judging by his work alone it is hard to gauge how he gained such prominence, but there is a clip of silent monochrome film footage from 1933 that suddenly makes sense of him.[*] He is at a garden party in Salzburg, deep in amused conversation with a woman and a man, while others nearby watch the famed author holding forth. Squeezing a cigar in his left hand, he laughs, looks to the camera with a grin, shakes the woman's hand then bends down to kiss it while she creases with laughter, switches the cigar to his right hand and smooths his hair with his left, his gaze remaining locked on the woman's face, glances to her male companion with a friendly gesture while swaying backwards, bobs forwards with a smile to someone else, then the film cuts out. He is charm in constant motion. Within ten seconds we see the vivacity, nervous energy, warmth and eagerness to please that propelled him through early-twentieth-century Austrian literary society.

His memoir *The World of Yesterday* is a detailed and valuable exposition of that era, but he relays his youthful successes with a faux-humility that undermines itself by urging the reader to think well of him. His insecurity wafts from the page. His prose is often engaging, but never irresistible. It is competent and smooth, but too smooth, too dispassionate, written with pathological reserve. What Roth, at a juncture that called for flattery, called its 'lovely epic calm' and 'superior dignity'[68] is its flaw. Zweig can hint at atmosphere, give the odd vivid

---

[*] Online at 1:21 into this YouTube clip: https://www.youtube.com/watch?v=pT-T6YrZJ2Xo Recordings of Zweig reading his poetry on Swiss radio in 1933 emphasise the same animated, stagey persona: https://www.mediathek.at/atom/01027411-0F4-0004D-000006DC-0101D962

description, conjure a suggestion of place, but the effect is like look-ing in at a lively coffee house through the windows. The scene is at a remove, muted and odourless. Where Roth is a double espresso, Zweig is a half-decent mocha, served lukewarm. Fellow writers in German mocked his grasp of grammar. Karl Kraus had an insult for him, of course: on being told that Zweig's widely translated novellas had con-quered all the languages of the world, he replied: 'Except one.'[69] But he was kind, patient, loyal and trustworthy, and his generosity would save Roth's skin many times over. He was fatherly to Roth, who was half a generation younger. It is necessary to appreciate the contrasts in their talents, disposition and background – all of which were apparent to both men – to understand the dynamic at play in their correspondence through the decade to come.

Early-twentieth-century photo of the Hôtel Foyot,
Rue de Tournon, in Paris's 6th arrondissement.

A week later Roth was back from Switzerland and briefly stayed at the Hôtel Foyot in Paris's Rue de Tournon, from where he departed for the industrial Saarland and Lorraine just over the Franco-German border. Friedl remained in Paris, alone. Roth was there to write a series of reports, to be titled 'Letters from Germany'. Owing to the political delicacy of Franco-German relations over this contested, economically important region, which had been under a specific international legal regime since the Treaty of Versailles, he wrote them under a pseudonymous byline, 'Cuneus', which means 'wedge' in Latin. This has two resonances, speaking to the Saar's position wedged between Germany and France, and Roth's as a man who felt himself caught between the two countries. If he hoped the pseudonym would shield him from flak on this contentious topic, he was to be disappointed: his reports prompted a flurry of criticism in newspapers such as the *Saarbrücker Zeitung*, which resented his unflattering portrayal of the industrial region: 'Saarbrücken station is the saddest of all the stations I have ever got off at,' Roth observed. The railway line's signals were 'colourless and pale in comparison with the fireworks the furnaces rain up against the sky', and the 'dark and threatening'[70] tunnels through which his train had passed were well lit compared to the black subterranean shafts clambered through daily by the local coal miners.

When Roth heard about the attacks on him in print by a *Saarbrücker Zeitung* writer pseudonymously bylined as 'Matz',[*] he told Benno Reifenberg of a retaliatory desire to 'beat him up good and proper'[71] (in print, not in person). He was so tired of journalism; he told Brentano that he intended soon to give it up as his principal occupation. He also advised his younger colleague to do the same in a couple of years' time, and suggested he stop moving 'in Jewish circles' and write for a heavy industry journal where he'd work with people 'more grateful than Jews', because if he stayed at the *Frankfurter Zeitung* he'd continue to be underpaid by 'scheming Jews'.[72] Roth's antisemitic expressions seem to have hardened and sharpened, to have progressed from disdain to fury.

He roamed the Saar's industrial areas, visited factories and a mine, then left because he felt unable to write. He told Reifenberg that this needn't matter – he already knew enough. 'I am steeped in the Saarland, and know it as well as I know Vienna. You will see.'[73] If he

---

[*] Later revealed as a journalist named Ludwig Bruch.

had trouble concentrating, perhaps this was connected to something else he mentioned to Reifenberg in a sudden digression from newspaper matters. It is a striking example of how their relationship veered between the professional and personal that Roth confesses to having got drunk one night and 'slept with an ugly hotel chambermaid from sheer wretchedness'.

In the next paragraph, he says that Friedl is 'very ill' in Saint-Raphaël, and he may need to take her to Frankfurt for treatment. This would conclude a year of frenetic activity even by Roth's standards: during 1927, having just returned from his long trip to Russia, he travelled between Poland, Berlin, Prague, Vienna, Frankfurt, Albania, Belgrade, the Harz mountains in northern Germany (a brief trip inspired by Heine's *Die Harzreise* published a century earlier), Marseilles, Switzerland, Paris and the Saarland. He felt in no need of a rest: the next question in his letter to Reifenberg is to ask where he should go next. And while he was back on professional matters, he'd spent 500 marks in four weeks – the paper really wasn't paying him enough. There is no acknowledgement that he was by now one of Europe's best-paid journalists, working at a rate that must have prompted envy and resentment among rivals: one mark per line, with a guaranteed minimum monthly income of 1,000 marks. (He handwrote his columns at a size whereby a line of his script equated to a line of newspaper type, so as to easily tot up his fees.) But what use was such a rate if it did not match his outgoings? There were his and Friedl's hotel and restaurant bills to pay, their medical bills too, and glasses of brandy to drink. He needed more money.

Chapter Eight

A man without an income is like a man without a name or like a shadow minus its body. One feels like a phantom.

Flight Without End

In 1928 Roth wrote a three-page ironic tale about the delicate art of positioning oneself near rich acquaintances. The narrator of 'The Grand House Opposite' ('*Das reiche Haus gegenüber*'), being not exactly poor yet in need of money, moves to a hotel in a neighbourhood where affluent types – bankers, newspaper editors – live in mansions. He had 'found [himself] in the sort of situation where a man is impelled to seek out the proximity of wealth in a sort of secret and carefully unacknowledged hope that it might somehow rub off on him'.[1] His window looks out on an impressive house that appears inhabited only by a few servants. He learns that the owner is an elderly man who only spends two months there a year. One day this man arrives. Every day he sits on his veranda, looking back towards the hotel. The two men eventually say hello across the street. Nothing more. We sense the narrator is playing a careful game, waiting for the moment to cultivate a friendship with someone who might prove a benefactor, or at least a talisman. Then one night the old man dies. After the funeral, a notary hands the narrator a letter from him. In it the man explains he had 'grown fond' of the narrator to the point of finding out his name, because 'even though you liked me, you kept your distance, and even though you were curious, you remained discreet. I leave only debts. Otherwise, you would have been my heir. Think of me with kindness.'[2] The next day, the narrator moves out of the hotel.

The tale has a bittersweet quality redolent of a Yiddish fable. 'Oy, what can you do?' it seems to ask, with a shrug and a terse laugh. Roth could work no harder. He was making himself ill; at the dawn of 1928 his liver was 'flushed with calvados',[3] he had neuralgia and he spoke of a desire to hibernate and 'sleep uninterruptedly'[4] from December to January. He felt entitled to more money from the *Frankfurter Zeitung* but his employers were reluctant: they already paid him well and they had other talented writers who also deserved their due.

Two options presented themselves. One was to focus on his novels. This way he might manoeuvre a publisher into paying a handsome advance, and perhaps he would at last write the bestseller that would bring in substantial royalties. At the end of 1927 this option offered cause for optimism, when he agreed a contract with the Kurt Wolff Verlag to publish *Zipper and His Father* and fund him through the completion of his next book. He wrote to Benno Reifenberg that he was 'glad for once to be able to give you some good news'.[5] They would pay Roth 700 marks for the month of April and, since a rival publisher, Zsolnay Verlag, had also expressed interest in his work in progress, he planned to use that as leverage to 'get more like 800–1,200 marks per month out of Wolff' through the first half of 1928. For once he had the prospect of financial independence. 'So for the next seven months, I'll be able to eat, with no newspaper work, almost like a pre-war novelist.'[6] Writing to Reifenberg again a week later, Roth added that he had another option in the form of interest from the major publishing house S. Fischer. 'In the event of a good offer, I'll swap Wolff for Fischer, if less good, I'll just play them off against each other.'[7]

The second option was to situate himself opposite 'the grand house' of wealthier acquaintances and hope for better luck than the narrator of his story. Roth had never been averse to receiving financial support from those he felt could afford it, ever since his uncle Siegmund Grübel underwrote his upbringing and education. Now the unjust position in which he found himself – confronted by bourgeois friends' inherited wealth juxtaposed with his and Friedl's misfortune – seemed to justify this approach. They didn't deserve all that money; he didn't deserve such hardship; a little redistribution was not only permissible but correct. This was not greed on Roth's part. When he had a stash of notes in his wallet he would do the same for others (even if this money had itself been a gift from a friend, intended to pay off his own debts). Such money as was available should be shared with those who needed it; and if he enjoyed a rare moment of good fortune, he would try to pass it on to others in equal need.

Soma Morgenstern remembered just such an instance in Paris in the 1930s, when Roth extracted a payment he was owed from a publication edited by the poet Louis Aragon. 'He adored Joseph Roth and apparently knew him well enough to have a bottle of cognac served right away,'[8] wrote Morgenstern. They talked politics for a while until a moment arrived when Roth could tactfully mention the paper's debt to him, which he believed was 300 francs. Aragon soon handed him money in an envelope. Outside, Roth opened it, counted the sheaf of notes and began to dance in the street. A thousand francs! He waltzed his way towards a taxi, which took them to the Café Weber on the Rue Royale, where they sat at a table on the terrace. An émigré poet passed by and Roth merrily beckoned him over. What did he fancy drinking? The poet accepted the offer but only asked for a coffee.

'*Ach was, Kaffee!*' said Roth – forget coffee! – and switched to French: '*Garçon, une fine!*' Waiter, a brandy! The poet ended up staying for a couple more, then made to leave, giving Roth his thanks. Roth took his hand, looked at him sternly and asked: 'Do you need money?' The poet was reluctant, but Roth would hear none of it. 'The first hundred-franc note was gone,' recalled Morgenstern. 'The second note went to another emigrant, a real blue-blooded prince ... I don't know who snapped up the third, since I had to answer the telephone.' For all that Roth had shed his illusions about Marxism, he retained the principle 'From each according to their ability, to each according to their need.'

The only way to make the novel-writing route a success was to work harder than ever. Literary success might also loosen his ties to the *Frankfurter Zeitung*, which were causing ever more stress; on 17 January 1928 he wrote angrily to Reifenberg saying that the political desk had edited and censored his work. This was intolerable, and if it didn't stop he would demand to edit their copy in return. The correspondence does not record how this suggestion went down. On 24 January he wrote to Zweig from Cologne. In response to Zweig's feedback on *Flight Without End*, Roth says that *Zipper* is coming out at Easter, and 'right now I'm busy on a third'[9] novel. A production line was being put in place. He mentions half-finished drafts going back to 1920. It sounds as if he is proposing to see what he can salvage. Earlier that month he'd told his Parisian friend Félix Bertaux* about this forthcoming novel, which he said should be finished in October 1928 and would be called *The Younger Brother*. It would take a different look at familial relationships from *Zipper*, this time examining siblings rather than parents and children. It concerned 'The generation of German secret associations, separatists, Rathenau murderers† – in short, of our younger brothers, today's 25-year-olds.'[10] In his early dealings with Zweig he sensed a promising friendship. Their correspondence had become warm and informal. They had not yet met, and Roth said he would love to make this happen. He had a new address in Paris – 152–4, Rue de la Pompe – which would be valid until mid-February, so perhaps Zweig could write to him there and arrange to meet in the spring?

At the beginning of 1928, then, Roth had what passed for hope, albeit the hope of a man swept out to a choppy sea who senses that, if he swims hard and he's correct that the winds are calming, he could yet make it home. Effort and a little good fortune could see him right. But by mid-February he would not still be in Paris. On the 13th he wrote from a pension in Saint-Raphaël, the Villa Alice, to tell Félix Bertaux that he'd had to 'up sticks and head south with my wife, who was feeling poorly'.[11] After the 16th he says he will take her to another place, yet to be determined, but somewhere untouched by the mistral, the cold northerly winter wind that blows through the Midi to the

---

* An eminent French scholar of German literature, and author of the influential *Panorama de la littérature allemande contemporaine*, which had just been published.
† I.e. those such as Erwin Kern, Ernst Werner Techow and Hermann Fischer, who were respectively twenty-three, twenty-one and twenty-six when they shot Walther Rathenau.

Mediterranean. When she showed signs of improvement, Roth left for a trip to Paris followed by Berlin, with Friedl remaining in Saint-Raphaël. In the first week of March 1928, Benno Reifenberg and his wife Maryla had an alarming visitation late at night at their home in Frankfurt. Someone knocked on the door, and when they opened it they saw a hunched woman with tangled hair, wearing crumpled clothing. They took a moment to realise who it was. In a panicked voice, gesticulating as she spoke, Friedl explained she had had to leave the Saint-Raphaël hotel because of the ghosts in the central heating pipes. The Reifenbergs booked her into a Frankfurt hotel and telephoned Roth, then stayed with her all night as she remained awake, talking frenziedly about her enemies. On other occasions she spoke with similar vitriol about her parents, referring to them dismissively as 'Them, them there'.[12]

An early-twentieth-century postcard of the Villa Alice, Saint-Raphaël.

If bitter resentment towards her parents was an aspect of Friedl's anguish, this fits with an analysis offered by Darcy Buerkle, a historian with an interest in Jewish women's mental health in 1920s Vienna. It is notable that her difficulties developed within the context of a mental-health crisis among Viennese Jews in the mid-1920s, during which a

meeting was held to discuss how to counter an 'epidemic of suicides'.*
'In general,' said Professor Buerkle, 'assimilated Jewish women in the
1920s suffered mixed messages, newly invigorated stereotyping and
ambitions that sometimes, not seldom, led to disorientation and a
sense of entrapment/helplessness. Systemic antisemitism and misogyny
combined to create a particular kind of unspoken vulnerable state.
Typically more educated than their mothers, there were nonetheless
significant limits on their lives. They were living a contradiction of
increased access to self-determination and ambition both profession-
ally and personally, and its thwarting ... Jewish parents generally, but
Jewish mothers in particular, felt the pressures related to their limited
capacities to protect their children from antisemitism.'

Such difficulties associated with the generation gap between
Orthodox Jewish parents and their children could have been exacerbated by entering a marriage such as Friedl's, added Professor Buerkle.
'Of course, it's difficult to answer your question without working out
the particularity of Friedl and Joseph Roth's dynamic and knowing
much more about Friedl's early life than I do. In general, though,
Jewish women of that generation were not prepared to be treated in
marriage the way that Friedl was apparently treated – and it caused
considerable fracturing of every kind for the women involved. It was
just too isolating and humiliating. Roth's lack of stability/familial
support and constant travel along with his (re-emergent?) alcoholism
would have been especially disconcerting.'[13]

As summer approached, Roth faced the prospect of another infirm
person becoming dependent on his care, though it is unclear whether
this ever transpired. Soon, he told Reifenberg in July, he would 'have
to move my old friend Frau Szajnocha in with me. Which means

---

* 'In February of 1926,' writes Professor Buerkle, 'the *Jüdische Rundschau*'s front-
page article informed its readers that B'nai B'rith had sponsored a meeting "filled to
capacity" to discuss the "suicide epidemic" in its midst ... A year later the newspaper
claimed that the number of Jewish suicides had risen sharply since 1922 and by 1927
had nearly doubled. In the same affective and political mode, a note in the same paper
just one week after the B'nai B'rith meeting reported alarming numbers for Vienna:
"In the last eight months seventy Jews have committed suicide in Vienna and among
them 45 percent were women."' Darcy Buerkle, *Nothing Happened: Charlotte Salomon
and an Archive of Suicide* (University of Michigan Press, 2013), pp. 169–70.

founding a household. She can't stay in Poland for many reasons –
and I am her only material prop. Secondly, I need to come up with
an arrangement for my wife. Where? What with? How? Where am I
going to put these two women?'[14]

Unprompted by any external event, only by 'perhaps ... one of those
hidden, inner, private things that sometimes cause a writer to raise his
voice, without him caring whether there is anyone listening to him
or not',[15] that is to say some secret turmoil that caused him to avert
his gaze from the present and dwell on the pre-war past, in March
1928 Roth described for *Frankfurter Zeitung* readers his memories of
those golden Viennese mornings when he watched Emperor Franz
Joseph I depart Schönbrunn by carriage for his summer residence at
Bad Ischl, the spa town where he signed the declaration of war in
July 1914. Roth had joined a crowd of onlookers who had taken the
specially laid-on early-morning trams to gather at the palace and
watch the high-stepping white horses clip down the gravel path,
guided by a coachman whose hands 'were two dazzling white spots
in the midst of the shady green of the avenue'. Roth claims he is
entitled to write now of the monarchy that ruled over his childhood
because he was 'so vehemently opposed to it then' – which is not how
his school peers remembered it. What matters is that his childhood
and the Imperial monarchy were entwined in his mind, regardless
of whether he approved of the Habsburgs' rule, and to think of
them at all was a warm retreat to a time when he was innocent and
hopeful. He recalls the great ceremony of the emperor's funeral. *The
cold sun of the Habsburgs had been extinguished, but it was a sun.* Now
the world is as dark as night to Roth, while across Europe he sees
crowds hail the false dawns of fascism and communism. And now
Franz Joseph 'lies buried in the Kapuzinergruft, and under the ruins
of his crown, while I, living, stumble about among them'. To reflect
on the emperor's passing is to reflect on his childhood's passing. He
mourns them both. He cannot resurrect the emperor, nor any other
lost father. But he can concentrate his intense imaginative powers
on reviving his childhood. They are such that he can, for a few

precious moments, surrender himself completely and believe that this imagined world is real.

The desperation in his letter about where 'to put these two women' was aggravated by his dubious acquisition of Austrian citizenship early in the decade having caught up with him. He had to return to Vienna to prove again that he was who he claimed to be, that he was not a Polish impostor. 'The unorthodox means by which I furnished myself with names, dates, schools, and army career,' he told Reifenberg, 'are to be tested to their destruction – and I've spent the past fortnight trying to establish my literary and journalistic existence to authorities who don't know anything about me ... Arguing that papers are *quite rightly bound* to have disappeared – hence the absence of conventional documentation. I'm living and improvising twenty novels. It's so exhausting, I haven't a hope of getting on with the one I'm trying to write. I've called a halt ... Without a passport, I'm toast.'[16] He was actually trying to write two novels during this period – *The Younger Brother* and the never-completed, Trotsky-inspired *The Silent Prophet* – but instead of pressing on with either, he spent his days touring between government offices and buttering up implacable functionaries by explaining his status, while dropping names of well-placed acquaintances. Another couple of weeks 'and I'll be done in',[17] he said. So besides these temporarily abandoned novels, he had his increasingly unstable wife to care for; newspaper articles to churn out when he felt drained dry and wanted to quit the *Frankfurter Zeitung*; and now a bureaucratic wrangle that could leave him without the passport on which his livelihood depended. This is not to mention his growing alcohol intake and consequent ill-health. Once again, his liver was giving him trouble.

In the summer of 1928 the population of Vienna swelled by around 100,000 people, more than 30,000 of them German men wearing white caps and singing songs by Schubert. It was the centennial of the composer's death, and people from around the world had swarmed into the city for a festival of his music performed by these '*Deutsche Sangesbrüder*', or 'German Brothers in Song'. 'The brothers were singing everywhere,' remembered Soma Morgenstern. 'They sat in the inns and drank beer and sang. They sat in the coffee houses and drank beer and sang. Their ladies drank coffee with cream and sang along. They sang in groups in the streets.'[18] They sang too in the Prater, in a huge temporary concert venue with capacity for more than 90,000 people, one-third of them choristers, two-thirds the audience. Morgenstern and Roth decided to attend one evening while Friedl was at her parents' in Leopoldstadt; Morgenstern said she never forgave them for going without her. Roth loved the concert – to witness 30,000 men singing Schubert's lieder in unison made for an overwhelming spectacle – but he was sceptical about the entire endeavour. It seemed plain to him that this mass arrival of Germans in Vienna was a political exercise, one designed to kindle support for *Anschluss*, the idea of German–Austrian annexation that had bubbled away since the late nineteenth century but had grown in popularity since the collapse of the Habsburg Empire. Like many left-wing publications, the *Frankfurter Zeitung* favoured the idea as the best way of strengthening the weakened Austria, but Roth hated it. Tying Austria to Germany would do it no good; the answer was to strengthen Austria itself, which he was coming to believe could only occur through the restoration of its monarchy. In any case, if that was the intention, the singers' behaviour did little to foster feelings of Germanic brotherhood among the Viennese. 'They drank too much beer,' said Morgenstern, 'and they threw up in all the coffee houses in the inner city.'[19]

Still, the concert itself made a happy change from his tiring pursuit of citizenship and a passport, the papers on which rested his continued career, his health and, to Roth's way of seeing things, his very existence. The trawl through the Viennese bureaucracy was a dull, genteel, protracted matter of life and death. Morgenstern said of himself that he had little trouble gaining citizenship as he was settled in Vienna, but 'Roth had great difficulties, because he had not been resident in Vienna for years.'[20] Eventually Roth succeeded in gaining a permanent passport, this time with the help of Martin Fuchs, a conservative, monarchist Austrian diplomat whom he had befriended.

Throughout this time he and Friedl stayed at the Hopfner Hotel in the Hietzing district of Vienna, near the Schönbrunn Palace. Sometimes he had to cancel appointments at the ministry because

Friedl would not leave the hotel and refused to be left there alone. At other times, Morgenstern helped by staying with her while Roth went out. He had never much liked Friedl's company, and these weeks did nothing to change that. 'Roth could not take the sick woman with him everywhere. In such cases she refused to be left alone and he was ashamed of her "hysterical" behaviour, for which she also blamed him. For hours I sat with her in the hotel room, and for hours she told me how he had made his trip to Russia and left her alone in Berlin. She gave the word "Berlin" such a sinister emphasis, as if he had left her alone in a dark forest, surrounded by wolves.'[21]

Morgenstern took her for walks in the park at Schönbrunn and showed her around the Imperial palace, which she enjoyed. He said it 'obviously did her a great deal of good, since at that time Roth was already having violent fits of monarchist sentiment, which she began to share snobbishly in the manner of petty-bourgeois wives'.[22] When it rained they sat in the Hopfner Hotel's café, where Friedl returned to her theme that Roth, whom she said she 'still loved very much', had provoked her debilitating anxiety. In 1924, she said, he had had to go on a trip for the *Frankfurter Zeitung* and that was fine: she understood, it took no toll on her. But she kept coming back to the long trip to Russia. That was another matter altogether. It was too much. And then there was his drinking, and she worried he was spending too much time with other women . . .

One day Morgenstern sat with the two of them in the café. When he, Roth and Friedl were together, Friedl usually remained in good spirits, he said. 'I seem to remember that that summer in Vienna she was not even under medical treatment. She read with interest everything we gave her to read. She had a good judgement about literature and an almost snobbish feeling for stylistic finesse.'[23] On this occasion, the atmosphere grew frosty. Friedl told Roth that she had explained his travels were the cause of her anxiety to Morgenstern, who now felt suitably awkward. Roth simply dismissed her opinion. He disagreed. She was wrong and he was right. He told Morgenstern later that he considered Friedl pathologically jealous, that the problem lay with her, not with him. But her insistence eventually wore him

down, Morgenstern said. 'I believed that the jealous woman was imagining an illness in order to control her husband with the power of her
weakness ... Unfortunately, the poor sick woman soon succeeded in
burdening her husband with the cause and guilt of her illness for two
or three years.'[24]

If she was jealous by summer 1928, and suspected that Roth had
had an affair in Russia, an article he wrote that April can hardly have
helped. In the Volksgarten, where in the green springtime an army
band played to an audience of young women and blackbirds, Roth
watched the trees sway in the breeze. It seemed to him that 'the excit-
able arms of the bandleader had not only the musicians at his beck and
call, but also the soughing leaves'.[25] Everywhere he looked were pretty
women. Because he was too poor to offer to buy one a coffee, instead
Roth ambled around the park imagining himself speaking with them.
He 'walked up and down the avenue, fell in love, despaired, got over it,
forgot, and fell in love again – all in the space of a minute'.[26] He spotted
a woman with whom he 'fell in love instantly', and as she rode away
in a carriage 'the dapper clopping of the horses mimicked my heart'.[27]
Evening fell, he heard more girls giggling in the darkness, the army
band struck up the 'Radetzky March', 'the Marseillaise of reaction'.
The composition seemed 'not to exist on paper' but had 'passed into
the players' flesh and blood, and they were playing it from memory, as
you breathe from memory'.[28] He considers returning to the park at the
same time tomorrow in hopes of seeing the lady again. Even if he were
spinning a half-fabricated tale solely for his readers' entertainment,
Friedl cannot have enjoyed reading this.

Her behaviour grew stranger and more troubling as the year went
on. She had spells of apparent paralysis, hallucinations, severe head-
aches, periods of confusion and absentmindedness. Her determination
not to be left alone strengthened in tandem with a belief that people
were persecuting her. She became obsessed with cleanliness, and after
menstruating would bathe over and again in a *mikveh*, the Jewish ritual
bath that purifies the body. She would become suddenly aggressive,
she spoke of suicide. That November in Frankfurt, Benno Reifenberg
saw her at the Hotel Englischer Hof; Roth was in Berlin at the time.

She had entered a catatonic state. 'We had the impression that she was deliberately paralysed. We took her to Dr Goldstein, a neurologist. The doctor said that she should not be left alone for a moment ... [for] if we left her alone, she could jump out of the window.'[29]

At this distance it is impossible to be sure about the interrelation in Friedl's mind between the general psychological pressures on Jewish women at this time (often pathologised by psychiatrists in gendered terms that Roth also used, e.g. 'hysteria'), the specific strains within her marriage, and the outbreak of a latent mental illness such as schizophrenia, which often derives from a genetic predisposition. After initially disregarding Friedl's opinion, Roth preferred to think of her symptoms as having an external cause and became convinced that he was responsible for her plight. If the condition had been triggered by his behaviour, then by his logic this meant it should be rectifiable: there had to be a cure. In Berlin, he summoned a doctor to examine her. Dr Ernst Wollheim later recalled: 'I first saw Friedl in a horrible corner room in the Hotel am Zoo. It was clearly a schizophrenic case; the woman lived in a private world and had lost contact with reality.'[30] She had been found walking naked in the hotel corridor, and tried to enter the lobby but was restrained by two parlour maids. Roth's insistence it could be cured led him to argue with doctors who suggested otherwise. 'About the word "schizophrenia", Roth became angry,'[31] Wollheim said.

First his father had succumbed to madness, but now his wife? The idea was too much to accept. He could not countenance the same devastating loss being visited upon him again, and perhaps too there was a sense of shame, a residue of the stigma attached to mental illness back in Brody. Roth was adamant that 'the illness was acquired and imagined that his wife could be cured', said Dr Wollheim. 'I persuaded him that schizophrenia is a hereditary disease in which current environmental factors do not play a decisive role, and he had no choice but to accept the case as incurable. But Roth remained completely unteachable. He continued to hold the opinion that he was to blame for his wife's condition, without giving any further reasons for this.'[32] Friderike Zweig witnessed the same behaviour. 'The situation was made worse for him by the fact that he indulged in self-reproach and studied many books on mental illness to see whether his behaviour could be to blame for her illness.'[33]

His guilt grew overwhelming and the pain unbearable. He sought to numb it whenever possible. In Soma Morgenstern's recollection, the summer of 1928 was when Roth's already excessive drinking escalated into something altogether more systematic and serious. 'In the time when the singing brothers in Vienna were singing, drinking beer and throwing up all over the city, Roth introduced me to one of his friends who had an influence on him in the early Twenties,' he said. At first the Social Democratic Party-supporting journalist Hugo Schulz had helped to shape Roth's political views, then he proved himself invaluable in 1921 when he submitted a supporting statement during Roth's previous wrangle over citizenship papers. Now he schooled Roth in another matter. On first seeing the two men together, Morgenstern was struck by Roth's 'almost disciple-like attitude' towards the two-decades-older Schulz. Initially he thought Roth simply admired his politics, intellect and wit. Soon he came to a different conclusion, 'that Roth was his student as a drunkard'. Schulz was an alcoholic, and Roth appeared to look up to him and follow his lead. 'He always ordered what Schulz ordered and drank in the intervals and in the order of the master. Drinking also needs to be learned before it becomes a way of life.'[34]

In this environment Roth's work rate began to resemble someone running on an accelerating treadmill. He was exhausted but he kept sprinting: chasing the money he needed, fleeing the dread that pursued him. He became volatile, and his innately suspicious outlook tipped over into paranoia. When Benno Reifenberg suggested at short notice that Roth make his previously mooted trip to Italy, he bristled. Why did they suddenly want him out of the way? What was Reifenberg planning to do in his absence? Were the editorial board using him as a pawn to open up commercial opportunities there?

He visited Rome in October 1928. This brought further problems. While there he produced a series of four articles, which appeared under the title 'The Fourth Italy', Mussolini's description of his new fascist state.* The first piece compared fascists Roth met there with the bolshevists he'd mixed with in Russia. The second noted the photographic portraits of Mussolini wherever one looked in Rome, and described the indoctrination of schoolchildren, who had to repeat a new catechism that almost all the bishops had approved: 'I am Italy, your mistress, your God'; 'I believe in the genius of Mussolini', 'in our Holy Father, fascism, and in the communion of martyrs' and 'in the conversion of the Italians and the resurrection of the Empire – Amen'. In the third, he described the porter at his hotel, who offers to post the guests' letters – but the solicitousness Roth usually admires in hotel staff does not apply here, for the man is almost certainly an informer to the secret police. On arrival guests were met by this man requesting they hand over their passports – a particularly sensitive matter for Roth, who had only just managed to regain his, and for whom it symbolised his freedom. Who did this man think he was, a porter or a border guard? The intrusion of the state into the international space of a hotel struck at Roth's core. You could not be a *Hotelpatriot* in Mussolini's Italy. The piece outlines how fascism was crushing liberty there, how every public meeting must first be approved by the police, how no one was issued a passport for foreign travel.

But readers would not have known all he wished them to know of this, because someone in the *Frankfurter Zeitung* office removed the comments most critical of Mussolini and his regime. The chronology is unclear, but it seems plausible that this happened during a month-long gap before Roth produced the final feuilleton on Italy, published on 22 December 1928. It is a broadside ostensibly attacking supine Italian journalism but containing remarks that those in the know must have read as barbs at his own editors. 'We know how fascism has taken hold of the Italian press,' he began with, later adding:

> The Italian journalist, being controlled, is no longer a journalist.
> Not only is he not free to write what he wants, in theory he must

---

* The previous three great Italian eras being the Roman period, the medieval period that saw the spread of Catholicism, and the Renaissance.

be shaped in a way that he is not able to write anything forbidden. As a consistent yes-man, he follows the decrees, orders, resolutions and measures of the government. He is not a critic, but an echo ...

A new species of journalist ... the boring journalist, is developing. (He also exists here, but not as an ideal.) Open any Italian newspaper! Their hallmark is boredom ... What does the reader find in the Italian newspaper? An exhibitionism of ideology, protected by law. Yet another report about a gallant gesture of the dictator. Here he visited, there he encouraged, there he shook hands with an ordinary man, clapped the shoulders of a soldier, helped an old mother back to her feet. All the imperial anecdotes from our old, disused school books have come back to life in modern Italian newspapers.[35]

Mussolini's admirers, like the Soviets, might argue that any capitalist-owned press was no better, and the newspapers were only a mouthpiece for the interests of capital, but Roth was having none of it: 'even journalists who are observed closely by the publisher can express their opinions better than writers employed by the government whose thoughts are fascistically pre-censored and to whom the censor is nothing but their own reflection'.[36]

No one would control Roth and stop him writing what he wanted. No one would transform him from a critic into an echo. No one would make him boring. No one would censor him. Even if he were 'observed closely' by the *Frankfurter Zeitung*'s editors, he would continue to express his own opinions. In late 1928 he wired Reifenberg to say that he proposed resigning over the editor Heinrich Simon's obstructive attitude towards him. The diplomatic Reifenberg seems to have enticed him back, once again assuming the unenviable role of mediator between the paper's most brilliant, tempestuous contributor and the senior staff he antagonised. Roth swallowed his pride. This contretemps coincided with a painful miscalculation concerning *The Younger Brother*. Roth abandoned Wolff Verlag because he thought S. Fischer would pay better, but this plan backfired when Fischer rejected his hastily completed manuscript. His finances gave him little other

option but to remain at the newspaper, aside from the precarious business of eliciting support from his friends. That Reifenberg was a good
friend as well as a colleague became clear by the end of this episode.
Perhaps he felt Roth had been hard done by and sympathised with his
predicament. His may not have been a 'grand house', but it was built
on stabler foundations than Roth's. By January 1929 a grateful Roth
had reason to write him these lines: 'I know how hard it is for you to
send me money, but still I have no option but to take it. I am simply
too wretched . . . I am still a wreck, a long way from being whole. Who
knows if I ever will be again.'[37]

For all his emotional intelligence and facility with words, numbers
had made him feel like a dunce since his schooldays. In his head or on
the page they jiggled and vanished; he never could keep them steady
under his gaze. 'Sometimes he tried to account for the money he got
through,' he would write of the drink–sodden, melancholic Lieutenant
Carl Joseph von Trotta in *The Radetzky March*. 'But he could never
remember the individual expenses, and sometimes he couldn't do the
simple addition. He couldn't do figures. His little notebooks told a tale
of desperate attempts to keep order. Endless columns of figures were
drawn up on every page. But they became muddled and confused, he
lost his grip on them, they added themselves up and misled him with
their wrong totals, they galloped away under his very eyes, to return
a moment later subtly altered and impossible to recognise. He wasn't
even able to keep track of his debts. The interest payments he didn't
understand. What he lent others was dwarfed by what he owed, as a
hill is dwarfed by a mountain.'[38]

It is not so hard to see why two publishers rejected Roth's manuscript.
In 1929 it was picked up instead by the Gustav Kiepenheuer Verlag in
Berlin, and published with a different title, *Right and Left* (*Rechts und
Links*). There are brilliant passages, of course, but the story barely hangs
together. It feels dashed off in places, uneven, imbalanced by the mis-
timed arrival of a character who then hogs centre stage. All told, it is a
markedly weaker book than *Rebellion* and *Zipper and His Father*. *Right*

and Left is another tale of a feckless father and rootless sons, set in bourgeois Berlin, where Paul Bernheim and his younger brother Theodor
enjoy a cossetted upbringing courtesy of the wealthy Felix Bernheim.
Again the story begins before the war. Paul is a talented, handsome,
conceited young man who moves skittishly between fads and pleasures:
art, dancing, fencing, visiting brothels, to name a few. Theodor is, like
Caesar in *Zipper*, the disappointing son, a talentless, self-aggrandising
liar. Like his namesake in *The Spider's Web*, Theodor seeks meaning and
direction in antisemitic, nationalistic politics, this despite the fact their
mother is Jewish. Frau Bernheim is a forlorn figure aggrieved by her
sons' reluctance to marry. Roth has her utter a foolish remark that must
have dripped with irony for friends who read the novel. 'The young
people are sensible,' she says to Paul. 'They marry quickly, which is
healthy and guarantees a long life.'[39] By the late 1920s, Roth considered
his hasty marriage more likely to accelerate him towards the grave.

The chief interest in *Right and Left* lies in realising the degree to
which, under pressure of time and as an exercise in psychological
self-analysis, Roth had begun overtly to mine his autobiography for
material that he could analyse through the actions of avatars for himself, in this case Paul Bernheim and a Russian–Jewish financier named
Nikolai Brandeis. It is thus a book of more interest to a biographer
than a reader. If Roth's creative process had become akin to a kalei-
doscope filled with colourful shards of autobiography, here he gives
it another twist. We've seen the elements before in his novels, letters,
autobiographical sketches and feuilletons; what has changed is their
arrangement and relation to one another.

Paul Bernheim has much in common with the image of himself
Roth preferred to project: born to a Jewish mother and gentile father,
he develops into a clever and precocious student, he is a chivalrous
and sophisticated urbanite in the habit of giving women roses, and he
serves with honour in the war. He is a combination of what Roth had
been and claimed to be. He is in some ways Roth's fantasy of himself,
a liberated alter ego without the disadvantages; he's born with similar
talents but into money instead of poverty, handsome instead of lugubrious, in cosmopolitan Berlin instead of a muddy *shtetl*, and with a father

whose financial success eases his start in life, rather than without a father, whose only legacy was his son's chronic feeling of abandonment.

Like Roth, at school Bernheim stood apart from the other boys, already having 'one foot in the bigger world outside. The voices of his classmates echoing in his ear, he sat in the classroom like a visitor. He never altogether belonged.'[40] But Roth's was a childhood of stigma and making do; Bernheim's one of ostentatious wealth. Early in the novel, while Paul is at the University of Oxford, his father Felix dies at sea after boarding a steamer at Marseilles in the company of a young woman, as Roth had wished he could instead of remaining tied to a sobbing Friedl. He grows distant from his widowed mother. He imagines her dead and feels no sorrow. He cannot quite understand his indifference to her, but there it is, there's no denying it.

The war uproots Paul from his university studies. As the Yiddish-speaking *Ostjuden* used to say – in a phrase that hangs over Roth's increasingly ironic and fatalistic works from hereon – *Mann tracht un Gott lacht:* Man makes plans and God laughs. Whereas Roth started the war as a pacifist and midway through enlisted to fight, Bernheim immediately volunteers, quits midway through as 'an embittered paci-fist', then returns to fight. When he travels to the eastern front, like Roth and Józef Wittlin he desires 'the most powerful experiences, the gravest dangers, the worst assignments'.[41] After the war he must make his way in the Berlin business world. Like Roth in Russia, Paul is crushed on days when he receives no post. It must mean no one is thinking of him, which means no one cares. Roth makes plain such imaginings are paranoid and egocentric, a wry self-chastisement per-ceptible to those informed readers (Friedl, Benno Reifenberg, Bernard von Brentano) whom he had berated for their failure to correspond with sufficient frequency. 'On days when his letter-box was empty, he felt doubly abandoned. Such days turned him to pessimism and superstition. He imagined there was some hostile power that kept his correspondents from writing to him, or imprisoned their letters at the post office, or caused them to disintegrate in the mailbags in the post-man's van ... So, all day yesterday and the day before, no one gave me a thought, Paul would say to himself when his letter-box was empty. I have many friends, but I am all alone. Not even [his girlfriend] Marga has written to me.'[42]

At one stage Paul is suicidal. He has a predisposition to melancholy. In a Berlin police station he stands aghast by a display case of photographs of disfigured, unidentified corpses, as Roth had done in 1923. 'So many people quit this life – and no one even knew who they were.'[43] Later he imagines his own face in that grim gallery. At different times he and Theodor need loans, whereupon Roth's narrator offers a defence of mendicancy that is almost admirable in its *chutzpah*. He claims that people who 'feel no compunction when asking for love or friendship'[44] but who have qualms about requesting financial support are actually inhumane, because it means they value money more than human connection. Money is nothing compared to love. And so a *Schnorrer* dons the mask of a *Mensch*.

One-third of the way in, Nikolai Brandeis appears, approaching Bernheim as a business partner. Brandeis is closer to the Franz Tunda aspect of Roth's fragmented self, a rootless traveller who ends the novel adrift, resolved to leave Berlin without knowing where he's bound. The great difference, though, between Brandeis and Bernheim on the one side, and Roth and Tunda on the other, is wealth. These men have money. Both are nouveaux riches: Brandeis is self-made, as was Felix Bernheim. Like Paul Bernheim, and in common with the falsified ancestry Roth liked to present in which his father was an Austrian or Polish nobleman, Brandeis too is half Jewish. He grew up in 'a little German settlement in the Ukraine', like the Schwabendorf colony that Roth claimed as his place of birth. He felt it 'had been a truer version of Germany than the country itself'. He remembers the 'Swabian faces of his playmates', and reflects on his father, 'whom he had lost at a relatively young age'.[45]

By sketching Brandeis's origins, Roth writes briefly for the first time about his homeland in the lyrical, nostalgic register that would predominate in his next book. For now, he spends a page lavishing on the reader the sensory delights of a February day in Ukraine: the cobalt sky with near-white tinges 'as if it had iced over there'; the wintry sun that makes the icicles drip until the north-east wind regathers itself to freeze them hard again; the silver birches shimmering in the twilit woodland; the aroma of burning twigs drifting into town from the fields where workers roasted potatoes on bonfires; the ice that 'would splinter like glass under your heel' when you walked the pathways across the marshes; the waning moon, the blue will-o'-the-wisps that hung over the fields 'like terrestrial stars'.[46] Brandeis's nostalgia is Roth's for Brody.

By now, Roth's scathing fictional depictions of nationalists and their notion of Germanness had made him a figure of loathing for their real-life equivalents, whose anger at him would surely only have intensified on reading *Right and Left*. The contemptible Theodor becomes a member of the God and Iron Society, intending to 'restore order in Germany, topple the government, ban the Bolsheviks and the Jews, light fires of celebration and declare war'.[47] But he ends up needing a job and, thanks to Brandeis pulling strings, he has no option but to accept one on a Jewish newspaper, the ultimate indignity. Paul marries into the wealthy Enders family, who own a chemical-making business; ammonia production was a growth industry in the new Germany, and a symbol of the 'progress' Roth had come to despise. The novel stumbles to its conclusion. It's as if Roth grew bored of his original premise midway and drifted into territory he found more engaging.

At the outset the novel promised to be a study of the making of a nationalist, presented in greater depth than *The Spider's Web* and examining the familial resentments and secret doubts over the authenticity of one's identity that might forge such an aggressive mindset. By the end it has mutated into one of a shady Jewish financier whose manipulations and callous self-preservation draw from the stereotypes promulgated by characters such as the two Theodors, Lohse and Bernheim. Brandeis is cold, cunning and ruthless, but he is also plainly a character with whom Roth identifies. If Roth gave credence to antisemitic stereotypes, perhaps this was because he felt they were true of himself. This caricature slips into view on his own agenda and vanishes again. Brandeis is a self-absorbed and solitary wandering Jew. He has no loyalty to people or places. In the end, his lover leaves him, and he decides to move on. 'I may not be back,' he says. 'I don't have the ability to stay in one place for a long time ... She left, and perhaps that's why I'm leaving too. I don't know what keeps me in a place, or what makes me leave it.'[48] At the end he thinks to himself: 'Where shall I go? All the world's ports are waiting for me.'[49] He'll head for a port, unmarried, and see where the tides take him. Roth, however, must return to securing his wife's psychiatric care, venturing back into her dark forest to keep her from the wolves.

The divisions within the self created by a hyphenated identity fracture further if you uproot from your homeland and try to assimilate into another. You feel peripheral to both, as if standing in a doorway between two crowded rooms, a double outsider; so you retreat into introversion, becoming akin to an inverted Janus where both faces look inwards. Marginality becomes central to your being: if you leave the *Ostjuden* to become Viennese, your centre lies at both groups' margins. You stand in doorways, you live on borders, you are a cuneus between nations, and as you try to bridge the two tribes within yourself you feel like a hyphen. You are neither one nor another, but familiar with both. With effort, you can pass for either (but the effort is greater than you let on, and secretly feels unsustainable; even if you return 'home' to your origins, you find it has changed in your absence and you feel estranged, like a returning soldier). This residency in a psychological borderland equips you well to be a double agent, a crafty transgressor slipping back and forth between realms like a Nikolai Brandeis, a Benjamin Lenz, or the furtive Kapturak who will scurry through your novels in the 1930s; but not to be a happy human being. Sure, you can step into a crowded room and mingle – alcohol will embolden you here – but you will always feel an outsider pulling off an act. You try to posit your separation as a virtue for a writer: a solitary onlooker can describe the form of a crowd better than someone in the crowd. You can look at France as if from Germany, at Galicia as a Viennese, at the Jews as a Catholic, at the socialists as a conservative; and for each vice versa. But you cannot stop looking within yourself too: you examine each fragment of your identity from its opposite perspective and find it incomplete, and your presentation as a member of that tribe unconvincing, even fraudulent.

Nothing is quite true and strong enough to withstand your fierce scrutiny. The eastern Jew in you detests your dilution of identity for social gain; the western metropolitan feels an antisemitic disgust that your 'voice smells of onions'. You can hate yourself from both perspectives. *It makes for an atrocious life.* You thus place immense value on personal relationships: if you are not an authentic part of a tribe or a nation, feeling wanted by individual friends becomes a vital source of security and validation. And a drink can kindle a fraternity with fellow drinkers; it can warm and soften the world into a home; but then comes the hangover, and the world cools and hardens, and you are isolated, alone, once again outside society. With a hangover you see too clearly. All illusions vanish, your failings are laid bare, everyone seems transparent. *I see through a magnifying glass. I peel the skins off people and things to see their hidden secrets.* In the Midi the limpid sunlight sharpened the world into revelatory clarity; but in the hungover Parisian dawn, everything is too sharp to touch. It may still be the morning, but you pour a cognac. To soften the world, to ready you for a new day, to start again.

Four letters written from the Hôtel Foyot in Paris in February and March 1929 pinpoint the peripatetic, chaotic, beleaguered condition that had become normalised for Roth. The first three elicit sympathy for his sadness. The last is shocking: it suggests a man in accelerating descent towards sociopathy, someone who has grown accustomed to dangerous thoughts and no longer cares who knows it.

'I haven't lived in a house since my eighteenth year, aside from the odd week staying with friends,' he told Stefan Zweig on 27 February, preferring to forget his and Friedl's spell in 1922 renting in Berlin. 'Everything I own fits into three suitcases. It doesn't strike me as at all odd, either. What is odd, though, to me, and even romantic, is a house, with pictures on the walls, and so on and so forth. In a fit of mindlessness, I took on the responsibility for a young woman. I need to keep her somewhere, she is frail, and physically not up to a life at my side.'[50]

On the same day he writes to Félix Bertaux. He says he's working on his novel twelve hours a day to finish the final thirty pages. The plan is to write one page a day for a month. He doesn't say which, but this is probably *Perlefter: The Story of a Bourgeois* (*Perlefter: Die Geschichte eines Bürgers*), which he would never complete. Friedl has been largely bedridden for weeks. They've recently returned from Marseilles, where he couldn't leave their hotel room. In response to Bertaux's proposal to translate Roth into French, he says: 'I cannot tell you what it would mean to me to be read by a generation of young Frenchmen.' For France he holds out 'the fond hope that simple human freedom will never be lost in this country, as it has been in others. Maybe I can convey to the odd young Frenchman what a terrible thing unfreedom is for the individual. By way of warning!'[51]

On 7 March, he wrote to Bertaux's twenty-one-year-old son Pierre, of whom he had grown deeply fond. He hinted at how his inner torment had begun to find expression in his published work. 'My grief leaks out of private things into the public realm, and that makes it easier to bear, just as, for instance, a war appears more bearable to an individual than a bout of pleurisy. So far as my wife is concerned, her present illness is only an acuter version of her chronic weakness, a complete lack of resistance, in which I am not without blame. There are various causes. These things, of which I have been unable to speak for months, if not for years, oppress me more than the form of the illness itself. Perhaps in another ten years I will be able to write about them, if I am still a writer then. For now, I drag them around with me, and torment myself.'[52]

Bernard von Brentano had been Roth's great hope among the younger writers on the *Frankfurter Zeitung*. He was 'decent',[53] he had 'talent',[54] he merited kindness: when Brentano's father died in 1927, Roth wrote a notably touching letter assuring him that 'If you feel too alone, then . . . I am standing at your shoulder – now, and in every enterprise in which you should feel in danger or alone.'[55] Roth's fear in Russia of having misjudged his character seemed unfounded. They rekindled contact after that trip, for a spell. But between 20 September 1927, when Roth praised his abilities and urged him to avoid 'scheming Jews', and 28 March 1929, when Roth wrote again to Pierre Bertaux, something changed. 'Your description of your meeting with Brentano was very amusing,' Roth told Bertaux:

I know exactly that you will have gotten excited to no end with him, because he is one of those people who will go on and talk to others, using your arguments, and simultaneously bad-mouth you. If Brentano is as unhappy as you say he is, then with every reason. No one has merited unhappiness as much as he. I only fear he won't be unhappy enough. Another thirty years of life for a creature like that are in my view too many. In thirty years, he can wreak much more destruction. He is one of three or four people I would happily murder, with no more compunction than putting out a cigarette. I don't know if you're acquainted with the feeling that removes any so-called humanity in you, and renders absurd the notion that killing a human being was anything special. Sometimes I feel the murderer in me is as natural as the writer, and if I were arrested and put on trial, I would be utterly perplexed.

I'm fairly sure that my name will have been sufficient cause for an argument between you and him. I am a red rag to him, just as he to me is a slavering dog. His brain is mad, his heart is weak, his tongue is glib and stupid. I have no sort of magnanimity or 'Christian feeling' for those who dislike me, and not sufficient dignity. I will hurt them as much as possible, with cunning and violence, and am only waiting for the opportunity of murdering them in a deserted alleyway.*[56]

In August 1929 Friedl's condition worsened. On 2 September Roth wrote from Berlin to Stefan Zweig in Salzburg with dire news: 'Since we last saw each other, a lot of very grim things have happened. My wife was taken to the psychiatric hospital at Westend in a very bad

---

* Michael Hofmann on this: 'Roth's friend, sometime roommate ... and editor, Hermann Kesten, is troubled by this letter, and gives it a long note, to the effect that one shouldn't take it seriously, and that Roth never actually hurt a fly. According to Kesten, Roth turned on most of his friends at some time or other, but more in the spirit of a literary joke, playing with them as with the characters in a novel. "He was more concerned with artistic truth than with reality. Roth had a very strict artistic conscience." While accepting this – especially the last sentence – one shouldn't shy away from accepting that Roth all his life was quick to take offence, and was ... a ferocious, gifted, principled, and implacable hater.' *A Life in Letters*, p. 138.

state, and for some weeks I've been unable to write a line, and compel myself to scribble just enough to keep body and soul together. I'll spare you any more detailed account of my condition. The word "torment" has just acquired a very real and substantial content, and the feeling of being surrounded by misfortune as by high black walls doesn't leave me for a second.'[57]

Roth went to Salzburg to stay with the Zweigs. Friedl spent the rest of the year in psychiatric care. In December, Roth told the writer René Schickele: 'I am writing in a desperate plight. Yesterday I fled to Munich. My wife has been very sick since August. Psychosis, hysteria, suicidal feelings, she's barely alive – and I'm chased and assailed by black and red demons, without a mind, unable to lift a finger, impotent and paralysed, helpless, with no prospect of ever getting out. Perhaps I can crawl away somewhere in Salzburg for a couple of weeks, alone with my misfortune. I don't know what the coming days will bring, but would like to see you.'[58] At the end of the year, despite showing little sign of improvement, Friedl was released from psychiatric care to stay with her parents in Vienna.

On 24 August 1929 Arab rioters in Hebron killed at least sixty-seven Jews in the belief that they were planning to seize the Temple Mount, a massacre that terminated centuries of Jewish presence in the city. Roth's response was to gauge the diasporic Jewish reaction by walking through Berlin's Jewish quarter; he would not in any case have wished to visit Palestine, but he deemed it 'better to be with the bereaved than the dead'.[59] Exacerbated no doubt by the trials in his personal life – the resulting piece's publication in September coincides with Friedl's hospitalisation – his tone is irritable and contemptuous until finally it is splenetic. On entering Grenadierstrasse he regretted the shop signs' mutation from 'the comely roundness of European Antiqua type' to the 'stiff, frozen, jagged seriousness' of Hebrew script. It was with those mournful letters that on Mount Sinai God had given the Jews the laws they were to spread among the 'cheerful, blithe peoples of the world'; but if they were God's chosen people, Roth reflected that it takes 'a truly divine love to choose' them. 'There were so many others that were nice, malleable, and well trained ... The weakest and far from loveliest of peoples was given the most dreadful curse and most dreadful blessing, the hardest law and the most difficult mission: to sow love on earth, and reap hatred.'[60]

Now they were heading collectively in the wrong direction, he said. Zionism had innate flaws: not only was it a nationalism, it was one for a people who were 'no nation [but] a kind of supranation'.[61] By pursuing it the Jews were demonstrating that 'the view of [them] as cleverer than other peoples is erroneous. Not only are they not cleverer, they are even sometimes more stupid. They aren't ahead of the times, but if anything lagging behind. They are aping the recently failed European ideologies.'[62] At the end of a decade that had seen nationalism fray the bonds of European civilisation, it was plain to Roth that the Jews today were not being led by the 'seven wise men of Zion', as dubiously claimed in the Protocols of the Elders of Zion. The Jews' constitution predisposed them to wander, he claimed, not settle – 'In seeking a "homeland" of their own, they are rebelling against their deeper nature.'[63] Roth wished to remain a wanderer, but he felt he was in a minority now, in opposition to 'several hundred thousand idiots of Zion, who have failed to understand the destiny of their people'.[64] His anger had grown volcanic: it boiled and churned within him until it burst out into view.

He would never settle, he knew that now. For all that he dreamed of a place where he felt at home, he had no expectation that one in the physical realm would make him happy for long: he would feel trapped and start to look towards the railway station. He favoured his imagination over reality and movement over stasis. Better to dream of home, better to wander: to travel in hope, rather than to arrive, settle and be disappointed. Better always to live from the three suitcases, packed and ready for departure. One man's rootlessness was another man's freedom. To assimilate but have the ever-present option to pull out and leave: that was the preferred condition, and one offered by hotel living. Those who did not assimilate – well, he despaired of their detachment while admiring their authenticity. Those who did assimilate – he sympathised, for he knew the loss it entailed and the pain of inauthenticity, the psychological exhaustion incurred in performing to 'pass'. To be a Jew was to stand at odds with the world; but to be an assimilated Jew was also to stand at odds with oneself. And suddenly the unassimilated eastern Jew seemed again to have the right idea. He ricocheted between which condition was worse, and seems never to have reached a conclusive position; perhaps this turmoil is what he meant when he told Soma Morgenstern that he suffered from 'assimilitis'. It would explain his outbursts of rejecting the whole fraught business of being a Jew, the moments when he seems to have thought . . . *to hell with it all – to hell with nations, with collectives, with tribes and the volk; damn the Jews, damn Jewishness, I won't be tied to anyone else, I'll sever all ties and assert my freedom, I'll be a true individual.* Then he felt terribly alone. He felt abandoned, isolated, adrift. Where were his friends when he needed them? Why did no one write?

The present looked grim from whichever angle he viewed it: personal, political, professional. The past looked preferable. He dwelled on the prelapsarian days before the trauma of the war. The days when childhood remained within reach, when a writer could make a living, when the Habsburgs' rule stitched together a swathe of Europe, when no one had heard of National Socialism, before drink, before he had heard of schizophrenia, when he was unmarried and free. To remember and reimagine the home he'd abandoned offered a few moments' retreat from the heavy sadness that weighed upon him. He toyed with the idea for a novel that had come to him in Russia, the great story that only he could tell. He had brushed against this territory in describing Nikolai Brandeis's homeland, and now his first pass at fleshing out this uniquely personal world took the form of a novel he proposed to call *Strawberries* (*Erdbeeren*). He took to storing the manuscript in the box his mother left him, with his prayer book and *tefillin*: it had become a reliquary of his abandoned Jewish childhood, the natural place to store this rumination on his Brody days. The manuscript peters out after thirty pages, but they contain some of the most gorgeous prose he would ever write, descriptive of youth in an unnamed eastern town. Roth's tone is soft, reflective, lyrical and sad, and yet also ironic, laconic, sly and drily funny: in every respect a striking contrast with the spiky lines that fill his letters at this time. What he describes is beautiful, which might make us happy were it not for the fact we sense it is irretrievably lost. This is his severed childhood of sparkling night skies. The little town was poor. People had no money, so they depended on miracles; that and assistance from the benevolent local count. The town is home to people like Pantaleimon, the gravedigger and thief; the patrician count, who doles out coins from his castle's veranda; and Manes Kroy, the narrator's flame-bearded, alcoholic father, who fell drunkenly from his sled one winter night and froze to death on the roadside ... the kind of characters Roth summoned up when telling his rapt Berlin friends tales of the east over drinks at a Kurfürstendamm café.

His narrator, Naphtali Kroy, lives in the west now but back in the home town he worked for a tailor, until a glazier of their acquaintance accused him of stealing a glass-cutting diamond. Kroy denies it, though soon after that he tells the reader he's a liar, and that he had 'learned there's no point telling the truth'.[65] Is that another lie? Where is the borderline between truth and fiction? Wherever it is, it is porous and Kroy slips back and forth like a Brody smuggler. If Kroy is dishonest, has this trait been cultivated by his experience of assimilated life in western Europe – in cities where Jews had to mask their identity to avoid persecution, and were thus accused of being liars? Where they needed false papers to prove their true identity? Kroy describes himself as a *Hochstapler* – an impostor or conman, an ironic self-description from an author who has just been driven half mad by the process of convincing the Viennese passport authorities he's not an impostor. 'That's what they call people in Europe who claim to be something other than what they really are. It's no different from what every Western European does. Only, they aren't conmen, because they have papers, passports, identity cards, birth certificates. Some even have family trees. Whereas I have a false passport, no birth certificate, and no family tree. So it's fair to say: Naphtali Kroy is a conman. In my homeland I didn't need any papers. Everyone knew who I was.'[66]

No proof of identity is needed in Roth's dream-home, because the authorities had no authority; there were policemen, but you could get drunk with them, and it was essentially a lawless town, therefore largely peaceful: people quietly sorted out their problems without recourse to the law. No intrusive state controlling people's lives such as he'd seen in Russia and Italy, no ideology. No talk of 'nationality' either; no one deferred to such foolish ideas – such arbitrary divisions were not recognised, 'because everyone spoke every language'.[67] There were no walls between people, they mingled like the Celts, Romans, Gauls, Germans and Phoenicians of Avignon. Well, almost. There was one exception. Only the Jews remained detached from this hybrid culture, preserving their own ways, distinctive in their hats and caftans, standing apart and alone, presenting a silent face to the gentile world. 'For a thousand years nothing good had ever come of it when a peasant asked a question and a Jew replied,'[68] as Roth observed elsewhere around this time. Distrust of Christians was wired into the eastern Jewish mindset by hard experience; *shtetl* Jews thus often kept to themselves, which led to their being labelled aloof and alien. Psychological walls and fences that aggrieved the goyim: what was over there, what were they hiding? What wealth, what sins, what strange practices? So here in the little town, as in any other *shtetl*, there were pogroms now and then. Roth implies that any town will occasionally kill its Jews, as if it's inevitable, a universal law, whether in Galicia or Palestine. They were soon forgotten. 'The murdered Jews were put in the ground, and the plundered ones denied they'd lost anything.'[69]

Those are the people; but now, more than before in his fiction, Roth attends to conjuring the place. Aspects of the landscape he describes sound idyllic, others bleak, but the language is always sensuous. He relishes evoking a pastoral setting in a way we haven't seen before in his novels. In winter, black trees stood stark against snowy fields and white skies, and the houses were festooned with icicles that hung from the roofs 'like tassels with rigor mortis'.[70] The frosted autumn landscape had tones of 'molten gold and molten silver', and ravens swarmed in the skies. In September fallen leaves filled the streets, no one bothered to sweep them away; he'd never seen such a thing until he came to the west. 'The sun was still very hot, and already very slant and very yellow. It went down in a red west, and rose every morning from a bed

of silver and mist.'[71] It rained often, but the 'rains were soft, water in
its most velvety form'. By May, the white skies had been painted a rich
blue. Nature enfolded and nurtured the townspeople, giving them sus-
tenance. The terrain supplied what their bodies needed, unlike a city.
In the autumn, they went to the fields to roast potatoes; in the spring,
stealthily to the forests to pick forbidden strawberries. Sometimes the
forester caught them, emptied their baskets and trampled the fruit
into the ground. The more he trampled, the more seeds embedded in
the mulch, the more strawberries would grow. This bountiful, wild
place thwarted German ideas about delineating and defining property
and identity.

Such rural scenes would figure in almost every novel to come, usually
summoned through a few recurrent aural symbols: the song of unseen
crickets, frogs and skylarks, the last of which may be understood in a
post-First World War context as a form of 'symbolic literary pastoral',
according to the critic Paul Fussell: 'What the lark usually betokens is
that one has got safely through another night.'[72] He remarks that 'Since
war takes place outdoors and always within nature, its symbolic status
is that of the ultimate anti-pastoral.'[73] To retreat to the pastoral in the
1920s was to recast the countryside as an idyll rather than a battlefield,
to fill the trenches and craters that still scarred and pocked the terrain. It was to erase the mining and petrochemical industries ravaging
swathes of the modern landscape, as Roth described in his journalism;
as such his new preoccupation mirrors the increasingly nationalistic
Wandervogel youth movement that reacted against industrialisation
by communing with nature. But in Roth's case the intention was, as
in *The White Cities*, to subvert the Nazi fixation on '*Blut und Boden*'
(blood and soil): in that book with a paean to the merits of mingling
bloodlines, and here by resurrecting a tolerant life on the land – not
an aggressive vision of the future to be realised by a *Lebensraum** policy

---

* The principle of 'living space', originating in the nineteenth century but popu-
larised by German nationalists from the First World War onwards, that proposed
aggressive territorial expansion as the only way to secure the resources necessary to
sustain German supremacy.

that would disperse the eastern Jews and Slavs, but by depicting a free, multi-ethnic rural past now obliterated by battle and 'progress', reachable solely by fiction or time travel across the chasm of war. Roth's return to the soil eschews Germany's strident nationalism for a sad conservatism; it is not a barked manifesto but a quiet, wistful gaze backwards. His pastoral vision conjures a pre-war world, dispels the smoke that joined up the towns and obscured the sun and the stars. It restores a kind of Austrian Arcadia.

But if a rural town met their physical requirements, only cities could fulfil the cleverest residents' intellectual needs. The little town had produced a stream of geniuses – doctors, astronomers, theologians and businessmen – but they must always move elsewhere to fulfil their potential. To the capitals, to the western nations. They always left a part of themselves behind, something that tugged them back from afar. The fragment concludes with successive visits by three men returning to their home town. One of them, Wolf Bardach, travels from Vienna after the death of his mother, who owned a lucrative steam baths; he inherits her money and builds a grand, New York-style hotel. The town has no need for it. No one stays there, its 200 rooms remain empty, as does the café on its ground floor, where classical music plays to a few canny townsfolk who stand out on the street, listening in free of charge. This folly is a towering symbol of the town's uninterest in western city life, big business, ostentation, and the America-infatuation of Weimar Berlin.

Another rich returnee, the dapper tea merchant Herr Britz, is a near-identical character to Henry Bloomfield in *Hotel Savoy*: he arrives in the frozen midwinter to visit his father's grave amid a hubbub of anticipation from poor folk hoping for money. He becomes the hotel's only resident, taking up five rooms on the ground floor. He distributes cash and goods wherever he goes, 'like an envoy from God'.[74] He amounts to Roth's vision of a Messiah, a returning, rescuing father figure with limitless ready money to bail out those in need. He leaves the townspeople so rich that they can finally pay a team including Naphtali Kroy and Pantaleimon to explore the dangerous seventeenth-century tunnels rumoured to run between the church and the count's castle, where in wartimes long ago the rich were said to have stashed their gold and jewels for safekeeping. They find skeletons, coffins, chests, but no treasure. Still, Kroy was so well paid for the work that it makes no difference to him.

The third wealthy returnee is a Herr Brandes, who comes back after twenty years in London with the aim of bringing better business practices to the old country. He constructs a strange, white-walled building with no windows. Someone who would build such a house must be insane, people murmur ... but it turns out to be a department store. We do not know whether it proves more successful than the hotel, because here that section of manuscript ends. Had it continued, it appears that a theme of the book would have been the lure and peril of homecoming, with an implication that one's home town is a place best visited in the imagination from afar. Roth would now never return to Brody in person, but from hereon would do so time and again in his fiction. *Strawberries* establishes the world he will fill in detail by detail: a little town in the east is the setting for half of his remaining ten novels and novellas. From now on he is like an artist compelled to repaint the same scene, emphasising different details, showing it in different lights, so endlessly fascinated by its possibilities that he can never consider any version as definitive.

In another loosely related fragment, referred to as 'This Morning, a Letter Arrived ...' ('Heute früh kam ein Brief ...') after its opening words, a different first-person narrator tells us Naphtali Kroy has relocated happily to Buenos Aires. This storyteller comes from the same town, a place where people 'have a good memory, because they remember with their hearts. I for my part had almost forgotten them, because I've been living, and still live, in western Europe, where the heart counts for nothing, the head for a little, and the fist for everything.'[75] A pithier summary of German life on the cusp of the 1930s would be hard to find. Roth revives Naphtali Kroy as a character in the other unfinished book he worked on in 1929, *Perlefter*, but that is a different story. As for *Strawberries*, this is all we have. We never learn who stole the glazier's diamond. Roth stowed the manuscript away in his locked box with the intention of returning to it. Friends who knew him through the 1930s said that he saw it as his great unfinished work, always hanging over him. He continued to redraft it but was never satisfied, and it was never completed.

Roth remained angered by his perceived mistreatment at the *Frankfurter Zeitung*. He had been angling to leave for some time, and had had a meeting in Paris with Reifenberg and Heinrich Simon in which they patiently asked the permanently dissatisfied Roth to explain the conditions he would find acceptable to work under, so they could do their best to bring them about. By then the damage had been done, and he was determined to leave. In spring 1929 he was approached by the *Münchner Neueste Nachrichten*, a monarchist, antisemitic, conservative publication owned by a right-wing industrialist named Paul Reusch, who had held talks with Hitler and agreed that the paper would not criticise the Nazi Party. Roth himself had ridiculed the *MNN* in the past, but now he was too disenchanted, depressed and broke to care. He wrote to Zweig: 'I have so little money, and hate all newspapers equally, I wonder if I shouldn't take their offer when it comes.'[76] He took the offer. After agreeing a one-year deal, he received widespread criticism from writers appalled at his hypocrisy. In the *Weltbühne*,* Hans Bauer wrote of recently opening a magazine from 1925 and happening upon 'a particularly excellent article by the excellent writer Joseph Roth'[77] that took a swipe at the lowbrow right-wing rag. The *MNN* had, Roth reported, just organised a lucrative novel-writing competition with a 100,000-mark prize, a sum way beyond any a German author could imagine. And why was it beyond their imagination? 'In a country where newspapers of the quality and ethos of the *Münchner Neueste Nachrichten* are published, writers of quality and ethos cannot fare well.'[78] Bauer wryly noted that after Roth had demonstrated his talent in his sharp 'criticism of the quality of a reactionary newspaper', it had been recognised by said newspaper offering him a job.

---

* The *World-Stage* – founded in 1905, a weekly political and cultural magazine that became a main forum for left-wing discussion during the Weimar years.

Roth hit back at Bauer: 'As we know, four years have passed since 1925, a period during which I might well be allowed to change my mind ... Wherever I write, it becomes "radical", that is: bright, clear and decisive ... I have never shared or even represented the worldview of any newspaper in which I was printed. The decent radicalism that two or three friends of mine, along with myself, have represented and continue to represent in the *Frankfurter Zeitung* is not the radicalism of the *Frankfurter Zeitung* ... Only two facts remain of Hans Bauer's commentary which I can acknowledge: first, that I made a lazy joke about the *Münchner Neuesten* in 1925 (and I regret it); second, that I am an "excellent writer".'[79] The argument was unconvincing, and he probably knew it. He demanded higher standards of other people than this. But the need for money now outweighed such considerations, so from spring 1929 the former '*rote Joseph*', one of the great liberal journalists of Weimar Germany, took the money of a paper that embodied his fears concerning the country's future direction. He would write around thirty apolitical articles for the *Münchner Neueste Nachrichten*, on topics such as Berlin's department stores, a stroll down the Kurfürstendamm, and a misanthropic appraisal of people he'd seen in the city's nightclubs (which he visited 'in a fit of incurable melancholy ... not to cheer myself up, you understand, but to take malicious pleasure at the phenomenon of so much industrialised merriment').[80]

By this time his *Frankfurter Zeitung* colleagues were at their wits' end. Roth had suggested to them that he could simultaneously write for both papers, but Reifenberg dismissed the idea out of hand. On 24 June 1929 Roth wrote them an angry letter, and five days later Reifenberg wrote a careful but damning reply. 'I am well disposed towards you,' he told Roth. 'But I have no intention of helping you to construct moral grounds for leaving the *Frankfurter Zeitung* ... [I] ask you to stop writing me letters like the last one, so that if, in the near or distant future, you should ever consider resuming your work at the *Frankfurter Zeitung*'[81] he should not jeopardise what remained of their relationship. Roth's response a few days later proves he had no interest in reconciliation. He remarks that Reifenberg's assurance that he remains 'well disposed' to Roth suggests the opposite is true, given that they have always been so well disposed to one another that it previously never needed stating; it was mutually understood. He said the *FZ*'s treatment of him had been 'immoral' whereas he was always 'moral', and that the paper's 'radicalism' and 'decency' was 'to a large extent my decency'. With his departure, the *FZ* would thus lose most of its decency. 'You yourself know very well that the glamour of my radicalism has embellished and even legitimised the whole *Frankfurter Zeitung* ... and wherever Joseph Roth writes, it becomes radical, in the privy or in parliament, just as it becomes cool wherever the wind blows. So I remain Joseph Roth as long as I write a line. But the *Frankfurter Zeitung* changes as soon as it loses the lustre of my lines.'

Reifenberg's letter had neglected to address two of Roth's questions, he thundered: a) why was he 'consulting with two dolts' about the publication of one of Roth's articles?, and b) who in the editorial team was responsible for this article not appearing? The two dolts are unnamed but could well have been the paper's film and literature editor Siegfried Kracauer, whom Roth considered likeable but inept, and the overall editor Heinrich Simon. He set out three conditions on which any future working relationship would depend: one, that he would no longer be expected to 'stand shoulder-to-shoulder with unworthy people'; two, that Reifenberg should succeed in advocating Roth's 'radical' work in this inhospitable newspaper that censored his criticisms of fascist states; and three, that he should 'finally acknowledge that a friend like me can be upright and even rude, and is still worth more than a shabby fellowship with rascals'.[82]

The immoral, unworthy dolts and rascals of the *Frankfurter Zeitung* decided at this point that they could survive without Roth's brand of decency, as did his great defender Benno Reifenberg.

As an increasingly volatile Friedl veered between aggression and catatonia, slipping ever further from reach into her own darkness, Roth began to see other women, torn between feelings of guilt, self-loathing and profound relief at the comfort of a lover's touch. Two women enter his story in 1929: one would know him only briefly but always remember him, the other would prove a dominant figure in the final decade of his life. The former was Sybil Rares, who told David Bronsen that 'Roth was my great love.' She was an actress, thirteen years younger than him. They became infatuated with one another. 'In the middle of the year Roth made me cancel my contract and go to Berlin with him,' she said. 'I also spent a few weeks with him in Paris, where we stayed in the enchanting Hôtel Foyot.' In Rares's eyes 'Roth was a wonderful person who saw to the bottom of things. Nothing fake could stand before him.' The combined lifestyles of a performer and a travelling reporter were not conducive to a sustained relationship. 'After a few months I was engaged elsewhere, and Roth for his part was always on the road. That is how we came apart.'[83] Roth gave a little more

Sybil Rares, photographed by Gerty Simon *c.*1929–32.

insight into the relationship's short duration to Géza von Cziffra: 'Sybil was an ideal partner, but not for too long. She was witty, always in a good mood and cheerful. But – do you have any idea how cheerfulness can get on one's nerves?'[84]

He met Andrea Manga Bell at the Berlin home of Lotte Israel, his friend Ernst Toller's partner. She was born Andrea Jimenez Berroa in Hamburg, of German and Afro-Cuban ancestry. Her Cuban father was a music teacher and composer who had studied under Franz Liszt, and her mother was of an old Hamburg family. After the war she married Alexandre Douala Manga Bell, a prince from Cameroon, which had been a German colony until 1916; he had fought for Germany in the war, lived for a spell at the Imperial court in Berlin and was now a medical student in Hamburg. They lived together in hotels in Paris, where Douala Manga Bell had an extravagant, debt-ridden lifestyle; Andrea was accustomed to such men before she met Roth. They had two children there, then she refused to accompany Douala Manga Bell when he returned to Cameroon, preferring to raise them in Germany despite having little money to do so, and despite the country's increasingly racist and intolerant atmosphere.

Roth admired her beauty and her intellect – she was a successful graphic artist and journalist on *Gebrauchsgraphik* magazine – and was

Andrea Manga Bell.

so smitten that her difficult domestic situation seemed a burden worth adding to his already complex life. He sent her a rose every day. She was charmed and equally desirous of him; she told Bronsen of an intense sexual charisma that exuded from him in person but did not register in photographs. 'Actually, Roth was ugly, but he attracted women strongly and there were always those who fell in love with him and who were after him. I have never known another man with so much sexual attraction. He walked slowly like a snail, everything slowed down on him, you never noticed any spontaneous movement, he lurked, every expression was deliberate. But he could be tender like no other and I was completely infatuated with him.'[85] Friedl remained with her parents in Vienna, and Roth continued to care about her, driving himself deeper into despair trying to understand her condition and arrange suitable treatment. This was a duty he would never shirk. But as the new decade began, he tried to justify to himself the idea that in such bleak circumstances, he also had the right to draw comfort from the love of another partner. 'As he saw it, he had been through hard times,' he would soon write of the melancholic, beleaguered Carl Joseph von Trotta in *The Radetzky March*. 'He thoroughly deserved the tender glances of a beautiful woman.'[86]

Chapter Nine

> I find it strange that people don't believe in miracles. They're prepared to believe in anything else, but not in miracles. I have experienced miracles.
>
> Nikolai Brandeis, *Right and Left*

When the nine-year-old Dan Morgenstern met Joseph Roth in Paris in 1938, he told Roth that his father, Soma, had read him passages from Roth's journalism. 'I thought you wrote very clearly,' said Dan. 'I understood everything.' Roth was delighted. As a writer and an individual, he liked to think of himself as someone who dealt in essentials and expressed himself in down-to-earth, accessible terms.

'I'm very pleased that you like things easy to understand,' he said. 'I and your father are *prosty Menschen*.'

The boy, who had been brought up in Vienna, asked what this Galician-sounding phrase meant.

'It's Yiddish for "simple people".'

'What is that word, "*prosty*"?'

Roth explained it had come from Polish and meant nothing more than 'simple'. 'I like that word very much and I say it very often. It's the sound of home for your father and for me.'[1]

Roth was anything but a simple man, but the more complex his life became, the more the idea of being one appealed to him. By the dawn of the 1930s it appealed very much indeed. He had known the story of Job since childhood, had drawn from it before in *Rebellion*, and had since then felt a growing affinity with the afflicted simple man whose faith God tests to near-breaking point. Having set *Strawberries* aside for now, he tried another way into the same territory. This time the little town would have a name, Zuchnow, and the central character would be straightforward and honest rather than a furtive impostor. The previous books were about sons' attitudes to their fathers: this one was from a father's perspective. *Job: The Story of a Simple Man* (*Hiob: Roman eines einfachen Mannes*) describes the trials endured by Mendel Singer – 'pious, godfearing, and ordinary, an entirely commonplace Jew'[2] – who lives with his wife Deborah and their children Jonas, Shemariah and Miriam. More than ever before, it is a story that lays bare Roth's pain; and never had he held such fervent hope for a novel's success, not only in much-needed financial terms but also as catharsis. This would be the most sustained leak of his private grief into the public realm. It marks the beginning of his peak years as a novelist.

The sound of Friedl shouting or screaming had begun to cause problems with her parents' neighbours. At the beginning of 1930, Roth arranged for her to move from the Reichlers' home in Vienna to his friend Stefan Fingal's in Berlin, where they would stay together. There, with her in bed in the next room, Roth worked on a story that examined his despair at her condition, yet risked exacerbating her decline by putting it into the public domain in thinly disguised form. On 20 January he wrote to René Schickele to thank him for an invitation, explaining that he could not

> leave Berlin before my wife's situation has stabilised, at least to the point that I know where she'll be looked after. At the moment, she's with a friend. Every day I need to scrape together money for her, for the nurse, for other necessities. I'm angling for a big travel assignment, so I can leave a couple of thousand marks here, at least in prospect, and wander off. The other thing, the emotional pressure, I shall have to deal with alone. Being an author is actually no help at all. That may be my official designation, but privately I'm just a poor wretch who's worse off than a tram conductor. Only time and not talent can provide us with distance, and I don't have much time left. A ten-year[*] marriage ending like this has the effect of forty,

---

[*] Actually a little less than eight years' marriage, though they had been a couple for a decade.

and my natural tendency to be an old man is horribly supported by external misfortunes. Eight books to date, over 1,000 articles, ten hours' work a day, every day for ten years, and today, losing my hair, my teeth, my potency, my most basic capacity for joy, not even the chance of spending a month without financial worries. And that wretch literature! I come from a time when you were a Greek and a Roman if you followed an intellectual occupation, and I stand there now like a stranger in the midst of this ghastly Anglo-Saxonism, that sentimental Americanism that rules the roost in Germany.[3]

Schickele too had been suffering with a debilitating ailment, in his case eczema. 'Go to a miracle man, not a doctor!' advised the man who despaired of medical professionals' ability to help his wife, before signing off: 'Kiss your dear wife's hand for me. In heartfelt warmth, your sad Joseph Roth.'[4]

Roth dreamed of finding a cure. In his imagined world Friedl stopped threatening suicide, recovered her lost self, and returned to him.* But in reality he was losing her, just as he had lost his father. On top of this, a new terror had begun to assert itself: that he would go insane too. He had used the word to describe himself in the 1926 letter to Bernard von Brentano that detailed his 'atrocious life' and would do so again with increasing fervour as the decade progressed; for now, the seed of the idea had taken root. At the dawn of the new decade, then, he found himself immersed in a reprise of his life's defining loss, and fearful of a worse one to come, that of his own mind. His initial dealings with the psychiatric profession had given no cause for hope of a medical solution to Friedl's plight, but still he tried to hope. Now she was back in his care, in bed, quite beyond

---

* R. D. Laing described the 'changes that the "inner" self undergoes' in schizophrenia as follows: '1. It becomes "phantasticized" or "volatilized" and hence loses any firmly anchored identity. 2. It becomes unreal. 3. It becomes impoverished, empty, dead, and split. 4. It becomes more and more charged with hatred, fear, and envy.' During this process, 'Anxiety creeps back more intensely than ever. The unrealness of perception' extends to 'feelings of deadness of the shared world as a whole, to the body, in fact, to all that is, and infiltrate even to the "true" self. Everything becomes suffused with nothingness.' R. D. Laing, *The Divided Self: An Existential Study in Sanity and Madness* (Penguin Books, 2010), Kindle edition, locations 2188 and 2166.

reach, while he sought to balance her needs with his writing commitments. He and Stefan Fingal decided to try a different approach. They brought in a Berlin wonder-rabbi, who proposed to drive out the demons that had taken possession of Friedl's mind. He failed. She crawled around on all fours, screamed that she despised her husband, and mocked him for being fatherless, pointedly calling him by his mother's surname, 'Grübel'. Roth could only continue to research the illness, while hoping that God would emerge from behind the stars and work a miracle.

The biblical Job is a righteous, wealthy man who lives in the land of Uz with many children, servants and animals. In Heaven, God asks Satan's opinion on Job's piety, and Satan replies that Job would soon curse Him if all he held dear were taken away. God permits Satan to test Job but not to kill him – so Satan's emissaries kill his livestock, children and servants. Job tears out his hair in grief but still prays to God. Satan tries again, this time inflicting Job with physical suffering in the form of a rash of sores. Still Job retains his faith, even when his wife tells him to curse God, give up and die. Job's friends Eliphaz, Bildad and Zophar offer counsel; but they anger him by suggesting he never understood others' pain, that he must have done something to merit such suffering, that he should seek God's forgiveness. Another friend enters, named Elihu: he contends that God communicates with humans through visions and physical pain. Recovery from suffering can lend understanding of God's love and care. The story moves from a series of dialogues to a reflection on wisdom: where is it to be found? Why does God afflict the righteous, where is his punishment for the wicked? Job wants to confront God with such questions, but He is elusive; He must be hiding in Heaven. Then He appears from a whirlwind to explain the extent and power of His Creation, mentioning two immense beasts, the Behemoth and Leviathan, that represent the disorder and chaos in His world. A humbled Job acknowledges His power and admits that human knowledge is minimal by comparison. We should accept our sufferings as part of a divine plan too great for us to understand. God asks for a burnt offering, and finally Job is restored – he has many more children, regains his wealth and health, lives to the age of 140 and dies content, 'being old and full of days'.[5]

Roth's Job is not wealthy, but the other significant elements of the biblical legend are present in the novel. Mendel Singer is humble and righteous, a taciturn man with a murmured prayer for every stage of the day. The book's first words tell us he lived 'Many years ago', but we soon gather that the story begins around twenty years before Roth wrote it. What he means is 'before the First World War', the chasmic temporal rift that divided him from a remote era. Mendel lives in a humble house, where he teaches religious studies to a dozen six-year-old boys. His beard is prematurely grey, like Jechiel Grübel's. His wife Deborah is bullish and acerbic, forever finding fault with him, a moveable mountain of a woman whose days are filled with chores and labour. He and Deborah are blessed with a fourth child, Menuchim, and here his trials begin. When the infant is laid down he emits strange, croaking cries during the young scholars' lessons, 'an ugly and profane noise above the Bible's holy verses'.[6] He has no cradle, but rests in a swinging basket suspended from the ceiling, such as Roth had seen in Odessa; his research for *The Wandering Jews* would colour his descriptions here of Jewish living conditions in Russia and America. At thirteen months Menuchim is diagnosed with epilepsy. By now he is grossly disfigured, a misshapen lump of barely animate flesh. Roth's description of his disability is informed by his response to the injured ex-servicemen he witnessed at the macabre funeral parade in Lwów in 1924: 'His great skull hung heavy as a pumpkin on his thin neck,'[7] he writes of Menuchim.* Deborah despairs of contacting God, who seems 'too lofty, too great, too far away, infinitely far away behind an infinite Heaven'.[8] She resolves instead to try an intermediary. She takes him to a wonder-rabbi in the nearby town of Kluczysk, who assures her: 'Menuchim, Mendel's son, will be healed. There will not be many like him in Israel. Pain will make him wise, ugliness good, bitterness

---

* In German: '*Sein grosser Schädel hing schwer wie ein Kürbis an seinem dünnen Hals.*' Compare this with his description in the article titled '*Die Krüppel*': 'Completely loose was his head, a heavy pumpkin on a thin chain of withered skin.' '*Ganz lose sass der Kopf, ein schwerer Kürbis an dünner Kette aus welken Hautlappen.*'

mild, and sickness strong. His eyes will see far and deep. His ears will be clear and full of echoes. His mouth will be silent, but when he opens his lips they will announce good tidings. Have no fear, and go home!'

The kind of words Roth had longed to hear from a doctor for at least two years. When, when, when? asks Deborah. 'After many years,'[9] says the rabbi, who ends the conversation saying he has no more time. He says she must never leave Menuchim's side, however great a burden he is to her. Deborah and Mendel know they can only support him as best they can, and hope and pray for fulfilment of the prophecy.

Their older children mature, while Menuchim does not; he can barely move or speak. He is indeed a burden, and at times his siblings abuse and mistreat him, even immersing him in a barrel where he almost drowns. As they reach adulthood, the army intrudes on all three healthy children's lives. The wall between this *frum* Jewish family and their neighbouring gentile world is breached to devastating effect.

Shemariah and Jonas must go for military training, where they mingle with Cossacks. Jonas, who has adopted the gentile habit of drinking to excess, wants to join the army; Shemariah does not, and the family scrape together the money to pay a notorious fixer named Kapturak,* whose services include arranging for deserters to escape by a silent late-night border crossing. Shemariah emigrates to America, and dispatches a friend named Mac to travel to Zuchnow and hand the family photographs and a letter, in which he explains that his name is now Sam. He has made a new life for himself. America! One way or another, the army has taken away two of Mendel's sons. But for him, the pretty, graceful Miriam's encounter with the Cossacks is more troubling still.

In his memoirs Soma Morgenstern related a conversation with Roth's friend and drinking partner Hugo Schulz, who asked him what he knew of Maria Roth.

'Did you read Roth's *Job*?' replied Morgenstern. 'The wife of Mendel Singer is exactly a portrait of his mother.'

---

* Who made a vivid debut in *The Silent Prophet*, extracts of which were published in newspapers in 1929 before Roth abandoned it; evidently he knew he had created one of his most memorable characters and resolved to work him into *Job* instead.

Schulz said he had imagined that Roth's mother resembled Miriam, 'Because he himself used to be so delicate.'*

'No,' said Morgenstern, 'Mendel Singer's daughter looks just like his wife Friedl.'

'Oh,' he said, 'the gazelle,' referring to Roth's description of Miriam.[10]

She wears a yellow shawl and radiates beauty. She has Mendel's 'black hair and his black, soft, and indolent eyes. Her limbs were tender and fragile. A young gazelle.'[11] The image suggests medieval Spanish Hebrew poetry, where the gazelle is a common symbol of erotic desire. One evening after prayers, as Mendel walks under the silver light of a sickle moon, he passes by a field where he hears lovers stir and laugh amid the rustling wheat. He fears they might murder him for discovering their tryst, so he hides and waits for them to pass before he can safely walk on. The stars sparkle, there is a hint of the swamp on the damp breeze, the fir forest looms dark and vast, the frogs croak and crickets chirp. Then he sees the ears of corn part to reveal a uniformed soldier holding the breasts of a yellow-shawled girl, who sinks lovingly into his embrace.

Miriam sleeps with Cossacks, Jonas joins their army. These are brutal symbols of assimilation that shake the foundations of Mendel's world. Sex and the military: one creates new life, the other deals in death, the very parameters of existence. Mendel could not feel more fundamentally betrayed. It transpires that Miriam has numerous such lovers from the barracks; sometimes she meets three men at a time. Her lover Ivan, a shy, bear-like man, credits her with teaching him all he knows of carnal matters: 'And what ideas she had had!'[12] She is impassioned, flirtatious, adventurous, a young woman unafraid to follow her libido: sexually 'lively and spirited', as Ludwig Marcuse said of Friedl. (The Roth scholar Ritchie Robertson notes that Miriam is also 'an extreme development of a well-known literary stereotype, that of the *schöne Jüdin* or, to put it bluntly, the sexy Jewess'.[13]) Mendel is aghast at

---

* To add to the connections between the Singers and Roth's family, recall that his mother Maria was also known as Miriam.

the path his daughter has taken; so with Sam established in the USA, he decides the family should join him. No Cossacks to corrupt Miriam in New York, he reasons.

Once Mendel has obtained departure papers, the family can leave – but what to do about Menuchim? Deborah is in torment. Like Job's wife, she asks her husband why God punishes them so, why He is so cruel; and Mendel tells her this is blasphemy. She agonises over whether to bring him to America. The rabbi had said never to abandon him. 'For long years, day and night, hour after hour, she had waited for the promised miracle. The dead, beyond, did not help; the Rabbi did not help; God did not want to help. She had wept an ocean of tears.'[14] Perhaps the miracle would yet occur before their departure ... She makes up her mind. 'Her son was to stay. She would go to America. There had been no miracle.'[15] Menuchim stays in Zuchnow while his family sail from Bremen to New York City, having again called upon Kapturak to make the arrangements. On the steamship, looking out to the great grey ocean, Mendel imagines the dark depths that hide the mighty Leviathan, the great biblical beast that signifies the vast, terrifying chaos in God's Creation that exists beyond human perception and comprehension, of which his own pain is but a fragment.

The Singer family move into a tenement on Essex Street. While his prose in the book's second half is paler than when describing the *shtetl*, without having visited New York Roth had a good grasp on the new Jewish world that had emerged in the Lower East Side; around one and a half million European Jews moved to New York between 1880 and 1920. Life brightens: they receive a letter from Zuchnow saying Menuchim has begun to speak a few words, and another from Jonas detailing his enjoyment of army life – he has become a fine horseman and 'can ride like the best Cossack'.[16] Miriam lives with and works for Sam, whose business is going well, and she goes out with Mac. For the first time, Mendel feels light-hearted. Late that night he sings psalms from his worn old prayer book and sways in a joyous dance, his movements flickering the candle flame that lights the little room.

Then the same rupture as in every Roth novel to date: the First World War. Sam, the Americanised boy who led them here, signs up to fight for the US Army. America was 'a real fatherland',[17] not like Russia. It was home now, and worth a Jewish boy fighting for, unlike the antisemitic tsar's army that held Jonas in its ranks, so Sam sets off for the front line. The story hinges on the following scenes, which Roth handles with exquisite care and which stand among his most devastating work. When Sam's friend Mac arrives again at their home, this time the news is bad. He brings Sam's watch and relays his last words. Deborah falls silent. Outside, snow falls. Inside, they hear the ticking of the clock. Suddenly, quietly, she begins to tear the hair from her scalp. Fistful by fistful she rips it out, while her face remains impassive. 'Her hands were like pale, fleshy, five-footed animals, feeding themselves on hair.'[18] Mendel looks on. Deborah begins to sing a strange, wordless song of mourning, 'a dark lullaby, for dead children',[19] delivered in a manly voice that suggests someone else stands unseen in the room. She falls quiet. Suddenly she screams, collapses to the floor and dies.

After this, Miriam does not want to be left alone. She says she is afraid. She begins to speak in strange, incomprehensible ways. On the eighth day of Mendel's mourning for Deborah, he hears that something has happened to his daughter. He is taken to the flat she shared with Sam, where he finds her lying in bed, her hair spread across the pillow, a nurse sitting at her side. Her formerly soft, indolent eyes are bloodshot and fiery. When she sees her father she begins to laugh. 'Her laugh lasted a few minutes. It sounded like the ringing of the clear, continuous signals at railway stations, and as though someone beat with a thousand brass hammers on a thousand thin crystal glasses.'[20] Abruptly she begins to cry. She kicks her legs and flails her fists until the nurse restrains her. Miriam begins to tell Mendel that she cheated on Mac with a boyfriend, Mr Glueck, then begins to say something worse: 'I like Mendel Singer too, and if you like—'[21] The nurse smothers her mouth to silence her.

A doctor comes. 'We will have to take her to a sanatorium,' he says. He forcibly anaesthetises her, and stretcher-bearers arrive by ambulance to take her away. At the institution, a doctor tells Mendel she has suffered a 'degenerative psychosis'. 'It can pass. But it can also appear as an illness which we physicians call dementia: dementia praecox – but even the name is uncertain. Anyhow, it is one of the rare cases that we can do little for.'[22]

Medicine cannot help her. The doctor advises Mendel to try asking God instead. All he can do, the doctor advises, is pray. 'Pray zealously to the good God.'[23] And hope for a miracle.

Mendel believes the devil entered her when the Cossack in the field entered her, and has resided within her ever since. He is distraught. He wants to go home. Sam is dead, Deborah is dead, Miriam is insane, Jonas might have died in the war, Menuchim lies helpless in a war zone and might, for all Mendel knows, be trapped this moment in a burning house, unable to move. If Friedl's condition informed Miriam's madness, in her catatonic episodes she was also akin to Menuchim: static, silent, locked inside herself. His soul, like hers, was 'buried in [his] impenetrable . . . mind', and 'who could say what storms of terror and misery [it] had to bear in these days'.[24] All Roth and Mendel could do was hope and pray that a locked door might suddenly unlock; now Mendel's psalms felt insufficient and futile. 'America has killed us,' he says, addressing his dead wife. It is still a fatherland, 'but a death-dealing fatherland'.[25]

The German tendency towards 'sentimental Americanism' is satirised by what the great modern nation does to the Singer family. Mendel becomes a shuffling, lopsided shadow of the authoritative man he used to be. His faith starts to crumble. He sets a fire in the fireplace, and prepares to burn his *tefillin*, *tallis* and prayer books. He imagines how they will curl into 'tiny, glowing spirals', and settle into silvery ashes. When his neighbours hear his crying and stamping, and see smoke escaping from the room, they call his friends to try to placate him. Menkes, Rottenberg, Groschel and Skovronnek arrive, the equivalents of Eliphaz, Bildad, Zophar and Elihu. Mendel sees his continued existence on Earth as an affliction to others: his 'presence brings misfortune . . . as a lonely tree in a level field draws down the lightning'.[26] Why, they ask, was he trying to burn his house? His intention was greater than that, he tells them. He did not only want to burn his house. They might think he is insane like his daughter, but in fact he is, at last, quite sane.

'For more than sixty years I have been mad, but today I am not.'

'Then tell us what you wanted to burn,' they say.

'I want to burn God.'[27]

Think of Job, says Rottenberg; reflect on how his sufferings were only a test by God. Skovronnek says that God's punishments always have a hidden purpose. We do not know why we are punished. Mendel says he does know why: it is because 'God is cruel, and the more one obeys Him, the more brutally He treats one.'[28]

The ending may seem an implausible contrivance to a secular twenty-first-century reader. Miracles do not happen, we say. The sick are not suddenly healed, those who are seriously disabled do not become fully functioning humans. And yet, the final pages of *Job* remain profoundly moving. We may not believe what we are being told, but we recognise the hopeful human spirit that wills such a resolution from such bleak circumstances. The author's fervent, touching belief in the value of hope rings louder than our sceptical thoughts. We are moved less by the story than by the bare humanity of the storyteller.

The war ends, and by way of celebration Mendel listens to a new gramophone record. It is a melody of rare and haunting beauty, and its title is 'Menuchim's Song'. The composer is an Alexis Kossak. Soon he conducts a concert in New York attended by a friend of Mendel's, where he lets on that he is from Zuchnow and wishes to find Mendel Singer. He has news to impart. Kossak asks for Mendel's address, which in time is relayed back to him. When Mendel joins the Skovronnek family for Passover Seder, the evening is interrupted by a knock on the door. A stranger enters, apologetic for disturbing them. He introduces himself as Alexis Kossak. He joins them at the table. He sits quietly through the singing of prayers, and through the feast. They come to the recitation of the miracles, which Skovronnek sings with especial fervour. After the cry of 'Next year in Jerusalem!', at last comes an appropriate moment for conversation. Mendel asks Alexis what brings him here. In a low voice, as the half-burnt candles cast their golden glow over the white tablecloth and the yawning faces of Skovronnek's grandsons, the stranger brings good news from the little town.

The Singers' old house had been empty since being occupied by

Austrian soldiers during the war. Alexis had bought it, and would now pay Mendel the $300 it had cost. There is news of Jonas: though he has not been seen for years, a couple of months ago Alexis met a man who had heard he was alive. There is cause for hope. Mendel wants to ask the great unanswered question that overhangs his life: what of Menuchim? But Skovronnek steers the conversation elsewhere, and Alexis relates his life story. As a child he had chronic illness and came from a poor family. Later he was sent to a medical institute in St Petersburg, where a doctor took an interest in his case and cured him. He came to live with this doctor, in whose home he became enraptured by music.

Over several pages Alexis relates his story, the audience at the table as rapt as readers of Roth's novel. Finally the question that lingers in the room can no longer be ignored, and Skovronnek speaks up to save his friend 'the misery of asking it'. After a pause, Alexis declares: 'Menuchim is alive!'[29] Mendel laughs, then he sobs; the moment echoes the insane, bedbound Miriam's response to seeing him, but here the emotion is an uncontrollable surge of joyous relief. He checks he is not mistaken. Alexis looks steadily back at him.

'Menuchim lives. He is alive, he is well, he is even prosperous.'[30]

And where is he now? asks Skovronnek.

'I am Menuchim.'

Mendel and Alexis Kossak embrace. No one speaks. The children silently cry. Alexis lifts Mendel and seats him on his lap, 'like a child'. The father has become the son. The weary Roth, beleaguered by his duties to Friedl, depicts an exhausted man at long last being treated with tender paternal care. Mendel looks into his friends' faces, and whispers the rabbi's prophecy: 'Pain will make him wise, ugliness good, bitterness mild, and sickness strong!'[31]

Skovronnek runs from house to house to gather Mendel's friends, crying: 'A miracle has happened!'[32] But it is not a miracle, not really, or not a divine one. Roth wants us to understand that no intervening deity was involved. Menuchim was cured by the Russian physician. This was no mystical transformation but one enabled by science; when pressed, Roth eschews the miracle-seeking he has fruitlessly pursued in his own life and comes down on the side of secular, rational modernity. Have faith in scientific progress, he tells his inner eastern Jew: there is more value in this than in beseeching a deaf God. He has not yet abandoned hope in a medical cure for Friedl and wants to believe that such things remain possible. Miracles may happen, but they are enacted by doctors, not gods.

Whatever its cause, the great dreamed-of resolution has come to pass. The last couple of pages have an otherworldly magic. After the story's progression from the *shtetl* to New York City, from the margins of an empire to the capital of the world, Mendel's delivery from suffering is confirmed by his transcendence from the shabby Jewish tenements to the Astor Hotel, an international space where the once-scorned and afflicted father will be treated like a cherished son. Hotels are where all becomes well, where the vulnerable are cared for by father figures. As Mendel climbs the floors of the high-rise building it is as if he were ascending to Heaven. He looks down on the New York nightscape, a dark expanse scattered with innumerable points of light – 'red, blue, green, silver, golden letters, pictures, and signs'.[33] American constellations, dazzling and unnatural. The city's rumbles and rattles fill his ears that were once accustomed to the croaks and rasps of frogs and crickets. He wants to go home. Menuchim tells him they can, after he has completed a concert tour it will be possible to return to Europe, and to the little town. And Menuchim suggests that if he could be healed, then so can Miriam be. They will visit her, get another doctor: she will recover.

Mendel can exhale now. He will go home. He can relax and retreat as Roth could only dream of doing. He sinks into contented sleep. 'And he rested from the burden of his happiness, and the greatness of the miracle.'[34]

The first half of *Job* is the first fully realised iteration of the imagined homeland Roth had begun to build. The previous novels were a mirror to Weimar society; this one is a painting of the past rendered in accentuated colour. The descriptions are rich in reds, blues, golds, yellows, greens. Every twist prior to the miraculous ending takes the Singer family into darker and sadder territory, but Roth's prose has a dreamy, luxuriant quality; you sense that the writing itself is a withdrawal, that respite lies in conjuring an alternative world, a refuge to revisit at will, created in what the critic Wolf Marchand termed an '*Ausdruck einer fortschreitenden Realitätsflucht*'[35]: the expression of a growing flight from reality.

Job's characters will recur – the crafty Kapturak will resurface in *The Radetzky March*, *Weights and Measures* and *The Emperor's Tomb*, flitting between the shadows. The Skovronnek family are likely some relation to Dr Skovronnek in *The Radetzky March*. Roth's creations begin to live through multiple stories. We glimpse the courtesan Mizzi Schinagl in that latter work, then she vanishes before drifting across view in *The Tale of the 1002nd Night* for long enough to reveal her character. The Captain of Horse Taittinger inhabits those books too. If we see *Strawberries* as an aborted iteration of the same project, Naphtali Kroy becomes another inhabitant of the dream-town who slips between that story and the also unfinished *Perlefter*. At the end of 1929 Roth mentioned an intention to write another novel about Nikolai Brandeis, to be called *No Entry*; in 1932 he spoke of 'resurrecting my old friend Franz Tunda',[36] that early restless avatar for Roth, to relate another episode in his ongoing flight. They ghost in and out of rooms, these transient characters; they materialise and you glimpse them, then they're gone.

Reading Miriam in the knowledge that she is modelled on Friedl gives a suggestion of what lies in the gaps between passing references to her behaviour in the psychiatrists' reports and Roth's letters. Miriam's nymphomania reads like an exaggerated version of the libidinous, spirited streak in Friedl that threatened Roth's feeling of control over her. At a press ball in Berlin, when Friedl made a complimentary remark about the band Roth's response was to stand up, erupt with anger and accuse her of sleeping with the violinist. She began to sob and he grabbed her arm and led her out. One factor in his insecurity was the impotence he had suffered since becoming a heavy drinker. He may have felt emasculated, fearing that Friedl would look elsewhere for fulfilment. There is no evidence that she did, only that she felt frustrated and this fed into her psychiatric distress. A letter he wrote to her sister Hedy refers to her overt sexual behaviour in a tone that suggests this was an acknowledged part of her condition. 'There is a beast in every person, in you, in me, in everyone, and when we become ill, it breaks out. Hölderlin and Strindberg were also crazy and cursed and masturbated.'[37] A later psychiatric report mentions 'sexual arousal' among her symptoms, and on one occasion the medics instructed Roth to have sex with her on the floor of a padded cell as part of her therapy.

Roth knew all too well that the material in *Job* was dangerously close to home. But however great his desire to help her, it was outweighed by his compulsion to work through their situation on the page. He went ahead and published a book that he hoped would raise the funds to alleviate his wife's suffering while knowing that if she were to read it, this was likely to undermine his, her parents' and the medical profession's efforts. 'Friedl had better not read my book,' he told her mother. 'It describes how Miriam becomes mentally ill, and she will understand that. As long as she remains in this spiteful mood and is angry with everyone, she will unfortunately remain ill, and you can't trust her with everything. Perhaps it will do her harm if she reads my book.'[38]

The hopeful spirit of the novel's final pages parallels the attitude Roth was determined to take concerning Friedl's condition. She had returned to her parents' in Vienna. While he was buffeted by waves of despair, he advised them to retain their hope. He may not have believed there was cause for optimism, but he saw the value in a positive attitude. 'Hope alone refused to die,'[39] as he wrote in *Job*. Without it, he and the family had nothing. On 3 May 1930 he relayed news to her parents from a consultation with a Dr Schacherl. 'It appears that the doctor is of one mind with me. Friedl seems, thank God, not to be suffering from any form of dementia. She probably has a hysterical psychosis. If it wasn't that she was so intelligent and so acutely sensitive, the whole thing might have been over in a few weeks. But she is obsessing on a certain point, can find no way out, and, out of despair at this, so to speak, is losing her mind. I am passing this on to you right away to get your hopes up. Dr Schacherl is an outstanding diagnostician, and a reliable fellow. Chin up, Friedl will one day speak clearly again.'[40]

Roth suggests they focus on her physical frailty rather than her mental condition, believing that the former aggravated the latter. Her weight had slipped below eight stone and she was anaemic. Both these matters needed urgent remedy. He suggested her parents give her 'liver, as much as possible, and slightly underdone', and perhaps blood soup. He was in correspondence with a psychiatrist in Marbach about the possibility of blood transfusions ('I'm expecting a detailed answer from him about the prospects of a cure'[41]), and hoped she might also receive a hormonal treatment. 'According to what Professor Kretschmer tells me, such attacks often heal quite suddenly, even after a long time. So please, please, don't lose patience! So long as I can manage to bring in enough money, I'm sure Friedl will get well without an asylum.'

The letter closes on the most plaintive of notes. Roth has one more suggestion for her care. 'If it's not too much trouble, why not give her a canary to keep in her room. It might distract her. You can always give it away, and they don't cost much. Can you run to a canary?'

In mid-May 1930, Friedl was admitted to a sanatorium at Hacking, western Vienna. 'Patient was healthy till 1928,' the institution noted. 'Then the mental illness started with a catatonic posture, knees pulled to the body, irritability, mutism, depression ... The contraction of the knees led to ankylosis [fusion of the bones] and surgery had to be done.'[42]

The following month, Roth's newspaper readers gained an insight into life inside an unnamed psychiatric hospital. The piece published in the Berlin weekly *Das Tagebuch* on 28 June 1930 was written by a man familiar with the workings of such an institution and the troubles faced by its patients, though he gave no indication as to how he'd gained such authority. It is not certain that he was writing about the specific institution at Hacking that currently housed Friedl; the piece may even represent an amalgam of such places he had seen in the past year while pursuing her treatment. Soma Morgenstern located the article's genesis in Roth's gradual realisation that he was not to blame for Friedl's schizophrenia, and his desire to understand its true causes and best treatment.

'For two or three years Roth believed, as the woman had persuaded him, that he was responsible for her illness. But it did not take that long before he had to realise that there are many and very expensive helpers, but no help. Many healers, and no healing. An active spirit that he always was, he started to study psychiatry. Not quickly reading a few relevant psychiatric works and immediately sarcastically voicing objections. It was not like that. At first he was driven by the urge to find a secret somewhere that could bring salvation to just his wife, which could not be expected from any specialist. Like all hopeless people, he began to believe in miracles, and he set out to find one.'

Morgenstern recalled that for this period Roth restricted his coffee-house visits to those that stocked the medical journals, which he would request from the waiter as soon as he entered. He would pore over them alone in his 'hunt for the miracle, the latest result of science'.[43] He took his research seriously. Morgenstern even claims Roth reduced his alcohol intake: in 'his desperation he remained sober and studied. One does not drink in libraries.' In the article Roth displayed a firm grasp of the journals he'd read, which left him unimpressed: 'The psychiatric literature bristles with unfruitful considerations, classifications, nomenclatures, some of them medically untenable. There are degenerative, reactive, endogenous, exogenous psychoses, Ganser's twilight states, manic-depressive insanity – not to mention the arbitrarily thrown together large symptom complexes such as schizophrenia. One could write volumes about the ridiculous methods of psychiatric diagnosis.'[44]

He pleaded for a more humane and empathetic approach to treating the mentally ill. He poured into the piece all his frustration at Friedl's treatment. The regime he had witnessed was more concerned with subduing than healing. It was a law unto itself, operating 'behind bars', unaccountable, unused 'to being controlled by the public, like all other departments of medicine'.[45] As he'd suggested to her parents, he was dismayed by the profession's disregard for the connection between the mental and the somatic. Patients were injected with sedatives that brought harmful physical side effects. He complained that 'practical psychiatry does not perform medical but police functions',[46] and even does this inadequately: 'Hundreds of lunatics are often watched over by only one miserably paid doctor. Nurses are inclined to mistake the patient's pain for the whims of a carefree mind and his or her wishes for wickedness. One rings in vain. The night nurse does not come. One is thirsty. One does not get any water . . . One starves. One receives too little and too bad food. Even the benevolent doctors are powerless.'[47]

The nurses feud among one another and mistreat the patients to undermine the doctors whom they do not like. 'The doctor can see everyone only once a day, in passing. He must be able to rely on the staff. Can he? – No! Does he? – Yes!'[48] What were these places for?, Roth asked, in evident despair. Not for healing, only for keeping insane people out of sight. This traumatised post-war world is in denial: it hides and ignores problems it does not wish to confront, whether they are psychiatric patients or the war-wounded.

He proposed a series of changes: open these institutions up to the light of public scrutiny. Admit that they have no solutions to many patients' conditions and are not in the business of healing them. Allow family as many visits as they wish. Take more care over analysis of the patients' tests. Increase staffing levels. And do so by employing the right people: 'Those who find it difficult to understand a "normal" person should not try to understand a mad person.'*[49]

The piece sparked furious debate, including defensive responses from prominent psychiatrists; but other experts conceded that he had made valid points. Morgenstern termed it 'a great victory for Roth. But the money that this victory earned him was not enough to pay for a month in a sanatorium where his sick wife was accommodated.'[50]

---

* Roth's vision of how such places ought to be run appears in his next novel, when he writes of a 'sanatorium on Lake Constance where pampered madmen from wealthy families were carefully and expensively treated, and the orderlies were as tender as midwives'. *The Radetzky March*, trans. Michael Hofmann (Granta Books, 2003), p. 205.

By late summer 1930 Friedl must have left the institution at Hacking and been back in her parents' care, for in September Roth wrote to Stefan Zweig that she had 'been taken to a sanatorium again'.[51] She had been refusing to eat. Her weight plummeted to five stone. She was too weak to move and had to be carried away on a stretcher to an expensive institution at Rekawinkel, a few miles west of Vienna. Whereas *Job* had been inspired by Friedl's situation, now life mirrored art: the scene sounds uncannily similar to Miriam's hospitalisation in the recently published novel. 'All my endeavours with my wife have failed,' he told Zweig. 'I'm exhausted, finished.'[52] A few weeks later he wrote in similar vein to Friedl's mother: 'I don't think there's anything to be done about my sadness. I'm through with life, for good. I can't wait around any more for miracles.'[53]

Friedl's hospitalisation was one of a series of blows that hit Roth in 1930, like an accelerated version of Mendel Singer's years of suffering, only without the miracle. Some were self-inflicted. In March, while writing *Job* and as her condition worsened, Roth had begun to write a novel for serialisation in the conservative *Münchner Neueste Nachrichten*. Soma Morgenstern recalled Roth telling him that he'd forgotten this commitment in the contract he'd agreed a year earlier, until the newspaper reminded him three weeks before the deadline. They were contracted to pay him 20,000 marks for the book, which he could ill afford to put at risk. Never mind that he had almost no time to fulfil his side of the deal – he said he would be fine to deliver the manuscript, which is thought to have been a version of his *Perlefter*. He began to work in a frenzy. Tormented by the impossible schedule he had created, and drinking still more heavily, in a moment of despair he scrawled repeatedly on the manuscript: 'Must finish novel in three weeks!' He completed the book and hastily packaged it for delivery to Munich, not realising that he had also scooped up the extra sheet. The editors were aghast. It was impossible, they said, to produce something good enough so quickly. Roth likely took this as further evidence of the Germans' unduly 'scientific' approach to writing, with its instinctive fear of inspiration and genius. Still, they tore up the contract. So ended Joseph Roth's brief spell in the employ of a downmarket right-wing newspaper.

On 13 May he wrote to Stefan Zweig from the Hotel am Zoo, on Berlin's Kurfürstendamm: 'Today, just an hour ago, I learned that a woman friend of mine shot herself. She was staying here in the hotel, had failed to find me yesterday, and I'm convinced I could have averted her death. All around me are suffering and death, and I could weep at my inability to find a little bit of goodness in myself, to save the life of a single human being.'[54]

The next day, Benno Reifenberg wrote to say that the *Frankfurter Zeitung* demanded exclusive rights to Roth's journalism if he were ever to work for them again. Roth's response to Hans Bauer in the *Weltbühne* magazine, where he had claimed that only his and a couple of friends' work lent the *FZ* any decency, was perceived as a 'defamation of the *FZ*, and you are therefore facing an extraordinary degree of suspicion and resentment'.[55] They suggested that Roth wrote another article for the magazine to resolve the matter. Roth replied that he was no longer in contact with the *Weltbühne*: 'I want nothing more to do with those *scum*.'[56] Géza von Cziffra reported that Roth was in the habit of disparaging '*Weltbühne* Jews', who fell into the subsect of disrespectful, liberal, *chutzpah*-afflicted Jews that he openly despised.

However much he earned from his writing, it felt insignificant set against the costs of Friedl's medical care. By June 1930 Kiepenheuer had already advanced him an immense total of 22,000 marks, it had all gone, and he admitted to Zweig they were 'rightly' refusing to give him any more. He needed 2,000 marks a month, and he was earning 500. 'The water is up to my neck ... I'm no longer equal to this *schmonzes** ... So you can imagine I'm sitting on coals. My wife's costs are fixed, I can do nothing to reduce them. I will work to the limits of possibility, even if it kills me.'[57]

In this context, the publication of *Job* in October felt like an afterthought. It would soon sell 20,000 copies – it was, both in sales and critical response, Roth's breakthrough novel. It brought him an

---

* 'Nonsense', Yiddish.

international profile.* It confirmed the respect of his peers: Robert Musil, with whom Roth did not always see eye to eye, would tell Morgenstern of his admiration for the scene where Mendel sees Miriam with her lover: 'How the poor Mendel Singer sees his daughter coming out of a cornfield with a Cossack entwined tightly around her, running away in his consternation and breathlessly reaching the synagogue after a long run and praying there – that is the idea of a poet.'[58] Stefan Zweig declared in the *Kölnische Zeitung*: 'One experiences instead of reading. And one is not ashamed to be shaken sentimentally for once by a real work of art.'[59] There were numerous translations, and Dorothy Thompson's English version opened up the American market. It was a book of the month in the USA, resulting in high sales. Hollywood even bought the film rights, though the resulting film, released in 1936 as *Sins of Man*, bears little resemblance to Roth's story. As he wrote in 1931, 'the prevailing antisemitism prevents the filming of any Jewish subject. A year ago I would have earned 100,000 marks with [*Job*]. But I have as scant good fortune as any other old Jew.'[60]

A screenplay by the Russian-Jewish writer Ossip Dymow was shelved, a new one commissioned, and eventually it was transformed from a Jewish fable into a Christian one, where the central character is a Tyrolean farmer and the wonder-rabbi a Franciscan monk. ('Mendel Singer Gets Baptised', jibed a Jerusalem publication's review.) In a British newspaper interview published in the year of the film's release, Marlene Dietrich would say that *Job* was her favourite novel. Roth was pleased that this publicity might increase his readership, but the book itself had by then long become meaningless to its author. On 22 September 1930 he wrote to Zweig and thanked him for reading *Job*. 'I for my part find it superfluous to have written it. I have no ties to it any more. I am tired of it, or I am simply tired.'[61]

*

---

* By the end of 1930 translation rights for *Job* had been sold to America, England, Denmark, France, the Netherlands, Poland, Sweden and Spain (as reported in Dutch newspaper *Het Vaderland*, 18 November 1930, cited in Els Snick, *Joseph Roth in den Niederlanden und Flandern. Vermittlung, Vernetzung und Orchestrierung eines vielseitigen Autors im niederländischsprachigen Kontext 1924–1940* (University of Utrecht Faculty of Arts, 2011)).

In Jewish mythology, a *dybbuk* is the disembodied spirit of a dead sinner that wanders until it can take possession of the soul of a living person who has erred, for instance by expressing religious scepticism. The notion clung to Roth long after he left Brody and influenced how he viewed his predicament. In 1930 Géza von Cziffra caught up with Roth at the Café Herrenhof in Vienna. 'I should never have married Friedl,' Roth told him. 'Or rather, she shouldn't have married me. She should have married the grocer's son on the corner, a confectioner or a clerk. In any case, someone who could have offered her peace and tranquillity, and not a homeless journeyman like me, who has no wardrobe, bed or mattress of his own, just three suitcases. The Hasid in me at first thought a *dybbuk* had haunted her, but no, I, Moische Joseph Roth, I haunted her!'[62]

Some time later, von Cziffra and Roth were eating at a Jewish restaurant, Neugröschl in Praterstrasse, when Roth leaped up with a cry of 'There sits my uncle!' He had spotted his relative – von Cziffra does not disclose the name – across the restaurant and the two men were soon embracing. Von Cziffra looked on as they fell into a conversation that he could not hear. Now the uncle appeared to be crying, and the restaurateur Herr Neugröschl giving Roth a consolatory handshake. Later von Cziffra asked Neugröschl why, to which the reply came: 'Didn't you know that his wife had died?' Von Cziffra was perplexed. He had seen Roth only that morning and he hadn't mentioned it. Friedl must have died in the afternoon . . . The next day, he asked Roth how she was.

'As always. Sometimes a little better, sometimes worse.'

An annoyed von Cziffra snapped at him: 'Why don't you admit that she is dead?'

'Dead?'

Yes, he said, he'd asked Neugröschl about the scene with Roth's uncle. Roth laughed and interrupted: 'That's what you mean?' Then he turned serious. 'My uncle is passing through here. He knew Friedl was ill, but I didn't want him to know what was really wrong with her. Being dead is not as bad for an Orthodox Eastern Jew as being possessed by the evil *dybbuk*.'[63] The sceptic in him may have looked askance at the irrational interpretations proffered up by his inner Hasid, but he respected the eastern tradition sufficiently to wish to avoid upsetting his family, and besides, he needed no more stigma heaped upon the shame he felt already. This shame combined with guilt, rage and sadness to drive him deeper into drink, which only reinforced these emotions and manifested them on his body.

The turn of the decade is a fulcrum point. The balance tilts. In four years Roth will age by twenty years. It is a drastic and terrible metamorphosis befitting Job, Mendel Singer or Andreas Pum. His face softens and slackens. His sharp features grow pudgy, his jowls pustulate, he grows a moustache that rests like a ragged moth above his fleshy lips. Photos from the 1920s usually show him wearing a fedora; now he goes bareheaded, which reveals thinning hair scraped back from his brow. His doleful eyes peep from between bulbous sacs and lids. A double chin sags over an askew bow tie. His gut overhangs his belt. He looks more susceptible to gravity. Only his legs retain their original physique, but now they appear comically ill equipped for the task of transporting this lumpen torso. He becomes reliant on his cane. He takes to wearing a cloak. Together they suggest an elderly aristocrat. If you had to define the difference between the two decades' photos, it would be in his energy. Before, he looked frozen in movement, spry and dynamic, intent on whatever he was doing, be it striding through Berlin or reading a newspaper. Now he looks still, passive, besieged by sadnesses; not yet defeated, but in thrall to torments and aware he is staving off the inevitable. It is heroic to fight to the last, though, and he knows this well, so a smile still plays at his lips.

Job was published by the Gustav Kiepenheuer Verlag in October, after its serialisation in the *Frankfurter Zeitung*: the first sign of their uneasy rapprochement with a writer whose need for money outweighed even his pride. (Roth to Zweig: 'I can hardly tell you how unwillingly I have attached myself to the newspaper again. What else could I have done? Kiepenheuer's money goes on [Friedl's care in] Vienna, there's almost nothing left for me.'[64]) Roth and Kiepenheuer had immediately hit it off. Kiepenheuer was a drinker too, and the pair became a regular sight at a reserved table in the evenings at Mampe's on the Kurfürstendamm. Kiepenheuer liked to make his authors feel cared for. He would welcome them in the mornings with a cognac. He would later recall: 'I first met Joseph Roth at Anhalter Bahnhof when he got off the Vienna D-train; from that moment on our friendship was sealed. He, the eternal passenger, came to Berlin for a few weeks or months and now a series of fruitful encounters of a human and publishing nature began for me ... Our meeting places were his room in the Hotel am Zoo, his corner in Mampe on Kurfürstendamm, in Paris the Café Deux Magots and above all the writing room of the Hôtel Foyot.'[65]

The summer of 1930 had seen the publisher's fiftieth birthday, which occasioned the most famous letter Roth ever wrote, one that is the closest we have to an autobiographical text. It is full of fabrications and candour, and contains many extraordinary passages, not least a fantastical account of his childhood. The boy who had barely left his mother's view was recast here as a wild rebel, the terror of Brody, feared by his peers, known for his bravado and malice. This flight of fancy shows that he was still dwelling in the landscape he'd sketched in *Strawberries*, but now not in a state of nostalgia so much as derangement:

> I loved freedom. The times I spent with my mother were my happiest. I got up in the middle of the night, dressed, and left the house. I walked for three or four days, slept in houses whose state I didn't know, and with women whose faces I was curious to see, and never did. I roasted potatoes on summer meadows, and on hard autumnal fields. I picked strawberries in forests, and hung around with a half-grown rabble, and was thrashed from time to time, so to speak, by mistake. Everyone who gave me a thrashing would quickly beg my forgiveness. Because he feared my revenge. My revenge could be terrible. I had no particular affection for anyone. But if I hated anyone, I would wish his death, and was prepared to kill him. I had the best slings, I always aimed for the head, and I didn't just use stones, but also broken glass and

razor blades. I laid traps and snares, and I lay in wait and lurked in bushes. When one of my enemies once turned up armed with a revolver, admittedly without ammunition, I felt humiliated. I started off by flattering him; gradually, in the teeth of my true feelings, made myself his friend; and finally bought the revolver from him, with bullets I had been given by a forester. I persuaded my friend that the ammunition on its own was much more dangerous than a weapon without ammunition.[66]

This bears no relation to any of his school peers' recollections of a studious and withdrawn boy. It is a retrospective projection of the freedom and reverence he wished he had enjoyed. He goes on to recount his early romantic adventures, his tutoring, his writing career, and finally he comes to his relationship with Kiepenheuer:

One Sunday we drank schnapps. It was bad schnapps, it made both of us ill. Out of sympathy, we became friends, in spite of the difference in our natures, which are such that only alcohol is capable of bridging them. Kiepenheuer is a West-Phalian, you see, while I am an East-Phalian. There hardly exists any greater contrast than that. He is an idealist, I am a sceptic. He loves Jews, I don't. He is an apostle of progress, I am a reactionary. He is ageless, I have been old ever since I can remember. He is turning fifty, I am two hundred. I could have been his great-grandfather, if I wasn't his brother. I am radical, he is conciliatory. He is polite and vague, I am ferocious. He is an optimist, I am a pessimist.

There must be some secret connection between us somewhere. Because sometimes we do agree. It's as though we each made concessions to the other, but we don't. Because he doesn't understand money. That's a quality we share. He is the most courtly man I know. So am I. He got it from me. He loses money on my books. So do I. He believes in me. So do I. He waits for my success. So do I. He is certain of posterity. So am I.

We are inseparable; that's his advantage.[67]

That final assertion was true. *Job* had suggested this; the next book would confirm it. Kiepenheuer's faith and his author's self-belief would be vindicated. That autumn, Roth began to write one of the greatest novels of the twentieth century.

PART THREE

Studio portrait of Joseph Roth, early 1930s.

Chapter Ten

> She ran the rule over Lieutenant Trotta. He looks old for his
> years, she thought: he's been through some sad experience,
> and failed to learn from it.
>
> *The Radetzky March*

When did the cold sun of the Habsburgs begin to set? When does
any sun begin to set? The instant after it reaches its zenith. But there
comes a moment when its descent hastens, then its light softens and
cools, and it gilds the clouds in its final blaze before it sinks below the
horizon. The Habsburg sun's decline began in 1859 when Franz Joseph
I led his troops to ignominy at the Battle of Solferino, and accelerated
in the mid-1860s. Defeat in the Austro-Prussian War of 1866 brought
territorial loss and political humiliation, tilted the balance of power
within the German Confederation,[*] and signalled Austria's vulnerabil-
ity to its rivals. The war left the empire in such financial ruin that its
future looked precarious, hence the following year's *Ausgleich*, whereby
Austria tried to fortify itself by forming the Dual Monarchy with
Hungary, which it had occupied since 1848.

Austria hoped that giving its neighbour semi-sovereignty and a
parliament would restore stability; instead, Hungary would spend
the next half-century sucking its resources and thwarting its ambitions. Dimming already, the sun faded further in the first decade
of the new century, as encapsulated by the condition of its military.
In 1866 Austria had had one of Europe's most impressive armies,
but by 1914 it was small by Russian, French and German standards,

---

[*] The group of thirty-nine German-speaking states in central Europe, formed in 1815
to replace the Holy Roman Empire.

woefully underequipped in modern weaponry, representative of an empire rooted in the past and led by an enfeebled octogenarian who had surrounded himself with yes-men. The sun set, and Austria-Hungary spent its twilight years almost rivalling the moribund Ottoman Empire for the unwanted title of 'the Sick Man of Europe'; and yet in these darkening times, this ailing monarchy launched a war it could never win.

The cover of *Radetzkymarsch* (*The Radetzky March*), published by Kiepenheuer & Witsch.

In Roth's greatest work, the empire's decline over the course of Franz Joseph's reign is traced through three generations of the Trotta family: Joseph, his son Franz and grandson Carl. Franz and Joseph share names with the emperor who ruled during their lifetimes; Carl, who ends the dynasty by dying childless, shares one with his successor, Karl I, who in 1916 became the last Emperor of Austria-Hungary, ruling for two years until its collapse at the end of the war. The story plays out in a succession of shadowy rooms – in homes, garrisons, brothels and bars – at the empire's edge, where the Viennese sun barely reaches. Again and again Roth writes of sunlight's passage into dingy chambers through half-curtained or blinded windows: a shaft highlights an intensely white bed coverlet, glints on a candlestick, gives bare floorboards a golden gleam while the walls stand in gloom. The last glimmer of day falls through a gap in the curtains. Damp and mustiness linger in the dusty air. If the sun is the Habsburg monarchy, it is obstructed from filling these distant Galician spaces; it cannot illuminate its entire territory. Out in the shady margins, bored officers try to overcome the futility felt by soldiers in peacetime: they drink their days away, defend 'honour' through petty feuds that expand to fill the space unoccupied by war, slip into their mistresses' bedrooms, carouse in bordellos; and all the while, fixers like Kapturak flourish in the shadows.

The novel opens at irresistible velocity on the bloody battlefield of Solferino, where Franz Joseph I led the Austro-Hungarian Army to defeat against the Franco-Sardinian Alliance. Among his troops is Joseph Trotta, an infantry lieutenant and platoon commander of Slovenian peasant stock. When the foolish emperor raises a field-glass to his eye, making himself a target for a sniper, Trotta pulls him to the ground and is hit in the shoulder by a bullet intended for the emperor's heart. A month later, Trotta has recovered enough to return to his Hungarian regimental headquarters, by which time he has been decorated, promoted and ennobled. When he next sees his father, the older man barely knows how to relate to him: instead of their traditional Slovenian he addresses Joseph in German, for 'the use of his mother tongue would have seemed like an undue intimacy with a son who, by the grace of fate and the Emperor, had moved so far'.[1] So by Imperial 'favour' a family is split between classes, the generations left unable to relate naturally, with Joseph displaced into the upper echelons of a hidebound Austrian military culture whose stultifying protocols only increase its inhabitants' isolation.

Joseph and his wife have a son, Franz. We never learn the wife's name and she will soon die young. The women who do feature in the story only exist in relation to lonely men's need for sexual gratification, either as mistresses or prostitutes; there are precious few female perspectives, and Roth instead looks overwhelmingly through male eyes to explore as never before his preoccupation with how fathers fail their sons.

At the age of five Franz is educated by a tutor. Joseph browses his son's primer and notices a section on the Battle of Solferino. The incident in which he saved the emperor's life has been transformed beyond recognition. The brave emperor had ventured deep into battle and was surrounded by enemy horsemen; the young Lieutenant Trotta, upgraded to the cavalry, rode to his rescue on horseback, slicing his sword down on enemy heads and necks until almost all were vanquished, at which point he was lanced in the chest. He shows the book to his wife and says: 'It's a lie!' She responds: 'It's for children.' The captain secures an audience with the emperor to press his concerns.

'"There's a lot of lying goes on," affirmed His Majesty.'[2] Such fictions sustain the faltering Austria: the empire's future rests on indoctrinating children with falsehoods that some will see through in adulthood. It is a crumbling institution propped up by patriotic mythology and anachronistic codes of behaviour. What troubles is it preparing for itself this way? Its rulers must hope that Austrians who realise they've been duped will agree the lies were worth telling to sustain the monarchy, that the truth was sacrificed for a worthwhile cause, and that few react with revolutionary fervour.

Still, the emperor has the section removed from the curriculum, and bestows two favours on Trotta: a 5,000-gulden award to fund his son's studies, and a baronetcy. He is now Captain Baron Joseph von Trotta und Sipolje. Franz grows up to become district commissioner of a Moravian town only identified as W.; he wanted to become a soldier but the disenchanted Joseph decides otherwise, and custom dictates that a father's will must be obeyed. The socially elevated Joseph sees the empire's flaws, but Franz, born into the aristocracy, has no perspective to become anything but an unquestioning functionary in the Austro-Hungarian bureaucratic machine. As a boy Franz befriends a promising artist named Moser, who painted Joseph's portrait. Now it hangs 'in the gloaming under the drawing room ceiling'[3], where later it will imprint itself on the mind of Franz's impressionable son, Carl Joseph, whom he sends to a military academy. The boy's vacations at home emphasise his father's obsession with hierarchy and rigidity. The house runs like clockwork, and its inhabitants are mechanised like the figures in a cuckoo clock: if it is lunchtime, then the housekeeper Fräulein Hirschwitz will emerge bearing platters before slipping back out of view. Carl struggles to eat his meals within the prescribed period and must bolt them down if he's to keep to the schedule. The house staff must know their place, and Carl Joseph always answers Franz with a dutiful 'Yes, Papa'. From his father's example he acquires emotional repression, and from his grandfather's an unattainable model of heroism. The Hero of Solferino's image and legend hang over the young soldier: 'That was what you did if you were a Trotta: you saved the life of the Emperor.'[4]

How can Carl Joseph live up to such expectation? If he cannot save the emperor's life, he dreams instead of laying his down to serve the empire. He imagines dying for the emperor in a hail of bullets, 'preferably to the music of the Radetzky March',[5] which he hears performed regularly by a military band that plays concerts beneath the district commissioner's veranda; they seem to produce the music automatically, like the band Roth watched in Vienna's Volksgarten. In the teenager's imagined death, his final actions will synchronise to Strauss's composition: in his mind 'the swift bullets whistled in time about Carl Joseph's head, his gleaming sabre flashed, and with heart and head filled with the gorgeous abruptness of the march, he would sink into its thrumming ecstasy, and a thin scarlet trickle of blood would run out over the shimmering golds of the cornets, the deep black of the drums and the victorious silver of the cymbals'.[6] This is music by which to die a neat, glorious death.

With this Roth establishes another of the novel's themes: how to live and die with meaning in a meaningless world; how to achieve a good and easy death. Later his publisher would claim to have suggested naming the book after the piece of music that resonates through the narrative. Gustav Kiepenheuer recalled: 'One day [Roth and I] were walking up and down Augustus Square in Leipzig and were looking for a title. When I called out "Radetzky March" he embraced me, took me by the arm and bore me off to Felsche's to celebrate the inspiration with a drink. Then he took his flat silver watch out of his waistcoat, opened the case, scratched the date, our names and Radetzky March with a penknife inside it, and gave it to me as a souvenir of this hour. I always had it with me, until I lost it in the war, just as I lost Roth himself.'[7]

The Radetzky March is largely bereft of the insistent energy of Strauss's celebration of Austrian military glory. There are dreamlike changes of pace, suspended moments where nothing happens but that a clock ticks, a fly buzzes, an officer looks out of a window; then it is as if, unbeknownst to the reader, the characters hear the opening drumroll of the march and are spurred into action: we hurtle into a battle scene, a drunken confrontation, an impassioned seduction. Then the last bullets fall, the glasses are drained, the lovers fall asleep, and all is quiet.

Stillness is the novel's default condition, from which its melancholic characters stir themselves before their sense of futility relapses them into inertia and silence. These silences are never dull, they are exquisite or fraught, and they accentuate the spasms of action by casting them in relief. 'Austria' is an idea that must be sustained by patriotic mythology because it bears no relation to the reality, which is a land of querulous ethnic groups abrasively jammed in together. Where the 'Radetzky March' plays, there for a few minutes it is still Austria, lit by a blazing sun. But when the march's last notes fade, reality reasserts itself.

Carl Joseph begins his military training. One day while out walking, he passes the home of an acquaintance, Sergeant Slama, and decides to call in. Slama's wife answers the door: her husband is out, but she invites him into her cool, dark sitting room. They sit beside one another and drink lemonade, while she smokes a cigarette. Carl Joseph is stiff and passive, his knees pressed together. He says little. Then she kisses him, sits astride him and unbuttons his tunic. He is at first horrified but offers no resistance, and once she has removed all of his uniform, then he is free to 'let himself fall. He received the woman like a great soft wave of delight, fire and water.'[8] Every other day Sergeant Slama delivers files to the district commissioner's office; while he is there, the commissioner's teenage son sleeps with his wife, drinks raspberry syrup with her, inhales her sweet perfume; and when they are apart he writes her love letters. Some time later, Franz and Carl Joseph are travelling by train to Vienna when it occurs to the father to pass on some news: 'You know Sergeant Slama, don't you? Unfortunately he's become a widower, just this year. Sad. His wife died in childbed. You ought to pay him a visit.'[9]

   Carl Joseph's world begins to collapse. Roth sets off the chain of events in one of his most masterly scenes. The code of honour dictates that Trotta should offer his condolences; in a culture as stiff and protocol-ridden as Austria's, there is no escaping this duty. First, he visits Frau Slama's grave, as 'the rain caressed his parted hair with damp tenderness'.[10] He arrives at the home he has furtively visited so often before, and sits quietly with the man he cuckolded. 'There's a smell of damp in the sitting room; of the two windows, one is curtained, the other admits the grey day's murky light.'[11] Carl Joseph senses that 'the Sergeant has some kind of grudge against him ... They were never taught in cadet school how an officer ought to behave in such a situation' – alas, the curriculum neglected to advise on the etiquette for consoling the bereaved husband of the woman who died giving birth to your child. There are protocols for almost every aspect of his world, and without them he is lost. 'To be on the safe side, then, Carl Joseph just smiles,'[12] a forced grin that clamps his lips together.

Sergeant Slama appears not to know of Trotta's relationship with his wife – or does he? The uncertainty hangs in the air. Trotta offers his condolences. He says she was a good woman. The sergeant responds, with due deference: 'She was beautiful, the Baron has seen her himself.' 'Yes, I've seen her, your wife. Did she have an easy death?'[13] It took two days, says Slama. A doctor might have saved her had he been called earlier, but it was too late. He offers Trotta a raspberry juice, which he accepts with pathetic alacrity, 'as though [it] would transform the situation'.[14] Soon Trotta makes his excuses and leaves. He has reached the street when he hears Slama say his name, and turns to find the man right behind him proffering a small package. When they are parted again, Trotta runs his fingers over it in his pocket, until he realises what it contains. His love letters. It transpires that Slama offered them first to the district commissioner, who ordered him to return them to his son himself. An order is an order, however humiliating it might prove for this newly bereaved man.

As Carl Joseph walks away in the rain, forlornly trying to loosen his tight collar, he can still taste the fruit juice in his mouth. He wants to be rid of it and all its associations. It occurs to him to drink a cognac in the town's café. He does not notice that officers from his garrison are sitting in the bar, nor even that his father is there; later, in a matter-of-fact manner, the father will check that Slama handed over the letters, then no more is said of it. But for now, writes Roth, 'Nothing is more urgent than the cognac.'[15] So Carl Joseph begins to drink. The beverages he imbibes throughout the book are an index of his condition.

In the early chapters it is sodas and raspberry juice; now he consumes alcohol every few pages.

One of *The Radetzky March*'s curious distinguishing qualities is the way that Roth repeatedly threatens then eschews a linear plot: instead, as Michael Hofmann has written, 'the scenes follow one another like broad discs overhanging one another, like the records cued on an old-fashioned gramophone'.[16] They have thematic coherence, they are a resonant series of vignettes offering diverse views on to the same world, and Roth achieves an extraordinary richness, depth and space while offering only sporadic narrative dynamism; the plot weaves like a homebound drunkard, and yet the result is compelling. If there is a consistent propulsive force to *The Radetzky March*, it is Trotta's urge towards the next drink. It is Roth's first conspicuously alcoholic novel. This pursuit gives Trotta direction and respite; he spends the middle third of the book largely inebriated, attempting to distract himself from a succession of blows. Barely a scene passes without Roth's characters downing a slivovitz, brandy or schnapps; the chemical scent of liquor hangs on their breath and rises from the page. The men in this book are isolated, straitjacketed in their stiff uniforms and ingrained formality, and only in the depths of a night's drinking do they form brief emotional bonds that melt away again by the morning. They are desperate men: desperate for human contact, and for the alcohol that engenders it, numbs their pain and warms the cold cavity within them.

Only an alcoholic could describe his characters' compulsion to drink with such stark authenticity. After an alarming encounter with the painter Moser, Trotta felt a sudden 'thirst for alcohol, a drinker's thirst, which is a thirst of the soul and the body. Suddenly you see as little as a short-sighted person, you have the feeble hearing of the deaf. You need a drink, right away.'[17] Elsewhere he 'drank a few glasses of schnapps. And straight away he felt at home in his incapacity. And then, like a man entering a prison or a monastery, the money he had on him seemed oppressive and unnecessary to the Lieutenant. He decided to spend it all at once.'[18] This was the alcoholic *Heimat* Roth had inhabited at least since his nights in the bars of Marseilles' old town in 1925, and the description gives an insight into why he fell repeatedly into such debt. Roth drank throughout the creation of the book, though at times he went on what he termed a 'diet': this consisted of sticking to wine instead of schnapps or brandy. He was worried by the chaos alcohol added to his life – for example, he left the fourth chapter of his manuscript, describing Trotta's visit to Frau Slama's widower, in a Paris taxi while drunk and, after a miserable afternoon's searching, had to write it again. The rewritten chapter is one of the best in his oeuvre. But the pressures that drove him to drink were unrelenting: for one thing, he had taken an advance from the publisher Phaidon in September 1930 to write a book about the *Orient Express*, but four months later, having spent it and instead immersed himself in writing *The Radetzky March*, he was showing no sign of delivering and Phaidon wanted the manuscript or their money back.

With his fellow soldiers an unwilling Trotta is compelled to visit a brothel, where the pianist defiles the 'Radetzky March' as a soundtrack to the officers' evening. The madam, Frau Resi Horvath, is grotesque, with 'false teeth [that] shimmered in her wide mouth, as yellow and as long as piano keys':[19] another of the sturdy, intimidating women who haunt Roth's imagination. Trotta and the regimental doctor, Max Demant, are the only two men who don't depart the salon with prostitutes, and they fall into conversation. As they make to leave, Carl Joseph notices on the mantelpiece one of the countless portraits of Franz Joseph that watch over his subjects across the Dual Monarchy. 'Scattered a hundred thousandfold throughout the whole great Empire was Emperor Franz Joseph, as omnipresent among his subjects as God in the world.'[20] And here it was in a bordello's grubby salon: 'in a bronze, fly-spotted frame was the Commander in Chief in miniature . . . in the snow-white uniform, with the blood-red sash and the Golden Fleece'.[21] As if the great man willingly conferred his dignity on such places. Something must be done about this tawdry state of affairs, thinks Carl Joseph, and with thudding heart he removes the picture from its frame, folds it and puts it in his pocket. The grandfather saves the emperor in a battle; the grandson saves his likeness from a brothel.

*

'I'm starting to enjoy myself,' Roth wrote to Zweig in March 1931 from the luxurious Hôtel du Cap d'Antibes, where he was staying at Zweig's expense. 'Only I miss you, your shrewd eye, your shrewd heart. Am writing the fourth chapter with the regimental doctor, in bold, strong lines.' This study of Max Demant would end up as the sixth chapter. 'Very good, I think. Don't worry about me! I'm more of a writer than I'm prepared to admit . . . Write back soon, even if it's just a line or two. My wife is doing badly. Credit to the girl, even so, that I'm not as burdened by it as usual. I may be a sonofabitch, but defloration in a literary setting, that's worth something to me.'[22]

'The girl' refers not to Friedl but Maria Gillès de Pélichy. In the South of France he had fallen in love again: overwhelmingly, rapturously – and dangerously, for he had 'deflowered' an underage girl who would not turn twenty-one until July. Roth writes of her in scandalous detail without mentioning her name to Zweig and to Friedrich Traugott Gubler,* and it was not until 2008 that the Belgian scholar Dr Els Snick uncovered her identity. De Pélichy was from a rich, Catholic Flemish family, and was in Antibes with her brother and uncle while recovering from an illness. Roth was dizzy with lust and sounds happily deranged in his correspondence. 'I'm caught in a terrible fix. I can't settle. I've fallen in love with a 20-year-old girl. It's impossible, it's a crime, I know it, to attach this girl to me, and to the dreadful tangle of my life. But I can't desist.' He told of how 'The little girl slips into my room at night, even though [her guardian is] sleeping next door, prays, crosses herself, and starts to sin.' She wanted to leave her family for him when she came of age, which he knew would be 'a huge scandal' in Bruges:

> I am perpetrating a cretinous stupidity at my age but for the first
> time since my wife's illness, I feel alive again. It's not something
> I can turn away. I think you'll understand. My novel is going
> nowhere, I don't have any income, I'm quite evidently insane. I

---

* A *Frankfurter Zeitung* colleague, newly appointed as feuilleton editor in place of Benno Reifenberg, who had moved to the Paris office.

can't work, and yet I know I'll become completely sterile if I can't have that girl. And then there's my still warm feeling for my wife. I would never have thought I could be so foolish as this ...

Dear friend, it's possible I'll need your calm, and your kind and helpful heart. Will you promise them to me! Don't mention this to anyone, except your good wife! – What shall I do? I have three chapters. I must be finished in July. I'm not enough of a novelist to go around thinking only of my book. With all my scepticism, for all my self-analysis, I'm in love. I'm incredibly fortunate. I need it as a thirsty man needs water. And I know it's poison.[23]

Maria Gillès de Pélichy confessed the affair to her family and was sent to a convent.* A monk wrote to Roth to inform him. Roth was bereft, crushed and full of self-recrimination. He continued to write the novel, and failed to meet his summer deadline.

Max Demant, a Jew of Galician origin, becomes Trotta's closest friend. He has poor vision and is ill-suited to army life. His eye trouble was informed by Roth's at this time. A couple of letters to Zweig in May 1931 detail its effect on him while he was (or rather, wasn't) working on The Radetzky March. May 13: 'I have an eye inflammation that stops me from writing',[24] and eleven days later: 'I am writing to you in a pair of dark glasses, prescribed by the doctor, very unpleasant, cornea apparently damaged. (Excuse any abruptness!) ... Eye is just expression of spiritual depression.'[25]

Demant has not long been back from sick leave, he is evidently

---

* A year later de Pélichy's family arranged for her to marry a respectable Belgian businessman, Jacques de Laveleye, with whom she moved to Brussels; later they lived in the Congo. They had five children in five years, and in 2016 the Belgian Roth scholar Els Snick met the two surviving daughters and one son. Snick wrote a remarkable account of this encounter in the form of a letter to the late Maria, who died in 1983. It tells of how she never loved her children, had to pay them to say they loved her, and spent much of her life drunk. Her affair in Antibes was a family secret whispered about by her sisters; her children knew she had had an illicit lover before marriage, but did not know his identity. 'For you,' Snick wrote to Maria of her time with Roth in Spring 1931, 'they were the last and only happy weeks of your life.' Els Snick, 'Briefgeheim', De Standaard, 28 August 2016.

troubled, and he and Trotta recognise each other's existential discomfort. They are united in their feelings of meaninglessness, and
of living in a grandfather's shadow: Demant's was a larger-than-life
character, famous in his Galician world as 'the silver-bearded king
of the Jewish innkeepers'.[26] One night Trotta walks Demant's cruel,
libidinous wife home from the theatre after the couple had argued
and a drunken Demant left prematurely. Trotta imagines his actions
to be chivalrous, but to the soldiers who oversee them it is an affront
to Demant's honour. The next day in the mess, Demant has a run-in
with a drunken Captain Tattenbach, who tells him to keep an eye on
his wife. 'I wouldn't let my wife go round at midnight on the arm of
a Lieutenant!' Demant tells him he's drunk; Tattenbach responds by
yelling at him: 'Yid!',[27] eight times over. The code of honour dictates
only one outcome to this affair. A duel is arranged for 7.20 a.m., with
pistols at ten paces.

Trotta must write a letter to his father explaining the situation in
which his foolishness has likely condemned his friend to death. He
has belatedly run into adulthood. 'It was the first difficult letter he
had ever had to write.' To write such a letter you would have to be as
strong as his grandfather – 'as straightforward, as decisive, as close to
the peasants of Sipolje. But if you were just his grandson!'[28] Vitality
and moral clarity come from authentic people, Roth implies, not from
those who have been uprooted and set adrift within the class system
by the dubious grace of Imperial decree. Like the would-be assimilator
Roth, Carl Joseph von Trotta is condemned to inauthenticity and its
corollary, constant self-doubt.

The culture of 'death before dishonour' meant that duelling persisted in Austria-Hungary, and especially among the aristocracy and
the army officer class, long after it had been consigned to history in
Germany and elsewhere. From outside it was seen as an insane relic
that embodied the empire's anachronistic culture. Displaying the brav-
ery to face death ranked above all else. Demant would fall victim to
the preposterous principles that Roth had seen within the antisemitic
societies of the University of Vienna. Demant's father-in-law, Herr
Knopfmacher, pinpoints the absurdity of the way this old Austrian

culture has outlived its time: 'There's something anachronistic, if you'll pardon my saying so, about this code of honour! We are in the twentieth century, remember! We have the gramophone, we can telephone people a hundred miles away, and Blériot and some other chaps are flying through the air!'[29] As the doctor himself says to Trotta while they drink away his final night before the duel: 'The cretinous stupidity of it! The honour that's invested in the silly tassel hanging on your sabre. You're not permitted to walk a woman home! Can you see how stupid that is?'[30] He knows that to die this honourable death will cast him as 'a hero', but that it is a futile and absurd heroism that pales beside the actions of the Hero of Solferino.

In the bar the clock ticks onwards, however much both men will it to stop. 'It would take a miracle if Demant was not to die,' Roth narrates. 'And there are no such things as miracles, as the Lieutenant already knew!'[31] Here, in the book after *Job*, he reasserts that there is no use in awaiting a divine intervention. And sure enough, there is no miracle. In the morning Demant and Tattenbach shoot each other, and both fall dead. A Major Prohaska casually imparts the news to Trotta: 'Both of them!' And, as an afterthought: 'Couldn't be helped!'[32]

Trotta is obliged to make another excruciating condolence visit, this time to Frau Demant; the way she seems to flirt with him, even as she sits by him in mourning dress with dried tear-trails on her cheeks, suggests there may after all have been an illicit side to their relationship. His role in the affair obliges him to transfer to a different regiment, from the elite Uhlans to a 'battalion of Jägers who were stationed no more than two miles from the Russian frontier'.[33] So Carl Joseph takes the eighteen-hour train journey to 'the most easterly station in the Austrian monarchy', to restart his career in the little town.

'In the years before the Great War,' Roth writes, 'at the time the events chronicled in these pages took place, it was not yet a matter of indifference whether a man lived or died.' Frau Slama, his grandfather Joseph, the family's trusty old servant Jacques, now Dr Demant: Carl Joseph cannot just lock away his memories of the dead, as those who survived the war would to retain their sanity. Roth adds: 'That's how it was then!

Everything that grew took long to grow; and everything that ended took a long time to be forgotten. Everything that existed left behind traces of itself, and people then lived by their memories, just as we nowadays live by our capacity to forget, quickly and comprehensively.'[34] The war altered collective time-perception and memory, Roth claimed: the only viable coping mechanism for such incalculable trauma was a policy of forgetting. The overwhelmed post-war mind could not bear the immensity of loss and horror, so reacted by shutting it out and looking ahead, rendering one's experience of life thinner, quicker, less engaged. Roth preferred a slower, deeper, richer quality of life, more easily attained in a pre-war era when people had the time and capacity to think and feel, when they could inwardly roam their memory at leisure, and outwardly gaze rather than glance at the world; much better that than this frantic modern condition that compelled him to snatch at passing ideas he would rather have given due contemplation.

His immersion in the little town of his memory was a bid to cultivate a mind-state at odds with the spirit of the times. The difference is analogous to that between the conditions that produce a fully realised novel and a hurried piece of putatively authoritative journalism whose author hopes the reader won't notice he's bluffing. Roth was familiar with both and strained for the former, achieving it somehow in the early 1930s by superhuman effort while being dragged by financial circumstance towards the latter. 'I need to write almost an article a day for the paper,' he told Stefan Zweig while creating *The Radetzky March*. 'I hope it doesn't stay that way.'*[35] He had struggled with journalism since beginning the book; in November 1930 he told Zweig: 'I can hardly access the newspaper tone any more – my head is full of the novel ("The Radetzky March," it'll be called).'†[36] The times called for

---

* As the German Roth scholar Klaus Westermann observes in his afterword to volume three of Roth's collected *Werke*, Roth simply could not sustain his earlier output: in 1921, after establishing himself in Berlin, he published about 160 articles; in 1924, almost 200; in 1930 just fifty and in 1932, when *The Radetzky March* was published, no more than twenty. *Werke*, vol. 3, pp. 1073–4.

† Gustav Kiepenheuer did not give a date for his conversation with Roth in which he claimed to have come up with the book's title, and there may have been a little myth-making in that anecdote given that Roth evidently knew what to call it as early as November 1930.

haste and amnesia but Roth strained to keep remembering the dead, whatever pain it might provoke; the brandy could numb that, as it did his painful present. To memorialise the little town was both a nostalgic retreat and a solemn honour to those he had lost. It was better to engage with their memory, even if it caused one as much suffering as it did Carl Joseph. Midway through the novel, Franz asks his son to be careful with his drinking and reminds him of the dissipated artist Moser, who is now an alcoholic: 'Schnapps will destroy you, you remember Moser, don't you?' Carl Joseph hesitates before confirming that he does, because Moser painted the portrait of his late grandfather. 'Had you forgotten?' his father gently asks.

'No, I haven't forgotten, I've always thought about that picture. I'm not strong enough for that picture. The dead! I can't forget the dead! Father, I can't forget anything! Oh, Father!'[37]

The little town had 10,000 inhabitants and 'a spacious Ring at the centre of it, the crossing point of its two principal streets. Of these, one went from east to west, the other north to south', like the *shtetl* in *The Wandering Jews*. The town is unnamed, referred to only as 'B.', but a clue to its inspiration lies in its tallest building, the Hotel Brodnitzer, modelled on Brody's Hotel Bristol on Goldgasse. The people were brilliant – gifted, hard-working – and could have conquered 'half the world' had they understood it, but they did not. 'Because they lived far away from it, between east and west, jammed in between night and day, a kind of living ghost that was sprung from the night and went about in the daytime.'[38] The bonds between the town's Jägers and nearby Russian border regiments were 'created and maintained by Count Wojciech Chojnicki, one of the wealthiest Polish landowners in the region'.[39] He is related to the Potockis, who owned Brody Castle and were connected to Andrzej Potocki, the Viceroy of Galicia assassinated in Lemberg by a Ukrainian nationalist during the 1908 election campaign. Chojnicki has the kind of freedom Roth desires: to work as and when he wishes, to follow his whims, to try to make money from nothing (he dabbles in alchemy). He has two castles, an 'old' and a 'new' one, but even the 'new' castle is lit by candles. No electricity, by order of the count. This castle is a bulwark against progress, a bastion of conservatism. Here he holds regular parties and soirees, where white-gloved servants in brick-red coats with black velvet collars lavish drinks on the guests: Roth takes pleasure in describing these evenings, which 'always began with vermouth and sherry. Then they moved on to Burgundy and Bordeaux. Then champagne was brought. And that was followed by cognac. They concluded, in apt tribute to the *genius loci*, with the local spirit, the ninety-proof.'[40]

Chojnicki bears more than a passing resemblance to his creator, with his 'bright, clever, slightly protuberant eyes ... his little blond moustache, his narrow shoulders'.[41] Friends of Roth's such as Soma Morgenstern recalled that he would have liked most of all to be a Polish count, and Chojnicki seems a projection of this. The count is a delegate in the Reichstag, where he has a critical word for everyone – in Roth's summary, 'the Emperor was a senile idiot, the government a bunch of morons, the Upper House an assembly of credulous and pathetic nitwits, the state authorities corrupt, villainous and lazy. Austrians of German stock crooned waltzes in their cups, Hungarians stank, Czechs were born to clean shoes, Ruthenians treacherously disguised Russians, Croats and Slovenes, whom he called "stoats and ravens", were broommakers and chestnut-roasters, and Poles, of whom he himself was one, fornicators, barbers and fashion photographers.'[42]

In the capital he ridicules the empire's rulers and its constituent groups; back in the little town, he predicts its demise. 'Whenever he came home from Vienna, or wherever else in the wide world he'd been disporting himself, he would deliver a lugubrious lecture, which would go roughly as follows: "This empire's had it. As soon as the Emperor says goodnight, we'll break up into a hundred pieces. The Balkans will be more powerful than we will. All the peoples will set up their own dirty little statelets, and even the Jews will proclaim a King in Palestine. Vienna stinks of the sweat of democrats, I can't stand to be on the Ringstrasse anymore ... The clergy's desperate to ingratiate itself with the people, you can hear the sermon in Czech if you please. In the Burgtheater, they put on Jewish garbage, and they ennoble one Hungarian toilet manufacturer a week. I tell you, gentlemen, unless we start shooting, it's all up. In our lifetime, I tell you.'"[43] He is insistent about this when Franz Trotta visits Carl Joseph in the little town: that it would be no less foolish to serve the Fatherland than for him to try to make gold from lead, 'Because the Fatherland no longer exists.' Herr von Trotta is perplexed. '"I thought you mightn't understand," said Chojnicki. "The fact is we're all dead!" It was very quiet. The last dim light of the day was long gone. Through the thin gaps in the blinds, you could have sighted a sprinkling of stars already out.'[44]

There are thirty references to the stars in a book of 363 pages (in English translation): that is, they are mentioned every dozen pages on average. They are 'so unattainably high in the sky',[45] they 'glinted in the sky'[46] and 'sparkled in gold and silver'.[47] They overhang *The Radetzky March*, as in Roth's other works, as an inescapable nightly reminder of God's unreachable distance and His indifference. As Trotta and Demant walked together on the night before the duel, 'From the quiet stars came no advice.'[48] Individuals come and go in moments, it takes little longer for great empires to fade and die, and the stars shine on, 'remotely and peacefully'.[49]

If one could only search for Him, instead of remaining rooted to Earth and awaiting a sign. If only one could be active instead of passive: it was tempting to believe a wonder-rabbi could intercede, but Roth had never seen one achieve any success. God remained distant and undetectable. Perhaps He moved through the galaxies as the writer Jean Paul speculated in 1820 in his 'Dream upon the Universe', a fantastical journey through space that embodies the German Romantic tradition behind Roth's fixation on the heavens: 'At length Sirius, and all the brotherhood of our constellations, and the galaxy of our heavens stood far below our feet, as a little nebula amongst other yet more distant neb-ulae. Thus we flew on through the starry wildernesses; one heaven after another unfurled its immeasurable banners before us, and then rolled up behind us; galaxy behind galaxy towered up into solemn altitudes before which the spirit shuddered; and they stood in long array through the fields of the infinite space, like triumphal gates through which the Infinite Being might pass in progress.'[50]

*

Franz is unsettled by the circumstances, the alcohol, his host's speeches. He glances at Carl Joseph merely to see someone familiar, but even his son seems strange to him now. He asks Chojnicki to explain what he means when he says the monarchy no longer exists. It is a notion he has refused to contemplate but must now confront. In a paragraph Roth has Chojnicki enunciate the anti-nationalist, conservative Catholic world view he'd settled on by the time of writing *The Radetzky March* that bemoans atheism while despairing of God's absence:

> 'Of course, taken literally,' Chojnicki replied, 'it still exists. We still have an army' – he nodded at the Lieutenant – 'and we have an officialdom' – with a nod back at the District Commissioner. 'But it's falling apart as we speak. As we speak, it's falling apart, it's already fallen apart! An old man with not long to go, a head cold could finish him off, he keeps his throne by the simple miracle that he's still able to sit on it. But how much longer, how much longer? The age doesn't want us any more! This age wants to establish autonomous nation states! People have stopped believing in God. Nationalism is the new religion. People don't go to church. They go to nationalist meetings. The Monarchy, our monarchy is founded on faith and devotion: on the belief that God has chosen the Habsburgs to reign over a certain number of Christian peoples. Our emperor is like a worldlier pope, his full title is His Royal and Imperial Apostolic Majesty, there is no other apostolic majesty anywhere, and no other royal family in Europe is as dependent on the grace of God and the people's belief in that grace. The German Kaiser will still rule if God deserts him; by the grace of the nation, it would then be. But the Emperor of Austria-Hungary may not be deserted by God. And now God has deserted him!'[51]

The 'apostolic' designation was conferred by the Pope on kings of Hungary in medieval times to recognise their role in spreading Christianity. Now, in the early 1900s, it was a hollow title that counted for nothing. God's desertion of humanity was complete – not only had He abandoned lowly sufferers like Roth, Andreas Pum and Mendel

Singer, but even His modern Apostle, the emperor. What hope was there, then, for anyone? What use was a deity who hid behind the stars? A little over a decade later, many would ask 'Where was God at Auschwitz?', but Roth had concluded Him criminally negligent by the early 1930s.

On parting from his troubled son, Franz wants to tell Carl that he loves him, but he cannot. Instead he just says: 'Chin up!' Male emotional illiteracy is hardly unique to the Habsburg Empire, but here it appears to embody the general culture. Franz cannot be seen to say he loves his son. For Roth, who so desired a father's love, there are few greater failings. This is the rigid Habsburg culture that stifles emotion and replaces it with formulaic behaviour that is intended to preserve the empire but deadens the people who live in it, until they are all walking corpses. Lacking substantial meaning in their lives, the soldiers in the little town are susceptible to the thin thrills of drink and gambling. Word spreads around that Kapturak, the fixer and moneylender whom we met in *Job*, will soon return to establish a casino. His return does not augur well – he is a steely, self-interested and furtive manipulator, one of many such men who haunted the frontier towns in those days, says Roth: 'they used to circle like those cowardly black birds that can see someone dying from an enormous distance'.[52] An unsettling man, dangerous yet somehow intangible, who ghosts across borders, vanishes into gloom, and suddenly stands right before you again when he wants his money back.

Trotta makes a new friend, Captain Wagner. At the casino, established in Brodnitzer's Café, Wagner loses a great deal of money. Kapturak is summoned. He agrees to grant a loan, only if it is guaranteed by someone who's not already in debt to him – someone like Trotta, he suggests. Captain Wagner urges Trotta to hurry up and sign, so he does as he is told. Over this period Trotta also often lends Wagner his own money. Chojnicki decides therefore that Trotta would benefit from being removed from Wagner's reach by taking a few days' break in Vienna with a married woman of his acquaintance, Frau von Taussig, who sleeps around to ward off her fear of ageing and mortality.

Trotta obediently agrees. Together in the capital the couple sit in the grandstand to watch the Corpus Christi procession, a grand spectacle whereby Roth can convey the aesthetic appeal of the monarchy's pomp and circumstance, even as he identifies its terminal malaise and the hollowness behind the shining façade.

Here, as throughout the book, Roth describes the soldiers' appearance with a relish for the telling detail informed in part by his army experience, and in part by his boyhood awe at the towering men in pristine uniform whom the little Muniu gazed up at when they visited Kalman Ballon's tailoring business. Roth conducted a rare amount of research for this novel, knowing he had to get it just right: he collected pictures of the *k. und k.* army and studied an illustrated book about its uniforms and insignia; then, on the manuscript's completion, another of Kiepenheuer's authors, Alexander Lernet-Holenia, was commissioned to check the military details for accuracy. The result is that Roth writes with a conviction and confidence that renders every description of the uniforms vivid. Here in Vienna, the couple watch 'gold-decked Knights of the Golden Fleece' and 'coffee-brown artillery', Bosnians in 'blood-red fezzes' and a squadron of dragoons whose 'black and grey helmets glinted in the sun'; and they see the 'china-blue eyes of the Supreme Commander' Franz Joseph, which 'filled out with new fatherly devotion and looked out at the grandson of the Hero of Solferino like a whole blue sky'.[53] And yet, dazzling as they are, the emperor and his parading troops are mechanical, lifeless, with all the presence of a cavalcade of ghosts: an ethereal superimposition from an otherwise vanished past, compelled by some occult mechanism to retrace the same route down the Viennese boulevards. They are all dead, only they do not yet realise it.

Now one of Roth's characteristic sudden intrusions by fate returns death from the metaphorical to the literal realm; the book consists of a pendulum-like series of swings between the two. Trotta's major asks that he lead his platoon of Jägers to assist local gendarmes in suppressing a brush factory workers' revolt, a task that at least echoes his grandfather's legendary moment, such that he can settle the question of how he'd act under pressure: he cannot save the elderly emperor, but he can protect his empire from a revolutionary threat. He comes to realise that his duty here places him as an oppressor. Trotta summons memories of the spectacle of Habsburg pageantry in Vienna to fortify him to suppress these impoverished men, who have for years been labouring in a factory where the dust causes a fatal lung condition. On the morning of the protest, in full uniform he enters a crowded local bar for a quick 'ninety-proof', and when the surrounding drinkers lapse into hostile silence he realises they are the protestors. One schnapps turns into several, before he departs with 'a hundred pairs of eyes stuck in his neck like darts'.

He lines up his platoon, and they too fall silent, eyeing him with sullen, taciturn faces. Neither side of this dispute admires him. He is quite alone. Now, Roth writes, 'the unhappy Lieutenant Trotta felt for certain that this was not the place for him. Where else?, he asked himself . . . Where do I belong? Not with those men sitting in the bar! In Sipolje? With my forefathers? With a plough in my hand instead of a sword?'[54] He discovers the urge towards the ancestral home and a healthy, natural, rural life on the land that Roth had toyed with at least since attempting to write *Strawberries*. Still his men stand frozen, until he orders them: 'At ease!' At last the decisive moment comes. The workers approach from the bar, singing the 'Internationale' in multiple languages, and Trotta orders his men to fall in. They shoulder arms. The workers yell and surge towards the gendarmes. Trotta orders his men to fix bayonets, then to march to the factory, whereupon the workers bombard them with lumps of metal and stone. Trotta freezes. He does not know what to do. Beside him appears the town's mayor, Horak, who urges him: 'Tell them to shoot, Lieutenant, for heaven's sake!' So the lieutenant does as he is told by the mayor. His men shoot their first salvo into the air, as their major had instructed. A woman cries out, some of her comrades think she has been hit, and soon they are all throwing rocks and nailed planks at the platoon. Trotta freezes. He does not know what to do. Again, Horak speaks up: 'Shoot! For God's sake, shoot!'[55] So Trotta repeats the order to fire, and is then knocked unconscious by a missile. He falls to the ground with a broken skull. His leaderless men shoot wildly until the highway is littered with bodies.

In the garrison hospital he urges the major not to tell his father of the events, then he falls ill with a brain fever and almost dies. As he drifts in and out of consciousness, Trotta is oblivious to the newspaper coverage that informs Franz Trotta of his son's culpability for the debacle. Carl Joseph is recovering when Captain Wagner appears at his bedside, asking that he act as guarantor for a loan from Kapturak. Again, Trotta signs. Two days later a doctor tells him that the deeply indebted Wagner has shot himself in the woods. If only Trotta had acted in his friend's interest, instead of weakly agreeing to help him further into debt. Trotta falls into more feverish dreams where the dead on his conscience try to summon him into their realm. What has he to show for his life but a trail of people whose deaths he has inadvertently brought about? The woman who bore his illicit child, the doctor he condemned to a duel, the striking workers who died because of his inert 'leadership', and now Captain Wagner ... He may be a soldier, but none of these deaths was intentional; he kills through being passive and suggestible. Unknown to him, as he lies in hospital, an investigation into his responsibility for the workers' deaths crawls through the military bureaucracy until an auditor connects his surname with the Hero of Solferino, and directs Trotta's file for the emperor's attention. The confused old emperor cannot remember why the name is so familiar. He asks a servant. The servant, himself elderly, vaguely recalls reading about the Battle of Solferino in a schoolbook ... 'Trotta!' he cries. 'That was the man who saved Your Majesty's life!' The emperor adds a final note to Trotta's file: 'To be settled favourably!'[56] Carl Joseph is rescued by his grandfather – a stroke of fortune that at the same time reinforces his life's meaninglessness, for once again his family's status protects him from experiencing consequences for his actions.

The emperor's vagueness justifies Chojnicki's terse description of his senility and infirmity. He has a 'head cold' such as the count described, but to prove it won't finish him off he decides to assert himself by making a surprise inspection of military manoeuvres out on the eastern frontier. There he is billeted in an old castle near the Russian border. Though his days are accounted for down to the minute, he can at least steal himself a few minutes' freedom and solitude by night. In his nightgown he creeps to his bedroom window and gazes out at 'the endless, deep blue, starry sky',[57] suddenly seeming 'very tiny to himself in front of the illimitable night'.[58] The next day brings a full roster of appointments that illustrate the pluralism of Austria–Hungary, flawed as it was. He must attend a service at the Greek Orthodox church, where a Roman Catholic and then a Greek Orthodox priest will say Mass. This done, someone whispers that the Jews are waiting for him too. 'They'd been completely forgotten. Oh dear, the Jews as well, thought the Emperor. All right! Have them come! But they'd better hurry. Otherwise he'd be late for the battle.'[59] He meets them at the edge of the village, where he sits on his white horse, clad in his blue cloak. 'Like a field full of strange black grain in the wind, the community of Jews bowed before the Emperor.'[60] An elder stops three paces before the emperor and holds up the Torah before giving a blessing in Hebrew. All is quiet but for the call of wild ducks flying by, a cockerel crowing in a faraway farmyard, and the gentle muttering of the Jews, whose 'long, silver-white, coal-black and fire-red beards ... were moving in the mild autumnal breeze'.[61] The elder issues his final benediction: 'Blessed art thou! Thou shalt not witness the end of the world!'[62] The emperor knows this all too well. He shakes the old Jew's hand and mounts his horse to ride away.

Here Roth works in his version of the example of Franz Joseph's benevolence towards Galicia's Jews taken from Brody folklore. The emperor overhears Captain of Horse Kaunitz saying he 'didn't understand a syllable of what that Jew was saying!'. The emperor turns to him on horseback: 'Never you mind, Kaunitz, he was talking to me!'[63] He rides on to inspect the battlefield exercise, which has been under way for two days. He does not understand what he is watching, though he tells his staff that he does. But he sees the bigger picture. When he looks out over the battlefield through a field-glass, this time the act brings him clarity rather than a sniper's bullet. He sees that his army will be 'defeated and broken up, distributed among the many peoples of his great empire. He could see the great golden sun of the Habsburgs sinking, smashing on the bottom of the universe, crumbling into various littler suns, which would shine as independent bodies to independent nations.'[64]

Now he must inspect the stationary regiments, which brings him to Trotta's battalion of Jägers. Trotta has only been out of hospital a few weeks. He is pale, drawn, apathetic and defeated, 'like a man who had lost not only his home, but also his homesickness, his nostalgia for that home':[65] Roth's epitome of desolation. The emperor asks if he is ill. Major Zoglauer explains the recent troubles suffered by Lieutenant Trotta, and the name sounds irritatingly familiar. He remembers the file that landed on his desk; but then also its connection with the Hero of Solferino. 'I remember your father very well!' he tells Trotta.

'Your Majesty,' Trotta replies, 'that was my grandfather!' The impact of how much time has passed, how very old he is now, sends the emperor reeling. He continues to make small talk but he has lost focus; he no longer sees Trotta before him but instead fixes his gaze on the distance, 'where the edges of infinity had come a little closer'.[66] As he contemplates eternity he is oblivious that a pendulous drop of mucus hangs from the tip of his nose. All the troops are willing it to fall, and at last it drips into his silver moustache. With that, the march past can begin. In a single tragicomic image, Roth lampoons the old man and his empire: both are pitiful, infirm and quietly mocked by onlookers.

Carl Joseph makes a rare independent decision: to leave the army. But Kapturak wants his money. It is the callousness of a man whom one of the soldiers later damns as a 'Jewish bloodsucker'[67] calling in a debt that spurred Wagner's demise and now sinks Trotta into yet deeper despair. His financial crisis is worsened by profligate spending on Frau Taussig. An imbroglio over a debt that must suddenly be repaid by a man left impoverished by the costs of maintaining a woman, entangled with resentment towards wealthy Jews whose favour dictates one's fortune: this was the stuff of Roth's life by now. His antisemitic remarks had become more vitriolic and provocative. In editing his letters for post-humous publication, his friend Hermann Kesten chose to remove a word from one Roth wrote to Zweig just after finishing The Radetzky March. He beseeches Zweig to forget about him, expresses regret for

ever embroiling him in his chaotic life, and bemoans his financial predicament. 'Possibly I am sinful, because I get through far more money
than more deserving persons require. I comfort myself with the (base)
thought that I have shorter to live than the deserving ones. I have no
plan for the rest of my life. If the [. . .] Jewish scribblers trash me, then
I have no money, Landauer has no money. I am 20,000 marks in hock
to the publisher. The publisher has done a lot for me. He needs money.
He doesn't have any. Please understand that I can do nothing. I cannot
live like this.'[68] The ellipsis stands in for '*saujüdischen*', meaning 'piggish-
Jewish'. The *Judensau* is an image dating from medieval Germany that
depicts Jews in sexual congress with, or suckling from, a pig. It is calculated to maximise insult to Jews. A desperate Roth, casting wildly
about in an abysmal depression, depicted his fate as hanging in the
balance at the mercy of all-powerful Jewish critics, whom he described
with a term steeped in Christian antisemitic tradition. The word is like
a grenade lobbed on to the page by a man out of control, later defused
by Kesten in an attempt to safeguard his friend's posthumous reputation. The well-to-do Zweig was no stranger to peddling disdainful
stereotypes of *Ostjuden*, but this word would surely have appalled him
and strengthened his concern for Roth's mental state.

Carl Joseph's descent into drink and debt takes a heavy toll on his
father, who ages rapidly like Andreas Pum and Mendel Singer, like
Jechiel Grübel, and now like Roth himself. Whereas the modest Joseph
Trotta sought an audience with the emperor because of his unease at
how he had been placed on a pedestal, now his desperate son Franz
seeks the same to exploit the family's elevated social position. He travels
to Vienna and trawls through a series of old contacts, all of whom are
shocked by his appearance: 'they were put in mind of a ghost, a ghost
from the olden days of the old Habsburg Monarchy; the shadow of history'.[69] Eventually he succeeds in arranging an audience at Schönbrunn.
He wears his full and finest uniform for a meeting in the palace. Here
in the heart of Habsburg power the sun shines undimmed, and it pours
through the high, open windows, between drawn and breeze-blustered
curtains, to highlight the district commissioner's perfect white gloves
and golden sword handle as he waits to be summoned to the emperor's

sanctum. The emperor glances at the file before him. Another Trotta! These people will keep bothering him. But which one was this – the Hero of Solferino? Franz politely explains. Finally he asks, three times over: 'Your Majesty! I beg you to have mercy on my son!' The two men reflect one another; they look near-identical now, with Franz Trotta's whiskers as white as Franz Joseph's, and when the emperor remarks on the fine weather and gestures to the window with his left hand, Trotta does so with his right, so the emperor is distracted by the odd feeling of standing before his own mirror image. Then he remembers how busy he is, and wraps up the conversation. 'That's fine then! It'll be taken care of! What has he got up to? Money? Taken care of! Regards to your Papa!'[70]

In the early summer of 1914, the military men in the little town are absorbed by their preparations for a grand party in Chojnicki's woodland, intended to give the troops a lift and serve as a rehearsal for the regiment's centenary celebrations the following year. Men of senior ranks spend their days fine-tuning an obsequious letter of invitation to a minor aristocrat, while charging their juniors with such tasks as hanging lanterns and garlands from the trees, making confetti, or checking that the serving staff's gloves are snug and spotless. Counts and barons from across Austria-Hungary are invited. No one hears the footsteps of war creeping up from behind, nor do they pay heed to the darkening weather. As the party begins, rainclouds gather. At first the military bands drown out the thunder and the fireworks are brighter than the lightning, but the storm comes too close to ignore. The symbolism is not Roth's subtlest work. The guests decamp into Chojnicki's castle, and none notices a dragoon on horseback gallop to the front door and ask to see Colonel Festetics. He hands a letter to the colonel, who withdraws to the castle's gloomy circular hall to read it: 'There are unconfirmed reports that the heir to the throne has been assassinated in Sarajevo.'[71]

Word of Franz Ferdinand's shooting reaches Chojnicki, who invites his higher-ranking guests – among them Lieutenant Trotta – one after another to a separate room where he tells them the news. None reacts strongly: some are too drunk, some are 'crippled as it were by their own inborn refinement',[72] the buttoned-up, emotionally repressive instinct of the Austrian upper classes. There is talk of abandoning the party. Some say it is only a rumour, others that a rumour is enough reason to cease their revelry. But not everyone is dismayed by the possibility of the archduke's death. The Hungarian contingent are in no mood to stop partying. Baron Nagy Jëno, a Hussar, loathed Franz Ferdinand because he was considered to prefer Slavs to Magyars. He 'had not come all the way to a party on this desperate frontier, only to have it called off because of some incident or another'.[73] Besides, he declares, even if the rumour were true, 'If one heir to the Monarchy has been assassinated, then there are other heirs to the Monarchy!'[74] The drunken Hungarians begin to talk among themselves in their own language, which no one else comprehends, but they do understand the intermittent bursts of laughter. Finally Master of Horse Jelacich, a Slovene who hated Hungarians as much as he did the Serbs, asks them to speak in German. 'All right,' a Count Benkyö replies, 'I can say it in German too: we were just agreeing, my compatriots and I, that it's a good thing if the son of a bitch is dead!'[75]

Trotta sways and grows paler. The fractures in his fatherland are now impossible to ignore, and he can see that it is breaking into pieces. At last, he locates his grandfather within himself and, with this, his voice. His grandfather, he declaims with fury to his drunken audience, saved the emperor's life, and Trotta, his grandson, would not stand by while the Habsburgs were insulted in this way. 'The behaviour of these gentlemen is scandalous!' he shouts. He threatens to shoot the next man to insult Franz Ferdinand's memory. He reaches for his gun. Benkyö starts to speak again – 'Be quiet!'[76] shouts Trotta. He is ordered from the room by Major Zoglauer; news of one murder is quite enough, and he does not want another. And as Trotta leaves, other guests pile into the room, and Benkyö calls out a request to the band: 'The Funeral March!' In the novel's grimmest tableau, the musicians strike up a ragged performance of Chopin's 'Marche Funèbre' and a horde of drunken, laughing guests, confetti still scattered on their heads and shoulders, form a circle to march and skip a *danse macabre*, going 'round and round, each one a mourner behind the corpse of the person in front',[77] accelerating as the band increases the tempo; and now it is Chopin's composition that dictates the mood, not Strauss's march for a dead empire.

Carl Joseph von Trotta leaves the army. He begins a new life among the peasants in the countryside near Chojnicki's castle. Here, as a civilian in the little town, living more like a proletarian than a baron, he feels at home:

> He knew the local language now. He could more or less under-stand what the peasants said. He traded with red-haired Jews, who were already beginning to buy in wood for the winter. He learned the different prices for birch, fir, pine, oak, linden and sycamore. He was mean. Just like his grandfather, the Hero of Solferino, the knight of truth, he counted out hard silver coins with his hard, bony fingers when he travelled into town of a Thursday, to the pig market, to buy saddles, hames, yokes and scythes, whetstones, reaping hooks, hoes and seed. When he chanced to see an officer passing by, he ducked his head. It was an unnecessary precaution. His moustaches grew and grew, the stubble stood tough and black and thick on his cheeks, he was unrecognisable. Preparations for the harvest were already in full swing, the peasants stood outside their huts, whetting their scythes on round, brick-red stones. All over the country sounded the chafe and scrape of steel on stone, drowning out the song of the crickets. At night, the Lieutenant would occasionally hear music and noise from Chojnicki's 'new castle'. He took those sounds into his sleep with him, they were no different from the occasional crowing of the cocks at night, or the dogs barking at the full moon. At last, he was contented, lonely and at peace. It was as though he had never led any other sort of life. When he couldn't sleep, he got up, picked up his stick, walked through the fields, through the polyphony of night, and awaited the morning when he'd greet the red sun and breathe in the dew and the gentle song of the wind that portends the day. He felt as fresh then as he did after a good night's sleep. Every afternoon, he walked

through the surrounding villages. 'Praise be to Christ Jesus!' said
the peasants. 'For ever and ever, amen!' replied Trotta. He had the
same bent-kneed walk as they did. That was the way the peasants
of Sipolje walked.[78]

He has returned to the condition of his Slovene ancestors. The
Trotta family has completed its deviation from its natural place. He is
restored, revived. He has come home.

The natural world detects the coming war before the humans; the
screaming ravens are more attuned than the peasants, who still work on
the fields and sharpen their scythes in anticipation of the harvest. The
bullet fired by Gavrilo Princip on 28 June led to the July Crisis, when
Austria wanted to retaliate against Serbia but feared Russian support for
the Serbs, and thus sought German backing. The Germans urged rapid
action by Austria to exploit sympathy for Franz Ferdinand's murder and
keep the crisis local, but instead Austria prevaricated. It finally issued
an ultimatum to Serbia on 23 July, listing demands such as a ban on
anti-Austrian propaganda publications; the outlawing of the nationalist
group connected to Princip; a joint Serbian-Austrian investigation into
the assassination plot; and removal of anti-Austrian individuals from
the military, government and civil service. Serbia could not accede to
every demand in the ultimatum, which Winston Churchill called 'the
most insolent document of its kind ever devised'.[79] On 28 July, a month
after Ferdinand's assassination, Emperor Franz Joseph declared war.

Carl Joseph rejoins the army. The Jäger battalion marches to the
north-eastern frontier at Woloczyska. They tramp on through a ghostly
landscape populated only by corpses of shot and hanged civilians. The
only sound is the howling of hungry dogs in abandoned farmyards.
The sun beats down, Trotta's platoon grows thirsty. They pass through
a couple of villages where the wells are 'choked with the corpses of
shootings and summary justice'.[80] At last they find another well, on the
raised ground of a railway embankment, but they can hear gunshots.
Some men are so thirsty they still run for water, and soon there are
more than a dozen bodies on the slope. Trotta orders his men to halt
and announces that he will fetch the water himself. It is a noble and

foolhardy gesture. As Max Demant turned to face Tattenbach's pistol, so Trotta walks into a firestorm. In his mind he is on his father's balcony hearing the band play the 'Radetzky March'. He takes a bullet in the skull. The Ukrainian peasants in his platoon call to him: 'Praise be to Christ Jesus!', but Trotta cannot muster the strength to respond. He cannot complete the Ukrainian blessing. It is left unresolved. He cannot even utter the dying words he wishes to speak. He has no resolution, no dignity. His body is left to be consumed by ravens and mud. Both Trotta and Demant die with honour, but to anyone looking in from outside Austria, the honour is outweighed by futility.

Carl Joseph asked Frau Slama's widower if she had an easy death. The night before his duel, Max Demant raised a glass: 'To an easy death!'[81] The Trottas' servant Jacques's quick and restful death prompts Franz to remark: 'That's how I'd like to die when the time comes.'[82] Carl Joseph's is not a good and easy death, it is pointless and pained. Just when he seemed to have found meaning to his life in the little town, the war condemned him to a meaningless demise. How can anyone expect to die well in a world so dictated by fate? Roth is, at the age of thirty-eight, when such questions should ideally remain abstract, analysing in earnest how best to take his leave of the world.

With Carl Joseph gone, his father succumbs at last to the emotion he has so long suppressed. He cries, then he begins to shake, and he roams the house and the streets informing anyone he encounters: 'My son is dead!' He continues to tremble for the remaining two years of his life. One day he receives a letter requesting that he visit Count Chojnicki in Vienna's Steinhof, the psychiatric hospital Roth described in his first published newspaper article back in 1919. The count has been confined there in a bare room since going insane on the battlefield. When Trotta arrives, the count says: 'Welcome to my mansion!' before promising to impart important news. 'You mustn't tell anyone! You and I are the only ones to know. The old man's dying!' He knows of the emperor's impending death, he explains, because God told him. Even in his insanity, the insanity that Roth feared he himself would succumb to, the all-seeing conservative count is correct. The emperor dies on 21 November 1916. Franz von Trotta dies only a few days later. The emperor is interred in the Capuchin Crypt, the district commissioner in a cemetery, where the ceaseless rain drums on the heads of the graveside mourners. Of the two men, Franz's friend Dr Skovronnek remarks: 'I don't think either of them could outlive Austria.'

Skovronnek goes to his café, where he and Franz used to play chess. The waiter looks to take the board away, but he says: 'No, leave it there!'[83] He plays against himself, an empty chair opposite. Outside the autumn rain sprays against the windowpanes. The skies, we infer, are grey and the air cold. The Habsburg sun is nowhere to be seen, and soon night will fall.

On 17 April 1932 the novel began its serialisation in the *Frankfurter Zeitung*, where it ran until 9 June. Roth had his new partner, Andrea Manga Bell, type up his chapters for submission to the newspaper. He wrote a foreword for his newspaper readers that clarified his affection for the lost father and fatherland he had satirised. The emperor and empire had many flaws, but few compared with those of the illiberal, nationalist demagoguery that was gaining control in Europe today. 'A cruel will of history has shattered my old fatherland, the Austro-Hungarian monarchy. I loved this fatherland, which allowed me to be a patriot and a citizen of the world at the same time, an Austrian and a German among all Austrian peoples. I loved the virtues and the merits of this fatherland, and today, when it is dead and lost, I love its faults and its weaknesses. It had many of them. It has atoned for them through its death.'[84]

On 11 July, Benno Reifenberg told him it was 'the first novel I read in serial form in the paper from beginning to end. Sometimes I even waited for the Reich edition* to come out, so that I could read the following instalment the evening before.'[85] There is something

---

* Reifenberg was reading the next day's instalment the evening before its publication. In the 1920s the *Frankfurter Zeitung* usually had three daily editions – two in the morning, one in the evening. Later they produced this *Reichsausgabe*, which combined news from all three editions and was printed in the evening for subscribers outside Frankfurt, brought to them by night train in time for the following morning.

poignant and touching in Reifenberg's attempt to build bridges with the former friend who had begun to shun him. It is a measure of the distance between them now that, where once they wrote by hand to each other's homes, this letter was dictated and sent to 'Mr J. Roth, c/o Kiepenheuer Verlag, 10 Kantstrasse, Berlin-Charlottenburg'.

The serialisation began before the novel was finished, Roth explained to Zweig, writing to him in August 1932 after a period of silence. He had written much of it slowly, his publisher recalled, sometimes only a single sentence a day, crafted to perfection; then at the end he had to hurry. Andrea Manga Bell said to Bronsen that Roth was still unsure how to end the story when he was three-quarters of the way through. In March 1932 he told Félix Bertaux he was still 'working desperately on the *Radetzky March*. The material is too much, I am frail, and unable to shape it.'[86] To Friedrich Traugott Gubler, Reifenberg's replacement as the *Frankfurter Zeitung*'s feuilleton editor, he described being immersed in the writing as 'like a mountain range in which I wander about in terror. One day, everything comes off, the next day it's all shit. Tricky, treacherous business. I don't even want to talk about the fact that in material terms I'm short of practically everything, I have nothing to eat unless someone asks me out, basically I don't care. I've tried to take refuge in the prewar era, but it's desperately difficult to write about when you feel the way I do [about those times]. I'm very much afraid I'm a bodger.'[87] He missed a deadline in September 1931, completed a version for serialisation, then made hasty changes before its publication as a book.

During this time he neglected his correspondence. 'I'm not sure that after such a long time, you don't have the right to set this letter aside, unopened,' he told Zweig. 'In 4 months this is the first week . . . that I can draw breath . . . Imagine, my novel had started to run in the paper before it was even finished. And, so to speak with the hot breath of pursuing time on my neck – of course to paralysing effect – I had to go on writing, revise, correct, and finally put in a flimsy ending. A Hamburg book club bought the book for August. I have to correct and revise, all at the same time, for 8 bloody hours a day and I'm completely enfeebled by it. My hands are still shaking.'[88] He explains that he has been staying with friends and acquaintances for months, 'and you know how ghastly that is for a habitual hotel dweller like me'.[89] He was subsisting on the five marks per day Kiepenheuer was paying him. 'I've had to stop paying back all my most pressing debts. Which made them press me all the more. There were places I couldn't even show my face. I owe the *Frankfurter Zeitung* 400 marks, I don't have the patience to write articles any more.' He said the only payments he had managed to keep up were the monthly instalments for Friedl's care: she remained in the sanatorium at Rekawinkel. 'Kiepenheuer can only keep going as long as its Jewish bankers stay in Germany. But everything suggests they're pulling out of Berlin. National Socialism will strike at the core of my existence.'[90]

On 18 September he wrote to Zweig again. The book had been published five days earlier and now Roth felt an immense absence within him. Zweig had read the book and congratulated Roth, who informed him by reply that 'your critical judgement let you down when you read my *Radetzky March*',[91] and his 'good luck message shames me'.[92] Roth felt he deserved nothing of the sort. 'I know my shortcomings in this novel, how I cried to the story itself to help me, embarrassing help for my "composition," which was rotten and deceitful of me. That's why I tinkered away at it for so long, two years, that's no proof of health, strength, and productivity.'[93] He emphasised: 'Believe me, I know all too well that my book hasn't turned out the way it should have. Of course I can tell you exactly why and wherefore. But what would be the point? I felt it while I was writing. I didn't write you that whole time. I know you have no fondness for wailing walls. They don't bring luck. Any friendship with me is ruinous. I myself am a wailing wall, if not a heap of rubble. You have no idea how dark it is inside me.' The affluent, cautious Zweig could never conceptualise such darkness, Roth explains, in a wounding insult dressed as a compliment. 'Because you are lucky enough – I've wanted to say this to you for a long time – not to be able to see certain depths of darkness, yes, you avert your eye. You have the grace to be able to avert your eye from darknesses that would do you harm.'[94] The word 'grace' was flattery: what Roth meant was blithe privilege, cowardice and complacency. In the next breath, he prostrates himself before Zweig, castigating himself as a harmful influence on a serene and good man. Roth's shame may be appropriate, but it is also dismaying. When he was in such a state – desperate, almost certainly drunk – he would permit no thought to go unexpressed. 'Believe me, it hurts me that I owe you money, for instance! – and it hurts me too that I am telling you this, I know exactly how much, I have it written down. I also know that you would otherwise give it to much more deserving individuals. I want to pay it back to you in slow instalments,' he promises. 'I tell you all this, shamelessly. I hope you will understand. Yes, you will understand.'[95]

In November, Roth wrote from Frankfurt to Félix Bertaux, explaining that he might be in Paris with Andrea Manga Bell for 'the dreary celebration of Christmas', in which case they might meet. 'Admittedly, I'll be short of money, and living in pretty reduced circumstances. The income from the Radetzky March won't come through until next spring.'

Even the congenitally pessimistic Roth was unduly optimistic here. It would not come through at all. In January 1933 Adolf Hitler became Chancellor of Germany, and in March the Enabling Act removed the Reichstag's ability to provide any opposition, granting him absolute power. Roth was on the Nazis' first list of prohibited writers. All his existing work was banned. He could not be published in German newspapers, thus abruptly severing his strained relationship with the Frankfurter Zeitung, and he could not have books published. Nor could he receive royalties for books already published. His career in Germany was finished. A man of brilliant talents who had expended much energy on transcending his eastern Jewish origin and assimilating into German–Austrian culture had been disabused of any lingering doubt as to his status. He was no more than a Jew.

Géza von Cziffra met Roth in Budapest in 1935, where he 'took out a copy of The Radetzky March from a briefcase and put it on the table.

'"I wanted to ask you if you wouldn't like to make a film of my novel. You were enthusiastic about it at the time."

'"I still am," I said, "but I'm afraid the material is far too elaborate, far too expensive for a purely Hungarian version. And in Germany . . ."'

'Roth cut me off: "... the dirty Jew Roth is banned."

'"I would have put it differently, Joseph," I said regretfully, "but that is undoubtedly the truth." Roth remained sullenly silent.'[96]

In late January 1933 Roth bumped into von Cziffra in a Berlin pub Roth did not usually frequent, the Café Hessler. Roth explained he was having to avoid his usual haunts having received threatening letters in which he was called a 'Jewish greaser' and a '*Saujud*', the term he himself had applied to Jewish literary critics in a letter to Zweig. The letter writers called Andrea Manga Bell 'a negro whore' who should be flayed alive. The couple spent that night staying with a friend of hers. Roth explained he would soon leave Germany for as long as Hitler was in charge. Hitler was not yet Reich chancellor and Hindenburg had not yet signed the Enabling Act, so von Cziffra 'didn't see Germany's future as bleakly as Roth did, and I told him so. But he waved it off.

'"Don't have any illusions, hell will reign here. Hitler's brownshirts will attack the Jews as the Cossacks did in Russia." He delivered his sentences so passionately that I fell silent, affected.

'"It doesn't matter to you," said Roth. "You are, after all, a goy." He paused for a moment, then added, "But still I advise you to leave."'[97]

He stowed two tied-up boxes of manuscripts, typescripts, galley proofs and newspaper clippings with Gustav Kiepenheuer. By chance they would survive looting by the Gestapo two months later. Had the Gestapo destroyed them, as they did two-thirds of the material in the Kiepenheuer archive, we would have lost the pre-published versions of *Hotel Savoy*, *Rebellion*, *Zipper and His Father*, *The Wandering Jews* and *Job*, and might never have known *The White Cities*, parts of *Strawberries*, 'Youth', 'The Private Tutor' and *Perlefter*, which were published post-humously from these fragmented drafts.

On 30 January 1933, the day Hitler took power as Reich chancellor, Roth fled Berlin for Paris, accompanied on the train by Andrea Manga Bell and her children. It was not intended as a grand, permanent exit, but he would never return to Germany. A fort-night later he wrote Zweig a note from the Hôtel Jacob in the 6th arrondissement in which he repeated his warning to von Cziffra. 'It will have become clear to you now that we are heading for a great catastrophe. Quite apart from our personal situations – our literary and material existence has been wrecked – we are headed for a new war. I wouldn't give a heller for our prospects. The barbarians have taken over. Do not deceive yourself. Hell reigns. Warmly, your old Joseph Roth.'[98]

The coming weeks would bring Zweig a deluge of letters from Roth, who told him the times demanded constant contact. On Friday, 17 March Roth asked him, given that there was no prospect of being published in Germany: 'Now do you understand why I always was, and am, presciently sad?'[99] Two days later came a request for an urgent loan by the middle of the week. In a long letter on 22 March he discussed their Jewish cultural inheritance, noted that the Jews were not the Nazis' only target, but 'as ever' were 'the ones that raise the most piteous lament', and told Zweig: 'It's not right that you want to stay even if things get dangerous.'[100] On 26 March, three days after the Enabling Act granted Hitler dictatorial power, he chided Zweig for his pacifism, for failing to take the fight to the Nazis. While it was vital not to give the impression of only caring for the Jews' fate in the face of such widespread oppression, it was incumbent on them as Jews to stand up for themselves. Zweig's seemingly elevated station and serene manner would offer no protection. 'There is a certain point where noblesse is disobliging, and doesn't help anyone. Because for the beasts over there, a filthy yid is what one remains. You opposed the war as a Jew, and I fought in it as a Jew . . . On the battlefield of humanity, you could say, there are such people as behind-the-lines Jews. We mustn't be like that.'[101]

The pugnacious Roth evidently considered Zweig's prevarication unconscionable. It was long past time to get out and speak up. Roth had apparently seen where events were heading as early as the previous summer: a line attributed to him in June 1932 by his cousin Fred Grübel is so prescient it smacks of restrospective myth-making. 'It's time to leave,' he is supposed to have said over drinks at Mampes Gute Stube. 'They will burn our books and mean us.'[102] Remarkable foresight if true, though he didn't pluck the idea from nowhere: it was suggested by Heinrich Heine's remark of over a century earlier, when he responded to a festival of book-burning by German students by writing: 'Where they burn books, they will also in the end burn people.'*

On 10 May 1933, around 40,000 people massed into Berlin's Opernplatz to hear a speech from Joseph Goebbels and hurl thousands of books on to a bonfire, among them *The Radetzky March* and Zweig's anti-war play *Jeremias*. And yet even after this, Zweig hesitated. In a letter two weeks later, Roth was blunter still: 'I am afraid, I fear for your immortal soul. You don't mind if I'm open with you? – I am afraid you don't quite see events straight. You're pondering your alternatives. You're making up your mind.'[103] Anyone with moral clarity would have made up their mind; Roth certainly had. He laid out the future for the dilatory Zweig's perusal. His projected timescales were awry, but otherwise Roth's vision was accurate. Nazism would last four years; Hitler would end in disaster or in a restored monarchy; within five months Jewish authors would no longer be published nor sold in German bookshops; there was no hope, they could only brace themselves for Hitler's inevitable war on the Jews. 'All authors of repute who stay will suffer their own literary death,' he warned. But perhaps Zweig was paralysed by considering this scenario alongside its alternative: any author so entirely invested in Germanic culture who left would suffer spiritual death. Either way he was confronted by a void. Now in his early fifties and starting to feel old, how could Stefan Zweig secure a future either inside or outside Germany and Austria?

From Paris, Roth wrote an article for the *Cahiers des Juifs* that echoes the lack of hope in his private correspondence but, unsurprisingly, takes a more philosemitic attitude than he displayed to his friends. Titled 'Auto-Da-Fé of the Mind' and published that autumn, it argues that 'Now, as the smoke of our burned books rises into the sky, we German writers of Jewish descent must acknowledge above all that we have been defeated. Let us, who were fighting on the frontline, under

---

* From Heine's play *Almansor*: '*Dort, wo man Bücher verbrennt, verbrennt man am Ende auch Menschen.*' Written after the 300th anniversary of Martin Luther's Ninety-Five Theses, in 1817, when nationalistic students who advocated the unification of German states burned books by authors they considered anti-German.

the banner of the European mind, let us fulfil the noblest duty of the defeated warrior: let us concede our defeat.'[104]

This stance was temporary. The article documents a moment of resignation, when his sadness overwhelmed him. In time he would rally, even as his morale continued to decline. He knew the odds were impossible, as he made plain to Zweig, but his sense of honour and moral duty compelled him to keep fighting, even from a position of powerlessness and almost inevitable defeat. He would not be a 'behind-the-lines' Jew like Zweig. He would remain an overt and vocal opponent of Nazism, even though he could no longer stand at the front line in Germany. From now he was compelled to fight in exile.

Chapter Eleven

There was at this time only one word that had any meaning: Flight!

One could flee. He felt as if he had been abstracted from
his own life for years and as if he were living somebody
else's. Somewhere his own waited like a good home, unjustly
abandoned.

The Silent Prophet

The Parisian literary journalist Frédéric Lefèvre watched his interviewee pace around a square salon with a grand fireplace, heavy
wooden furniture, vases of rare yellow flowers and golden-spined
books against the walls, then pause to sit in silence and sip absentmind-
edly from a glass of cognac. Dr and Mme Gidon's Louis Philippe-era
apartment stood high above the Rue des Martyrs, so little of the city's
street noise competed with Roth's answers to Lefèvre's questions
for a profile in the June 1934 edition of *Les Nouvelles littéraires*. The
success of *The Radetzky March* had led to its translation into French
by Blanche Gidon, and here in her home Roth gave Lefèvre insight
into its creation. Lefèvre was a perceptive observer, whose article
captured Roth on the page in a few deft lines. He compared Roth's
'sharp gaze' to that of 'a cunning and suspicious Norman peasant',
while the 'sudden melancholy that shadows the gleam of his blue,
slightly protruding eyes makes him resemble a fatalistic Russian who
wonders what all this is for'.[1] At first glance, he wrote, Roth was a
surprising, even worrying presence. 'It takes time to decipher him.
His slender figure is shrouded in mystery. Gradually, one gets used
to it, understands and is reassured: he is a complex being, a superimposition of almost contradictory personalities that express themselves

in his posture, a gesture, a look, a wrinkle of his expressive face, a
tone of voice. These different personalities are full of deep humanity.
The shoulders thrown back, the stiffness are reminiscent of the former
officer of the Austro-Hungarian Army. How I wish Joseph Roth were
still in uniform. He likes to act martial and at the same time tries in
vain to twirl his blond, unruly, too-short moustache between thumb
and forefinger.'

Old postcard of the Rue des Martyrs, Paris.

The claim to have been an officer was one of many fabrications
Lefèvre dutifully included in his article, among them inaccurate
descriptions of Roth's birthplace (on this occasion it was 'Schwaby'
again), education, career path and parentage; today his father was a gentile Viennese, a dissolute artist much like Professor Moser in his latest
novel. More useful were Roth's observations on his creative process –
he described his ten-hour working days, his redrafting and corrections
to the proofs, how his novels emerged from a sensation rather than a
plot: 'a place, an atmosphere [that] won't let me go',[2] he explained. He
wrote with a musical motif in his ear that bled into the novels' rhythm
and tone (Jewish sacred music for *Job*, and latterly Strauss's 'Radetzky
March' in the eponymous novel). Though he reviewed other authors'
books, he rarely read novels for pleasure, and never his own once they

were published.* Equally noteworthy are his remarks on his religious stance – 'I do not believe that man can save man. I am a believer, and as such I believe that man can only be saved through heaven ... If one believes that man can be saved by man, one is ripe for communism or for National Socialism.'³ Writers could only rely on 'divine grace', and without God's help they were lost. Catholicism, he declared, 'is Judaism for Christians'. If Viennese Jewish women would only convert to Catholicism, he jibed, they would not have to confess their sins to Sigmund Freud ... 'I have Jewish origins and therefore I love Catholicism,' he concluded. 'But I am not completely happy because I am not completely Catholic. I would be completely happy as a monk, but I lack the strength for that.'⁴

Now that Habsburg Vienna was a fading memory, the only place he loved was Paris, he said. 'I love my Latin Quarter, my Hotel Foyot. It is my hotel. They give me money and food there when I am in need. It is discreet, quiet, elegant, like an old provincial place ... Rilke showed it to me. He was confined there by a serious illness.'⁵

He turned in candid fashion to the recent events' impact on his livelihood. *Job* was a success and earned him a good income, he said. 'My publisher Kiepenheuer gave me 3000 marks a month, which together with my journalist's salary made a nice sum. But it was never enough. My lifestyle of a *grand seigneur* is expensive.'⁶ Roth preferred to be seen as financially crippled solely by his extravagant tastes rather than by his wife's illness; in December 1933, because of his inability to meet the private sanatorium's expensive fees, Friedl had been transferred to the state-run Steinhof psychiatric hospital on the western fringes of Vienna, where Count Chojnicki had ended up in *The Radetzky March*. The reduced fees continued to rack up. 'And now the Nazis have robbed me of most of my income. They have also confiscated the 30,000 marks that my publisher still owed me because I wrote an

---

* J. M. Coetzee: 'Roth is not a modernist. Part of the reason is ideological, part temperamental, part, frankly, the fact that he did not keep up with developments in the literary world. Roth did not read much; he liked to quote Karl Kraus: "A writer who spends his time reading is like a waiter who spends his time eating."' *Inner Workings: Literary Essays 2000–2005* (Vintage Digital, 2015), Kindle edition.

article against them. National Socialism is abhorrent to me, as is every collectivist mysticism, under whatever name it appears. I am an individualist ... I am Austrian, I have a Jewish mother, and I cannot forgive the National Socialists for their attitude towards Austria, nor for their persecution of the Jews: you don't spit on your mother's grave.'[7] He grew increasingly agitated and began to stride around again, pulling at his moustache and shouting: 'I hate the Prussians. That's why I fearlessly went to war as a liaison man. Why do I hate them? It's instinctive. Do you know why you love or hate someone?'[8]

After sharp disagreement over the quality of her translation ('utterly unusable',[9] he declared), Blanche Gidon had become a friend of Roth's. During 1934, articles such as 'The Third Reich: Agency of Hell on Earth' and 'Europe is Possible Only Without the Third Reich'* made plain that he would not be cowed in exile, and Gidon would play a valuable role in translating such works for French magazines, broadening the audience for his campaign against Nazism. It was a measure of his curious ability to distinguish between professional and personal respect that he somehow sustained this relationship. As he explained to her in response to an angry letter, in which she evidently accused him of impugning her character, 'I have always been grateful to you for going to so much trouble over my book. I never doubted that you took on the translation for no selfish motive. However, I cannot avoid saying to you that your translation is a bad translation, and – in spite of my debt to you for going to so much trouble over the book, and in spite of the friendship I feel for you – it remains a bad translation. I fail to understand how a perfectly objective criticism should strike you in light of a personal grievance. Anyone is free to tell me that such and such a book of mine is no good. I would *never* draw personal conclusions from it.'[10] Here as elsewhere, he argued that candour was a truer expression of friendship than a false compliment.

Their connection survived, as did the novel's translation, which

---

* Published in the *Pariser Tagblatt* on 6 July 1934 and in *Die Wahrheit* on 20 December 1934.

remains in print in France. However, this attitude did not extend to those whose professional conduct proved themselves, to Roth's mind, immoral in character. It was to Blanche Gidon that he declared in September 1933 that he no longer counted their mutual friend Benno Reifenberg worthy of continued association. Reifenberg's sin was to remain at the *Frankfurter Zeitung* under Hitler's dictatorship, in the hope that he could help it remain a dissenting liberal voice. Roth told Gidon that it was now 'impossible for me to have any sort of fellow feeling with my friend Reifenberg. Persons who neglect their honour cannot remain my friends. Whoever enters into a relation with the Third Reich, and a public one at that, like my poor friend Reifenberg, is struck out of the book of my friends.'[11] Reifenberg would concede after the war, on surveying the paper's Nazi-era output for a mooted anthology, that any opposition it had offered was so subtle as to be ineffectual.

Since shortly after his arrival in Paris in early 1933, the expensive Hôtel Foyot had become Roth's home, which he shared with Andrea Manga Bell and her two children, José Emmanuel (1920–47) and Andrea Tüke Ekedi (1921–2003). They lived in premises on the first floor, which gave a view over the Jardin du Luxembourg. Soma Morgenstern and his wife Inge were staying on the same floor. Inge and Andrea got on well, and in the evenings the two couples would go out together, walking via the Boulevard Saint-Germain and the Place de la Concorde for dinner in Rue Lincoln, a side street of the Champs-Élysées. At that time, Morgenstern recalled, Roth still usually ate at least one meal a day and could remain sober for several hours at a time. He liked to let on that much of his meagre income had to be diverted to Manga Bell, who he said had no income at all. 'But such information was not to be taken seriously with him,' wrote Morgenstern. 'For he always liked to boast about the number of people close to him whom he allegedly had to "support". This was one of his tricks to make his financial situation seem even more difficult than it was.'[12] Sometimes Roth would compose 'very inventive'[13] letters to Manga Bell's husband, who owned plantations in Cameroon, begging him for money, and she would copy them out in her own hand.

His letters at this time refer to his efforts to find a permanent residence and school for her son, whom he repeatedly refers to as 'my little pickaninny'.[14] Elsewhere he writes of living with his 'tribe of Negroes'. His terminology will be offensive to most twenty-first-century readers, and during this year he would put in print some descriptions of 'racial' characteristics that perpetuate stereotypes: he mentions 'the wondrous singing voice of the African, the subtlety and also the fervour of the Mongol, the nobility of the Indian, the intelligence of the Jew'.[15] Two factors mark him as relatively progressive by the standards of his time. For one, he was in an interracial relationship in the Nazi era, when this would attract considerably more hostility than today, and he devoted much time and energy to the welfare of these black children whom he had opted to take into his care. He told Blanche Gidon that he loved them as if they were his own. Two, that in his next book, while setting out the stereotypes above, he also sought to cast racism as a grave sin.

The Antichrist (*Der Antichrist*) is by some distance Roth's strangest book. An unclassifiable mixture of polemic, philosophical treatise, memoir and fiction, it is at once an explicit setting-out of Roth's conservative world view and an oblique, narrative-light diatribe that baffled many of the readers he'd gained with the success of *Job* and *The Radetzky March*. It was published in September 1934 by Allert de Lange, which along with the Querido Verlag was one of two Amsterdam-based imprints that were signing up émigré writers who could no longer be published in Germany. Both had set up German-language divisions headed by ex-Kiepenheuer editors to distribute the work of German and Austrian exiles. If this unfocused and strange book lacks the rigour that had characterised Roth's best work to date, then this had much to do with his decision to break ties with Benno Reifenberg, whose calm and patient counsel had curbed his excesses during their years collaborating at the *Frankfurter Zeitung* and influenced his novel-writing too. The Roth scholar Jon Hughes identifies the split with the *FZ* and 'the values represented by its Feuilleton . . . as a critical juncture for Roth. There are many practical reasons why Roth's post-1933 texts never quite attain the completion, even perfection, sensed by many readers of *Radetzkymarsch*. One might cite the trauma of his wife's

mental illness, the experience of exile, and the descent into complete
dependency upon alcohol. But the best evidence of the effects of the
absence of editorial guidance is perhaps to be found in Roth's final
attempt at a sustained piece of non-fiction (albeit with fictionalized
and mythological elements), his polemical text *Der Antichrist* (1934),
published in exile to general bemusement from what remained of his
reading public.

'This text is strikingly distant from the rational tone, sharp observations, and gentle humour of Roth's best work for the *Frankfurter
Zeitung*,'[16] Hughes concludes. It wouldn't be Roth if there weren't the
odd striking observation, but too much of the book is repetitive, undis-
ciplined and self-indulgent. While it is a dissatisfying work to read, *The
Antichrist* is of biographical interest. It lays bare Roth's all–consuming
anger and alienation by 1934, and likewise his determination to revolt
against modernity. It develops his ongoing debate with God and confirms his moral courage in taking a public stand against racism. Its
publication came a month after President Paul von Hindenburg's death,
which Hitler exploited by combining the chancellorship and presidency
and calling himself *Führer*. The Antichrist is never named, but its cross
has four hooks: it is the *Hakenkreuz*, the Nazi swastika. The Antichrist
is not merely Nazism, though: more the heathen spirit that Nazism
and Hitler embody, as does communism. Roth's narrator is a spurned
prophet, wandering through the world, arguing with and rejected by
all he encounters. He meets one misguided character after another and
fails to persuade them to take a righteous path. The lasting impression
one takes away from *The Antichrist* is of a despairing man whose values
stand counter to the dreadful direction of his times.

'I have written this book as a warning and exhortation, that one
might recognize the Antichrist in all the forms in which he appears,'[17]
he proclaims in an epigraph. In a portentous biblical tone he describes
the Antichrist's camouflaged presence across the modern world, from a
heathen Hollywood (or as he terms it '*Hölle-Wut*', meaning 'hell-fury')
that takes the liberty of stealing actors' 'shadows' and preserving them
on screen after their deaths, to the newspaper industry that peddles
lies and censors honest journalists' reports, the effect being to soothe a

dying world that it is in good health, much as the family of an ill man might urge a doctor not to tell him of his terminal prognosis. The conceit is that Roth's narrator is a reporter dispatched around the world as an emissary of a figure he terms the Mighty Master of a Thousand Tongues: a newspaper editor, commander of all the voices that speak within his publication. Along the way Roth takes repeated swipes at his enemies: communists, Nazis, racists, agents of godless modernity. The opening pages see Roth scolding himself, answering his own earlier works' pleas for God to explain His apparent dereliction of duty. He argues against those who would doubt and interrogate God without acknowledging that he himself numbered among those sceptics. It was human arrogance, he said, to declare that God did not exist just because we do not see Him. His wisdom is 'fathomless' and it is not for us to question His ways. Some men who had travelled in the new aeroplanes had returned to Earth crowing that they'd seen no sign of Heaven up there in the skies, but flight had merely 'lifted the earth upwards, so to speak; however, in no way have we brought Heaven downwards. And if we were able to climb even higher, to some unnamed planet, Heaven would recede even further away.'[18] It will always remain behind the stars. It is inherent in God to operate at a level beyond our comprehension. And yet, 'arrogant as we are, many of us believe that we can deny Him because we are powerless to know Him. We therefore take revenge for His severity. If He withholds the grace of knowing Him, we say He doesn't exist.'[19]

On racism, Roth is impassioned and unforgiving. 'The worst are the half-breeds,' someone tells his narrator. 'No,' comes the response, 'the worst are those who would think and say such a thing.'[20] It is worth bearing in mind that not only was Andrea Manga Bell of Cuban, African and German heritage, but by now Roth wanted people to think of him as, like her, being of mixed ethnicity, in his case gentile Austrian and Jewish. He goes on: 'it is clearly written that God created man in His image: man, not his colour. He created grey, black, greenish and reddish trees and plants, and they are all trees and plants.' The same goes for animals, fish and birds: all come in a variety of colours. So it is with humans. Given that God created us in His image, 'We therefore blaspheme Him when we mock or disparage the hooked nose of the Jew, the slanted eyes of the Mongol or the large lips of the African.'[21]

By the book's midway point he is rambling like a drunken mono-maniac, muttering to anyone who's still listening about how the palm trees in Hollywood are really statues, and actors there who bear a likeness to Napoleon or Caesar 'sell the shadows of their noses'.[22] The arguments make more sense in context, but only a little. Sections in which his narrator discusses the mining, oil-drilling and chem-ical production industries were lightly reworked from newspaper articles he'd written a few years earlier. (By the end of the year he acknowledged he had 'made a silly mistake by padding the book with journalistic work. It should have been half the length.'[23]) Then towards the end his narrator is dispatched to report on the Jews. The book developed from a work he had proposed to call *The Jews and Their Anti-Semites* (*Die Juden und ihre Antisemiten*). Its legacy becomes apparent here. He rails against antisemites who would call themselves Christian, when Jesus himself was a Jew, so 'Whoever thinks little of the Jews, thinks little also of Jesus Christ' and 'is not a Christian and mocks God himself'.[24] Rather, 'He who is a Christian esteems the Jews.' It is hard to reconcile this with the man whose letters are lit-tered with hateful comments about his fellow Jews – but perhaps this section of *The Antichrist*, like the assertion we should trust in God, was a form of a self-reproach. It is with a return to the importance of accepting and trusting God that the book concludes.

'God is our only home,' Roth writes. 'In His sublime presence there can be no evil but only love and justice.

'Outside of His sublime presence He has given us no home other than paradise and after that the entire earth.

'The whole earth is *temporarily* our home. Our real home, however, is the eternal presence of God.'[25]

Earth is but a hotel in which we are guests. Only God is home and, just as we saw in *The Radetzky March*, Roth is starting to prepare for this homecoming.

*

'I finished *The Antichrist* an hour ago,' he wrote to Zweig from the Hôtel Foyot on 26 March 1934. 'At last, for the first time in my life, I'm satisfied with a book.

'You too, I'm sure, will be satisfied with it. It's a thousand times better than *Tarabas*. I spent 10–12 hours on it every day, 8 on the writing, 2–4 preparing it.

'I'm at the end of my tether, but very happy.'[26]

It may well have been the most satisfying book to produce, but this was the ego-oriented satisfaction of catharsis, a satisfaction for the writer more than the reader. He had said everything he had to say without being constrained by the conventions of plot and characterisation, or by the guidance of a watchful editor who knew how to direct him towards his strengths. *Tarabas: A Guest on Earth* (*Tarabas: Ein Gast auf dieser Erde*), his ninth published novel, had also come out that year with Allert de Lange. He'd finished writing it in late 1933 in Rapperswil, Switzerland, and soon afterwards travelled to Amsterdam to make corrections to the proofs and negotiate with the publisher, Gerard de Lange. It was an ill-fated combination, for de Lange was an alcoholic too. Roth had arrived in Amsterdam with almost no money, and claimed to have spent three days in the American Hotel without eating. Then he extracted 1,000 francs from Fritz Landshoff, an ex-Kiepenheuer editor who now worked for Querido, and started to drink on an empty stomach. 'I had a supper invitation from Mr de Lange, for which I turned up completely drunk,' he wrote to Zweig. 'Now, Mr de Lange is a mighty drinker, and he wasn't sober either. But something happened that I thought would never happen to me. For the first time in my life I experienced a complete blackout. My recollection of the evening is absolutely nonexistent. It's possible I've wrecked my chances with de Lange.'[27]

After that, Landshoff wrote a letter to Hermann Kesten: 'Roth is, I believe, really about to lose the remnants of a once royal mind,' he said. 'He drinks like a fish. This will not end well.'[28]

As Roth knew, the novel is not among his best works. It has all the drink-soaked dissolution of his previous novel, but none of its coherence or depth.* It traces the rise of the ruthless Nicholas Tarabas, whose troubled relationship with his father turns him into a feckless wanderer who flits between New York and Russia. Serving in the army during the war offered him a 'wide and bloody home',[29] but when he is ejected into society he remains adrift. Eventually he reaches the little town of Koropta, where he becomes a terrifying leader of a band of men. He and his men stay at the White Eagle inn, run by a Jew named Nathan Kristianpoller. The building has an outhouse that was rumoured once to have been a Christian chapel, a hazy story clarified to devastating effect when some of the men start drunkenly to use it as a shooting gallery, which causes wall plaster to fall away to reveal an icon of the Virgin Mary. A miracle! The Jew must have defiled the image of the mother of God ... in truth Kristianpoller is quite innocent, but with horrifying plausibility a pogrom breaks out. The town's Jews are savagely beaten and humiliated, their houses burnt down, and Tarabas fails to intervene. In the aftermath, when the little town is under curfew, he encounters a feeble, red-bearded Jew creeping out to bury their damaged holy books, as dictated by Jewish law, and is so enraged by this breech of the curfew that he rips out the man's beard.† In the final part of the book he tries to atone for his sins and heal the rifts in his personal relationships. He seeks to go home, but his parents and their

---

* Among contemporary reviews, Peter Monro Jack's in *The New York Times* put it well: 'It would take a book twice the size of this to do what Herr Roth evidently intended. Tarabas as a character falls between the parable and novel. Neither side is fairly worked out ...'. The book is 'sketchy and confusing', but into this weak construct he has 'shot, with an almost tremulous excitement, scenes of Russian drama of extraordinary verve and veracity. It is for these only that one must read *Tarabas*.' 'A Parable in Fiction', *The New York Times*, 2 December 1934, accessed at https://archive. nytimes.com/www.nytimes.com/books/99/10/31/specials/roth-tarabas.html

† One of Roth's cousins remembered that Roth based this on a First World War officer he had met from the Polish Blue Army, aka the Haller Army, which 'had acquired dismal notoriety for a series of atrocities, often in the form of Jewish pogroms, against the civil population in its home country. In the course of one such action the officer in question had ripped the red beard off a man he came across in the street. He came to regret this misdeed to such an extent that he could not rest until he succeeded in finding the injured party, asking for forgiveness and offering the victim a fortune in recompense.' David Bronsen, *Joseph Roth: Eine Biographie* (Kiepenheuer & Witsch, 1993), p. 237.

servant do not recognise him: his father thinks he is a tramp and has him kicked off their property. Such are the perils of attempting to reclaim a home on this Earth, as Roth had suggested five years earlier in the aborted attempt at *Strawberries*. Tarabas dies and the tale concludes with an epilogue fifteen years later, in which the wise innkeeper Kristianpoller is asked whether the town's Jews still live in fear. They do not, he says – people have a remarkable capacity to let their sufferings slip into the past. 'You know how it is,' he shrugs, 'people forget. They forget fear and they forget the terrors that they go through. They want to live at all costs; they make themselves get used to everything, because they want to live!'[30]

To live . . . the tale effectively ends with the old Jewish toast, *l'chaim* – to life! Murderous antisemites come and go, but the Jewish people endure. It was a note to hearten Roth's Jewish readers in 1934, one that would prove correct, but only just.

The novel's publication almost ended his friendship with Soma Morgenstern. On reading a newspaper extract from *Tarabas* during a train journey, Morgenstern was furious that Roth had used the name Kristianpoller for his Jewish innkeeper. Morgenstern had used the surname for a character in an unpublished novel that Roth had read.* As soon as Morgenstern got home he wrote Roth an indignant letter demanding an explanation for this apparent theft. Roth wrote back explaining that he had an old friend named Kristianpoller and had named the innkeeper after him, not after Morgenstern's character. Morgenstern was not persuaded. 'It was not entirely new to me that Joseph Roth had a tendency to adorn himself with other people's feathers, although he himself was richly feathered,'[31] he wrote in his memoirs. Still, he was prepared to let the matter drop until he received another letter from Roth a week later. 'What really made me angry was a passage in the letter which he had apparently scribbled down in a good frenzy, which read something like that he – Roth – was like a river which, as nature has it, is enriched by its tributaries. And one should leave him alone!'[32] Morgenstern was not amused by this

---

* Eventually published in 1946 as *The Son of the Lost Son*.

description of his status relative to Roth's, and a friendship of more than two decades' standing collapsed.

Roth's relationships were falling apart wherever he looked. His love affair with Frau Manga Bell – as he always referred to her to his friends – had always been tempestuous, the flipside of a sexual passion Roth had never before known: he told Morgenstern that 'She made a man out of me'; or rather, as Morgenstern put it in his memoirs, 'He expressed himself more drastically than I would like to write down here.'[33] Roth would tell his friends that much of the tension derived from her children's demanding and ungrateful attitude. She was as volatile as him and they made a combustible combination. Under his influence she began to drink heavily. He told friends that he could 'see the signs already' that she would go mad, 'just like my wife'.[34] In Paris, Roth told Ludwig Marcuse that she carried a revolver in her handbag, and when the couple were due to see one another in the Café Selecte after a few days' separation, Roth asked Marcuse to accompany him in case she pulled out the gun. She didn't. For his part, Roth's increasing anxiety about physical attack led him to develop what Manga Bell called 'a defence complex'.[35] She said he began to carry sharp little shoemaker's knives on his person, and that he once wrapped an iron ball in a handkerchief and asked her if she thought it could smash someone's skull, before hitting her on the head with it. Manga Bell's daughter had a similar recollection of Roth showing her this and claiming it could easily be deployed to 'smash somebody's skull'.[36] Roth wouldn't let Manga Bell out alone, and even the hairdresser had to come to them. 'The hair salon is a brothel,'[37] he informed her. Judging by the daughter's remarks to David Bronsen, Roth's jealousy and paranoia plagued the relationship. She was fourteen years old when, during a spell in the South of France, Roth told her: 'Your mother can't be left alone for a moment or she gets into bed with the nearest taxi driver or lift boy.' 'I hit him so hard on the mouth that he bled,' Andrea Tüke Ekedi said. 'Afterwards Roth told anyone who would listen, "If I don't constantly buy the children presents then they go ahead and hit me on the mouth."'[38]

In 1935 Géza von Cziffra talked with Roth about Friedl and Manga

Bell while they walked through Vienna to the Hotel Bristol, where Roth was staying. He had become a legendary figure among the staff there, having consumed so many bottles of Hennessy that the bar waiter remarked: 'We have not had a guest like this since the late Count Adalbert Sternberg',[39] a notoriously wild alcoholic aristocrat and politician. (In the twenty-first century the Roth scholar Ilse Josepha Lazaroms visited the hotel and spoke with the current staff, who mentioned that Roth's debts at the bar remain unpaid to this day.) On reaching the bar, Roth ordered a cognac and von Cziffra asked him: 'What about Andrea? Would you marry her?' 'Manga Bell? Never! She is not a woman with whom you can start a family. She would never acknowledge a man as her husband, as the man in charge. We are on the same level, our life together is not a duet but a constant duel.'[40]

She, on the other hand, told David Bronsen that Roth had suggested they marry. 'I teased him, "Roth" sounds so harsh after "Andrea".' Her husband would in any case never have agreed to a divorce, she said. He was still insisting she and the children should join him in Africa, and at one stage he tried to arrange their transport there. Roth could not get divorced either, she added, for he 'was married to an insane woman from whom he could not escape'.[41] The pair's burden of inescapable ties to their ex-spouses formed a substantial part of the adversity that tied them to one another.

His remaining friends were worried for his health. Hermann Kesten assumed a role as the convenor and guardian of the émigré writers; Zweig would call him the 'protective father of all those who had been scattered across the world'.[42] He invited Roth (who told Zweig it was 'Because he's seen how wretchedly off I am'[43]) and Manga Bell to join him, his wife Toni, Heinrich Mann and his partner Nelly Kröger (a fellow alcoholic, and soon to be Roth's drinking companion) for an extended spell in Nice in summer 1934. Roth reluctantly accepted. It was his idea of hell, he wrote to Zweig a couple of hours before departing from Marseilles: 'After two days I'll have to move into a hotel. I can't share a toilet with acquaintances, and be seen in pyjamas and see others so dressed. Grisly! Sooner be completely destitute, as once before.'[44] Kesten had a three-storey house at 119, Promenade des Anglais. Roth and Manga Bell had the first floor, with Mann and Kröger above them, and the Kestens below. In Kesten's recollection it was a blissful summer. 'On blue evenings we stood on our balconies and watched the sun set in the sea and its reflection reddened the waves and the sky and the cheeks of our women. We spent the following months together cheerfully, meeting around the corner in a small bistro to eat or drink, or sitting in front of the Café de France or on the Place Massena in the Café Monnot under the arcades, sometimes wandering back to our house under the stars by the sea, in a fervent discussion of the laws of the historical novel.'[45]

Roth's correspondence with Zweig over the summer of 1934 tells a different story. At the end of May he travelled south from Paris to Marseilles, and the Hôtel Beauvau where he'd stayed with Friedl almost a decade earlier. The coming months would vindicate Landshoff's assessment of his mental condition: Roth's mind was coming apart, and his letters detail its disintegration in devastating fashion. His debts had sunk him to new depths of despair and anger. The letters are the howls and gasps of a man sinking in quicksand, who cannot see that his violent thrashing is only pulling him further under. On 14 June he begged Zweig to get him an advance from an English publisher. 'They will listen to you. I beg you, I implore you to take this trouble upon yourself! Take the rope off my neck that's on the point of choking me! Please, please understand. I'm going down, I'm already wallowing in filth. All sorts of ugly private painful humiliating things on top of that. I cannot WRITE to you about them. In spite of that, I've completed 2 novellas, each of 40 pages. I'm working like a pack-ass. I have worries, such worries, and I'm so UNHAPPY. Please, please secure a little freedom for me. I can't live like this any more, it's killing me. Absolutely. Is that what you want? Do you think I'm blackmailing you? I'm writing to you in desperate need. Please will you talk to the publishers.'[46]

A week later he was pleading that Zweig should 'continue to think of me as a sensible person subject to occasional fits of madness but broadly in control, and as a conscientious friend who only writes like this in hours of clarity'. He had 'debased and humiliated' himself,

and 'borrowed money from the most impossible places, despising
and cursing myself as I did so', all because he had never had a bank
account or savings, only ever cash in hand. In Paris his debts were
2,000 francs; now they had risen to 11,000 francs,* 'urgent, pressing,
terrible debts'. He was consumed with self-loathing at his selfishness
in clinging to Zweig 'like a drowning man clinging to his rescuer'.
He returned to the rope metaphor a few lines later: 'I've felt the rope
around my neck for months now – and if I haven't been throttled,
it's purely because every now and then some good-natured individual comes along and allows me to push a finger in between my neck
and the rope. And straight after, the rope draws tight again.' In such
a state he had been working all day, every day, and now he needed
to be free: 'the relaxing of the noose isn't enough, it has to be taken
off. Oh, please, I need 12,000 francs by the end of August. Maybe an
English publisher will provide them. Maybe, maybe! I am working,
it's all I can do, I can't do more! Please, please don't forsake me! Don't
take anything here amiss! Picture me lying flat out on my deathbed.
Forgive me. I have drunk nothing while writing this to you. I am
stone-cold sober.'[47]

Zweig, who had relocated to London, kindly agreed to serve as
an intermediary to sell the translation rights for *The Antichrist* to the
Viking Press. Roth had told him the rights were available. Zweig
began to negotiate on his behalf. It transpired they were not available; they were held by William Heinemann, which had published the
English translation of *Job* and had the rights to his next two titles. An
exasperated Zweig relayed this to Roth, who pleaded ignorance of his
own contractual obligations – quite plausibly, but just as likely he had
thought to chance his arm at extracting an extra advance from Viking.
There were also negotiations with Victor Gollancz, who had expressed
an interest in the book; Roth seized on this, before a contract had
been signed, and asked Gollancz to wire him money. Zweig was now
embroiled in rebuilding bridges on his friend's behalf. By 13 July Roth
was in Nice with the Kestens and Manns, distraught at the likelihood

---

* Around £8,000 in today's prices.

of being considered 'a swindler'. His honour, he said, meant everything to him. His misinformation derived from ineptitude, not deceit.

He had left Marseilles in despair, telling Zweig that he was beset with a recurrent fear he'd had since boyhood: that he would go mad at the same age as his father. This itself smacks of confusion, as Roth was now almost forty, and his father had gone insane in his mid-twenties. Whatever, the fear of insanity gripped him. 'If only you knew how I felt! How ringed with darkness! For days at a time, I fear for my reason,' he said. 'My dear friend, my sufferings are appalling! Work is flight, for me.'[48]

As Kesten's reminiscence of their time in Nice suggests, the work he sought to escape into was a historical novel. Each of these three exiled authors was writing one: Mann was working on his *Henri IV* manuscript, and Kesten's *Ferdinand and Isabella* was set in Spain at the time of the Inquisition. Roth was writing *The Hundred Days* (*Die hundert Tage*), which tells the story of the period between Napoleon's return from Elba and his defeat at Waterloo. The narration alternates between Napoleon and his servant Angelina Pietri, a Corsican immigrant who is infatuated with him. It was a change of direction for Roth, one that he explained, perhaps half-jokingly, arose 'Out of envy of Stefan Zweig', according to von Cziffra's recollection. Zweig had become well known for his biographies of great historical figures, and was immersed in what would become a ten-year project to write the life of Balzac. 'He writes about queens like Mary Stuart and Marie Antoinette,' said Roth, 'he moves in castles among distinguished people when he sits at his desk, and I'm constantly surrounded by Eastern Jews.' Von Cziffra reminded him that the Trottas weren't eastern Jews, to which Roth responded: 'No, but small, bourgeois spirits next to Zweig's Balzac. Without any real aspiration for more, or even for something higher. Hence Napoleon.'[49]

While attempting to balance writing this book with haranguing Zweig and placating Frau Manga Bell, he descended into violent paranoia. Wherever he looked he saw betrayal: every publisher he dealt with was ripping him off, seeking to offend him, to impugn his honour. In the face of this barrage, the beleaguered Zweig was unsure how best to change his friend's ways. Too often in their correspondence he offers unsolicited, well-meant but patronising advice. He implores Roth to stop marketing himself to multiple publishers simultaneously ('What you're doing is crazy, negotiating with firms on three unwritten books at once') and proposes that Roth draw up an at-a-glance table of 'all your obligations to various publishers' so he can 'look it over'.[50] The tone is that of a wearied but indulgent father offering to take his son's affairs in hand. It would be no surprise if Roth felt demeaned. But the prevailing advice is that Roth stop drinking. Several times, he offers to pay for a spell at a drying-out clinic. 'I beg you: please calm down! Don't drink. Alcohol is the Antichrist and money, not the wretched cinema. They're not stealing your shadow, it's you making yourself into a shadow, a pale shadow of yourself, by your drinking – please, my friend, take my offer, take a cure for a month, and under strict supervision.'[51]

Roth is stung and turns accusatory. The letters veer between pleas and reproaches, compliments and slaps. 'You're smart,' he flatters Zweig, 'I'm not. But I see things you can't, because your smartness blinds you to them. You have the grace of reason, and I of unhappiness. Don't give me any more advice – help me, act for me. I'm going under.' Of the famed biographer, he asks: 'Is it possible you have so much brilliant insight into dead figures – and none for your living friend? Or am I dead to you? Listen, I am still alive, I am a human being ...'. Later, having learned of Zweig's plan to leave London – which would not eventuate until 1940 – he bombards him with recriminations: 'You're leaving Europe, and you're my only real friend!' Then an invitation: 'How would you like to write my obituary?' and a veiled threat: 'I'll send you my will.'[52]

These epistolary missiles fired their way from the Côte d'Azur to Zweig's flat in Hallam Street, near Portland Place, throughout the summer. On 13 July, just after he'd arrived in Nice, Roth was 'beside myself, at the end of my tether, finished, I am feeling close to suicide, for the first time in my life'.[53] July 19: 'I am doomed, that much is clear. You think I'm mad, when I'm rational ... It's too late, I'm sick of this world.'[54] July 20: 'I'm getting horrible demands by mail every day.'[55] August 2: 'I don't know what next week will bring: bread or dead.'[56]

Later that month he made similiar complaints to Blanche Gideon: 'My finances are going from bad to worse . . . I'm in need of a miracle.'[57]

Life had tightened into an unpickable knot of obligations. The only solution was to work harder to earn more money; the only respite lay in drinking more. By September he admitted, 'I don't know, I don't know what to do,' before taking a swipe at the man who, however gauchely at times, had spent the summer trying to help him. 'You all drop me, you are so worldly, and so canny, and I am guilty of so much "foolishness". I have helped so many people, I am left so alone. I was so nice to people, they are so mean. I am so much your friend, in spite of all, I remain Your Joseph Roth.'[58]

It was a compulsion. Roth forced his friends away as if driven by an unconscious urge to vindicate his belief that eventually everyone would abandon him, a belief that had taken root in childhood and now dominated his thoughts. But this need to portray himself as the victim of others' callousness and ingratitude led him at times to be plain disingenuous. On 14 September he wrote a remarkable letter from Hermann Kesten's villa in Sanary-sur-Mer to Friedl's parents in Vienna, perhaps in part informed by his knowledge that her resentment of them was a factor in her mental illness. The Reichlers had been considering a move to Palestine, along with Friedl's sister Erna, her husband and their child, but were agonising over the prospect of moving so far from Friedl, who remained at the Steinhof. Roth's view of the matter was unambiguous. He prefaced the letter by saying he was staying with Kesten because nowadays he was reliant on the goodwill of friends, and he did not know how long he would remain so. 'But that is not the most important thing. It is more important that you go to Palestine and that poor dear Friedl remains alone.'

'This letter I am writing now is the most difficult of my life. For I must, with a heavy heart and in all conscience, advise you, dear parents, to do what your healthy children advise you to do. You no longer have any business in Vienna. In Palestine you will at least have something to eat. I cannot help, neither you nor Friedl, I am literally a beggar myself . . . I have become an old Jew, without hair, without teeth, my health is badly affected. God has beaten me and you, my dear ones.' He said that it was against his own interests, but he must advise them to take the opportunity to live with Erna and their grandchild. He could sense that they were conflicted and still hoped that Friedl would recover and make their decision easier. But the medical consensus was clear, he said: 'Friedl cannot suddenly get well. And, if God performs a miracle and makes her well, you will be informed of it,' and they could always then return from Palestine. They should bear in mind, though, that Friedl's costs were only covered for another six weeks, and he could not commit to covering them in future. So he asked one thing of them before they leave: that they arrange for a reliable man – not a woman, a man – to supervise her situation in Vienna and keep Roth constantly informed. They had previously suggested some of Friedl's aunts could fulfil this role, but Roth insisted on 'a reliable male personality in Vienna with whom I can correspond; not women, not, above all, several women … As soon as this person is determined, you can leave with a clear conscience … I myself waited for a miracle and ruined myself. I love the memory of Friedl as I have always loved her myself. But it's no use. Spend your years in peace when the opportunity is there. That's all I know to say. I am very unhappy, I try to bear it. I am always your faithful son.'[59]

In this light, the letter Roth wrote to Zweig four days later demonstrates the trait Morgenstern noticed whereby he would cast himself as unfairly burdened to elicit sympathy and financial support. 'With me,' he told Zweig, 'terrible things are happening on top of terrible things. *My parents-in-law are emigrating to Palestine.* It was for the sake of those old people that I undertook so much for my wife, now the mother is leaving her daughter, and I alone will be the mother.'[60]

Sure enough, the suggestion that he had been abandoned was followed by an explanation of his present financial predicament. If it fell on him to pay the Steinhof's fees of about 150 schillings a month from November onwards, he would have to work harder still, which seemed also to offer an acceptable solution to his suicidal urges. 'I think it's more respectable,' he explained to Zweig, 'to drown in the sea of work than in the actual sea, and I have hit upon a method to cheat my faith, which forbids suicide. So I will die with my pen in my hand. Soon, soon, I won't see you again, my dear friend.'[61]

The plan was to work himself into the grave. Drinking enabled him to write, or so he thought. If he drank at a suicidal rate, he could justify it as a catalyst for working himself to death: a far more honourable way to go. The self-deluding, self-justifying logic of the alcoholic had fixed itself in his mind. It was in this mindset that he later offered Zweig the following contorted rationale for his alcohol consumption. 'Don't worry about my drinking, please,' he wrote. 'It's much more likely to preserve me than destroy me. I mean to say, yes, alcohol has the effect of shortening one's life, but it staves off immediate death. And it's the staving off of immediate death that concerns me, not the lengthening of my life. I can't reckon on many more years ahead of me. I am as it were cashing in the last 20 years of my life with alcohol, in order to gain a week or two. Admittedly, to keep the metaphor going, there will come a time when the bailiffs turn up unexpectedly, and too early. That, more or less, is the situation.'[62]

When the eminent Vienna Secession movement architect Otto Wagner's 'Lower Austrian Provincial Institution for the Care and Cure of the Mentally Ill and for Nervous Disorders at Steinhof' opened in 1907, the vast complex of villas set in parkland by the Vienna Woods was hailed as the biggest and most beautiful asylum yet built in Europe. Among its sixty buildings that housed up to 3,000 patients were communal kitchens and laundries, a farm, a plant nursery, a hospital wing, offices and a mortuary. The intention was to create a calming therapeutic environment, akin to a rural colony, whereby the patients would feel themselves close to nature. To judge by what is known of Roth's visits to Friedl's room in Building Number 8, at the front-right of the complex, in her case this failed; at least, any calmness she otherwise felt was dispelled by the sight of him. Once he found her in an aggressive state and she threatened to attack him. On another occasion he ignored advice not to upset himself by visiting her, and on doing so was only able to look at her through the spyhole in her door. She was overweight, barely recognisable, with her formerly lustrous hair crudely cropped short. We have a good idea of how she must have appeared, for staff at the Steinhof photographed her after her arrival in

1933. Her once-alert features look tired and distressed, her stylish out-fits have been replaced by a loose, narrow-striped institutional blouse. In the first shot her lips are slightly parted – just slack-mouthed, or is she about to protest to the photographer? These are the last known images of Friedl Roth.

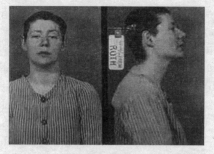

Friedl Roth photographed after admission to the Steinhof, Vienna, 1933.

After that visit, Roth was so depressed by the sight that a friend asked why he had forced this traumatic experience on himself. 'Once in a lifetime,' he replied, 'you have to hold yourself to account.'[63]

But having done so, he could leave again, while Friedl remained alone in her cell. How did she feel: consumed by fury, confusion, betrayal? She had given her life over to this man and his needs: this man who had forcibly moulded her personality into a shape he deemed appropriate, who did as he pleased without reference to her needs; who took off alone and slept with other women, yet would rather render himself impotent with drink than give her the intimacy she needed to feel loved; who lived in violent terror of her desiring another man; and who wanted to show off her beauty but was embarrassed by her ignorance. She was akin to a butterfly that he wanted to pin on display, for fear that she might fly beyond his reach: he never trusted that she would return, so he dared not grant her freedom. His freedom had required her constraint. The lack of liberty she felt in her marriage had calcified into a formal confinement within a psychiatric hospital. In the Steinhof, the choices were the company of people in derangement or solitude in her room with her terrifying thoughts. But better this than a visit from the man she blamed for her madness, an intrusion she could not bear. After she threatened to attack him, Roth reported back to his friends: 'I have visited her, she hates me.'[64]

It was during the summer of 1935 that Roth wrote his most notorious letter, a diatribe to Zweig in which he chastised him for considering working with Chaim Weizmann. 'A Zionist is a National Socialist, a National Socialist is a Zionist,'[65] Roth asserted. That one was persecutory and the other emancipating in intent was an insignificant distinction in his uniform loathing for all nationalisms. The Zionist leaders' engagement with the Nazis – born of a desperation with which Roth refused to empathise – amounted to an unforgivable complicity, much like Benno Reifenberg's continued tenure at the *Frankfurter Zeitung*. Roth refused to engage with anyone tainted by association with the Third Reich and chose instead to reject – or 'defect' from – both his Jewishness and the Germanic culture into which he had once tried to assimilate. Having been forced by Germany into physical exile, to turn the tables and proclaim a self-imposed spiritual exile from Germanness was a small reclamation of agency that granted a modicum of dignity. He posited his marginality as a virtue, but in so doing also cast Jewishness as a straitjacket one must escape to be fully human. 'Don't forget that the Jewish boycott has collapsed; that the Zionists – unlike all the other Jews – are in some proximity to the Nazis; that there are relationships between them of all kinds; that even sympathies between them exist, as might be expected among nationalists of various stripe; but that the most powerful urge of the Nazis is anti-Semitism, because Jews are not liked anywhere, and, if there were to be a world conscience anywhere it wouldn't be roused by Jews; if a goy is a friend to Zionists, then it will be out of anti-Semitism,' i.e. because both wanted the Jews out of Europe:

> Whereas if we, you and I and the likes of us, support Zionism, it's because we're human beings, not Jews or non-Jews. In this point there is no understanding between Mr Weizmann and me. (To be concrete, if we were to meet, I would be in his eyes – magnanimity

here or there – I would be a 'defector.') I am delighted to be a defector, from Germans and Jews. I am proud of it. *As a consequence* I am *not* a defector from the lists of Christians and human beings . . . [W]hat I want to do is protect Europe and humanity, both from the Nazis and from the Hitler-Zionists. I don't care about protecting the Jews, except as the most imperilled advance guard of mankind. If *that's* what Mr. Weizmann has in mind, then I will agree to participate, with my feeble strength – which isn't a manner of speaking.[66]

The three couples remained in Nice for eight months. Roth missed his October deadline for *The Hundred Days* and finished it the following spring. In the South of France he had also been writing two short stories. Chiefly narrated by the psychiatrist Dr Skovronnek whom we met in *The Radetzky March*, 'The Triumph of Beauty' traces the collapse of a relationship between a courtly, well-bred man and his beautiful wife, who develops 'hysteria' and drives him to suicide. 'It's simply not possible to treat incurables,' Skovronnek says of him. 'You cannot keep alive someone who is set on killing himself, and the husbands of certain women I view as incurable suicides.'[67] Skovronnek is Roth's ideal psychiatrist: he 'treats the husbands, who suffer more at the hands of their wives than their wives do from their illnesses, as his patients too – and he is right to do so'.[68] Eventually the man dies young from what Skovronnek calls 'the deadliest and (pardon me) commonest of all afflictions: he died of a woman, his own wife'.[69] After his suicide, she makes a sudden recovery and is finally seen dancing gaily in a Montmartre nightclub with her new lover.

The woman's name is Gwendoline. Géza von Cziffra was with Andrea Manga Bell at the Hôtel Foyot when she passed him a copy of *Les Nouvelles littéraires* and said it contained a story by Roth, in a French translation by Blanche Gidon. Manga Bell translated it back into German for von Cziffra as his French was poor. 'Does this Gwendoline remind you of anyone?' she asked after reading it aloud. He decided to feign ignorance and not give her the pleasure of a conversation about Friedl, whom she loved to denigrate. Later Roth told him with a laugh that 'Manga Bell would love to take the novella on a lecture tour just to badmouth Friedl.' He added: 'So you know, the character of Gwendoline only resembles Friedl in her illness, but not in her nature. Gwendoline was a nymphomaniac who slept with countless men, which Friedl never did, not even in her imagination.' 'How would you know?' asked von Cziffra. Roth gave him a thoughtful look and said: 'Anyway, Friedl's illness is the greatest defeat of my life, and I wanted to convey that to posterity in "The Triumph of Beauty".'[70]

Like Miriam in *Job*, Gwendoline is another character who's inspired by Friedl but given a promiscuous nature. These women embody his jealous, paranoid fantasies about his wife. They could also be seen as a form of revenge, portraying a woman as she would least like or deserve to be seen, just as he fabricated tales of his mother's neglect as a response to her stifling solicitude. The lasting impression a reader takes from 'The Triumph of Beauty' is its ugliness of spirit; it was not beauty but ugliness that had triumphed over Roth's mind. The story is like nothing else he wrote, not least because of its misogyny. While previously it was plain that Roth objectified women, here he appears to despise them. He describes how beautiful women always end up old and unattractive. When Gwendoline sticks out her tongue, it reminds Skovronnek of a snake's. When ladies smile, the narrator remarks, they 'look exactly like a poor whore', and when they say 'a well-bred goodbye', they smile 'like a girl giving a man the glad eye'. Women's constitution is 'incompatible with firm arrangements': they cannot be relied upon. And so on. Roth wrote to Blanche Gidon that 'If women were to think my novella is directed against them, I would be sorry. It's not informed by misogyny – it's simply my conviction that a woman finding a man incapable of loving her as she would like to be loved will one day become a plaything of the devil's.'[71] But the story is informed by misogyny, whether or not Roth cared to admit it. Like antisemitism, *in extremis* he found it offered a framework for organising his rage at the world. What was wrong with Gwendoline?, asks the narrator, before answering: 'God alone knows, He made Eve.'[72] Women's flaws have been inherent and general since Creation. The story is an ugly blemish on his oeuvre.

'The Bust of the Emperor' is a conservative paean to the graceful virtues of the old aristocracy. Much like Count Chojnicki, its main character Count Morstin reflects Roth's beliefs, in this case his faith in the emperor and the traditional hierarchy. Morstin lives near Brody – a rare mention of the town – and is a gentle, courtly old Austrian of the sort Roth revered and aspired to emulate. Like the lost empire, he is multinational in character: he lives above nationality, part of an international network of aristocrats rather than a plebeian nationalist. Such families straddle many borders – he has cousins in Paris, Hungary and Peking – for such people float around the world freely, courtesy of their money and connections. Created two years into Roth's life in exile, the count represents a world that did not divide and exclude people by imposing borderlines between them, and did not encourage nationalistic chauvinism with its aggressive othering of 'outsiders'. As Ilse Josepha Lazaroms puts it in her thoughtful and stimulating study of Roth's life, *The Grace of Misery*, in Roth's responses to exile 'time and again he came to the same conclusion: that discomfort, disaster, and a pervasive kind of existential homelessness are structural elements in a world divided along national lines.'[73]

The count is anti-democratic, as Roth had become by now in the face of the collective madness engulfing the European populations, who he thought needed saving from being able to exert their worst impulses. By early 1935 he had reached a decisive view on where the blame lay, as he explained to Blanche Gidon. 'It's the Jews – you know I have the right to speak frankly about the Jews – who have introduced Socialism and catastrophe into European culture,' he informed Gidon, who was also Jewish. His perceived maltreatment and disrespect from 'progressive' Jews at the *Frankfurter Zeitung* would only have heightened his anger at such people. '"*Novarum rerum cupidissimi*":* that's the Jews for you. They are the real cradle of Hitler and the reign of the janitors. One shouldn't always believe that "the Left" is good and "the Right" is wicked ... The Jews have unleashed the plebs.'[74]

---

* 'Greedy for novelty', a neophiliac mindset entirely at odds with the wary and misanthropic conservatism that Roth had slumped into by the mid-1930s.

Democracy would be a fine thing in a better world, but it was too great a risk in this one, where in the past few years the 'plebs' had ushered fascists into governments that became dictatorships. Jewish revolutionaries had fomented the instability in which nationalism flourished, Roth believed.* To his mind, the left-wing Jews who advocated for democracy and liberation of the proletariat had enabled the masses to express their baser instincts: they had created monsters that were now preparing to eat them. In the past year Austria had seen a civil war that led to a ban on left-wing parties. An emergency fascist government led by the dictator Engelbert Dollfuss was almost brought down by a Nazi attempted coup on 25 July 1934, in which Dollfuss was murdered; it limped on under the leadership of Kurt Schuschnigg, a fellow nationalist whom Roth disparaged by calling Schuschniak, to imply he was of lowly Slovene origin. The situation was a travesty but, as Bronsen noted, Roth had oddly little to say on the subject. He did not denounce the Austro-fascist government for its attacks on the Social Democrats nor its 'bloody suppression of the workers' uprising',[75] for two reasons. First, the government was opposed to the Nazis and might keep them at bay. Second, he believed it could form a transitional stage towards restoration of the Habsburg monarchy, which he had for the past year described to all who would listen as 'the only possible salvation for Austria'.[76] This obsession had come to distort his old principles. The young Otto von Habsburg, with whom he had become acquainted, sought to reclaim the throne with the aid of a band of Austrian legitimists that included Roth. How best to turn Habsburg's claim into reality was a question that would consume him for the rest of his life.

---

* The Marxist writer Bruno Frei, Roth's friend from early-1920s Berlin, told Bronsen how he confronted him on the issue of his conversion from socialist to conservative monarchist. Roth told him that communist troublemakers had rendered stable government impossible in Germany and paved the way for the Nazis. The two men could not agree, and Roth, who had been drinking schnapps throughout the conversation, became so angry that he began to smash the furniture.

Chapter Twelve

... the hatred which I now felt for myself was hatred of a
different kind. For the first time I felt a contempt for myself.
Previously I had never realised that a false existence, founded
on a borrowed and stolen name, could destroy one's own,
one's real existence.

Confession of a Murderer

A collection of colour photographs taken in Ostend during the
summer of 1936 indicates why the Belgian coastal town was known as
the *Reine des Plages*. It had been a lure for the aristocracy and *jeunesse
dorée* since the nineteenth century; Stefan Zweig had grown enraptured with the town before the First World War. From the vantage
point of a café on the promenade, all human life played out before
Joseph Roth's squinting eyes. The photos depict a bright, breezy
summer: holidaymakers huddle by red- and yellow-striped wind-
breaks and cast crisp shadows on the pale sand; the flags of Britain,
Italy and France furl from poles planted on the beach. A black-hulled
liner steams by a long pier. A lady strolls by beneath a powder-blue
parasol, a red-bathing-suited child by her side. Bathers paddle and
splash, children laugh and shriek in the cold North Sea. Roth could
hear the veering gulls, watch the grey and white marbled waves crash
on the ribbed sand, smell the salt in the air. His friends would venture
through the crowds to swim in the sea, but Roth only looked on from
afar. He said he felt as much at home in the water as a fish would in
a café. On occasion he might shuffle along the promenade, but he
would rather stay put with his schnapps.

The beach at Ostend, summer 1936, with the Kursaal
casino in the background.

He had travelled there alone from Amsterdam. He was alone
because he had become estranged from Andrea Manga Bell; or at
least from her children, and her children were always at her side.
From the Hôtel de la Couronne near Ostend's railway station he
wrote to Blanche Gidon that 'Mrs Manga Bell has steadily refused
to adapt to the rules of my life.' The way those rules had affected
Friedl seems not to have caused Roth to reconsider his approach to
romantic relationships. It is hard, too, to feel much sympathy when
he complains that his partner of five years' children 'are much more
important to her than I am'. They weren't children any more, he
pointed out, but 'two adults who call me *boche*' – him, the eastern
Jew persecuted by Germany. 'I myself am the lost, sick child,' he
said. 'I can keep Mrs Manga Bell on her own, but I've had it with
the children. I'm standing on the brink of the abyss. I can no longer
bear the least psychological pressure, it would kill me. And I don't
want to die.'[1]

In tandem with this, his relationship with Zweig had reached a
nadir four months earlier. To understand how, it is necessary first to
rewind to June 1935 and the death from a heart attack of Gerard de
Lange. 'Whoever was his friend could count on his loyalty,' Roth

declared in an obituary. Fellow émigré authors published by his Allert de Lange press would have raised their eyebrows on reading those words, for Roth's connection with the late publisher was the source of much resentment. If you had mentioned Roth's poverty to René Schickele, for instance, he would have choked with indignation. In a letter from May 1935 to the art historian Julius Meier-Graefe, Schickele fumed that Roth had gone 'to Amsterdam to sit beside the till ... For us de Lange authors, Roth is a sort of vacuum cleaner. No speck of dust, no crumb from the master's table that doesn't get sucked into that bottomless hole. What's left for the rest of us?'[2]

De Lange's death dealt Roth a double blow – not only did he lose a friend and drinking partner, but a lucrative stream of income. Whoever replaced de Lange in running the imprint was less likely to indulge his financial demands. Via a lawyer, Roth demanded that the editor Walter Landauer give him an accurate summary of his books' advances and earnings. Landauer replied: 'Following Mr Roth's request, we have now carefully considered the situation ... As friendly as the publishing house is to Mr Roth, I have to tell you frankly that this settlement makes a catastrophic impression on the publishing house. Mr Roth was paid hfl 16635.83 (including the February payment). The only amount received was hfl 2975.66 ... We are therefore in the greatest embarrassment at the moment. It is commercially impossible for us to conclude a new contract with Mr Roth, which is only approximately on the same financial basis as his previous contract with us.'[3]

Roth was beside himself with fury and responded, as was his wont by now, with an antisemitic reference to the younger Berliner Landauer who had developed ideas above his station. 'A callow Kurfürstendamm Jew,' he thundered in an August 1935 letter to Zweig, 'who has done nothing makes so bold as to write to me, who gave him his start in life, in that tone. It's of a piece with those Jewesses with lacquered nails you see in Marienbad. Please read the letter. The *chutzpah* of it! Exacerbated by the circumstance that L. let it lie for a long time, before sending it off, and forgot to change the date. The *chutzpah* was stronger than he was. So I am facing my end.

I don't want to have anything more to do with those shits from the Kurfürstendamm.'[4]

Zweig and Landauer exchanged letters in February 1936 in which, at their wits' end, they deliberated over how to handle their friend. On 11 February a weary Zweig informed Landauer that he was 'busy here cleaning the Augean stables of Roth. I am doing what I can. I gave him 3000 frcs the previous month, and this month I intend to give him considerably more, but on condition that he leaves the Foyot. We can't tolerate weekly bills accumulating there that would be burdensome even for rich people – either he changes his lifestyle or I don't do it anymore. Roth is, after all, only one of the many I keep afloat today with the chance income of a bestseller book [sic], but he cripples my arm. Why don't other writers live in the Foyot all the time? Because it's too expensive and Roth also has the art of needing four times as much everywhere as someone else. So now we are forcing him to move.' He would issue two conditions for future assistance, he said: that Roth curbed his expenditure and no longer ran up drinks bills on credit at his future hotel. 'He must live cheaply, appear more willing and we must be very strict with him (although he will repay us most rudely), precisely because we want to help him and continue to help him.' He asked Landauer to impose similar conditions, and Landauer confirmed that Allert de Lange were considering how to draw up a viable arrangement for the future, while knowing that having 'paid out about 15,000 guilders to Roth in the course of the last 2 years', 'a sum that exceeds many times over what authors with good names receive under the present circumstances',[5] it might not be possible to sustain the relationship at all.

In March 1936, finally tested to breaking point by Roth's belligerence, paranoia and profligacy, Zweig snapped. He told him to stop blaming his publishers and friends, and 'finally have the courage to admit that however great you are as a writer, in material terms you're a poor little Jew, almost as poor as seven million others, and are going to have to live like nine-tenths of the human beings in the world, on a small footing and with a tightened belt'.[6] The Viennese millionaire had at last made explicit the difference between him and the little

Ostjude. He knew it would stop Roth in his tracks. He proceeded to give a paternal lecture: stop complaining that life is unfair, stop comparing his financial situation to that of less talented writers, stop moaning about his obligations. 'You have ONE obligation, which is to write decent books, and not to drink too much, so that you remain among us for as long as possible. I implore you not to waste your strength in futile rebellions, don't go accusing other people, decent businesspeople who calmly and quite rightly do their sums, which is something you never learned to do.' Zweig tried to shake Roth into changing tack; the time for gentle guidance had passed. 'Now or never is the moment for you to change your life, and maybe it will have been a good thing that you were finally brought to a point where the old road didn't go on any more, and you were forced to turn back.' [7]

The words stung Roth just as Zweig intended, but they had little other impact. 'You know you've no need to tell *me* of all people what it is to be a poor little Jew,' he replied. 'I've been that since 1894, and with pride. A believing eastern Jew from Radziwillow.* I would drop it if I were you. I've been small and poor for 30 years. Heck, *I am poor*. But nowhere is it written that a poor Jew may not try to earn a living.'[8]

Testy messages crossed the North Sea, between Zweig's 'rather dark and slightly gloomy'[9] service flat in London and Roth's 'wretched red light hotel',[10] the Hotel Eden in Amsterdam, where he had been working hard despite various maladies – 'dropsical feet',[11] high temperature, vomiting what little food he ate. He had been trying again to write *Strawberries* – among his demands in this correspondence was that Zweig find it a publisher – but was now frantically transplanting chunks of it into a new short novel, *Weights and Measures* (*Das falsche Gewicht*), at the same time as editing another, *Confession of a Murderer* (*Beichte eines Mörders*). 'I'm chucking all the material into it

---

* A small town now known as Radyvyliv, a couple of miles north-east of Brody. At that time it lay just across the Russian border. It is as if Roth could not say the word 'Brody' to Zweig. It may also be, as Sidney Rosenfeld suggests, that he wished to imply a connection with the noble Radziwiłł family.

that I wanted to save for my great book *Strawberries*. It's a shame, but what else can I do? I'm living off the last of the money that Querido paid me for the stories: 5 weeks ago, 200 gulden, for all rights, it's extortionate. But what could I do?'[12]

Zweig continued to negotiate with Landauer on Roth's behalf, despite everything. Helping those less fortunate than him was what he did. In 1932 he had even exerted influence on Mussolini: the renowned author wrote the dictator on behalf of an anti-fascist named Giuseppe Germani, who had been imprisoned with ten years' hard labour, and Mussolini commuted the sentence. It was in part a case of *noblesse oblige*, part genuine humanitarianism, and in Roth's case also a sincere desire to help a man whom he considered a 'genius', as he told Hermann Kesten. Acting from a distance on Roth's behalf was simpler, in any case, than dealing with him in person at this point. He claimed in April that he would have visited Roth in Amsterdam but the only flights were with German airlines, 'and frankly I'd sooner drown. But we must see one another soon.'[13] Roth saw through Zweig's blandishments. It was plain he was lying – and sure enough, Zweig gave a more honest account of his feelings to his American publisher, Ben Huebsch: he could not face visiting Roth and wished 'he would commit some minor infraction that would get him jailed for two or three months. There's no other way to stop him drinking.'[14] In his reply Roth mentions that Walter Landauer had abandoned him, leaving him 'all alone',[15] and now he levelled the abandonment accusation at Zweig: 'You won't come either. It's not true that only German planes fly here.'[16] He'd inspected the flight timetables. As well as a single daily Lufthansa flight, there were five operated by Dutch airlines. Zweig could easily have visited. 'But you don't want to, and it would be better if you said so. But I can empathise with you, I can sense that you have no desire to see a man in utter distress.'

The following weeks saw a barrage of long letters in which Roth detailed his concept of friendship, which was 'UNCONDITIONAL', with

---

* A wild overreaction, of course: a few weeks later he described the 'kind' Landauer looking after him 'like a brother'.

'no criteria'. He had already assured Zweig that 'friendship is our true home,' and he would 'observe it more faithfully than anyone else';[17] now he promised that he would 'let myself be cut into tiny pieces for you, literally'. In return, he hoped that Zweig might 'save me from my doom'.[18] Perhaps such remarks triggered Zweig's easily stimulated sense of guilt, for, magnanimous as ever, he invited Roth to Ostend, where a group of émigré writers were to gather for the summer. Egon Erwin Kisch had lived there for a while, and brought with him a retinue of communist friends. The charismatic, depressive playwright Ernst Toller came with his young actress wife Christiane, who always had to pack a length of rope in his suitcase in case he decided finally to act on his suicidal urges. Hermann Kesten would join them to spend another coastal summer writing a historical novel, this time about the Spanish Habsburg king Philippe II. Zweig arrived with his new lover, Lotte Altmann, for whom he had recently left his wife, Friderike. The simple charms of a seaside resort offered an escape from his marriage and from his critics, who had seized upon the errors in his recent study of Calvin, hastily published under pressure from his publisher, Reichner, whom Roth despised and had unsuccessfully warned Zweig to avoid. Roth had encouraged him to switch to Allert de Lange; Zweig hoped, contemptibly, that sticking with the Viennese publishing house would allow his books to retain a readership in Nazi Germany.

While in Ostend, Zweig intended to finish his next book, a 'Jewish legend' that would be published the next year as *The Buried Candelabrum* (*Der begrabene Leuchter*). His invitation to Roth in late June was a nostalgic attempt to rewind their relationship, even as he suspected that Roth's plight was beyond reversal. 'It would be wonderful to have you there as a sort of literary conscience for my legend. We could test one another in the evenings, and lecture each other, as in the good old days.'[19] This they did: Roth critiqued Zweig's work, and spent evenings in an Ostend bistro revising *Confession of a Murderer* as per Zweig's suggestions. The book was nearing publication, but now Roth wrote to Landauer to explain that substantial late changes would be required.

The completed novel remained weak, for all of Zweig's assistance. At 190 pages in English translation it is hardly long, but it still feels stretched and uneven. It should have been a short story. Over the course of a night's drinking in a Russian restaurant called the Tari-Bari, in Paris's Rue des Quatre Vents, the secret agent Semyon Golubchik confesses his story to the narrator and gathered friends. Golubchik is the illegitimate son of the wealthy Prince Krapotkin, but was raised in humble circumstances by his mother and her husband, a forester. It is at first a tale of a man in search of his negligent father, under the impression that finding him and establishing a relationship will set his life in order. He is assisted here by Jenö Lakatos, an untrustworthy Hungarian (in Roth there is no other kind) whom we previously met in 'The Triumph of Beauty', and who will reappear in 'The Leviathan'. On confronting the absent man in Odessa, he is disabused of his illusions: the prince resents the young man tracking him down. 'What do you want of me?' he asks, in a threatening tone. His birthright, says Golubchik. The prince calls him a fool, and says that if he is his son, he is but one of many scattered across Russia. He feels greatly wronged by his father's rejection.

Roth is still scratching away at the personal resentments that coloured *Zipper and His Father* and passages from *The White Cities* concerning fathers' failings around a decade earlier. The rejection is heightened by the fact that the prince treats his wife's illegitimate son as his own. This resentment culminates in Golubchik finding his lover, Lutetia, and this young man in bed together, whereupon he attacks them both and leaves them for dead. Woven into this plot is his duty as a police spy to ensnare a Jewish revolutionary, Channa Lea Rifkin, whom he considers one of the most spiritually, if not physically, beautiful women he has met. His guilt is such that, when the First World War makes its typical disruptive intrusion into a Roth plot, he hopes to be killed in action. 'At that time I longed for [death]. For I believed then that death was an agony by which one could atone. Only later did I begin to realize that it was a deliverance. I had not earned it; and therefore it had not come to deliver me.'[20]

In theme and setting the novel has much in common with *Tarabas*.

Both are largely set in Russia, involve a protagonist who wrongly believes he has committed murder and see him belatedly reckon with his moral failings. Both are beset with guilt over their treacherous treatment of eastern Jews: in *Tarabas* the sexton Shemariah, and in *Confession of a Murderer* the social revolutionary Channa Lea Rifkin. As Sidney Rosenfeld notes, 'That both victims are *Ostjuden* ... is surely more than coincidence.'[21] Rosenfeld is doubtless correct that this reflects Roth's certainty by the mid-1930s that Europe's Jews faced disaster, which 'led him to express compassion with his east European kin by portraying them as the defenseless victims of violence at the hands of evil perpetrators'. Likewise, it seems plausible that Roth hoped to 'assuage feelings of personal guilt at having abandoned his fellow Jews when he left Brody with the intent to assimilate in the west'.[22] As his dreams of assimilation evaporated, he gestured amends through his fiction to those compatriots he'd left behind in his flight from the east. That barely any would be able to access a banned, exiled author's books would only have strengthened his sense of impotence and futility. Any substantial effort to spring the *Ostjuden* from the trap closing around them would require more liberty, power and time than he possessed.

'You just need to put yourself in my shoes,' he had informed Zweig in one of the desperate deluge of letters mailed to London in early 1936:

> you can do that, in my typical day, I've told you what that's like. I have no more nights. I wander around till 3 a.m., lie down fully dressed at 4, wake up at 5, and start wandering around again. I haven't been out of my clothes for two weeks. You know what time feels like, an hour is a lake, a day is a sea, the night is an eternity, waking up is a thunderclap of dread, getting up a struggle for clarity against fevered nightmares. That's what it's all about, time, time, time, and I don't have any. In two weeks I'll have a contract, in three weeks, I'm told, there'll be a reply from America – and how much of my life do I lose in those 2 weeks! For nothing! For nothing! Humiliated, disgraced, indebted, smiling, smiling through gritted teeth – an acrobatic stunt – so that the hotel proprietor

doesn't notice, my pen clamped, cramped in my hand, desperately clinging to the idea I've just had, because it's galloping away from me, sometimes starving, falling asleep in my chair after 3 sentences, but what do you want, what do you want from a man who's half madman, half corpse? What else am I to do, if I don't write books? I'm old and sick, I can't go back to the army, which is the only job I ever had. Debts, ghosts, privation, and writing, talking, smiling, no suit, no shirt, no boots, hungry open mouths, and scroungers to stuff them, and ghosts, ghosts, wall-to-wall ghosts. And what a life behind me![23]

Time, time; finite, diminishing time. Roth's childhood fascination with clocks and watches grew into an obsession, and a compulsion to disassemble them. What machinery lay behind the face? He could never pass a watchmaker's without pausing at the window, Manga Bell recalled, and he collected dozens of timepieces. He would remove the casing, unscrew the movement, prise up the face to reveal the mechanism, the wheels, spring and pinion, lay them out and marvel at how they combined to record time as it ticked away second by second, then day by day. Such an exquisite creation of human ingenuity. If he scrutinised them long enough, he might understand their workings . . . But fascination pivoted into dread. Sometimes the incessant ticking left him aghast at what he called 'the powerlessness of men against the unalterable laws of time'.[24] The 'long since fulfilled' boyhood desire he felt in the Brody horologist's shop to measure time now '[gave] way to a new wish to know nothing more about it'.[25] Manga Bell remembered that the Hôtel Beau in Paris had too many clocks for his liking, so he threw them out of the window.

Being around Zweig could bring out Roth's conciliatory side: in conversation his expressive, melancholic face and self-deprecatory streak presented a more engaging prospect than the furious screeds written when he was alone and drunk in a hotel room. In mid-July Roth told Blanche Gidon that Zweig had been 'so sweet' to him, 'like a brother'.[26] That summer in Ostend Lotte Altmann took a photograph of them that captures this moment in their relationship, at the same time as indicating the stark differences in their character. Both men wear suits, both sport a moustache and a side-parted scrape of thinning hair, and there the similarities end. They are sitting on the sunlit terrace of the Hôtel Helvetia on the seafront. Zweig leans in to Roth in fond, protective fashion; Roth bristles and does not reciprocate. Zweig is active, Roth inert. Zweig gazes benevolently and smiles at Roth; Roth squints and scowls at the camera. Zweig looks beseeching, Roth sceptical. Zweig appears the younger man, but he is thirteen years older: he looks to be in fair health, whereas Roth is pudgy and immobile, a half-drunk glass of wine before him, a cigarette squeezed between his slim fingers. Here are two men who a few months earlier exchanged furious correspondence in which one belittled the other and told him to change his ways. Perhaps it is not fanciful to see in Zweig's doting expression a relief at reconciliation and a need to feel liked by his maddening friend, and in Roth's implacable surliness a determination not to reciprocate, for fear of appearing as weak and needy as he did in the letters where he begged Zweig to save his life.

Stefan Zweig and Joseph Roth on the terrace of the Hotel Helvetia, Ostend, in 1936, photographed by Zweig's partner Lotte Altmann.

He liked to keep Zweig on his toes, to prove he wasn't entirely beholden to his rich friend. When Zweig took him to a tailor to be fitted for a new pair of suit trousers, Roth was pleased with them, even though the tailor declined his request to cut them in the narrow style of an Austro-Hungarian Army officer. The next day, sitting at a bistro table in the market square, he ordered three glasses of liqueur and poured one over his jacket. 'What are you doing?' asked Hermann Kesten. 'Punishing Stefan Zweig,' said Roth. He explained, while emptying the other glasses over himself, that he intended to shame Zweig by turning up for dinner that evening in a stained jacket. 'Millionaires are like that! They take us to the tailor, and buy us a new pair of trousers, but they forget to buy us a jacket to go with them.'[27]

So Zweig bought him a new jacket too, and Roth was pleased with it. What was more, he was pleased that, if he must move around clad in a reminder of his dependence on charity, at least he had not abased himself again in the process. Leading the laughter at the bistro table when Roth doused himself was a young woman who had joined the circle of exiled writers, one whom he had never met before. The novelist Irmgard Keun arrived as the only non-Jewish émigrée from Germany, and as soon as they met Roth interrogated her over the circumstances of her departure.

'Egon Erwin Kisch and his wife Gisela took me to the Café Flore in Ostend,' she told Bronsen, but she misremembered: there was no Café Flore in the town, and the Belgian scholar Els Snick believes it must have been the Brasserie Floréal, on the ground floor of the guesthouse where Zweig stayed. 'A little later Stefan Zweig came in with a gentleman who was swaying drunkenly and whose jacket was covered with cigarette ash. Kisch, looking at his jacket, said in amusement, "What! No crown? No ermine?"' – the communist's friendly barb at this shabby monarchist – 'and introduced Joseph Roth to me. I had left Germany at the age of twenty-five, but Roth was not satisfied with this, he wanted to know on the very first evening why I hadn't emigrated in 1933 already. During our first conversation I noticed his delicate, narrow hands with their unusually long fingers. They didn't go well with his terribly fat stomach, and I later discovered that his portliness and his skinny legs made him look a bit like a garden spider.'[28]

This did not deter her from finding him strangely attractive; nor did the 'reddish blond moustache [he had grown] to cover up his defective teeth', nor his 'somewhat protuberant eyes', nor his overwhelming aura of melancholy. 'When I first met Roth in Ostend, I felt here was someone who was simply about to die of sadness. His round blue eyes were almost blind with despair, and his voice sounded as though buried under tons of grief. Later on, that impression blurred a little, because at that time Roth wasn't just sad, he was also the greatest and most impassioned of haters . . .'.[29]

Keun had a husband, Johannes Tralow, whom she had left among other reasons because he was a Nazi sympathiser, and a lover, Arnold Strauss, a Jewish doctor who had already fled to New York. She was clever, funny, vivacious and already well regarded for her novels *The Artificial Silk Girl* and *Gilgi, One of Us*. Since she had been blacklisted for her anti-Nazi views and 'immoral' literature, her third novel had just been published by Allert de Lange. With the Atlantic lying between her and Strauss, she considered herself single. She soon joined Roth at the Hôtel de la Couronne and they became a couple, of sorts: Keun specified later that they were not in love, it was no great passion, more a temporary convergence of two uprooted people with common enthusiasms, and for a time this was just what she desired.

Among those enthusiasms was alcohol. They drank together. She tended him during his morning routine. For a couple of years it had required him to retch until he vomited, which latterly had produced

Irmgard Keun in 1932.

blood and bile, and this symptom of advancing alcoholism was joined now by an expanding litany of ailments: heart pains, migraines, haem-orrhoids, palpitations, swollen feet that made walking difficult, and gums that had lost their grip on his teeth, which the moustache could not disguise. In the evenings he had nausea and pains that felt like knife wounds in his neck, as Keun told a friend while despairing of how to help him. The nights offered little relief: insomnia, terrors akin to the sufferings of Job: 'In intense thoughts out of visions of the night, when deep sleep falleth on men: / Dread came over me, with trembling, and it caused all my bones to shudder.'[30] The mornings entailed a painful sift through the blackouts, piecing together fragments of embarrassing memories from the night before, trying to remember what he'd rather forget. Once he was ready for a new day they would study the *Paris Soir* horoscope, which Roth informed her, 'half seriously . . . would tell us where the next money would come from'. Sometimes they pawned their possessions. Their lives together were lived hand–to–mouth. 'But somehow money always turned up,' Keun said, 'just when things looked worst.'[31]

They wrote together at the same table, but he never discussed literature with her, preferring to do so with Hermann Kesten. More often he talked about Friedl. Keun said he spoke of her all the time. She haunted him. So many people he wanted in his life had, as he saw it, abandoned him or let him down; but he remained chained by moral and financial obligation to the one person from whom he wished he could sever himself. The women who replaced Friedl in his affections knew that they were living with a man who spent much of his time preoccupied by an invisible woman. Friedl existed out of sight in her cell in Vienna, but she was a ghostly presence in Andrea Manga Bell and Irmgard Keun's lives.

He had begun the previous year to issue divorce proceedings, but found the process too complex and costly. That summer, June 1935, Soma Morgenstern and Walter Landauer had arranged Friedl's transfer to the free–of–charge Mauer-Öhling state care facility near Amstetten, just as her parents emigrated to Palestine. However dubious Roth's claim that they had abandoned him, he was obliged at this critical time to increase rather than reduce his interest in her care and act as her 'mother', as he had put it to Zweig. The rope around his neck tightened. The terror of further abandonment that led him to control people whom he valued once again proved counterproductive. Keun began to feel trapped. He could not bear the thought of her abandoning him too. What if she tried to steal away from him in the small hours? He could not allow this to happen. She must not move beyond his reach. As they lay together in bed at night, he would fall asleep gripping a fistful of her hair, and in the morning when she awoke his fingers still held it tight.

The Hotel Eden, Amsterdam, pictured in the 1930s, and
the former hotel – now apartments – pictured in 2022.

By night, the windows of Amsterdam's canal houses cast golden
reflections over the black depths. The waters mirror your mood. Those
comfortable within themselves feel the city's cosy *gezelligheid* in the
shimmering glow on the ripples, and those prone to dread gaze over
into the dark expanses, growing still more disconcerted by how the
curved waterways steer them awry as they try to walk home.

Roth never felt at home in Amsterdam, but he resided there for
four months in 1936, divided by his summer in Ostend. In exile the
Dutch capital and Brussels became the hubs of his publishing network,
much as Berlin and Vienna had been before the Third Reich. He
chose a hotel near the thirteenth-century Oude Kerk, so he could
hear its carillon chime the hours. The wide Damrak canal spans to
the back wall of the Hotel Eden at 24 Warmoesstraat, and in the 1930s
the owners would ferry their guests across the water to the door. The
brothers Piet and Antonius Blansjaar and their receptionist Andries
van Ameringen became Roth's temporary family. Van Ameringen
took care of his needs, from arranging appointments at the hairdresser
to looking after his cash. Roth accompanied the Blansjaars for meals
and they read him newspaper articles, translating into German as he
understood little Dutch (this and the country's Calvinist heritage

were reasons he felt more comfortable in French-speaking, Catholic Brussels).

Zweig's hope was fulfilled that Roth would live under supervision somewhere cheaper than the Foyot, but the Blansjaars did not stop him drinking. He worked in their writing room, where they kept him stocked with jenever. Sometimes Roth wandered to the nearby Nieuwmarkt and then south to the streets that formed the *Jodenbuurt*, the Jewish quarter: Jodenbreestraat, Waterlooplein, places where he might meet people who would make him feel more at home. Piet Blansjaar once read him a report from *De Telegraaf* about a police action against traders at the Nieuwmarkt who were using weighted scales, so that customers who paid for a kilogram received only 800 grams of goods. Roth was fascinated and sat himself down at a table in the hotel with a bottle of Bols-Jenever, a small glass, an ashtray for the long Russian cigarettes he had taken to smoking, a sheaf of paper, an inkwell and his leaky Swan fountain pen. 'The ink on his fingers was wiped off on our cat,' recalled Blansjaar, 'the cat and Roth were very fond of each other. Roth needed an ink wiper and that was our black and white cat.'[32] He began to write his novel *Weights and Measures*. It was here that he also completed *Confession of a Murderer*, which features a hotel modelled on the Eden in its final pages. The narrator returns from a walk with the memory of church bells resounding in his head, speaks with the perspiring owner in the sunlit lobby and settles himself in a writing room with 'a dried-up ink pot and a majolica vase filled with celluloid violets which reminded me of All Souls Day'.[33] The Hôtel Foyot it was not, but the Blansjaars cared for him.

Irmgard Keun came to stay for a month in the autumn, along with his cousin Paula Grübel, who was working for the family's hop- and malt-dealing business and had meetings with the Heineken brewery. Roth and Keun worked on their books: she was writing *After Midnight* (*Nach Mitternacht*), a story of a love affair under Nazi rule in Frankfurt, which would be published by Querido in 1937.* They walked by the

---

* She had had a three-book deal with Allert de Lange but, despite their support for exiled writers, they wanted also to sustain their commercial interests in Germany, which led them to reject *After Midnight* for fear that its powerfully anti-Nazi satirical message would jeopardise this.

canals and drank in cafés. Roth gave an interview to the newspaper *Het Volk* in which he politely spoke of his love for Amsterdam, in whose residents he claimed to see 'Spinoza and Rembrandt; I still meet them here today. On the outside, the people are still the people Rembrandt painted. Inside they are still like Spinoza. They live in his spirit.'[34] But for much of his time Roth remained at the hotel, receiving his visitors there. 'In Amsterdam he was absolutely isolated,'[35] said Johan Winkler, a Dutch Christian Socialist journalist. Winkler said Roth did not fit the city's café culture: its inhabitants had little appetite for being harangued about Austria, God, the emperor and the Antichrist.

Aside from the hoteliers, among the few people close to him at this time were Anton van Duinkerken, a Catholic journalist and writer of religious poetry, a young art historian named Frans Hannema, and Walter Landauer, who redoubled his efforts to promote Roth. Allert de Lange's premises on the Damrak thoroughfare between the railway station and the city centre combined a bookshop on the ground floor and offices upstairs. Passers-by could hardly remain unaware of *Confession of a Murderer*.

The window display was filled with black-and-orange-jacketed copies of the book, and Landauer pasted up newspaper reviews with the critics' praise underlined in red. On 12 June 1936 the bookshop hosted a lecture by Roth, a conservative analysis of society's ills titled 'Faith and Progress'. He agreed to speak on the conditions that only people he knew would be invited and he would have a carafe of schnapps on the lectern. Public speaking had terrified him for a long time; three years earlier he politely declined an invitation to give a talk in Zurich, explaining that 'Unfortunately I suffer from so-called psychological barriers, I am unable to read aloud in front of an audience, and have thus lost many opportunities of earning money over many years.'[36]

When the evening came, the room filled with people, many of them strangers. The Blansjaar brothers helped freshen him up and make him look presentable before he attempted to overcome his fear and face the eager audience. 'Roth stepped up to the lectern,' Piet Blansjaar recalled, 'and his first act was to fill the glass with what was in the decanter. Roth took a sip, stiffened, got all red in the face, then very pale, ran out of the room and was very indignant'. What a disgrace, he said, that it was filled with water! He refused to return until the situation was remedied. An apologetic Allert de Lange representative had to explain to the audience that Roth had been suddenly indisposed and there would be a short delay. 'I had to run home,' said Blansjaar, 'get half a litre of jenever, the carafe was filled again and the lecture started and was a success.'[37]

Afterwards around thirty of those present decamped to Café Reynders on Leidseplein, where Roth had become a familiar figure. Reclusive and lonely as he may have been at times, he made his mark on the town. Amsterdammers grew accustomed to seeing this small, rotund man in a cape pottering down Damrak, kissing the hands of women he met and clicking his heels together when bidding them farewell, and it became known that if you wished to meet him, there was every chance you would if you frequented that café. Roth was often seen there drinking with Frans Hannema. On one occasion, the pair of them knocked back ten gins each before closing time, at which point they were asked to leave and Hannema fell off his stool, overturning a table laden with glasses. Roth, being more practised in such matters, stood up straight-backed like a soldier and calmly walked out of the door.

He became known as a regular in at least half a dozen bars. De Pool, another of the city's traditional 'brown cafés', at 42–43 Damrak. De Engelse Reet in the Begijnensteeg. De Amstelstroom at 204 Kalverstraat (where Roth had only to call out *'Noch einer!'* [another!] and the barman Frits Gerth would rush to refill his glass). Café Scheltema on Nieuwezijds Voorburgwal, where journalists from the nearby newspaper offices drank. The all-night bar at the Lido restaurant on Leidsekade. The artists' society De Kring, on the Kleine-Gartmanplantsoen. Within a few months he imprinted himself on Amsterdam's cultural memory, and several of the cafés now bear plaques commemorating his presence. Everywhere he drank he wrote, filling notebooks with his tiny script. But nowhere was he more associated with than the Café Reynders, where he caroused with Anton van Duinkerken, a luminary of Dutch literature. They liked to toast their friendship by buying drinks for everyone in the bar. On Koninginnedag (Queen's Day) in August, Roth even invited in a brass band that was performing on Leidseplein and treated all the musicians to orange bitters. But often his drunken generosity ran aground at the end of the night. On several occasions the two Reynders sisters who ran the café had to summon Fritz Landshoff from his bed, so that the publisher could pay his author's bar bills. Then the shamefaced walk home across the black canals: over the bridges on Prinsengracht, Keizersgracht, Herengracht and Singel, then perhaps a swaying meander down the broad boulevard of Rokin before adopting his upright officer's gait for the final march along Warmoesstraat, past the Gothic silhouette of the Oude Kerk to the Hotel Eden.

Landshoff had known Roth for years; he knew what to expect. Back in Berlin before the Third Reich, he had worked with Landauer and Hermann Kesten at the Gustav Kiepenheuer Verlag. In exile Kesten joined Landauer at Allert de Lange, which recruited him at Stefan Zweig's suggestion as their editor of German émigré writers, while Landshoff went to Querido. Landshoff later described how Roth's works were published alternately by the two houses, each taking over the monthly payments to Roth when the other could not afford to increase his debts to them. Without Roth always realising it, in this way his friends cooperated to keep offering him financial support; but a time came when neither publisher could continue to subsidise him, nor deal with his abusive ingratitude. At this point Anton van Duinkerken introduced him to the Catholic publisher De Gemeenschap, a connection that at first excited both publisher and author. De Gemeenschap had acquired a famed writer, and Roth a new source of advances. By summer 1937 the publishing director Henri Nelissen realised that his hopes had been wildly optimistic, as the firm's accounts came under assault from Roth's demands.

In the middle of November 1936, newspaper readers were informed that Roth's finances had taken a still more disastrous turn. It was reported that the Hotel Eden's receptionist Andries van Ameringen had disappeared on 11 November with a large sum of money he had been looking after for Roth. Two days later Roth filed a report with the police in which he detailed the circumstances of the theft, explaining how he trusted van Ameringen and had no choice but to press charges. It seemed an acute betrayal. Roth told the Dutch writer Maurits Mok: 'Never mind about the money, I have lost a friend.'[38] But some of those close to Roth suspected that all was not as it seemed. Keun, who was living at the hotel at the time, believed that he engineered the 'theft' to engender sympathy and financial support. Van Ameringen had fled (Keun said Roth assisted him in this) and the money could not be retrieved, so Roth requested the lost sum as compensation from De Gemeenschap. Either way, it was time to move on from Amsterdam. A few days later he left the city. He returned for publishing negotiations in July and September 1937, but would never live there again. De Gemeenschap reimbursed him the 'stolen' money. In 1940, owing to the numerous debts the publishers incurred in dealing with Roth, they went bankrupt.

Joseph Roth, Frans Hannema, Charles Nypels, Otto B. de Kai, Joop Sjollema and Maurits Mok in a café in Amsterdam, 1936.

Before he left, he met a few Dutch friends for a parting drink at the Noord-Zuid Hollandsch Koffiehuis near Centraal Station, where the only known photograph of him in Amsterdam was taken. Where the others look alert, he looks bleary and forlorn. Frans Hannema remembered Roth as an alternately gregarious and silent figure: he would sit without speaking for hours at a time. He seemed 'so defeated, both mentally and physically, that I sometimes had to hold his arm while he was walking', said Hannema.

Roth was so crushed by his time in Amsterdam that he could hardly bear to return. He only did so reluctantly for publishing negotiations the next year, whereupon he gave Hannema a farewell gift, a dedicated copy of *Confession of a Murderer*. He borrowed the train fare back to Paris from the Blansjaars and bought a first-class ticket. Spending someone else's money on the most expensive option was, he acknowledged, 'typical of me, my dear Frans'. Hannema only said: 'Joseph, I hope we'll meet again soon.' 'No, we'll never see each other again.' Hannema hugged him on the platform at Amsterdam Centraal and noticed he was crying. 'I've got something in my eye, Frans,' he said. 'I would like you to go now, I can't stand parting these days.'[39] With that, Roth took his seat in the carriage and stared straight ahead without looking out of the window.

In 1936 Roth agreed a contract with De Gemeenschap for a novel to be called *The Tale of the 1002nd Night* (*Die Geschichte von der 1002. Nacht*). The idea arose from his time in Ostend: Stefan Zweig took him to smart locations on the seafront such as the Venetian Galleries, the Royal Villa and the former Royal Palace Hotel, which in 1900 and 1902 had hosted the Shah of Persia, Mozaffar al-Din Shah Qajar, and his vast entourage. People in the town still spoke of those times – the shah practising his rifle-shooting on the beach, the gala ball at the casino, the gymkhana, the military torchlight procession in his honour. Perhaps in the knowledge that the shah's predecessor had visited Vienna during the World's Fair in 1873, Roth was inspired to write a story imagining his introduction to the Habsburg Imperial capital back in the late nineteenth century, one that reaffirms how Roth's extraordinary powers of fantasy only intensified in reaction to a growing need to take flight from excruciating reality.

The Tale of the 1002nd Night is a beautiful, sensuous, tangled and overpopulated tale of old Vienna that traces the downfall of three lives, set in motion by a visit from the shah in an unspecified year in the 1800s. He sets sail in part to recover from illness, but also because he is bored of his harem of 365 wives and wants instead to fall in love with a western woman. Vienna swoons at his arrival. Weary as Roth may have been, he fortified himself in dreams of a time when the Habsburg sun remained just above the horizon, and found the strength to recapture his full descriptive powers when describing the military parade, equine display at the Spanish Riding School and lavish society ball laid on in the shah's honour. There the Persian ruler falls for the renowned beauty Countess W. and decides that he must sleep with her that night. Among the various practical and ethical obstacles is the fact that she is married, but, in something of an orientalist trope, the shah is a man whose every whim and desire must be fulfilled or else there will be dire consequences. An eccentric collection of Persian servants and Austrian officials anxiously scurry off to satisfy his demand. Among them is the Ninth Dragoons' Captain of Horse, Baron Alois Franz von Taittinger, whom Roth reincarnated from *The Radetzky March*. He has a bright idea: Countess W., whom he once courted, has a near-doppelgänger in his sometime lover Mizzi Schinagl (another character revived from Roth's masterpiece), who is now a prostitute at a brothel run by Frau Josephine Matzner. Some hurried dressing-up ensues: Schinagl in a sky-blue silk ballgown to match the countess's, the brothel as a mansion. This ingenious solution seems to work perfectly.

To thank the 'countess' for their night together, the shah gives her a fabulously valuable string of pearls; and from there begins the collapse, which Roth narrates with the disorienting briskness and flashing intensity of a fever dream. The fantasy world he constructed during his progressive retreat from reality here finds its most ornate expression, replete with silks and velvets, candlelight and perfume, trotting Lippizaners and cantering cavalry, oriental rugs and fine lace. This sensuous aesthetic combines with Roth's fixation on how rapidly the threads of our lives unravel to create an unsettling tonal flicker of light and shade, keeping the reader intrigued even when the plot feels strained.

Mizzi already has a son from her past liaison with the baron, but Taittinger is an absent father who shows no interest in his child (he cannot even remember if it is a boy or a girl). He had grown bored of her: in his view, people could be divided into those who are 'bores', 'so-so' and 'charmers'. Despite his contempt, she remains in love with him. Taittinger, who hitherto considered himself a charmer, is wracked with regret for his part in the sordid episode with the shah and slumps into alcoholic torpor. On selling the pearls and retiring from prostitution, Mizzi is thrilled by her sudden wealth, ignores sensible advice about how to invest it, and gives much of it away to associates including Frau Matzner, while embarking on an orgiastic lifestyle: 'Men had been her daily, her nightly bread. She was like a poor quarry seeking its own hunters.'[40] She is lured by a lover into a scam to sell counterfeit Brussels lace, and is sent to jail.

Everything had changed 'from the moment Taittinger had seen the cropped head of Mizzi Schinagl,'[41] writes Roth's narrator in describing his visit to his imprisoned former lover; another sexually liberated woman whom Roth brings to ruin, this one even incarcerated and short-haired like the institutionalised Friedl. A great beauty so transformed that, in the process, the world seemed transformed too into something ugly and malign. It enhanced the suspicion that the world is grim beneath its cosmetic dressing, which fate conspires to sweep away at critical moments.

Worried by the prospect of losing her money when her banker unexpectedly dies, Frau Matzner dies of a fever, moments after thinking she had recovered. Taittinger is blackmailed and betrayed by a gutter journalist who hears of his illegitimate child and writes scandalous, gossipy reports in which the thinly disguised protagonists are identifiable to those in the know. He is ejected from the cavalry, and at the same time learns that his estate out in the cold Carpathian mountains is falling into ruin, so he must embark on the forced excursion to the Austrian periphery that is now customary for Roth's anti-heroes. The family pile is a large house with many doors and many rooms. The deaf Hungarian footman has neglected his duties: there are toads in the kitchen, mould in the dining room, cardboard in broken windows, and in the study the ancestral portraits hang crooked.

In the local inn Taittinger is at last confronted by his abandoned, damaged son. He takes the train back to Vienna. There is nowhere left to run, and nothing to be done; his debts are insuperable, he cannot adapt to civilian status, he becomes a lost man out of place. The shah also returns to Vienna and brings the tale full circle, and among the tributes this time is a panopticon, a display of waxwork figures such as had always enchanted Roth. After Mizzi's release from jail, Taittinger had helped her buy shares in this show at the Prater. When it opens with a tableau depicting the shah's original visit, in which Mizzi performs as ruler of his harem, Taittinger is humiliated. The indebted, disgraced ex-soldier runs out of options, is refused readmission to the army (not even the infantry will have this old cavalryman) and shoots himself in the head. 'I think he lost his way in life,' a colleague observes. 'It happens. A man can lose his way!'[42]

Roth felt himself lost by now, but *The Tale of the 1002nd Night*[*] is touched with genius. The scenes are jumbled but luminous; the characters are thin, but on occasion their inner numbness yields to instants of devastating pain. The rigidities of Habsburg military life left Taittinger unable to think for himself or take a moral stance. He had grown so accustomed to lying that he barely noticed he was doing it any more; he only noticed when he didn't. In discussing his dire situation with his fellow soldier Zenower, the closest person he has to a friend, Taittinger 'caught himself telling the truth; and for the first time in many years he blushed, the way he had once blushed as a boy when he'd been caught telling a lie'.[43] But this is the old Vienna, where disreputable artifice is integral to sustaining a reputable appearance. So much of it is fake, so little bears scrutiny. A prostitute dressed up as an aristocrat, a brothel as a mansion, the shah rendered in wax, the world ugly beneath its cosmetic veneer. The waxworks maker is given the last words, ones that we can hear Roth saying as he looked over Europe at the end of the 1930s. 'I might be capable of making figures that have heart, conscience, passion, emotion and decency. But there's no call for that at all in the world. People are only interested in monsters and freaks, so I give them their monsters. Monsters are what they want!'[44]

For all that Roth satirises the old Austria, he does so with affection.

---

[*] Published in English in 1999, trans. Michael Hofmann, with the title *The String of Pearls*.

To the legitimist in him, the enervating military and bureaucratic culture he critiqued had to be weighed against the empire's tolerant, multi-ethnic character and the merits of a strong monarchy. Besides, Habsburg passivity and inefficiency was far preferable to the terrifying resolve of Nazism. Gentle atrophy would always trump aggressive virility for the conservative Roth. Bores, charmers, or monsters? There was no debate to be had.

When Roth gave a talk to a group of Jewish students, a member of the audience asked why he had chosen a Catholic publisher for *The Tale of the 1002nd Night*. 'Because I have been baptised,'[45] was the terse response. But many of those close to him remained sceptical that he had, noting that he often seemed lacking in understanding of Catholic doctrine and worship. Pierre Bertaux thought it a political position, and this is supported by Fred Grübel, who recalled a plan devised by Roth.

'He had the idea, characteristic of him, that only a union with what he considered the greatest and wisest power on earth, the Roman Catholic Church, could save us,' said his cousin. Roth proposed that in return for a large sum of money from Jewish donors, handed over by a Catholic convert – 'he had in mind the industrialist Louis Hagen, who had just become papal chamberlain' – the Church would ban the heathen NSDAP. 'If the church bells fell silent in Catholic Germany, if no mass was said, if no sacraments were given to the Nazis, then at least the Catholic part of Germany would come to its senses and Germany and the Jews would be saved from the anti-Christian and anti-Jewish catastrophe.'[46]

Others close to him considered Roth's 'Catholicism' no more than a snobbish affectation, and not something to take seriously. Andrea Manga Bell and Soma Morgenstern shared this view. She once asked him: 'Do you know where Roth is?'

'At Mass,' he replied, adding: 'at Latour-Maubourg', the Parisian boulevard where the Catholic Association of Former Austrians worshipped at a private Dominican chapel.

'And when will he be back?'

'When the communion wine is finished.'[47]

It was a good line, but unsympathetic and glib. Roth's friend Hans

Natonek once accompanied him to a Christmas Midnight Mass at that chapel, where 'after confession, [he] went to the communion pew and received the Host. He came back with such a transfigured expression, that I had to think it was genuine.'[48]

At other times he is thought to have attended the famous Church of Saint-Sulpice, a couple of streets away from the Hôtel Foyot. To step into the vast baroque interior with its Delacroix murals and sublime painted ceilings, its shadowed stone, marble and gilt, must have moved Roth's soul. Picture him as he trudges into one of its twenty-one chapels' wooden confessionals, lowers himself to the seat and sighs. He stares blankly ahead, the paternal priest sees his sagging profile through the lattice. '*Pardonnez-moi, mon père, pour les péchés que j'ai commis,*' says Roth. Forgive me, Father, for my sins. Whether or not he had faith in God, the act would have had psychological value. Who could doubt that he sought forgiveness, or that he needed a father?

The church of Saint-Sulpice, Paris: a confessional
in one of its twenty-one chapels.

Perhaps his 'Catholicism' reduces to these factors. The aesthete in him was seduced by its imagery and incense, the snob in him by its nobility, the politician in him by its role in his scheme to reinstall the Habsburg monarchy, the internationalist in him by its transcendence of borders, the sinner in him by the absolution of confession, and the lost child in him by its provision of father figures. But in his essence, he was always an eastern Jew, and it was only among his fellow *Ostjuden* that he felt at home.

'The eastern Jews did not unwind at the end of their day by drinking,' wrote the rabbi Abraham Heschel. Roth was a cultural aberration: alcoholism was almost unknown among them. In 1925 in Warsaw, where they formed one-third of the population, arrests for drunkenness numbered eighty-seven for Jews and 11,994 for non-Jews. 'After a day's physical labour, they rested their bodies and engaged their minds by studying books.' Poor Jews who lived on a diet of potatoes, said Heschel, 'sat there like intellectual princes. They possessed whole treasuries of thought – the knowledge, ideas, and sayings of many ages. When a problem came up, there was immediately a crowd of people to offer opinions, proofs, quotations ... The stomachs were empty, the homes overcrowded – but the minds were replete with the riches of the Torah.'[49] In 1936 Roth made one of his most important late friendships. Joseph Gottfarstein was a Talmudic scholar from Lithuania, a learned and humble *Ostjude* of the kind Heschel described and Roth so admired, not one of the deracinated western liberal Jews he held in such contempt.* They discussed God and belief, or else would sit in companionable silence. They spoke Yiddish together, Gottfarstein fluently, Roth just well enough. Gottfarstein lived near Roth in Paris, but he was a man one might have found in the little town.

Over the winter of 1936–7, Roth embarked upon a lecture tour across Poland funded by the country's PEN Club, accompanied by Keun. It was the same talk he had given in Amsterdam, titled 'Faith and Progress'. He found the trip gruelling and demeaning: 'I go from

---

* Robert Wistrich offered a persuasive account of Roth's differing attitude to eastern and western Jews: 'The modernity of the Western Jew was fundamentally suspect to Roth and identified with a loss of both Jewish and human substance ... In Roth's conservative transvaluation of values, the world of the shtetl re-emerged as the ideal embodiment of a lost intimacy and innocence; the materialist values of the Western *Bürgertum* [bourgeoisie] (Jewish and Gentile) represented its self-alienated antithesis. In the inherited traditions, hopes, and fears of the Ostjuden, Roth found a more convincing metaphor for an authentically human universalism than in the sublimated sophistication of Western Bildung.' *The Jews of Vienna in the Age of Franz Joseph* (Plunkett Lake Press, 2016), Kindle edition, locations 14585 and 14595.

place to place like a traveling circus, every other evening in penguin suit, it's terrible, every other evening the same talk.'[50] But it enabled him to do something he had long wished to do, something he needed to do before he ran out of time. It had been 'an eternity' since he'd been to Galicia, he told her. 'I have to see it one more time.'[51]

They stayed at the Hotel Europejski in icy Lwów, where he reconnected with his cousins Paula, Resia and Heini Grübel; their father Siegmund had died. He declined their offer of accommodation at the flat in Ulica Hofmana, telling Keun: 'It is frightful to live with relatives. Besides, Jews have terribly small schnapps glasses, the size of thimbles.' In Lwów he seemed to Keun for the first time to be at home. Though he didn't wish to stay with family, he introduced her to his cousins and delighted in reacquainting himself with his frail old friend Frau von Szajnocha-Schenk. 'You must meet her, a noble lady,' he said. Relations were frostier with his cousin Paula, who tried to dissuade him from drinking and was shouted at in return. When she noted the state of his teeth and suggested she order him some dentures, he abruptly declined the offer. Later he explained to Keun: 'If Paula pays for my teeth, she'll own a bit of me too.'*[52]

Still, back in the former Galicia Keun saw a different Roth from the one she had hitherto known, a man who could be himself, which meant fully inhabiting his Jewishness. 'Only there,' Keun recalled, 'where he came from, was he not splintered into a thousand fragments. He was demonstrably proud of the poorest Jews, like the ones he took me to once, who lived in a cellar where the candles burned even by day. He sat down at their table and spoke Yiddish with them; you could feel the love emanating from him, and I had to love him for it.' She said that he 'revived in Poland among the Jews. He ate properly again there and was healthy and natural.'[53]

There was only one place in the region he did not wish to visit. As he had written of the anti-hero in *Tarabas* a couple of years before, 'Often during his wanderings he had found himself near his native

---

* 'Too' – Zweig paid for his clothes, he owed any money he earned to his creditors, and his ideas were owed to publishers who had paid him advances for promised but unwritten books. Which elements of himself could Roth truly call his own by 1937?

village, but he had always made a wide detour around it. He was not yet sufficiently prepared; for it needs much preparation before one is ready to go home again.'[54] He was still not prepared, said Keun. He never would be. 'When I asked him why he didn't go to Brody, he became silent and withdrawn. He was afraid of seeing it again. I believe he felt drawn towards it but the memories, good and bad alike, which would have taken hold of him there would have been too upsetting.'[55]

Their time together in Poland gave a glimpse of the man in his natural environment, where he could relax instead of having to sustain a 'false existence' that gradually destroyed one's 'real existence'.[56] Back in Vienna, he returned the mask to his face. In the east, he had spoken standard German with his relatives. Now she found him more affected again, adopting a form of German littered with Viennese dialect. He would never again return to the east. He would spend what remained of his life in places where he had adopt a persona to pass for normal; but acting is hard work, and he had barely the energy or willpower to play these roles for much longer.

On a late summer Monday 'in the fourth year of the German apocalypse', Roth received two large brown paper parcels tied with string, containing complimentary copies of his new novella *Weights and Measures* to inscribe for friends. He decided for now not to open them. Most of his friends were writers and he would rather they read 'the works of the immortal dead', he noted in a diary article for *Das Neue Tage-Buch*, a German émigré newspaper published in Paris. It was, he said, his eighteenth book.* 'Of the previous seventeen, fifteen have been forgotten. In Germany the forgotten ones have also been banned. Outside Germany you're hardly likely to come across one in a bookshop.'[57] He doubted his friends would want a signed copy, anyway:

---

* Remarkably, this is correct. Roth must have counted the unpublished *The White Cities*, *The Silent Prophet* and *Perlefter*, and *Panoptikum: Gestalten und Kulissen*, a collection of his feuilletons published in 1930 as part of the contract with the *Münchener Neueste Nachrichten*. Otherwise: *The Spider's Web*, *Hotel Savoy*, *Rebellion*, *Flight without End*, *The Wandering Jews*, *Zipper and His Father*, *Right and Left*, *Job*, *The Radetzky March*, *The Antichrist*, *Tarabas*, *Confession of a Murderer*, *The Hundred Days*, and now *Weights and Measures*.

books with personalised dedications were harder to sell on, he said. He was depriving them of one of his best works.

Weights and Measures hasn't the depth and heft of *The Radetzky March* nor the emotional clout of *Job*, but it is precise, lucid, immersive in its evocation of the little town and devastating in its depiction of a virtuous man's collapse into drink-sodden obsession. Anselm Eibenschütz leaves the routine and structure of his beloved Austro-Hungarian Army at his wife's behest, to take a civilian role as the inspector of weights and measures in Szwaby, a border town of smugglers and crooks. The little town's name derives from the German colony in Brody Roth claimed as his birthplace, and it lies in the district of Zlotogrod, which recalls the street where Roth grew up, the Vulytsya Zolota or Goldgasse.

Weights and Measures' origin as a fragment of *Strawberries* is apparent. Its setting and characters hint at the great novel – a final laying of childhood ghosts, an apotheosis of his literary preoccupations – that Roth hoped *Strawberries* would be. We move through the shadows and mud of a Galician *shtetl*, with its screeching poultry market, its tavern of card-playing smugglers and Russian deserters drinking themselves unconscious on schnapps. We feel the bone-chilling cold of a Brody winter, the rejuvenating springtime warmth that cracks the ice into floes on the river, the cold light of the overhanging stars. We reacquaint with Mendel Singer, whose wife runs a store by his *cheder*; with the people-smuggler Kapturak; even the gendarme Herr Slama, whose wife died giving birth to Carl Joseph von Trotta's child. Its cast and setting are Roth's childhood world distilled into 100 pages with an almost uniformly brilliant lightness of touch. Zweig was amazed to find Roth's talent so intact. 'It's a miracle how his brain remains so undamaged,' he said. 'He is the same great artist he was before. It almost looks as if he could be saved.'[58]

The vacancy arose with the death of a heavy-drinking, well-loved inspector – well-loved because he didn't do the job – and his sober replacement is met with suspicion. The upright Eibenschütz intends to establish order and check the town's traders are not defrauding their customers by using false weights on their scales. He immediately makes an enemy in Leibusch Jadlowker, whose tavern is a hub of illicit behaviour, a natural home for Kapturak. Eibenschütz is undone by the women in his life, of course: by now Roth's protagonists usually are. His wife is impregnated by his junior colleague. He sends the man to another office; as for his unfaithful spouse, she and the illegitimate child continue to share his home but he shuts them away in another room, out of sight. Sometimes he hears the baby crying, just as sometimes Roth heard reports of Friedl's suffering.

As Eibenschütz spends an increasing amount of his time in the town's tavern, he falls for Jadlowker's lover, a beautiful, seductive gypsy woman named Euphemia. When she admits that she hates Jadlowker, it seems as if the once 'cold and pitiless' stars 'had moved a little closer to the earth'.[59] They become lovers, but when another lover returns to town, she rejects him. He is first cuckolded by one woman, then abandoned by another. When a cholera outbreak sweeps the little town, killing his wife and her baby, Eibenschütz welcomes the prospect of dying too: 'Actually he yearned for death.' The prospect of falling prey to the disease comforts him. 'But how to await death, when one did not know if it would really come, without stupefying oneself? So Inspector Eibenschütz drank.'[60] Eventually he 'fell into alcohol as into an abyss, into a soft, alluring, feather-bedded abyss'.[61]

Roth often told Soma Morgenstern that without alcohol, he would merely have been a good journalist. He once offered to point out the great passages in his books that 'I owe to a good Calvados', but Morgenstern said there was no need: he could identify the episodes written when drunk, and in truth they were the books' weak spots. In Roth's hotel room he took one of the now-unwrapped copies of *Weights and Measures* and indicated certain sections as an example. 'How can you tell?' asked an indignant Roth. Morgenstern explained they were the books' most sadistic passages. Roth concurred, but lashed out at his friend: 'You don't like that for didactic reasons. You want to cure me. You want me to become a teetotaller like you. A paragon of virtue like you and Hitler!'[62] Unlike Hitler, Morgenstern was not teetotal and he did not appreciate the comparison.

Such passages probably included the book's denouement, in which Kapturak and Jadlowker plot to ambush and murder Eibenschütz by hitting him over the head with a stone wrapped in a handkerchief. It is the same technique for skull-smashing that Roth mentioned to Manga Bell and her daughter as his proposed method of self-defence. Perhaps this explains why a delicately wrought and restrained fable of a good man's corruption and ruin is marred at the last by a lurch into bloodshed, as an inebriated Roth succumbed to the urge to purge himself in print of a keenly nurtured fantasy of violence against his own enemies.

From Brussels' Grand Hotel Cosmopolite on 10 July 1937, Roth wrote a damning letter to Zweig in which he recalled that since their 'melancholy goodbyes' in Ostend the previous summer, Zweig had all but ignored him. Their reconciliation seemed to have foundered. Roth deplored the inadequacy of his pacifist idealism – 'The nonviolence of Mahatma Gandhi is just as unhelpful to me, as Hitler's violence is detestable'[63] – his privileged complacency, his naïvety, his egocentricity, his dazed confusion. Zweig had faced widespread criticism from Jewish émigrés during the previous few years for not only refusing to speak out against Hitler and call for international action to save Germany's Jews, but even continuing to collaborate with people now complicit in the Nazi regime. He had written libretti for Richard Strauss, who since 1933 had been the president of the Nazis' Reich Chamber of Music.

In 1935 during a trip to New York, the US publisher he shared with Roth, Viking Press, called a press conference where a horde of newspapermen gathered, eager to hear the international celebrity author finally condemn what was happening in Germany. Repeated questions yielded no forthright response. Zweig said he hadn't been to Germany for three years so he couldn't presume to give an informed comment on the situation there. Eventually he said he would not be drawn on what he thought would happen. The new Germany was too unpredictable. 'I will make no prophecy. I would never speak against Germany,' Zweig declared. 'I would never speak against any country.' His biographer George Prochnik explains Zweig's rationale: he was wary that, as a man in exile, he should choose his words carefully for fear of aggravating the situation of Jews in Germany who were effectively 'hostages, and anything we who are free say or do will be revenged on these defenceless people'.[64]

But Roth would surely have countered that the Nazis would soon attack them in any case: they were already consumed by irrational and fathomless fury at Jews, and who was Zweig to think that he might delicately reason with and pacify such people? He was unforgivably inert and confused at a critical moment that demanded action. 'Because you notice it getting darker,' Roth jibed in the letter from Brussels, 'you stand there bewildered by the approach of night.'[65] As darkness fell over Europe, Zweig seemed to Roth to think that he could make a difference by shouting: 'Down with politics!' Roth despaired of him. 'Why do you do these things?!'* He added a terse postscript. 'I am going to Ostend again. It will remind me of you.'[66] He and Keun returned to the Belgian coast the following week at the invitation of Hermann Kesten. It wasn't the same as the previous summer, he told Zweig mournfully on 28 July. 'Ostend without you, the same bars, completely different. Very familiar, very remote, terrifyingly both at once. I stagger from one week to the next.'[67]

Four days later, a 'wonderfully comforting'[68] reply from Zweig prompted Roth to speak of the 'umbilical cord of friendship'[69] between them. He remained 'all washed up', was writing his fifth book in three years,† and, with a cool detachment, as if viewing his life from such distance that he could see its entirety, noted that it was entering its conclusive stage: 'The ending is a little protracted. I take more time dying than I ever had living.'[70] He mentioned that the owner of the Brasserie Floréal 'asks after you every day',[71] and said he would be happy to meet Zweig anywhere that suited him.

In a terse, single-line letter on 26 August, he was 'VERY disquieted'[72] that Zweig had not replied. Three days later he asked directly:

---

* Five years later, at the end of his life, Zweig would concede he was wrong: 'We are none of us very proud of our political blindness at that time, and we are horrified to see where it has brought us ... I had inhibitions [about being outspoken] ... feeling mistakenly that I had no right to join in discussions of the present situation when I was in a foreign land.' *The World of Yesterday*, p. 419.

† *The Antichrist, Tarabas, Confession of a Murderer, The Hundred Days* and *Weights and Measures*. He doesn't even mention starting work on *The Tale of the 1002nd Night*.

'Dear friend, where will you be going? Perhaps we could meet anyway?'[73] On 4 September, 'if you want to see me, it will be possible only in Brussels ... Place? Hotel? Time and place? – If you can't, then please drop me a line to say so. I'm on tenterhooks.'[74] On 21 September, a final letter from Ostend: 'I am leaving today. I have hung on in vain, in the hope of seeing you.'[75] Then two days later, another sent from Amsterdam in which Roth mentioned he that he'd finally received a letter from Zweig that had been delayed in the post for a week. He inferred from it that Zweig was instead planning to meet the Italian conductor Arturo Toscanini, who had become a prominent anti-fascist. Roth could not understand why Zweig would see an acquaintance at the expense of a close friend.

On 25 September came a long response from Zweig. 'Why, oh why,' he asked, 'are you so easily offended – aren't we beaten about enough without baring our teeth at one another?' After filling Roth in on his activities and plans, on how tired he was, how a friend had betrayed him, and how much he wanted to meet Roth, a true friend, he concluded: 'Roth, don't become bitter, we need you, for the times, however much blood they drink, remain anaemic in terms of their intellectual force. Preserve yourself! And let's stay together, we few!'[76] Zweig wrote again soon afterwards. The overriding emotion prompted by Zweig's belated letters to Roth that autumn is sympathy. Zweig sounds like a man disabused of his naïve faith in humanity. He is crushed, every bit as melancholy as his friend; not as furious, but as wounded, both by the state of the world and their friendship.

'My dear fellow,' he wrote, 'got your letter a moment ago. It saddens me. I remember how we once wrote to each other; telling each other of our plans, celebrating our friends, and rejoicing in our mutual understanding. I know nothing now of what you are working on, what keeps you busy; in Italy people were telling me of a new novel of yours, and had read it, and I didn't know about it ... No, Roth, I was never disloyal to a true friend for a second. If I wanted to see Tosc., then it's because I honour him, and because one should take every opportunity one gets of seeing a 72-year-old,' a crass remark given that Roth's life expectancy was shorter than the spry Italian's. Toscanini would live to eighty-nine, dying in 1957. Roth, by 1937, felt himself at death's door, and had repeatedly told Zweig so. In any case, said Zweig, 'in the end I didn't even see him (you must have missed that in my letter) because I had to go, Amsterdam wasn't anywhere on my route, and I had no idea if you were there or in Utrecht.' Roth seems to have been seeking confirmation of his belief that Zweig would abandon him.

> Roth, there are so few of us and you know, however much you push me away, that there can be hardly anyone who is as devoted to you as I am, that I feel all your bitterness without opposing it with any bitterness of my own: it doesn't help you, you can do what you like against me, privately, publicly diminish me or antagonize me, you won't manage to free yourself of my unhappy love for you, a love that suffers when you suffer, that is hurt by your hatred. Push me away all you like, it won't help you! Roth, friend, I know how hard things are for you, and that's reason enough for me to love you all the more, and when you're angry and irritable and full of buried resentments against me, then all I feel is that life is torturing you, and that you're lashing out, out of some correct instinct, perhaps against the only person who wouldn't be offended thereby, who in spite of everything and everyone will remain true to you. It won't help you, Roth. You won't turn me against Joseph Roth. It won't help you!
>   Your St. Z.[77]

That autumn, Soma Morgenstern received a surprising telephone call from Zweig, who got straight to the point: Joseph Roth had arrived in Vienna and the three of them were going to meet in the bar of the Hotel Bristol. He announced the plan with such conviction that Morgenstern heard himself agree, for all that he had remained angry with Roth since their dispute over *Tarabas* three years earlier, the longest they had ever gone without contact. They would meet at the grand hotel by the opera house at 4 p.m. 'Although I entered the bar at four o'clock sharp,' remembered Morgenstern, 'the two were already in lively conversation. Joseph Roth rose as quickly as he could manage at that time. We hugged in silence.' Zweig said that the tension between them was the last thing he needed. Roth replied that it had taken Zweig's presence to lure Morgenstern there, and pushed Morgenstern towards him with a mixture of tenderness and aggression. Morgenstern thanked Zweig for arranging the rapprochement and asked Roth if he really believed he wouldn't have come without Zweig's mediation; at this, Roth laughed that Morgenstern was capable of anything, and now Morgenstern 'heard for the first time the already hoarse alcoholic laughter interrupted by coughing, which in the last years of his life should

A signed portrait of Joseph Roth, 1938.

plague him more often and more painfully'.[78] As well as the drink, Roth had been smoking up to eighty cigarettes a day. Morgenstern studied Roth's face as he took a calming sip of cognac:

> The changes in his face and posture shocked me. He was less than forty-three years old, and – my heart won't forgive me for writing it down – he looked like a sixty-year-old drunkard. His face with its distinct cheekbones, his too-short chin once enlivened by constantly alert eyes, was now bloated and saggy, his nose reddened, his blue eyes bloodshot, the hair on his head looked plucked-out in places, his mouth completely covered by a dark red moustache that hung in Slovakian style. But as he was now called to the telephone, walking slowly bent over his cane, on thin legs in narrow, old-fashioned, tight-fitting trousers, with a sagging belly that did not seem to belong to his slender frame, this East Galician Jew gave the impression of a noble, but depraved, Austrian aristocrat of the old school – exactly the impression that he had aimed for with

all his might throughout his life – sometimes honestly, and sadly sometimes dishonestly.[79]

Another friend from this period noted what a strange figure he cut by now, owing to his fear of losing his manuscripts while drunk, as he had done when writing *The Radetzky March*. 'He often carried them with him, rolled up in his jacket pocket,' said Joseph Constant, a Russian-Jewish sculptor in Paris. 'He carried a fat MS on one side and his swollen liver extended from the other, being noticeable through his suit coat, giving him a deformed look.'[80]

With Morgenstern settled into the room, Roth returned his attention to Zweig. It was a rare visit to Vienna for both men: whenever Roth returned, it was with the perpetual fear of running into Friedl's relatives and being obliged to visit her in the asylum. As for Zweig, he was now well established in London, and Roth wanted his opinion on how England would react if Hitler tried to annex Austria. Zweig said it would depend entirely on the response of the Austrian government and its neighbouring states. Roth said that if Schuschnigg remained in charge, then 'Austria is lost';[81] while he accepted the right-wing anti-democratic government as the best way to resist *Anschluss* with Germany, he thought Schuschnigg was a weak character. He asked Morgenstern's view. Morgenstern said he was no expert on English politics, but he relayed the opinion of his friend Abraham Sonne, who had been secretary in London to Chaim Weizmann. When Chamberlain became prime minister, Sonne sat in Vienna's Café Museum with Morgenstern and told him: 'This Birmingham steel trader will deliver Europe piece by piece to Hitler.'[82] Roth declared that he wanted to meet this Dr Sonne. Morgenstern said that they met almost daily between 6 p.m. and 7 p.m. in the Café Museum. Zweig regretted not being able to come, because he had an invitation to a meal at Sigmund Freud's and might remain there all evening.

'Thus the conversation came to Freud,' Morgenstern recalled. 'Actually, it was more of an argument than a conversation.' Roth began to jibe at Zweig and Morgenstern tried to arbitrate: he disapproved of Zweig's 'boundless admiration' for Freud, but nor did he enjoy Roth's 'spitefulness', which 'was hard to accept because it also had a personal motive'.[83] Roth goaded Zweig by ridiculing Freud and citing Karl Kraus, who had died a year ago. 'As you know, I am not an admirer of Karl Kraus. But his definition of psychoanalysis as "the art of living on one patient for a whole year" is apt.'[84] To approvingly quote Kraus in Zweig's presence seemed to Morgenstern a cruel provocation, because Zweig had often been a victim of Kraus's vitriolic wit.

'Zweig, obviously glad that he could break off an embarrassing conversation about Freud, pretended to only have waited for the opportunity to ask me what he had probably wanted to ask for a long time: "You were part of Kraus' circle of friends for a while, weren't you?"'

'Not true,' Roth answered on Morgenstern's behalf. 'Soma and I, we have never been Krausian. We were spared this illness of the Viennese youth. We two belong, perhaps for that reason, to the few writers whom Kraus never attacked. He even praised me once.' When Kraus was alive, said Roth, 'I felt as if he were standing behind me while I wrote, taking care that I didn't sin against the language. Now that he is dead, I miss him. And I begin to worship him.'[85]

Morgenstern was appalled at Roth's needling of the ever-patient Zweig. 'But Zweig was a tolerant liberal,' Morgenstern reflected. 'He was downright infatuated with Joseph Roth, and he also accepted this confession.' 'And you,' he asked Morgenstern, 'will you now also begin to worship him posthumously?' Morgenstern said he'd been wise to Kraus's character ever since reading *Die Fackel* and learning that he sided with the antisemites in the Dreyfus Affair. 'What?!' Roth yelled, turning to Zweig, 'is this supposed to be true?'

Zweig confirmed it. He listed the famous names who had professed positions for and against the persecuted Jewish officer, who died in 1935. He mentioned that Marcel Proust was a Dreyfusard, unbeknown to Roth and Morgenstern, though he was mistaken in adding that Proust had fought duels over the matter. Roth spluttered: 'Marcel Proust, the half-Jew, fights duels for Dreyfus in Paris! Wonderful! Karlchen Kraus, the Czech Jew, shoots at him in Vienna with antisemitic jokes. Disgusting!' 'Disgusting' – *ekelhaft* – had become a word Roth used with increasing frequency. He repeated it now: '*Ekelhaft* . . .'[86]

Zweig quoted the former French prime minister Clemenceau, who said that until the end of his life Dreyfus never fully understood what the affair named after him was about. Then he quoted Anatole France, who said that if the central figure in the affair had not been Dreyfus but another Jew – 'Karl Kraus, for example,' Roth chipped in – then Dreyfus himself would have been an anti-Dreyfusard. 'That is the blessing of assimilation,'[87] was Roth's sarcastic conclusion. His posthumous veneration for Karl Kraus was as dead as his faith in assimilation.

They returned to discussing the Schuschnigg government and agreed that the Catholic *Heimwehr* coup in February 1934 had left Austria powerless and at the mercy of Mussolini. Roth declared there was only one way to save the country: to proclaim the young Otto von Habsburg Emperor of Austria.

'Indulgent and silent,' Morgenstern recalled, 'Zweig stood up, and with a hasty glance at the clock he indicated that he was already a little late for the meal at Freud's.' Freud was at that time writing what would become his final book, *Moses and Monotheism*, which he would finish on his deathbed in 1939. In it Freud would make the controversial claim, as Roth and his peers must already have known, that Moses was not born a Hebrew but an Egyptian. In mock-tearfulness, Roth begged Zweig to persuade Freud not to also, 'for God's sake, come up with a theory that Hitler was of Jewish descent'. Zweig bristled. 'You do him wrong,' he told Roth. 'Freud once confessed to me how sad he was that he had to take the Jews' greatest figure from them at a time when they were so cruelly persecuted.'[88]

Morgenstern continued:

> He had not yet finished speaking, when Roth burst into such con-vulsive laughter that I grasped his hands with both hands to prevent him from slipping off his chair and getting hurt. For a long time we held each other's hands, and we laughed in fraternal solitude against the world, which can hardly fathom how laughable it is if a man imagines he can take Moses away from the Jews.
>
> Peter Altenberg speaks somewhere of Mozart's sacred laughter.

This here was the sacred laughter of Joseph Roth. I joined in heartily and I didn't mind that this scene took place in a bar and that the
alcohol played its part.

When we looked around, with tears in our eyes, we saw that
Stefan Zweig must have laughed with us, because he looked
very amused.[89]

Roth composed himself. Never in his life, he said, would he have
imagined that he would come to think of Sigmund Freud as a *nebbish*, the Yiddish term for someone pitiful and laughably ineffectual.
Then another barb at Zweig, the Viennese bourgeois Jew: 'How
would you translate the word "*nebbish*"?' he asked Morgenstern, his
fellow Galician. 'Mr Zweig certainly does not know the word.'[90]
Zweig explained that actually he knew very well what the word
meant. As he left to meet Freud, Roth asked Morgenstern to escort
Zweig from the hotel, explaining that his swollen feet prevented him
from walking.

Outside, Zweig said how pleased he was that the two old friends
were reconciled, and that Roth's willingness to bury the hatchet
augured well for his mental state. 'Only a thorough weaning cure can
still save him,' Zweig added. 'I will gladly pay the cost of a cure.'[91]

As they prepared to leave for the café where they hoped to meet Dr
Sonne, Roth told Morgenstern he knew what Zweig would have said
while they were out of his earshot: 'That I'm in urgent need of rehab.
He'll pay for everything!' Zweig would pay for him, Roth explained,
not out of friendship alone but 'because he thinks I'm a genius. So,
because he's a schmuck.'[92]

Roth settled the bill at the bar, parted from the waiter as if from an
old friend, and walked at snail's pace through the hotel lobby. He had
loosened his shoelaces because of his swollen feet, but now he had to
try to bend down and retie them, which took several attempts. 'Your
son would laugh if he saw me like this,' he told Morgenstern. 'In the
rue de Tournon, the children already laugh when they see me walking
down the alley.'[93] Perhaps it brought to mind Job 19:18, in which Job
complains that even little boys ridicule him. The Café Museum is less

than five minutes' walk from the Hotel Bristol, but Roth wanted to
call a taxi. Morgenstern said no cab driver would take him for such a
short distance.

When they finally arrived at the café, Dr Sonne was nowhere to
be seen. It was a Thursday, and the waiter reminded Morgenstern
that he never called in at the Café Museum on Thursdays. It did not
matter, though – another mutual acquaintance was here. Morgenstern
took daily walks on the Ringstrasse with Dr Josef Löbel (1882–1942),
a well-known gynaecologist and medical writer. Roth knew him
well too, but their relationship had soured when he used Löbel as the
model for Dr Skovronnek in *The Radetzky March* and 'The Triumph
of Beauty'. Dr Löbel was a prolific and famed author, friend of many
artists and bohemians; Dr Skovronnek was the chess-playing partner
of a provincial Habsburg commissioner; but both were gynaecologists
in the Czech spa town of Franzensbad. Löbel took exception to his
relegated status and his unexpected appearance in print. After *The
Radetzky March* was published he asked Roth whether the character
really was based on him, and Roth told the truth. In Morgenstern's
words, Roth 'had obviously not yet had the experience that a man
confronted with his portrait in a novel suffers the same shock as one
who hears his voice for the first time on a gramophone or on the
radio'. Still, the two men embraced, and sat down with Morgenstern
for dinner.

Roth ordered a Stanislauer schnapps, then a double shot of the same
liqueur. He downed them both in single gulps. Soon he was in raucous
high spirits, and his loud laughter made their table the centre of attention in the café. He moved the conversation on to Austria's situation,
and Löbel felt uneasy; he was under the impression that Roth, the anti-
democratic Catholic monarchist, actively supported the Catholic-fascist
regime. Roth denied this. Löbel and Morgenstern could see no cause
for hope; Vienna was lost, it was only a matter of time. But Roth, awash
in drink in the middle of a crowded Viennese café, avowed that there
was one cause for hope, one way of saving Austria, and with it Europe:
to reinstate the Habsburg monarchy and declare war. He had become
obsessed by the idea. Anyone who still thought they could get rid of

Hitler without war was insane, he proclaimed. 'That is true,' agreed Dr Löbel, 'but you don't have to do a thing, Hitler will provoke his own war.' 'I want the honour of being a warmonger,' barked Roth with hoarse laughter, as people on the neighbouring tables fell quiet. 'You have to do something about it. The earlier the war breaks out, the better.'[94]

Morgenstern suspected he'd forgotten he was no longer in Paris, where he could speak German loudly in public without being understood. Dr Löbel abruptly changed the subject to the state of the Parisian publishing house Flammarion, which published his books; Roth knew an editor there and could answer his questions. Then Löbel made his excuses and left.

'We'll be here at the same time tomorrow,' Roth called after him, but Löbel pretended not to hear. As soon as he was in the café's revolving door, Roth told his old friend: 'He too was angry with me years ago. As you were.'

Morgenstern said he had previously explained to Löbel that he had no cause to feel offended. At this, 'to my shuddering surprise,' Morgenstern said, Roth 'suddenly kissed me right on the mouth, with his wet moustache smelling of Stanislauer'.[95] Morgenstern saw the funny side of it, but still, he was relieved when a few moments later a waiter called him to the telephone. It was Dr Löbel. He wished to know how much longer Roth would stay in Vienna. Another week or so, Morgenstern replied. 'You are his boyhood friend,' said Löbel. 'You still see in him the young, bright, charming, noble Joseph Roth. But he is nothing but an old alcoholic, one step away from delirium, in a state which is not very different from a madman. Thank God that he will only stay here for a week. Otherwise, as a doctor, I would advise you to stay away from him.'[96]

When Morgenstern and Zweig met Roth the next afternoon, they found him in a gloomy mood. His fear had proved correct – it was impossible to visit Vienna without crossing paths with Friedl's relatives, and he had been obliged to pay them a visit. Now he was drinking Hennessy to recover from the experience. It was a golden autumn

afternoon with deep-blue skies, and Zweig suggested dinner somewhere outdoors. He would invite Abraham Sonne too. Roth began
to protest about his swollen feet, but he livened up when Morgenstern
suggested the Prater. 'Splendid, let's go there right away,' he said, and
began to retie his shoelaces.

They took a taxi, and when they reached the park they took
a *Fiaker*, the traditional Viennese horse-drawn carriage. Roth
demanded that it take them to the Wurstelprater, the world's oldest
amusement park. On arriving he strode energetically ahead. It seemed
to Morgenstern that Roth had been rejuvenated by the Prater, a place
that held happy memories for him. He walked so much faster than
his two friends that they lost sight of him. When they found him
again, it was at the amusement park's shooting gallery, where Roth
was wielding a rifle.

'As he heard us coming, he turned his happy face towards us with
beaming, albeit bloodshot eyes. "I've already scored two hits," he
bragged to Zweig,' and he had won a trophy. He invited Morgenstern
to have a go; then his intentions became clear when he made the same
suggestion to Zweig. Morgenstern tried to pass him the rifle, but
Zweig shrank back 'as if I had offered him a red-hot iron', and Roth
shook with noisy laughter. 'I only wanted to prove to you that Mr
Zweig, true to his pacifism, will not even touch a shotgun.' Whereas
Roth wanted to start a war against the Nazis, Zweig blanched at
holding a fairground air rifle. With Zweig suitably ridiculed, it was
time to adjourn for dinner. They made for the Prater's Eisvogel restaurant, where all the white-painted chairs were empty but for one at
a white-clothed table in the furthest corner, occupied by Dr Sonne.

What began as a cheerful evening ended in solemn discussion of
where Morgenstern and Sonne should flee to when, as now seemed
inevitable, they had to leave Vienna. Roth and Zweig felt at a safe
distance in Paris and London, but the other men faced a quandary.*
When Roth and Morgenstern departed, they left Zweig and Sonne

---

* Morgenstern would soon reunite with Roth in Paris; Sonne escaped to Jerusalem,
where he became known as a poet under his Hebrew name, Avraham ben Yitzhak.
He died in Israel in 1950, aged sixty-six.

behind, and walked together for a while down Praterstrasse until they reached the Ferdinandsbrücke. Morgenstern was dismayed again by Roth's behaviour towards Zweig, and asked him to explain himself.

'When we are alone,' Roth replied, 'we get along very well. We are good friends indeed. But his overheated philanthropy provokes me. It can't be genuine. The hatred for Jews affects him personally,' he said, meaning that Zweig was angered to be a target of it himself, rather than by the Nazis' loathing for Jews of all kinds. 'I sometimes have the feeling that he wouldn't be so angry with the Nazis if they would differentiate. Between Eastern Jews and Western Jews. Between rich and poor Jews. Between famous and non-famous Jews. The rich German Jews always believed at first that Hitler meant only us, us Eastern Jews.'

Even if that were the case, Morgenstern told him, he had no reason to be so unkind to him. Zweig had nothing but admiration for Roth, he said – and that was genuine.

'I have for him no admiration, and that's genuine, too. I am incorruptible.'

'But the money he gives you, you take it.'

'Yes,' Roth snapped back, 'I take it. I take it because he has it. But I do it like Anton Kuh. I take a bribe, but I don't deliver.'

The writer Anton Kuh, he said, had accepted the gift of ties from a tie dealer, the expectation being that he would then praise them in his journalism. Sure enough, Kuh mentioned the ties in an article, and in brackets he added: 'In return for payment', as prescribed by Austrian advertising laws. Roth would take Zweig's money, and he would be open about doing so and do him no favours in return – that way, no one could accuse him of being corruptible. By Roth's logic, his rudeness demonstrated his integrity.

As they parted outside the Hotel Bristol, their conversation returned to Morgenstern's need to get out of Vienna. Roth instructed him: 'Give notice on your flat and prepare for your emigration.' Morgenstern said he had been thinking it over and planned to stay until his flat's lease expired in the spring. But he admitted he was undecided. All he knew was that they were approaching a time that would be like their experiences in the First World War, when 'one wrong move makes the difference between life and death'.

'So don't make any wrong moves,' Roth told him. 'Otherwise we will never see each other again. Because the war is coming. Hopefully soon!'[97]

Chapter Thirteen

My spirit is broken, my days are cut short, the grave is ready for me.

Job 17:1

From the table in the Café Tournon where he had spent the day, Joseph Roth gazed across the street at the demolished remains of the hotel that had for sixteen years been his Parisian home. As he drank, he thought about place, time and memory, how they entwine and interrelate; that when a cherished place disappears and an era thus ends, we grasp our memories and they grow brighter in the mind, just as the reality fades away. He drank and ruminated, he watched people come and go: a woman whom he used to love, an elderly man shuffling in slippers, a taxi driver who paused from his work for a glass of red wine, a few boisterous men who laughed at the waiter's antics. He sensed that they would like him to laugh too, so he stood up and joined in, and silently observed this within himself: 'Who's that laughing in me?' And he advised his misery: be patient, you will soon regain my attention.

Yesterday one wall had remained standing, the back wall, which had formed part of his bedroom, and he saw a patch of its sky–blue and gold wallpaper. It had been far from grand. Géza von Cziffra described it as 'a hole of a room in which, apart from fleas and bedbugs, which he called his permanent guests, he could at most have accommodated a canary'[1]. But it was his domain in Paris; it was his refuge there. He watched then as two workers on scaffolding attacked the wall with a pickaxe and sledgehammer, tied ropes around it, clambered down and pulled until it collapsed in a great cloud of white dust.

'Now I'm sitting facing the vacant lot, and hearing the hours go by,' he wrote in June 1938 in an article for *Das Neue Tage-Buch*. 'You lose one home after another, I say to myself. Here I am, sitting with my wanderer's staff. My feet are sore, my heart is tired, my eyes are dry. Misery crouches beside me, ever larger and ever gentler; pain takes an interest, becomes huge and kind; terror flutters up, and doesn't even frighten me any more. And that's the most desolate thing of all.'[2]

The Hôtel Foyot had been condemned as unsafe in 1937. It was deemed at risk of collapse. Roth was the last guest to leave. Even the night porter left before him. After it had been stripped bare, with the carpets ripped out, mirrors taken from the walls and pot plants removed from the foyer, still he refused to give up his room. With the other residents and staff departed, almost the only sound he would hear as he shuffled around was an auction of the furnishings in the back room. Only when the workmen began to remove the roof did he give up and pack his suitcases. He moved temporarily to the neighbouring Hôtel Paris-Dinard, then over the road to the Hôtel de la Poste, which was above the Café Tournon. His new room had a view over the Foyot's ruins.

The day darkened, and still Roth sat in the café opposite the rubble of his former home. The newspaper vendor brought the evening papers, which contained 'all the terrors of the world', and placed them on his table. Street lights flickered on over the Rue de Tournon. Through their silver glow came a refugee, who said he knew a place that served good, cheap meals. Roth was pleased for the man, but did not stir. He rarely ate now. The refugee receded into the darkness and Roth realised he had taken the newspapers with him. The table was empty. The site of the Hôtel Foyot was empty. Everything was empty.

Irmgard Keun had ended their relationship at the beginning of the year. Her explanation of why she left recalls his obsession with clockwork and his treatment of Friedl. 'Roth aspired to dissect human beings into their component parts and then to put them back together again, in order to possess them completely. He wanted to have command of human beings, to try out his hypnotic powers on them. When he had achieved his goal, he lost interest in them. He wanted to make me into something that I wasn't. He often said to me: "A lady doesn't do that kind of thing." For reasons of propriety I was not permitted to speak to the taxi driver. I was not allowed to carry a parcel. He wanted to make a devoted maid out of me, to educate me into "delicateness". He forced me into the role of someone people pitied, until I believed in it myself. He wore me down so much that I had to weep.'

She found his paranoia terrifying; she watched him amass a collection of more than forty pocket knives to keep about his person in case he was attacked. He made her promise never to leave him. She could barely leave the hotel without triggering his 'insane jealousy'. She felt more and more trapped, she said, 'until I absolutely had to break free. In Paris I left him with a great sigh of relief and went with a French naval officer to Nice. I had the sensation of having escaped from an intolerable burden.'[3]

She promptly embarked on writing her novel *Child of All Nations* (*Kind aller Länder*), in which the young female narrator, Kully, gives a child's-eye view of a transient life trekking across Europe in the period after her parents are forced to become émigrés owing to the father's criticisms of the Nazi regime. Her father, Peter, is a quite monstrous character: a sexist, alcoholic writer, published in Amsterdam after his exile from Germany, whose life is consumed by the business of extracting advances from publishers and loans from acquaintances while attempting now and again to repay debts, who expects those in his orbit to bend to his will, and one of whose favourite pastimes is disassembling clocks and watches to try to understand their mechanism.

After Keun left him, Roth tried to go back to Andrea Manga Bell. He turned up at her apartment. He had, said Manga Bell, kept in contact throughout his time with Keun and now he hoped to walk back into her life. 'I suffered terribly, and for months on end, when Roth left me,' she said. 'The whole time I said to myself, "one of my hands has been chopped off".' She was not about to let him back after he'd deserted her for another woman. 'During the time when Roth was with Irmgard Keun, he didn't stop writing to me. Several times he asked me for advice and said: "You can always find ways of doing everything." At the beginning of 1938 it was at last all over between the two of them. Then Roth suddenly turned up at my door and wanted to come back to me, but I controlled myself and did not let him in.'[4]

And so Roth sat all day in the Café Tournon. He would drink alone, or with acquaintances at the bar, or at his *Stammtisch* with his Catholic monarchist friends, for whom the Hôtel de la Poste had become a meeting place. The more he drank, the more he would laugh, a hoarse, raucous laugh that echoed down the silent Rue de Tournon after midnight and attracted attention from the gendarmes who guarded the Senate at the end of the street. He would write letters of reference on behalf of fellow émigrés who sought work in Paris after their escape from Germany or Austria; his old friend Stefan Fingal was now safe in the Hôtel de la Poste after Roth persuaded the French Foreign Ministry to issue him a travel permit, repaying a decade-old favour Roth felt he'd owed since Fingal accommodated Friedl in his flat after the onset of her schizophrenia. Or he would sit alone and brood, scan the newspaper headlines and fulminate. Between sips of cognac he could look back over his forty-four years – he could think of Friedl in her room in Vienna, of the white sunlight of Provence and the oil-wells of Baku, of the skull-strewn battlefields and the war-wounded in Lemberg, of the stars that twinkled over the arena in Nîmes, of distant snowbound Brody. He could think back to childhood, then to the spring of this year and the debacle that had dealt his hopes for Europe a terminal blow.

He had for some time been adamant that Austria's future could only be safeguarded against Nazi occupation by the restoration of the Habsburg monarchy; as he had told the wearily indulgent Stefan Zweig in Vienna, it was vital to instal Otto von Habsburg as emperor.* Roth had visited the exiled Otto's royal court in Steenokkerzeel, Belgium,

---

* While the scheme itself showed a lack of judgement, Roth was not wrong in his assessment of Otto's capabilities. In his long life – he died in 2011 aged ninety-eight – von Habsburg was, as Martyn Rady says, 'probably the best emperor the Habsburgs never had'. His devotion to peace and justice in Europe spanned the twentieth century: he opposed Hitler and Mussolini, intervened to save thousands of French Jews in 1940, became a Member of the European Parliament and worked to bring former Soviet states into the EU, and after the Bosnian War he defied death threats from Serbian gangsters to visit Sarajevo in the name of establishing peace. His body was laid to rest in the Capuchin Crypt in Vienna in July 2011, but his heart is interred in a Benedictine monastery in Hungary, a symbol of his lifelong commitment to both halves of the lost Austro-Hungarian Empire. See Martyn Rady, *The Habsburgs: The Rise and Fall of a World Power* (Allen Lane, 2020), p. 326.

and brimmed with pride at their becoming acquainted: Roth took to referring to him as 'my Emperor'. Otto appreciated Roth's support, but felt he would be of more assistance in good health. It is said that he summoned up his most imperious voice to declare: 'Roth, I, as your Emperor, order you to cease drinking.'[5] Roth was sufficiently reverent to his emperor that he obeyed the command, but only briefly.

The fact that the republican government had barred the exiled heir from returning to Austria was a hindrance, but not insurmountable, for Roth had devised an elaborate plan. He would smuggle the heir to the throne to Vienna in a coffin, then, with the help of Austrian patriots, monarchist politicians and the army, proclaim the new emperor. Otto von Habsburg's private secretary, Count von Degenfeld, was involved in this scheme, according to Manga Bell. However, there remained the question of procuring a corpse; Roth's intention seems to have been to locate a terminally ill Austrian living abroad and, when the time came for the body to be repatriated, replace it with the living emperor-in-waiting. With the monarchy thus restored, Roth believed that the British monarchy would ally with their Austrian peers and France to present a strong front against an expansionist Germany.

The first step was to persuade Schuschnigg to relinquish power. Roth had known this for some time, but with the Berchtesgaden agreement that came into effect on 18 February 1938, it was time to act. The deal between Hitler and Schuschnigg saw a pardon issued to all National Socialists in Austrian custody, and Arthur Seyss-Inquart installed as the *Gauleiter* of Vienna. Roth could stall no longer: the opportunity had come for him to direct the course of history.

After gaining approval from Otto von Habsburg, he travelled from Paris to Vienna to persuade Schuschnigg to hand over the chancellor-ship and thus thwart the *Anschluss*. His sister-in-law, Hedy Reichler,[*] said he travelled under a false name. Just before boarding the train, he wrote to his young friend Pierre Bertaux, by now a politician and broadcaster, with the brisk air of an Imperial Army officer about to

---

[*] Hedy escaped Vienna and went to London, where she married an Alfred Davis and settled in Maida Vale.

enact a military operation. His advice to France: side with Russia; declare a military alliance with Czechoslovakia; proclaim active support for Austria. He expected to find the country in a state of siege, he said. German troops were already massed at the border.

When he arrived in Vienna, he found the city desolate. It was a cold, rainy February evening when Soma Morgenstern answered the telephone to hear a voice say: 'If you recognise me by my voice, don't say my name. I am here incognito.' Morgenstern recognised his old friend's voice immediately and replied with Karl Kraus's greeting to Bertolt Brecht on his flight from Germany to Vienna in 1933: 'The rats are boarding the sinking ship.' 'We must meet immediately,' said Roth, 'but not at the Café Museum. We'll meet in the Mainl-Stube,' another bar. 'I only have to cross the street. I do not want to be seen.'[6] Once they had met and Roth had extracted a promise that Morgenstern would tell no one of his presence in the city, he explained he was on a secret mission on behalf of Count von Degenfeld and outlined the plan.

Roth's initial attempts to contact senior politicians came to nothing. His fame as a writer brought less influence than he had hoped. He headed to the Hotel Bristol, where he saw the expressionist writer Franz Theodor Csokor, a long-time opponent of Nazism. '[You] stood there,' he recalled of Roth later, 'tired already and struggling with the destruction around you and in you, a sentry guarding an idea.'[7] The idea would not gain traction. No one would grant him an audience. Schuschnigg had more pressing matters on his agenda. Roth became convinced he was being shadowed by Seyss-Inquart's henchmen, and this seems not only to have been his paranoia.

Géza von Cziffra was in Vienna at the time, and describes a conversation with a monarchist he named only as 'Count W.' – perhaps Friedrich von Wiesner, a Jewish-born Catholic leader of the Austrian legitimists, who would later be placed under house arrest. This count told him Roth had moved out of the Bristol again because he was being persecuted by Nazis. He was drinking himself to death and kept saying: 'I can't be saved any more!' After a moment's silence, the count concluded: 'Roth, in his present state, does our movement more harm than good. Since he arrived in Vienna he has been acting madly. He is desperate to speak to Schuschnigg.'

'What does he want from the Chancellor?' asked von Cziffra.

'He demands of him that he should resign. Nothing more, nothing less!'

The two men agreed that they felt sorry for Roth, but the count was clear: '[He] is a fantasist. We have to do realpolitik, we have to see where we are.' Then he added hopefully: 'I think Skubl pointed him in the right direction today.'[8]

Michael Skubl was the chief of police, the one official with whom Roth had by now secured a meeting. Roth requested protection from the Nazis who were pursuing him, and that the police would side with Otto von Habsburg if the coup went ahead. But Skubl could make him no such promises. He had only a blunt warning for Roth: he could not guarantee his safety, his life was in great danger and he should leave Vienna immediately. Roth drank a slivovitz and headed to the railway station.

On 11 March, Schuschnigg ordered the Austrian people not to resist a German invasion; the next day, the *Wehrmacht* occupied Vienna and Seyss-Inquart announced the *Anschluss*. Hitler arrived the day after that, touring through a Vienna bedecked with swastika flags, his cavalcade proceeding between jubilant crowds who *sieg-heil*ed while chanting: '*Ein Volk, ein Reich, ein Führer!*' By then Roth was back in Paris, defeated. If the collapse of the Habsburg Empire had killed the old Austria, the *Anschluss* removed any hope of its resurrection. 'A world has passed away,' he noted a week later in a journal article titled 'Requiem Mass', 'and the world that survives can't even grant itself a fitting funeral.'[9]

It was soon after this that a Parisian newspaper reported that the famed author Joseph Roth had relinquished his lieutenant rank in the Austro-Hungarian Army in protest at the *Anschluss*. Soma Morgenstern had fled Vienna and come to stay at the Hôtel de la Poste, where he read the article with eyebrows raised. Over a Calvados that evening he discussed it with Roth, who reacted with a mischievous smile. Then he turned serious and pointed his cane in Morgenstern's face: 'You're one

of the few who knows I was never a lieutenant.' Morgenstern said he
understood Roth's highest rank was sergeant. 'That's right,' he replied,
'but if you joke about it, I'll kill you.'[10]

Another cognac, another look at the ruins. He might think back two
months further, to January 1938, when Zweig reproached him for his
refusal 'to understand how painful your remoteness and silence are
to me' and said the cooling of their friendship made no sense. Zweig
announced he would soon be off to Portugal, 'where there are no
newspapers and no mail'. Though Roth's letters to him in the past six
months had been few and curt, Zweig's intention to go incommuni-
cado hit Roth as an abandonment. He had fired back a sarcastic reply:
'It's good that you're going somewhere where you won't get letters.
That way, you'll be spared possible news of me. Go with God! It's in
His hands whether we see each other again or not.'[11]

'*Garçon!*' Another Pernod goes down in one. Blanche Gidon's husband
said he knew that Roth had lost the fight when it became his favourite
drink. Perhaps he thinks back to mid-June 1938, when he received a
letter from De Gemeenschap regarding *The Tale of the 1002nd Night*.
'We received your letter of the 8th of this month but we did not
receive the corrections to the 1002nd Night promised in your letter
of 23 May *at the latest within ten days*. This is the umpteenth time that
you have failed to keep your promises. It is your own fault that the
management of our foundation . . . no longer has full confidence in
your promises.'[12]

Eventually Roth convinced the publisher to postpone this book
owing to the political circumstances and bring forward publication
of the topical *The Emperor's Tomb* (*Die Kapuzinergruft*), which came
out in December 1938: the last novel Roth wrote and the last he
saw published. It was half the length he'd promised the publishers.
It is beautiful and slapdash; but given Roth's state by late 1938, its
existence is a marvel. He began writing it in the third person, then
decided on a first-person narrative, the better to channel his desolation into his main character, Franz Ferdinand Trotta.

Spanning from before the First World War to a late-1930s Vienna breached by Nazis such as those who had pursued Roth during his doomed venture in the spring, *The Emperor's Tomb* is not so much a sequel to *The Radetzky March* as a companion piece. Where the latter is 'done in oils'[13] (Michael Hofmann's phrase) and bookended by battle scenes, it has a brisk, sketchy quality and hinges on the now-predictable arrival of the First World War midway through its 180 pages, after which Roth grafts his *Heimkehrerroman* style of the 1920s on to his present preoccupation with eulogising the lost world of Austria-Hungary.

Franz Ferdinand Trotta is the grandson of a brother of Joseph Trotta, the Hero of Solferino. His first-person narrative details the post-monarchy decline of Austria through his own gradual degeneration. Where Anselm Eibenschütz's collapse was triggered by the malevolence and callousness of a few individuals, Trotta is undone by the forces of history. His friendships with a Slovenian cousin, the chestnut roaster Joseph Branco, and a Jewish coachman from Zlotogrod, Manes Reisiger, embody the fraternity between Austrians, Slavs and Jews that the nostalgic Roth saw fostered by Habsburg rule.

Reisiger invites him to Zlotogrod, a trip to the empire's periphery that sparks joyful speculation. The little town has just the imaginative hold over Roth's protagonists as it did over him: an inscrutable place on the distant margins where myth and legend flourish. 'Our life before the Great War was idyllic, and a journey to the faraway town of Zlotogrod seemed like an adventure to all of us ... And we started to paint an imaginary picture of the remote little town of Zlotogrod, to such a degree that even while we were describing it, we were convinced we were painting wholly inaccurate pictures; and we couldn't stop distorting this place none of us had ever seen.'[14] In the event, they call by Jadlowker's frontier tavern. In their repeat visits to the little town where we encounter the same people and places, these late books feel more like chapters in the same epic than individual novels.

With the First World War, his world begins to unravel. Right to the last in Roth's oeuvre, the war reliably arrives in almost every novel to disrupt plans and ruin lives. Like a trauma victim who suffers flashbacks, Roth could not stop replaying the moment that aborted his adolescence and rerouted his life, repeatedly working it through in hope of making sense of it. Whether he witnessed bloodshed in person is irrelevant – he was horrified by the hell unleashed on others who were less fortunate, and by the cataclysm that obliterated his homeland, and never again trusted the world. Here, Trotta is taken prisoner of war and sent to Siberia, which allows Roth to flesh out his old fantasy that he'd had such an experience before escaping back to Vienna. His wife Elisabeth, who is Austrian, abandons him for another woman, a domineering Hungarian. Their scandalous coupling is hardly Roth's subtlest critique of Hungary's parasitic role within the Dual Monarchy.

Back at his mother's after the war, she gives him some old packets of his cigarettes she found while tidying the house. Trotta can make out a girl's name on the lid in his faded handwriting: Friedl Reichner. 'I remembered straightaway. It was the name of an attractive girl who worked in the *Trafik* where I must have bought these cigarettes.' His mother smiles and asks who this Friedl is. 'A nice girl, Mama!' he replies. 'I never tried to look her up again.'[15]

There are two things to say of that odd and superfluous paragraph in which, as with the abrupt reference to Mizzi Schinagl's cropped hair in *The Tale of the 1002nd Night*, Roth's private grief does not so much leak as burst into the public realm. One, that the single letter's difference from Reichler seems so minor as to be barely worthwhile, until you recall that Roth loathed Zweig's publisher Herbert Reichner (a 'little man', a '*Weltbühne* Jew') and would have enjoyed emasculating him by attaching his name to an inconsequential female character. Two, that as Roth looked back on the twenty years since he had first spoken to Friedl at the Café Herrenhof in Vienna, and the decade since she had gone insane, he brooded over an alternative reality whereby they met, he thought she was pretty, then he shrugged and walked away.

Trotta loses his wife twice over – first to homosexuality, then, after he has won her back and they have had a son, to the accursed cinema. Elisabeth is lured away by a career in Hollywood. Then his dear mother dies. He loses his friends, he has to send his son to live with a friend in Paris, and he loses his home. 'At that time, I didn't realise that it wasn't the last time I would lose my home,'[16] he reflects. *You lose one home after another.* He retreats to his coffee shop, but a strange man enters wearing an absurd uniform. Trotta takes him for a toilet attendant; it transpires he is a Nazi. Ridicule was the last weapon available to Roth. The Nazi declares the establishment of a new German people's government. The people Trotta is sitting with vanish. The café's Jewish owner turns out the lights, pulls down the shutters and flees, telling Trotta he can finish his schnapps by candlelight and let himself out.

Of all Roth's *Heimkehrerromane* the novel most resembles *Flight Without End*. The endings parallel one another: indeed, at one stage they were near-identical. As the publisher wrote to Roth in September 1938, 'It has come to our attention that the last chapter of *The Emperor's Tomb* which you sent us is almost word for word the same as the last chapter of your *Flight Without End*. Is that an error? Surely one can't use exactly the same chapter in two different books?'[17] Roth's life by now was both chaotic and desperate enough that it is equally plausible he intended to dupe his publisher or wrote it in such drunken confusion that he'd forgotten it was near-identical to a book from eleven years earlier.

The published ending still echoes Tunda's fate, but is yet bleaker, for it denotes the demise not only of a man but of a country, and where Tunda has an excess of freedom, Trotta is in newly Nazified Vienna unable to move. The 'superfluous' Tunda stood for the individual whom war rendered unfit for the new society; the Trottas are emblematic of the vanishing old Austria. When, having lost everything, Trotta wanders from the café to the Capuchin Crypt to visit the tomb of Franz Joseph, it is a valedictory gesture for a lost country by a man who has nowhere left to turn. 'Where can I go now, I, a Trotta?'[18] he asks in the novel's final line. Like the protagonists of Roth's early books, and like its author by late 1938, he had come to the end of his story with no sense of resolution, only adrift, gazing not so much into the future as into a void. Where could he go now? Not to the beloved Zlotogrod, for we learn it was destroyed in the war. Such was the fate of the little town.

Joseph Roth and Soma Morgenstern in the Café Tournon, Paris, 1938.

It is tempting to imagine Roth muttering '*Hölle-Wut!*' to himself as he leaned over the manuscript and described Elisabeth's career in the movie business, but, in need of money and with an eye on escaping the Nazi threat, he had started to consider a move to Hollywood. Since March 1938 he had had a new source of income, a $30-a-month award from the American Guild for German Cultural Freedom, but it wasn't enough. He worked unsuccessfully on film treatments with the playwright, screenwriter and director Leo Mittler, who also lived on the Rue de Tournon.* He hoped to capitalise on Marlene Dietrich's admiration for his work: at one point she seemed interested in filming his novella *Stationmaster Fallmerayer* (*Stationschef Fallmerayer*), a stylishly executed tale of how a beautiful woman can send a man's life spinning into the abyss. On 8 June 1938 he wrote to Barthold Fles, an American literary agent with whom he had had friendly correspondence: 'Help me to America at once! Instead of writing me sentimental letters.'[19] Nothing came of the request.

Roth remained in Paris, and increasingly in the Café Tournon;

---

* Roth and Mittler wrote two drafts of films together, to be titled *The Last Carnival of Vienna* (*Der letzte Karneval von Wien*) and *Children of Evil* (*Kinder des Bösen*), which concerned memories of Habsburg Vienna and Jewish persecution. See Heinz Lunzer and Victoria Lunzer-Talos, *Leben und Werk in Bildern* (Kiepenheuer & Witsch, 1994), and the Literaturhaus Wien website: http://www.literaturhaus.at/index.php?id=10276

except when the hoteliers Monsieur and Madame Alazard refused to serve him, at which he would heave himself up and make the short walk to the Au Petit Suisse, where he could always get another drink. The day's drinking at the Tournon usually ended in conversation about the state of a continent poised on the cusp of war, as he described in an article from November 1938 titled 'In the Bistro After Midnight', published just as the *Kristallnacht* pogroms erupted across Germany. It describes an exchange between habitués of the bar that turns to the question of conscience in the modern world. People no longer follow their consciences; instead, they follow orders. Conscience is history, now: today people are governed by authorisation. Roth attributes a speech on the difference between the two to a taxi driver, but if this were accurate, the man precisely shared Roth's conservative disdain for technological progress. Compare a horse-drawn carriage with a motor cab confronted by someone running out into the road, he says. The horse would instinctively stall; the taxi would speed on,

unless authorised by its driver to stop. The dictators' achievement, he says, is to kill off conscience. 'No more conscience in the world! No more horses!'

The Senate's clock chimes two o'clock in the morning. Mme Alazard says: 'Time for bed, gentlemen,'[20] and stacks the chairs on the tables. Then the slow climb up the narrow staircase of wooden steps and hexagonal tiled landings to his bedroom on the top floor. A few hours' unconsciousness, snoring, lying fully clothed across the bed that takes up most of the tiny room.

The Senate viewed from the terrace of the Café Tournon, Rue de Tournon, Paris.

In 1938 a heart attack rendered Roth weaker still. After this he struggled to walk more than a short distance, and became increasingly rooted in the hotel and its immediate environs. He wrote occasional articles. He still had books he wished to write. His correspondence grows thinner from now, but he would write to old friends; Józef Wittlin said that whereas their youthful letters often closed with the poetic line 'Raise the violin,' now his preferred valediction was 'Lower the violin.'[21]

Soma Morgenstern had become a close companion again now that they lived together at the Hôtel de la Poste. If the weather was cool they would sit on an upholstered bench by the café's window, Roth set up for the day with his fountain pen, paper and cognac. If it was warm, he would move to a green table on the terrace and feel the life of the city blowing by. The café faces east. Fifty yards away to the right is the columned entrance to the Senate, surmounted by a dome bearing a cupola and a clock. But it would be wrong to say that this formed part of Roth's view when he sat on the terrace. Morgenstern joined him there one morning and after they'd read their newspapers, Roth asked:

'What time is it? I have an appointment.'

Morgenstern pointed to the clock. Roth looked morose.

'I haven't seen that clock for a long time,' he said.

'You can't see the clock?' asked Morgenstern. 'You must get yourself a new pair of glasses.'

'It's been like that a long time. Glasses won't help.'[22]

His eyesight had been fading for years and now the world was a blur to him, whether or not he was drunk. He no longer had interest in receiving treatment for his ailments, from his fading eyes to his swollen feet. When friends told him to seek medical help, he would retort: 'I don't need a doctor, I need a priest.'

Another day, and Roth traipses from his bedroom down the tightly winding wooden staircase to the bistro and his seat by the window. An émigré acquaintance of theirs, a Social Democratic journalist named Jakob Altmaier, asked Morgenstern to pass on his book manuscript for Roth to critique. Morgenstern was reluctant – he remembered a previous occasion when a mild-mannered schoolteacher had asked this favour of Roth. When the man came to reclaim his manuscript and Roth's verdict, Morgenstern had never seen Roth so furious, 'apart from when his former friend Bernard von Brentano was mentioned'. 'It is an imposition to give me such a scribble to read,' he shouted. 'You insult me! You humiliate yourself! You insult literature and your profession!'[23] So Altmaier bypassed the hesitant Morgenstern and left the parcelled manuscript for Roth at the hotel. Roth was content to take a look. 'Dear Altmaier,' he thought to himself, 'he can't write. His articles are mediocre even for a Social Democratic journalist. But maybe he has something to tell. He knew the whole world in Germany.'[24]

Two days later Morgenstern came down from his room to find a great commotion in the bistro. The hotel's owners, Monsieur and Madame Alazard, were embroiled in a loud argument. Germaine Alazard doted on Roth and loved to mother him; her husband hated him but recognised his value to their bar takings and that he attracted a crowd of fellow émigrés and monarchists. Roth stood on the terrace holding his cane, looking frightened and pale. He beckoned Morgenstern over: 'They have given me notice. I have to move out. Let's go.'[25]

At a bar around the corner he explained what had happened. That afternoon, he had read a section of Altmaier's manuscript. It drove him into such a frenzied rage that he ripped it into pieces and tried to flush it down the toilet. This only succeeded in blocking the toilet, and now workmen had had to be called in, or else the bistro would have to close. Roth did not dare return there, so Morgenstern mediated on his behalf and persuaded the owners to reverse their decision.

Money had come to preoccupy him more than ever. 'He spoke of money every hour of the day,' said Morgenstern. 'He needed money. He expected a cheque. A cheque arrived late. A money transfer did not arrive in time. A publisher cheated him. His publisher will cheat him.'[26] But when he had it, he continued to distribute it among his fellow émigrés. It was around this time that he received the surprise 1,000 francs from Louis Aragon's journal. Having passed much of it on to others in need, he took Morgenstern to the nearest bar, Café Weber. They were not much enamoured of its clientele – too many of the French intelligentsia there subscribed to the prevalent view: '*Mieux Hitler que Blum*', referring to the Jewish socialist prime minister Léon Blum, whose Popular Front had taken power in 1936.

Sketch of Roth with Klaus Dohrn at the Café Tournon, 1939, by Bil Spira.

The afternoon grew hazier as Roth drank Pernod and brandy with passing friends. Morgenstern hoped to entice him to a nearby Czech restaurant, this being one of the few cuisines he enjoyed, but Roth had ordered more drinks, which the waiter now placed carefully before him. Just then, a fascist newspaper vendor wearing stormtrooper boots marched by the terrace. He cried out his paper's name in French with a German accent, each time adding: '*Mort aux juifs!*' As drunk as he was, Roth still noticed the amusement on the faces of the café's other customers. He shouted with a voice that drowned out the newspaper seller: '*L'addition, garçon, l'addition!*' Then he overturned his glass. '*J'en ai assez!*'[27] I've had enough!

A letter from Stefan Zweig to Joseph Roth at the end of 1938:

Dear Josef [sic] Roth,
*   I have now written to you three or four times, always without reply,*
and think our old friendship gives me the right to ask you what you mean

by this obstinate and hopefully not ill-intentioned silence. It is probable
that I will pass through Paris on my way out or back, in January or
March, and I would simply like to know which you prefer: that I try to
visit you, or that I avoid you (as you so sedulously avoid me). I write
without the least trace of chilliness, but purely and simply for information;
your silence is too striking, too protracted and oppressive for me to be able
to explain it away, say, by business on your part.

All best wishes and that the year ahead (in spite of everything) may be
no worse than the one just gone.

Your Stefan Zweig[28]

There is no record of a reply from Roth.

Among the Jewish exiles who gathered at the Café Tournon was
the artist Wilhelm 'Bil' Spira, who fled Vienna after the *Anschluss*
and would later turn his skills to counterfeiting visas and passports
to enable people to escape Vichy France. His sketches of a paunchy,
lachrymose Roth drinking in the
café convey the lethargic demeanour that had become characteristic
of him by the end of 1938. In one
he has an arm around Klaus Dohrn,
one of his Catholic monarchist
friends. Another artist drew him
at this time, too, a Dutch illustrator named Mies Blomsma. Roth
admired the way her drawing
caught his personality, and when
it was complete he added an
approving annotation: '*Das bin ich*
wirklich; böse, besoffen aber gescheit.'
In Michael Hofmann's translation,
'This is me all right. Pissed off,
soused but clever.'

Sketch of Joseph Roth by Mies
Blomsma, November 1938,
with Roth's inscription.

When Géza von Cziffra and Roth met for the last time, Roth said he was working on a novella to be called *The Legend of the Holy Drinker* (*Die Legende vom heiligen Trinker*).

'Why is your drinker holy?' asked von Cziffra. 'For the same reason I am,' Roth replied. 'Because the good Lord blessed him the same way he blessed me. He once lent my drunkard, a *clochard*, two hundred francs to pay back to Saint Thérèse of Lisieux, via a priest at the Chapel of Sainte-Marie des Batignolles. The *clochard*, of course, squandered the gift on drink, but the loving God found a way to send him money again and again – just as He kept rekindling my poetic talent whenever the inner flame threatened to go out.'[29]

The chapel of Sainte-Marie des Batignolles,
Place du Docteur Félix Lobligeois, Paris.

One day in late 1938, as Roth sat in his usual place on a cushioned bench in the bistro, he listened to a story told by Serge Dohrn, brother of Klaus and a fellow Catholic monarchist. It concerned a drinker whose troubled life had been touched by a succession of miracles before he died. Roth spun it into his own story, which he worked on until the spring of 1939. It is extraordinary that in such an abject physical and mental condition he created one of his finest works. *The Legend of the Holy Drinker* is small, smooth and polished, a gem of the kind that his readers might have deemed him no longer capable of producing. Its creation was akin to the sudden visitation of grace.

The *clochard*, a vagrant, is Andreas Kartak, a former miner from Polish Silesia who sleeps beneath the bridges of the Seine. He has a chance encounter on a spring evening in 1934 with a well-dressed older gentleman, who insists on giving him 200 francs despite Andreas's admission that he would have no way of repaying the debt. The older man has recently become a Christian after reading the story of little Thérèse of Lisieux, the famed nineteenth-century saint. He believes he has been sent by God, and says that Andreas need only return the money to Thérèse's statue in the Chapelle de Sainte-Marie des Batignolles. Andreas, being 'a man of honour albeit of no fixed address',[30] has every intention of doing so. This financial blessing is the first miracle he experiences. Roth, whose fervent hopes for a miracle during the past decade had been dashed over and again, grants his alcoholic protagonist several more: an unexpected offer of work where he can name his price; a wallet that unexpectedly contains 1,000 francs; a reunion with a schoolfriend, Kanjak, who's now a famous footballer. Kanjak offers to send him a smart suit in the mail; when he says he has no postal address, Kanjak insists on renting him a hotel room.

After a fortnight he again meets the well-dressed benefactor, who has no memory of their previous encounter and insists on giving him another 200 francs. But whenever Kartak tries to visit the church to repay the debt, circumstances prevent him from doing so. He is thwarted, for instance, by a bar landlord who forces him finally to pay his bills, and exploits his innumeracy to extract a little extra money besides. He meets an old mining friend who persuades him to drink when he was planning to repay the debt. Kartak means well but he is doomed by fate, the machinations of others and his own weakness. It is all too familiar, just as his benefactors bear more than a resemblance to Stefan Zweig. But finally, when waiting in a bistro outside the church for Mass to finish, he seems – to himself, at least – to settle his account. There he meets a girl in a heavenly-blue dress, who says her name is Thérèse and that she's waiting for her parents to leave the service. In his drunken stupor he imagines that she is the little saint incarnate. She refuses his money and gives him some more of her own.

As Kartak heads for the bar to collect another of the many Pernods he's consumed with his newfound wealth, he collapses to the floor. It is clear he is dying, so the waiters carry him over the road into the church's vestry, accompanied by Thérèse. In his final moments, barely capable of speech like the dying Joseph von Trotta, but in an entirely opposite state of resolution and contentment, he reaches for his wallet and musters two final words: 'Miss Thérèse!' And with his debt satisfied, he dies. He may be delusional, but he is happy. The narrator's final line is a desperate plea: 'May God grant us, all of us drinkers, such a good and easy death!'[31] Kartak's is the kind of swift, painless demise enjoyed by Jacques in *The Radetzky March*, aspired to by Franz Trotta, denied to Frau Slama, and by now prayed for by Joseph Roth.

In January 1939 he received a letter from Dorothy Thompson, the American journalist who had translated *Job*. She wrote on behalf of PEN America to invite him as a 'special guest' at the World Congress of Writers, which would be held in May in New York City. At a time when the basic rights to speak, publish, worship and assemble were 'being denied and threatened over an increasingly large part of the world', she said, 'it seems to us particularly urgent that writers from all countries should gather to consider ways and means of defending free expression under difficult circumstances'.[32] Roth agreed to attend, and wrote again to the American literary agent Barthold Fles: 'I hope that you will wait for me at the ship. Strive already today to make as much publicity as possible for my arrival.'[33]

Around now, his cousin Fred Grübel was released from internment in Buchenwald, then fled to England with his young family from where he wrote to tell Roth of their intended move to America. Roth spoke of his joy that the family were safe and said he hoped to meet them in New York. Then he lost his will to escape and succumbed to resignation. Hans Sahl, a fellow émigré and poet, wrote of seeing Roth at the Hôtel de la Poste at this time. Roth no longer wanted to go to America: he said he was a European, 'and I want to die with Europe, here, on a street in Paris, in front of this hotel'.[34]

*

May 3 1939 was Soma Morgenstern's forty-ninth birthday. He was not a man for celebrating birthdays, but he was pleased when Roth suggested a midday walk in the Jardin du Luxembourg, not least because Roth so rarely wished to walk anywhere these days. The gardens were no more than 100 metres away, but by the time they arrived Roth was exhausted. When they found a bench on a secluded pathway in the shade, he said: 'Do you know why I dragged you here? I wanted to ask you to sing me my two favourite songs.'[35]

Morgenstern sang him an old Ukrainian song called 'Hyla', and the Yiddish folk song 'Amol iz Geven a Mayse' ('Once Upon a Time There Was a Story'). It is about a Jewish king who dies, leaving his wife desolate. Its refrain is a mournful '*Vey iz mir un vind*': woe is me, and pain. Its final verse:

> Where can one find a wise person
> That can count the stars?
> Where can one get a doctor
> Who can heal my heart?

Roth listened with both hands resting on his cane, his head lowered. He remained silent after the song had finished, and Morgenstern saw teardrops on his fingers. They made their way back slowly to the hotel, pausing often so that Roth could sit down and adjust his shoes.

On 22 May Roth wrote a brief, ironic observation on the 'Goethe Oak' – one of several around Germany associated with the poet – that stood in Buchenwald. It would be his last article. 'The inmates of the concentration camp pass by this oak every day; that is, they are passed by there,' he wrote. The tales of atrocities connected to this tree had been much exaggerated, said Roth, and he wished to set the record straight: not one of the inmates had been tied to this tree and shot. That would be sacrilege, he implies. No, such horrors were restricted 'to the other oak trees, of which there is no shortage in this forest'.

*

That day, in the Mayflower Hotel in New York, Ernst Toller took the rope from his suitcase. His brother and sister had just been sent to a German concentration camp. When news of his suicide reached the Café Tournon, Roth was devastated. Stammering with shock, he cried: 'How stupid of Toller to hang himself now, just when our enemies' end is nigh!'[36] Others in the café at the time included his friends Stefan Fingal, who was also living at the Hôtel de la Poste, Hans Natonek and Eduard Broczyner, and they confirmed to Bronsen that Roth was not alone in believing that the Nazis might be losing their grip on power.

Reports differ on what happened next. Morgenstern's account of the day is as follows. He said that he and Roth were perplexed at what could have driven their friend to take such a step. 'We don't have the right to exterminate ourselves,'[37] Roth said. He looked as pale and scared as when he'd been evicted from the hotel. Now he sat with his eyes closed and whispered: 'That's disgusting,' speaking to himself. When he reopened his eyes, he reached for his newspaper; then he thought better of it, and suggested to Morgenstern they go somewhere else, where they wouldn't have to make conversation with acquaintances. Morgenstern suggested a nearby gramophone store where one could pay to listen to records. As they slowly walked there, he warned Roth that the store did not serve alcohol. This was fine, said Roth:

'I have no need for it.'

'I've never heard that from you before.'

'Really?' Morgenstern recalled Roth looked proud of himself and had suddenly come alive. 'Let's remember this day,'[38] said Roth.

In the store Morgenstern mentioned the affecting scene in *Job* when Mendel Singer plays 'Menuchim's Song' on the gramophone. In response Roth only asked whether they could listen to Jewish folk songs here, and Morgenstern told him of a song by Rabbi Yitzchak of Berdichev. They listened to a recording of the rabbi's song 'Dudele', in which to a minor-key melody the singer asks of God: 'Where can I find you?', and answers himself: 'Where can I *not* find you?' God, the rabbi tells us, is not hiding. He is everywhere we look, so omnipresent we do not notice Him. 'A beautiful song,' said Roth. 'It is partly like a folk song and partly like a prayer.' He seemed much recovered from the morning's trauma – so much so that, to Morgenstern's surprise, he suggested lunch. They were near the Boulevard Saint-Michel. 'I remember a little restaurant there from the time when I still ate every day,' he said. He offered to make his friend 'a Galician déjeuner ... a dish for us from the homeland'.

On the way he bought a bunch of spring onions from a greengrocer. At the restaurant he ordered three eggs, boiled potatoes and curd cheese. When the food was served, he crushed the potatoes with a spoon and fork, mixed them with the eggs and cheese, chopped in the onions and shared the dish with his friend. He looked almost cheerful. 'The only food I really like is what I ate when I was young,' he said. Galician food with a Galician friend had proved the tonic he needed. Aside from a little beer with the meal, he still seemed in no need of a drink. He was content, calm and sober. Morgenstern had an appointment to try to gain a visa at the American Consulate, so they parted and agreed to reconvene at the hotel.

The entrance to the Hôpital Necker, Paris.

Bronsen makes no mention of this outing, and suggests that what came next immediately followed the news of Toller's death. Regardless, by four o'clock that afternoon Roth was sitting on the Café Tournon's terrace with his young monarchist friend Max Riccabona and Stefan Zweig's ex-wife Friderike, who had taken it upon herself to care for him, though Roth secretly considered her pompous and patronising. When Morgenstern belatedly rejoined them, he noticed the number of empty drinks saucers on his table. 'What took you so long?' Roth barked. This was not the jovial drunk whose hoarse laughter was part of the soundtrack to the Rue de Tournon, but one simmering with anger and aggression. Mme Alazard called Roth to the telephone, and with his cane he wearily levered himself up from his seat. '*J'y cours,*

Madame,' he called. When he returned he carefully resettled himself. Then he suddenly reached forwards, looked around and slumped on to the table, unconscious.

Morgenstern and Riccabona carried him into the bistro and laid him on the floor. Mme Alazard placed a cushion under his head. They called an ambulance, but Morgenstern knew Roth would resist being taken to hospital, so he went to phone a doctor friend of theirs. When he returned, Riccabona told him that Roth was repeatedly mumbling to himself: 'I think he's saying: "I am not baptised."' Morgenstern leaned down and listened to Roth whisper, with his eyes closed, 'I am not baptised.'

When the ambulance arrived, Roth was conscious enough to be escorted on foot to its door, which, chivalrous to the last, he held open for Mme Alazard and Friderike Zweig – '*Les dames d'abord*' – before climbing in himself.

At the Necker Hospital for the poor, he told the medics he wanted to leave and refused to go to bed. They gave him an injection that sent him to sleep. He was installed in a bed separated by a glass wall from a large general ward. Blanche Gidon, whose radiologist husband knew the medical staff, visited and told him he would soon be out again, but neither she nor Roth believed this. A succession of other visitors followed: Morgenstern, Fingal, Natonek, Broczyner, Friderike Zweig, Jean Janes, and Pauline Kulka, a relative on Roth's mother's side. When Fingal visited, Roth had begun to develop bronchitis and struggled to speak. He rasped: 'I've got to get out of here.'[39] When Frau Kulka arrived she gave him a lecture: the alcohol was to blame, it had destroyed him.

When Morgenstern visited, Roth asked from his bed how he could leave. With trembling fingers, he kept playing with a fountain pen that he could never quite grip; the pen seemed to have a life of its own. Morgenstern said he needed a weaning cure. Roth said he did not need to be in hospital for that.

Broczyner, a doctor whom Roth had known since schooldays in Brody, was appalled to find that the medics had forbidden him alcohol. He told a Professor Fissinger that Roth was seriously alcoholic and must be given regular small doses to ward off delirium tremens. The doctors then gave him a little, said Broczyner, but not consistently, and they paid him scant attention. One said later that if she had known who her patient was, she would never have left his bedside; but she did not, so Roth lay there alone.

On 26 May 1939, Morgenstern found Roth conscious and lucid. Roth beckoned him to the bedside, pulled him close and whispered in his ear that he needed to bring him a suit and shoes and get him out of the hospital. 'They give me nothing to drink, not even milk,' he said. 'I am dying of thirst. I'm beginning to feel feverish.'[40]

That day Fingal visited him too. The fever had taken its grip: Roth had a temperature of forty degrees and was delirious. In a weak voice, he said: 'I must see Chaplain Osterreicher,' a Jewish convert to Catholicism who had become a spiritual mentor to Roth. After this, he became incoherent. His hands were shaking again, and before Fingal left he observed how Roth clenched his fists to try to stop the tremors, then gave up. When Friderike Zweig came again to his bedside, she found him unconscious but crying out in a strangulated voice to his favourite wine waiters: '*Mon cher Victor, une fine . . . Jean, un bock.*'

No one responded, neither the imagined *garçons* nor the doctors. The delirium tremens worsened. He had tried to escape, so the medics strapped him to the bed. 'Is this necessary?' Fingal had asked, and was told: 'Well, if he won't behave, it's necessary.'[41] He could not move. He muttered to himself in German, but the nurses spoke only French. He had screaming fits and was heard to shout: 'I have to get out of here!' Just before 6 a.m. on 27 May, he fell silent. It was not a good and easy death.

Preparations for the funeral forced upon Roth's friends the impossible task of resolving the question of his religious identity. To his Jewish friends he was Jewish; to his Catholic friends, a Catholic; each had seen in him what they wanted to see, and to each he had emphasised the facet of himself he thought they would like. But a funeral demanded a decision one way or the other. The contradictions and tensions within this Catholic Jew could not be reflected within the service. Or could they? The next day the Hôtel de la Poste hosted a furious debate. Frau Kulka, a convert to Catholicism, said that as the only relative present her wishes should be followed, and she insisted they honour Roth's desire for a Catholic burial. His Jewish friends had to defer to this and seemed to accept that there would be no rabbi at the service. Morgenstern and Gottfarstein agreed that the latter would say Kaddish at the graveside. Three days later, on 30 May 1939, they gathered at the Cimetière de Thiais to the south of Paris. Montmartre had proved too expensive, so they were forced to choose this cemetery on the outskirts known as the last resting place of the city's poor. Stefan Fingal is documented as having reserved and paid for the grave.

The question lingered as to whether he had been baptised – despite Roth's admission that he hadn't, Catholic friends such as Serge Dohrn remained convinced otherwise. There was no proof either way, so he could only be permitted a 'conditional' Catholic service. This meant that Roth's coffin was not allowed into the church, and no Mass would be read at the altar, but he could be buried with Catholic rites. At the graveside the chaplain, Johannes Osterreicher, was starting the ceremony when a gathering of Galician Jewish friends began to mutter and cry. They insisted that Roth remained a Jew and a rabbi should be fetched who would bury him in accordance with Jewish ritual. Osterreicher persevered, but a goods train rumbled past on a nearby embankment, drowning out his words. *Mann tracht und Gott lacht* . . .

Otto von Habsburg sent a group of Austrian legitimists to lay wreaths at the grave. One of them delegated this task to Friderike Zweig, who tossed earth into the grave and declared: 'To a true fighter for the Monarchy, in the name of His Majesty, Otto von Habsburg.' In the face of this provocation, the communist contingent tried to reclaim their erstwhile comrade – Egon Erwin Kisch angrily heaved in a spadeful of soil and tossed in a bunch of red carnations, shouting: 'In the name of his colleagues from the SDS,' an organisation of exiled writers.

The atmosphere had grown so fraught that Joseph Gottfarstein's intentions to say Kaddish came to nothing: he felt too intimidated in the face of Catholic ceremony and political tension. He and

Morgenstern agreed that in the circumstances it would have seemed 'too demonstrative', so they performed the rite on a later occasion at a synagogue in Paris.

Stefan Zweig had been so dismayed by the prospect of seeing Roth buried by a priest that he did not leave London. Instead, Zweig wrote a funeral address that shows how the rancour and sadness he felt at the decline of their friendship gave way, after Roth's death, to his instinctive tenderness and generosity:

> Saying goodbye, this difficult and bitter art, has offered us ample, indeed abundant, opportunity in recent years. How much and how often have we emigrants and outcasts had to say goodbye to our homeland, to our own proper sphere of activity, to our homes and possessions and to all the security we have fought for over the years. How much have we lost, lost again and again ... Whenever we lose a person, one of the rare ones we know to be irreplaceable and irretrievable, we feel affected and delighted at the same time at how much our trampled heart is still capable of feeling pain and revolting against a fate that robs us prematurely of our best, our most irreplaceable.
>
> Such an irreplaceable person was our dear Joseph Roth, unforgettable as a human being and for all times not to be expelled from the annals of German art as a poet by any decree. The most diverse elements were uniquely mixed in him for creative purposes.[42]

Zweig declared that there was within Roth 'a Russian man – I would almost say a Karamazovian man – a man of great passions, a man who tried the utmost in everything; a Russian fervour of feeling filled him, a deep piety, but fatally also that Russian drive to self-destruction'. Then there was 'a second person in Roth, the Jewish person with a bright, uncannily alert, critical prudence ... who looked with fright and at the same time with secret love at the wild, the Russian, the demonic person within himself'. And a third character operated within him too, 'the Austrian man, noble and chivalrous in every gesture, just as obliging and charming in his daily nature as he was musical in his art. Only this unique and unrepeatable mixture explains to me the uniqueness of his being, of his work.'[43]

He spoke of Roth's humble upbringing, how his experience of poverty had forged his generosity towards others in need, and how the darkening world turned a gentle man into someone bitter, angry and addicted to the drink that helped him forget his pain. Finally, Zweig came to his anguish at being unable to prevent Roth's 'self-murder' by alcohol, and how he absolved Roth of responsibility for his death. The blame lay not with Roth but with 'this nefarious and lawless time, which pushes the noblest into such despair that they know no other salvation out of hatred for this world than to destroy themselves'.[44] Yet even in Roth's darkest days, Zweig observed, 'In everything he did, said and wrote, one sensed an irresistible and unforgettable goodness, a magnificent, a Russian exuberant self-exhaustion. Only those who knew him in those times will be able to understand why and how infinitely we loved this single person.'[45]

A week earlier, Germany had agreed a pact with fascist Italy and vowed to invade Poland at the earliest opportunity. Refugees were desperately trying to flee Europe, in some cases reaching the USA by ship only to be returned to Europe, where they would within a couple of years be murdered. As Hitler manoeuvred towards war, Zweig concluded by likening the mourners' task to that of soldiers who, after their army has suffered a defeat on the battlefield, are sent to face the advancing victorious force and buy time while the remainder of the troops regather themselves for future battles. Roth and Ernst Toller had fallen, and it was time to step to the front line, just as Roth had told Zweig in 1933 when he chided him for being a 'behind-the-lines Jew' on the 'battlefield of humanity'. The living should fulfil this role 'uprightly and manfully to the bitter end, as these two lost comrades showed us in advance, like our eternally effusive Ernst Toller, like our unforgettable, unforgettable Joseph Roth'.[46]

Sybil Rares was there to listen to Zweig's tribute, so too was Andrea Manga Bell, who made her presence felt: Morgenstern later made the barbed remark that her loud and sustained crying 'stole

the show'.[47] Irmgard Keun did not attend. Instead she wrote a poem
for Roth named for the city where they spent much of their time
together, and asked Walter Landauer to drop it into the grave:

'*Für Joseph Roth (Amsterdam)*'

Die Trauer, Freund, macht meine Hände dumm,
Wie soll ich aus dem schwarzen Blut der Grachten Kränze winden?
Das Leid, mein Freund, macht meine Kehle stumm,
Wo bist du, Freund, ich muss dich wiederfinden.

Grief, friend, makes my hands dumb,
How shall I make wreaths from the black blood of the canals?
Sorrow, my friend, makes my throat silent,
Where are you, friend, I must find you again.[48]

As Germaine Alazard had cared for Roth in his final months living
at her hotel, so she did in his death, tending his grave throughout the
war. In 1946 Roth's cousin Fred Grübel paid a fee to the paupers' cemetery to ensure the grave would be preserved and not reused. In 1970
a permanent gravestone was at last installed. It is made of grey marble
and inscribed in gold capitals: in translation, JOSEPH ROTH, AUSTRIAN
WRITER, DIED IN PARIS IN EXILE, 2.9.1894–27.5.1939.

The grave of Joseph Roth at the Cimetière de Thiais, Paris.

Though Roth lies interred in a Catholic section of the cemetery, the marble slab often bears a scattering of stones placed out of respect by Jewish visitors, alongside cellophane-wrapped bouquets, and sometimes a bottle of wine. A conifer stands at the foot of the grave, emerging from a tangle of ivy and grass. It is a quiet place where birdsong dances over a low hum of traffic, secluded by trees against the urban mess of an ugly *banlieue*. It feels far from Paris, let alone from Brody. To the west you can see the sunset, then, overhead, the stars.

Chapter Fourteen

Give my love to your children and do not complain me
[*sic*] – remember the good Josef Roth and Rieger,[*] how
glad I always was for them, that they had not to go through
those ordeals.

Love and friendship and cheer up, knowing me quiet
and happy.

Stefan

Final letter from Stefan Zweig to his ex-wife Friderike, written in English, 22 February 1942

Friedl Roth's fate remained unclear for seven decades until 2011, when
it was clarified in devastating detail in a study by the late Austrian
author Andreas Hutter.[†] The Heil- und Pflegeanstalt at Mauer-Öhling[‡]
in Lower Austria, to which she was sent in June 1936, was a progressive
institution where ten doctors and 200 nurses cared for around 2,000
patients, who could enjoy cultural events, read newspapers and books,
go on supervised summer outings and play sports. In May 1940 a
committee of doctors and clerical assistants arrived from Berlin. They
asked for all the patients' files to assess their fitness to work. Between
13 June and 12 July, twelve transports took 693 patients on a forty-mile
westward journey to a nursing home for the mentally ill in the Linz

---

[*] Erwin Rieger (1889–1940), Viennese author who had been Zweig's friend
since 1918.
[†] '*Friederike Roth (1900–1940). Über Die Letzten Tage, Die „Sie Nicht Überlebt Hat'''*
('About the Last Days, "Which She Did Not Survive"'), in *Zeitschrift für Germanistik*,
vol. 21, no. 3 (Peter Lang, 2011), pp. 599–604. See: http://www.jstor.org/
stable/23979372
[‡] It exists today as the Landesklinikum Mostviertel Amstetten-Mauer in
Lower Austria.

district of Niedernhart. Among them was a patient listed as Friederike Roth, an 'author's wife' with a 'schizophrenic disorder'. Niedernhart was only a front, from where they would be transported to their true destination. One day in early July she was among fifty patients driven by coach to Castle Hartheim, a facility led by the SS-doctor Rudolf Lonauer and his deputy MD Georg Renner, as part of the *Aktion T4* euthanasia programme for psychiatric patients and people with disabilities. It is believed that the institution's staff photographed Friedl after her arrival, but these images were destroyed towards the end of the war. Moments later, she was led naked with up to sixty other psychiatric patients into a gas chamber.

The obliteration of Jewish life in Europe during the early 1940s need not be outlined here beyond its specific application to those characters who feature in Roth's story. On 9 September 1942 his cousin Paula Grübel was murdered at Auschwitz. Her older sister Resia is thought to have been killed too, but the details of her death are unconfirmed. In 1942 Emil Faktor, the editor of the *Berliner Börsen-Courier*, was killed in the Łódź ghetto after being refused entry to the USA. In 1944 Walter Landauer starved to death at Bergen-Belsen.

Others escaped but did not survive. Stefan Zweig moved to New York, at least in physical terms; those who met him there noted that mentally he seemed still to be living in the ruins of Europe. In the summer of 1941 Klaus Mann encountered him looking dishevelled and unshaven on Fifth Avenue, but Zweig was too preoccupied by some troubling reverie to notice Mann. Thinking himself unobserved, Zweig had dropped the smile he usually wore in company. It was only when Mann hailed him that Zweig came to, 'like a sleepwalker who hears his name', and adopted his characteristic lively demeanour, 'able to smile, chat, joke, be as engaging and animated as ever: the suave and elegant, somewhat too smooth, somewhat too amiable *homme de lettres*'.[1] A few weeks later, Zweig took dinner with another refugee, the playwright Carl Zuckmayer, and asked what point there was in living as a shadow. 'We are just ghosts – or memories,'[2] Zweig told him.

With his second wife, Lotte, Zweig moved to the Brazilian city of Petrópolis, where they lived in a bungalow by the jungle, a surreal dislocation too far for a man so rooted in his identity as Austrian. On his bedroom wall he hung a framed copy of a verse by the sixteenth-century Portuguese poet Camões: 'Ah! Where shall weary man take sanctuary, where live his little span of life secure?'[3] He played chess, listened to his radio, smoked his pipe, read his diminished collection of books, and eventually completed his memoir *The World of Yesterday*. In the letter he wrote to Friderike Zweig on 22 February 1942, he said his depression had become so acute he could no longer concentrate. He foresaw no end to the war. He had liked Petrópolis at first but the solitude, which once soothed him, now felt oppressive. She shouldn't worry, he said: by the time the letter reached her, he would feel much better. The following day, Stefan and Lotte Zweig killed themselves by overdosing on barbiturates. He left a suicide note saying that at sixty, after years of homeless wandering, he had not the energy to begin a new life. 'I send greetings to all of my friends,' he wrote. 'May they live to see the dawn after this long night. I, who am most impatient, go before them.'[4]

Andrea Manga Bell survived the war in hiding. In 1950 she gave an interview to *Der Spiegel* in which she described how her ex-husband, Alexandre Douala Manga Bell, had shot dead their son, who had gone to Cameroon to confront his father about abandoning his children. She remained in Paris, where she died in 1985 in at the age of eighty-three. In 1945 Irmgard Keun emerged after also hiding through the war, in her case in Berlin, protected by false rumours that she had committed suicide. In the 1960s, alcoholic and homeless, Keun was committed to psychiatric care. In 1977 her work was rediscovered and she enjoyed a financial and critical revival late in life, until her death from lung cancer in Cologne in 1982.

Among Roth's Jewish friends, some managed to rebuild their lives. Stefan Fingal survived a French concentration camp and lived through the German occupation under a false name in the South of France. Soma Morgenstern and Józef Wittlin separately left France for New York City, where they both died in 1976, aged eighty-five and seventy-nine respectively. Wittlin was assisted by Hermann Kesten, who had also found refuge in NYC; Kesten lived until 1996, when he died aged ninety-six, having in later life become treasured as a rare survivor from the literary culture that the Nazis destroyed.

Without Kesten, Joseph Roth's work might not have discovered the readership that it did in the second half of the twentieth century. Aside from *Job*, *The Radetzky March*, *Confession of a Murderer* and *The Legend of the Holy Drinker*, Roth's novels and short stories were largely out of print by the 1950s. Of the thousands of newspaper articles he wrote, few were anthologised. In 1956 publication of the first three-volume edition of Roth's works, edited by Kesten, created the foundation on which a new post-war audience discovered him. From there, collections of his journalism and then his letters (again edited by Kesten, in 1970) consolidated interest in his life, as did the 1974 Bronsen biography that helped determine facts about the man whom Bronsen termed a 'mythomaniac'. At this point Roth was perceived more as a novelist than a journalist. The next year brought an extended four-volume edition of Roth's writing, but it was not until the comprehensive six-volume *Werke* was published between 1989 and 1991, edited by Klaus Westermann and Fritz Hackert, that his newspaper work was granted the same prominence as his fiction. By the turn of the twenty-first century, seven decades on from when Germany banned and incinerated his books, Roth was re-established as a canonical German-language author. The collapse of the communist bloc and opening up of eastern Europe also rekindled western readers' interest in its history and literature. It was around this time that Roth regained prominence among anglophone readers: Michael Hofmann's translations, published by Granta (in the UK) and Norton (in the USA), spurred a revival of admiration for his work and fascination with his life.

Aside from the innate quality of Roth's storytelling, other allures emerged as the twenty-first century witnessed echoes of his time: resurgent bloodshed, displacement of refugees, populist demagoguery, aggressive ethnonationalists agitating against rickety supranational projects all lent Roth's prose an uncannily topical air. Readers today connect with the moral clarity of his robust opposition to nationalism; admire his empathy with the exiled and dispossessed; recognise his crisis of identity; and, not least, are primed for a nostalgic pull towards the aesthetics and perceived values of his *Mitteleuropa* as its last inhabitants fade from view.* Austria-Hungary's high culture, its diversity, its grandeur, its vibrant Jewish intellectual and artistic life: all were yearned for once they were destroyed.

Back in the 1960s, the Italian critic Claudio Magris identified the Habsburg Myth, the delusion detectable in post-Second World War Austrian literature that the Dual Monarchy era was one of tolerance and prosperity: a view propagated by Roth's ironic but ultimately reverential treatment of the vanished Austria of his childhood. Now his writing, with its bittersweet evocation of the Habsburg Empire whose loss he mourned, entices readers in at least three respects. It sustains that myth by evoking for twenty-first-century readers a tolerant, multi-ethnic civilisation that becomes a dreamlike refuge from our own times' intolerance and division. In its examination of the traumas that manifested during the empire's collapse – the rise of nationalism and exclusion; the attendant feelings of rootlessness, marginalisation and outsider status – we find resonances with and instruction for our current condition. By turns Roth withdraws us from and confronts us with our modern world. This singular mixture of retreat into an imagined past and unflinching engagement with the present, heightened by his fantastical mingling of truths and fabrications in both his 'fictional' and 'non-fictional' works, creates a third allure: a beguiling brew of tensions that we desire to resolve, even as we suspect they are intractable. A man who smuggled so many autobiographical facts into his fiction, and so often applied a poetic sheen to his reportage, plainly does not recognise a borderline between fact and fiction. Under scrutiny this border soon fades away. What kind of man creates such work, we wonder, and are satisfied to learn that it was one who detested national boundaries and instead erected inflexible moral lines that, once crossed, earned trespassers his irreversible contempt (despite the appalling immorality of

---

* Stefan Zweig's work enjoyed a resurgence in popularity too, for instance in stylish republications by Pushkin Press, whose cover designs appealingly invoke a Habsburg aesthetic. By the time of Wes Anderson's successful 2014 film *The Grand Budapest Hotel*, which draws from Zweig's works and bathes the viewer's eyes in a gently dilapidated, pastel-toned Mitteleuropean world, it was clear that an aestheticised presentation of the Habsburg era could prove a potent balm for twenty-first-century sores.

his own conduct at times, which only strengthened his self-contempt). Freedom of movement, rigidity of conviction: those were integral to Roth's ethos. He challenges us to understand him; often we suspect we never will, but perhaps this biography has helped its readers to feel they have studied him long enough to draw conclusions.

There are few artefacts of Joseph Roth's life extant in the world. There is no record of what became of his collections of knives and watches, his walking canes, or the clothes bought for him by benefactors such as Zweig. Such items as still exist are now carefully preserved. In 1946, Roth's young cousin Fred Grübel was in Paris, working for the international Jewish relief organisation that helped Holocaust survivors, when he visited Blanche Gidon. 'On a grey-silver Parisian winter morning, I climbed the steep Rue des Martyrs on Montmartre, where Mme Gidon lived,' he said. 'The kind, petite, snow-white old lady handed me an old worn-out coupe case.'[5] It contained many of Roth's manuscripts, books and letters. Walter Landauer had salvaged them from Roth's hotel room and passed them to Germaine Alazard, who gave them to Gidon. When Grübel asked her where she had kept them during the Gestapo's reign of terror, she smiled and answered: 'Sous le lit de la concierge!' Grübel knew he needed a safer place for these treasures than beneath a bed. He took them to New York City and later placed them in the archives of the Leo Baeck Institute, of which he was a director. They remain there today in the Center for Jewish History, and form a sizeable part of its Joseph Roth Collection; other papers, including the Job manuscript, are in the Deutsches Literaturarchiv in Marbach, Germany. As well as much of his literary output, the Joseph Roth Collection contains relics of his personal life. Calling cards in his and Friedl's names that hint at their happier years in France. Yiddish theatre programmes from his time in Russia and Ukraine, the great journey that sundered their marriage and diverted them into separate abysses. Photographs of them together that he kept safe in his suitcase long after their separation. Receipts and notepaper from hotels, traces of temporary homes, remnants of a life lived in endless flight.

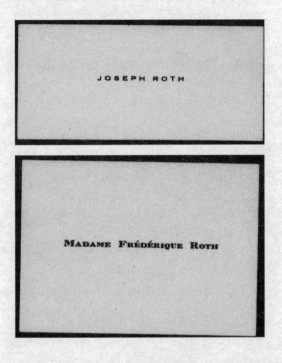

JOSEPH ROTH

Madame Frédérique Roth

Acknowledgements

This study of Joseph Roth's life could not have been published without the help of a great many people who gave generous encouragement, advice and support over the course of five years. I am indebted to Bella Lacey at Granta Books for her belief in the project and her sensitive, thoughtful editorial suggestions. Profound thanks go to Matthew Hamilton, my literary agent, for his kind support and wise advice, not only during the creation of this book but over the past decade. I am most grateful to Emeritus Professor Helen Chambers of the University of St Andrews, who helped me in the initial stages of my research by allowing me to quote from her unpublished English translation of David Bronsen's biography of Roth. At the outset I also approached Michael Hofmann to see whether he would permit me to use his translations of Roth's novels and journalism. Since giving his consent, Michael has been a valuable source of encouragement and advice. I am deeply grateful for his numerous astute observations on a draft of the manuscript.

Dr Jon Hughes, Reader in German and Cultural Studies at Royal Holloway, University of London, has been a consistently generous-spirited source of authoritative knowledge of Roth and his world. I am most thankful to him for reading my manuscript and pointing out errors that I would have been embarrassed to include. Likewise, my thanks go to my military historian friend Steve Pope for his close reading of my manuscript. Again, Steve's insights and expertise saved me from including some historical inaccuracies, and his assistance and friendship are greatly appreciated. Any errors that remain are my responsibility alone.

A note on Michael Hofmann's translations: they were originally published in American English, but for consistency with the rest of my text, and with Michael's consent, I have changed the spellings to British English. I would also like to thank Richard Panchyk and Will Stone for kindly agreeing to let me quote from their translations of Roth's work.

On the topic of translation, I should mention that I am not a scholar of German literature. I read Roth in English translation first, then refer to the German. I have studied previously untranslated articles by Roth with the help of my German tutor, Michael Struppek, a kind man to whom I owe deep thanks for his generosity of spirit in assisting me with this project. I have written this book in the hope that my love for Roth's writing and fascination with his personal, historical and cultural context has allowed me to tell his story in a way that compensates for my inexpertise in the German language and its literature.

One of the great pleasures of my research was speaking and corresponding with Dan Morgenstern. It was a thrill to talk to someone who remembers Roth, and what's more, who received my approach in such a warm and helpful spirit. I would like to thank Dan for sharing his memories and giving permission to quote translated passages from his father Soma Morgenstern's memoir *Joseph Roths Flucht und Ende*, a book that merits a complete translation in English. I would like to thank the German publisher zu Klampen Verlag for also granting me permission to quote from this book, and the Munich-based author and journalist Claus Lochbihler, who alerted me to Dan's existence and suggested numerous useful sources of information over the course of my research. I am equally grateful to Bonnier Media Deutschland for granting permission to quote from *Der heilige Trinker: Erinnerungen an Joseph Roth* by Géza von Cziffra. All attempts have been made to contact other copyright holders for permission to reproduce material. If you believe material for which you hold rights is reprinted in this book, please contact the publisher and we will acknowledge this in future editions.

When I began work on this book, I imagined I would follow in Roth's footsteps across Europe. Then came the Covid-19 pandemic, and my ambitions receded. Proposed trips to Vienna and Berlin had to be abandoned, but still, I managed to visit Ukraine in early 2019, Paris in late 2021, and Ostend and Amsterdam in early 2022. In each of those places people gave me generous assistance. In Ukraine, I was delighted to meet Ihor Sharyak, who gave me a comprehensive tour of Brody; Myroslava Zakharkiv, who showed me around Lviv and gained me access to the Grübel family's apartment block in Ulica Hofmana;

and Natalie Dunai, who along with her husband Alex Dunai has been a crucial source of information on Roth's family history. I am most appreciative of the Dunais' efforts on my behalf in the Ukraine National Archives, and would direct anyone seeking to research family history in the former Galicia to visit www.alexdunai.com. In Paris, Patrick Herpe (https://leparisdepatrick.com) gave me a very enjoyable and informative tour of Roth's old haunts, and in Ostend Els Snick went above and beyond in hosting me and showing me the places where Roth, Stefan Zweig, Irmgard Keun and their friends lived and social-ised during the summer of 1936. I am deeply grateful to Els for her generosity and her belief in the value of my book. In Amsterdam I had a memorable day exploring Roth locations with Ilse Josepha Lazaroms and Femke Foppema, both of whom have been a steady source of kind encouragement and enthusiasm for my project, and whose help I greatly appreciate. It was a pleasure to walk around Roth's Amsterdam with Emile Brugman, the founder of Atlas Contact, which is publishing this book in Dutch translation. Similarly I am most grateful to Jessica Nash of Atlas Contact for her enthusiastic support, and for organising the research trip along with her colleague Maaike Broere. At Granta, Christine Lo, Dan Bird, Lamorna Elmer and George Stamp have also provided invaluable help, and I am most grateful to Linden Lawson for her meticulous, diligent and thoughtful copy-editing.

Many more photographs from my travels in Ukraine, Paris and the Low Countries, including locations such as Roth's school, the Grübels' apartment in Lviv, and his favourite hotels and bars, can be found on my website, www.keironpim.co.uk.

In the face of the obstacles created by Covid, my research was made immeasurably easier by the wonderful Society of Authors, which gave me two grants: an Emergency Grant during the first year of the pan-demic, and one from their Authors' Foundation that funded my trips to Ukraine and Paris. I am, as ever, deeply appreciative of all the Society does to support writers.

I am also grateful to two institutions that assisted me. The Leo Baeck Institute in Manhattan, and particularly its archivist Michael Simonson, gave me generous support, especially with regard to my picture research. In London, the Wiener Holocaust Library gave me similarly kind assistance with picture research. My thanks to both these vitally important organisations.

This book has been a labour of love that happily also gave me a better understanding of my family history. My maternal great-grandparents were from Cieszanów in Poland, Mostyska in Ukraine, Saaz in Bohemia, and Vienna: their world was Roth's world. I have always had a fascination for the *Mitteleuropa* that half my ancestors inhabited, and it has been revealing and rewarding to explore that world through the prism of Roth's life. I owe a debt to my grandparents, Josef and Ruth Meller, both of whom died years before this book was written. The books of theirs I have inherited on subjects such as Vienna, Karl Kraus, Jewish folklore and pre-war European Jewish culture in general have been invaluable to my research.

Above all, however, I must thank my immediate family. My wife, Rowan, has been an incredible support. Her observations on my manuscript always alerted me to perspectives I had not considered, and I appreciate the understanding she showed when I needed to travel overseas for research trips. Our younger daughters Lottie and Rosa have been a delight and a happy distraction from my labours over a book that Lottie renamed *Endless Work*. And I owe especial thanks to our oldest daughter, Isla, whose remarkable empathy and insights in our conversations about Joseph and Friedl Roth led me to analyse their relationship in ways I would not otherwise have considered. My love and thanks go to all my brilliant, beautiful girls.

Finally I would also like to thank these people, each of whom offered help, encouragement or advice: Robbie Aitken, Stuart Anderson, Jonathan Arnold, Devorah Baum, John Bernat Roth, Jason Blake, Jonathan Brooker, Nashi Brooker, Darcy Buerkle, Brian Case, Jo Catling, Anthony David, Jon Dennis, Samantha Ellis, Samuel Gottfarstein, Jason Hazeley, Amanda Hopkinson, Philipp Hubmann at the Dokumentationsstelle für neuere österreichische Literatur in Vienna, Robert Jackman, Torsten Jugl at the Wiener Holocaust Library in London, Sean Kaye-Smith, Kirk Laws, Lilian Levy at the *AJR Journal*, Peter Lobbenberg, Andrew Male, Jean McNeil, Daniel Meller,

Rachel Meller, Andy Miller, Ben Miller, Sascha Neuberger, Jeremy Noel-Tod, Sveta Payne, my parents Malcolm and Claudia Pim, Andrew Pippos, the late Barbara Probst Solomon, David Rechter, Paul Saxton, Paul Scraton, Rivka Ben-Shochet of the Tracing the Tribe group on Facebook, Rainer-Joachim Siegel, Steve Snelling, Evelyn Toynton, James Vaughan, Sabine Wieber and Paul Willetts.

Notes

Works by Roth with titles longer than one word are referred to by their initials, e.g. *The Antichrist* is *TA*, *Collected Shorter Fiction* is *CSF*, *Confession of a Murderer* is *COAM*, *Flight Without End* is *FWE*, *The Hotel Years* is *THY*, *A Life in Letters* is *ALIL*, *The Radetzky March* is *TRM*, *Report from a Parisian Paradise* is *RFAPP*, *The Wandering Jews* is *TWJ*, *What I Saw* is *WIS* and *Zipper and his Father* is *ZF*.

Introduction

1   *Joseph Roth: A Life in Letters*, ed. and trans. Michael Hofmann (Granta Books, 2013), p. 151, letter to Gustav Kiepenheuer on his fiftieth birthday.
2   Joseph Roth, *The Wandering Jews*, trans. Michael Hofmann (Granta Books, 2001), p. 34.
3   Ibid., p. 38.
4   Ibid., p. 39.
5   Ibid., p. 22.
6   Ibid., p. 25.
7   Ibid., p. 52.
8   Interview with the author, 7 December 2018.
9   Fritz Hackert and Klaus Westermann (eds) *Werke*, 6 vols (Cologne, 1989–91), accessed at https://archive.org/details/josephrothwerke0000roth, vol. 3, p. 352, 'Beim Uhrmacher', Frankfurter Zeitung, 21 June 1931.
10   Ibid., p. 351.
11   Ibid., p. 352.
12   David Bronsen, *Joseph Roth: Eine Biographie* (Kiepenheuer & Witsch, 1993), p. 34. From an unpublished translation by Helen Chambers. All translations from Bronsen are by Helen Chambers.

13   https://shtetlroutes.eu/en/brodi-putvnik/

14   David Bronsen with Irmgard Keun, cited in David Bronsen, 'Austrian vs. Jew: the Torn Identity of Joseph Roth', accessed at https://digipres. cjh.org/delivery/DeliveryManagerServlet?dps_pid=IE8995465& (last accessed 9 March 2022).

15   Dennis Marks, *Wandering Jew: The Search for Joseph Roth* (Notting Hill Editions, 2011), p. 86.

16   Volker Weidermann, *Summer Before the Dark: Stefan Zweig and Joseph Roth, Ostend 1936*, trans. Carol Brown Janeway (Pushkin Press, 2017), p. 26.

17   *TWJ*, p. 21.

18   Ibid., p. 126.

19   Ibid., p. 124.

20   'The Cradle', in *The Hotel Years*, trans. Michael Hofmann (Granta Books, 2016), pp. 259–60. First published as 'Die Wiege' in *Die Literarische Welt*, 17 December 1931.

21   Bronsen, p. 340.

Chapter One

1   D. Kampa and D. Keel (eds), *Joseph Roth. Leben und Werk* (Diogenes, 2010), p. 176.

2   Géza von Cziffra, *Der Heilige Trinker. Erinnerungen an Joseph Roth* (Ullstein Taschenbuch Verlag, 1989), pp. 33–4.

3   Roman Vishniac, *Polish Jews: A Pictorial Record*, intro. by Abraham Joshua Heshchel (Schocken, 1965), p. 16.

4   Ritchie Robertson, 'Roth's *Hiob* and the Traditions of Ghetto Fiction', in Helen Chambers (ed.), *Co-Existent Contradictions: Joseph Roth in Retrospect* (Ariadne Press, 1991), p. 187.

5   Amos Elon, *The Pity of it All: A History of the Jews in Germany, 1743– 1933* (Metropolitan Books, 2002), p. 4.

6   Ibid., p. 5.

7   Ibid., p. 4.

8   Robertson, p. 187.

9   Ibid., p. 190.

10   Elon, p. 5.

11   Bronsen interview with Moses Wasser, quoted in Wilhelm von Sternburg, *Joseph Roth: Eine Biographie* (Kiepenheuer & Witsch, 2010), pp. 107–8.

12   Von Cziffra, pp. 44–6.

13   'Aus dem Tagebuch des Schülers Joseph Roth', *Die Literarische Welt*, 11 July 1930, in Bronsen, p. 53.

14   Ibid., p. 51.

15   Ibid., p. 45.

16   Ibid., pp. 45–6.

17   Simon Winder, *Danubia: A Personal History of Habsburg Europe* (Picador, 2013), p. 1.

18   Bronsen, p. 56.

19   David Bronsen interview with Klaus Dohrn, Bronsen, p. 59.

20   Ibid.

21   Ibid.

22   Joseph Roth, *The String of Pearls*, trans. Michael Hofmann (Granta Books, 1998), p. 229.

23   'Rede über den alten Kaiser', *Werke*, vol. 3, pp. 939–40, *Die Österreichische Post* (Paris), 1 July 1939.

24   'Seine k. und k. apostolische Majestät', ibid., p. 911, *Frankfurter Zeitung*, 6 March 1928.

25   Soma Morgenstern, *Joseph Roths Flucht und Ende: Erinnerungen* (Aufbau-Taschenbuch-Verlag, 1998), p. 60.

26   Joseph Roth, *Job: The Story of a Simple Man*, trans. Dorothy Thompson (Granta Books, 2013), p. 5.

27   Ibid., p. 216.

28   Bronsen, p. 41.

29   Ibid., p. 40.

30   Marks, p. 86.

31   *ALIL*, p. 3.

32   Ibid., p. 6.

33   Ibid., p. 7.

34   Ibid., p. 6. Schwabendorf, holidays, 1911, to Resia Grübel.

35   Bronsen, p. 52.

36   Ibid.

37   Ibid.

38   *ALIL*, p. 7, Brody, 2 September 1912, to Resia and Paula Grübel.

Chapter Two

1   Sternburg, p. 123.

2   *Hotel Savoy*, by Joseph Roth, trans. John Hoare (Granta Books, 2000), p. 53.

3   *Hotel Savoy*, p. 16.

4   *Hotel Savoy*, p. 102.

5   *Hotel Savoy*, p. 107.

6   *ALIL*, pp. 16–17, Vienna, 24 February 1918, to Paula Grübel.

7   Bronsen, p. 60.

8   Józef Wittlin, Reminiscences of Joseph Roth, undated, Box 4, Folder 46, Joseph Roth Collection, AR 1764, Leo Baeck Institute, New York. See: https://archives.cjh.org/repositories/5/archival_objects/672542

9   Sternburg, pp. 103–4.

10   Addendum to a letter to Felice Bauer, 13 September 1913, quoted in Reiner Stach, *Kafka: The Decisive Years*, vol. 2 (Princeton University Press, 2021), p. 361.

11   Ibid.

12   Letter to Max Brod, 16 September 1913, accessed at: https// homepage.univie.ac.at/werner.haas/1913/bk13-008.htm

13   Bronsen, p. 62.

14   *TWJ*, p. 31.

15   Ibid., p. 15.

16   Ibid., pp. 15–16.

17   Ibid., p. 19.

18   Devorah Baum, *Feeling Jewish (A Book for Just About Anyone)* (Yale University Press, 2017), pp. 40–1.

19   Józef Wittlin, *The Salt of the Earth*, trans. Patrick Corness (Pushkin Press, 2018), Kindle edition.

20 Sidney Rosenfeld, *Understanding Joseph Roth* (University of South Carolina Press, 2001), pp. 8–9.

21 Robert Musil, *The Man Without Qualities*, trans. Sophie Wilkins (Picador, 1997), p. 1. (NB: to quote from a book implies that one has read it, and it would be more honest to say that, at the time of going to press, I am a quarter of the way through *The Man Without Qualities* – so, only another 750 or so pages to go.)

22 Arthur Schnitzler, *Dream Story*, intro. by Frederic Raphael (Penguin Books, 1999), p. v.

23 *Werke*, vol. 3, p. 898, *Die Österreichische Post* (Paris), 1 March 1939.

24 Adam Kirsch, 'The Torch of Karl Kraus', *The New York Review of Books*, 23 October 2008: https://www.nybooks.com/articles/2008/10/23/the-torch-of-karl-kraus/

25 Walter Benjamin, 'Karl Kraus', in *Reflections: Essays, Aphorisms, Autobiographical Writings* (Houghton Mifflin Harcourt, 1978), p. 254.

26 *Werke*, vol. 3, p. 1034.

27 *Ver Sacrum*, issue 1, p. 10, accessed online at https://anno.onb.ac.at/cgi-content/anno-plus?aid=vsa&datum=1898&size=35&teil=0101&page=12

28 Stefan Zweig, 'Buchmendel', in *The Invisible Collection/Buchmendel*, trans. Eden and Cedar Paul (Pushkin Press, 1998), p. 46.

29 Ibid., p. 47.

30 Marjorie Perloff, *Edge of Irony: Modernism in the Shadow of the Habsburg Empire* (University of Chicago Press, 2018), p. 10.

31 Bronsen, p. 66.

32 Edward Crankshaw, *Maria Theresa* (Viking Press, 1970), p. 313.

33 Carl E. Schorske, *Fin-de-Siècle Vienna* (Vintage Books, 1981), p. 187.

34 *ALIL*, p. 11, Vienna, a Thursday, 1916, to Paula Grübel.

35 Ibid., p. 223, Hotel-Pension Savigny, Berlin, 15 December 1932, to Stefan Zweig.

36 Joseph Roth, *What I Saw: Reports from Berlin 1920–33*, ed. Michael Bienert, trans. Michael Hofmann (Granta Books, 2004), p. 47.

37 *TWJ*, p. 22.

38 Heinz Lunzer and Victoria Lunzer-Talos, *Joseph Roth im Exil in Paris*.

1933 bis 1939 (Dokumentationsstelle für neuere österreichische Literatur, 2008), p. 55.

39 Perloff, p. xiii.

40 Stefan Zweig, *The World of Yesterday: Memoirs of a European*, trans. Anthea Bell (Pushkin Press, 2011), p. 125.

41 *ALIL*, p. 42, Hôtel de la Place de l'Odéon, Paris, 14 June 1925, to Bernard von Brentano.

42 Rosenfeld, p. 11.

43 Theodor Lessing, *Jewish Self-Hate*, trans. Peter C. Appelbaum (Berghahn Books, 2021), p. 27.

44 Robert Wistrich, *The Jews of Vienna in the Age of Franz Joseph* (Plunkett Lake Press, 2016), Kindle edition.

45 Alma Mahler, *Gustav Mahler: Memories and Letters*, ed. Donald Mitchell, trans. Basil Creighton (University of Washington Press, 1975), p. 109.

46 *ALIL*, p. 105, Hotel Excelsior, Munich, 21 December 1927, to Félix Bertaux.

47 Bronsen, p. 68.

48 Ibid.

49 *ALIL*, p. 150, letter to Gustav Kiepenheuer on his fiftieth birthday, 10 June 1930.

50 Baum, pp. 28–9.

51 'Leaving the Hotel', in Joseph Roth, *The Hotel Years: Wanderings in Europe Between the Wars*, trans. Michael Hofmann (Granta Books, 2016), p. 187, *Frankfurter Zeitung*, 24 February 1929.

52 Bronsen, p. 84.

53 'Where the World War Began', *THY*, pp. 85–6, *Frankfurter Zeitung*, 3 July 1927.

54 Bronsen, pp. 68–9.

55 Morgenstern, p. 22.

56 Bronsen, p. 81.

57 *TWJ*, p. 89, p. 57.

58 David Bronsen interview with Heinz Kindermann, quoted in Sternburg, p. 153.

59 Zweig, *The World of Yesterday*, p. 116.

60 All quotes from Wittlin's reminiscence of Roth held in the Leo Baeck

Institute, viewable online at http://www.archive.org/stream/josephroth
_07_reel07#page/n209/mode/1up (last accessed 9 March 2022).

61 *Werke*, vol. 2, p. 996, '*Geschenk an meinen Onkel*', *Frankfurter Zeitung*,
18 November 1928.

62 Sylvia Asmus, Heinz Lunzer and Victoria Lunzer-Talos (eds), '*So wurde
ihnen die Flucht zur Heimat*': *Soma Morgenstern und Joseph Roth, Eine
Freundschaft* (Weidle Verlag, 2012), p. 49.

63 Bronsen, p. 72.

64 *Werke*, vol. 2, p. 914, 'Seine k. und k. apostolische Majestität',
Frankfurter Zeitung, 6 March 1928.

65 Bronsen, p. 70

66 Bronsen, p. 71.

67 *ALIL*, pp. 10–11, Vienna, a Wednesday (1915 or 1916), to Paula Grübel.

68 Bronsen, p. 78.

69 Ibid.

70 S. Pesnel, E. Tunner, H. Lunzer and V. Lunzer-Talos (eds), *Joseph Roth –
Städtebilder: Zur Poetik, Philologie und Interpretation von Stadtdarstellungen
aus den 1920er und 1930er Jahren* (Frank & Timme, 2015), p. 33.

71 *Werke*, vol. 1, p. 5, *Österreichs Illustrierte Zeitung*, 5 December 1915.

72 *Collected Shorter Fiction of Joseph Roth*, trans. Michael Hofmann (Granta
Books, 2002), pp. 14–15.

73 Wittlin, Reminiscences of Joseph Roth, Leo Baeck Institute.

74 Joseph Roth, *The Radetzky March*, trans. Michael Hofmann (Granta
Books, 2003), pp. 73–4.

75 *ALIL*, p. 207, fn 1.

76 Bronsen, p. 79.

77 Ibid., p. 80.

78 Baum, pp. 27–8.

79 Rosenfeld, p. 5.

80 Joseph Roth, *Right and Left*, trans. Michael Hofmann (Granta Books,
1999), p. 111.

81 *TWJ*, p. 29.

82 *Right and Left*, p. 224.

Chapter Three

1   Bronsen, p. 87.

2   Wittlin, Reminiscences of Joseph Roth, Leo Baeck Institute.

3   *ALIL*, p. 153.

4   Wittlin, Reminiscences of Joseph Roth, Leo Baeck Institute.

5   Bronsen, pp. 86–7.

6   Bronsen, p. 88.

7   Wittlin, *The Salt of the Earth*, Kindle edition, p. 54.

8   Wittlin, Reminiscences of Joseph Roth, Leo Baeck Institute.

9   Bronsen, p. 89.

10 Ibid.

11 Wittlin, *The Salt of the Earth*, Kindle edition.

12 Wittlin, Reminiscences of Joseph Roth, Leo Baeck Institute.

13 Bronsen, p. 90.

14 Wittlin, Reminiscences of Joseph Roth, Leo Baeck Institute.

15 Bronsen, p. 91. 'Seine k. und k. apostolische Majestät', *Frankfurter Zeitung*, 6 March 1928.

16 *ALIL*, p. 56, Marseilles, 30 August 1925, to Benno Reifenberg.

17 Bronsen, p. 91.

18 Von Cziffra, p. 9.

19 *ALIL*, pp. 220–1, Caffè Centrale Ascona, as of: Englischer Hof, Frankfurt am Main, 28 October 1932, to Otto Forst-Battaglia.

20 Ibid., p. 16, Vienna, 24 February 1918, to Paula Grübel.

21 Bronsen, p. 92.

22 *ALIL*, p. 14, Field Post 632, 24 August 1917, to Paula Grübel.

23 Joseph Roth, 'Die Krüppel. Ein polnisches Invaliden begräbnis', *Frankfurter Zeitung*, 23 November 1924.

24 Sternburg, p. 177.

25 *Der Friede*, no. 52, 17 January 1919, cited in 'Staatsfiktionen. Bilder eines künftigen Österreich in der Wiener Wochenschrift Der Friede (1918/1919)', in Klaus Amann, *Die Dichter und die Politik. Essays zur österreichischen Literatur nach 1918* (Edition Falter/Deuticke, 1992), p. 16.

26 Werke, vol. 1, p. 1105, *Prager Tagblatt*, 10 February 1918

27 Bronsen, pp. 100–1.

28 *CSF*, p. 18.

29 Barbara Probst-Solomon, 'Some Notes on My Father's Cousin, Joseph Roth', *Tablet*, 27 May 2016, accessed at www.tabletmag.com/sections/arts-letters/articles/notes-on-joseph-roth (last accessed 9 March 2022).

30 *The White Cities*, in *RFAPP*, p. 73.

31 Bronsen, p. 103.

32 *Werke*, vol. 1, pp. 21–2, 'Menschliche Fragmente', *Prager Tagblatt*, 17 April 1919.

33 Isaac Babel, *The Complete Works of Isaac Babel*, ed. Nathalie Babel, trans. P. Constantine, intro. by Cynthia Ozick (W. W. Norton, 2005), pp. 412–13.

34 Bronsen, p. 101.

35 *ALIL*, p. 153 to Gustav Kiepenheuer on his fiftieth birthday. June, 1930.

36 Bronsen, p. 101.

37 Deborah Holmes, 'Joseph Roth's Feuilleton Journalism as Social History in Vienna, 1919–20', *Austrian History Yearbook*, 48 (2017), pp. 255–65, doi:10.1017/S0067237816000667, accessed at https://www.cambridge.org/core/journals/austrian-history-yearbook/article/joseph-roths-feuilleton-journalism-as-social-history-in-vienna-191920/1CF0235386EFEAAEE6B0F5AB84158AE5#fn33

38 'Alte und neue Berufe' ('Old and New Professions'), *Der Neue Tag*, 31 July 1919, p. 5, as translated by Deborah Holmes in ibid.

39 *Werke*, vol. 1, p. 24, *Der Neue Tag*, 20 April 1919.

40 Bronsen, p. 105.

41 'Of Dogs and Men', *THY*, pp. 7–8, *Der Neue Tag*, 1 August 1919.

42 Zweig, *The World of Yesterday*, p. 123.

43 'Die kleine Form' ('The Small Form'), 1926, accessed at http://depts.washington.edu/vienna/literature/polgar/Polgar_Form.htm (last accessed 9 March 2022). Original text in Alfred Polgar, *KIeine Schriften*, vol. 3, pp. 369–72.

44 'Literature and Close Reading: An Interview with Andreas Huyssen – Eric Bulson interviews Andreas Huyssen', *LA Review of Books*, 19 February 2016, see: https://lareviewofbooks.org/article/literature-and-close-reading# (last accessed 9 March 2022). For an entertaining

summary of the various strands of Viennese feuilleton that had developed by the mid-nineteenth century see Ferdinand Kürnberger, 'The Feuilletonists', in Helen Constantine (ed.), *Vienna Tales*, trans. Deborah Holmes (Oxford University Press, 2014), pp. 103–18.

45   From his essay 'The Painter of Modern Life', published in *Le Figaro* in 1863, and reproduced online at https://courses.nus.edu.sg/course/elljwp/Baudelaire%20on%20the%20flaneur.htm

46   Bronsen, pp. 102–3.

47   Ibid., p. 101.

48   Ibid., p. 108.

49   Deborah Holmes, 'Joseph Roth's Feuilleton Journalism as Social History in Vienna, 1919–20'.

50   Bronsen, p. 105.

51   Ibid., p. 101.

52   *TWJ*, p. 67.

53   *CSF*, p. 176.

54   *RFAPP*, p. 18.

55   Sternburg, p. 481.

56   Von Cziffra, p. 55.

57   Joseph Roth, *The Emperor's Tomb*, trans. Michael Hofmann (Granta Books, 2013), p. 40.

Chapter Four

1   Bronsen, p. 111.

2   Von Cziffra, pp. 10–11.

3   *WIS*, pp. 14–15.

4   Bronsen, p. 112, from 'Die Tyrannei der Stunde', *Der Neue Tag*, 5 October 1919.

5   Ibid., pp. 108–9, from "Versuchsklassen", *Der Neue Tag*, 21 March 1920.

6   Ibid., p. 113. To Gustav Kiepenheuer on his fiftieth birthday. June, 1930.

7   Words spoken fifteen years later in Paris, to the French critic Frédéric Lefèvre: '*L'inflation m'a chassé de Vienne, on n'y pouvait plus vivre. Je suis parti pour où il y avait quelque chose à gagner.*'

8   Bronsen, p. 113.

9   *TWJ*, p. 68.

10 *ALIL*, p. 153. To Gustav Kiepenheuer on his fiftieth birthday. June, 1930.

11 Morgenstern, p. 149.

12 Bronsen, p. 114.

13 Karl Scheffler, *Berlin. Ein Stadtschicksal* (E. Reiss, 1910), p. 266.

14 *WIS*, p. 11.

15 *TWJ*, p. 68.

16 Bronsen, p. 115.

17 Ibid., p. 116.

18 Morgenstern, pp. 149–50.

19 Bronsen, p. 118.

20 *WIS*, p. 23, 'Going for a Walk', *Berliner Börsen-Courier*, 24 May 1921.

21 Ibid., p. 23.

22 Ibid., p. 24.

23 Ibid., p. 37.

24 Ibid., p. 38.

25 *Werke*, vol. 2, p. 351, *Der Drache*, 24 February 1925.

26 *WIS*, p. 76, 'Schiller Park', *Berliner Börsen-Courier*, 23 October 1923.

27 *THY*, p. 10, 'Millionaire for an Hour', *Neue Berliner Zeitung 12-Uhr-Blatt*, 1 April 1921.

28 *THY*, p. 12, 'The Umbrella', *Neue Berliner Zeitung 12-Uhr-Blatt*, 29 May 1921.

29 *WIS*, p. 180, 'The Tour Around the Victory Column', *Neue Berliner Zeitung 12-Uhr-Blatt*, 15 March 1921.

30 *WIS*, p. 82, 'The Unnamed Dead', *Neue Berliner Zeitung 12-Uhr-Blatt*, 17 January 1923.

31 Ibid., p. 81.

32 Ibid., p. 82.

33 Ibid., p. 80.

34 *WIS*, p. 53, 'Nights in Dives', *Neue Berliner Zeitung 12-Uhr-Blatt*, 23–28 February 1921.

35 Ibid., p. 58.

36   Ibid., p. 57.

37   Ibid., p. 61.

38   Ibid., pp. 60–1.

39   Bronsen, p. 118.

40   Sternburg, p. 191.

41   The document is viewable online at https://archive.org/details/
      josephroth_06_reel06/page/n407/mode/1up?view=theater (last
      accessed 9 March 2022).

42   Bronsen, p. 122.

43   Bronsen p. 120.

44   Sternburg, p. 245.

45   Gustav Kiepenheuer, 'Eine Reverenz vor Joseph Roth', in Kampa and
      Keel, p. 51.

46   Von Cziffra, p. 28.

47   Bronsen interview with Bruno Frei, Bronsen, p. 123.

48   THY, p. 48, 'The Mother', Berliner-Börsen Courier, 25 April 1922.

49   Ibid.

50   Ibid., p. 49.

51   Werke, vol. 1, p. 871, Leipziger Mittag, 2 October 1922.

52   Robert Waite, Vanguard of Nazism: The Free Corps Movement in Post-
      War Germany 1918–1923 (W. W. Norton, 1969), p. 214.

53   Jewish Chronicle, 9 November 1923, p. 19.

54   Bronsen, p. 122.

55   Ibid.

56   ALIL, p. 26, Berlin, 17 September 1922, to Herbert Ihering.

57   Joseph Roth, The Silent Prophet, trans. David Le Vay (Peter Owen,
      2002), p. 43.

58   Jon Hughes, 'Joseph Roth and Benno Reifenberg: Aspects of the
      Author–Editor Relationship', The Modern Language Review, vol. 101,
      no. 4 (October 2006), p. 1045.

59   Bronsen, p. 129

60   Von Cziffra, p. 32.

61   ALIL, p. 25, Friederike Reichler to Paula Grübel, Berlin, 28
      December 1921, half past eleven at night.

62   WIS, p. 17.

63 Ibid., pp. 153–4, 'The Philosophy of the Panopticum', *Berliner Börsen-Courier*, 25 February 1923.

64 Bronsen, p. 126.

65 Martyn Rady, *The Habsburgs: The Rise and Fall of a World Power* (Allen Lane, 2020), p. 327.

66 Bronsen, pp. 127–8.

67 '... über alle Dinge, die Deutschlands Wohl und Wehe [betreffen], die Arbeit, das Brot und den Tod seines Volkes, ... über die barbarischen Formen des öffentlichen Lebens'. 'Schweigen im Dichterwald', *Prager Tagblatt*, 16 November 1923, quoted in Lazaroms, pp. 19–20, fn 69.

68 Bronsen, p. 129.

69 Sternburg, p. 31.

70 Von Cziffra, p. 31.

71 Morgenstern, p. 100.

72 Joseph Roth, *The Spider's Web*, trans. John Hoare (Granta Books, 2004), p. 4.

73 Ibid., p. 6.

74 Ibid., p. 7.

75 Ibid., pp. 16–17.

76 Ibid., p. 16.

77 *WIS*, p. 56, 'Nights in Dives'.

78 *Job*, p. 21.

79 'April', *CSF*, p. 81.

80 *Hotel Savoy*, p. 40.

81 Joseph Roth, *Rebellion*, trans. Michael Hofmann (Granta Books, 2000), p. 75.

82 *The Spider's Web*, p. 4.

83 Ibid., p. 11.

84 Ibid., p. 53.

85 Ibid., p. 71.

86 Ibid., p. 58.

87 Ibid., p. 53.

88 Ibid., p. 64.

89 Rosenfeld, p. 19.

90 *THY*, p. 32, 'Germany in Winter', *Frankfurter Zeitung*, 9 December 1923.

91 'The Dream of a Carnival Night', *Vorwärts*, 2 March 1924, in Joseph Roth, *On the End of the World*, trans. Will Stone (Pushkin Press, 2019), p. 4.

Chapter Five

1   *Hotel Savoy*, p. 9.

2   Ibid.

3   *THY*, p. 155, 'Arrival in the Hotel', *Frankfurter Zeitung*, 9 January 1929.

4   *ALIL*, p. 527 (Paris), 10 October 1938, to Stefan Zweig.

5   *THY*, p. 155.

6   *THY*, p. 77, 'Hotel Kopřiva', *Prager Tagblatt*, 4 December 1923.

7   Ibid., pp. 79–80.

8   *Hotel Savoy*, p. 9.

9   Ibid., p. 11.

10   Ibid., p. 72.

11   Ibid., p. 47.

12   Ibid., p. 53.

13   Ibid.

14   Ibid., p. 56.

15   *WIS*, p. 77, 'Schiller Park'.

16   *Hotel Savoy*, p. 72.

17   Ibid., p. 37.

18   Ibid., p. 28.

19   Ibid., p. 54.

20   Ibid., p. 77.

21   Ibid., p. 114.

22   Ibid., p. 67.

23   Ibid., p. 107.

24   *TWJ*, p. 11.

25   *Hotel Savoy*, p. 118.

26   Ibid., p. 123.

27   Joseph Roth, *Flight Without End*, trans. David le Vay (Peter Owen, 2000) p. 5.

28 *ALIL*, p. 42, Hôtel de la Place de l'Odeon, Paris, 14 June 1925, to Bernard von Brentano.

29 *TWJ*, p. 1.

30 Von Cziffra, pp. 19–20.

31 *THY*, p. 20, 'Baltic Tour', *Frankfurter Zeitung*, 6 July 1924.

32 Ibid., p. 22.

33 *ALIL*, p. 27, Friederike Roth to Paula Grübel, Berlin, 14 July 1924.

34 Ibid., p. 28. (Berlin, 15 July 1924), to Paula Grübel.

35 *Rebellion*, pp. viii–ix.

36 Ibid., p. 2.

37 Ibid.

38 Ibid., p. 72.

39 Ibid.

40 Ibid., p. 37.

41 Ibid., p. 32.

42 Ibid., p. 42.

43 Ibid., p. viii.

44 Ibid., p. 45.

45 Susan Miron, 'On Joseph Roth', *Salmagundi*, no. 98/99 (1993), p. 202.

46 *Rebellion*, p. 48.

47 Ibid., p. 52.

48 Ibid., p. 64.

49 Ibid., p. 73.

50 Ibid., p. 94.

51 Ibid., p. 76.

52 Ibid., p. 108.

53 Job 16:8.

54 *Rebellion*, p. 108.

55 Ibid., p. 119.

56 Ibid., p. 138.

57 Ibid., p. 142.

58 Rosenfeld, p. 102.

59 *THY*, p. 69, 'Journey Through Galicia: People and Place', *Frankfurter Zeitung*, 20 November 1924.

60 Ibid., p. 68.

61 Ibid., p. 69.

62 Ibid., p. 66.

63 Ibid., p. 68.

64 Bronsen, p. 144.

65 *Werke*, vol. 2, pp. 289–92, 'Die Krüppel', *Frankfurter Zeitung*, 23 November 1924.

66 Ibid., p. 290.

67 *THY*, p. 70.

68 Ibid., p. 70, *Frankfurter Zeitung*, 20 November 1924.

69 Sternburg, pp. 289–90.

Chapter Six

1   *RFAPP*, p. 92, 'Tournon', *The White Cities*.

2   *ALIL*, p. 38, Paris, 16 May 1925, to Benno Reifenberg.

3   *FWO*, pp. 104–5.

4   Ibid., p. 107.

5   Bronsen, p. 186.

6   Sternburg, p. 246

7   Von Cziffra, p. 22.

8   Ibid., p. 23.

9   Ibid., pp. 24–5.

10 Jon Hughes, *Facing Modernity: Fragmentation, Culture, and Identity in Joseph Roth's Writing in the 1920s* (Maney Publishing for the Modern Humanities Research Association and the Institute of Germanic and Romance Studies, 2006), p 14.

11 *ALIL*, p. 39, Paris, 16 May 1925, to Benno Reifenberg.

12 *RFAPP*, p. 79, 'Lyons', *The White Cities*.

13 Ibid., p. 102, 'Avignon', *The White Cities*.

14 Ibid., pp. 127–8, 'Tarascon and Beaucaire', *The White Cities*.

15 Jon Hughes, 'Joseph Roth in France: Re-assessing *Die weißen Städte*', *Austrian Studies*, vol. 13 (2005), pp. 138–9: www.jstor.org/stable/27944764 (last accessed 22 October 2020).

16   *RFAPP*, p. 109, 'Avignon', *The White Cities*.
17   Hughes, 'Joseph Roth in France: Re-assessing *Die weißen Städte*', p. 139.
18   *RFAPP*, p. 18.
19   Rosenfeld, p. 26.
20   *ALIL*, p. 44, Lyons, 25 July (1925), to Benno Reifenberg.
21   Ibid., p. 105, Hotel Excelsior, Munich, 21 December 1927, to Félix Bertaux.
22   Hughes, 'Joseph Roth in France: Re-assessing *Die Weißen Städte*', p. 138.
23   *ALIL*, p. 42, Hôtel de la Place de l'Odéon, Paris, 14 June 1925, to Bernard von Brentano.
24   Ibid., p. 61, Frankfurt, 19 December 1925, to Bernard von Brentano.
25   Ibid., p. 42, Hôtel de la Place de l'Odéon, Paris, 14 June 1925, to Bernard von Brentano.
26   Ibid., p. 58, Paris, 11 September (1925), to Bernard von Brentano.
27   Ibid., p. 50, Hôtel Beauvau, Marseilles, 26 August (1925), to Benno Reifenberg.
28   Ibid., p. 47, Marseilles, 22 August 1925, to Bernard von Brentano.
29   Ibid., p. 47.
30   Ibid., p. 40, Paris, 2 June 1925, to Bernard von Brentano.
31   Ibid., p. 47, Marseilles, 22 August 1925, to Bernard von Brentano.
32   *RFAPP*, p. 132, 'Marseilles Revisited', *The White Cities*.
33   Ibid., p. 133.
34   *ALIL*, p. 51
35   *ALIL*, p. 48, Marseilles, 22 August 1925, to Bernard von Brentano.
36   Ibid., p. 29, Berlin, 22 January 1925, to Erich Lichtenstein.
37   Ibid., p. 46, fn 1, Hôtel Beauvau, Marseilles, 18 August (1925), to Benno Reifenberg.
38   Ibid., p. 47, Marseilles, 22 August 1925, to Bernard von Brentano.
39   *RFAPP*, pp. 97–8, 'Avignon', *The White Cities*.
40   *RFAPP*, p. 35, 'Lyons', *Frankfurter Zeitung*, 8 September 1925.
41   Ibid., p. 61, 'Nice', *Frankfurter Zeitung*, 26 October 1925.
42   Ibid., p. 62.
43   Ibid., p. 39, 'The Cinema in the Arena', *Frankfurter Zeitung*, 12 September 1925.
44   Ibid., p. 40.
45   Ibid.

46   Ibid., p. 37, 'Lyons', *Frankfurter Zeitung*, 8 September 1925.

47   Ibid., p. 73, introduction, *The White Cities*.

48   *ALIL*, pp. 53–4, Hôtel Beauvau, Marseilles, 30 August (1925), to
     Benno Reifenberg.

49   Ibid., p. 54.

50   Ibid.

51   Ibid., p. 55.

52   *RFAPP*, p. 84, 'Lyons', *The White Cities*.

53   Ibid., p. 91, 'Tournon', *The White Cities*.

54   Ibid., p. 86, 'Vienne', *The White Cities*.

55   Ibid., p. 98, 'Avignon', *The White Cities*.

56   Ibid., p. 123, 'Nîmes and Arles', *The White Cities*.

57   Ibid., p. 98, 'Avignon', *The White Cities*.

58   Ibid., p. 72, introduction, *The White Cities*.

59   Ibid., p. 71.

60   Hughes, 'Joseph Roth in France. Re-assessing *Die Weißen
     Städte*', p. 128

61   Ibid., p. 73.

62   Ibid., p. 76.

63   *ALIL*, p. 59, 29 November 1925, to Bernard von Brentano.

64   Ibid., p. 59.

65   *THY*, p. 25, 'Melancholy of a Tram Car in the Ruhr', *Frankfurter
     Zeitung*, 9 March 1926.

66   *ALIL*, p. 66, undated, to Bernard von Brentano.

67   Ibid., p. 67.

68   Ibid., p. 63, Frankfurt, 30 December 1925, to Bernard von Brentano.

69   Ibid., p. 74, Benno Reifenberg to Joseph Roth, *Frankfurter Zeitung*
     editorial, 7 April 1926.

70   Ibid., p. 76, 8 April 1926, to Bernard von Brentano.

71   Ibid.

72   Bronsen, p. 188

73   *RFAPP*, pp. 159–62, 'Report from a Parisian Paradise', *Frankfurter
     Zeitung*, 14 April 1926.

74   *ALIL*, p. 78, 22 April 1926, to Benno Reifenberg.

75 Ibid.
76 Ibid.
77 *ALIL*, p. 79, 22 April 1926, to Benno Reifenberg.
78 *Job*, afterword, p. 222.

Chapter Seven

1 Read online on Project Gutenberg: https://www.projekt-gutenberg. org/roth/reisruss/chap017.html, translation by Michael Struppek.
2 Ibid.
3 Walter Benjamin, 'Moscow Diary', *October*, vol. 35 (1985), pp. 9–135: www.jstor.org/stable/778471 (last accessed 10 March 2022).
4 Ibid., pp. 29–30.
5 Ibid., p. 29.
6 *ALIL*, p. 447, 17 February 1936, to Stefan Zweig.
7 Ibid., p. 84, 30 August 1926, to Benno Reifenberg.
8 Ibid.
9 Ibid., p. 86.
10 Ibid., p. 84.
11 *THY*, p. 119, 'The Wonders of Astrakhan', *Frankfurter Zeitung*, 12 October 1926.
12 Ibid.
13 *Werke* vol. 2, p. 1019
14 *TWJ*, p. 110.
15 Ibid., pp. 113–14.
16 Lunzer and Lunzer-Talos, *Joseph Roth im Exil in Paris. 1933 bis 1939*, p. 183.
17 *Werke*, vol. 2, pp. 1008–22.
18 *ALIL*, pp. 90–1, (October 1926?), to Benno Reifenberg.
19 Ibid., p. 88, Odessa, 1 October 1926, to Benno Reifenberg.
20 Ibid., p. 90.
21 *Werke*, vol. 2, p. 1009.
22 Morgenstern, pp. 36–7.

23   *ALIL*, p. 85, Hôtel Foyot, Paris, 27 February 1929, to Stefan Zweig.

24   Ibid., p. 93, 23 April 1927, to Benno Reifenberg.

25   Ibid., p. 221, Caffè Centrale Ascona, as of: Englischer Hof, Frankfurt am Main, 28 October 1932, to Otto Forst-Battaglia.

26   *FWO*, pp. 30–1.

27   Ibid., p. 35.

28   Ibid., p. 36.

29   Ibid., p. 38.

30   Ibid., p. 36.

31   Ibid., p. 54.

32   Ibid., p. 55.

33   Ibid.

34   *ALIL*, p. 69

35   *ALIL*, p. 98, Hôtel Helvetia, Paris, 14 June 1927, to Ludwig Marcuse.

36   Ibid., p. 69, fn 3.

37   Ibid., p. 93, 23 April 1927, to Benno Reifenberg.

38   *FWO*, p. 129.

39   Ibid., p. 130.

40   Ibid., p. 144.

41   *THY*, p. 135, 'Arrival in Albania', *Frankfurter Zeitung*, 11 June 1927.

42   Ibid., p. 130, 'A Meeting with President Ahmed Zogu', *Frankfurter Zeitung*, 29 May 1927.

43   Ibid., p. 146, 'Article about Albania (Written on a Hot Day)', *Frankfurter Zeitung*, 30 July 1927.

44   *TWJ*, p. 29.

45   *Joseph Roth – Städtebilder: Zur Poetik, Philologie und Interpretation von Stadtdarstellungen aus der 1920er und 1930er Jahren* by S. Pesnel, E. Tunner, H. Lunzer and V. Lunzer-Talos (eds), (Frank & Timme, 2015), p. 162

46   Bronsen, p. 186.

47   *ALIL*, p. 99, Grenoble, 17 August 1927, to Benno Reifenberg.

48   Ibid., p. 100.

49   Joseph Roth, *Zipper and his Father*, trans. Michael Hofmann (Granta Books, 2005), p. 1.

50   Rosenfeld, p. 31.

51 *ZF*, p. 5.

52 Ibid., p. 13.

53 Ibid., p. 8.

54 Ibid., p. 32.

55 Ibid., p. 42.

56 Ibid., p. 38.

57 Ibid., p. 52.

58 Ibid., p. 62.

59 Ibid., p. 65.

60 Ibid., p. 75.

61 *ALIL*, p. 107, 152–4, Rue de la Pompe, Paris, 27 December 1927, to Benno Reifenberg.

62 See *RFAPP*, p. 74.

63 *ZF*, pp. 127–8.

64 Ibid., p. 129.

65 Ibid., p. 133.

66 *ALIL*, p. 100.

67 Zweig, *The World of Yesterday*, p. 139.

68 *ALIL*, p. 143.

69 Michael Hofmann, 'Vermicular Dither', *London Review of Books*, vol. 32, no. 2, 28 January 2010.

70 *Werke*, vol. 2, pp. 779–80, '*Bahnhof von Saarbrücken*', *Frankfurter Zeitung*, 22 November 1927.

71 *ALIL*, p. 111, Paris, 8 January 1928, to Benno Reifenberg.

72 Ibid., p. 102, Frankfurt am Main, 20 September 1927, to Bernard von Brentano.

73 Ibid., p. 103, Strasbourg, Tuesday (1927), to Benno Reifenberg.

Chapter Eight

1 *CSF*, p. 130.

2 Ibid., p. 133.

3 *ALIL*, p. 108, 152–4, Rue de la Pompe, Paris, 27 December 1927, to Benno Reifenberg.

4   Ibid., p. 111, Paris, 8 January 1928, to Benno Reifenberg.

5   Ibid., p. 107, 152–4, Rue de la Pompe, Paris, 27 December 1927, to Benno Reifenberg.

6   Ibid.

7   Ibid., p. 111, Paris, 8 January 1928, to Benno Reifenberg.

8   Morgenstern, p. 199.

9   *ALIL*, p. 116, Cologne, 24 January 1928, to Stefan Zweig.

10 Ibid., p. 109, Paris, 5 January 1928, to Félix Bertaux.

11 Ibid., p. 117, Saint-Raphaël, 13 February 1928, to Félix Bertaux.

12 Bronsen, p. 192.

13 Email correspondence with the author, January 2022.

14 *ALIL*, p. 124, Hotel Imperial, Vienna, 30 July 1928, to Benno Reifenberg.

15 *THY*, p. 91, 'His K. and K. Apostolic Majesty', *Frankfurter Zeitung*, 6 March 1928.

16 *ALIL*, p. 124, Hotel Imperial, Vienna, 30 July 1928, to Benno Reifenberg.

17 Ibid., p. 125.

18 Morgenstern, p. 53.

19 Ibid., p. 56.

20 Ibid., p. 51.

21 Ibid., p. 52.

22 Ibid., p. 146.

23 Ibid., p. 53.

24 Ibid., p. 147.

25 *THY*, p. 206, 'Music in the Volksgarten', *Frankfurter Zeitung*, 8 April 1928.

26 Ibid., p. 207.

27 Ibid., p. 208.

28 Ibid.

29 Sternburg, p. 227.

30 Ibid.

31 Sternburg, p. 228.

32 Ibid., pp. 228–9.

33 Friderike Maria Zweig, *Spieglungen des Lebens* (1964), cited in Sternburg, p. 231

34 Morgenstern, pp. 57–8

35 *Werke*, vol. 2, p. 988–92, trans. Michael Struppek

36 Ibid., p. 988.

37 *ALIL*, p. 129, 6 January 1929, to Benno Reifenberg.

38 *TRM*, p. 271.

39 *Right and Left*, p. 39.

40 Ibid., p. 7.

41 Ibid., p. 35.

42 Ibid., p. 68.

43 Ibid., p. 96.

44 Ibid., p. 165.

45 Ibid., p. 108.

46 Ibid., p. 118.

47 Ibid., p. 57.

48 Ibid., p. 231.

49 Ibid., p. 234

50 *ALIL*, p. 133, Hôtel Foyot, Paris, 27 February 1929, to Stefan Zweig.

51 Ibid., p. 134.

52 Ibid., p. 135–6, Hôtel Foyot, Paris, 7 March 1929, to Pierre Bertaux.

53 Ibid., p. 58, Paris, 11 September (1925), to Bernard von Brentano.

54 Ibid., p. 102, Frankfurt am Main, 20 September 1927, to Bernard von Brentano.

55 Ibid., p. 99, Marseilles, 31 July 1927, to Bernard von Brentano.

56 Ibid., pp. 137–8, Hôtel Foyot, Paris, 28 March (1929), to Pierre Bertaux.

57 Ibid., pp. 139–40, Berlin, 2 September 1929, to Stefan Zweig.

58 Ibid., p. 141, 10 December 1929, to René Schickele.

59 *WIS*, p. 45, 'Wailing Wall', *Das Tagebuch*, 14 September 1929.

60 Ibid., p. 47.

61 Ibid., p. 48.

62 Ibid., p. 49.

63 Ibid., p. 47.

64 Ibid., p. 50.

65 *CSF*, p. 145.

66 Ibid., p. 135.

67 Ibid., p. 136.

68   *Job*, p. 31.

69   *CSF*, p. 136.

70   Ibid., p. 160.

71   Ibid., p. 137.

72   Paul Fussell, *The Great War and Modern Memory* (Oxford University Press, 2000), pp. 241–2.

73   Ibid., p. 231.

74   *CSF*, p. 160.

75   Ibid., p. 166.

76   *ALIL*, p. 139, Hôtel Foyot, Paris, 29 March 1929, to Stefan Zweig.

77   Sternburg, pp. 354–5.

78   Ibid., p. 355.

79   Ibid.

80   *WIS*, p. 171, 'The Berlin Pleasure Industry', *Münchner Neueste Nachrichten*, 1 May 1930.

81   Sternburg, p. 352.

82   Ibid., p. 353.

83   Sternburg, p. 379.

84   Von Cziffra, p. 78

85   Bronsen, pp. 206–7.

86   *TRM*, p. 214.

Chapter Nine

1   Morgenstern, p. 174.

2   *Job*, p. 3.

3   *ALIL*, p. 142, 20 January 1930, to René Schickele.

4   Ibid., p. 143.

5   Job, 42:17.

6   *Job*, p. 7.

7   Ibid.

8   Ibid., p. 13.

9   Ibid., p. 15.

10   Morgenstern, p. 60

11 Ibid., p. 4.

12 Ibid., p. 101.

13 Chambers, pp. 196–7.

14 *Job*, p. 96.

15 Ibid., p. 108.

16 Ibid., p. 135.

17 Ibid., p. 149.

18 Ibid., p. 153.

19 Ibid., p. 153.

20 Ibid., pp. 157–8.

21 Ibid., p. 158.

22 Ibid., p. 161.

23 Ibid., p. 162.

24 Ibid., p. 105.

25 Ibid., p. 156.

26 Ibid., p. 170.

27 Ibid., p. 166.

28 Ibid., p. 167.

29 Ibid., p. 207.

30 Ibid., p. 208.

31 Ibid., p. 209.

32 Ibid., p. 210.

33 Ibid., p. 214.

34 Ibid., p. 220.

35 *Joseph Roth und völkisch-nationalistiscshe Wertbegriffe* by Wolf R. Marchand (Bouvier Verlag, 1974) p. 7.

36 *ALIL*, p. 222, Hotel Englischer Hof, Frankfurt am Main, 14 November 1932, to Félix Bertaux.

37 Sternburg, p. 232, 12 April 1930, letter to Hedi Reichler.

38 Heinz Lunzer and Victoria Lunzer-Talos, *Joseph Roth: Leben und Werk in Bildern* (Kiepenheuer & Witsch, 1994), p. 113.

39 *Job*, p. 96.

40 *ALIL*, pp. 145–6, Hotel Stein, Salzburg, 3 May 1930, to his parents-in-law.

41 Ibid., p. 145, Hotel Stein, Salzburg, 30 April 1930, to Hedi Reichler.

42   Report by Dr Rosenthal, Sanatorium Wien–Hacking, mid–May 1930. In Andreas Hutter, 'Friederike Roth (1900–1940). Über Die Letzten Tage, Die "Sie Nicht Überlebt Hat"', Zeitschrift für Germanistik, vol. 21, no. 3 (2011), p. 600.

43   Morgenstern, p. 152.

44   Werke, vol. 3, p. 220, 'Psychiatrie', Das Tagebuch, 28 June 1930.

45   Ibid., p. 219.

46   Ibid., p. 218.

47   Ibid., pp. 218–19.

48   Ibid., p. 219.

49   Ibid., p. 221.

50   Morgenstern, p. 156

51   ALIL, p. 163, Hotel Englischer Hof, Frankfurt am Main, Tuesday (23 September 1930), to Stefan Zweig.

52   Ibid., p. 165, a Thursday in September 1930, to Stefan Zweig.

53   Ibid., p. 169, Hôtel Foyot, Paris, Thursday (October 1930), to Jenny Reichler.

54   Ibid., p. 147, 13 May 1930, to Stefan Zweig.

55   Ibid., p. 148, Benno Reifenberg to Joseph Roth, 14 May 1930, c/o Gustav Kiepenheuer, Altonaerstrasse 4, Berlin NW 87.

56   ALIL, p. 149, 17 May 1930, to Benno Reifenberg.

57   Ibid., p. 155, 20 June 1930, Hotel am Zoo, Berlin, to Stefan Zweig.

58   Morgenstern, p. 77.

59   Lunzer and Lunzer-Talos, Joseph Roth: Leben und Werk in Bildern, p. 187.

60   Bronsen, p. 218.

61   ALIL, p. 161, Hotel Englischer Hof, Frankfurt am Main, 22 September 1930, to Stefan Zweig.

62   Von Cziffra, p. 54.

63   Von Cziffra, pp. 74–5.

64   ALIL, p. 161, Hotel Englischer Hof, Frankfurt am Main, 22 September 1930, to Stefan Zweig.

65   Gustav Kiepenheuer, 'Eine Reverenz vor Joseph Roth' in Kampa and Keel, p. 51

66   ALIL, p. 151, to Gustav Kiepenheuer on his fiftieth birthday.

67   Ibid., pp. 153–4.

Chapter Ten

1   *TRM*, p. 8.
2   Ibid., p. 13.
3   Ibid., p. 45.
4   Ibid., p. 76.
5   Ibid., p. 26.
6   Ibid., p. 26–7.
7   Kampa and Keel, p. 53.
8   *TRM*, p. 34.
9   Ibid., p. 40.
10   Ibid., p. 57.
11   Ibid., p. 55.
12   Ibid., p. 58.
13   Ibid., p. 56.
14   Ibid., p. 57.
15   Ibid., p. 61.
16   Ibid., p. x.
17   Ibid., p. 217.
18   Ibid., p. 220.
19   Ibid., p. 80.
20   Ibid., p. 75.
21   Ibid., p. 82.
22   *ALIL*, p. 181, Hôtel du Cap d'Antibes, 24 March (1931), to Stefan Zweig.
23   Ibid., pp. 178–9, Hôtel du Cap d'Antibes, Sunday (February or March 1931?), marked: 'Very personal. Antibes (A-M.) Please deliver immediately!'
24   Ibid., p. 184, 13 May 1931, to Stefan Zweig.
25   Ibid., p. 185.
26   *TRM*, p. 115.
27   Ibid., p. 101.
28   Ibid., pp. 104–5.
29   Ibid., p. 131.
30   Ibid., p. 114.
31   Ibid., p. 114.

32   Ibid., p. 119.

33   Ibid., p. 138.

34   Ibid., p. 120.

35   *ALIL*, p. 191, Frankfurt am Main, 28 August 1931, to Stefan Zweig.

36   Ibid., p. 171, Hotel Der Achtermann and Niedersächsischer Hof, 20
      November 1930, to Stefan Zweig.

37   *TRM*, p. 183.

38   Ibid., p. 139.

39   Ibid., 146.

40   Ibid., p. 147.

41   Ibid., p. 146.

42   Ibid., p. 148.

43   Ibid., pp. 148–9.

44   Ibid., p. 175.

45   Ibid., p. 276.

46   Ibid., p. 69.

47   Ibid., p. 67.

48   Ibid., p. 115.

49   Ibid., p. 216.

50   'Dream upon the Universe', from *Der Komet* by Jean Paul Richter
      (1820), trans. Thomas de Quincy, quoted in Frank Seafield, *The
      Literature and Curiosities of Dreams* (London: Chapman & Hall), 1865.

51   *TRM*, p. 176.

52   Ibid., p. 188.

53   Ibid., p. 211.

54   Ibid., p. 227.

55   Ibid., p. 229.

56   Ibid., p. 234.

57   Ibid., p. 238.

58   Ibid., p. 239.

59   Ibid., p. 242.

60   Ibid.

61   Ibid.

62   Ibid., p. 243.

63   Ibid.

64   Ibid., p. 245.

65   Ibid., p. 246.

66   Ibid., p. 247.

67   Ibid., p. 284.

68   *ALIL*, p. 212, Hotel Schwanen, Rapperswil am Zürichsee, 24
      September 1932, to Stefan Zweig. The unexpurgated letter is
      reproduced in M. Rietra and R. J. Siegel (eds), *'Jede Freundschaft mit
      mir ist verderblich': Joseph Roth und Stefan Zweig – Briefwechsel 1927–1938*
      (Wallstein, 2011), pp. 84–5.

69   *TRM*, p. 299.

70   Ibid., p. 308.

71   Ibid., p. 320.

72   Ibid., p. 322–3.

73   Ibid., p. 324.

74   Ibid., p. 325.

75   Ibid., p. 327.

76   Ibid., p. 328.

77   Ibid., p. 329.

78   Ibid., pp. 338–9.

79   David Fromkin, *Europe's Last Summer: Why the World Went to War in
      1914* (Heinemann, 2004), p. 188.

80   *TRM*, p. 349.

81   Ibid., p. 110.

82   Ibid., p. 166.

83   Ibid., p. 363.

84   Sternburg, p. 393.

85   *ALIL*, p. 203, Benno Reifenberg to Joseph Roth, 11 July 1932:
      'To Mr J. Roth, c/o Kiepenheuer Verlag, 10 Kantstrasse, Berlin-
      Charlottenburg 2'.

86   Ibid., p. 199, 20 March (1932), to Félix Bertaux.

87   Ibid., pp. 199–200, Sunday, to Friedrich Traugott Gubler.

88   Ibid., pp. 203–4, Baden-Baden, c/o Fabisch, Yburgstrasse 21, 7
      August 1932, to Stefan Zweig.

89   Ibid., p. 204.

90   Ibid.

91 Ibid., pp. 208–9, Hotel Schwanen, Rapperswil am Zürichsee, 18 September 1932, to Stefan Zweig.

92 Ibid., p. 208.

93 Ibid.

94 Ibid.

95 Ibid., p. 209.

96 Von Cziffra, p. 68.

97 Ibid., p. 63.

98 *ALIL*, p. 237, Hôtel Jacob, Paris (mid–February 1933), to Stefan Zweig.

99 Ibid., p. 245, Hôtel Foyot, Paris, 17 March 1933, to Stefan Zweig.

100 Ibid., p. 247.

101 Ibid., pp. 249–50.

102 Sternburg, p. 401.

103 *ALIL*, p. 256. [Paris], 22 May 1933, to Stefan Zweig.

104 *WIS*, p. 207, 'The Auto-da-Fé of the Mind', *Cahiers Juifs* (Paris), September/November 1933 (from the French).

Chapter Eleven

1 *Werke*, vol. 3, p. 1032, 'VON DEUTSCHER LITERATUR. Eine Stunde mit Joseph Roth, von Frederic Lefevre'.

2 Ibid., p. 1034.

3 Ibid., p. 1035.

4 Ibid.

5 Ibid., p. 1034.

6 Ibid., p. 1033.

7 Ibid., pp. 1033–4.

8 Ibid., p. 1034.

9 *ALIL*, p. 236, 11 February 1933, to Félix Bertaux.

10 Ibid., p. 243, 16 March 1933, to Blanche Gidon.

11 Ibid., p. 272, Hotel Schwanen, Rapperswil am Zürichsee, 27 September 1933, to Blanche Gidon.

12 Morgenstern, pp. 105–6.

13 Bronsen, p. 208.

14 *ALIL*, p. 241, Café des Deux Magots (Paris), 24 February 1933, to Félix Bertaux. See also *ALIL*, pp. 226, 234 and 237.

15 Joseph Roth, *The Antichrist*, trans. Richard Panchyk (Peter Owen, 2010), p. 75.

16 Hughes, 'Joseph Roth and Benno Reifenberg: Aspects of the Author-Editor Relationship', p. 1053.

17 *TA*, p. 25.

18 Ibid., p. 34.

19 Ibid., p. 35.

20 Ibid., p. 37.

21 Ibid., p. 75.

22 Ibid., p. 102.

23 *ALIL*, p. 386, 121 Promenade des Anglais, Nice, 11 November 1934, to Carl Seelig.

24 *TA*, p. 136.

25 Ibid., p. 164.

26 *ALIL*, p. 318, Hôtel Foyot, Paris, 26 March 1934, to Stefan Zweig.

27 Ibid., pp. 291–2, Hôtel Foyot, Paris, 22 December 1933, to Stefan Zweig.

28 Sternburg, p. 412.

29 Jospeh Roth, *Tarabas: A Guest on Earth*, trans. Michael Hofmann (Granta Books, 2004), p. 40.

30 Ibid., pp. 272–3.

31 Morgenstern, p. 119.

32 Ibid., p. 123.

33 Ibid., p. 106.

34 Bronsen, p. 306.

35 Lunzer and Lunzer-Talos, *Joseph Roth im Exil in Paris*, p. 52.

36 Bronsen, p. 306.

37 Lunzer and Lunzer-Talos, *Joseph Roth im Exil in Paris*, p. 53.

38 Bronsen, p. 260.

39 Morgenstern, p. 143.

40 Von Cziffra, p. 77.

41 Bronsen, p. 207.

42 Weidermann, pp. 69–70

43 *ALIL*, p. 343, Dégustation Cintra, Marseilles, 11 July 1934, to Stefan Zweig.

44   Ibid.

45   Sternburg, p. 437.

46   *ALIL*, p. 338, Hôtel Beauvau, Marseilles, 14 June 1934, to
     Stefan Zweig.

47   Ibid., pp. 339–40, Hôtel Beauvau, Marseilles, 22 June 1934, to
     Stefan Zweig.

48   Ibid., p. 343, Dégustation Cintra, Marseilles, 11 July 1934, to
     Stefan Zweig.

49   Von Cziffra, p. 86.

50   *ALIL*, p. 357, Stefan Zweig to Joseph Roth (July 1934).

51   Ibid., p. 350, Stefan Zweig to Joseph Roth (July 1934).

52   Ibid., p. 351, (summer 1934).

53   Ibid., p. 346, Nice, 13 July 1934, to Stefan Zweig.

54   Ibid., p. 356, (Marseilles), 19 July 1934, to Stefan Zweig.

55   Ibid., p. 359, Nice, 20 July 1934, to Stefan Zweig.

56   Ibid., p. 363, Nice, 2 August 1934, to Stefan Zweig.

57   Ibid., p. 366, Nice, 20 August 1934, to Stefan Zweig.

58   Ibid., p. 373, Nice, 9 September 1934, to Stefan Zweig.

59   Lunzer and Lunzer-Talos, *Joseph Roth: Leben und Werk in Bildern*, p. 213.

60   *ALIL*, p. 374, 121 Promenade des Anglais, Nice, 18 September 1934,
     to Stefan Zweig.

61   Ibid., pp. 374–5.

62   Ibid., p. 429, Hôtel Foyot, Paris, 12 November 1935, to Stefan Zweig.

63   Bronsen, p. 194.

64   Bronsen, p. 194.

65   *ALIL*, p. 414, Hôtel Foyot, Paris, 14 August 1935, to Stefan Zweig.

66   Ibid., pp. 414–15.

67   *CSF*, p. 209.

68   Ibid., p. 208.

69   Ibid., p. 211.

70   Von Cziffra, pp. 76–7.

71   *ALIL*, p. 335, Hôtel Beauvau, Marseilles, 14 June 1934, to Blanche
     Gidon (written in French).

72   *CSF*, p. 219.

73   Lazaroms, p. 167.

74 *ALIL*, p. 399, Hôtel Imperator, Nice, 27 February 1935, to Blanche Gidon (written in French).

75 Bronsen, p. 278.

76 *ALIL*, p. 267, Hotel Schwanen, Rapperswil am Zürichsee, 31 August 1933, to Stefan Zweig.

Chapter Twelve

1   *ALIL*, p. 485, Hôtel de la Couronne, Ostend, 15 July 1936, to Blanche Gidon.

2   Ibid., p. 444, fn 1.

3   Sternburg, p. 425.

4   *ALIL*, pp. 419–20, Hôtel Foyot, Paris, 21 August 1935, to Stefan Zweig.

5   Els Snick, *Joseph Roth in Den Niederlanden Und Flandern: Vermittlung, Vernetzung Und Orchestrierung Eines Vielseitigen Autors Im Niederländischsprachigen Context 1924–1940* (University of Utrecht, Faculty of Arts, 2011), p. 146.

6   *ALIL*, p. 460, Stefan Zweig, 49 Hallam Street, London W1, to Joseph Roth, 31 March 1936.

7   Ibid., p. 461.

8   Ibid., pp. 461–2.

9   https://theartsdesk.com/books-theatre/private-life-stefan-zweig-england

10 *ALIL*, p. 468, Eden Hotel, Amsterdam, 8 May 1936, to Blanche Gidon.

11 Ibid., p. 468, Eden Hotel, Amsterdam, 7 May 1936, to Stefan Zweig.

12 Ibid., pp. 466–7, Eden Hotel, Amsterdam, 4 May 1936, to Stefan Zweig.

13 Ibid., p. 464, Stefan Zweig to Joseph Roth (undated).

14 Weidermann, p. 52.

15 *ALIL*, p. 464, Eden Hotel, Amsterdam, 30 April 1936, to Stefan Zweig.

16 Ibid.

17 *ALIL*, p. 413. Hotel Foyot, Paris 6e, 24 July 1935, to Stefan Zweig.

18 Ibid., p. 469, Eden Hotel, Amsterdam, 11 May 1936, to Stefan Zweig.

19 Ibid., p. 479, Stefan Zweig to Joseph Roth, Hotel Regina, Vienna (end of June? 1936).

20   Joseph Roth, *Confession of a Murderer: Told in One Night*, trans. Michael Hofmann (Granta Books, 2003), p. 182.

21   Rosenfeld, p. 67.

22   Ibid.

23   *ALIL*, pp. 445–6, Hôtel Foyot, Paris, Wednesday (February 1936?), to Stefan Zweig.

24   *The String of Pearls*, p. 175.

25   *Werke*, vol. 3, p. 352.

26   *ALIL*, p. 485, Hôtel de la Couronne, Ostend, 15 July 1936, to Blanche Gidon.

27   Ibid., p. 232.

28   Bronsen, p. 265.

29   Ibid., p. 264.

30   Job 4:13–14.

31   Bronsen, pp. 265–6.

32   Snick, pp. 196–7.

33   *COAM*, p. 188.

34   Sternburg, p. 447.

35   Snick, p. 148.

36   *ALIL*, pp. 269–70, Hotel Schwanen, Rapperswil am Zürichsee, 5 September 1933, to Carl Seelig.

37   Snick, p. 155.

38   Lunzer and Lunzer-Talos, p. 189.

39   Bronsen, pp. 295–6.

40   *The String of Pearls*, p. 72.

41   Ibid., p. 157.

42   Ibid., p. 244.

43   Ibid., p. 159.

44   Ibid., p. 256.

45   Bronsen, p. 270.

46   Fred Grübel, 'Mein Vetter Muniu', in Walter Zadek and Christine Brinck, *Sie flohen vor dem Hakenkreuz. Selbstzeugnisse der Emigranten: ein Lesebuch für Deutsche* (Rowohlt, 1981), p. 234.

47   Bronsen, p. 271.

48   Lunzer and Lunzer-Talos, *Joseph Roth im Exil in Paris*, p. 90.

49 Vishniac/Heschel, p. 10.

50 *ALIL*, p. 488

51 Bronsen, p. 272.

52 Ibid., p. 273.

53 Ibid.

54 *Tarabas*, p. 230

55 Ibid., p. 274.

56 *COAM*, p. 113.

57 *RFAPP*, p. 276, 'From an Author's Diary', *Das Neue Tage-Buch* (Paris), 4 September 1937.

58 Bronsen, p. 319.

59 Joseph Roth, *Weights and Measures*, trans. David Le Vay (Penguin Classics, 2017), p. 33.

60 Ibid., p. 69.

61 Ibid., p. 79.

62 Morgenstern, p. 148.

63 *ALIL*, p. 495, Grand Hôtel Cosmopolite, Brussels, 10 July 1937, to Stefan Zweig.

64 George Prochnik, *The Impossible Exile: Stefan Zweig at the End of the World* (Other Press, 2014), Kindle edition.

65 *ALIL*, p. 495, Grand Hôtel Cosmopolite, Brussels, 10 July 1937, to Stefan Zweig.

66 Ibid., p. 496, Grand Hôtel Cosmopolite, Brussels, 10 July 1937, to Stefan Zweig.

67 Ibid., p. 498, (Ostend), 28 July 1937, to Stefan Zweig.

68 Ibid., p. 499, 2 August 1937, to Stefan Zweig.

69 Ibid.

70 Ibid., p. 500.

71 Ibid.

72 Ibid., p. 506, Hôtel de la Couronne, Ostend, 26 August 1937, to Stefan Zweig.

73 Ibid., p. 507, Hôtel de la Couronne, Ostend, 29 August (1937), to Stefan Zweig.

74 Ibid., p. 508, Hôtel de la Couronne, Ostend, 4 September 1937, to Stefan Zweig.

75   Ibid., p. 512, Hôtel de la Couronne, Ostend, 21 September 1937, to
     Stefan Zweig.

76   Ibid., p. 513–14, Stefan Zweig to Joseph Roth, 25 September 1937.

77   Ibid., p. 514–15, Stefan Zweig to Joseph Roth (autumn 1937).

78   Morgenstern, p. 142.

79   Ibid., p. 142–3.

80   Lunzer and Lunzer-Talos, *Joseph Roth im Exil in Paris*, p. 38.

81   Morgenstern, p. 144.

82   Ibid.

83   Ibid., p. 145.

84   Ibid., p. 159.

85   Ibid., p. 160.

86   Ibid., pp. 160–1.

87   Ibid., p. 162.

88   Ibid., p. 163.

89   Ibid.

90   Ibid., p. 164.

91   Ibid.

92   Ibid., p. 165.

93   Ibid., p. 167.

94   Ibid., p. 170.

95   Ibid., p. 171.

96   Ibid., pp. 171–2.

97   Ibid., p. 184.

Chapter Thirteen

1   Von Cziffra, p. 72.

2   *RFAPP*, p. 239, 'Rest While Watching the Demolition', *Das Neue
    Tage-Buch* (Paris), 25 June, 1938.

3   Bronsen, p. 280.

4   Ibid., p. 263.

5   *The Habsburgs: Embodying Empire* by Andrew Wheatcroft (Penguin,

1996), p. 292. Wheatcroft's source is an interview Otto von Habsburg gave to Dutch television.

6   Morgenstern, p. 185.

7   Bronsen, pp. 281–2.

8   Von Cziffra, pp. 110–11.

9   *On the End of the World*, 'Requiem Mass', p. 33. *Das Neue Tage-Buch* (Paris), 19 March 1938.

10   Morgenstern, pp. 189–90.

11   *ALIL*, p. 521, Hôtel Paris-Dinard, Monday (postmarked 10 January 1938), to Stefan Zweig.

12   Sternburg, p. 471.

13   *TRM*, p. x.

14   Roth, *The Emperor's Tomb*, p. 36.

15   Ibid., p. 111.

16   Ibid., p. 105.

17   Ibid., p. xiii.

18   Ibid., p. 183.

19   Lunzer and Lunzer-Talos, *Joseph Roth: Leben und Werk in Bildern*, p. 249.

20   *RFAPP*, p. 250, 'In the Bistro After Midnight', *Die Zukunft* (Paris), 11 November 1938.

21   Wittlin, Reminiscences of Joseph Roth, Leo Baeck Institute.

22   Morgenstern, p. 248.

23   Ibid., p. 227.

24   Ibid.

25   Ibid., p. 228.

26   Ibid., p. 197.

27   Ibid., p. 201.

28   *ALIL*, p. 529, Stefan Zweig, 49 Hallam Street, London W1, to Joseph Roth (end of 1938).

29   Von Cziffra, p. 15.

30   Joseph Roth, *The Legend of the Holy Drinker*, trans. Michael Hofmann (Granta Books, 2013), p. 8.

31   Ibid., p. 99.

32 Lazaroms, p. xxiii.

33 Lunzer and Lunzer-Talos, *Joseph Roth: Leben und Werk in Bildern*, p. 250.

34 Hans Sahl, *Das Exil im Exil* (Luchterhand Literaturverlag, 1990), p. 61, as cited in Sternburg, p. 481.

35 Morgenstern, p. 286.

36 Bronsen, p. 335.

37 Morgenstern, p. 266.

38 Ibid., p. 267.

39 Sternburg, p. 19.

40 Morgenstern, p. 275.

41 Bronsen, p. 338.

42 Stefan Zweig, 'Joseph Roth', in Kampa and Keel, pp. 174–5.

43 Ibid., p. 175.

44 Ibid., p. 185.

45 Ibid., p. 182.

46 Ibid., p. 189.

47 Morgenstern, p. 278.

48 First published in Irmgard Keun, *Bilder und Gedichte aus der Emigration* (Epoche-Verlag, 1947), p. 35, translation by Michael Struppek.

Chapter Fourteen

1 Klaus Mann's diary accessed at https://www.projekt-gutenberg.org/ mannk/wendepun/chap012.html (last accessed 11 March 2022).

2 Prochnik, Kindle edition.

3 Oliver Matuschek, *Three Lives: A Biography of Stefan Zweig*, trans. Allan Blunden (Pushkin Press, 2013), p. 354.

4 The letter is held in the Stefan Zweig archive at the National Library of Israel, and reproduced online here: https://web.nli.org.il/sites/nli/english/ collections/personalsites/archive_treasures/pages/stefan-zweig.aspx

5 Zadek and Brinck, p. 235.

Bibliography

Works by Joseph Roth

Collected Shorter Fiction of Joseph Roth, trans. Michael Hofmann (Granta Books, 2002).

Confession of a Murderer: Told in One Night, trans. Michael Hofmann (Granta Books, 2003).

Flight Without End, trans. David le Vay (Peter Owen, 2000).

Hotel Savoy, trans. John Hoare (Granta Books, 2000).

Job: The Story of a Simple Man, trans. Dorothy Thompson (Granta Books, 2013).

Joseph Roth: A Life in Letters, ed. and trans. Michael Hofmann (Granta Books, 2013).

Rebellion, trans. Michael Hofmann (Granta Books, 1999).

Right and Left, trans. Michael Hofmann (Granta Books, 1999).

Tarabas: A Guest on Earth, trans. Michael Hofmann (Granta Books, 2004).

The Antichrist, trans. Richard Panchyk (Peter Owen, 2010).

The Coral Merchant: Essential Stories, trans. Ruth Martin (Pushkin Press, 2020).

The Emperor's Tomb, trans. Michael Hofmann (Granta Books, 2013).

The Hotel Years: Wanderings in Europe Between the Wars, trans. Michael Hofmann (Granta Books, 2016).

The Hundred Days, trans. Richard Panchyk (Peter Owen, 2011).

The Legend of the Holy Drinker, trans. Michael Hofmann (Granta Books, 2013).

On the End of the World, trans. Will Stone (Pushkin Press, 2019).

Perlefter: The Story of a Bourgeois, trans. Richard Panchyk (Peter Owen, 2013).

The Radetzky March, trans. Michael Hofmann (Granta Books, 2003).

Report from a Parisian Paradise: Essays from France, 1925–1939, compiled by Katharina Ochse, trans. Michael Hofmann (W. W. Norton, 2004).

The Silent Prophet, trans. David Le Vay (Peter Owen, 2002).

The Spider's Web, trans. John Hoare (Granta Books, 2004).

The String of Pearls, trans. Michael Hofmann (Granta Books, 1998).

The Wandering Jews, trans. Michael Hofmann (Granta Books, 2001).

Weights and Measures, trans. David Le Vay (Penguin Classics, 2017).

Werke, ed. Fritz Hackert and Klaus Westermann, 6 vols (Cologne, 1989–91), accessed at https://archive.org/details/josephroth werke0000roth

What I Saw: Reports from Berlin 1920–33, ed. Michael Bienert, trans. Michael Hofmann (Granta Books, 2004).

Zipper and his Father, trans. Michael Hofmann (Granta Books, 2005).

Roth, Joseph and Stefan Zweig, *Jede Freundschaft mit mir ist verderblich: Joseph Roth und Stefan Zweig. Briefwechsel 1927–1938*, ed. Madeleine Rietra and Rainer J. Siegel (Wallstein, 2011).

Studies of Roth's life and work

Asmus, Sylvia, Heinz Lunzer and Victoria Lunzer-Talos (eds), *'So wurde ihnen die Flucht zur Heimat': Soma Morgenstern und Joseph Roth, Eine Freundschaft* (Weidle Verlag, 2012).

Bienert, Michael (ed.), *Joseph Roth in Berlin: Ein Lesebuch für Spaziergänger* (Kiepenheuer & Witsch, 1996).

Bronsen, David, *Joseph Roth: Eine Biographie* (Kiepenheuer & Witsch, 1993).

Chambers, Helen (ed.), *Co-existent Contradictions: Joseph Roth in Retrospect; Papers of the 1989 Joseph Roth Symposium at Leeds University to Commemorate the 50th Anniversary of His Death* (Ariadne Press, 1991).

Coetzee, J. M., 'Joseph Roth, the Stories', in *Inner Workings: Literary Essays 2000–2005* (Vintage Digital, 2015).

Grübel, Fred, '*Mein Vetter Muniu*', in Walter Zadek and Christine Brinck, *Sie flohen vor dem Hakenkreuz. Selbstzeugnisse der Emigranten: ein Lesebuch für Deutsche* (Rowohlt, 1981).

Kampa, Daniel and Daniel Keel (eds), *Joseph Roth: Leben und Werk* (Diogenes, 2010).

Lazaroms, Ilse Josepha, *The Grace of Misery: Joseph Roth and the Politics of Exile, 1919–1939* (Brill, 2012).

Lunzer, Heinz and Victoria Lunzer-Talos, *Joseph Roth 1894–1939. Ein Katalog zur Ausstellung im Jüdischen Museum der Stadt Wien* (Dokumentationsstelle für neuere österreichische Literatur, Vienna, 1994).

Lunzer, Heinz and Victoria Lunzer-Talos, *Joseph Roth. Leben und Werk in Bildern* (Kiepenheuer & Witsch, 1994).

Lunzer, Heinz and Victoria Lunzer-Talos, *Joseph Roth im Exil in Paris. 1933 bis 1939* (Dokumentationsstelle für neuere österreichische Literatur, 2008).

Magris, Claudio, *Lontano da dove: Joseph Roth e la tradizione ebraico-orientale* (Giulio Einaudi, 1971).

—— *Danube*, intro. by Richard Flanagan, trans. Patrick Creagh (Collins Harvill, 1990).

Marks, Dennis, *Wandering Jew: The Search for Joseph Roth* (Notting Hill Editions, 2011).

Morgenstern, Soma, *Joseph Roths Flucht und Ende. Erinnerungen* (Aufbau-Taschenbuch-Verlag, 1998).

Pesnel, S., E. Tunner, H. Lunzer, and V. Lunzer-Talos (eds), *Joseph Roth – Städtebilder: Zur Poetik, Philologie und Interpretation von Stadtdarstellungen aus den 1920er und 1930er Jahren* (Frank & Timme, 2015).

Rosenfeld, Sidney, *Understanding Joseph Roth*, ed. James Hardin (University of South Carolina Press, 2001).

Sebald, W. G., '*Ein Kaddisch für Osterreich – Über Joseph Roth*', in *Unheimliche Heimat. Essays zur österreichischen Literatur* (Fischer E-Books, 1991).

Snick, Els, *Joseph Roth in Den Niederlanden Und Flandern. Vermittlung, Vernetzung Und Orchestrierung Eines Vielseitigen Autors im*

Niederländischsprachigen Context 1924–1940 (University of Utrecht, Faculty of Arts, 2011), accessed at https://dspace.library.uu.nl/bitstream/handle/1874/214871/snick.pdf?sequence=2&isAllowed=y. (last accessed 12 March 2022).

von Cziffra, Géza, *Der Heilige Trinker. Erinnerungen an Joseph Roth* (Ullstein Taschenbuch Verlag, 1989).

von Sternburg, Wilhelm, *Joseph Roth. Eine Biographie* (Kiepenheuer & Witsch, 2010).

Weidermann, Volker, *Summer Before the Dark: Stefan Zweig and Joseph Roth, Ostend 1936*, trans. Carol Brown Janeway (Pushkin Press, 2017).

Williams, C. E., *The Broken Eagle: The Politics of Austrian Literature from Empire to Anschluss* (Paul Elek, 1974).

Essays and articles

Acocella, Joan, 'European Dreams: Rediscovering Joseph Roth', *The New Yorker*, 19 January 2004.

Holmes, Deborah, 'Joseph Roth's Feuilleton Journalism as Social History in Vienna, 1919–20', *Austrian History Yearbook* 48, 2017, pp. 255–65.

Hughes, Jon, 'Joseph Roth and Benno Reifenberg: Aspects of the Author-Editor Relationship.' *The Modern Language Review*, vol. 101, no. 4, 2006, pp. 1044–54. *JSTOR*, www.jstor.org/stable/20467028. Accessed 22 Oct. 2020.

—— 'Joseph Roth in France: Re-Assessing 'Die Weißen Städte'. *Austrian Studies*, vol. 13, 2005, pp. 126–41. *JSTOR*, www.jstor.org/stable/27944764. Accessed 22 Oct. 2020.

—— *Austrian Studies*, vol. 17, 2009, pp. 206–208. *JSTOR*, www.jstor.org/stable/27944923. Accessed 19 Jan. 2021

—— 'Violence, Masculinity and Self: Killing in Joseph Roth's 1920s Fiction', https://repository.royalholloway.ac.uk/file/9742f627-8da8-58b5-ad95-d7182ebd427d/1/GLL_53.2__2000_.pdf

—— Hutter, Andreas, 'Friederike Roth (1900–1940). Über die

letzten Tage, die "sie nicht überlebt hat"' *Zeitschrift für Germanistik*, vol. 21, no. 3, 2011, pp. 599–604. *JSTOR*, www.jstor.org/stable/23979372. Accessed 27 May 2021.

Jaffin, David, 'Joseph Roth: The Poet Of Silence', *European Judaism: A Journal for the New Europe*, vol. 10, no. 1, 1975, pp. 47–48. *JSTOR*, www.jstor.org/stable/41442495. Accessed 12 March 2021.

Miron, Susan, 'Austrian Nights', *The American Scholar*, vol. 68, no. 1, 1999, pp. 144–6. *JSTOR*, www.jstor.org/stable/41212844. Accessed 27 May 2021.

—— 'On Joseph Roth.' *Salmagundi*, no. 98/99, 1993, pp. 198–206. *JSTOR*, www.jstor.org/stable/40548646. Accessed 12 March 2021.

Snick, Els, 'Defloratie Met Literaire Omranding: Een Speurtocht Naar De Romance Tussen De Oostenrijkse Schrijver Joseph Roth En De Brugse Jonkvrouw Maria Gillès De Pélichy', *Zacht Lawijd,* 11.1 (2012): pp. 2–17.

Topp, Leslie, 'Otto Wagner and the Steinhof Psychiatric Hospital: Architecture as Misunderstanding', *The Art Bulletin*, vol. 87, no. 1 (Taylor & Francis, Ltd., College Art Association), 2005, pp. 130–56, http://www.jstor.org/stable/25067159. Accessed 13 May 2022.

Other sources

Babel, Isaac, *The Complete Works of Isaac Babel*, ed. Nathalie Babel, trans. Peter Constantine, intro. by Cynthia Ozick (W. W. Norton, 2005).

Benjamin, Walter, *Reflections: Essays, Aphorisms, Autobiographical Writings* (Houghton Mifflin Harcourt, 1978).

—— 'Moscow Diary', October, vol. 35, 1985, pp. 9–135, accessed at www.jstor.org/stable/778471

Cesarani, David, *Final Solution: The Fate of the Jews 1933–1949* (Pan Books, 2017).

Constantine, Helen (ed.), *Vienna Tales*, trans. Deborah Holmes (Oxford University Press, 2014).

Crankshaw, Edward, *Maria Theresa* (Viking Press, 1970).

David, Anthony, *Into the Abyss: A Neuropsychiatrist's Notes on Troubled Minds* (Oneworld, 2020).

Elon, Amos, *The Pity of It All: A Portrait of the German-Jewish Epoch* (Picador, 2003).

Field, Frank, *Last Days of Mankind: Karl Kraus and his Vienna* (Macmillan, 1967).

Friedrich, Otto, *Before the Deluge: A Portrait of Berlin in the 1920s* (Michael Joseph, 1974).

Fussell, Paul, *The Great War and Modern Memory* (Oxford University Press, 2000).

Goffman, Erving, *The Presentation of Self in Everyday Life* (Penguin Books, 1990).

Herzl, Theodor, *The Jewish State* (Penguin Classics, 2010).

Keun, Irmgard, *Child of All Nations*, trans. Michael Hofmann (Penguin Classics, 2009).

Laing, R. D., *The Divided Self: An Existential Study in Sanity and Madness*, intro. by Anthony David (Penguin Classics, 2010).

Lessing, Theodor (ed.), *Jewish Self-Hate* (Berghahn Books, 2021).

Musil, Robert, *The Man without Qualities*, trans. Sophie Wilkins and Burton Pike (Picador, 1997).

Nirenberg, David, *Anti-Judaism: The Western Tradition* (Head of Zeus, 2015).

Perloff, Marjorie, *Edge of Irony: Modernism in the Shadow of the Habsburg Empire* (University of Chicago Press, 2018).

Rady, Martyn, *The Habsburgs: The Rise and Fall of a World Power* (Allen Lane, 2020).

Remarque, Erich Maria, *All Quiet on the Western Front*, trans. Brian Murdoch (Vintage Digital, 2010).

Sahl, Hans, *Das Exil Im Exil. Memoiren Eines Moralisten II* (Luchterhand, 1990).

Sands, Philippe, *East West Street* (Weidenfeld & Nicolson, 2017).

Schorske, Carl E., *Fin-de-siècle Vienna* (Random House, 1980).

Stach, Reiner, *Kafka: The Decisive Years*, trans. Shelley Laura Frisch (Princeton University Press, 2021).

Sennett, Richard, *The Foreigner: Two Essays on Exile* (Notting Hill Editions, 2011).

Vishniac, Roman, *Polish Jews: A Pictorial Record*, intro. by Abraham Joshua Heschel (Schocken Books, 1988).

von Goethe, Johann Wolfgang, *Faust, Part One*, trans. Anna Swanwick (David McKay, 1898).

Walsh, Joanna, *Hotel (Object Lessons)* (Bloomsbury, 2015).

Wassermann, Jakob, *My Life as German and Jew*, trans. S. N. Brainin (Coward-McCann, 1933).

Wasserstein, Bernard, *On the Eve: The Jews of Europe before the Second World War* (Profile Books, 2013).

Wawro, G., *A Mad Catastrophe: The Outbreak of World War I and the Collapse of the Habsburg Empire* (Basic Books, 2014).

Werfel, Franz, *Twilight of a World*, trans. H. T. Lowe-Porter (Viking Press, 1937).

Wiener, Alfred, *The Fatherland and the Jews: Two Pamphlets by Alfred Wiener, 1919 and 1924* (Granta Books, 2021).

Williams, Cedric, *The Broken Eagle: The Politics of Austrian Literature from Empire to Anschluss* (Elek, 1974).

Winder, Simon, *Danubia: A Personal History of Habsburg Europe* (Picador, 2014).

Wistrich, R. S. (ed.), *Austrians and Jews in the Twentieth Century: From Franz Joseph to Waldheim* (Palgrave Macmillan, 1992).

—— *The Jews of Vienna in the Age of Franz Joseph* (Plunkett Lake Press, 2016, Kindle edition).

Wittlin, Józef and Philippe Sands, *City of Lions* (Pushkin Press, 2016).

Zadek, Walter and Christine Brinck, *Sie flohen vor dem Hakenkreuz. Selbstzeugnisse der Emigranten: ein Lesebuch für Deutsche* (Rowohlt, 1981)

Zweig, Stefan, *The Invisible Collection and Buchmendel*, trans. Cedar Paul and Eden Paul (Pushkin Press, 1998).

—— *The World of Yesterday: Memoirs of a European*, trans. Anthea Bell (Pushkin Press, 2011).

Websites and online material (all last accessed 12 March 2022)

Abraham Sonne biographical details: https://www.soma-morgenstern.
     at/userfiles/file/Sonne%20SM%20W%20v121113.pdf

Adam Kirsch, 'Half Human', *Tablet*, 1 February 2012: https://www.
     tabletmag.com/sections/arts-letters/articles/half-human

Alfred Polgar, *The Small Form*: https://depts.washington.edu/vienna/
     documents/Polgar/Polgar_Form.htm

Austrian short film depicting men signing up for the war: https://
     ww1.habsburger.net/en/media/vienna-war-film-extract-1916

Austro-Hungarian Army barracks in Lemberg/Lwów / Lviv: http://
     forgottengalicia.com/austrian-military-barracks-in-lviv-part-i/

Barbara Probst Solomon, 'Some Notes on My Father's Cousin,
     Joseph Roth', *Tablet*, 27 May 2016: https://www.tabletmag.
     com/sections/arts-letters/articles/notes-on-joseph-roth

Benjamin Ivry, 'Still Wandering', *Tablet*, 18 October 2011:
     https://www.tabletmag.com/sections/arts-letters/articles/
     still-wandering

—— 'Tragic in Novels, Lucky in Friends', *Forward*, 19
     February 2012: https://forward.com/culture/151474/
     tragic-in-novels-lucky-in-friends/

Berlin, the Centropa Source Book, vol. 1: https://www.centropa.
     org/sites/default/files/centropasourcebook-berlin-small.pdf

Berlin: Symphony of a Metropolis (Walter Ruttmann, 1927): https://
     www.youtube.com/watch?v=_YSDgruADlE

Brody, 'Ukraine road trip: In Brody, New Signage at Fortress
     Synagogue ruin & New Recognition of Jewish History':
     https://jewish-heritage-europe.eu/2017/07/31/ukraine-road-
     trip-new-signage-in-brody/

Brody, Vanished World blog, 'Jews Have Never Lived in Brody':
     https://vanishedworld.blog/2013/03/08/jews-have-never-
     lived-in-brody/

Brody as depicted on Władysław Kocyan's postcards: https://
     forgottengalicia.com/brody-as-depicted-on-wladyslaw-
     kocyans-postcards/

Brody page on Shtetl Routes website: https://shtetlroutes.eu/en/town/brody/

Brody page on the Holocaust Historical Society's website: www.holocausthistoricalsociety.org.uk/contents/ghettosa-i/brody.html

Brody research sources listed in abstract for Börries Kuzmany, 'Brody always on my mind: the mental mapping of a Jewish city', *East European Jewish Affairs*, 43, 2 (2013): https://www.tandfonline.com/doi/abs/10.1080/13501674.2013.813130?src=recsys&journalCode=feej20&

Brody, Jewish Gen Kehila Links page: https://kehilalinks.jewishgen.org/brody/brody.htm

Brody, the Ghetto, Holocaust Education & Archive Research Team (HEART), the Holocaust Research Project: http://www.holocaustresearchproject.org/ghettos/brody.html

Center for Jewish History/Leo Baeck Institute contents of Joseph Roth Collection digital archive: https://archives.cjh.org//repositories/5/resources/6801

Chris Wilkinson, 'The Only Thing New in the World: Galician Slaughter 1846', 31 August 2019: https://forgottengalicia.com/the-only-thing-new-in-the-world-galician-slaughter-1846/

Film shot from a tram in 1906: https://www.youtube.com/watch?v=pN6SrB6r3MA

Great Synagogue of Brody: https://uma.lvivcenter.org/en/photos/1663

Iain Bamforth, 'Scheherazade in Vienna', *The New York Times*, 15 November 1998: https://archive.nytimes.com/www.nytimes.com/books/98/11/15/reviews/981115.15bamfort.html

International Encyclopaedia of the First World War – *The Last Days of Mankind*: https://encyclopedia.1914-1918-online.net/article/the_last_days_of_mankind_play

James Wood, 'Empire of Signs', *London Review of Books*, vol. 21, no. 5, 4 March 1999: https://www.lrb.co.uk/the-paper/v21/n05/james-wood/empire-of-signs

JewishGen.org 1897 Galician Business Directory, Brody Portion (by occupation): https://kehilalinks.jewishgen.org/brody/sherins_brody_occupations.htm

Jillian Saucier, 'Letters in Flight: The Peripatetics of
    Joseph Roth', *Critical Flame*, 21 (September–
    October 2012): http://criticalflame.org/
    letters-in-flight-the-peripatetics-of-joseph-roth/

Józef Wittlin entry in the YIVO Encyclopaedia of Jews in Eastern
    Europe : https://yivoencyclopedia.org/article.aspx/Wittlin_Jozef

Józef Wittlin, Reminiscences of Joseph Roth, undated, Box: 4,
    Folder: 46. Leo Baeck Institute. Series IV: Grubel, Fred
    (Grübel, Fredrick). Leo Baeck Institute. https://archives.cjh.org/
    repositories/5/archival_objects/672500 (accessed 3 November
    2021).

Karl Kraus reading his work in 1934: https://www.youtube.com/
    watch?v=rg-uGpBhs2g

Kingdom of Galicia map, Wikipedia: https://en.wikipedia.org/
    wiki/Galicia_(Eastern_Europe)#/media/ File:Map_of_the_
    Kingdom_of_Galicia_1914.jpg

Literaturhaus Wien page on Joseph Roth: http://www.literaturhaus.
    at/index.php?id=7003

Michael Hofmann, 'On translating Joseph Roth', *Dublin Review*,
    autumn 2002: https://thedublinreview.com/article/on-
    translating-joseph-roth/

Military medals of the Austro-Hungarian Imperial Army:
    https://ironcrossmilitaria.co.uk/collections/austro-hungarian-
    empire-militaria

'Mission of Inquiry to the Jews of Brody', excerpted from *Narrative of
    a Mission of Inquiry to the Jews from the Church of Scotland in 1839*,
    William Whyte & Co., Edinburgh, 1844: https://kehilalinks.
    jewishgen.org/brody/mission_of_inquiry.htm

Monovisions – Black & White Photography Magazine, on Emil Mayer:
    https://monovisions.com/emil-mayer-biography-city-
    life-documentary-photographer/

Ostend seafront and Hotel Helvetia photographs:
    https://www.beeldbankkusterfgoed.be/
    zoeken?keywords=%E2%80%98Overbevolkte%20terrassen%20
    op%20de%20zeedijk%20voor%20hotel%20Helvetia

'Rediscovering Europe's War-Time Writers',
by Tobias Grey, *The Wall Street Journal*, 3
September 2010. https://www.wsj.com/articles/
SB10001424052748704206804575468391455834072?mod=WSJ_
Books_LS_Books_5

'Rekawinkel Sanatorium': https://oldthing.de/Rekawinkel-
Sanatorium-Kat-Pressbaum-0024044765

Roth's time in Amsterdam: Els Snick, 'Het kroegleven
van Joseph Roth in Amsterdam', published
18 May 2014 at: https://onsamsterdam.nl/
het-kroegleven-van-joseph-roth-in-amsterdam

Sigmund Freud, *The Interpretation of Dreams*, Classics in the History
of Psychology, Chapter 4: Distortion in Dreams: https://
psychclassics.yorku.ca/Freud/Dreams/dreams4.htm

Silent footage from 1911 held by Film Archiv Austria, viewable here:
https://www.youtube.com/watch?v=FbMwd1CHMhI.

Soma Morgenstern estate: https://www.soma-morgenstern.at/

'The Shah to visit Ostend', *Nottingham Daily Express*, Wednesday
8 August 1900, p. 6, accessed via the British Newspaper
Archive: https://www.britishnewspaperarchive.co.uk/viewer/
bl/0001896/19000808/159/0006

'The Shah at Ostend', *Nottingham Daily Express*, Tuesday 21
August 1900, p. 4, accessed via the British Newspaper
Archive: https://www.britishnewspaperarchive.co.uk/viewer/
bl/0001896/19000821/085/0004

'The Torch of Karl Kraus', by Adam Kirsch, *New York Review
of Books*, October 23, 2008: https://www.nybooks.com/
articles/2008/10/23/the-torch-of-karl-kraus/

'Von Wiesner, Austrian Monarchist Leader, Dead in Vienna', *Jewish
Telegraphic Agency*, 1 February 1940: https://www.jta.org/
archive/von-wiesner-austrian-monarchist-leader-dead-in-vienna

'Weisser Mann immer schlecht', *Der Spiegel*, 23 August
1950, accessed at: https://www.spiegel.de/politik/
weisser-mann-immer-schlecht-a-f8ca9ce2-0002-0001-0000-
000044449496?context=issue

Illustration Credits

All photographs by the author unless otherwise stated

Index

Keep in touch with
Granta Books:

Visit granta.com to discover more.

GRANTA